'MANTHAN'
"Not Just Effective but Efficient: A New Blueprint for Management in 21st Century"

"Learn...
...to Lead"

Edited by

Dr. S. H. Gawhane
M.Sc. (Stat.), Ph.D. (Stat.)
Professor/Chief Executive Officer
SSPM, Kondhapuri Campus

Dr. Omprakash Haldar
DETE, BE, M.A., M. Sc., MBA, M.Phil,
Ph.D. (Marketing),
Professor/Convener National Conference

Himalaya Publishing House

MUMBAI • NEW DELHI • NAGPUR • BENGALURU • HYDERABAD • CHENNAI • PUNE • LUCKNOW • AHMEDABAD • ERNAKULAM • BHUBANESWAR • INDORE • KOLKATA

First Edition : 2011

Published by : Mrs. Meena Pandey for **Himalaya Publishing House Pvt. Ltd.,**
"Ramdoot", Dr. Bhalerao Marg, Girgaon, **Mumbai - 400 004.**
Phone: 022-23860170/23863863, Fax: 022-23877178
E-mail: himpub@vsnl.com; Website: www.himpub.com

Branch Offices :

New Delhi : "Pooja Apartments", 4-B, Murari Lal Street, Ansari Road, Darya Ganj, New Delhi - 110 002. Phone: 011-23270392, 23278631; Fax: 011-23256286

Nagpur : Kundanlal Chandak Industrial Estate, Ghat Road, Nagpur - 440 018. Phone: 0712-2738731, 3296733; Telefax: 0712-2721215

Bengaluru : No. 16/1 (Old 12/1), 1st Floor, Next to Hotel Highlands, Madhava Nagar, Race Course Road, Bengaluru - 560 001. Phone: 080-32919385; Telefax: 080-22286611

Hyderabad : No. 3-4-184, Lingampally, Besides Raghavendra Swamy Matham, Kachiguda, Hyderabad - 500 027. Phone: 040-27560041, 27550139; Mobile: 09848130433

Chennai : No. 85/50, Bazullah Road, T. Nagar, Chennai - 600 017. Phone: 044-28144004/28144005

Pune : First Floor, "Laksha" Apartment, No. 527, Mehunpura, Shaniwarpeth (Near Prabhat Theatre), Pune - 411 030. Phone: 020-24496323/24496333

Lucknow : Jai Baba Bhavan, Church Road, Near Manas Complex and Dr. Awasthi Clinic, Aliganj, Lucknow - 226 024. Phone: 0522-2339329, 4068914; Mobile: 09305302158, 09415349385, 09389593752

Ahmedabad : 114, "SHAIL", 1st Floor, Opp. Madhu Sudan House, C.G. Road, Navrang Pura, Ahmedabad - 380 009. Phone: 079-26560126; Mobile: 09327324149, 09314679413

Ernakulam : 39/104 A, Lakshmi Apartment, Karikkamuri Cross Rd., Ernakulam, Cochin - 622011, Kerala. Phone: 0484-2378012, 2378016; Mobile: 09344199799

Bhubaneswar : 5 Station Square, Bhubaneswar (Odisha) - 751 001. Mobile: 09861046007

Indore : Kesardeep Avenue Extension, 73, Narayan Bagh, Flat No. 302, IIIrd Floor, Near Humpty Dumpty School, Narayan Bagh, Indore - 452 007 (M.P.). Mobile: 09301386468

Kolkata : 108/4, Beliaghata Main Road, Near ID Hospital, Opp. SBI Bank, Kolkata - 700 010, Phone: 033-32449649, Mobile: 09910440956

DTP by : HPH, Editorial Office, Bhandup (Sunanda, Pooja, Avinash)

Printed by : Prabhat Book Binders, Mumbai.

From the Editorial Team

Dr. S.H. Gawhane

M.Sc. (Stat.), Ph.D. (Stat.)
Professor/Chief
Executive Officer
SSPM, Kondhapuri Campus

Dr. Omprakash Haldar

DETE, BE, M.A., M.Sc., MBA, M.Phil, Ph.D. (Marketing),
Professor/Convener National Conference

Shrinath Shikshan Prasarak Mandal (SSPM) was established in the year 1984 and taken over by Hon. Prof. M.N. Navale, a dynamic leader and philanthropist, with an objective of providing quality education in the field of Management, Computer Sciences and Education from Kindergarten onwards specially in the rural area. Sinhgad Management School (SMS) is under the umbrella of SSPM which has set precedence with its excellence academic track and unique teaching learning process. Sinhgad Management School was established in the year 2008 with the MBA Programme with following features: Courses are affiliated to University of Pune; State-of-the-art infrastructural facilities, eco-friendly environment, lake view site; Fulltime highly qualified and experienced faculty; unique pedagogy.

The present management issues made a basis for organizing a national level forum where such issues would be discussed and experiences will be shared. SMS, Kondhapuri made an attempt to offer such platform for organizing a National Conference - 'MANTHAN' "Not Just Effective but Efficient: A New Blueprint for Management in 21st Century." with the slogan, 'Learn to Lead' on 16th -17th Feb. 2011 at Kondhapuri, Tal. Shirur, Dist. Pune, India.

In 21st Century, the aim of all managers is to say that they must be productive. The need for productivity requires the importance of performing effectively and efficiently the basic managerial activities in this modern era. Successful companies create surplus through productive operations, which implies effectiveness and efficiency in individual and organizational performance also. Effectiveness is the achievement of objectives. Efficiency is the achievement of the end results with the least amount of resources. To know whether managers are productive, they must know their goals and maintaining the management system to upgrade the conditions to achieve the best position.

The Conference will be a landmark for the activities which will be marking their presence across the boundaries of the Corporate and the Academics. The conference will foster the much awaited issues which do need attention from every walk of corporate and academic life, and education Sector. The conference aimed at braining together academia, Corporates, researchers, research scholars, students and practitioners for sharing and exploring the emerging areas of research in management practices in corporates and to suggest providing solutions for business to survive and grow in adverse condition also.

The objectives of the conference is deliberations and presentations of research work and management practices in the areas of Opportunities and Challenges, Weaknesses and Threats for developing the New Age, Efficient Managers and Effective Management System in present scenario. It will offer a unique opportunity for research scholars to present their work, seek suggestions/recommendations and improve upon their work.

In response to the call, about 100 full research papers/case studies/articles are reviewed from all over India. After a rigorous process of review, 56 papers were selected for publishing in the form of a book. All the papers included in this book represents the creative, innovative, efficient and effective manner of management practices in 21st century. It is a proud moment and a great pleasure for collecting the research papers of different field from different states of India, which are tireless efforts put by every member of the team.

Foremost we are grateful to our president Hon. Prof. M.N. Navale and secretary Dr. (Mrs.) Sunanda Navale for their continuous support, motivation and enthusiasm in organising this conference.

The entire team of Sinhgad Management School, Kondhapuri worked hard for achieving great success of the National Conference. On behalf of SMS, Kondhapuri, we are grateful to all the staff teaching and non-teaching those who helped directly and indirectly for getting success of this national conference.

We are grateful to the authors of research papers/articles/case studies for their quick response and sharing their knowledge to this mega event.

We appreciate Himalaya Publishing Company who worked hard with interest and devotion to ensure that the book is made available in time to the delegates at the inaugural function.

We welcome your comments on the coverage and the contents of this book at smsknationalcon@gmail.com.

Editors

Contents

ISBN – 978-93-5024-769-3

1 "CSR and Ethics of Job Search Portals – A Myth or A Reality"

Dr. A. Ravi & Ms. Dhanya
The Oxford College of Engineering, Bommanahalli, Bangalore-68.

Introduction

Business ethics also known as corporate ethics is a form of applied ethics or professional ethics that examines ethical principles and moral or ethical problems that arise in a business environment. It applies to all aspects of business conduct and is relevant to the conduct of individuals and business organizations as a whole. Competition, rivalry among the firms, lack of autonomy of the persons at different levels of marketing hierarchy, nature of the products marketed, nature of the persons to whom products are marketed, the profit margin claimed, and everything relating the marketing field does make the agency of a marketing person just a cog in the wheel. Deprived of agency, the hierarchy of marketing hardly lets one with an opportunity to autonomously decide to be ethical. Without one having agency, one is deprived of the ethical choices. Equally Challenging is a company's ability to adhere to CSR. CSR policy functions as a built-in, self-regulating mechanism whereby business monitors and ensures its active compliance with the spirit of the law, ethical standards, and international norms. The goal of CSR is to embrace responsibility for the company's actions and encourage a positive impact through its activities on the environment, consumers, employees, communities, stakeholders and all other members of the public sphere. Furthermore, CSR-focused businesses would proactively promote the public interest by encouraging community growth and development, and voluntarily eliminating practices that harm the public sphere, regardless of legality. CSR is the deliberate inclusion of public interest into corporate decision-making, and the honouring of a triple bottom line: people, planet, profit.

The paper is based on the research and survey conducted on the topic "**CSR and Ethics of a Job Search Portals – A Myth or A Reality?**"_ Today, there are more than 40,000 job sites available to job seekers. Apart from these job sites there are numerous government websites that have jobs available on them; thousands of newspapers with job classified sections online and also almost 100,000 companies' websites that have job openings on them. But having access to all these is not possible for job seekers. The job seeker uses only traditional ways to look for jobs that suit them the best. These people eventually do not end up with quality job results. They either register with any job portal or look in the classified sections of the newspaper's website but these do not help them much for they miss many job openings that are available in the market. **Job boards** wait for the employers to come and publish the job openings on their site. For every job opening that is to be posted they charge employers with a huge amount of fees. Since the jobs available on these sites are accessed by all free members, the applications for these jobs are also higher and this reduces one's chance of being employed.

Job portals wait for the employers to come up to them. Getting access to all the jobs in the market is not possible by a single person as claimed by the Job Portals. Job portals look for the employers who are willing to pay, to post the job openings in their website. In good economic conditions, they have many companies in their portals who advertise on job openings but in bad economic conditions they have very few jobs to offer to their clients. This is so because during these bad economic times employers prefer posting the openings on their own sites and not on the job portals. Having these serious impediments and many tall claims being made which is opposed to the business ethics and CSR, the report is a study on how effective a job portal would be in helping a registered client get the 'Right Job at the Right Time at the Right Place'.

Objective of the Study

- To evaluate the reliability of the various Resume services provided by the job portals.
- To determine to what extent the job portals adhere to Ethics and CSR in Business.
- To understand the general perception of public about the active role played by job portals in job searching and improving chances of employment.

Scope of the Study

- Defining appropriate functioning of Job portals
- Establishing organizational values
- Nurturing individual responsibility
- Providing leadership & oversight
- Relating decisions to stakeholder interests
- Developing accountability
- Relating consequence with respect to Criminal behavior and legal framework – every business needs to have a code of ethics pertaining to criminal behavior and legal issues. The employees in a business need to be trained sufficiently regarding legalities of the business and the consequences their actions would have upon them and the business.
- Human values and personal behavior – every business needs to have an ethical framework or policy for human values and behavior. Employees should be given training on how to interact with different people, be it customer, suppliers or competitors. They need to be aware of how they are expected to behave with people at different levels and that inappropriate behavior will have consequences.
- Corporate and business ethics – though we are discussing business ethics, this strictly pertains to the corporate ethics, ethical policies for business and actions that are going to be under check and need to be in compliance with legal framework and standards.

Limitations of the Study

- Time constraint posed a serious limitation to gathering accurate results pertaining to the study.
- Though Judgment sampling is the sampling technique used for the purpose of research the sample size of 100 may not include respondents from different Job portals in the exact proportion.

Research Methodology and Research Design

Sample Size: 100

Nature of Data: Primary Data

Target Audience: Job Seekers who have hired Resume services of Job Portals in Bangalore

Sampling Technique: Judgment Sampling

Research Design: Descriptive Research

Analysis and Interpretation of Data

For the purpose of analysis and interpretation of data statistical methods and tools like Tabulation, pie charts and graphs are used in this research. Analysis and interpretation of data enables the process of filtering and editing of data. It also throws light on what are the different categories or unit of Analysis involved in the Research. Thus at the end of interpretation process all the raw data gets transformed into useful facts and information that facilitate decision making.

TABLE 1 – Resume Development by Professionals

SL No:	*RESPONSE*	*PERCENTAGE*
1	STRONGLY DISAGREE	0%
2	DISAGREE	0%
3	NEUTRAL	62%
4	AGREE	8%
5	STRONGLY AGREE	30%

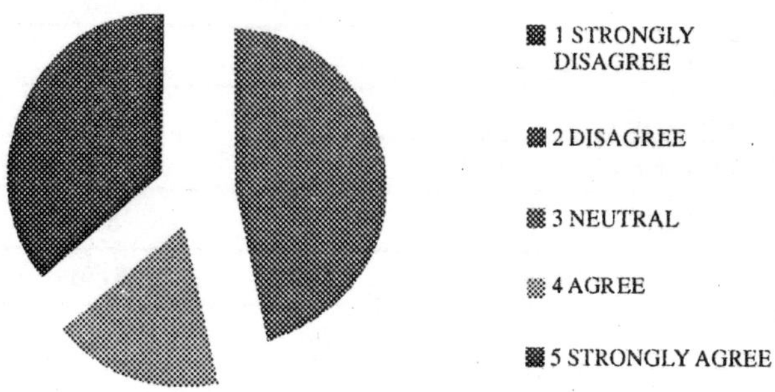

Fig. 1 : Resume Development by Professionals

- **INFERENCE:** The study reveals most of the respondents have an indifferent attitude towards Resume development by professionals. They opined that their resume seemed to have no major difference from the resume they developed on their own despite being developed by professionals.

TABLE 2 – Premium Resume Service is worthwhile

SL No:	*RESPONSE*	*PERCENTAGE*
1	STRONGLY DISAGREE	0%
2	DISAGREE	2%
3	NEUTRAL	58%
4	AGREE	9%
5	STRONGLY AGREE	31%

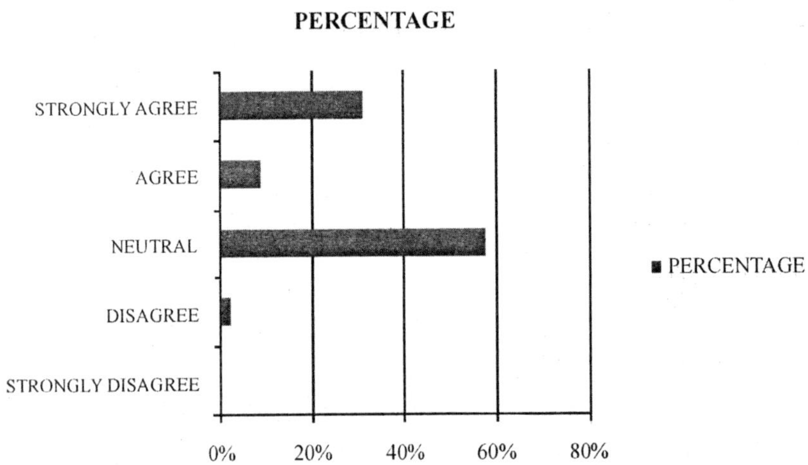

Fig. 2 : Premium Resume Service is worthwhile

- **INFERENCE:** Majority of the respondents feel Premium Resume Development would hardly enhance the Quality of the resume. Some of the respondents strongly believe it would definitely improve quality of the resume.

TABLE 3 – Super Express Resume/ Express Resume were delivered on time

Sl No:	*RESPONSE*	*PERCENTAGE*
1	STRONGLY DISAGREE	0%
2	DISAGREE	8%
3	NEUTRAL	3%
4	AGREE	8%
5	STRONGLY AGREE	81%

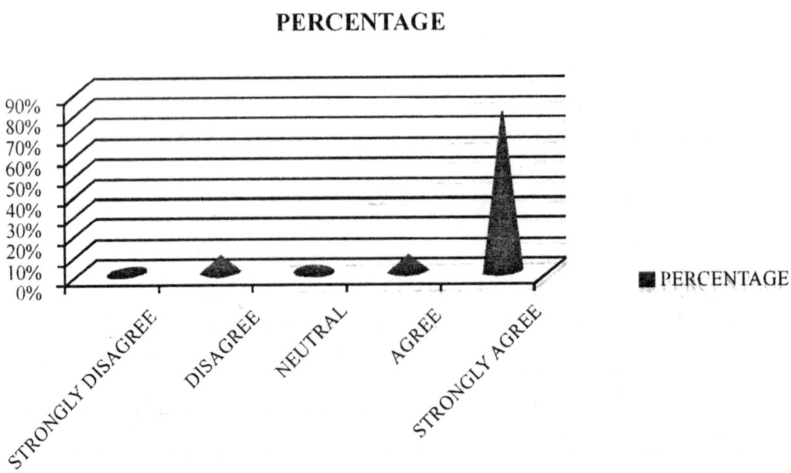

Fig. 3 : Super Express Resume/ Express Resume were delivered on time

- **INFERENCE:** Majority of the respondents feel Express and Super Express resume were delivered on time as promised by the job portals.

TABLE 4 – Relevance of Professional Write - up

SL No:	*RESPONSE*	*PERCENTAGE*
1	STRONGLY DISAGREE	0%
2	DISAGREE	14%
3	NEUTRAL	52%
4	AGREE	34%
5	STRONGLY AGREE	0%

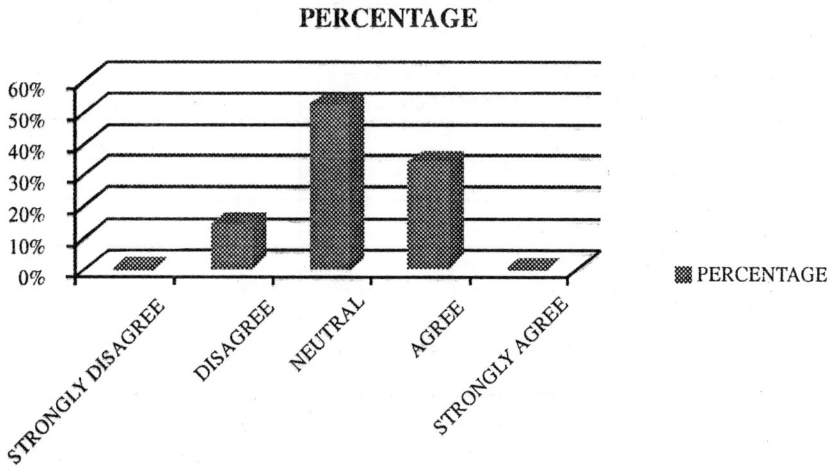

Fig. 4 : Relevance of Professional Write - up

- **INFERENCE:** Majority of the respondents had a neutral opinion about relevance of Professional Write ups.

TABLE 5 – Resume Display improves the visibility of the Resume by Recruiters

SL No:	*RESPONSE*	*PERCENTAGE*
1	STRONGLY DISAGREE	69%
2	DISAGREE	10%
3	NEUTRAL	11%
4	AGREE	11%
5	STRONGLY AGREE	0%

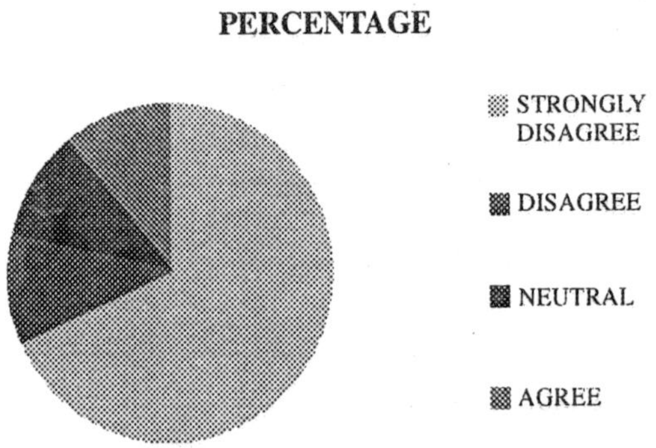

Fig. 5 : Resume Display improves the visibility of the Resume by Recruiters

TABLE 6 – Job Mail informs about the most relevant openings

SL No:	RESPONSE	PERCENTAGE
1	STRONGLY DISAGREE	6%
2	DISAGREE	71%
3	NEUTRAL	13%
4	AGREE	3%
5	STRONGLY AGREE	7%

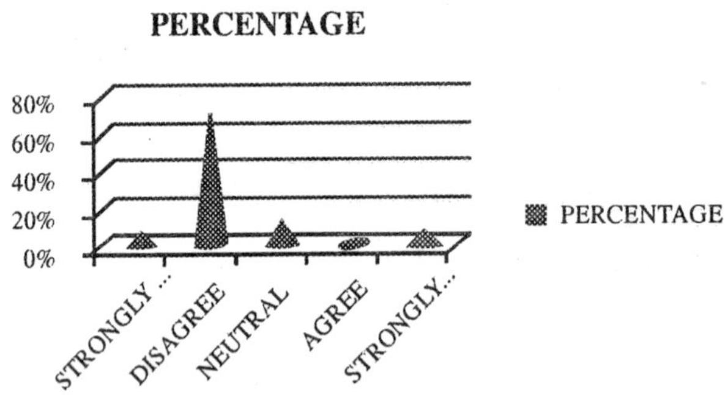

Fig. 6 : Job Mail informs about the most relevant openings

- **INFERENCE:** Majority of the respondents opined that Job mail hardly helps in being informed about the most relevant openings in various companies.

TABLE 7 – Resume Services improves the chances of employment

SL No:	RESPONSE	PERCENTAGE
1	STRONGLY DISAGREE	0%
2	DISAGREE	82%
3	NEUTRAL	0%
4	AGREE	38%
5	STRONGLY AGREE	0%

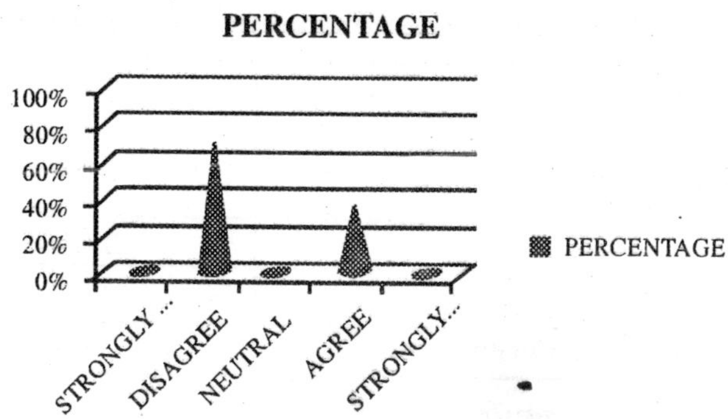

Fig. 7 : Resume Services improves the chances of employment

- **INFERENCE:** Majority of the respondents opined that Resume Services are in no way improving the chances of employment. Thus all the claims made by them seem to be just tall claims.

TABLE 8 – Rates are reasonable

SL No:	*RESPONSE*	*PERCENTAGE*
1	STRONGLY DISAGREE	43%
2	DISAGREE	38%
3	NEUTRAL	19%
4	AGREE	0%
5	STRONGLY AGREE	0%

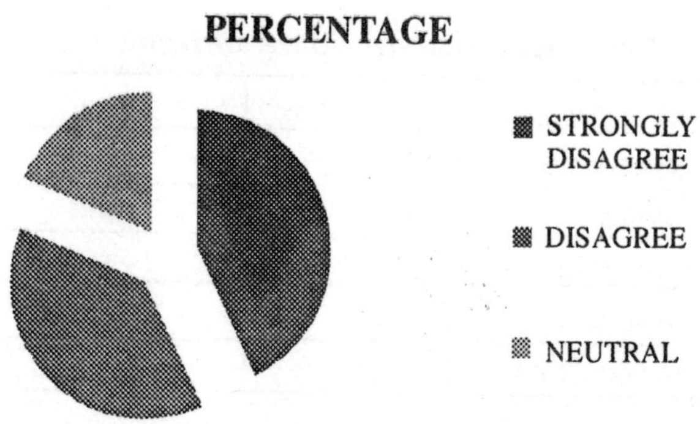

Fig. 8 : Rates are reasonable

- **INFERENCE:** Majority of the respondents opined that the rates charged for the various services offered to the job seekers are not reasonable.

TABLE 9 – Branches offer superior service as compared to HO

SL No:	*RESPONSE*	*PERCENTAGE*
1	STRONGLY DISAGREE	0%
2	DISAGREE	33%
3	NEUTRAL	18%
4	AGREE	49%
5	STRONGLY AGREE	0%

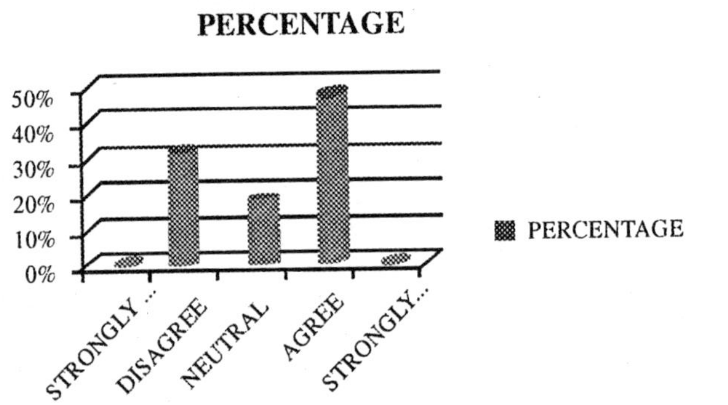

Fig. 9 : Branches offer superior service as compared to HO

- **INFERENCE:** There is a mixed opinion among the respondents about the branches offering better service when compared to the Head office. This inevitably proves despite the customer having the opportunity to speak to the officials personally their plight remains more or less the same.

TABLE 10 – Online transactions are secure

Sl No:	*RESPONSE*	*PERCENTAGE*
1	STRONGLY DISAGREE	0%
2	DISAGREE	10%
3	NEUTRAL	24%
4	AGREE	57%
5	STRONGLY AGREE	9%

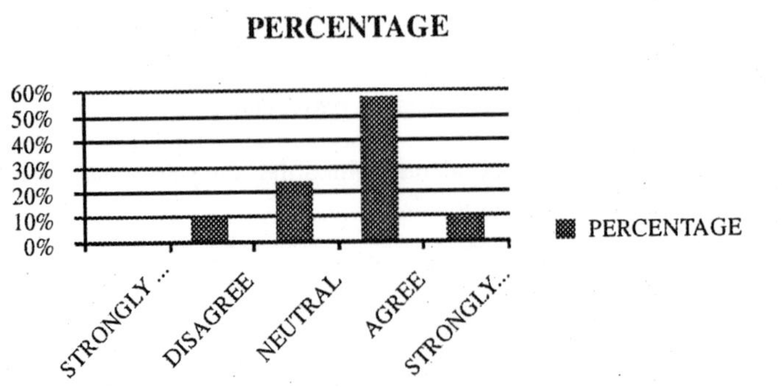

Fig. 10 : Online transactions are secure

- **INFERENCE:** There is a mixed opinion among the respondents about the online transactions being safe whether it is by providing the card details or by sending a link. When it comes to providing the card details they are even more skeptical.

Findings

- The study reveals most of the respondents have an indifferent attitude towards Resume development by professionals. They opined that their resume seemed to have no major difference from the resume they developed on their own despite being developed by professionals.
- Majority of the respondents feel Premium Resume Development would hardly enhance the Quality of the resume. Some of the respondents strongly believe it would definitely improve quality of the resume.
- Majority of the respondents feel Express and Super Express resume were delivered on time as promised by the job portals.
- Majority of the respondents had a neutral opinion about relevance of Professional Write ups. It suggests that Write ups have very trivial role to play.
- Majority of the respondents opined that Resume Display service is of no good in improving the visibility of the resume to the recruiters. There is absolutely no difference between the paid member and a free member in this regard.
- Majority of the respondents opined that Job mail hardly helps in being informed about the most relevant openings in various companies.
- Majority of the respondents opined that Resume Services are in no way improving the chances of employment. Thus all the claims made by them seem to be just tall claims.
- Majority of the respondents opined that Resume Services are in no way improving the chances of employment. Thus all the claims made by them seem to be just tall claims.
- Majority of the respondents opined that the rates charged for the various services offered to the job seekers are not reasonable.

Recommendation and Suggestions

- The study has proved that ethics & CSR seems to have taken a backseat in the case of functioning of job portals. The public is being deceived by job portals by making tall claims which never turns out to be true. Stringent action needs to be taken and there is an eminent need for precise and clear rules that compensates for the damage caused to any registered member of a portal.
- The management needs to take responsibility for a comprehensive plan that includes educating the employees about the importance of ethics in business.
- Obtain adequate resources to support Business ethics initiatives. Incorporate culture, values & programs that support ethical practices in Business.
- Recognition of the role of co-workers & managers and balancing stakeholder interests.
- Management of situational pressures and providing special rewards beyond short-term performance.
- Discretion needs to be applied before spending a considerable amount of money on services like Display and Job mail. Resume writing is most appropriate if a resume has to be prepared very urgently.
- It would be appropriate to hire the service by personally making a visit to any of the branches of the portal in the city rather than hiring it via telephone and making online payment. Grievance redressing is better in the farther case. Lodging a complaint also becomes simpler.

- It is advisable not to disclose the card details to anyone who claims to be an employee of the job portal and assures all online transactions are secure.

Conclusion

Using a stakeholder and an organizational decision making framework helps to link societal, organizational, and individual interests. The use of critical thinking is an important part of ethical decision making especially in ambiguous areas. While the development of personal character is important, it must be linked to competence in understanding risks and approaches to managing ethics and compliance in a complex organizational context. The national culture and regulatory system is also an important area that can affect ethical decision making. Business ethics in organizations requires values-based leadership from top management, purposeful actions that include planning and implementation of standards of appropriate conduct, as well as openness and continuous effort to improve the organization's ethical performance. Although personal values are important in ethical decision making, they are just one of the components that guide the decisions, actions, and policies of organizations. The burden of ethical behavior relates to the organization's values and traditions, not just to the individuals who make the decisions and carry them out. A firm's ability to plan and implement ethical business standards depends in part on structuring resources and activities to achieve ethical objectives in an effective and efficient manner. Enron and Daewoo provide excellent examples of highly visible firms who have failed to provide the ethical leadership necessary to avoid misconduct that has damaged their reputation, and created ethical disasters that have damaged many stakeholders.

References

1. Strong Is the Tendency to Treat Top Sales Performers Leniently?" *Journal of Business Ethics*, Vol. 43, pp. 337-351.
2. Ferrell, O.C. (2005), "A Framework for Understanding Organizational Ethics," in *Business Ethics: New Challenges for Business Schools and Corporate Leaders*, R.A. Peterson and O.C. Ferrell, eds. Armonk, New York: M.E. Sharpe, pp. 3-17.
3. Ferrell, O.C. (2006), "The Fall of Enron: A Stakeholder Failure," Forthcoming in Ferrell, O.C, Fraedrich, John, Ferrell, Linda, *Business Ethics,* Boston: Houghton Mifflin 2007.
4. Freeman, R.E. (1984), *Strategic Management: A Stakeholder Approach* (Boston: Pitman, 1984).
5. Harrison, J.S. and Freeman, R.E. (1999), "Stakeholders, Social Responsibility, and Performance: Empirical Evidence and Theoretical Perspectives," *Academy of Management Journal*, Vol. 42, No. 5, pp. 479-485.
6. Hart, S.L , and Sharma, S. (2004). "Engaging Fringe Stakeholders for Competitive Imagination," *Academy of Management Executive*, Vol. 18, No. 1, pp. 7-18.
7. Jones, T.M. (1991), "Ethical Decision Making by Individuals in Organizations: An Issue- Contingent Model," *Academy of Management Review*, Vol. 16, pp. 366-395.
8. Maignan, I., and Ferrell, O.C. (2004), "Corporate Social Responsibility and Marketing: An Integrative Framework," *Journal of the Academy of Marketing Science*, Vol. 32, No. 1, pp. 23-19.
9. Maignan, I., Ferrell, O.C. and Ferrell, L. (2005) "A Stakeholder Model for Implementing Social Responsibility in Marketing," *European Journal of Marketing,* Vol. 39, #9.10, pp. 956-977.
10. Miller, R.L. and Lewis, W.F. (1991), "A Stakeholder Approach to Marketing Management Using the Value Exchange Models," *European Journal of Marketing*, Vol. 25, No. 8, pp. 55-68.

ISBN – 978-93-5024-769-3

2 Evaluation of Training Programmes for Rural Development Study w.r.t. Hatkanagale Taluka, Dist. - Kolhapur, Maharashtra

Mrs. Rajashree N. Badage
Asst. Prof. – SKN Sinhagad Business School.
Dr. Sambhaji V. Mane
Reader, (SRTMU, Nanded Sub Centre Latur).

Introduction

Management experts concentrate on effective and efficient performance of the employees in the organisation. Training refers to programs designed to help new employees adjust to the workplace successfully. In addition, they include the formal on-going efforts of corporations and other organizations to improve the performance and self-fulfillment of their employees through a variety of methods and programs. Training has emerged as formal corporate functions, integral elements of corporate strategy, and is recognized as professions with distinct theories and methodologies as companies increasingly acknowledge the fundamental importance of employee growth and development, in order to improve the success and efficiency of their organizations. This technique is also useful for the rural people.. As maximum of population lives in rural area and depends on agriculture it affects total productivity of the country. The Department of Rural Development implements schemes for generation of self-employment and wage employment, provision of housing and minor irrigation assets to rural poor, social assistance to the destitute and Rural Roads. Apart from this, the Department provides the support services and other quality inputs such as assistance for strengthening of DRDA Administration, Panchayati raj institutions, training & research etc. the main purpose of this study is to identify rural people awareness regarding this concept , to determine the effectiveness and usefulness of this programme for rural development.

Objectives

Following are the objectives of the present study.

1. To know the awareness of rural people about the existing training programmes.
2. To as certain the effectiveness of existing training programmes.
3. To study the usefulness of training programmes regarding development of rural people.

Hypothses

1. Training is useful for self-employment
2. Traininghelps to increase rural productivity.

Research Methodology

For accomplishing the above objectives, collection of both primary and secondary data has been called.

1. Primary Data

Primary data is first-hand information which has been directly collected by the researcher from the following research tools-

(a) Questionnaire

Researcher has collected data through well-structured questionnaire. It is useful to collect factual information as - facts about the respondent like-sex, age, marital status etc, Psychological information such as attitudes, opinions, beliefs etc. and behavioral information like social participation and so on.

(b) Interview

Researcher has conducted well-structured interviews with respondent. It enables to grasp the behavioral context of the data furnished by the respondent.

(c) Observation

Researcher has been systematically observed a specific phenomenon in its proper setting for the specific purpose of gathering data.

2. Secondary Data

Researcher has collected data from Gazetteers department Kolhapur, Collector office Kolhapur, Grampanchayat of villages in Hatkanagale Taluka, Panchayat Sammitee, government publications etc.

Sample Design

In sample design, sufficient care has been taken to embody the universe comprehensively. As per the 1991 census, total population of Hatkanagale Taluka is 321275 as Hatkanagale Taluka constitutes of five circles, Researcher has taken into account rural population for the sampling purpose from these circles. Proportionate stratified sampling method has been used for sample design. This sampling involves drawing a sample from each stratum in proportion to the latter's share in the total population.

- ***Sample size*:** Sample size has been determined by considering (1) Degree of accuracy required, (2) Degree of variability or diversity in the population and (3) The number of different variables examined simultaneously in data analysis.

Sr. No.	*Name of the Circle*	*Name of the villages*	*Sample size*
1	Vathar	Talsande, Kini, Ghunki	10
2	VadgaonKasba	Ambap, Bhendvade, Khochi	10
3	Hatkanangale	Hingangao, Kumbhoj, Nej	10
4	Ichalkaranji	Tardal, Rui, Chandur	10
5	Hupri	Talandge, Yalgud, Rangoli	10

Data Presentation and Interpretation

TABLE 1 – Age distribution of respondents

Age- Group	*No. of Respondents*	*Percentage (%)*
30 years or less	20	40
Between 30-40 years	22	44
41 years and above	8	16
Total	50	100

(Source: Author's Field Work, 2011.)

Above table shows that, 40 percent (20) respondence are below the age of 30 years. Whereas 44 percent (22) respondents are between the age group of 30-40 and only 16 percent (08) respondents age is 41 and above.

TABLE 2 – Respondents educational qualification.

Education Qualification	*No. of Respondents*	*Percentage (%)*
Below 10th	05	10
HSC	12	24
Graduation	20	40
Post-graduation	13	26
Total	50	100

(Source: Author's Field Work, 2011.)

It is observed that, only 10 percent of respondents are less qualified, 20 percent of respondents have completed HSC, 40 percent of respondents are graduates and 26 percent of respondents are postgraduates.

TABLE 3 – Awareness of training programmes

Response	*No. of Respondents*	*Percentage (%)*
Yes	22	44
No	28	56
Total	50	100

(Source: Author's Field Work, 2011.)

The researcher has tried to find out the awareness about the training programmes. 44 percent respondents know about the training programmes run by the government, whereas 56 percent respondents are unaware about the programmes.

TABLE 4 – Schedule of training programme communicates properly

Response	*No. of Respondents*	*Percentage*
Strongly Agree	00	00
Agree	05	10
Strongly Disagree	20	40
Disagree	25	50
No Opinion	00	00
Total	50	100

(Source: Author's Field Work, 2011.)

The above table clearly indicates that, 20 percent respondents are strongly disagree and 25 percent respondents are disagree that they are not getting any prior information regarding training activity.

TABLE 5 – Existing training programmes are useful to improve knowledge of agriculture

Response	*No. of Respondents*	*Percentage*
Strongly Agree	08	16
Agree	10	20
Strongly Disagree	20	40
Disagree	12	24
No Opinion	00	00
Total	50	100

(Source: Author's Field Work, 2011.)

From the table it understood that only 16 percent respondents were strongly agree ,20 percent were agree, 40 percent were strongly disagree and 24 percent were disagree regarding usefulness of existing training programme. They required update knowledge for improvement.

TABLE 6 – Methods of Existing training programmes are efficient to provide latest knowledge

Response	*No. of Respondents*	*Percentage*
Strongly Agree	08	16
Agree	10	20
Strongly Disagree	14	28
Disagree	18	36
No Opinion	00	00
Total	50	100

(Source: Author's Field Work, 2011.)

As per the analysis of collected data 28 percent respondents were strongly disagree, 36 percent were disagree about the effectiveness of existing methods training. Whereas only 16 percent were strongly agreed and 20 percent were agree regarding the statement.

TABLE 7 – Existing training programmes are providing knowledge of new technology to increase productivity

Response	*No. of Respondents*	*Percentage (%)*
Strongly Agree	06	12
Agree	10	20
Strongly Disagree	15	30
Disagree	15	30
No Opinion	04	08
Total	50	100

(Source: Author's Field Work, 2011.)

It clearly shows from the above table that 12 percent respondents were strongly agreeing with the opinion 20 percent were also agree, 30 percent were disagree, and 30 percent were strongly disagree while 08 percent have not given their opinion on this.

TABLE 9 – Before conducting training need assessment carried out

Response	*No. of Respondents*	*Percentage (%)*
Strongly Agree	00	00
Agree	05	10
Strongly Disagree	18	36
Disagree	20	40
No Opinion	07	14
Total	50	100

(Source: Author's Field Work, 2011.)

The table shows that only 10 percent respondents were agreeing that need of rural people consider before conducting training activity. 36 percent were strongly disagreed, 40 percent were disagreed and 7 percent have not given their opinion on this.

TABLE 10 – Existing training programme promotes self-employment

Response	*No. of Respondents*	*Percentage (%)*
Strongly Agree	10	10
Agree	12	24
Strongly Disagree	14	28
Disagree	12	24
No Opinion	02	04
Total	50	100

(Source: Author's Field Work, 2011.)

The table shows that 10 percent respondents were strongly agreeing that existing training programmes encourages self- employment, 24 percent agreed, 28 percent were disagreed and 4 percent have not given their opinion on this.

Results

As the researcher has observed that there is requirement for rural people to cope with the changing situations and involve themselves in self- employment. Training activities are conducted for rural people development by government. For the purpose of measuring effectiveness of such programmes the study is conducted.

The analysis showed following results.

1. It is observed that maximum respondents are young aged.
2. It is found that, literacy level of rural people is satisfactory as more respondents have a good educational qualification.
3. It has been observed that, maximum of rural people are unaware about the training programmes. Some people are
4. There is no proper information channel through which people can get knowledge about such programmes. Rural people themselves should go through the Zillah Parishad for getting information. Schedule of training programme is also not declared time to time. Particular time period is not decided.
5. According to the respondents existing training programmes are not that much of useful for updating knowledge regarding agriculture.
6. Traditional training methods are using which are not that much of useful for improvement of skills.
7. Existing training programmes are failed to reach satisfactory level as need assessment is not carried out.
8. People those who wants to involve themselves in self- employment they only go through the related offices and do the same. Existing training programmes are not that much of encouraged rural people.

Conclusion and Recommendations

Based on the findings of the study it could be concluded that existing training programmes are quite effective in terms of development. There is a requirement to make it more effective in context to the development of rural people as well as development of self-employment. For making training programmes more effective there is requirement of need assessment . Proper information channel and scheduling should be developed for making aware of the people. New methods of training should be adopted for introducing new technologies. There is requirement to promote self- employment through effective training programmes.

Suggested Training Model

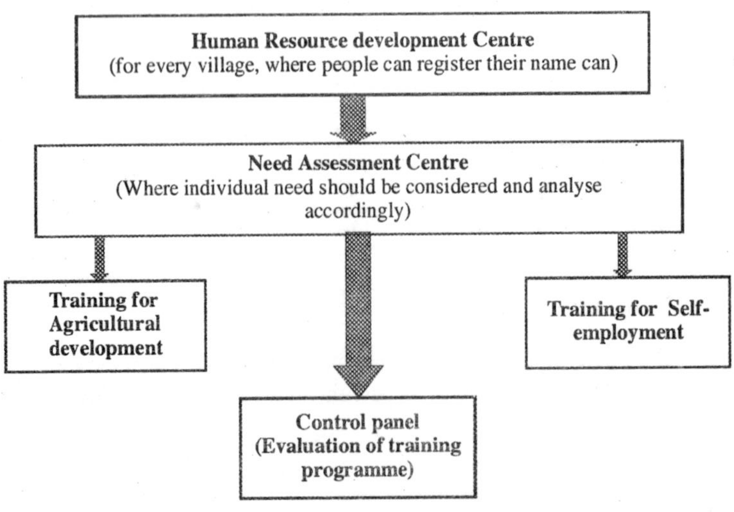

References

1. Monappa, A. (1999). Saiyadain, M. (1999). Personnel management. New Delhi: Tata McGraw-Hill Publishing.
2. Decenzo, D.A. (1998). Stephen, P.R. (1998). Personnel Human Resource Management. New Delhi: Prentice Hall Of India.
3. Gary Dessler. (2000). Human Resource Management. New Delhi: Prentice Hall Of India.
   http://blogs.siliconindia.com/Abhishek1003/INDIAN_RURAL_AREAS_PROBLEMS-bid1opCX3yn28782565.html Retrieved on 21/12/2010.
4. http://www.rediff.com/money/2006/dec/11iit2.htm Retrieved on 21/12/2010
   http://www.outreach-international.org/our-work/where-we-work/asia/india/?gclid=CJyX1Zb4854CFccvpAodvnlT3A Retrieved on 22/12/2010
5. http://www.moneycontrol.com/news/business/people%92s-participation-key-to-sustainable-development_316835.html Retrieved on 22/12/2010
6. http://infochangeindia.org/Urban-India/Cityscapes/Promoting-people%E2%80%99s-participation-in-urban-governance.html Retrieved on 23/12/2010.
7. Social development - India - problem, average, system Retrieved on 24/12/2010.

◈◈◈

ISBN – 978-93-5024-769-3

3 Deposits Repayable by Banks through Equated Monthly Installments: A Proposal for an Innovative Product and its Potentiality Study

Dr. V. S. Mangnale, Prof. D.B. Bhoite, Prof. S. S. Khandal & Ms. Asha Bajaj
Sinhgad Institute of Business Management, Kamlapur.

Introduction

The proposed deposit scheme is based on the popular concept of annuity. The term Annuity is used to describe a series of periodic flows of equal amounts which can be either receipts or Payments. Such flows will be in form of receipts coming to the depositors as repayment of their deposits with interest so far as the proposed deposit scheme is concerned. If you have a certain amount of money and you want to place it in a bank, you have only one option to get regular periodic income: place the money for a certain period under a fixed deposit scheme of a bank and get regular interest every month. At the end of the chosen period the principal amount will remain intact. You can again renew the deposit and continue to get interest leaving the principal amount intact. This can happen till the end of your life time but ironically the fact remains that you will never be able to use the principal amount which after your death would go into the hands of your legal heirs. You do not use the principal amount because that will reduce your deposit amount and you will get lesser regular income that is interest. Is it possible to use the principal amount even during the life time without sacrificing the interest otherwise receivable? The proposed scheme comes with an affirmative answer. As known to every one, the Equated Monthly Installment (EMI) in the context of any bank loan recovers from you not only the interest part of the loan but also the principal amount on pro-rata basis over a period of time leaving zero balance at the end of the period. Here in the context of proposed deposit scheme you are recovering not only the interest from the bank but also a part of the principal amount of deposit every month. This means higher liquidity in your hands. Of course, at the end of the life you will have zero balance in your deposit account. But does it matter? To find an answer to this question first it would be interesting to compare the proposed deposit scheme with the Reverse Mortgage Loan Scheme as there are certain commonalities.

Comparison with the Reverse Mortgage Loan Scheme

The Reverse Mortgage loan scheme introduced by many banks following the proclamation of the government in the 2007- Budget of its desire to have the scheme taken up by the Indian banks and as we know now, the Reverse Mortgage Loan Scheme is a loan against own house given to a senior citizen, he can continue to occupy the house through out his life and use the borrowed money coming his way from the banks in form of regular monthly cash flows for maintaining his standard of living without botheration of repaying the loan or interest any time during his life time. The bank will recover the loan with interest only after his death or the death of the last surviving spouse by selling the house. This is a broad idea about the Reverse Mortgage Loan scheme (Ruparelia M.V.2008).

The acceptance of the loan scheme largely depends upon whether a person possesses emotional attachment with the home and the kids and whether he has the traditional Indian mentality to leave a legacy behind him for the kids. If there is no such attachment and the mentality, it would also matter whether the kids would come in the way of making a decision to take the loan by mortgaging the house. Again, we have to see as to what extent the fast erosion in the social values and how the kids are treating the parents in the modern times have a changing impact on the traditional mentality. Since the acceptance of the proposed deposit scheme is also likely to be influenced by almost similar factors a comparison of both products has been considered as useful to clear these points. It may not be out of place to mention here that the findings from survey on potentiality study of the Reverse Mortgage Loan Scheme were quite in favour of success of the scheme in form of viable number of people likely to accept the same. There may be some additional features coming to fore once we start thinking more about the proposed deposit scheme. We will have to take an overall view. But before we talk about the other implications let us start first with the comparison. Both the schemes are basically aimed at enhancing the purchasing power of a senior citizen with the use of some asset on the premise that the asset in each case is no longer useful to him after his death and any additional liquidity that can be generated during one's life time is certainly beneficial.

The apprehended obstacles in acceptability of the Reverse Mortgage Loan Scheme are discussed above. While some of the obstacles apply also to the proposed deposit scheme, whether the degree of attachment to home is equal to the attachment to other own assets like bank deposit is a question. The author feels that the Indians' emotional attachment to home, may be greater than the attachment to any other asset. If this sounds true, the things go more in favour of the deposit scheme getting accepted by many people including even the homeowners who might reject the reverse Mortgage Loan Scheme due to their strong emotional attachment to home.

Another obstacle which was apprehended in respect of Reverse Mortgage Loan Scheme was: what would happen, if the senior citizen outlives the loan period. Although, the scheme promised to allow the senior citizen to continue to occupy the house till death of both the spouses, the monthly regular inflow would be discontinued. This feature is also applicable in case of the proposed deposit scheme. We shall discuss this later when we critically analyze all the features of the scheme. One remarkable feature which can also be drawn from the comparison is that a person is not averse to the Reverse Mortgage loan Scheme but he cannot accept it simply because he does not have any home of his own. This individual having some amount of savings will have no difficulty in readily availing the proposed deposit scheme.

Both the schemes generally come without the obstacles discussed above to the senior citizens who are unmarried, divorcees/married but having no issue, having male/female kids not needing/interested in parents' property. This is so because of irrelevance of the issues pertaining to attachment to home or other assets after death, leaving a legacy for the kids or likely interference of the kids. (Madhu T 2009).

Comparison with Existing Pension Schemes

None of the existing pension schemes have the features is matching with the proposed deposit scheme. It can be explained as under representatively.

1. Jeevan Suraksha (Lakhotia & Subash Lakhotia) Pension continues to the legal heirs. Hence it does not repay principle like EMI.
2. ICICI Pru forever Life: The maximum entry level age is 55. The purchase price is returnable to the legal heir. Hence it does not repay principle in EMI.

3. UTI Retirement Benefit Plan is a mutual fund scheme and does not match with the features of the proposed deposit scheme. The maximum entry level age is 58.
4. Jeevan Dhara and Jeevan Akshay (LIC): The corpus is passed on to the nominee after death. Hence it, too, does not repay principle like EMI.
5. Kothari Pioneer's Pension Plan: The corpus is kept intact. Hence it does not entail EMI-based payment.

The Advantages of the Proposed Deposit Scheme

It would be useful to enumerate the likely benefits that can be derived from the scheme. These can be enlisted as under with little repetition to have full list of benefits presented at one go.

1. The scheme will enhance the purchasing power of the senior citizen to combat the ever rising inflation, with no matching increase in the interest rates.
2. The scheme will instill a sense of security as financial security has a considerable bearing on the overall security concerns.
3. The homeless people who could not accept the Reverse Mortgage loan scheme would find an alternative solution available.
4. The people who may not accept the Reverse Mortgage loan Scheme because of the strong traditional attachment to own home may not have problem to accept this scheme as the other assets like deposits may not fall in the category of the same degree of strong emotional attachment as in the case of home.
5. Some people may not accept the Reverse mortgage loan scheme due to the strong emotional attachment with own home. However some of them may not be able to actually stay in their own home. They may have to compulsorily stay together with the kids settled at some other place because maintaining two establishments may not be possible for the kids. These senior citizens may have a strong feeling to go back to their original place where they lived throughout their life if some alternative source of income is available. The proposed deposit scheme offers this.
6. The above advantage is also applicable to homeless people staying elsewhere with the kids. Although they cannot dream of staying in an own house at original place but can at least fulfill the dream to stay at 'own' town (may be in a rented house) with the help of additional liquidity coming their way through the deposit scheme.
7. The class comprising of unmarried people, people with no issue and people with issue but kids not interested/needing anything from parents will find no problem in accepting the scheme unless there are some other reasons discussed later on.
8. The people who do not want to pass on anything to the kids because of latter's ill treatment may accept the scheme with no problem.
9. The people can get additional liquidity to the extent ranging from 15% to 61% depending upon their estimated residual life span as explained in Appendix 1 to this article which is based on presumption of interest rate of 10% p.a.
10. Despite the socio-economic obstacles in the Reverse Mortgage Loan Scheme, the survey came out with viable number of people in its favour. The obstacles having commonality with the proposed deposit scheme cannot deter the same from having equally viable number or even larger than that.

Likely Effects of Outliving on Adopting the Proposed Deposit Scheme and the Proposed Solutions

The calculations in the table appearing at Appendix I is based on the deposit term chosen by an individual. This choice will depend on the expected residual life span in each case. The senior citizens in the age group of

80-90 years may choose a 5 years term. The people in the 75-80 years age group may choose a 10 years term. Those in the age group of 70-75 years may go for 15 years term. The people in the still lower age group may go for a term of 20 years or more. Longer the term, lesser will be the amount of EMI. Of course, whatever term is chosen, the EMI will always be bigger than mere interest Life expectancy of an Indian citizen was just over 40 years in 1947. Today it is 64 years. But this is a general average. A particular individual may live more than that. If the assessment for the expected residual life-span differs when it comes to reality and the person outlives the deposit term, he would be left with zero balance of deposit before death and the EMIs would stop coming his way. The similar problem can be visualized in respect of Reverse mortgage scheme, too. But looking to the popularity of the said scheme in the western countries it appears that the careful choice of the term and some additional protective measures can eliminate the problem in respect of the deposit scheme, too.

The possible solution to this problem in respect of the proposed deposit scheme can also be adding some reasonable cushion to one's expected mortality level and placing the deposit for a little longer period. Here, monthly annuity may go little lower than the one shown in the table. Again, it is certain that it will be always more than mere interest.

The choice of the term can be made only after seeking opinion of the medical experts. Even the medical advice may not be 100% accurate. The risk of surviving can be mitigated by making it a subject matter of insurance. The insurance company can play a vital role to offer a foolproof protection. It can become a viable insurance product considering that Insurance co. may have to pay in few particular cases as against large no. of cases which will fall in the zone of average longevity period. If the government can see the scheme as an effective social security measure, it can play a constructive role in respect of the last two suggestions. The government can also consider how the interest rates can be protected to ensure only positive and no negative impact of the interest rate fluctuations on the amount of EMI.

The Need and Objectives

Although the likely benefits of the scheme are discussed at length, how the people would weigh them in the context of the perceived problems was considered a subject matter of a survey. The success or failure of the scheme in emerging as acceptable depends upon the size and scale of the problems. The best way to ascertain the same was to go to the senior citizens, ask them and find the facts. The survey was conducted with the following objectives.

1. To estimate the magnitude of the senior citizens to whom the scheme can be prima facie beneficial.
2. To carve out the percentage of the people (out of the likely beneficiaries) who may actually opt for the scheme without any self-generated or external obstacles.
3. To derive conclusion about the potentiality of the scheme.
4. To put forth rational recommendations.

The Methodology and Limitations of the Survey

1. A questionnaire based sample survey of 200 senior citizens in Solapur, Maharashtra after getting the questionnaire validated by first conducting a pilot survey of 25 senior citizens belonging to different socioeconomic class.
2. Since the target location of the survey was city of Solapur, the Solapur-specific features may, to an extent, dilute the objectivity of the findings.
3. To minimize the impact of the above mentioned limitation the samples were chosen from different localities in proportion to their relative weightage in the total population of Solapur. This was aimed at minimizing at least any area-specific impact on the findings.

Findings

1. Basic Information

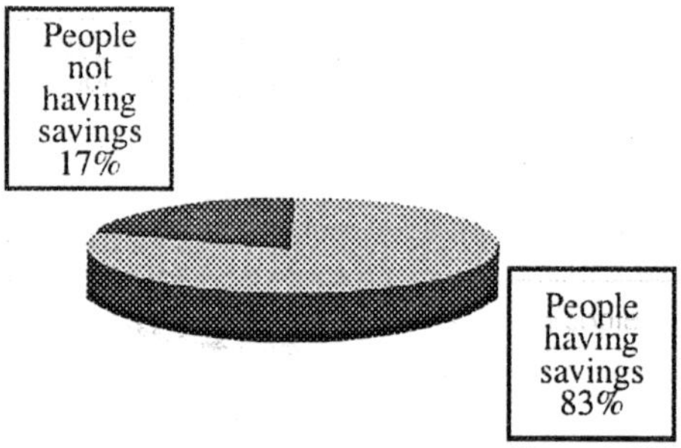

- 83% people were having savings.
- 17% people were having no savings and hence not considered relevant for the purpose

Fig. 1 : Status of Savings

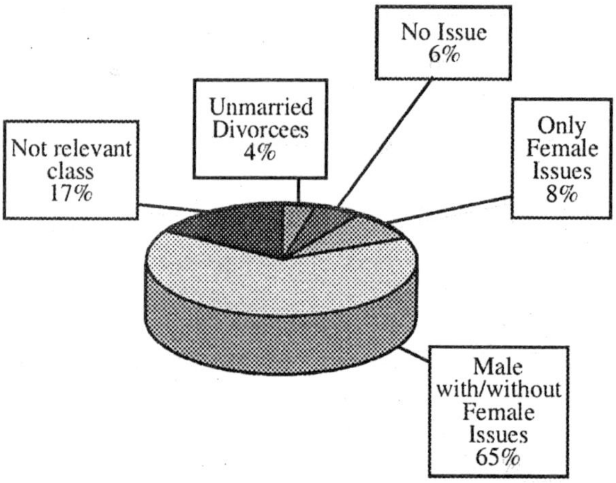

Divorcees
6% People having no issue
8% People having only female issues
65% People were having only male male + female issues.
17% People were not eligible and hence ignored.
This classification was later on useful to ascertain the percentage of people who were dependent only on their own income/only on kids' contribution/ both/living with kids spending for the parents. It was also useful to analyze which class responds how

Fig. 2 : Status Regarding Kids

4% senior citizens unmarried

2. Need Identification

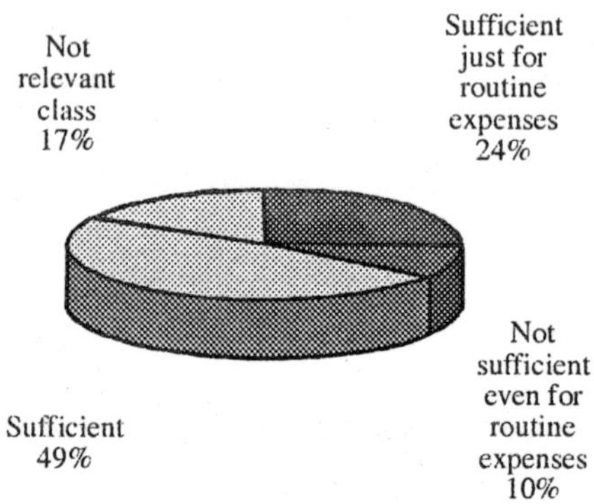

aimed at providing additional purchasing power to supplement the resources presently available with the senior citizens need analysis was done on that line.
-24% people said that they had funds enough just to meet bare minimum expenses for living but not for any comfort, entertainment or contingencies.
-10% people informed having funds insufficient even to meet routine expenses
49% people said that they were happy with their present financial status.
17% people: Not eligible for the scheme.
The 34% (24+10) people were identified as potential beneficiaries,
49% people who said they were happy with the present standard of living were further analyzed as follows.

Fig. 3 : Present Resources Position

Since the proposed scheme is basically

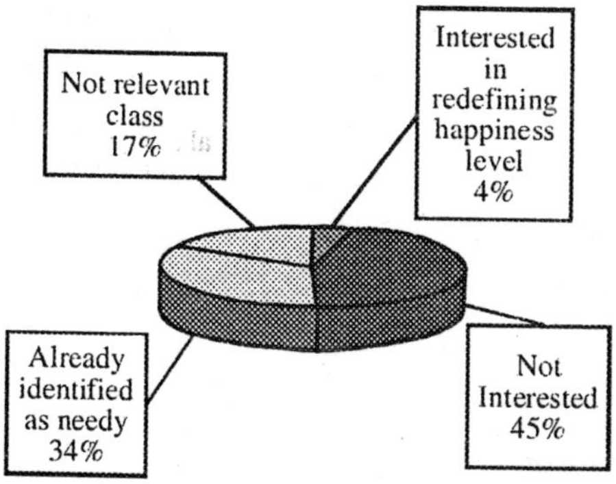

a self-complacently perceived happiness level. But when asked whether they could think of raising their standard of living further, had they even more resources e.g. they can employ some workers to help them in domestic affairs or cooking, use auto rickshaw to go to temples etc.; 4% of them showed interest. Thus total percentage of likely beneficiaries got increased from 34% to 38% The remaining 45% self-proclaimed happy people were put to further analysis as under

Fig. 4 : Desire to upgrade Living Standard

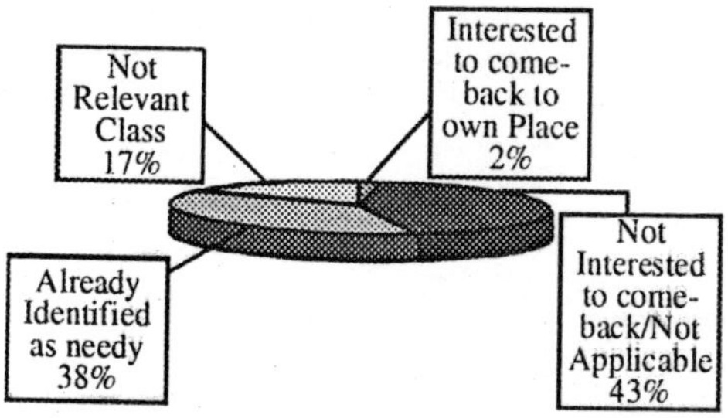

Out of the above mentioned 45% people, there may be people not staying at their original place in own home but with kids at some other place due to the reason that their kids can not manage double establishments but can manage well, if parents go to stay with them. These senior citizens may not have financial problems but they may not be comfortable with the climate of the new place or with the climate of the new place or with the life style of the young generation or may be having emotional attachment with the original place where they lived throughout their life-time. When asked whether they would like to back to own home. If they find an attractive source of finance 2% of them showed interest. Thus total percentage of likely beneficiaries got increased to 40%. This was the ultimate picture emerging out of the need analysis.

But the big question was: Whether all these 40% people will really opt for the schemes? What about the apprehensions like strong mentality to leave a legacy, no-risk mentality at old age and likely interference from kids? So we put all these likely beneficiaries through filtration process based on likely obstacles

Fig. 5 : Socio-Economic Need : Home-coming

3. Obstacles in Decision Making

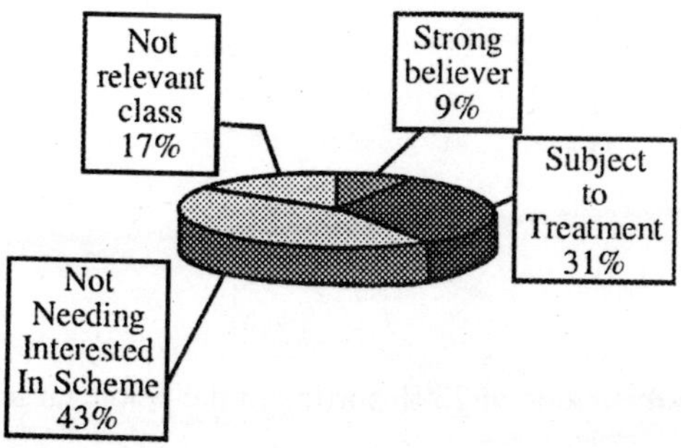

The first filtration process was pertaining to mentality to leave a legacy behind

The survey reveled that out of 40% people, 9% people may be benefitted by the scheme but will not opt because of this reason.

The remaining 31% people were put to a second test pertaining to perceived complications in the scheme.

Fig. 6 : Mentality to Leave Legacy

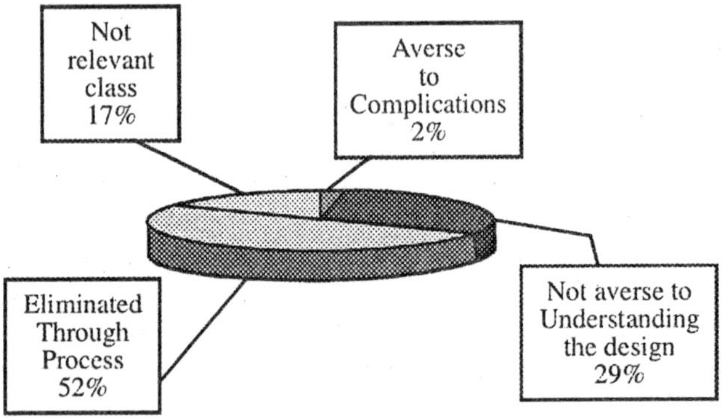

emerging as above, there were 2% people reluctant to opt for the scheme as they found the product complicated, reducing the percentage of potential takers to 29%. These 29% were put to one last test as under

Fig. 7 : Perceived Complication

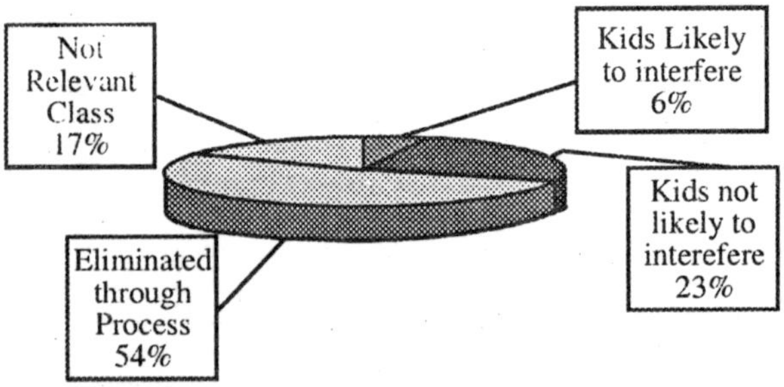

As you can see here out of the balance potential takers comprising of 29% of the people , 6% people apprehended kids' interference and only 23% people were found to be representing the ultimate firm potential takers so far as present scenario is concerned.

Fig. 8 : Likelihood of Kid's Interference

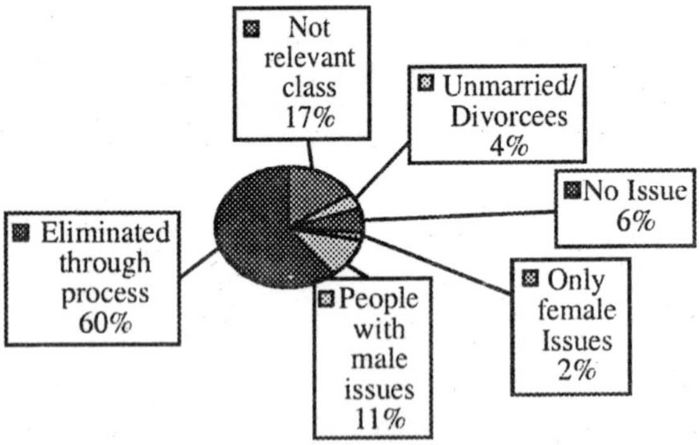

If we look at the composition of the likely optees of the scheme we find that 50% of them are from unmarried, divorcees, people with no issues and people with only female issues. The remaining 50% people are from people with usual features.

Fig. 9 : Who are They?

Conclusion

The basic Scope of the Scheme –

1. The groups containing almost confirmed takers form total of 23 % portion of the whole target group, which is not a negligible figure to start with.
2. There is a scope to market this scheme in India considering the viability emanating from the magnitude of the potential optees.

The Scope in Future –

1. There is a group of people who need additional fund inflow but do not opt now because of reasons like desire to leave a legacy, no risk mentality or anticipated disinclination from kids etc. The needy people having kids but ill-treated are likely to have a second thought and become strong contenders of the scheme. This is a class which offers hidden potential in the medium to long run.
2. It is a human tendency not to accept any new thing immediately but to change the mind set over a period of time after watching others enjoying fruits of that thing.

Recommendations and Suggestions

The proposed deposit Scheme offers sufficient scope in India for the present to be taken up as a viable product by the banks, which can see enlarged scope in medium to long term. For this creation of sufficient awareness among the people and fine tuning the terms of the scheme to suit both the ends are the major initiatives required to be taken by the government and banks.

The proposed scheme should be seen as an important social security measure and when it is a matter of striking a balance between feasibility/viability and social security, the government should take necessary supportive and motivational measures like insuring the risk as to timing of death in a specific time-slot to ensure additional protection in case of depositor outliving the deposit term.

The Senior Citizens' forums in India can play a constructive role in creating awareness among the people about the benefits of the scheme as also arranging for some medical consultancy services to help the senior citizens choose a right term and adequate cushion. They can also follow up with the government for relevant issues like insurance and interest rates.

References

Government Website, viewed 1st March 2007 <http://www.cbec.gov.in/budget0708/speech-e.htm>

Indian Banks' Association official website page of support services, viewed 20th February, 2009 <http:www.iba.org.in/Mon_Inc_Dep_disc_inter.asp>

Lakhotia & Subhash Lakhotia "Jeevan Suraksha-Personal Pension Scheme" Wednesday, 04 December, 2002,

18:16 Last Updated: Wednesday, 14 May, 2003, 20:18, viewed 25th February 2009 <http://sify.com/finance/

tax/fullstory.php?id=12190721>

Madhu T, "Sunset Funds - A regular income on your retirement, and more tax savings", viewed 25th February

2009http://www.outlookmoney.com/olmnew/article.aspx?sid =6&cid=30&articleid=705>

Official webpage of LIC: Scheme Details on Jeevan Akshay –III, viewed 28th February 2009 < http://www.licindia.com/pension_plans_002_features.htm>

Official webpage of LIC: Scheme Details on Jeevan New Jeevan Dhara-I, viewed 28th February 2009 <http://

www.licindia.com/pension_plans_004_features.htm>

Vipin Desai, Journal of Management / December 2009.

Ruparelia,M.V., "Reverse Mortgage Loan by M.V.Ruparelia", viewed 1st February 2008 < http://mvrup.rediffiland. com/scripts/ xanadu_diary_view.php?postId=1187852589>

Khan M.Y., "Indian Financial System", < http://www.mhhe.com/khanifs>

Financial Markets and Financial Services, Vasant Desai.

◈◈◈

ISBN – 978-93-5024-769-3

4 New Criteria for Marketing Segmentation and Differentiation: An Expedient in the Competitive Era

Asmita G. Patwe & Prashant B. Wagh
Matrix School of Management Studies.

Introduction

"The greatest opportunity for creating competitive advantage often comes from new ways of segmenting, because a firm can meet buyer needs better than Competitors or improve its relative cost position" By Porter

There is no traditional recipe for choosing the variables to be utilized while segmenting. Identifying & picking up the right segmentation variables is among the most creative parts of the Segmentation process, because it provides conceiving parameters along which products are designed or differed.

The traditional segmentation bases do not provide the best way to segment markets. Most crucial segmentation parameters to marketing objectives are differences in buyer attitudes, motivations, values, usage patterns, aesthetic preferences, and extent of susceptibility. In today's volatile & furiously competitive market a method of analysis that cuts through the general details revealed by the market research is very important to focus sharply on new opportunities. It is believed from old times that discovery of the most useful ways of segmenting a market produces the beginnings of a sound marketing strategy.

Today, market segmentation is no more based upon the routine segmentation bases but one also has to consider catching the first sign of a major trend in a swiftly changing market and thus gain sufficient time to prepare to take advantage of it & also understanding otherwise seemingly meaningless demographic market information and apply it in innovative and effective ways.

What is Segmentation?

To state the meaning of market segmentation, it is a process of defining and sub-dividing a large heterogeneous market into clearly identifiable, smaller & homogeneous markets having similar needs, wants, or demand characteristics. Its objective is to design a marketing mix that precisely matches the expectations of customers in the targeted segment.

Purpose of market segmentation is the concentration of marketing efforts & forces only on the optimally profitable sub-markets to gain competitive advantage. The main purpose of segmenting a market is to allow a market or sales program to focus on the prospects that are most likely to purchase the products or services on offer. If it is done properly it ensures that the best return for the marketing expense is outlaid. There are definite differences and these depend on whether you are selling to individual consumers or to business customers.

Traditionally, market segmentation-strategies are based on four basic criterion **(a)** Demographic- using variables such as age, race, sex, income, occupation, education, geographic location, household status etc., **(b)** Psychographic, **(c)** Geographical differences and **(d)** Behavioral.

Changes in the Air: Why We Need New Criterion for Market Segmentation

Since a long time we are using the above mentioned segmentation bases, but now the situation is changing and marketers require some new tool to attain the competitive advantage in today's era.

The criterion, on which the conventional segmenting methods are based on, shows its roots in the distant past, and in the evolution of our civilization. In the traditional societies, characterized by bigoted adherence to a viewpoint, the people were highly influenced by their affiliations. Their gender, nationality, religion (tribe/race), socio-economic status, profession, and age group had greater impact on their behavioural pattern than today. There were clear group basis fundamentals pertaining to manifestation, general manners and particularly utilization or consumption. Then, back in those days, if you knew one facet of a particular group, you could quite easily presume the others.

But all this has transformed. People are becoming steadily more individualistic, and less definable. A survey conducted by me & my colleague revealed a fascinating results. The 100 respondents when studied bases demographic information did not show a typical preference pattern & shown contradicting opinions as well as choices.

The research was conducted on Consumer preferences while buying a new mobile handset.

The research result leads to a conclusion that there is a need to revise & review the segmentation bases & techniques. While segmenting we can not go on individual level, study each & every individual & then customize products for them. This is practically not possible for all product categories.

The details of the research conducted are discussed below.

Hypothesis: Demographic segment do not show identical consumer preferences.

Research Methodology

Type of research: It is a strategic marketing research, conducted using exploratory research techniques.

Sampling plan: Sample drawn using 3 distinct demographic parameters wiz educational qualification, income groups & age group. The sample was collected from employees of 3 different management institutes in Pune.

Sample size: 100 respondents

Sampling method: Non-probability sampling

Data: Primary Data

Data collection method: Survey

Data collection instrument: Questionnaire with close ended question

Research Limitation: Time constraint was the major difficulty while conducting this research. It posed the following situations which appeared to be the foremost.

Limitations for the Research

1. Smaller sample size.
2. Less personal interaction may have resulted into confused responses.
3. Consumers & respondents whom the research are carried out behave artificially when they are aware that their attitudes, beliefs, views etc are observed
4. Strategic market research is not a exact science though it uses the techniques of science, thus the results & conclusions draw upon by using MR are not very accurate.
5. The research conclusions cannot be verified. The reproduction of same project on the same class of respondents can give different results.

Data Analysis

Consumer Preferences Vs. Positions held in Occupation

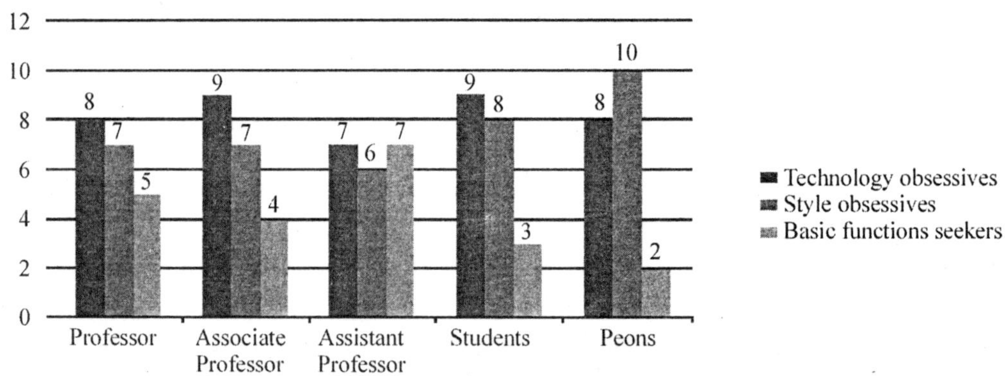

The data analysis indicates that no consumer preference can be correlated to the positions of the respondents, as there is a negligible difference between people opting for a particular product feature over other.

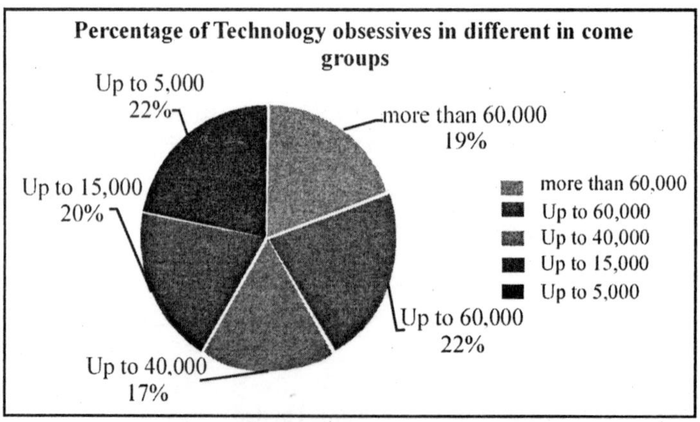

If we consider that recent & upgraded technology comes with a high price, the above graph shatters the concept of targeting high income group people with such products . As we can see that 22 % of people from the group- income up to Rs. 5,000 are technology obsessive over other high end income groups.

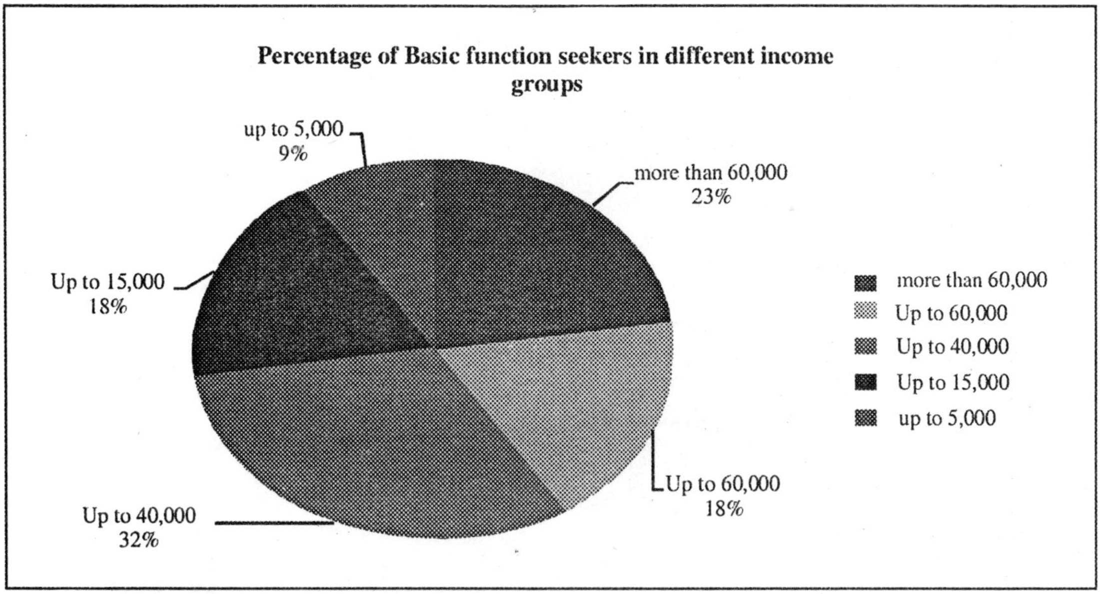

The basic function seekers where in the cost of product remains comparatively lesser than that of product with recent technology or styles. But more number of people from income group- up to 40,000 are not interested in new technology or style but they consider mobile as a source of communication & look for only basic function in their handsets. Now if we refer the graph given below in the income category "income group- up to 40,000" 18 people out of 20, are from age group 26-35 which is suppose to be the techno savy generation than those in the age group 56 & above.

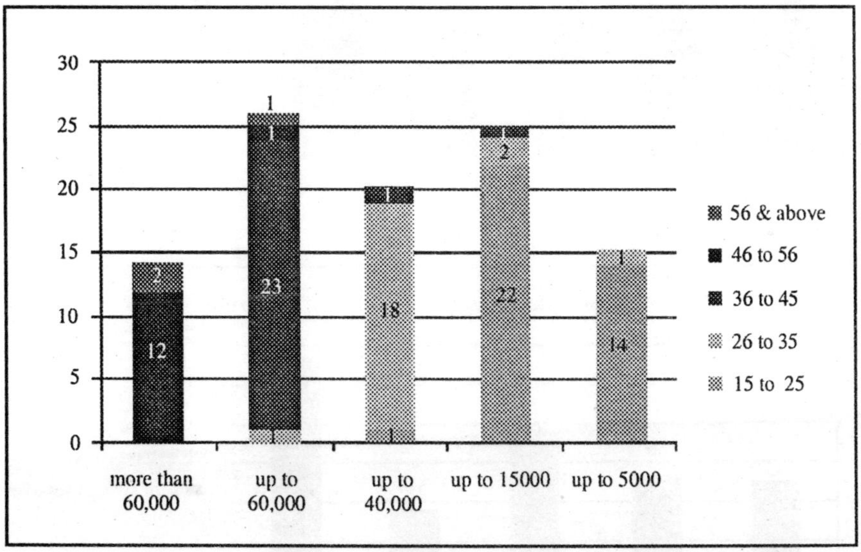

The graph indicates that almost equal number of people from low & middle income group perceive high prices of mobiles as a constraint in purchasing. The difference is very marginal (not more than 5% in all the income groups). Also the lowest income group has the least number of people considering price for not buying a handset.

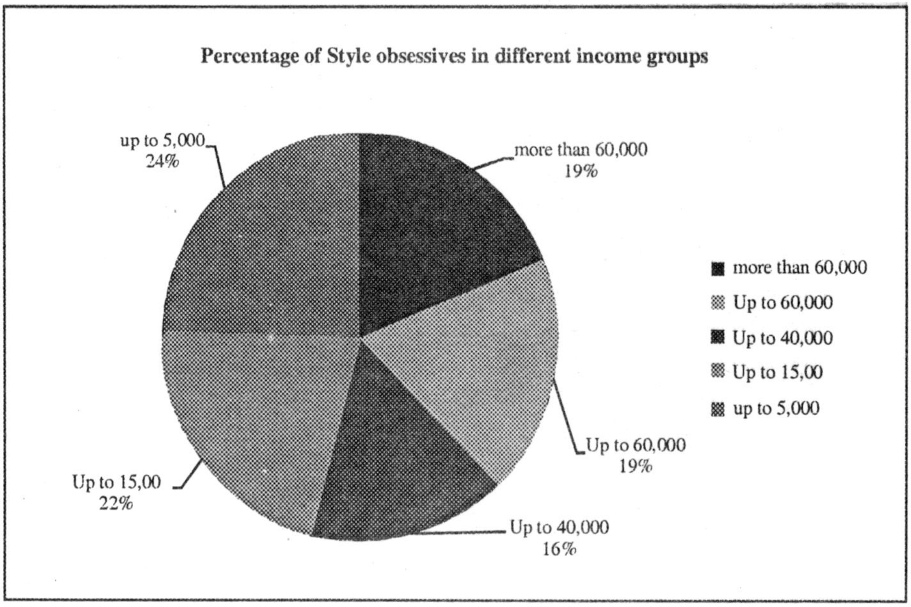
Percentage of Style obsessives in different income groups
up to 5,000 24%
more than 60,000 19%
Up to 60,000 19%
Up to 40,000 16%
Up to 15,00 22%
more than 60,000
Up to 60,000
Up to 40,000
Up to 15,00
up to 5,000

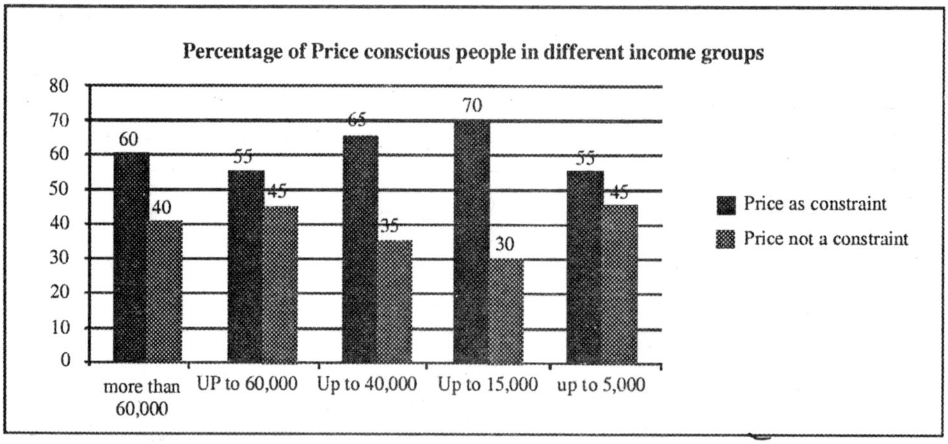
Percentage of Price conscious people in different income groups
80
70
60
50
40
30
20
10
0
60
40
55
45
65
35
70
30
55
45
more than 60,000
UP to 60,000
Up to 40,000
Up to 15,000
up to 5,000
Price as constraint
Price not a constraint

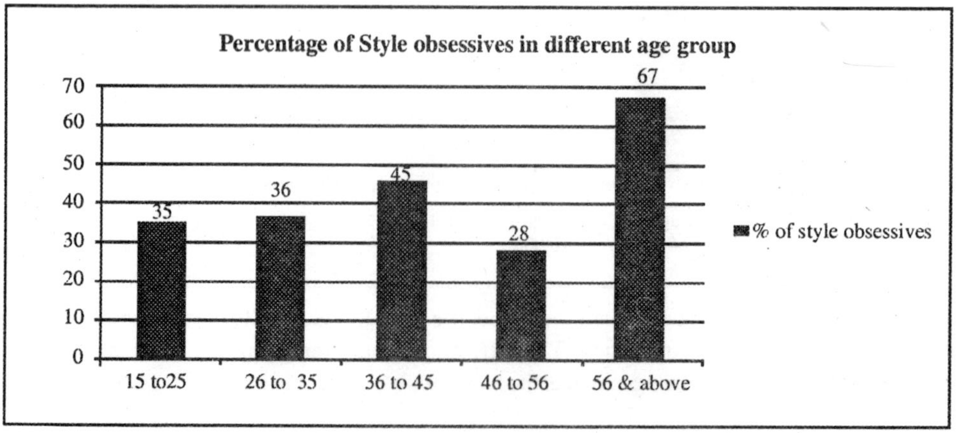
Percentage of Style obsessives in different age group
70
60
50
40
30
20
10
0
35
36
45
28
67
15 to25
26 to 35
36 to 45
46 to 56
56 & above
% of style obsessives

If we say that as a person become older he tends towards simplicity, then it is not true at least in stylish mobile handset as the result indicates.

67% people from age group 56 & above has voted for style as the most important question while purchasing a mobile handset followed by age group 36-45 with 45%

Inference of the Data Analysis:

The data analysis shows that irrespective of the demographic & socio-cultural class, people are opting for high priced, multi-function mobiles with latest technology.

Wide differences in choices & opinions suggests that the trusted segmentation criterion like demographics cannot be used utterly & has to be supported with some new concepts

New Criterion for Market Segmentation

This has generated the demand of drastic change in approach to segmentation & eventually few new are added to the wagon such as-

Price segmentation: It is not a much unknown segment base as price wars has already made it a huge success. In this, customers are grouped according to their sensitivity towards prices. We should not mistake this with segmentation based on income groups.

Distribution segmentation: Yet another quite routine segmentation criterion today is distribution segmentation. Companies using this parameter, sell their product by different brand names through different distribution channels. This is normally used to cater high profile customers using some particular outlets.

Time segmentation: Many people visit stores at a particular time of day or a particular day of week.

Few people are night walkers & shop late than general customers. There are certain stores who serve these Night walkers, remain open later than others. This gives the marketing professionals another idea to use as a segmentation base. Customers can be segmented on the basis of their shopping time.

Fear of losing out: A large group of people which always has a fear in mind of missing out something that others are doing or availing or enjoying. An epidemic has hit world's top MBA programs. Harvard Business School has christened it as FOMO: fear of missing out. The Symptomatic representation include a chronic inability to turn down invitations to any party or dinner, or shopping at a high profile place, buying recent hits (products/technologies/clothe brand and much more) which may give an access to anyone who might be a valuable addition to one's network—no matter the cost.

Living Large: The old saying- You can pretend anything but cannot pretend having money is no more applicable. Today a huge number of people can be categorized as Living Large. People who do not have sufficient income have the want & desire & are spending heavily to fulfill it. This group is contradicting the trusted demographic segmentation base & originating the concept of new criteria for segmentation called as people who want to Live Large.

e.g. today's students are splurging like the high-paid executives they expect to & may become tomorrow. "I wanted to live more comfortably" is there dictum, which is opening a door of enormous opportunity for the marketing professionals.

Media segmentation: This particular criterion is not very widely used. The theme behind is if a particular media is used exclusively for promoting a product, the company can tab the group of people using that media e.g. Radio channel or news papers if used devotedly, people patronized to that media forms a special segment.

This is practiced by the companies that have some control over a media & can discourage competitors from using that media

In addition to the preceding, markets can be segmented by hobbies, by political affiliation, by religion, by special interest groups, by sports team loyalties, by universities attended, and hundreds of other variables. You are only restricted by your imaginations.

Product Differentiation

If the three keys to selling real estate are location, location, location, then the three keys of selling consumer products are differentiation, differentiation, and differentiation.

— Robert Goizueta, former Chairman, Coca-Cola Company

Not only newer criterion for market segmentation is required to sustain in the competitive era but also product differentiation. As the market is flooded with a type of product, a minute differentiation also gives an edge over others.

Differentiation and Segmentation

Differentiation is different from segmentation. Differentiation is concerned with *how* a firm competes – the ways in which it can offer uniqueness to customers. Such uniqueness might relate to consistency (McDonald's), reliability (Federal Express), status (American Express), quality (BMW), and innovation (Sony). Segmentation is concerned with *where* a firm competes in terms of customer groups, localities, and product types. Whereas segmentation is a feature of market structure, differentiation is a strategic choice by a firm.

What Does Product Differentiation Mean?

Differentiation makes a product more striking by its divergent & unique qualities with other competing products. Unbeaten product differentiation creates a competitive advantage for the seller, as customers view these products as unique or superior.

Product differentiation can be accomplished in many ways. It may be a simple packaging change wherein the goods are packed in a creative way, or as sophisticated as incorporating new well-designed features. Sometimes differentiation does not involve changing the product at all, but creating a new advertising campaign or other sales promotions instead.

Product differentiation is a competitive business strategy whereby firms attempt to gain a competitive advantage by increasing the perceived value of their products and services relative to the perceived value of other firm's products and services.

Products sold by two different firms may be exactly the same, but if customers believe the first is more valuable than the second, then the first product has a differentiation advantage. The existence of product differentiation, in the end, is always a matter of customer perception but firms can take a variety of actions to influence these perceptions.

Purpose of Product Differentiation

Incorporate differentiating features that will cause buyers to prefer the company's product/service over the brands of rivals. A firm pursuing such a strategy thus focuses on higher revenues/margins for achieving enhanced economic performance.

The Challenges

Finding ways to differentiate in a way that craft VALUE for buyers and that are difficult to imitate or harmonized by rivals

Differentiation Strategies Firms Can Adopt

The theoretical tool of dealing with diversity or variety is ***product differentiation***.

The differentiation of products can be vertical differentiation, i.e. each product may exist in a number of qualities or horizontal differentiation- product exists in a number of variants of equal quality. Anything a company can do to craft value for buyers represents an impending basis for differentiation.

Being inimitable in the market endow with distinct rewards. In fact, if you do not provide something unique, your business will be ruthlessly challenged. So, it's out of question whether product differentiation is required or not.

One can differentiate ones product based on various ideas .Following are the few-

1. Expediency or timing
2. Product features
3. Linkage between functions
4. Customization as per requirements or trends
5. Product mix
6. Cost recuperation
7. Links with other firms
8. Reputation
9. Product customization
10. Distribution channels

Expediency or Timing

Nobody has time to wait these days. In order to differentiate your product from your competitors', delivery of goods and services precisely when they are needed needs to be considered. Differentiating through delivery of goods or services doesn't always mean being faster than competitors — but exactly on time! If I order long curtains for renovating and redecorating the house, I probably don't want them at the beginner's day of the work. I may need them once I finish with other preliminary tasks such as coloring. If I get them too soon, I block my funds by paying for them or they might get damaged waiting to be dangled. However, I do want them when the time is right for me. The company that can deliver what I need -when I need it will certainly be better positioned to earn my continued business.

Customization as Per Requirements or Trends

When I order those curtains, I don't want just any old prototype. They need to fit flawlessly to my windows, and I want them in the fashion and color pattern that goes best in my house and as per the recent trends.

Customization is an element of product differentiation that cannot be over-emphasized. The more you know about your customers' needs — and the better you do in serving those needs to your customers' satisfaction — the stronger your competitive position will be in the market.

Service-based businesses are particularly capable of customization.

Even with a product-based business, there are still techniques available for individualizing your firm, such as customizing your billings, or special packaging for your best customers.

Product customization is a rapidly growing field for clothing, footwear (ex. sports shoes in school colors), backpacks in the color you want, cosmetics, automobiles, motorcycles, etc.

Product Features

A way in which firms can attempt to influence customer perceptions is to modify the objective chattels of the products or services.

Association Between Functions

To differentiate products, linking the functions within the firm in a non conventional way can be used. E.g. linking the sales and service function in a way that it influences the product sale.

Product Mix

The mix of products or services sold by a firm can be a foundation of product differentiation.

For example, HP discovered in 1960' that its customers were purchasing HP instruments and attaching them with cables made by other firms to computers made by other firms. The value of these instruments, in combination with cables and computers, was greater than the value of instruments, cables and computers sold separately.

A second kind of connection among a mix of products: many customers choose to go to one location to shop at several stores at ones, rather than traveling to a string of locations to shop. This one-stop shopping trim downs commuting time and cost. The value of a number of stores brought together in a meticulous location is greater than the value of those stores if they were one-off.

Cost Recuperation

Cost recuperation does not mean paying the cheapest price. It does mean gaining the highest leverage per rupee spent. It often makes more brains to fritter a little more to acquire a product or service that most closely aligns with your requirements and brings contentment. Too frequently, "I got it cheap" is the consolation prize when you end up with something that really doesn't properly serve your needs

Links with Other Firms

Another basis of product differentiation is linkages between one firm's products and the products or services of other firms. For example, links between credit card companies with car rental firms or Insurance companies.

Reputation

One of the most powerful foundations of product differentiation is the repute of a firm and of its products. Reputation is often very difficult to build up. However, once developed, it tends to last a long time. In the end, the ability of a firm to develop, maintain and improve its reputation depends on customer occurrences with that firm's products and services.

Product Customization

Products are differentiated in the extent to which they are customized for particular function.

Distribution Channels

Products have been differentiated on the basis of nonconventional distribution channels. For example, Coca-Cola distributes its drinks through a network of independent and company-owned bottlers. Coca-Cola manufactures key ingredients for its soft drinks and ships these ingredients to local bottlers, who add carbonated water, package the drinks in cans or bottles, and distribute the final product to soft-drink outlets in given geographic vicinity.

By using above mentioned ways of product differentiation, a firm can adopt a suitable strategy & earn an edge over the competitors.

Conclusion

There is no traditional recipe for choosing the variables to be utilized while segmenting & differentiating. Identifying & picking up the right segmentation variables & perfect differentiation strategy is among the most creative parts of the Segmentation process, because it provides conceiving parameters along which products are designed or differed.

The traditional segmentation bases do not provide the best way to segment markets. Most crucial segmentation parameters to marketing objectives are differences in buyer attitudes, motivations, values, usage patterns, aesthetic preferences, and extent of susceptibility. In today's volatile & furiously competitive market a method of analysis that cuts through the general details revealed by the market research is very important to focus sharply on new opportunities. It is believed from old times that discovery of the most useful ways of segmenting a market produces the beginnings of a sound marketing strategy.

Today, market segmentation is no more based upon the routine segmentation bases but one also has to consider catching the first sign of a major trend in a swiftly changing market and thus gain sufficient time to prepare to take advantage of it & also understanding otherwise seemingly meaningless demographic market information and apply it in innovative and effective ways.

Similarly product differentiation in an innovative way provides a wild card to enter the nontraditional market segments.

Thus, it won't at all be an exaggeration to say that the New Criteria for marketing segmentation and differentiation are an expedient in the competitive era!

Bibliography

1. **Market Segmentation**, Jerry W. Thomas, Decision Analyst- http://www.decisionanalyst.com/publ_art/marketsegmentation.dai

   Strategic Management, Raphael Amit, Professor at Wharton University of Pennsylvania, US.
2. **Strategy formulation and implementation**: Tasks of the General Manager, by Arthur A. Thompson, Jr & A.J. Strickland III, 1992.
3. **Competitive Advantage**, Michael E. Porter, 1985.
4. **Competitive Strategy**, Michael E. Porter (1980) and Thompson & Strickland (1992).

5. **Gaining and Sustaining Competitive Advantage**, Jay. B. Barney, Addison-Wesley, 1997.

6. **Contemporary Strategic Analysis**, Robert M. Grant, 3th edition, Blackwell, 1998.

7. **"A Theory of Human Motivation," Psychological Review 50(1943):** Abraham Maslow.

8. **"God, What a Blunder: The New Coke Story, "December 17, 1993, Michael Bastedo and Angela Davis,** (http://members.lycos.co.uk/thomassheils/newcoke.htm).

9. **Tom Peters,** *op. cit.*: 149.

10. The Japanese Way of Marketing: (New York: HarperBusiness, 1996),Johny K. Johansson and Ikujiro Nonaka, Relentless.

11. Michael E. Porter, *op. cit.*:

12. **"Competitive Industrial,Marketing Strategies," Long Range Planning** (1984), Shiv Mathur.

13. **"Turbulent times for air charters,"** Financial Times (October 21, 2003): 21.

◈◈◈

ISBN – 978-93-5024-769-3

5 "Disclosure of Corporate Governance-Building Investor Protection: Case Studies on INFOSYS Technologies Ltd. and RELIANCE Industries Ltd."

Dr. Yashasvi Rajpara & Prof. (Dr.) Sandip Bhatt
SGM (EM) College of Commerce & Management (SEMCOM), Gujarat.

Introduction

Former World Bank President James Wolfensohn "has equated the importance of the governance of corporations to that of the governance of countries." According to the Organisation for Economic Co-operation and Development ("OECD"), "Corporate governance deals with the rights and responsibilities of a company's management, its board, shareholders and various stakeholders." The spectacular collapses of Enron and WorldCom in the United States, where shareholders lost a combined $245 billion, and the collapse of Italian dairy giant Parmalat in Europe, have transformed corporate governance from an afterthought to the cornerstone of any firm's or country's long-term success.

Corporate governance in a developing-country setting takes on additional importance. Good corporate governance is vital because of its role in attracting foreign investment. The extent of foreign investment, in turn, shapes the prospects for economic growth for many developing countries. This Note presents an in-depth inquiry into corporate governance in one such developing country, India. While India's corporate-governance framework is advanced for a developing country, it still can be significantly improved. Part II discusses the importance of corporate governance for developing countries. Part III provides a brief history of corporate governance in India. Part IV examines the current standards of corporate governance in India. Finally, Part V recommends improvements to India's corporate-governance framework.

The importance on Corporate Governance increased with the result of business scams and failures in the World as well as India. This concept is neither new nor has acquired any novel or special meaning, all of a sudden. It is as old as the corporate themselves. It broadly defines the Scope, responsibility and accountability of the concerned affected by the structure of the corporate entity. It encompasses the relationship of the members of the company inter- se as well as with the outsiders. The impact of globalization of the business has also necessitate the corporate entities to lay emphasis on transparent reporting and to clearly define the role of the financial institutions, non-executive directors, managing directors, chairman, audit committee, relationship of stock exchange and the companies.

Corporate Governance the buzzword today, is tidily becoming a determining factor in investment decision globally. A good Corporate Governance is the key of efficiency in a competitive environment and improvement in the prospects for attaching long term capital by installing confidence in the investors. It is rightly stated by

Basudeb Sen. That "The improvement in Corporate Governance is to serve me shareholders' interest alone because, it is out of the shareholders money that the employees, suppliers and the government will derive the benefits."

Meaning Of Corporate Governance

Corporate governance refers to the mechanism and arrangements employed by financiers - shareholders and lenders, so that their interest is taken care of by the agents who have considerable residual control rights in practice.

Traditionally, corporate governance focused on conflict of interest between managers and owners, i.e the agency problem that arises from the separation of management and finance. But increasingly, several forms of agency problems became recognised. Management may act in their own self-interest, which may lead to corporate failure. Problems were reported at various reputed companies like Enron, WorldCom, Global Crossing, Adelphia and others. This gave birth to the need for formal regulation on corporate governance.

"Corporate Governance is about promoting corporate fairness, transparency and accountability" J. Wolfensohn, President, World Bank

"The fundamental objective of corporate governance is the enhancement of long-term shareholder value while, at the same time, protecting the interests of other stakeholders."

- Kumar Mangalam Committee report on corporate governance, 1999.

Corporate governance represents the value framework, the ethical framework and the moral framework under which business decisions are taken.

Corporate governance therefore calls for three factors:

(a) Transparency in decision-making

(b) Accountability which follows from transparency because responsibilities could be fixed easily for actions taken or not taken, and

(c) The accountability is for the safeguarding the interests of the stakeholders and the investors in the organization. This means the company is fair in its dealings i.e. not involved in unethical practices.

As defined by The Institute of Chartered Accountants of India, Corporate governance is the system by which companies are directed and controlled by the management in the best interest of the stakeholders and others ensuring greater transparency and better and timely financial reporting. The Board of Directors are responsible for governance of their companies.

The system of corporate governance consists of various checks and balances. It also asks for appropriate input into the management of the company.

It deal with questions like how do financiers exercise control over managers, and how do financiers ensure that managers do not steal the resources placed with them, or squander them on uneconomical projects.

More specifically, corporate governance covers issues like the legal rights of the financiers, the role of large investors, the method of electing boards of directors, the composition of the board, the composition of various sub-committees of the board, the appointment of the auditors, the ability of the board to maintain the surveillance, the system of checks and balances instituted over managerial behaviour, the incentives offered to managers to protect financiers from dissipation of capital, the standards of financial reporting and corporate disclosure and so on.

Corporate Governance has different perspective in different economies. The focus of the activities depends on the financial system of the economy. Whatever the definition is, but there is a global consensus about the objective of 'good' corporate governance – maximizing long-term shareholder value. Since shareholders are residual claimants, this objective follows from a premise that, in well performing capital and financial markets, whatever maximizes shareholder value must necessarily maximize corporate prosperity, and best satisfy the claims of creditors, employees, shareholders, and the State.

Need for Corporate Governance

Good corporate governance practices are important to encourage investment in a country. The company in a global economy where access to capital markets is in the interest of economy assumes greater significance. Strong corporate governance is indispensable for growth of capital market and is an important instrument of investor protection. Studies of companies all over have shown that markets and investors do take notice of well managed companies, respond positively to them and reward such companies with higher valuations. Good corporate governance makes to the efficiency of a business enterprise, to the creation of wealth and to the country's economy. The need is for the entire corporate word to follow the principles of corporate governance.

There is need to monitor the functioning of corporate and also guiding the interest of investors and creditors. With increasing awareness and access to information, investors do not depend on regulators to protect them. They are conscious of their rights and strive to maximize their wealth, so does a company. The key differences, with everything else being common, will be the ability to create self driven, self assessed, self regulated organization with a conscience. That ultimate is all about corporate governance in India and elsewhere.

Recently, there have been a large number of scams in the companies of India, involving corers of rupees. They have shaken the investors' confidence in the Indian companies considerably. So much of primary stock market is quit dull and the funds raised by Indian companies from the investors in the primary market have got to lowest ebb. The various aspirant companies are even afraid of raising funds by issuing shares to the public. The need for effective Corporate Governance, as enumerated by Devi Singh, are as follows; Assertion of rights by the shareholders, significant presence of foreign institutional investors who are demanding greater professionalism in the management of Indian corporate, Concern Integration of India with the world economy, which demands that Indian Industry conforms to the standard set of international rules.

Investors primarily consider two variables before making investment decisions—the rate of return on invested capital and the risk associated with the investment. In recent years, the "attractiveness of developing nations" as a destination for foreign capital has increased, partly because of the high likelihood of obtaining robust returns and partly because of the decreasing "attractiveness of developed nations." The lure of achieving a high rate of return, however, does not, by itself, guarantee foreign investment; the attendant risk weighs equally in an investor's decision-making calculus. Good corporate-governance practices reduce this risk by ensuring transparency, accountability, and enforceability in the marketplace.

While strong corporate-governance systems help ensure a country's long-term success, weak systems often lead to serious problems. For example, weak institutions caused, at least in part, the debilitating 1997 East Asian economic crisis. The crisis was characterized by plummeting stock and real-estate prices, as well as a severe erosion of investor confidence. The total indebtedness of the countries affected by the crisis exceeded one-hundred billion dollars. While the presence of a good corporate-governance framework ensures neither stability nor success, it is widely believed that corporate governance can "raise efficiency and growth," especially for countries that rely heavily on stock markets to raise capital.

In an open market, investors choose from a variety of investment vehicles. The existence of a corporate-governance system is likely a part of this decision-making process. In such a scenario, firms that are "more open and transparent," and thus well governed, are more likely to raise capital successfully because investors will have "the information and confidence necessary for them to lend funds directly" to such firms. Moreover, well-governed firms likely will obtain capital more cheaply than firms that have poor corporate-governance practices because investors will require a smaller "risk premium" for investing in well-governed firms.

Also, sound corporate-governance practices enable management to allocate resources more efficiently, which increases the likelihood that investors will obtain a higher rate of return on their investment. Finally, leading indices show that developing countries that have good governance structures consistently outperform developing countries with poor corporate-governance structures. Thus, in an efficient capital market, investors will invest in firms with better corporate-governance frameworks because of the lower risks and the likelihood of higher returns. At a macro level, if firms in developing countries attract investment, they will stimulate growth in the local economy. If they "cannot attract equity capital, they are doomed to remain on a small, inefficient scale," and they will be unable to stimulate growth in their host country.

"With competition raising the bar for survival, it is parameters like corporate governance that will set firms apart" Mr. Kumar Mangalam Birla.

Good corporate governance is the degree to which companies are run in an open and transparent manner. The importance of good governance thus, can be listed as:

1. Reduces the chances of reputational hazards.
2. Helps in attracting talent in terms of non-executive manager directors.
3. Good governance and a disciplined attack to financial controls can reduce the amount of frauds.
4. Leads to reduction in both audit fees and insurance premiums through changing the command outlook of an organisation.
5. Reduces the likelihood of operational dislocation, litigation and fraud arising out of improper evaluation of business hazards and controls.

Corporate Governance in India

Corporate governance reform in India has focused primarily on the "role and composition of the board of directors." Each of the three sets of recommendations (the CII Code recommendations from 1997, The Kumar Mangalam Birla Committee recommendations from 2000, and the Murthy Committee recommendations from 2003) has advanced a more nuanced and sophisticated understanding of corporate governance in this respect. For example, while the CII Code was silent on the financial-literacy levels expected of directors, the Murthy Committee recommended that companies train their "Board members ... in the business model of the company as well as the risk profile of the business parameters of the company." Another notable recommendation of the Murthy Committee was that the Audit Committee be comprised entirely of "financially literate non-executive members with at least one member having accounting or related financial management expertise." The Birla Committee, in contrast, required only that the "majority and chair" of the audit committee be independent and that at least one director be well-versed in finance.

The SEBI laws that took effect on January 1, 2006, are based in part on the Murthy Committee's recommendations and represent a substantial improvement over the laws that previously were in effect. The new laws require that when the "Chairman of the Board is a non-executive director, at least one-third of the Board should [be] comprise[d] of independent directors," and when "[the chairman] is an executive director, at least half of the Board should [be] comprise[d] of independent directors.") The definition of independent directors is sufficiently strict. Further, the law mandates that "two-thirds of the members of [the] audit committee shall be independent directors." Finally, every firm must "submit a quarterly [corporate-governance] compliance report to the stock exchanges."

The new laws are a welcome addition to India's corporate-governance arena and likely will address a number of concerns identified by the Information and Credit Rating Agency ("ICRA"), a Moody's affiliate, in its February 2005 survey of Indian firms. The survey discovered that in ten companies, "independent directors accounted for just twenty-five percent to thirty-three percent of the board strength." The selection of independent directors, in keeping with traditional staffing norms, was largely through friends and relatives. Thus, the boards of directors were not independent in a meaningful sense. The survey also found that the financial literacy of the individuals comprising the audit committees was unsatisfactory. The OECD 2004 Corporate Governance Country Assessment painted a similarly mixed picture—while India's corporate-governance structure met several key requirements, it did not succeed in ensuring participation of institutional investors or safeguarding the rights of minority shareholders. Thus, while the new law that took effect on January 1, 2006 considerably improves prior law, it falls short on a number of key criteria. It creates no official requirement for whistle blower protection, it does not address the problem of institutional-investor apathy in India, and it does not require director retraining, to name just a few shortcomings. The remainder of this Note presents suggestions for enhancing corporate governance in India.

Corporate Governance and Investor Confidence

Corporate governance affects the "portfolio investment climate" i.e. how investors view the risks and returns of investing in companies and in markets. This is very important now when we have global investors investing their money in global markets.

A number of countries across the globe have undergone investor confidence crisis and India is no exception to this. It was in response to various primary and secondary market scams and the investors' confidence crisis that the need to induct global standards was immensely felt. May be the scope of scams might not be mitigated but at least be reduced to the minimum.

Whenever companies fail to follow good corporate practices, minority shareholder are badly affected as they are the weakest segment of the capital market and are rarely able to protect their own interests and investments. It is the issue of global concern today that the average investor should come back to the capital market considering the same as a safer investment option.

Improvements in the quality of financial reporting as well as corporate governance practices would instil investor confidence and trust in the capital market. This is evidenced by the willingness of investors to pay a 'corporate governance premium' for securities of a well-governed company.

An 'Investor Opinion Survey on Corporate Governance' conducted by McKinsey & Co. in June 2000, indicated that more than 80% of the investors were willing to pay a premium for well-governed companies with the premium ranging from 11% to 40% for companies exhibiting high governance standards. In their view a company with good governance would turn in a superior performance over time, which would result in higher valuations.

Corporate Governance at INFOSYS Technologies Ltd.

Mr. Nandan Nilekani, CEO and MD, Infosys Technologies Ltd., said that Infosys is a flat world company. One major change in the business landscape is the new regulatory environment, which is driving greater accountability and transparency.

The Company's Vision is: "To be a globally respected corporation that provides best-of-breed business solutions, leveraging technology, delivered by best-in-class people."

The corporate governance philosophy at Infosys is based on the following principles:

- Satisfy the spirit of the law and not just the letter of the law. Corporate governance standards should go beyond the law.
- Be transparent and maintain a high degree of disclosure levels. When in doubt, disclose.
- Make a clear distinction between personal conveniences and corporate resources.
- Communicate externally, in truthful manner, about how the company is run internally.
- Comply with laws in all the countries in which company operates.
- Have a simple and transparent corporate structure driven solely by business needs.
- Management is the trustee of the shareholders' capital and not the owner.

There is a long list of various awards received by the company. Following is just an indicative list:

- CRISIL and CARE have developed unique models to assess the quality of corporate governance on a sustainable basis. CRISIL assigned "CRISIL GVL Level 1" rating and "CGR 1" rating given by ICRA. The rating indicates the capability of the company to create wealth for all its stakeholders while adopting sound corporate governance practices. Infosys is the first company to be assigned the highest CGR by ICRA.
- Infosys won Silver in the 2006 Vision Awards Annual Report competition of the League of American Communications Professionals LLC (LACP).
- Ranked as the "Business World Most Respected Company" (2007, 2004 and 2001).
- It was rated as **'Best Company to Work for in India 2006'** by BT-Mercer-TNS survey published in 'Business Today'. It was considered as the most admired company for the 6th consecutive year in a survey by Asia Wall Street Journal (2006).
- Infosys topped the regional rankings for best corporate governance in Asia Money's Corporate Governance Poll in 2005.
- Ranked second in corporate governance among 495 emerging companies in a survey conducted by Credit Lyonnais Securities Asia (CLSA) Emerging Markets. It was voted India's best-managed company five years in a row (1996-2000) by the Asia Money poll (2001).
- In 2000, Infosys had been awarded the "National Award for Excellence in Corporate Governance" by the Government of India.
- In 1999, Infosys had been selected as one of Asia's leading companies in the Far Eastern Economic Review's REVIEW 2000 Survey and voted India's most admired company by The Economic Times. It also won the Bombay Stock Exchange's **Corporate Award for excellence** in corporate governance.

"Multinational companies have started studying Infosys as a role model for disclosure. The company gives details about everything related to it under the sun in seven international languages, making it most investor friendly," Ghanshyam Dass, Director (South Asia), NASDAQ, said.

In its presentation on Infosys titled "This is not Fantasy", NASDAQ has pointed out that the company provides segmented information to not only the shareholders and other stakeholders but also customers, clients, suppliers, media and analysts. "Infosys has maintained transparency beyond regulatory reporting requirements," NASDAQ adds.

At the core of Infosys' corporate governance practice is, the Board, which oversees how the management serves and protect the long-term interests of all stakeholders of the company.

Talking about the members on the Board, 8 out of 15, are independent members. Apart from that, further following the mandatory and non-mandatory requirements specified by SEBI in the Code, they have audit, compensation, investor grievance, nominations, and risk management committees, which comprise independent directors.

As a part of the company's commitment to follow global best practices, Infosys complies with the Euro shareholders Corporate Governance Guidelines 2000, and the recommendations of the Conference Board Commission on Public Trust and Private Enterprises in the U.S. The company also adheres to the UN Global Compact Programme.

The annual report of the company includes financial statements, which are presented in substantial compliance with GAAP requirements of various countries and International Financial Reporting Standards. It also comprises reports of substantial compliance with the corporate governance standards of various countries viz. Australia, Canada, France, Germany, Japan and the United Kingdom.

Corporate Governance at RELIANCE Industries Ltd.

The company is meeting the aspirations of all the stakeholders. This is demonstrated in shareholder returns, high credit rating, governance processes and an entrepreneurial, performance focused work environment. The customers of the company have benefited from high quality products delivered at the most competitive prices.

The employee satisfaction is reflected in the stability of the senior management, low attrition across various levels and substantially higher productivity. Above all the company feels honoured to be an integral part of India's social development.

Traditional view of governance as a regulator and compliance requirement has given away to adoption of governance tailored to the specific needs of the company. Clause 49 has set the benchmark compliance rules for a listed company and the baseline for governance standards. Reliance not only adheres to the prescribed corporate practices as per clause 49 but is constantly staying to adopt emerging best practices worldwide. It is the endeavour of the company to achieve higher standards and provide oversight and guidance to management and strategy implementation and risk management and fulfillment of stated goals and objectives.

Corporate Governance has indeed been an integral part of the way the company has done the business for several decades. This emanates form strong belief that strong governance is integral to creating value on a sustainable basis. Since IPOs of 31 years back, the company have grown revenues and net profit Compounded Annual Growth Rate (CAGR) of 28 % and 32 % respectively. The financial markets have endorsed this sterling performance as is reflected in a 38 % CAGR growth in our market capitalization in the past five years. In terms of distributing wealth to shareholders, a part from having a truck record of uninterrupted dividend payout, it have also delivered a consistent unmatched shareholder returns since listing. What epitomizes the impact of all that the company does is fact that the shareholders of the company base has grown from 52,000 after the IPO to around 3.5 million now.

Corporate Governance is a journey for constantly improving sustainable value creation and is an upward moving target. The company has undertaken several initiatives towards maintaining the highest standards.

It is the companies' constant endeavourment to adopt the best governance practices as laid down in international codes of Corporate Governance and as practiced by well known global companies. Some of the best global governance norms put into practice at Reliance include the following:

- The company has designed Lead Independent Director with a definer role.
- All securities related findings filings with Stock Exchange and SEBI are reviewed every quarter by the Shareholders'/Investors Grievance committee of Directors of the company.
- The company has established policies and procedures for corporate communication and disclosures.
- The company has an independent Board committee for matters related to Corporate Governance and Stakeholders' Interface and nomination of Board members.

Conclusion

In the era of globalization and changing scenario of global business, there is considerable debate about what actually constitutes Corporate Governance. The investors in present scenario will not depend on the regulators to protect their interest and will shift their allegiance with those companies which maximize their wealth. Only the better and sound governed and professionally managed companies will be able to attract the investor's money and the momentum of corporate growth and substance, in future, would solely depend on how well a company is being governed. The issue of Corporate Governance has now become a necessity rather than a matter of choice.

Infosys is always known for its investor friendly approach. Not only this it has received various awards and ranked amongst the top in various rankings given by leading magazines / associations. It has been rated as the best company to work with in India, best employer and also pro investor company. It was one of the first companies in India to publish a compliance report on corporate governance, based on the recommendations of a committee constituted by the CII. Infosys maintained a high degree of transparency while disclosing information to stakeholders. It was the first Indian company to comply with USGAAP – long before other Indian companies started practicing. The company's disclosure and corporate governance practices are now being taken up as a role model by companies in the US. Indeed, NASDAQ itself has selected two companies - Infosys Technologies and USA Networks - as the "best value reporters".

Corporate Governance in Reliance Industries Ltd (RIL), RIL believes in adopting the best global practices in the area of Corporate Governance, & follows the principles of fair representation & full disclosures in all its dealings & communications thereby protecting rights and interest of all its stakeholders. RIL recognize the proper communication as a key element of the overall Corporate Governance frame work, and therefore, emphasizes continuous, efficient, & relevant communication to all external constituencies. The company has constitution of Audit committee, comprising four independent, Non- Executive Directors. The constitution of Audit Committee also meets with the requirements under section 292A of the companies Act, 1956.

References

1. Bansal C.L: Boardroom practice in India, (1989) Aditya Books, New Delhi.
2. Ghosh T.P: The Role of Chartered accountant, The three pillars of wisdom, (2000), The Chartered Accountant Aug.
3. Haldia Ashok : Corporate Governance in the year 2000, Frame-work The South Asian Experience, (2000), The Chartered Accountant April.
4. Maheshwari G.C & Sunita Sharma: Independent Directors:What & Why, (2000), Indian Journal of Accounting, Vol. XXXI Dec.
5. S.Sundaram : Corporate Governance Accountability: The Global view. (2000), The Chartered Accountant Aug.

6. Sharma. K. R : Accountants & Corporate Governance. (2000), Need for a paradigm shift Chartered Secretary Nov.
7. T.S. Krishna Murty : Intrview with Krishna Murty on Corporate Governance. (2000), The Chartered Accountant Aug.
8. Dr R.K.Sharma "Accountants and Corporate Governance", (2000), Indian Journal of Accounting, Vol. XXXI.
9. Dr G.L.Dave & Manisha Dave "The Role of Accounting Professionals", (2002), Indian Journal of Accounting, Vol. XXXII.
10. Deepak Gupta & D.D. Meena "Corporate Governance: Strategic issues", (2003), Indian Journal of Accounting, Vol. XXXIV (1).
11. Brijeah Kumar, R.K. Singh and Vinay K. Seivastav "Corporate Governance Practices", (2004), Indian Journal of Accounting, Vol. XXXIV (2).
12. Chakraharty. M "Corporate Governance in India" (2005), ICFAI Journal of Corporate Governance, Vol. IV, No.4, October.
13. Ravi, M "The ownership of Reliance: A case study of corporate practices", (2005),The ICFAI Journal of Corporate Governance, Vol. IV, No.4.
14. Naresh Kumar Corporate Governance: Role of Independent Directors in Indian companies", (2006), The Accounting World.
15. Neetu Parkash "Corporate Governance in Asian Nations", (2007), Indian Journal of Accounting, Vol. XXXV II (2).
16. "Business Ethics and Corporate Governance": Published by ICFAI Center for Management Research
17. "India Today": Vol. XXXIV Number 4; for the week Jan-20-26, 2009.
18. "Indian Management": Volume 48 issue 2, February-2009.
19. "The Chartered Accountant: Volume 56 NO. 01 July 2007, Volume 55 Number 12 June-2007.
20. "Professional Banker": Published by ICFAI Press, issue of April- 2009.
21. "Portfolio Organizer": Published by ICFAI Press, issue of April- 2009.
22. "Chartered Secretary": Vol. XXXIX, issue of January- 2009.
23. "Organizational Management": Vol. XXII Number 4, Jan-Mar-2007.
24. Annual Reports of Reliance Industries Ltd.
25. Annual Reports of Infosys Technologies Ltd.

◇◇◇

ISBN – 978-93-5024-769-3

6

"Consumer Satisfaction in Retail Through Effective Supply Chain Management: A Case Study for Perishable Food Product in Pune"

Nityanand Singh
Research Scholar, Indira Institute of Management (UoP) Thatawade, Pune.

Introduction

The Indian retail sector is highly fragmented with 94% of its business being run by the unorganized retailers like traditional family run mom & Pop and corner stores. The organized retail however, in a very nascent stage but last few years witnessed immense growth by this sector. An analysis by A.T. Kearney reveals that organized retail in India accounts for only 6 % of the total retail market. In 2009, A.T. Kearney's Global Retail Development Index (GRDI), ranked India as the most emerging destination for retail. Today's vibrant consumers are not only apprehensive about price, quality and service but also concern with corporate social responsibility of business which is the area of concern as it contributes as good as 72% loss of perishable food product in terms of quality and 35% wastage in terms of quantity.

A prime disturbing feature of the retailing industry is the lack of proper supply chain perspective. A chain tying-up with a set of exclusive, loyal suppliers and manufacturers for themselves has not really been practiced. Supply chain management of perishable food products are very typical issue which is to be adequately managed to gain the competitive advantage for optimum profit in current scenario by enhancing more value towards consumer satisfaction. Supply chain effectiveness is the tool which can provide a source for enhanced profitability. In today's era of modern marketing where competition is on peak level, supply chain integration is the only way left which not only provides the satisfaction to consumer in terms of price and quality, but also provide an opportunity to reduce cost of product by stopping wastage and also offer reasonable price to the farmer for their produce. This will also helpful in controlling of price fluctuation and inflation.

Objective of The Study

To assess the level of customer satisfaction and value creation through Supply chain management in organized Vs un-organized retail for perishable food product in Pune.

Review of Literature

There are ample of literature available on supply chain management but very little work has been done on supply chain of perishable food product. In this study researcher has tried to gather and extract information on various areas of supply chain as well as retailing and compile them to prepare a base for this research. Demeter & Gelei in their article advocates about the extension of coordination and integration of value creating processes. They also defines that there are three types of SCM models: 1) Transaction dominated 2) Internally integrated & 3) Externally integrated. After analyzing these models in Indian perspective it can be said that Un-organised retail are coming under first models where as organized retail are fulfilling the criteria mentioned in second model (i.e. Internally Integrated) and in some case i.e. partially it also fulfills few criteria of third model (i.e. Externally integrated). Here it is quite relevant to mention that very small numbers of organized retail companies are Externally integrated (For e.g. Wall Mart) whose automatic replenishment system is highly shared by their supplier/manufacturers.

Retailing industry focus on a different aspect of SCM, that is location and logistics issues are more often than transformation. A supply chain can reduce its inventory efficiently redistributing its stock within the supply chain (Davis 1993). The role of supply chain management is seen as important element in the strategy (Fuller *et.al.* 1993). The IT enabled logistics management not only enhanced the quality of product & services but also reduce operating cost, eliminate wastage, optimum utilization of available resources and also able to provide mechanism to collect and store huge amount of data for decision making.

Ajay Dwivedi, director, Crisil Research advocates that less layers and less wastage of food occurs in organized retail.

The majority of middle class Indian consumers are wary of large retail formats with well-stocked shelves (Aggarwal, Singh, 2004). They are considered to have overpriced goods, even though they sell at the government mandate Maximum Retail Price (MRP). Smaller stores often stay open beyond normal working hours and work on low margins because they employ cheap labor and have lower overheads. Such outlets attract customers in large numbers. Also consumers have the notion that large shops spend on promoting themselves and pass on the cost to the consumer. Retail format should be one of the factors which should be taken into consideration since; this is one of the reasons for failure of Wal-Mart in Indonesia (Robert Slator, 2002).

Research Methodology

The descriptive research study carried out which are concerned with describing the characteristics of a retail consumers in terms of supply chain management. Care has been taken during collection of data so that the respondent must have taste and knowledge of both type of retailing to avoid any biased or prejudice comparison of organized and un-organized retail. An optimum sample size of 200 respondents is deemed fit to fulfill the requirements of efficiency, representativeness & reliability data for the purpose of research. In order to collect primary data, a pre-tested structured questionnaire has been used as an instrument. The area of study is restricted to pune and the period of study was Sep-Dec 2010.

Hypothesis Testing with Chi-square Test

This hypothesis testing will verify the objective of research where we have to make assessment of consumer satisfaction and value creation through effective SCM of perishable food product in organized vis-à-vis un-organized retail stores.

In the following section we will analyze the impact of the supply chain management of perishable food products on consumer satisfaction in organized vis-a-vis un-organized retail stores. The questions in consumer segment numbered from B1 to B18 will be analyzed to get the requisite information. We have grouped these questions in four major variable which are considered as important indicators of consumer satisfaction known as customer offering viz product, price, quality and service. Question no. B12 & B15 covers the aspects related to product, Qu B1 & B16 gives information about price, Qu B3 & B6 tales about quality and Qu B2,B4, B5, B7,

B8, B9, B10, B11 & B13 covers various aspects of service, which are considered major factor in retail marketing like ambiance, merchandizing tools like offers, facility to consumer etc. In above mentioned questions, we have enquired about various factors affecting consumer satisfaction and value creation. For this purpose chi-Square test as a test of goodness of fit will be applied which enables us to explain whether or not above named four variable/ attributes are having any significance in enhancement of SCM which will give more satisfaction and value creation for consumer . Here we are interested to know whether four attributes/ variables viz product, price, quality & service are significant for supply chain management of perishable in organized and un-organized retail or not. In this situation we proceed with the null hypothesis that these four attributes (viz product, price, quality & service) are similar in both type of retail system which means that there are no difference in organized and unorganized retail on the basis of above mentioned four attributes and consumers are equally satisfied with their supply chain practices. (Kothari, 2004 pg 236,237).

Null- Hypothesis: (Ho): The product, price, quality & services *i.e. customer offering* are similar in organized and un-organized retail stores.

Alternate Hypothesis: (H1 The product, price, quality & services *i.e. customer offering* are ***not*** similar in organized and un-organized retail stores.

Chi-square test as a test of goodness of fit enables us to see how well does the assumed theoretical distribution fit for the observed data. In order that we may apply the chi-square test as a test of goodness of fit, it is necessary that the observed as well as theoretical or expected frequencies must be grouped in the same way and the theoretical distribution must be adjusted to give the same total frequency as we find in case of observed distribution. The following table depicts the observed data in respect of Investment for up-gradation/ integration in both type of retailing. (Kothari, 2004 pg 237, para-3).

TABLE 1 – Table of Observed Frequency for Customer Offering

Retail System	*Product*	*Price*	*Quality*	*Service*	*Total*
Organized Retail	562	410	485	1870	3327
Un-organized Retail	35	175	51	601	862
Total	597	585	536	2471	4189

Response marked as 'strongly agree' & 'agree' considered in favour of organized retail and given weightage with 2 and 1 respectively.

Response marked as 'Disagree' & 'strongly disagree' considered in favour of un-organized retail given weightage with 1 and 2 respectively.

For Product Qu number B12 & B15 are considered and calculations are as follows:

TABLE 2

QU NO	*ORG RETAIL*			*UN-ORG RETAIL*		
	ST AGR FREQ x 2	AGREE FREQ X 1	TOTAL	DISAGREE FREQ X 1	ST DISAGREE FREQ x 2	TOTAL
B12	108 X 2=216	82 X1=82	298	6 X1=6	4X2=8	12
B15	85X2=170	94X1=94	264	19X1=19	2X2=4	23
			562			35

Shah Janat, "Supply Chain Management: Text and Cases" 2009, Pearson Education, New Delhi, pp249-250

For price Qu number B1 & B16 are considered and calculations are as follows:

TABLE 3

QU NO	*ORG RETAIL*			*UN-ORG RETAIL*		
	ST AGR FREQ x 2	AGREE FREQ X 1	TOTAL	DISAGREE FREQ X 1	ST DISAGREE FREQ x 2	TOTAL
B1	29 X 2=58	59 X 1=59	117	103 X1=103	9X2=18	121
B16	109X2=218	75X1=75	293	16X1=16	19X2=38	54
			410			175

For Quality Qu number B3 & B6 are considered and calculations are as follows:

TABLE 4

QU NO	*ORG RETAIL*			*UN-ORG RETAIL*		
	ST AGR FREQ x 2	AGREE FREQ X 1	TOTAL	DISAGREE FREQ X 1	STR DIS-AGREE FREQ x 2	TOTAL
B3	69 X 2=138	99 X1=99	237	28 X1=28	4X2=8	36
B6	61X2=122	126X1=126	248	11X1=11	2X2=4	15
			485			51

For Services Qu number B2, B4, B5, B7,B8, B9, B10, B11 & B13 are considered and calculations are as follows:

TABLE 5

QU NO	*ORG RETAIL*			*UN-ORG RETAIL*		
	STR AGR FREQ x 2	AGREE FREQ X 1	TOTAL	DISAGREE FREQ X 1	STR DISAGREE FREQ x 2	TOTAL
B2	65X 2=130	108 X1=108	238	23 X1=23	4X2=8	31
B4	76X2=152	99X1=99	251	17X1=17	8X2=16	33
B5	15X2=30	51X1=51	81	99X1=99	35X2=70	169
B7	7X2=14	37X1=37	51	76X1=76	80X2=160	236
B8	82X2=164	92X1=92	256	22X1=22	4X2=8	30
B9	64X2=128	119X1=119	247	13X1=13	4X2=8	21
B10	59X2=118	123X1=123	241	15X1=15	3X2=6	21
B11	95X2=190	76X1=76	266	23X1=23	6X2=12	35
B13	61X2=122	117X1=117	239	19X1=19	3X2=6	25
			1870			601

Now, the expectation from organized retail classifying on the basis of four variable / attributes are as follows:

For product = (3327 x 597) ÷ 4189 = 474.15

For Price = (3327 x 585) ÷ 4189 = 464.62

For Quality = (3327 x 536) ÷ 4189 = 425.70

For Service = (3327 x 2471) ÷ 4189 = 1962.52

Now, the expectation from Un-organized retail classifying on the basis of four variable / attributes are as follows:

For Product = (862 x 597) ÷ 4189 =122.85

For Price = (862 x 585) ÷ 4189 = 120.38

For Quality = (862 x 536) ÷ 4189 = 110.30

For Service = (862 x 2471) ÷ 4189 = 508.48

TABLE 6 – Table Of Expected Frequency For Customer Offering

Group	*Observed Frequency (O ij)*	*Expected Frequency (E ij)*	*O ij - E ij*	*(O ij - E ij)²*	*(Oij - E ij)²/ E ij*
Organized retail preferred by consumer for product	562	474.15	87.85	7717.62	16.28
For Price	410	464.62	-54.62	2983.34	6.42
For Quality	485	425.70	59.30	3516.49	8.26
For Service	1870	1962.52	-92.52	8559.96	4.36
Un-Organized retail preferred by consumer for product	35	122.85	-87.85	7717.62	62.82
For Price	175	120.38	54.62	2983.34	24.78
For Quality	51	110.30	59.30	3516.49	31.88
For Service	601	508.48	92.52	8559.95	16.83

$X^2 = \Sigma(Oij - Eij)^2 / Eij$

$= 171.63$

Since, Degree of freedom = (c-1) (r-1)

= (4 -1)(2 -1) =3

The calculated value of chi- square for three degree of freedom at 5 % level of significance is 7.815.

The calculated value of chi-square is 171.63 is much higher than the table value which means that calculated value can't be said to have arisen just because of chance. It is significant. Hence the hypothesis does not hold good and null hypothesis (H0) is rejected meaning thereby alternate hypothesis (H1) is accepted. This means that the attributes/ variable viz. product, price, quality & service are not similar at organized and un-organized retail stores and therefore preferences of consumer are based on product, price, quality and service offered by organized and un-organized retailers which are integral part of supply chain management.

Data Analysis Through Pearson Product Moment Correlation Coefficient

To analyze the data collected through questionnaire from consumer, we will utilize the Pearson product moment correlation coefficient which helps us to determine the linear correlation between two variables one by one. It means that we will check the relationship of each variable with respect to other individually i.e. occupation, qualification, monthly income, frequency of visit to organized retail/ shopping mall, monthly purchasing of perishable and frequency of purchase of perishable food product.

The Pearson product moment correlation coefficient, r, a dimensionless index that ranges from -1.0 to +1.0 inclusive and reflects the extent of a linear relationship between two data sets.

We will use the correlation analysis tool to examine each pair of measurement variables to determine whether the two measurement variables tend to move together — that is, whether large values of one variable tend to be associated with large values of the other (positive correlation), whether small values of one variable tend to be associated with large values of the other (negative correlation), or whether values of both variables tend to be unrelated (correlation near 0 (zero)).

The formula for the Pearson product moment correlation coefficient, r, is:

$$r = \frac{\Sigma(x - \bar{x})(y -)}{\sqrt{\Sigma(x - \bar{x})^2 \Sigma(y - \bar{y})^2}}$$

where x and y are the sample means average (array1) and average (array2) for two considered variables.

Each array represents the 200 item (as the sample size is 200) corresponding the response marked against respective question in questionnaire. These questions are replicating the demographic information enabling researcher to frame out the consumer behavior pertaining to purchase of perishable in organized as well as un-organized retail stores.

The values assigned for different group of response are as follows:

Qu A 5:	Employee =5	business =4	housewife =3	studying =2	any other =1	
Qu A6	Matriculate=1	graduate=2	post grad =3	prof. edu=4		
Qu A7	up to 10000=1	10k-20k = 2	20k-30k=3	30k-40k=4	40k-50k=5	above 50k=6
Qu A8	Daily =1	Thrice in week = 2	Twice in week = 3	once in week = 4	occasionally = 5	
Qu A9	up to 2000=1	2k-4k=2	4k-6k=3	6k-8k=4	above 8k=5	
Qu A10	Daily=1	Thrice in week=2	Twice in week=3	once in week=4	occasionally=5	

TABLE 7 – Coefficient of Correlation

	Occupation qU.a5	*Qualification qU.a6*	*Montly Income qU a7*	*Frequency of Visit qU a8*	*Monthly Purchasing of Perishable qU a9*	*frequency of purchase of perishable qU a10*
	C1	C2	C3	C4	C5	C6
R1 Occupation	1					
R2 Qualification	0.365311	1				
R3 Montly Income	0.457368	0.494066	1			
R4 Frequency of Visit	-0.06751	-0.20638	-0.24014	1		

R5 Monthly Purchasing of Perishable	0.463113	0.510137	0.698913	-0.27152	1	
R6 Frequency of Purchase of Perishable	-0.00366	0.040012	-0.04149	0.463665	-0.1185	1

In the cell C1R2 the value of r = 0.365311 which is showing the positive correlation between occupation and qualification.

In cell C1R3 the value of r=.457368 which denotes the high degree of positive correlation. It means that the respondent who have higher level of occupation like employee/ business people, have higher level of income in respect of student etc.

In cell C2R3, the value of r is 0.494066 which indicates the positive correlation between qualification and income of respondent i.e. more qualified people are earning more.

In cell C1R4, C2R4 & C3R4, the value of r are -0.06751, -0.20638 & -0.24014 respectively. This indicates the negative correlation between occupation, education, monthly income and frequency of visit to organized retail by which we can infer that the highly educated employed person or business people who falls under high income group, are getting less time in respect to student and housewife to visit organized retail shop for purchasing of perishable due to their busy schedule. This further necessitates the requirement of effective supply chain management in order to enhance quality of product for its optimum utilization and reducing wastage at the same time. This necessity becomes more pulsating as the numbers of working women are rising in society.

In cell C1R5, C2R5, C3R5 & C4R5, the value of r are 0.463113, 0.510137, 0.698913 & -0.27152 respectively. These value of r indicates that monthly purchasing of perishable food products are positively correlated with qualification, occupation and monthly income of respondent but negatively correlated with frequency of visit to retail shop for purchasing of perishable products. This fortifies our objective for providing optimum satisfaction and value creation through supply chain management in the dynamic environment of consumer behavior and speckled taste.

In cell C1R6, C2R6, C3R6, C4R6 & C5R6, the value of r are -0.00366, 0.040012, -0.04149, 0.463665, -0.1185 respectively. By seeing these value we can infer that frequency of purchasing is negatively correlated with occupation but magnitude is quite small. The frequency of purchasing is positively correlated with qualification which shows the consciousness and awareness of consumer towards quality and perishability of food product. The frequency of visit is negatively correlated with monthly income which indicates that high income people doesn't have more time to spent for shopping which compels them to look forward for better packaging and processed food which is an integral part of efficient SCM. The frequency of purchasing of perishable food product is positively correlated with frequency of visit to retail shop but negatively correlated with average total monthly purchasing of perishable product. Therefore we can derive the information that the people who have time (but falls under comparatively lower income group), they are purchasing the perishable food product more frequently where as people of comparatively high income group with less available time for frequent visit to retail shop having more consumption of perishable food product. We can provide more value for such consumer by enhancing SCM of perishable food product with longer durability and self life.

Validation of Objective Through Karl Pearson's Coefficient of Contingency (C)

Karl Pearson has suggested a measure known as coefficient of Mean Square contingency for studying the association in contingency tables of Chi-square (÷²) to study the magnitude of the relation between attributes. (Kothari, 2004 pg 147, 250, para-1).

$$C = \sqrt{\chi^2 /(\chi^2 + N)}$$

Where C = Coefficient of contingency

$$\chi^2 = \Sigma(Oij - Eij)H2 / Eij$$

i.e. chi-square value based on observed and expected frequency

N = Number of items

In our study, we are interested to measure the magnitude of correlation between the two attributes viz., investment plan/ awareness for up-gradation & integration by retailers vis-a-vis effective SCM practices of organized and un-organized retail.

Now, $C = \sqrt{\chi^2 /(\chi^2 + N)}$

$$= \sqrt{171.63/171.63 + 4189}$$

$$= 0.039$$

Here the value of C is showing positive correlation which attest and strengthen our belief that product, price, quality and service (as integral part of SCM) deeply affecting the consumer satisfaction at organized and un-organized retail stores. Therefore, the consumer will attracted towards the retail system which will provide effective supply chain management for perishable food product. It is obvious from the hypothesis testing and derived positive correlation that organized retail are practicing the better SCM and hence offering more value and satisfaction to consumer in comparison to un-organized retail.

Conclusion

Effective supply chain management of perishable food products by retailer is influencing the consumer satisfaction. Today's vibrant consumers are not only apprehensive about price, quality and service but also concern with corporate social responsibility of business in which is the area of concern as it contributes as good as 72% loss of perishable food product in terms of quality and 35% wastage in terms of quantity. Optimum satisfaction and value creation through supply chain management in the dynamic environment of consumer behavior and speckled taste. The requirement of effective supply chain management in order to enhance quality of product for its optimum utilization and reducing wastage is of paramount importance in consumer's mind. The development of efficient supply chain management will certainly helpful for government as it will reduce embracement for government in controlling inflation and price fluctuation, improve credibility of government, reduce wastage, provide better remuneration to farmer and enhance their quality of life and availability of food as basic necessity to general/ poor people.

References

1. Bhattacharya SK, Logistics Management, 2nd Edition-2008, S. Chand.
2. CII – Mckinsey "Indian Retail Environment." (2004), pp. 21- 42.
3. Donald & David, Logistical management, edition 2000, TMH.
4. Dubey & Sai kumar, Supply Chain Management, Inst of Public Entp. Hyd.
5. Ernst & Young, The Great Indian Retail Story, 2006.
6. http://www.msamb.com/english/about/default.htm Maharashtra State Agricultural Marketing Board Schemes.htm.
7. Janat Shah, Supply chain Management, Text and Cases, 2009, Pearson Education pp. 13-20.
8. National Seminar on Logistics &Supply Chain Management, IASMS, BANGALORE, INDIA.
9. Piyush Kumar Sinha & Sanjay Kumar Kar An Insight into the Growth of New Retail Formats in India W.P. No.2007-03-04 March 2007.
10. Proceedings Of The Fourth Asia Pacific Retail Conference *College Of Management, Mahidol University,Bangkok,* Thailand 4th-6th September 2007.
11 Singhal, Arvind (Chairman, KSA Technopak) "Indian Retail: The Road Ahead" www.eretailbiz.com
12. Skill Gap In Logistics Sector, KPMG Report 2007.
13. USTDA Report-2008, Building capacity in Cold Chain Infrastructure.

◈◈◈

ISBN – 978-93-5024-769-3

7 A Study on Master Data Management

Mr. Shishir Goswami
Corporate, IBM.

Introduction

Data is one of the essential and basic elements for Information and knowledge management in organization.

The pain that organizations are experiencing around consistent reporting, regulatory compliance, strong interest in Service-Oriented Architecture (SOA), and Software as a Service (SaaS) has prompted a great deal of interest in Master Data Management (MDM).

Today Master data management solutions providing ample business opportunities across large organization working across different sectors like Banking, Insurance, Supply chain management etc.

Master data can be defined as the information required to create and maintain an enterprise-wide "system of record" for your core business entities, in order to capture business transactions and measure results for these entities. Obviously, this master data spans all organizational business functions.

For example, in the sales, marketing and customer service functions, master data can consist of customer numbers, service codes, warranty information, distribution information and partner information. In the supply chain function, master data might include information on products, item codes and suppliers. In the finance function, master data might include information on cost centers, department codes and company hierarchies. As you can see, master data is really the core data about your company. Despite its importance, master data is often woefully inconsistent across the company. Data values that should uniquely describe entities are often different in different business units. Relationships between entities such as products and suppliers are often defined differently in different information systems. Numerous hierarchies also exist for master data entities. Further, identifiers that are supposed to be unique to each entity are sometimes either used multiple times or used incorrectly.

The sales and marketing functions revolving around the customer are critical to the business, and any enhancement to this capability can be of great value to the organization.

Customer, in the majority of instances, is the most widely used concept across an organization. It crosses several functional lines across most organizations. As a result, the customer function takes a very high priority because quality and integrity of the information cannot be compromised. Any deviations from this principle will result in degradation in the customer experience. Inaccurate information will quickly lead to a loss of confidence in the information. This lack of confidence could eventually lead to an abandonment of the solution or result in increased costs in problem resolution. Either scenario results in a lack of confidence in the solution.

Any MDM program will need to focus on providing greater insight into customer behavior, enhancing the customer experience, the ability to identify patterns around the customer, and opportunities to identify new customers and grow the customer base. Most importantly, the program needs to provide a consistent and reliable source of customer information across the enterprise.

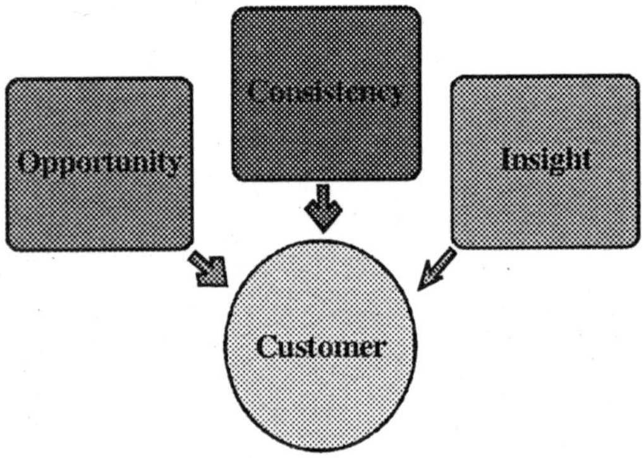

Having identified "customer" as a central theme to the MDM program, let us take a closer look at the various processes and possibilities that exist within the space. Customer, in the majority of instances, is the most widely used concept across an organization. It crosses several functional lines across most organizations. As a result, the customer function takes a very high priority because quality and integrity of the information cannot be compromised. Any deviations from this principle will result in degradation in the customer experience. Inaccurate information will quickly lead to a loss of confidence in the information. This lack of confidence could eventually lead to an abandonment of the solution or result in increased costs in problem resolution. Either scenario results in a lack of confidence in the solution.

Today in a growth driven environment large organizations are having various operations (department) and each operation has its own IT infrastructure or database. This leads to many problems like

- Quality of data
- Consistent classification and identification of data
- Data-reconciliation issues.
- Data redundancy

What is Master Data?

Most software systems have lists of data that are shared and used by several of the applications that make up the system. For example, a typical ERP system as a minimum will have a Customer Master, an Item Master, and an Account Master. This master data is often one of the key assets of a company. It's not unusual for a company to be acquired primarily for access to its Customer Master data.

There are some very well-understood and easily identified master-data items, such as "customer" and "product." In fact, many define master data by simply reciting a commonly agreed upon master-data item list, such as: customer, product, location, employee, and asset. But how you identify elements of data that should be managed by a master-data management system is much more complex and defies such rudimentary definitions.

In fact, there is a lot of confusion around what master data is and how it is qualified, necessitating a more comprehensive treatment.

There are essentially five types of data in corporations:

Unstructured - This is data found in e-mail, white papers like this, magazine articles, corporate intranet portals, product specifications, marketing collateral, and PDF files.

Transactional - This is data related to sales, deliveries, invoices, trouble tickets, claims, and other monetary and non-monetary interactions.

Metadata - This is data about other data and may reside in a formal repository or in various other forms such as XML documents, report definitions, column descriptions in a database, log files, connections, and configuration files.

Hierarchical - Hierarchical data stores the relationships between other data. It may be stored as part of an accounting system or separately as descriptions of real-world relationships, such as company organizational structures or product lines. Hierarchical data is sometimes considered a super MDM domain, because it is critical to understanding and sometimes discovering the relationships between master data.

Master - Master data are the critical nouns of a business and fall generally into four groupings: people, things, places, and concepts. Further categorizations within those groupings are called subject areas, domain areas, or entity types.

For example, within people, there are customer, employee, and salesperson. Within things, there are product, part, store, and asset. Within concepts, there are things like contract, warrantee, and licenses. Finally, within places, there are office locations and geographic divisions. Some of these domain areas may be further divided. Customer may be further segmented, based on incentives and history. A company may have normal customers, as well as premiere and executive customers. Product may be further segmented by sector and industry. The requirements, life cycle, and CRUD cycle for a product in the Consumer Packaged Goods (CPG) sector is likely very different from those of the clothing industry. The granularity of domains is essentially determined by the magnitude of differences between the attributes of the entities within them.

Why Should I Manage Master Data?

Because it is used by multiple applications, an error in master data can cause errors in all the applications that use it. For example, an incorrect address in the customer master might mean orders, bills, and marketing literature are all sent to the wrong address. Similarly, an incorrect price on an item master can be a marketing disaster, and an incorrect account number in an Account Master can lead to huge fines or even jail time for the CEO- a career-limiting move for the person who made the mistake!

Here is a typical master-data horror story: A credit-card customer moves from 2847 North 9th St. to 1001 11th St. North. The customer changed his billing address immediately, but did not receive a bill for several months. One day, the customer received a threatening phone call from the credit-card billing department, asking why the bill has not been paid. The customer verifies that they have the new address, and the billing department verifies that the address on file is 1001 11th St. N. The customer asks for a copy of the bill, to settle the account. After two more weeks without a bill, the customer calls back and finds the account has been turned over to a collection agency. This time, they find out that even though the address in the file was 1001 11th St. N, the billing address is 101 11th St. N. After a bunch of phone calls and letters between lawyers, the bill finally gets resolved and the credit-card company has lost a customer for life. In this case, the master copy of the data was accurate, but another copy of it was flawed. Master data must be both correct *and* consistent.

Even if the master data has no errors, few organizations have just one set of master data. Many companies grow through mergers and acquisitions. Each company you acquire comes with its own customer master, item master, and so forth. This would not be bad if you could just Union the new master data with your current master data, but unless the company you acquire is in a completely different business in a faraway country, there's a very good chance that some customers and products will appear in both sets of master data—usually, with different formats and different database keys. If both companies use the Dun & Bradstreet number or Social Security number as the customer identifier, discovering which customer records are for the same customer is a straightforward issue; but that seldom happens. In most cases, customer numbers and part numbers are assigned by the software that creates the master records, so the chances of the same customer or the same product having the same identifier in both databases is pretty remote. Item masters can be even harder to reconcile, if equivalent parts are purchased from different vendors with different vendor numbers.

Merging master lists together can be very difficult. The same customer may have different names, customer numbers, addresses, and phone numbers in different databases. For example, William Smith might appear as Bill Smith, Wm. Smith, and William Smithe. Normal database joins and searches will not be able to resolve these differences. A very sophisticated tool that understands nicknames, alternate spellings, and typing errors will be required. The tool will probably also have to recognize that different name variations can be resolved, if they all live at the same address or have the same phone number. While creating a clean master list can be a daunting challenge, there are many positive benefits to your bottom line from a common master list:

A single, consolidated bill saves money and improves customer satisfaction.

Sending the same marketing literature to a customer from multiple customer lists wastes money and irritates the customer.

Before you turn a customer account over to a collection agency, it would be good to know if they owe other parts of your company money or, more importantly, that they are another division's biggest customer.

Stocking the same item under different part numbers is not only a waste of money and shelf space, but can potentially lead to artificial shortages.

The recent movements toward SOA and SaaS make Master Data Management a critical issue. For example, if you create a single customer service that communicates through well-defined XML messages, you may think you have defined a single view of your customers. But if the same customer is stored in five databases with three different addresses and four different phone numbers, what will your customer service return? Similarly, if you decide to subscribe to a CRM service provided through SaaS, the service provider will need a list of customers for their database. Which one will you send them?

For all these reasons, maintaining a high-quality, consistent set of master data for your organization is rapidly becoming a necessity. The systems and processes required to maintain this data are known as *Master Data Management.*

What is Master Data Management?

For purposes of this article, we define Master Data Management (MDM) as the technology, tools, and processes required to create and maintain consistent and accurate lists of master data. There are a couple things worth noting in this definition. One is that MDM is not just a technological problem. In many cases, fundamental changes to business process will be required to maintain clean master data, and some of the most difficult MDM issues are more political than technical. The second thing to note is that MDM includes both creating and maintaining master data. Investing a lot of time, money, and effort in creating a clean, consistent set of master data is a wasted effort unless the solution includes tools and processes to keep the master data clean and consistent as it is updated and expanded.

While MDM is most effective when applied to all the master data in an organization, in many cases the risk and expense of an enterprise-wide effort are difficult to justify. It may be easier to start with a few key sources of Master Data and expand the effort, once success has been demonstrated and lessons have been learned. If you do start small, you should include an analysis of all the master data that you might eventually want to include, so you do not make design decisions or tool choices that will force you to start over when you try to incorporate a new data source. For example, if your initial Customer master implementation only includes the 10,000 customers your direct-sales force deals with, you don't want to make design decisions that will preclude adding your 10,000,000 Web customers later.

An MDM project plan will be influenced by requirements, priorities, resource availability, time frame, and the size of the problem. Most MDM projects include at least these phases:

1. **Identify sources of master data.** This step is usually a very revealing exercise. Some companies find they have dozens of databases containing customer data that the IT department did not know existed.
2. **Identify the producers and consumers of the master data.** Which applications produce the master data identified in the first step, and—generally more difficult to determine—which applications use the master data. Depending on the approach you use for maintaining the master data, this step might not be necessary. For example, if all changes are detected and handled at the database level, it probably does not matter where the changes come from.
3. **Collect and analyze metadata about for your master data.** For all the sources identified in step one, what are the entities and attributes of the data, and what do they mean? This should include attribute name, datatype, allowed values, constraints, default values, dependencies, and who owns the definition and maintenance of the data. The owner is the most important and often the hardest to determine. If you have a repository loaded with all your metadata, this step is an easy one. If you have to start from database tables and source code, this could be a significant effort.
4. **Appoint data stewards.** These should be the people with the knowledge of the current source data and the ability to determine how to transform the source into the master-data format. In general, stewards should be appointed from the owners of each master-data source, the architects responsible for the MDM systems, and representatives from the business users of the master data.
5. **Implement a data-governance program and data-governance council.** This group must have the knowledge and authority to make decisions on how the master data is maintained, what it contains, how long it is kept, and how changes are authorized and audited. Hundreds of decisions must be made in the course of a master-data project, and if there is not a well-defined decision-making body and process, the project can fail, because the politics prevent effective decision making.

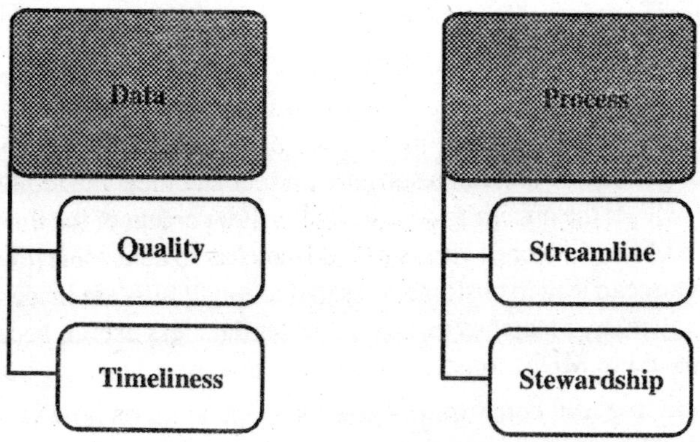

6. **Develop the master-data model.** Decide what the master records look like: what attributes are included, what size and datatype they are, what values are allowed, and so forth. This step should also include the mapping between the master-data model and the current data sources. This is normally both the most important and most difficult step in the process. If you try to make everybody happy by including all the source attributes in the master entity, you often end up with master data that is too complex and cumbersome to be useful. For example, if you cannot decide whether weight should be in pounds or kilograms, one approach would be to include both (WeightLb and WeightKg). While this might make people happy, you are wasting megabytes of storage for numbers that can be calculated in microseconds, as well as running the risk of creating inconsistent data (WeightLb = 5 and WeightKg = 5). While this is a pretty trivial example, a bigger issue would be maintaining multiple part numbers for the same part. As in any committee effort, there will be fights and deals resulting in sub-optimal decisions. It's important to work out the decision process, priorities, and final decision maker in advance, to make sure things run smoothly.
7. **Choose a toolset.** You will need to buy or build tools to create the master lists by cleaning, transforming, and merging the source data. You will also need an infrastructure to use and maintain the master list. These functions are covered in detail later in the paper.
8. You can use a single toolset from a single vendor for all of these functions, or you might want to take a best-of-breed approach. In general, the techniques to clean and merge data are different for different types of data, so there are not a lot of tools that span the whole range of master data.
9. The two main categories of tools are Customer Data Integration (CDI) tools for creating the customer master and Product Information Management (PIM) tools for creating the product master. Some tools will do both, but generally they are better at one or the other.
10. The toolset should also have support for finding and fixing data-quality issues and maintaining versions and hierarchies. Versioning is a critical feature, because understanding the history of a master-data record is vital to maintaining its quality and accuracy over time. For example, if a merge tool combines two records for John Smith in Boston, and you decide there really are two different John Smiths in Boston, you need to know what the records looked like before they were merged, in order to "unmerge" them.
11. **Design the infrastructure.** Once you have clean, consistent master data, you will need to expose it to your applications and provide processes to manage and maintain it. This step is a big-enough issue, I devote a section to it later in the document. When this infrastructure is implemented, you will have a number of applications that will depend on it being available, so reliability and scalability are important considerations to include in your design. In most cases, you will have to implement significant parts of the infrastructure yourself, because it will be designed to fit into your current infrastructure, platforms, and applications.
12. **Generate and test the master data.** This step is where you use the tools you have developed or purchased to merge your source data into your master-data list. This is often an iterative process requiring tinkering with rules and settings to get the matching right. This process also requires a lot of manual inspection to ensure that the results are correct and meet the requirements established for the project. No tool will get the matching done correctly 100 percent of the time, so you will have to weigh the consequences of false matches versus missed matches to determine how to configure the matching tools. False matches can lead to customer dissatisfaction, if bills are inaccurate or the wrong person is arrested. Too many missed matches make the master data less useful, because you are not getting the benefits you invested in MDM to get.
13. **Modify the producing and consuming systems.** Depending on how your MDM implementation is designed, you might have to change the systems that produce, maintain, or consume master data to

work with the new source of master data. If the master data is used in a system separate from the source systems—a data warehouse, for example—the source systems might not have to change. If the source systems are going to use the master data, however, there will likely be changes required. Either the source systems will have to access the new master data or the master data will have to be synchronized with the source systems, so that the source systems have a copy of the cleaned-up master data to use. If it's not possible to change one or more of the source systems, either that source system might not be able to use the master data or the master data will have to be integrated with the source system's database through external processes, such as triggers and SQL commands.

14. The source systems generating new records should be changed to look up existing master record sets before creating new records or updating existing master records. This ensures that the quality of data being generated upstream is good, so that the MDM can function more efficiently and the application itself manages data quality. MDM should be leveraged not only as a system of record, but also as an application that promotes cleaner and more efficient handling of data across all applications in the enterprise. As part of MDM strategy, all three pillars of data management need to be looked into: data origination, data management, and data consumption. It is not possible to have a robust enterprise-level MDM strategy if any one of these aspects is ignored.
15. **Implement the maintenance processes.** As we stated earlier, any MDM implementation must incorporate tools, processes, and people to maintain the quality of the data. All data must have a data steward who is responsible for ensuring the quality of the master data. The data steward is normally a business person who has knowledge of the data, can recognize incorrect data, and has the knowledge and authority to correct the issues. The MDM infrastructure should include tools that help the data steward recognize issues and simplify corrections. A good data-stewardship tool should point out questionable matches that were made—customers with different names and customer numbers that live at the same address, for example. The steward might also want to review items that were added as new, because the match criteria were close but below the threshold. It is important for the data steward to see the history of changes made to the data by the MDM systems, to isolate the source of errors and undo incorrect changes. Maintenance also includes the processes to pull changes and additions into the MDM system, and to distribute the cleansed data to the required places.

As you can see, MDM is a complex process that can go on for a long time. Like most things in software, the key to success is to implement MDM incrementally, so that the business realizes a series of short-term benefits while the complete project is a long-term process. No MDM project can be successful without the support and participation of the business users. IT professionals do not have the domain knowledge to create and maintain high-quality master data. Any MDM project that does not include changes to the processes that create, maintain, and validate master data is likely to fail. The rest of this paper will cover the details of the technology and processes for creating and maintaining master data.

While packaged products are a viable means of quickly implementing a solution, it is worth noting that some products are more customizable than others. This can sometimes limit the optimal implementation of an MDM solution. Most products offer a set of entities related to the customer function, but there needs to be a certain amount of extensibility to the schema. Some products allow for this. Others require numerous configuration changes and limit the ease of use, which is important. These are reasons why some organizations build homegrown solutions to suit their needs.

Examining customer attributes leads to familiar concepts like name, address, segmentation, affiliation, type, etc. Each of these concepts needs to be accommodated for in the model. From this point, the management of the solution is no different from a regular data project. All of the same functions apply to MDM as well. Quality of the information, data load-related challenges, timing, real time versus near real time, high availability, historical data needs, change data capture are all familiar requirements that apply to an MDM solution.

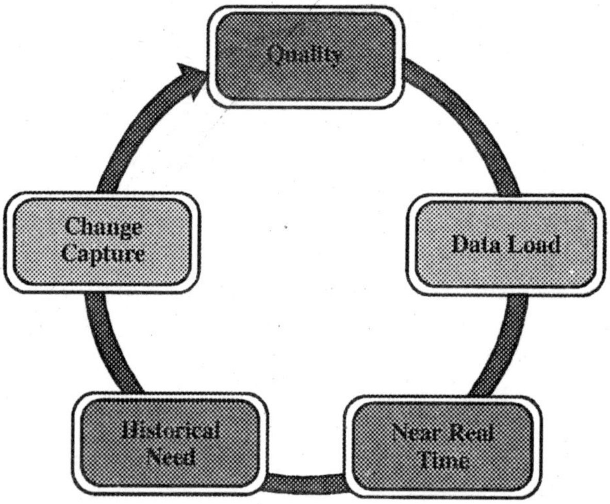

How Do I Create a Master List?

Whether you buy a tool or decide to roll your own, there are two basic steps to creating master data: clean and standardize the data, and match data from all the sources to consolidate duplicates. Before you can start cleaning and normalizing your data, you must understand the data model for the master data. As part of the modeling process, the contents of each attribute were defined, and a mapping was defined from each source system to the master-data model. This information is used to define the transformations necessary to clean your source data.

Cleaning the data and transforming it into the master data model is very similar to the Extract, Transform, and Load (ETL) processes used to populate a data warehouse. If you already have ETL tools and transformation defined, it might be easier just to modify these as required for the master data, instead of learning a new tool. Here are some typical data-cleansing functions:

- **Normalize data formats.** Make all the phone numbers look the same, transform addresses (and so on) to a common format.
- **Replace missing values.** Insert defaults, look up ZIP codes from the address, look up the Dun & Bradstreet number.
- **Standardize values.** Convert all measurements to metric, convert prices to a common currency, change part numbers to an industry standard.
- **Map attributes.** Parse the first name and last name out of a contact-name field, move Part# and partno to the PartNumber field.

Most tools will cleanse the data that they can, and put the rest into an error table for hand processing. Depending on how the matching tool works, the cleansed data will be put into a master table or a series of staging tables. As each source is cleansed, the output should be examined to ensure the cleansing process is working correctly.

Matching master-data records to eliminate duplicates is both the hardest and most important step in creating master data. False matches can actually lose data (two Acme Corporations become one, for example) and missed matches reduce the value of maintaining a common list. The matching accuracy of MDM tools is one of the most important purchase criteria. Some matches are pretty trivial to do. If you have Social Security numbers for all your customers, or if all your products use a common numbering scheme, a database JOIN will find most of the matches. This hardly ever happens in the real world, however, so matching algorithms are normally very complex and sophisticated. Customers can be matched on name, maiden name, nickname, address, phone number, credit-card number, and so on, while products are matched on name, description, part number, specifications, and price. The more attribute matches and the closer the match, the higher degree of confidence the MDM system has in the match. This confidence factor is computed for each match, and if it surpasses a threshold, the records match. The threshold is normally adjusted depending on the consequences of a false match. For example, you might specify that if the confidence level is over 95 percent, the records are merged automatically, and if the confidence is between 80 percent and 95 percent, a data steward should approve the match before they are merged.

Most merge tools merge one set of input into the master list, so the best procedure is to start the list with the data in which you have the most confidence, and then merge the other sources in one at a time. If you have a lot of data and a lot of problems with it, this process can take a long time. You might want to start with the data from which you expect to get the most benefit having consolidated; run a pilot project with that data, to ensure your processes work and you are seeing the business benefits you expect; and then start adding other sources, as time and resources permit. This approach means your project will take longer and possibly cost more, but the risk is lower. This approach also lets you start with a few organizations and add more as the project demonstrates success, instead of trying to get everybody on board from the start.

Another factor to consider when merging your source data into the master list is privacy. When customers become part of the customer master, their information might be visible to any of the applications that have access to the customer master. If the customer data was obtained under a privacy policy that limited its use to a particular application, you might not be able to merge it into the customer master. You might want to add a lawyer to your MDM planning team.

At this point, if your goal was to produce a list of master data, you are done. Print it out or burn it to a CD, and move on. If you want your master data to stay current as data is added and changed, you will have to develop infrastructure and processes to manage the master data over time. The next section provides some options on how to do just that.

How Do I Maintain a Master List?

There are many different tools and techniques for managing and using master data. We will cover three of the more common scenarios here:

- **Single-copy approach** - In this approach, there is only one master copy of the master data. All additions and changes are made directly to the master data. All applications that use master data are rewritten to use the new data instead of their current data. This approach guarantees consistency of the master data, but in most cases it's not practical. Modifying all your applications to use a new data source with a different schema and different data is, at least, very expensive; if some of your applications are purchased, it might even be impossible.
- **Multiple copies, single maintenance** - In this approach, master data is added or changed in the single master copy of the data, but changes are sent out to the source systems in which copies are stored locally. Each application can update the parts of the data that are not part of the master data, but they cannot change or add master data. For example, the inventory system might be able to change quantities and locations of parts, but new parts cannot be added, and the attributes that are included in the product master cannot be changed. This reduces the number of application changes that will be required, but the applications will minimally have to disable functions that add or update master data.

Users will have to learn new applications to add or modify master data, and some of the things they normally do will not work anymore.

- **Continuous merge** - In this approach, applications are allowed to change their copy of the master data. Changes made to the source data are sent to the master, where they are merged into the master list. The changes to the master are then sent to the source systems and applied to the local copies. This approach requires few changes to the source systems; if necessary, the change propagation can be handled in the database, so no application code is changed. On the surface, this seems like the ideal solution. Application changes are minimized, and no retraining is required. Everybody keeps doing what they are doing, but with higher-quality, more complete data. This approach does have several issues:
- **Update conflicts are possible and difficult to reconcile.** What happens if two of the source systems change a customer's address to different values? There's no way for the MDM system to decide which one to keep, so intervention by the data steward is required; in the meantime, the customer has two different addresses. This must be addressed by creating data-governance rules and standard operating procedures, to ensure that update conflicts are reduced or eliminated.
- **Additions must be remerged.** When a customer is added, there is a chance that another system has already added the customer. To deal with this situation, all data additions must go through the matching process again to prevent new duplicates in the master.
- **Maintaining consistent values is more difficult.** If the weight of a product is converted from pounds to kilograms and then back to pounds, rounding can change the original weight. This can be disconcerting to a user who enters a value and then sees it change a few seconds later.

In general, all these things can be planned for and dealt with, making the user's life a little easier, at the expense of a more complicated infrastructure to maintain and more work for the data stewards. This might be an acceptable trade-off, but it's one that should be made consciously.

Versioning and Auditing

No matter how you manage your master data, it's important to be able to understand how the data got to the current state. For example, if a customer record was consolidated from two different merged records, you might need to know what the original records looked like, in case a data steward determines that the records were merged by mistake and really should be two different customers. The version management should include a simple interface for displaying versions and reverting all or part of a change to a previous version. The normal branching of versions and grouping of changes that source-control systems use can also be very useful for maintaining different derivation changes and reverting groups of changes to a previous branch.

Data stewardship and compliance requirements will often include a way to determine who made each change and when it was made. To support these requirements, an MDM system should include a facility for auditing changes to the master data. In addition to keeping an audit log, the MDM system should include a simple way to find the particular change you are looking for. An MDM system can audit thousands of changes a day, so search and reporting facilities for the audit log are important.

Hierarchy Management

In addition to the master data itself, the MDM system must maintain data hierarchies—for example, bill of materials for products, sales territory structure, organization structure for customers, and so forth. It's important for the MDM system to capture these hierarchies, but it's also useful for an MDM system to be able to modify the hierarchies independently of the underlying systems. For example, when an employee moves to a different cost center, there might be impacts to the Travel and Expense system, payroll, time reporting, reporting structures, and performance management. If the MDM system manages hierarchies, a change to the hierarchy in a single place can propagate the change to all the underlying systems. There might also be reasons to maintain hierarchies in the MDM system that do not exist in the source systems. For example, revenue and expenses might need to be rolled up into territory or organizational structures that do not exist in any single source system. Planning and forecasting might also require temporary hierarchies to calculate "what if" numbers for proposed organizational changes. Historical hierarchies are also required in many cases to roll up financial information into structures that existed in the past, but not in the current structure. For these reasons, a powerful, flexible hierarchy-management feature is an important part of an MDM system.

Conclusion

The recent emphasis on regulatory compliance, SOA, and mergers and acquisitions has made the creating and maintaining of accurate and complete master data a business imperative. Both large and small businesses must develop data-maintenance and governance processes and procedures, to obtain and maintain accurate master data. While it's easy to think of master-data management as a technological issue, a purely technological solution without corresponding changes to business processes and controls will likely fail to produce satisfactory results. This paper has covered the reasons for adopting master-data management, the process of developing a solution, and several options for the technological implementation of the solution. Future papers in this series will explain the technological and procedural issues that must be resolved to implement an MDM system.

References

1. http://www.information-management.com/issues/20050501/1026072-1.html
2. http://www.sap.com/solutions/enterprise-information-management/master-data-management/index.epx
3. http://www.information-management.com/infodirect/2009_184/master_data_ management_business_ intelligence_data_quality-10019193-1.html?portal=master_data_management.

◈ ◈ ◈

ISBN – 978-93-5024-769-3

8 "A Critical Study of Implementation of TQM and Six Sigma in Multinational Organizations"

Prof. Milind A. Kulkarni
Smt. Kashibai Navale College of Engineering, Department of Management Studies, Vadgaon, Pune-411041.
Dr. Vilas D. Nandavadekar
Sinhgad Institute of Management, Sinhgad Road, Vadgaon, Pune-411041.
Mr. Rahul S. Rokade
Sinhgad College of Pharmacy, Sinhgad Road, Vadgaon, Pune-411041.

Introduction

Libraries, information providers, information intermediaries, online hosts, database producers, software designers, interface designers and telecommunications agencies can all be regarded as providing a service. In general terms, organizations and individuals may be viewed as offering their customers a product which might be either a good or a service. The most challenging question confronting business leaders and managers in the new millennium is not "How do we succeed?" It's; "How do we stay successful?"Business today offers the spectacle of a succession of companies, products, and even industries getting their peak for a short period of time and then fading away. It's like riding the wheel of fortune as consumer tastes, technologies, financial conditions and competition change ever more quickly.

Many quality models and frameworks have been proposed to improve the competitiveness of businesses in the modern world. Total Quality Management (TQM), Business Process Reengineering (BPR), Kaizen, Benchmarking, Balanced Scorecards, Business Excellence models, and other improvement programs have been adopted and implemented by various organizations. All these frameworks advocate the concept that everyone in an organization is responsible for the quality of goods and services produced by the organization. All of them focus on process improvement, need for organizational and cultural change, radical improvement in organizational performance in terms of quality and cost, education and training, focus on customer needs, and team-based approach.

However, research studies indicate that organizations implementing these different frameworks have exhibited mixed results. Taking the example of BPR which claims amazing results on performance improvement. Companies like Ford Motor Co., CIGNA, and Wal-Mart are all recognized as having successfully implemented BPR. However, not every BPR project is successful. Hammer and Champy (1993) claim that 70 per cent of organizations failed to achieve any benefit from their own reengineering efforts. In addition, Price Waterhouse performed a survey of the experience of Fortune 500 companies and large British companies with reengineering. They found that executives were only partially pleased with their results (Berman, 1994). A number of critical factors for BPR success have been identified by various researchers (Choi and Chan, 1997; Al-Mashari and Zairi, 1997; O'Neill and Sohal, 1998).

Similarly, TQM has been a popular business strategy in many organizations over the past 15 years. However, research data show that only one-fifth or at best one-third of TQM programs in the USA and Europe have achieved significant or even tangible improvements in quality, productivity, competitiveness or financial returns (Harari, 1993). Brown (1995) found that more than two-thirds of the companies which adopted TQM ended up failing or dropping the system initiative before it could really take hold. This caused many managers to rethink their belief in TQM. A number research studies on the critical success factors of TQM implementation have been carried out by academicians and researchers (Yourself and Zairi, 1995; Lau and Idris, 2001; Sohal and Terziovski, 2000).

Six Sigma is another approach aimed at achieving significant improvements in business performance and popularized by the success stories of Motorola, GE, and Allied Signals. Motorola, where Six Sigma was developed in the 1980s, claims to have made amazing results. From 1987 to 1997, Motorola achieved a fivefold growth in sales with profits climbing nearly 20 percent per year, cumulative savings at US$14 billion and stock price gains compounded to an annual rate of 21.3 percent. Motorola was also cited as the first winner of America's Malcolm Baldrige National Quality Award in 1988. Similarly, GE and Allied Signals achieved savings of US$2 billion and US$1 billion in five and three years, respectively. Looking at the exemplary achievements of these companies, many other leading organizations have embarked upon the implementation of Total Quality Management and Six Sigma. However, not all companies can claim to have had the same benefits. A study by Deloitte indicates that fewer than 10 per cent of the companies are implementing Total Quality Management and Six Sigma to the point where it is significantly affecting the balance sheet and the share price in any meaningful period of time. These mixed and varying results of Six Sigma implementation poses some very serious questions:

- What are the factors which contribute to the successful implementation of Total Quality Management and Six Sigma?
- What are the problems faced in implementing a Total Quality Management and Six Sigma program?
- What are the tangible and intangible benefits of Total Quality Management and Six Sigma implementation?

This research is aimed at answering these questions from the MULTINATIONAL's perspective. It Investigates the critical success factors for Total Quality Management and Six Sigma implementation, the problems

faced, and the benefits attained through Total Quality Management and Six Sigma.

Objective of Research

- The purpose of the research is to study the implementation of TQM & Six Sigma in the Multinational organizations.
- Based on the results of the study, it then aims to identify the critical factors which contribute to the successful implementation of & TQM Six Sigma implementation.
- In addition, it also attempts to investigate the different problems faced in the Six Sigma implementation, and the benefits attained through implementing TQM & Six Sigma.
- The research findings will then be used to propose a Six Sigma framework which addresses the key factors necessary for TQM & Six Sigma implementation.

Scope of Study

The research covers the national and multinational organizations in Multinational which have implemented or are implementing Total Quality Management and Six Sigma. They population of study includes both manufacturing and service organizations.

Research Questions

The research aims to answer the following research questions:

1. What is the implementation status of TQM & Six Sigma in Multinational organizations?
2. What are the problems faced or barriers in implementing TQM & Six Sigma?
3. What are hard and soft factors which impact on the successful implementation of TQM and Six Sigma?
4. What are the key benefits attained through Total Quality Management and Six Sigma implementation?

Overview of Research Methodology

The research methodology is based on quantitative approach which involves collection of research data and interpretation of results using statistical tools.

The primary research data was collected using the questionnaire tool. The scope of research was Multinational companies which are implementing or have implemented Total Quality Management and Six Sigma. The list of companies and the corresponding contact information were collected through Six Sigma conferences, published literature references, and internet sources. The questionnaire along with a covering letter and returned envelop was sent to 75 organizations through postal mail. In addition, the covering letter and questionnaire were sent to some companies through e-mails where the mailing address was not available.

Literature search was done using the secondary data in the form of articles published in international journals on Six Sigma, quality and others. Electronic journals in the library resources, such as, Emerald, were intensively used for collecting secondary data for literature review. In addition, books and publications from leading authors on. Total Quality Management and Six Sigma were also used for literature review. Case studies of various organizations implementing Total Quality Management and Six Sigma published in journals and available on net were also consulted for literature review and analysis of research findings.

Summary

The chapter covered the introduction and background of research, identifying the need for a study to investigate critical factors of Total Quality Management and Six Sigma implementation owing to the mixed results of TQM & Six Sigma implementation in different organizations. The objective of the research is to study the implementation of TQM & Six Sigma in Multinational organizations and identify the critical success factors along with problems faced and the benefits gained. The research employs quantitative approach using cross-sectional survey of Multinational organizations.

What is Six Sigma?

Some scholars and practitioners have attempted to describe Six Sigma in one or two definitions (e.g., Breyfogle, Cupello, & Meadows, 2001; Dambolena & Rao, 1994). However, many have concluded that there are at least three definitions (e.g., Adams, Gupta, & Wilson, 2003; Brue, 2002; Eckes, 2001; Pande & Holpp, 2002): Six Sigma can be viewed as a metric, a mindset, and a methodology. The first logical and commonly heard definition for Six Sigma is that it is a statistical expression – a metric (Breyfogle et al., 2001; Brue, 2002; Dambolena & Rao, 1994; Hahn et al., 1999; Harry, 1998; Pande & Holpp, 2002). The lowercase Greek symbol ó (sigma) is the metric or fundamental statistical concept that denotes a population's standard deviation and is a measure of variation or dispersion about a mean. Mikel J. Harry (1998) and Forrest W. Breyfogle et al. (2001) among others explained how Six Sigma can be defined as a term for process performance that produces a mere 3.4 defects per million opportunities (DPMO). According to Paul (1999), Six Sigma is a statistical term that refers to 3.4 defects per million opportunities (or 99.99966 percent accuracy), which is as close as anyone is likely to get to perfect. A defect can be anything from a faulty part to an incorrect customer bill (Paul, 1999). In simple terms, Six Sigma is a metric representing a process that is performing virtually free of all defects. In fact, there is a difference in the true value of Six Sigma and Motorola's value of Six Sigma (Billups, 1993). To understand the definition of Six Sigma, it is important to differentiate between these. The sigma value of a process describes the quality level of that process. A quality level of K sigma exists in a process when the half tolerance of the measured product characteristic is equal to K times the standard deviation of the process: K * process standard deviation = half tolerance of specification However, this definition alone does not account for the centering of a process. A process is centered when X = T, where X is the process average or mean and T is the target value, which is typically the midpoint between the customer's upper. Specification limit (USL) and the lower specification limit (LSL). A process is off centered when the process average, X, does not equal the target value T. The off centering of a process is measured in standard deviations or sigma.

Definitions

Pedestal (2000) defines Six Sigma as:

"A comprehensive and flexible system for achieving, sustaining, and maximizing business success. Six Sigma is uniquely driven by close understanding of customer needs, disciplined use of facts, data, and statistical analysis, and diligent attention to managing, improving, and reinventing business processes."

According to Antony and Banuelas (2001), Six Sigma is:

"A business improvement strategy used to improve business profitability, to drive out waste, to reduce costs of poor quality and to improve the effectiveness and efficiency of all operations so as to meet or even exceed customers' needs and expectations"

TQM and Six Sigma's Implementation Methodologies

A **methodology** is an organized set of methods, techniques and tools, developed to guide the whole cycle of a process to achieve its objectives (Saracelli and Bandat, 1993). According to Preece and Peppard (1996), a methodology is simply theory put into practice aiming at dealing with real world situations. Valiris and Glykas (1999) define a methodology as a structured set of guide-lines (or principles) which enable an analyst to derive ways of alleviating a problem. The use of a methodology is essential for a number of reasons. First, a methodology provides a means of codifying experience, knowledge and ideas, in a form that not only can be easily applied, but also can be evaluated and tested. Second, a methodology offers a certain level of organization, and facilitates planning and monitoring. Third, a methodology enables those who are involved to understand their tasks and clarify their roles. Finally, adoption of a methodology allows a standard set of required skills to be identified and developed. The main focus of six sigma is to reduce potential variability from processes and products by using either a continuous improvement methodology, abbreviated as **DMAIC**, or a design/redesign approach known as design for six sigma (**DFSS**). Let us discuss these two methodologies one by one:

DMAIC

DMAIC methodology is used for improving the existing processes. It consists of five stages which are abbreviated as DMAIC: Define, Measure, Analyze, Improve, and Control.

Define (D) is the first step of the Six Sigma methodology where leaders are expected to select projects, set initial goals or targets, and develop a project charter or statement of work (SOW). Costs of poor quality associated with the new or existing process being analyzed are estimated. Improvement targets are set often in terms of sigma and cost (Pedestal. 2002). Leadership selects the appropriate team members. The team then determines more precisely the criteria that are critical to the customer. Run charts, interviews, or surveys, for example, are utilized to obtain leads and use able figures (Eckes, 2001). A high-level process map of the existing process is to be developed with start and end-points clearly illustrated. Strategic deliverables are a process map, a working project charter, a team roster, and the costs of poor quality. A progress report to leadership normally concludes each step (Eckes, 2001; Pedestal. 2002).

Measure is the second step of the Six Sigma methodology and is denoted by the capital letter **M**. This is where a baseline measure is taken using actual data (Eckes, 2001; Pande et al., 2002; Snee, 2003). The measure then becomes the origin from which the team can gauge improvement. The team develops measures or utilizes existing ones, such as SPC data or database information, and pairs them accordingly with critical customer criteria. Pareto diagrams and controls charts as well as methods mentioned above in the define step are possible data sources for baseline measures. Testing repeatability and reproducibility (R&R) of a measurement system is recommended throughout a Six Sigma project wherever critical measures are taken. A data gathering plan or sampling plan can be followed for greater accuracy (Eckes, 2001; Pande et al., 2002). The project charter or SOW should be refined based on the data gathered in the measure step. The process map can be revised based on new discoveries of value added or non-value added steps in the existing process. Strategic deliverables for the measure step are baseline figures, R&R results, process capability, an improvement goal, a refined process map, and a refined project charter (Eckes, 2001; Pande et al., 2002).

The third step, **A**, is **Analyze**. Here teams identify several possible causes (X's) of variation or defects that are affecting the outputs (Y's) of the process. One of the most frequently used tools in the analyze step is the cause and effect diagram (Eckes, 2001; Snee, 2003). A Six Sigma team explores possible causes that might originate from sources, such as people, machinery and equipment, environment, materials, and methods. Another highly effective technique to expose root cause is asking "why" to a possible cause at least five times (Eckes, 2001). Team member suggestions may need clarified before proceeding further, so each and every team member has a clear understanding of the cause being presented. The resulting list should be reduced to the most probable root causes. Causes can be validated using new or existing data and applicable statistical tools, such as scatter plots, hypothesis testing, ANOVA, regression, or design of experiments (DOE). Experts warn not to assume causation or causal relationships unless there is clear proof. Furthermore, validating root causes can help teams avoid implementing ineffective improvements and wasting valuable resources (Eckes, 2001).

The team then enters the **Improve (I)** step. Here a team would brainstorm to come up with countermeasures and lasting process improvements that address validated root causes. The tool most preferred for this process is the affinity diagram, which is a brainstorming technique where a topic or issue is presenteu to a small team who then quickly list ideas or solutions (Eckes, 2001). The team should narrow the list to one or two potential improvements that are step deliverables for small-scale implementation. Improvements should be selected based on probability of success, time to execute, impact on resources, and cost (Eckes, 2001; Pande et al., 2002). If newly gathered data indicates the small-scale implementation is a legitimate success, teams should proceed to full-scale implementation (Pande et al., 2002).

The final step for at least the black belt and many of the team members is **Control**, which is signified by the capital letter **C**. At this point devices should be put in place to give early signals when a process is heading out of control. Teams may develop poka-yokes or mistake proof devices that utilize light, sound, logic programming, or no-go design to help control a process (Breyfogle et al., 2001). The ultimate goal for this step is to reduce variation by controlling X's (i.e., the inputs) and monitoring the Y or Y's (i.e., the outputs) (Pande et al., 2002).

In approximately three to six months, the sigma levels or process capability figures, that should be routinely measured and documented by workers, are then checked by the process owner to make certain that the installed improvements are lasting. Any documentation and project reports should be finalized. With a control plan in place, the project is delivered to the rightful owner who is usually the project champion or a sponsor from leadership. It is the owner's duty to then manage the new or improved process (Eckes, 2001; Pande et al., 2002).

Research Methodology

The research method selected for this research project is **Survey**. A survey is defined as The collection of data on a number of units and usually at a single juncture in time, with a view to collecting systematically a body of quantifiable data in respect of a number of variables which are then examined to discern patterns of association (Bryman, 1989). The survey was conducted using the **Questionnaire method**. According to Robson and Colin (1998), the advantages of questionnaire are as follows:

- It can be one of the least resources intensive.
- It is simple to use – basic awareness training being sufficient to get things Started.
- It can readily involve many people within the organization.
- The questions asked can be customized to suit the organization.
- It enables the organization to receive feedback which can be segmented by function and by level.
- It can be used in parallel with the workshop approach to provide a more Balanced view of deployment team.
- It can give a good visual reference if results are graphed.

The Figure 4-2 gives an overall picture of the research design for this research project.

Data Collection

Design of Questionnaire

To collect data for the research project in quantitative terms, a research questionnaire was designed and then distributed to the companies. The questionnaire (APPENDIX 2) included different sections seeking information on various aspects of Six Sigma. Multiple-choice and scale-type questions were used to collect response in an objective manner. In addition, open questions were used to collect subjective information. Licker scale of 1 to 7 was used to rate the critical success factors and the benefits of Six Sigma implementation. The various sections of the questionnaire are outlined as follows:

- **Introduction of organization** – this part sought information about the company in terms of company name, nature of business and number of employees
- **About Six Sigma Program** – this part included questions regarding the history of Six Sigma program in the company, such as, the starting year of Six Sigma program, the reasons for initiating Six Sigma program, other improvement initiatives being implemented, etc.
- **TQM AND Six Sigma Implementation** – this part included questions regarding the status of Six Sigma implementation, such as, the implementation stage of Six Sigma program, number of Six Sigma projects implemented, number of Six Sigma qualified persons, percentage of people involved in Six Sigma projects, etc.
- **Problems in Six Sigma implementation** – this part included questions regarding the problems faced in implementing Six Sigma and the level of organizational resistance to Six Sigma program
- **Critical Success factors** – this part included a list of critical success factors for Total Quality Management and Six Sigma, identified through review of literature and previous researches on Total Quality of India and Six Sigma. Licker Scale was used to rate the factors in the order of this significance.

- **Benefits of Six Sigma** – this part included a list of potential benefits of Six Sigma, identified through literature review. Licker scale was used to rate the significant benefits achieved through Total Quality Management and Six Sigma implementation.

Validity and Reliability Testing

The validity and reliability of the data collected and the response rate achieved depends on the design of the questions, the structure of questionnaire, and the rig our of the pilot testing. A valid question will enable accurate data to be collected and one that is reliable will mean that these data are collected consistently. Foddy (1994) argues that: "The question must be understood in the way intended by the researcher and the answer given by the respondent must be understood by the researcher in the way intended by the respondent" (Foddy, 1994)

Population and Sampling

Population refers to the group that forms the subject of study in a particular survey. **Sampling Frame** refers to a list, or other record of a population from which a sample can be selected, e.g., Register of Electors, Kompass Directory (Collis & Hussey, 2003). The population of the research consisted of MULTINATIONAL organizations, manufacturing and services, which are implementing or have implemented Six Sigma. Due to limited control over the choice of the companies, non-probability sampling techniques, i.e., **Convenience sampling** and **snow-ball sampling** methods, were used for selecting the companies. A total of 75 MULTINATIONAL companies from a diverse range of sectors were selected based on the data available through Six Sigma web portals, conferences, events, news releases, articles, and print media. After selecting the companies and identifying contact persons with addresses, the questionnaire along with covering letter and return envelope was mailed to them at their postal addresses. In some cases where the postal addresses were not available, emails were sent to companies by attaching the covering letter and questionnaire.

Data Analysis and Discussion of Findings

This chapter covers the analysis of data collected through research questionnaire and the discussion of the results. The analysis of data has been done by compiling the data and presenting the findings using graphs and tables. The findings have then been discussed by comparing with literature review and similar researches. Some best practices have also been identified through review of case studies. Finally, a framework has been proposed for effective implementation of Total Quality Management and Six Sigma based on the literature review and discussion of findings.

Data Analysis

As discussed in the previous chapter, a total of 75 questionnaires were sent to different companies in MULTINATIONAL for collecting primary data related to the Six Sigma research project. Out of 75 questionnaires, 19 valid responses were received and 6 questionnaires were returned undelivered. It represents a response rate of 25% which is satisfactory in this type of research and corresponds well with the similar surveys done in other academic researches. The respondents were mainly Six Sigma Project Leaders, Master Black Belts, or Quality Managers.

Classification of Respondents

The first part of the questionnaire was designed to classify the responding companies in terms of the nature of business and size of organization by number of employees. Figure 5-1 and Figure 5-2 present the classifications of respondents by nature of business and number of employees, respectively. (Ref. Figure 4.2.1)

TABLE 1 – Respondents by Businesses

Particular	Percentage
Power & Energy	12%
Utility	12%
IT/Telecom	13%
Consulting	13%
Others	13%
Banking and Finance	37%

TABLE 2 – Respondents by Number of Employees

Particular	Percentage
1-100	13%
501-1000	25%
2500	62%

It can be seen that the primary businesses of respondents in the survey included bot. Manufacturing and services sectors. Rather services sectors make more than 50% of the respondents. This indicates that Six Sigma, though initiated from the manufacturing sector, has equally been adopted by the services firms in MULTINATIONAL. Also, the majority of organizations implementing Six Sigma are large organizations having more than 2500 employees. This can be explained by the fact that Six Sigma is a resource intensive program requiring significant initial investment in developing the Six Sigma organizational infrastructure and training of Total Quality Management Six Sigma specialized team members (MBB, BB, GBB). In 1998, GE spent US$400 million on Six Sigma (most of it for training). At 3M, more than 23,000 3M employees were trained in Six Sigma methodologies and processes by the end of 2003. (**Ref. Figure 4.2.2**)

About Six Sigma Program

In the first question about the history of Six Sigma program, the respondents were asked when the Six Sigma Program was initiated. Figure 5-3 shows the results of responses received from the companies. (Ref. **Figure 5.1)**

TABLE 3 – Initiation of Six Sigma Program

Particular	Percentage
1990-1992	14%
1999-2001	29%
2002-2005	57%

As can be seen from the figure, more than 50 companies started the Six Sigma program during or after 2002 and more than 85% started it during or after 1999. This supports the findings made by Antony and Banuelas (2002) in a similar research of MULTINATIONAL organizations and indicates that Six Sigma is still a relevantly newer management approach being adopted by MULTINATIONAL companies, as compared to ISO 9000, TQM, and BPR, which were adopted in early and mid 90s. This finding has to be viewed in the context that the Six Sigma concept was pioneered in USA by Motorola in mid 80s and popularized by GE in the mid 90s. In the next question, the respondents were asked about the events that triggered the initiation of Six Sigma program. Figure 5.4 shows the graphical presentation of the results received from the respondents. (Ref **Figure 5.2**)

TABLE 4 – Initiation of Six Sigma Program

Particular	*Percentage*
Competitor Pressure	22%
Drive Change for Improvement	34%
Poor Customer Satisfaction	22%
Headquarter Directive	11%
Increase Business	11%

Figure indicates that the biggest trigger for Six Sigma Program in MULTINATIONAL organizations was the need to drive change for continuous improvement. The much publicized successes of Motorola, GE, and other leading US companies presented Six Sigma as a successful tool for driving change in the organizational culture and striving for continuous improvement. Other significant drivers were competitors' pressure and poor customer satisfaction. These findings can be compared with similar findings for BPR where the major drivers were found to be an intense need to cut cost and competitor pressure (O'Neill and Sohal, 1998). In the next question, the respondents were asked as what other quality initiatives had been implemented or were being implemented at the time of initiation of Six Sigma program. Figure 5-5 shows the results of the responses. (Ref. **Figure 5.3)**

TABLE 5 – Initiation of Total Quality Management and Six Sigma Program

Particular	*Percentage*
ISO 9000/QA	40%
TQM	20%
BPR	20%
Lean Manufacturing	10%
None	10%

It can be seen that 40% companies had adopted ISO 9001 before implementing Six Sigma. This finding reinforces the arguments made by Preferential (2004) that ISO 9000 can serve as the stepping stone for Six Sigma and can be integrated with Six Sigma to achieve maximum benefits from the two approaches. 20% of companies had either implemented TQM or BPR in addition to ISO 9000 before embarking on the Six Sigma program. These results suggest that all these quality initiatives help in developing a quality-oriented culture in the organization which emphasizes customer orientation, teamwork, employee development and involvement, and continuous improvement – all essential components of Total Quality Management and Six Sigma. Thus they pave the way for implementing Total Quality Management and Six Sigma. The next question asked the respondents as who was the primary sponsor of Six Sigma Program in the organization. Figure 5-6 shows the results of the responses from the companies. (Ref. Figure 5.4)

The figure indicates that in more than 50% cases the Director was the primary sponsor of the Six Sigma Program, followed by GM in 22% cases. CEO was the primary sponsor in only 11% cases. Thus, it reinforces the concept that Six Sigma initiative should be driven from the top with active management support and involvement. The findings suggest that sponsor must be from the executive management but not necessarily the CEO of the organization. (Ref.Figure 5.4.)

This section included a list of critical success factors for Six Sigma implementation, arranged in random order. These critical factors were identified through literature review and study of previous researches on Six Sigma. A semantic differential scale from 1 to 7 was provided against each factor, with score 1 indicating no criticality and score 7 indicating the maximum criticality. The respondents were asked to rate the success factors based on their experience of Six Sigma implementation in their organizations, in order of their criticality.

TABLE 6 – Gives the Ranking of Success Factors Based in Terms of Mean and Standard Deviation of the Rating Given by the Respondents.

Ranking	*Success Factors for Six Sigma*	*Mean*	*Standard Deviation*
1	Creating an effective change culture	6	1.4
2	Top Management support	6	1.4
3	Effective communication	5.8	0.7
4	Teamwork	5.6	1.1
5	Employee education and training	5.5	1.4
6	Effective use of Six Sigma methodology	5.5	0.95
7	Organizational infrastructure for Six Sigma	5.2	0.9
8	Effective use of Six Sigma tools	5	1.6
9	Project Management skills	4.8	0.9
10	Liking incentives with Six Sigma	4.5	2.2
11	Role of IT	3.8	1.9
12	Use of consultants	2.2	1.0

Conclusion and Recommendation

This chapter presents the conclusions of the research based on the analysis of data and discussion of research findings. The conclusion briefly describes the objective of research and the methodology used for research. It then summarizes the key findings leading to the proposed framework. Finally, the recommendations for effective implementation of Total Quality Management and Six Sigma have been proposed and the potential areas for future research have been identified.

Conclusion

The aim of the research project was to study the implementation of Total Quality Management and Six Sigma in MULTINATIONAL organizations, assess the problems faced in Total Quality Management vs. Six Sigma implementation, identify the critical success factors, and enumerate the significant benefits achieved through Six Sigma implementation. The research was unique in the sense that such a broad analysis of Total Quality Management and Six Sigma implementation was never carried out before in the MULTINATIONAL. Previous researches focused primarily on the identification of critical success factors for Six Sigma but did not focus on the status of Six Sigma implementation in MULTINATIONAL organizations and the problems faced in the Total Quality Management and Six Sigma implementation. The research led to some interesting, yet important, findings. First, Six Sigma has been adopted in both manufacturing and services organizations in MULTINATIONAL, thus dispelling the myth that Six Sigma is more applicable in the manufacturing environments. Second, though Six Sigma was pioneered in mid 80s, it was mainly adopted by MULTINATIONAL organizations during or after 2000. Third, the major drivers for Total Quality Management and Six Sigma implementation are a need for change for continuous improvement, competitors' pressure, and poor customer satisfaction. Fourth, most of the organizations had implemented ISO 9000 and, in some cases, TQM or BPR before embarking on implementing the Six Sigma program. Regarding the implementation status of Total Quality Management and Six Sigma, most of the organizations have initiated Six Sigma program on a wider scale, starting and implementing more than 15 projects in various functions of the organization. One significant finding was the average time of the Six Sigma project which ranged between four to nine months, thus implying that Six Sigma projects are short-term projects. Another important finding showed that around 1-20% of employees have been involved in Six Sigma projects, thus indicating that Six Sigma program so far has been focused on a selected group of people, which include the Champions, Sponsors, MBBs, GBBs, and team members. Also it was found that the percentage of time devoted by Six Sigma project team members vary from role to role, with Six Sigma leaders, MBBs and BBs devoting 100% of their time on Six Sigma projects while other team members spend around 1-20% of time. The major roles of top management in the Six Sigma program have been in the form of commitment and support, championship and leadership, and resource provision. The study also revealed that most of the organizations used external consultants, mostly for training of Six Sigma team members, to facilitate the implementation of Total Quality Management and Six Sigma.

Regarding the problems faced in Six Sigma implementation, the study indicated that most common problems faced by the organizations included lack of resources, poor data collection and analysis, lack of management commitment, measurement problems, and organizational resistance to change. Most of the organizations faced moderate level of resistance to Six Sigma initiative. To overcome this resistance, the most common communication media used included kick off meetings with managers, workshops, and individual communication with employees. The core theme of the project was to identify and categorize the Critical Success Factors for Total Quality Management and Six Sigma implementation. The research concluded that the most critical factors for successful Total Quality Management and Six Sigma results are top management support and creating an effective organizational culture of change. Also, effective communication, teamwork, and employee education and training are considered as important factors for Six Sigma implementation. On the other hand, role of IT and use of Total Quality Management and Six Sigma consultants are less significant in the successful implementation of Six Sigma though the study also indicated that majority of companies used the services of external consultants for Total Quality Management and Six Sigma training and implementation. The study also classified the critical factors into soft factors and hard factors and concluded that soft factors play a more significant role in Six Sigma success than the hard factors.

Regarding the potential benefits achieved through Total Quality Management and Six Sigma implementation, the survey results showed that the most significant benefits attained through Total Quality Management and Six Sigma implementation were cost reduction, reduced defects/errors, cycle time reduction, and minimization of waste and non-value-added activities. Another significant finding of the research was that most of the companies are satisfied with the implementation results of Six Sigma.

Based on the literature review and the analysis of results of the survey, a Six Sigma framework has been proposed incorporating the key elements for effective implementation of Six Sigma. At the core of the framework is the DMAIC methodology which is supported by interlinked hard factors and soft factors. The critical hard factors include organizational infrastructure for Total Quality Management and Six Sigma, project management, process management, and statistical tools. The soft factors impacting on them are top management support and commitment, effective culture of change, education and training, effective communication, and teamwork.

Figures

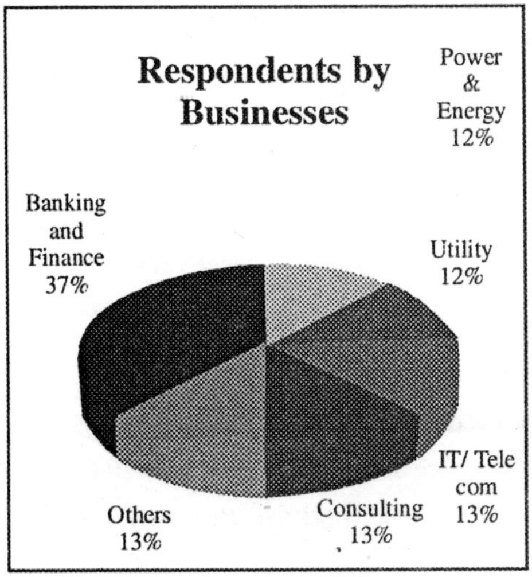

Fig. 1 : Respondents by Businesses

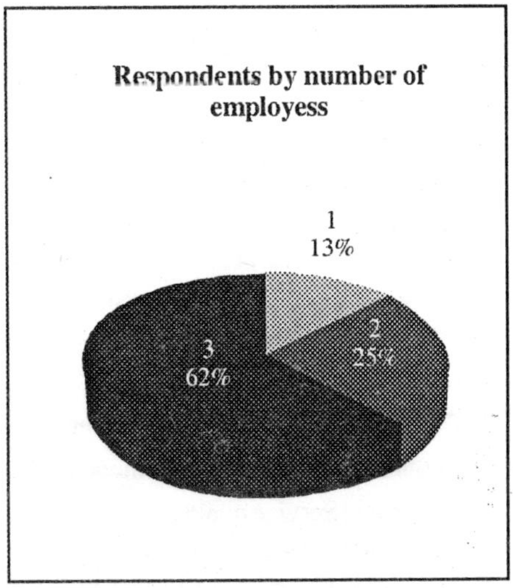

Fig. 2 : Respondents by number of employees

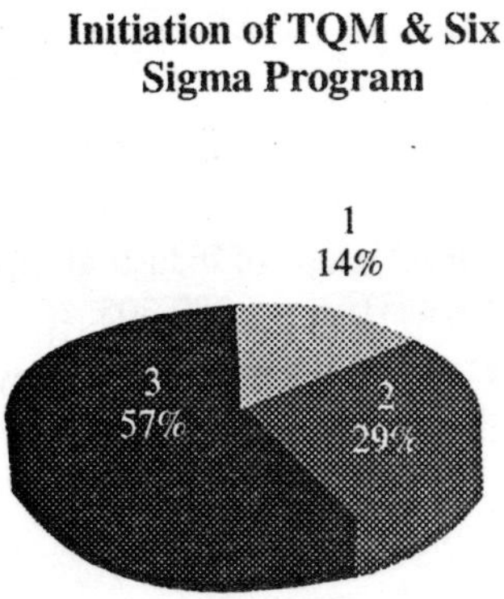

Fig. 3 : Initiation of Six Sigma Program

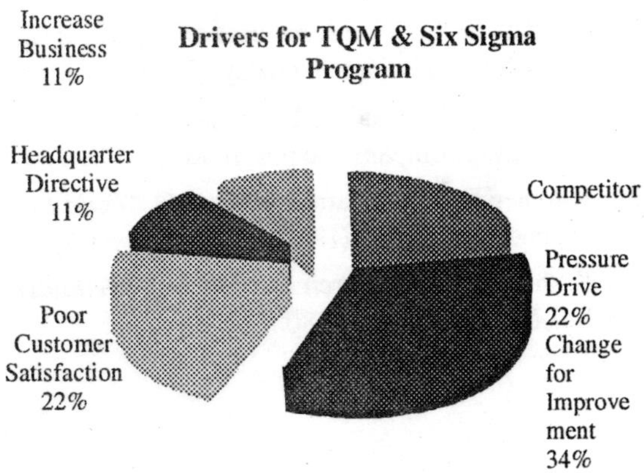

Fig. 4 : Drivers for Six Sigma Program

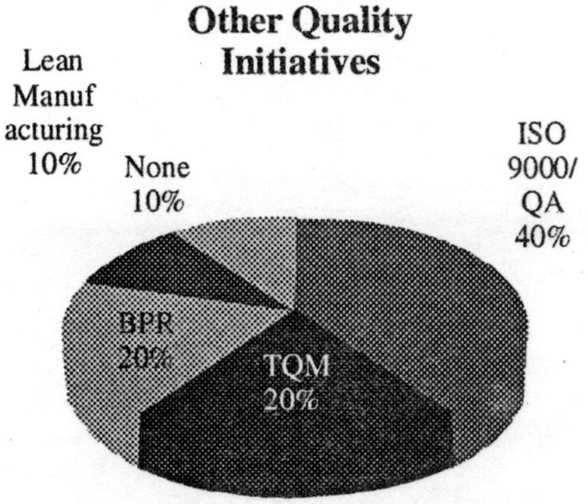

Fig. 5 : Other Quality Initiatives

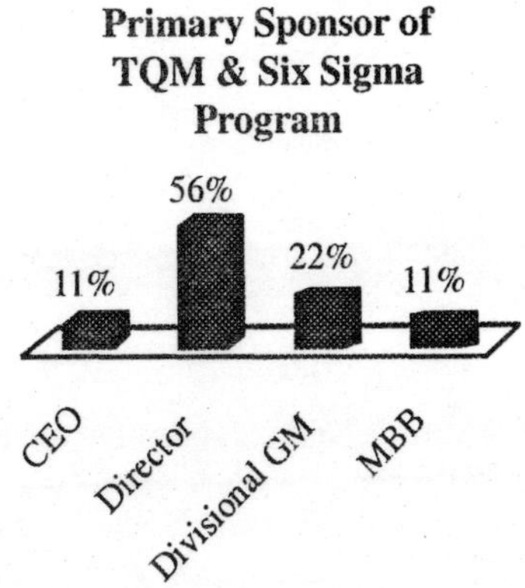

Fig. 6 : Success Factors for TQM & Six Sigma

References

1. R.B. Chase and N. J. Aquilano, *Productions and Operations Management: A Live Cycle Approach, Irin,* 1992, Homewood, IL.
2. B.G. Dale, D.M. Lascelles and J.J. Plunkett, The process of total quality management, in: *Managing Quality,* D.G.Dales and J.J. Plunkett, eds, Philip Allan, 1990, Oxford, pp. 3-18.
3. T.A. DeCotiis and T.P. Summers, A path analysis of a model of antecedents and consequences of organizational commitment, *Human Relations* 40(7) (1987), 445-470.
4. J.A. Dotchin and J.S. Oakland, Total quality management is services. Part 1: understanding and classifying services *international Journal of Quality and Reliability management* 11(3) (1994), 9-26.
5. J.A. Dotchin and J.S. Oakland, Total quality management is services. Part 2: Service quality, *International Journal of Quality and Reliability management* 11(30 (1994), 27-42.
6. N.L. Enrick, Quality, Reliability and Process Improvement, 1985, Industrial Press, New York,
7. D.A. Garvin, Quality on the line, Harvard Business Review 61 (September-October, 1983), 65-73.
8. C. Gronroos, Strategic management and marketing in the Service Sector Bromley, Chartwell Bratt, 1984.
9. C. Gronroos, Service quality: The six criteria of good perceived quality service, *Review of Business* 9(3) (Winter, 1988), 10-13.
10. L. Harvey and D. Green, Defining quality, *Assessment and Evaluation in Higher Education 18 (1993), 9-34.*
11. Dandapane. S. ***'Fundamentals of Social survey and Research Methods'*** The Scholars Foundations, (1971)Second Edition, Himalaya Publication, pp. 307-310.
12. Briner Wendy, Geddes Michael, hastings Colin, ***'Project Leadership'***, (1979),Third Edition, Grower publishing company old post road, pp. 112-120.
13. Kimbler D. L. and Farrell William G. ***'TQM Based Project Planning'*** Dept. of Industrial engineering clemoon University, (1987), Sixth Eidition, Clemson South California USA. pp. 289-305.
14. Kothari C. R., ***'Research Methodology Methods and Techniques'***, (1987),Fourth Edition, Wiley Eastern Ltd, New Delhi, pp. 75-80.

◈◈◈

ISBN – 978-93-5024-769-3

9

A Comparative Study on Effective and Efficient Appraisal System in Present Scenario Adopted by Few Companies

Dr. O.P. Haldar
Sinhgad Management School, Kondhapuri, Pune.
Mr. Amit Dube
Dr. E.B. Khedkar

Introduction

Performance appraisals are essential for the effective management and evaluation of staff. Appraisals help develop individuals, improve organizational performance, and feed into business planning. Formal performance appraisals are generally conducted annually for all staff in the organization. Each staff member is appraised by their line manager. Directors are appraised by the CEO, who is appraised by the chairman or company owners, depending on the size and structure of the organization.

Annual performance appraisals enable management and monitoring of standards, agreeing expectations and objectives, and delegation of responsibilities and tasks. Staff performance appraisals also establish individual training needs and enable organizational training needs analysis and planning.

Performance appraisals also typically feed into organizational annual pay and grading reviews, which commonly also coincide with the business planning for the next trading year.

Performance appraisals generally review each individual's performance against objectives and standards for the trading year, agreed at the previous appraisal meeting.

Performance appraisals are also essential for career and succession planning - for individuals, crucial jobs, and for the organization as a whole. Performance appraisals are important for staff motivation, attitude and behavior development, communicating and aligning individual and organizational aims, and fostering positive relationships between management and staff.

Performance appraisals provide a formal, recorded, regular review of an individual's performance, and a plan for future development.

Job performance appraisals - in whatever form they take - are therefore vital for managing the performance of people and organizations. Managers and appraises commonly dislike appraisals and try to avoid them. To these people the appraisal is daunting and time-consuming. The process is seen as a difficult administrative chore and emotionally challenging. The annual appraisal is maybe the only time since last year that the two people have sat down together for a meaningful one-to-one discussion. No wonder then that appraisals are stressful - which then defeats the whole purpose.

In view of the above scenario where performance appraisal is of utmost important I took the research on performance appraisal in four different companies so that to extract information and same can be given to these companies for their betterment and general use for other organizations

Performance appraisal is necessary to measure the performance of the employees and the organization to check the progress towards the desired goals and aims.

The latest mantra being followed by organizations across the world being - "get paid according to what you contribute" - the focus of the organizations is turning to performance management and specifically to individual performance. Performance appraisal helps to rate the performance of the employees and evaluate their contribution towards the organizational goals. If the process of performance appraisals is formal and properly structured, it helps the employees to clearly understand their roles and responsibilities and give direction to the individual's performance. It helps to align the individual performances with the organizational goals and also review their performance.

Performance appraisal takes into account the past performance of the employees and focuses on the improvement of the future performance of the employees. Here at naukrihub, we attempt to provide an insight into the concept of performance appraisal, the methods and approaches of performance appraisal, sample performance appraisal forms and the appraisal software available etc. An attempt has been made to study the current global trends in performance appraisal.

Objective

Objective behind the research is to know the present performance appraisal system adopted by these four companies and the effectiveness of the appraisal system in these companies. Also to extract the information on the appraisal system so that it can be made more effective and efficient in present scenario for the above said companies and to other organizations

Significance

Present scenario being dynamic in nature where competitiveness is at cut throat level ,it is very difficult to retain valuable employees and keep them loyal and committed towards the organization performance appraisal system is the one of the important tool available with management. By providing the comparative information on the appraisal system adopted by the four different companies of different sectors not only to management of these companies but also to other organizations interested in the field. The performance appraisal system ,as we know is one of the basic tool for the management to keep their employee motivated and committed for the organization the research report has its importance in the management of human resource in the organizations

Potential appraisal, a part of Performance appraisal, helps to identify the hidden talents and potential of the individuals. Identifying these potential talents can help in preparing the individuals for higher responsibilities and positions in the future. The performance appraisal process in itself is developmental in nature.

Performance appraisal is also closely linked to other **HR processes** like helps to identify the training and development needs, promotions, demotions, changes in the compensation etc. A feed back communicated in a positive manner goes a long way to motivate the employees and helps to identify individual career developmental plans. Based on the evaluation, employees can develop their career goals, achieve new levels of competencies and chart their career progression. Performance appraisal encourages employees to reinforce their strengths and overcome their weaknesses.

Research Methodology

1. For all the four companies sample size was 100, 25 from each company area covered was within pune city with locations as Kharad, Viman Nagar, Chandi Chowk and Shivaji Nagar.
2. With the Questionnaire we adopted Personal Schedule techniques for Primary Data and for secondary data documentations of respective companies and other references.

Limitations

1. Very less time for collection of data and fund also limited for research.
2. The area of study also limited to certain companies.
3. Sometimes the response is coming in duplicity.

Analysis and Findings

As I have taken four different companies from different sector I would like to give brief introduction of these companies.

Bharati AXA

Bharti AXA Life Insurance is a joint venture between Bharti, one of India's leading Business groups with interests in telecom, agri business and retail, and AXA, world leader in financial protection and wealth management. The joint venture company has a 74% stake from Bharti and 26% stake of AXA. The company launched national operations in December 2006. Today, it has over 5200 employees across over 12 states in the country. Our business philosophy is built around the promise of making people is "Life Confident".

The organizational structure of bharati AXA:

As we expand our presence across the country to cater to your insurance and wealth Management needs with our product and service offerings, we continue to bring 'life Confidence' to customers spread across India. Whatever your plans in life, you can be Confident that Bharti AXA Life will offer the right financial solutions to help you achieve them. The vision of Bharti AXA Life Insurance Company Limited is to become the preferred life insurance company in India. This vision extends to our recruitment philosophy as well. Both the Bharti Group in India and AXA globally enjoy the status of being a very employee focused organization. At Bharti AXA Life Insurance, we are determined to achieve our vision through talented manpower that are empowered, focused on customer service, and champions of strategic and operational excellence.

Apart from life insurance Bharati AXA has launched its operation in general insurance business. It starts its general insurance business in July 2008. It has its first office at Hyderabad. So Bharati AXA deals with both General insurance and Life insurance sector and providing best services to its clients among all other service providers.

Bharti AXA Values :

- Team Spirit
- Integrity
- Innovation
- Pragmatism
- Professionalism

The guiding Human Resources principles at Bharti AXA are:

- Clearly define scope of responsibilities and empower people to deliver.
- Provide people with the means to develop their competencies.
- Consider individual training and development a priority investment.
- Build organizations that are conducive to teamwork and that involve everyone.
- Promote ongoing dialogue between managers and the people who report to them.
- Make cultural difference a key source of strength.

India INFOLINE Ltd.

The IIFL (India Infoline) group, comprising the holding company, India Infoline Ltd (NSE: INDIAINFO, BSE: 532636) and its subsidiaries, is one of the leading players in the Indian financial services space. IIFL offers advice and execution platform for the entire range of financial services covering products ranging from Equities and derivatives, Commodities, Wealth management, Asset management, Insurance, Fixed deposits, Loans, Investment Banking, GoI bonds and other small savings instruments. IIFL recently received an in-principle approval for Securities Trading and Clearing memberships from Singapore Exchange (SGX) paving the way for IIFL to become the first Indian brokerage to get a membership of the SGX. IIFL also received membership of the Colombo Stock Exchange becoming the first foreign broker to enter Sri Lanka. IIFL owns and manages the website, www.indiainfoline.com, which is one of India's leading online destinations for personal finance, stock markets, economy and business.

IIFL has been awarded the 'Best Broker, India' by Finance Asia and the 'Most improved brokerage, India' in the Asia Money polls. India Infoline was also adjudged as 'Fastest Growing Equity Broking House - Large firms' by Dun & Bradstreet. A forerunner in the field of equity research, IIFL's research is acknowledged by none other than Forbes as 'Best of the Web' and '...a must read for investors in Asia'. Our research is available not just over the Internet but also on international wire services like Bloomberg, Thomson First Call and Internet Securities where it is amongst one of the most read Indian brokers.

A network of over 2,500 business locations spread over more than 500 cities and towns across India facilitates the smooth acquisition and servicing of a large customer base. All our offices are connected with the corporate office in Mumbai with cutting edge networking technology. The group caters to a customer base of about a million customers, over a variety of mediums viz. online, over the phone and at our branches.

V Customer India

V Customer believes that our clients are looking for a partner who can help them strengthen their relationship with their customers. V Customer provides a unique focus around the customer that helps you gain insight into customer behavior and leverage the solutions and services to improve the customer support experience. We ensure that people, process and technology are always centered around the goal of increasing customer satisfaction.

In the traditional model of outsourced contact center or CRM services, clients provide all the customer intelligence, business platforms and process knowledge. Today, we believe that our clients are looking forward to us to deliver a world-class solution that enables their customers to get the benefit of not only the best of class industry practices, but also the latest innovations in customer communication and outreach.

V Customer partners with its clients to ensure that their customers have a consistently great experience in the course of every interaction with the support team. Our goal is to provide the most cost-effective solution that leverages a global workforce that enables customers to get the help they need, when they need it and via the communication channel they choose.

V Customer has developed some of the most flexible and adaptive customer communication tools designed to support both inbound and outbound communications. Whether it is ensuring the customer is never on hold, or assuring the customer with follow-up status updates after they have made a request, our solutions assure the customer is always handled in a quality fashion and provided the information they need.

We understand that our clients have a limited budget within which they would like to support their customers. While their budget is limited, they also want the customer to feel like they care. This is why in addition to our flat pricing structure, we provide state-of-the-art speech-based IVR solutions and web-based self-service solutions, with fully integrated messaging that ensures customers only make an inquiry just once.

Finally, we understand that not all customers have the same needs or the same comfort levels with communication channels. Our CRM solutions help us identify which customer profiles map best to which communication channel and we help guide the customers to the channel that best suits them. By having a common knowledge base across all channels we are able to ensure that regardless of the channel the customers choose, they will get the identical information in the fastest and most effective way possible.

V Customer is a leading provider of customer care contact center solutions and services. We leverage the right blend of innovative technology, business analytics and industry expertise to consistently deliver customized, high quality, cost-saving services and solutions. We offer a unique combination of best-in-class contact center services and an integrated, feature-rich CRM suite to help increase your customers lifetime value. We provide industry expertise in Communications, Retail and Consumer Technology sectors. Our focus allows us to understand your business, help you reduce operating costs, and improve quality levels by deploying self-service and automation to optimize customer care.

Established in 1999 and privately held, vCustomer provides its high quality customer lifecycle solutions through state-of-the-art facilities in the United States, India and the Philippines. V Customer's North American headquarters is located in Kirkland, Washington 1999, Sanjay founded vCustomer Corporation, headquartered in Kirkland, Washington, providing Customer Support and Business Process Outsourcing services with operations in the US, UK, Philippines and India. Before founding vCustomer, Sanjay was the Network Architect at Teledesic Corporation, a visionary LEO Satellite venture backed by Bill Gates and Craig McCaw. Prior to that, he worked at Microsoft Corporation, where he created and managed the Broadband and Internet Telephony Group. Over the years, he has participated in a number of technical groups in the area of Broadband and Internet standards at the ITU, the ATM Forum and IETF. He has co-authored diverse standards including Voice over ATM and Quality of Service for TCP/IP networks.

Zensar Ltd.

Zensar Technologies is a global information technology services and business process outsourced headquartered in Pune, India. It is a software wing of RPG Group , and offers a range of integrated information technology (IT) and BPO products and services to Fortune 500 clients.

Zensar has a marketing presence in the US, Europe, Asia Pacific and Australia. The company has operations and a customer base spanning across 18 countries including software development centers at Pune and Hyderabad in India and Gdansk in Poland

At Zensar, we innovate to enhance the customer's competitive advantage to add agility to their business. With Zensar's wave of collaborative capabilities ensures global integration of the enterprise. Innovations like the pre-configured SAP solutions, hosted ERP for SMEs, Platform BPO and shared IT services model ensures that various benefits like cost reduction, performance improvement, optimal resource utilization and service enrichment are readily passed on to the customers making their business and

IT operations globally competitive. Zensar recognizes Cloud Computing as an economical computing style to cut the infrastructural cost and maximize entrepreneurial scalability. We enable organizations to efficiently deploy custom applications, manage network and provision cloud computing environments with the flexibility to meet sudden changes in demand through peaks and troughs

Zensar is an Information Technology and Business Process Outsourcing (BPO) Services Company with a unique point of view - a company that can engage with some of the world's largest businesses and still provide personalized care; where innovation is routine and distinction, is regular! Zensar provides end-to-end services from Consulting to Implementation to support to over 300 active Fortune 500 and other customers. We have adopted a mature framework to sustain and accelerate growth by diversifying into territories and managing business opportunities across horizons on a 24X7 format. We consistently deliver business value and innovation to customers, while creating a sustainable competitive advantage for ourselves.

ZENSAR Technologies' third global delivery centre in the country and sixth in the world was inaugurated at EON free zone, Kharad on Monday. With an area of 34,422 square feet, the facility has been built with an investment of Rs 4 crore and will accommodate over 400 professionals. This is the company's first foray into a Special Economic Zone (SEZ).

Ganesh Natarajan, Vice Chairman and MD, Zensar Technologies said, "This newly established centre will be the innovation hub for the Company and will host all of Zensar's new and innovative offerings which will drive the growth of the Company's business in the coming year." He also said that Pune would continue to be the focal point of our global expansion.

In line with its focus on innovation, the Company also launched Solution BluePrint (SBP) on the web for the community at large. SBP is Zensar's initiative to incorporate engineering practices in software development. Zensar's approach goes a step ahead towards enabling the building of components and focusing on building reusable platform-agnostic models.

Zensar has been headquartered in Pune and has over 3000 professionals working out of its Pune facility. The Company also has its Development Centres in Hyderabad in India, Slough in UK, San Jose in USA and Gdansk in Poland which are fully functional and have over 1000 professionals working out of these centres.

John Levack of Electra partners, who is also a board member of Zensar Technologies was also present for the inauguration.

Tools Used

e modern approach to performance development has made the performance appraisal process more formal and structured. Now, the performance appraisal is taken as a tool to identify better performing employees from others, employees' training needs, career development paths, rewards and bonuses and their promotions to the next levels.

Appraisals have become a continuous and periodic activity in the organizations. The results of performance appraisals are used to take various other HR decisions like promotions, demotions, transfers, training and development, reward outcomes. The modern approach to performance appraisals includes a feedback process that helps to strengthen the relationships between superiors and subordinates and improve communication throughout the organization.

The modern approach to Performance appraisal is a future oriented approach and is developmental in nature. This recognizes employees as individuals and focuses on their development.

During the research ,data collected from four different companies on various factors . The factors are :-
Communication - Organizes and expresses ideas and information clearly, using appropriate and efficient methods

of conveying the information. **Interpersonal Skills-** Is sensitive to the needs, feelings and capabilities of others. Approaches others in a non-threatening and pleasant manner and treats them with respect. **Conflict resolution -** Expresses alternative points of view in a non threatening way. Knows when it is appropriate to compromise and when it is important to take a stand. **Teamwork-** Works on projects as part of a team, exchanging ideas and contributing skills that complement those of the other team members; Fulfills commitments to team members. **Ethics-** Maintains high level of character and a professional attitude. Is able to conform and promote the company's standards of conduct. **Job Knowledge-** Possesses skills and knowledge to perform the job competently. **Desire to Improve efficiency- Continually** looks for ways to improve performance. **Quality-** Completes high quality work according to specifications. Thoroughly follows standards and Procedures. Keeps complete records. Pays attention to details. Has a strong sense of quality and knows how to. **Initiative-** Strives to learn and improve, Seeks out ways to better themselves and the company, Takes on responsibilities, Does not remain idle – is hard working. Self-motivated **Discipline -** Whether following all the rules , regulations and procedures In a positive ways

PERSONAL ATTRIBUTES (Extended Matrix format) Score: / 5.0 %

R = Ratings Scale 5 – Exceptional; 4 – Exceeds Expectations; 3 – meets Expectations; 2 – Below Expectations; 1 – Needs Improvement. And results are:-

Communication

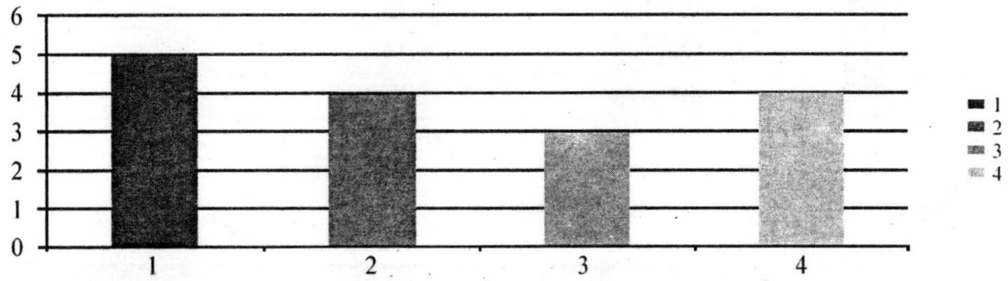

Interpersonal Skills

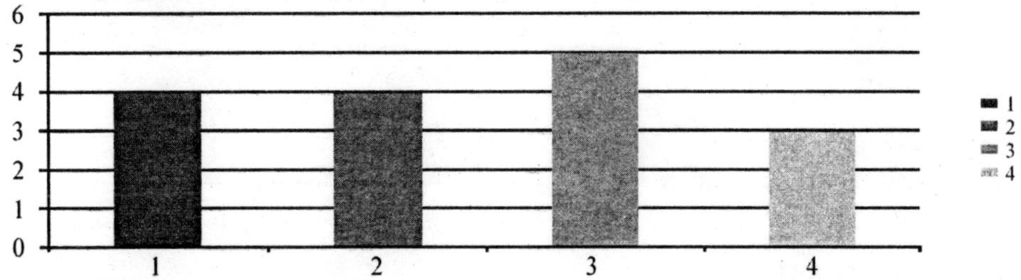

Conflict Resolution

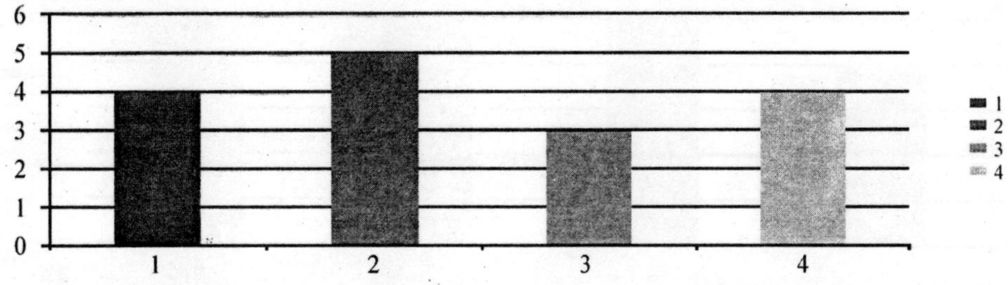

Teamwork

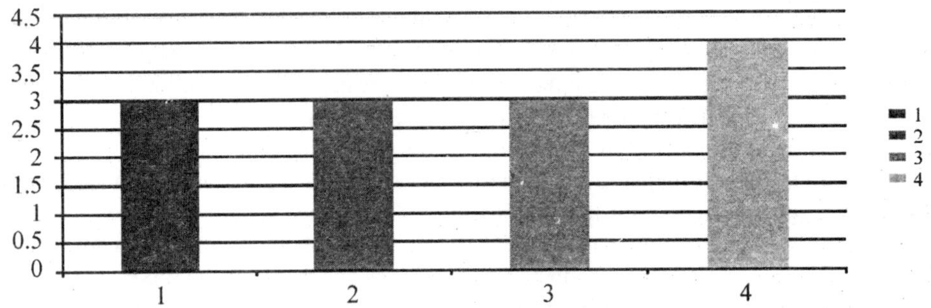

Ethics

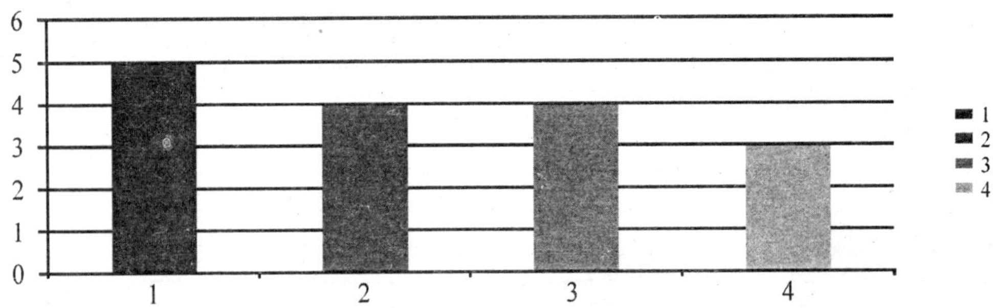

Job Knowledge

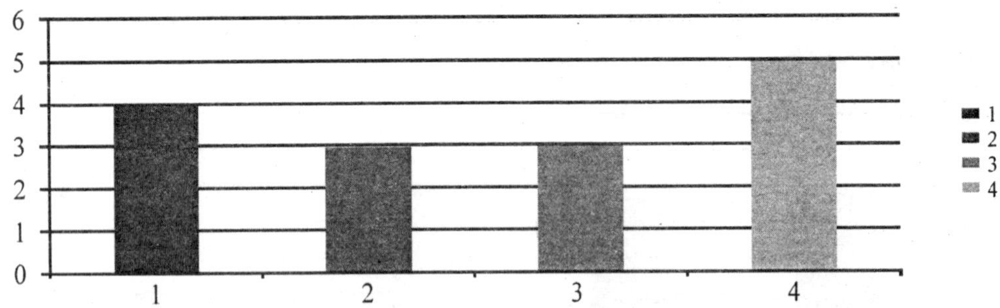

Desire to Improve Efficiency

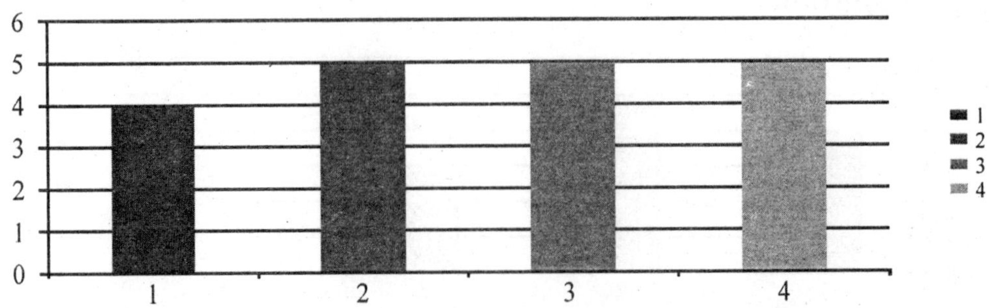

Quality

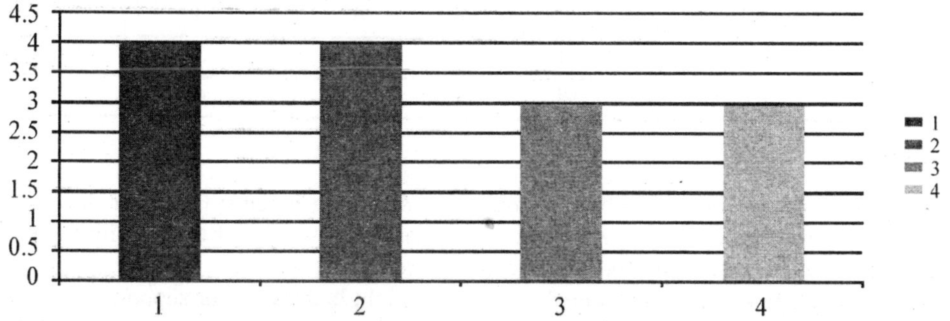

Initiative

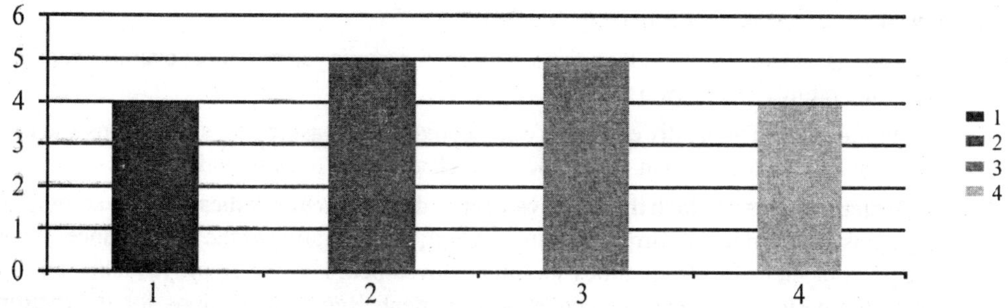

Discipline

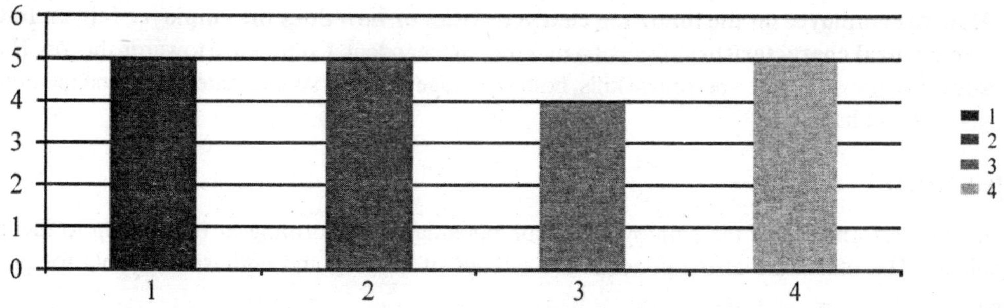

Summary

Factors	*India infoline*	*Bharti AXA*	*Zensar*	*V customer India*
communication	5	4	3	4
interpersonal skill	4	4	5	3
conflict resolution	4	5	3	4
team work	3	3	3	4
ethics	5	4	4	3
job knowledge	4	3	3	5

desire to improve efficiency	4	5	5	5
quality	4	4	3	3
initiative	4	5	5	4
discipline	5	5	4	5

Conclusion

The current responsibilities held by the employee; Accomplishments; Goals for the next appraisal period; Areas for improvement; Training requirements felt for the present job; Responsibilities the employee would like to add to his current responsibilities; Problems faced; Solutions tried; Measures taken for personal and professional development; Best and worst aspects of the job; Is the superior supportive.

- **The form also includes a section where the employee rates himself on various behavioral parameters like**: Communication skills, Inter-personal skills, Problem-solving, Team work, Adaptability/Flexibility, Initiative, Decision Making, Leadership, Maturity

  The self appraisal form also includes a section where the employee can quote examples and incidents to support his ratings and answers.

  The self appraisal form generally ends with a subjective section asking for suggestions and the choice of discussing any other topic that the employee feels the need to raise and discuss:-
- **The performance areas in which the improvement or development is indicated**:-The accomplishments and the targets achieved in the current appraisal period; Overall rating of the performance; What skills, knowledge, competencies and qualities should be developed; Has the employee taken any steps for improving his performance and his career development; Recommendations for the **training and development** of the employee; Updating knowledge on the latest developments on their job related and subject areas.
- **Rate the employee on the following characteristics or how does the employee fair on following behavioural characteristics:** Decision making, Independent, Confidence towards the job, Handling stress and pressure, Inter-personal skills, both with superiors and subordinates, Leadership, motivating and conflict handling

Suggestions

The past performance of the employee and the potential of performing in future help to identify the hidden talents. The others are also can adopt these types of modern and enthusiastic tools for personnel appraisal.

References

1. http://www.zensar.com/zensar-media/inthenews/370-zensar-tech-opens-delivery-centre-in-kharadi#ixzz1AqKfrXMo.
2. Walker & Boyd; Marketing strategy; 2008,5th Edition, Tata McGraw-Hill, New Delhi.
3. Sheth & Parvatiyar; Relationship Marketing; 2002, 10th printing, Sage Publications, New Delhi.
4. Philip Kotler; Marketing Management; 2008, 10th Edition, Tata McGraw-Hill, New Delhi.
5. Richard Batterley; Leading Through Relationship Marketing; Tata McGraw-Hill.
6. Internet:- whereisdoc.com, www//Google.com.
7. Browser and Documents of different Companies and service providers.
8. Vinod V Sople, Logistics Management, 2008, 2nd Edition, Pearson Education, New Delhi.

◈◈◈

ISBN – 978-93-5024-769-3

10 "Customer Relationship Management in Banking Industry"

Mr. Abhishek A. Khadtare, Mrs. Meghna A. Navale, & Mr. Vasim S. Kalavant
Sinhgad Institute of Business Management, Kamlapur, Solapur.

Introduction

Customer focus and relationship management have become fundamental marketing and business philosophies for many companies seeking competitive advantage. Establishing, maintaining and enhancing customer relationships have always been an important aspect of business. Although CRM is considered to be a business philosophy closely related to relationship marketing, it is the linkage with technology that is particularly of great interest. Marketing academics have begun to explore and understand the linkage between CRM technology, relationship marketing and business relationships as providing opportunities for sustainable competitive advantage.

Due to rapid development of the Internet, e-commerce and self-service customer support, there are increased expectations from customers for improved, personalized service and immediacy. Marketing practitioners are now using technology to their advantage and working closely to deliver value to the organization and to the customer. This has prompted marketing practitioners to use technology to capture and use customer information in order to better meet customer demands. Customer relationships are considered superior to transactional exchange in their ability to create sustainable competitive advantage and superior business performance.

The service sector is receiving much deserved attention resulting from its inevitable role in a country's economic de-elopement. Despite all the efforts gaps such as the relationship between technological advances and service development are yet to be revealed from the perspective of new applications that organizations want to develop and implement.

Objectives of the Study

(1) Comparative analysis of CRM strategies are used by Public sector bank and Private sector bank.

(2) To find out how public sector banks and private sector banks are using Information Technology (IT) application for relationship marketing.

(3) To find out which facilities are need to give by Public sector banks in order to delight their customers and employees.

Research Methodology

Research design constitutes the blue print for the collection, measurement and analysis of data. In this research to understand CRM and Banking industry we have taken ICICI bank who already adopted CRM in their business.

Sources of Data

A case Study on ICICI Bank has been selected for the purpose of conducting study.

Secondary Data

Secondary data are those data, which are already published. It may be useful for many other people than the researcher who has published it. There are various sources of secondary data collection.

- Articles on CRM taken from journals, magazines published from time to time.
- Through internet.
- Magazines
- Library Records

Theoretical Background

Customer Relationship Management

Customer relationship management (CRM) is developing into a major element of corporate strategy for many organizations. CRM, also known by other terms such as relationship marketing and customer management, is concerned with creation, development and enhancement of individualized customer relationships with carefully targeted customers and customer groups resulting in maximizing their customer life time value.

Industry leaders are now addressing how to transform their approach to customer management. A new form of cross-functional marketing, i.e. CRM is replacing narrow functionally based traditional marketing. The traditional approach marketing has been continuously questioned in recent years. This approach emphasized on the management of the key marketing mix elements such as product, price, promotion, and place within the functional context of the marketing department.

Phases of CRM

The three phases in which CRM can help to support the relationship between a business and its customers is explained below:

- Acquire: A CRM initiative can help a business in acquiring new customers through excellent contact management, direct marketing, selling and fulfillment.
- Enhance: A web-enabled CRM combined with customer service tools offers customers excellent service from a team of trained and skilled sales and service specialists, which offers customers the convenience of one-stop shopping.

Benefits of CRM

These CRM initiatives have been shown to help companies attain the following objectives:

- To provide better customer service.
- To increase customer revenues.
- To discover new customers.
- To cross sell/up sell products more effectively.
- To help sales staff close deals faster.
- To make call centers more efficient.
- To simplify marketing and sales processes.

The advantages can also be summarized according to the domain it contributes to:

Marketing

- To make intelligent business decisions with enhanced customer insights.
- To increase marketing velocity and speed to market.
- To maximize visibility into and control of your entire marketing process.
- To drive customer demand up.
- To increase returns on the marketing investments.

Sales

- To grow profitable relationships.
- To maintain focus on productive activity.
- To eliminate barriers to productivity.
- To improve sales efficiency service.
- To transform service into a profitable line of business.
- To increase customer loyalty.
- To increase the sales revenue.
- To reduce costs of customer service and field service
- To decrease service give aways/ Poka yokes.

Web channel enablement

- To drive revenue and extend market reach.
- To increase customer convenience and satisfaction.
- To reduce the cost of sales and support.
- To build lasting customer loyalty.
- To improve sales and service profitability.

Running and customer interaction center

- To increase customer satisfaction.
- To improve credibility with your customers.
- To increase revenue and productivity.
- To manage the customer interaction life cycle.

Why Now?

What makes CRM appropriate for today's environment? While there are many number of environmental factors and business advancement that impact and enable the real importance for CRM in today's environment is competitive and differentiation. CRM promises to be competitive and differentiation in today's environment.

Organization today is finding it difficult to compete on the basis of product. Technology advancement has enabled the near immediate replication of product features and functions. It is just a matter of weeks between a product launch and saturation of the market. Just think about it, are there many products out there that are truly unique.

Price, which has traditionally been another basis of competitive differentiation, is no longer a means for many to compete. Complex channel networks have caused parity pricing.

Promotion strategies have similarly lessened as a means of differentiation. Clubs abound, special offer are the norm, and sales are continual.

Place of distribution has likewise become less influential in the success or failure of a business. The Internet has created an avenue for even the smallest business to compete.

While all these factors are still important, none of them can alone support the success of most business. CRM –the ability to provide a more meaningful sales and service experience promises to be means of differentiating, of providing customers with a reason to frequent your business rather than that of your competitors.

Ownership of customer relationship provides exponentially greater rewards than differences in product, price, promotion or place of distribution could ever offer. All of these factors can even be mitigated if you can serve as the one stop provider that can identify. Quantify, and service customer's need.

Implementation of CRM in Banking Sector

Implementing a customer relationship management (CRM) system at a bank takes careful planning. Banks need to involve key employees in the vendor decision so that they choose a system which will give them the most for their investment. Ease of use and ability to view information quickly are equally important to employees and managers.

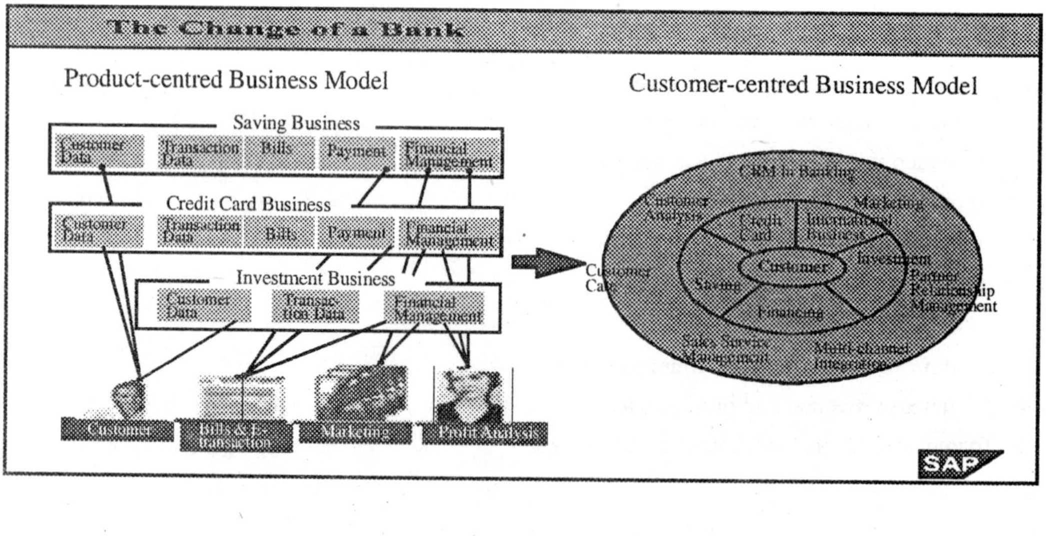

Implementing a CRM system at a bank is a first step toward improved customer relationships. Computer system on blue circle ground image by patrimonio designs from Fotolia.com

1. **Step 1-** Gain employees' opinions. Ask bankers which data is important to them when tracking customers and prospects. Most bank CRM systems include contact information, account information and potential sale amounts. They also include an estimate of how likely it is that the banker will convert a prospect into a new customer. When employees provide input into the new system decision, they will be more willing to use the CRM when it is rolled out.
2. **Step 2-** Research vendors: Ask similar sized banks for vendor recommendations. Find out if the vendor provided appropriate CRM features for the bank's specific needs. Ask if the company delivered the system on time and if the firm provided sufficient support and training to employees after the sale. Create a spreadsheet comparing vendor features and pricing.
3. **Step 3-** Narrow the choices to three or four vendors. Meet with department managers that will use the CRM system. Review the vendor choices and make a vendor decision as a group. Arrange training by combining vendor resources and internal training resources. Allow ample time for employees to learn the CRM system before holding them accountable for using it

Campaign Management - Banks need to identify customers, tailor products and services to meet their needs and sell these products to them. CRM achieves this through *IMPORTANCE OF CRM IN BANKING SECTOR*

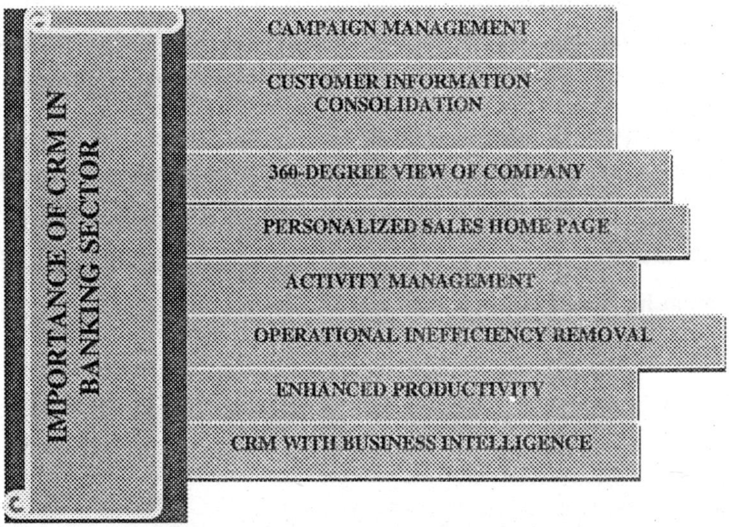

Customer Relationship Management deals with the interactions with the customers (current or potential) across multiple touch points including the Internet, bank branch, call center, field organization and other distribution channels. It helps banks in the following ways:

1. Campaign Management by analyzing data from banks internal applications or by importing data from external applications to evaluate customer profitability and designing comprehensive customer profiles in terms of individual life style preferences, income levels and other related criteria. Based on these profiles, banks can identify the most lucrative customers and customer segments, and execute targeted, personalized multi-channel marketing campaigns to reach these customers and maximize the lifetime value of those relationships.
2. *Customer Information Consolidation* – Instead of storing customer information in product centric manner (for e.g. separate databases of savings account & credit card customers), CRM stores the

information in a customer centric manner covering all the products of the bank, thereby integrating various channels to deliver a host of services to customers.

3. *360-degree view of company* – Means that who so ever the bank speaks to, irrespective of whether the communication is from sales, finance or support, the bank is aware of the interaction. CRM removes inconsistencies in data, thereby making the client interaction processes smooth and efficient, thus leading to enhanced customer satisfaction.
4. *Personalized Sales Home Page* – CRM provides a single view where Sales Mangers and agents can get all the most up-to-date information in one place, including opportunity, account, news, and expense report information. This would make sales decision fast and consistent.
5. *Activity Management* – CRM helps managers to assign and track the activities of various members. This improves transparency and leads to improved efficiency.
6. *Operational Inefficiency Removal* – CRM helps in Strategy Formulation to eliminate current operational inefficiencies. An effective CRM solution supports all channels of customer interaction including telephone, fax, e-mail, the on-line portals, wireless devices, ATMs, and face-to-face contacts with bank personnel. It also links these customer touch points to an operations center and connects the operations center with the relevant internal and external business partners.
7. *Enhanced Productivity* – CRM helps banks in enhanced productivity of customers, partners and employees. It enables customer service agents to provide uniform service across multiple channels such as phone, Internet, email, Fax.
8. *CRM with Business Intelligence* – Banks need to analyze the performance of customer relationships, uncover trends in customer behavior, and understand the true business value of their customers. CRM with business intelligence allows banks to assess customer segments, which help them calculate the net present value (NPV) of a customer segment over a given period to derive customer lifetime value. Customers can be evaluated within a scoring framework. With such knowledge, banks can efficiently allocate resources to the most profitable customers and reengineer the unprofitable ones.

A Case Study on Public Sector and Private Sector Bank

Customer Relationship Management in State Bank Of India

Products and services by SBI

- Personal Banking
- NRI Services
- Agriculture
- International
- Corporate
- SME
- Domestic Treasurer

Need for CRM

The need for system automation became critical at SBI Life Insurance. The challenge was to meet the demanding service and fulfillment levels of the growing insurance sector. SBI Life was on the lookout for a technology solution that was easy to implement, cost-effective and robust to expand its presence in the insurance sector and achieve a higher degree of service differentiation. Although the organization had a centralized system, most of the work was done manually. They needed client/server architecture in place. But it was not integrated with the legacy systems.

Early on, the top management realized that technology was a crucial driver for product and service delivery. Although using the extensive SBI group platform for cross-selling products and services was a viable option, reaching and engaging the customer cost effectively required a technology backbone. The portal initiative started sometime in 2003. Earlier, the insurance major had little enterprise software to support its business and the processes were carried out in an ad hoc manner. The system went live in 2004, taking just four to five months to go online.

It was clear as far back as 2002 that a durable and scalable system was going to be essential, and it was felt that a Web portal would be the best solution as a part of SBI's CRM initiative. Various options were taken into consideration-recreating their entire operations in-house, allowing a vendor to provide the basic platform and then build applications on it, etc. SBI also spoke to some leading providers in the industry, did some spadework, and finally decided to go for BEA Web Logic.

Benefits of CRM in SBI Life

- Reduction in TAT (Turn Around Time)
- SBI Life can now integrate and manage content, campaigns and merchandising to patrons via the Web
- Streamlined product delivery and support processes with a single contact point on the Web
- Site offers a one-stop-shop for customers' insurance needs

The insurer was looking at a system that would be up and ready in the shortest span of time, in a stable manner, and roll out business-critical applications. The other concern for SBI Life was connectivity; it decided to use the Internet to tackle the problem of linkage across locations in India. (SBI has a network of over 9,000 branches.) Since laying out the network, application and infrastructure is time consuming and not very cost-effective, using the Internet fits perfectly into their scheme of things.

BEA faced tough competition from industry biggies who were also bidding for the project. Sanjay Dhingra, BEA's Director of Sales believes that the most challenging part of the project was to put a technology backbone in place that could handle SBI's transactions and also scale up as and when required-the insurer was looking at a system that could be upgraded every six months.

When looking for vendors SBI sought cutting-edge technology that did not cost the earth. Another important issue was support. Typically, Indian service providers do not have the capability to deliver the required services. They believe that the product by itself should be mature enough to manage both its own complexity as well as that of the business, and also offer ease of use for those who work on it. Most importantly, the vendor had to have a roadmap extending well into the future.

In India, many implementations are not up to the mark due to cultural aspects of business. Acceptance among staff and familiarity of employees with the system were two of the things we considered before they decided to go in for a full-fledged implementation.

There were hiccups as various centers had problems connecting to the CRM portal, which have been solved. They are using multiple types of connectivity, leased lines that terminate at the central data centre in Mumbai, broadband connections, dial-up connections, telephone lines, etc. The type of connectivity depends on the number of users in that particular branch and the kind of work being done there.

Outcome: Saving Time and Money

Process improvements are evident. All of this happened with minimal system changes without adding to the existing infrastructure. As a result, SBI has been able to decentralize 36 branches. The solution has also brought down by 50 percent the time taken for specific processes like cash management, insurance claims, and accounting. The insurer has managed to save about 30 percent of costs on infrastructure, with better utilization of manpower. Unlike separate frameworks for integration and custom application development, the BEA solution was a model that enabled faster customization and development of applications.

With almost 30 functions already running on the site, they feel that in future the portal has the capability to scale up to handle a much bigger transaction load. The company is to add applications in a phased manner, and is looking at service oriented architecture (SOA) in the future. They are still adding new functionalities, and with an SOA (using WebLogic Integration 8.1) they can maintain the value provided to our customers while minimizing investments in maintenance and development.

ICICI Bank's CRM Initiatives

ICICI Bank has to manage more than 13 million customers. The bank has over 550 branches, a network of 2025 ATMs, multiple call centers, Internet banking and mobile banking. Its customers often use multiple channels, and they are increasingly turning to electronic banking options. Business from the Internet. ATMs and other electronic channels now comprise more than 50 per cent of all transactions.

In the process of making its business grow to this level, ICICI Bank has distinguished itself from other banks through its relationship with customers.

The Teradata solution focuses on a Customer Relationship Management (CRM) platform. Information from various legacy and transaction systems is fed into a single enterprise called wide data warehouse. This allows the bank to generate a single view of its customers. The warehouse has the capability to integrate data from multiple sources comprising Oracle and flat files. The Behaviour Explorer enables profiling of customers and querying on various parameters. These enable the bank staff create suitable campaigns for targeting individual customers on the basis of their requirements.

The logistics in the system have also led to other benefits like interactive reports, unearthing cross-selling opportunities as well as finding out about the channel usage undertaken by a segment. The data access was facilitated through the use of Cognos Power Cubes.

Customer Relationship Management (CRM) has been deployed in retail banking. The challenges in managing customer relations in retail banking are due to the multiple products being offered and the diverse channels being used for the distribution of the products. Customer expectation from banks can be summed up as:

The use of Customer Relationship Management (CRM) in banking has been essentially done for the following purposes:

Targeting Customers

- It is necessary for banks to identify potential customers for approaching them with suitable offers. The transactional data that is generated through customer interactions and also by taking into account the profile of the customer (such as the lifecycle stage, economic background, family commitments, etc.) needs to be collated into one database to facilitate its proper analysis. For example, a customer interacts with the banks for savings accounts, credit cards, home loans, car loans, demat accounts, etc. the data generated through all these services needs to be integrated to enable effective targeting. After the integration is done, a profitability analysis of the customer needs to be undertaken to acquire an understanding of the profit-worthiness of the customer before targeting him with new offers.
- **Sales reference material**: A consolidated information database on all products, pricing, competitor information, sales presentations, proposal templates and marketing collateral should be accessible to all the people concerned. These prove to be very helpful in Sales Force Automation (SFA) wherein the

salesperson gets instantaneous access to all relevant material as and when it is required (especially when he/she is in a meeting with a client.)

- **Consistent interface with customers**: The communication to customers from various departments like sales, finance, customer support, etc. should be consistent and not contradictory. Therefore, all departments should be privy to a unified view of the customer to enable a consistent approach. Removal of inconsistencies is necessary to ensure that customers are not harassed and frustrated owing to poor internal co-ordination. This is bound to enhance customer satisfaction. The contact centres used to interface with customers should ensure consistency in customer interaction, irrespective of the medium used for the interaction such as telephone, Internet, e-mail, fax, etc.

Banks can use the data on customers to effectively segment the customers before targeting them. Proper analysis of all available data will enable banks to understand the needs of various customer segments and the issues that determine "value" for that segment. Accordingly, suitable campaigns can be designed to address the issues relevant for that segment and to ensure higher loyalty from these customers. When data analysis is done in the right manner, it helps in generating opportunities for cross-selling and up-selling.

The Benefits of CRM

- **Customers' usage pattern**: ICICI's CRM data warehouse integrates data from multiple sources and enables users to find out about the customer's various transactions pertaining to savings accounts, credit cards, fixed deposits, etc. The warehouse also gives indications regarding the customer's channel usage.
- **New product development**: Analysis at ICICI guide product development and marketing campaigns through Behaviour Explorer, whereby customer profiling can be undertaken by using *ad hoc* queries. The products thus created take into account the customer's needs and desires, enabling the bank to satisfy customers through better personalization and customization of services.
- **Central data management**: The initial implementation of CRM allowed ICICI to analyse its customer database, which includes information from eight separate operations systems including retail banking, bonds, fixed deposits, and retail consumer loans, credit cards, custodial services, online share trading and ATM.

Some Noteworthy CRM Initiatives of ICICI Bank

Mobile ATMs: Customers of ICICI Bank can access their bank accounts through mobile ATMs. These ATMs are kept in vans and parked at locations that have a high traffic of bank customers such as the commercial areas in a city or upmarket residential areas ICICI Bank now provides standard ATM facilities through ATM vans. This facility has been tried at Mumbai, Chandigarh and various places in Kerala during specified timings.

Bulk Deposits: The ICICI Bank's Bulk Deposit ATMs enable customers to deposit large amounts at one time. Unlike conventional ATMs, which are able to accept only 30 notes at a time, these ATMs allow the deposit of huge amounts. The Bulk Deposit ATM is available in Mumbai's Vashi sector branch office of ICICI. The bulk deposit facility can be availed of by select customers who need to deposit huge amounts of cash. ICICI Bank issues a special card called the 'Deposit Only Card' to facilitate this service. This card allows for deposit transactions only. The service is further facilitated by the provision of special bags at ATMs in which a customer can put his money. After the deposit slip is filled, the bag can be inserted in the ATM. The transaction slip is then generated by the ATM as an acknowledgement of the deposit. ICICI Bank also has cash pick-up service for business customers under the business banking segment.

ATMs for the visually challenged: ICICI Bank has launched ATMs with special voice-guided systems, which guide a visually challenged person to access ATMs without any help. The jack on the terminal enables headphones to be connected to it and voice commands enable the customer to transact business. Customers may choose a suitable language to get voice commands. After the language selection is done, the customer is guided to ensure that the ATM card is inserted in the right slot and thereafter, guidance is provided for entering the PIN by using the keypad.

References

1. Strong Is the Tendency to Treat Top Sales Performers Leniently?" Journal of Business Ethics,.
2. Ferrell, O.C., "A Framework for Understanding Organizational Ethics," in Business Ethics: New Challenges for Business Schools and Corporate Leaders, R.A. Peterson and O.C. Ferrell, (2005), eds. Armonk, New York.
3. Ferrell, O.C. "The Fall of Enron: A Stakeholder Failure," Forthcoming in Ferrell, O.C, Fraedrich, John, Ferrell, Linda, Business Ethics, (2006),Boston: Houghton Mifflin 2007.
4. Freeman, R.E. Strategic Management: A Stakeholder Approach (1984), (Boston: Pitman, 1984).
5. Harrison, J.S. and Freeman, R.E. "Stakeholders, Social Responsibility, and Performance: Empirical Evidence and Theoretical Perspectives," (1999), Academy of Management Journal.

◈ ◈ ◈

ISBN – 978-93-5024-769-3

11 Risk of System Failure under Dependent Set Up

Dr. Soma Roychowdhury
Indian Institute of Social Welfare and Business Management, Kolkata.
Debasis Bhattacharya
Visva-Bharati University, Santiniketan.

Introduction

Managing risk in system performance is a very important problem in business and industry. By a system we mean a functionally related group of components forming a complex whole. We may consider it like a machine composed of a number of components. A system can be of any kind. Not only the engineered systems like stereo system or sprinkler system, the transmission or distribution system of a power supply agency, the management information system or an HR information system, a social system (a system composed by people in a society, organized by a characteristic pattern of relationships), our body system (such as respiratory system, digestive system, nervous system etc.) etc. are also the examples of a system. If the failure times of the components, which the system is composed of, are random and dependent in nature, then the problem of evaluating the risk of failure or comparing different systems becomes difficult. Under the dependent set-up, it is also an important issue to study the behaviour of failure times of the systems. In this paper we have studied the effect of dependence on the risk of failure of a system and compared the risks of failure of some coherent systems, functioning in a business or social or health or some other random environment. The systems become more complex under dependent set-up. Here by system failure we mean the failure of a system to function properly. Likewise a component failure indicates some disruption in proper functioning of a component. If the failure times of components are random, assumption of independence might not be appropriate always. This is a very restrictive assumption. The components of a system may share the same environment or share the same load or may be subject to the same set of stresses. If one component fails, then stress of other components may increase, or the risk of system failure or failure time of the system may be affected in some other way. We have seen that this assumption of independence may over- or under-estimate the true risk of system failure, when actually the failure times of the components are dependent. For details on different kinds of dependence see Lehmann[2], Shaked[4], Barlow and Proschan[5], Roussas[3]. Ma[1] considered a system with n non-renewable dependent components sharing a common random environment and discussed the environmental effect on the performance of the system. The systems become more complex under the dependence set-up, and the dependence of components is difficult to describe even for simple systems consisting of more than two components. Ignoring the effect of dependence may lead to overestimation or underestimation of the risk of system failure. It is necessary to study how the failure time of the system and the risk of system failure are affected if the failure times of the components are dependent. Incorporating the aspect of dependence in a risk model will definitely improve the risk analysis. How the risk of system failure depends on the failure time distribution of the components has also been studied in this paper.

The organization of this paper is as follows. Section 1 introduces the work, while Section 2 discusses some preliminaries required for the present study. Section 3 discusses how 'dependence' affects the failure time of the system and the risk of system failure. Section 4 compares the risks of failure of the systems having dependent components A comparison of failure times of the system has been made under dependence and independence set-ups, to study the effect of dependence on system reliability at different time points, for some frequently used distributions of the failure times of the components, Section 5 includes some discussion and concluding remarks.

Some Preliminaries

A system is a functionally related group of elements or components. More technically, it is a physical entity that achieves in its domain a defined objective through the functions of its parts. Thus the risk of a system failure will be a function of the risks of its component failures. A system is said to be coherent if its every component has some contribution towards the system performance and if the performance of the system improves with the improvement of any component or a subset of components. A coherent system contains no component whose functioning or failure has absolutely no effect on the system performance irrespective of what state the remaining components might be in. The risk of system failure decreases with the decrease in the risk of failure of any component. The performance of a system can be measured by its time-to-failure or its risk of failure. In a random environment, the times-to-failure of the components are random, and hence an uncertainty is involved in determining the time-to-failure of a system. Here we make an attempt to determine the time-to-failure of a system as well as the risk of failure of the system using the idea of cut sets of a coherent system. The time-to-failure of a system can be determined from the times-to-failure of its components. A coherent system can be considered to be a collection of minimal cut sets. A set of components in the system whose failure causes the system to fail is called a cut set of the system. A cut set is said to be minimal if the set cannot be reduced without losing its status as a cut set. The number of components in a minimal cut set is its cardinality.

Let $X_1, X_2, \ldots, X_n$ be the random times-to-failure of the components of an n-component system which has m minimal cut sets, $K_1, K_2, \ldots, K_m$ of sizes $N_1, N_2, \ldots, N_m$, respectively. $\sum_{i=1}^{m} N_i \geq n$. Then the time-to-failure of a system is given by

$$T = \min_{1 \leq i \leq n} \max_{j \in K_i} X_j = \min_{1 \leq i \leq n} Y_i \qquad \ldots (1)$$

where $Y_i = \max_{j \in K_i} X_j$ is the maximum of the times-to-failure of the components of the ith minimal cut set.

Let us call it the time-to-failure of the ith minimal cut set, since the component having maximum time-to-failure among the times-to-failure of all components in the ith minimal cut set, by faiing, will cause the system to fail. The time-to-failure of a system, as given in (1), will be the minimum of the times-to-failure of all minimal cut sets.

A minimal cut set will be called the most likely minimal cut set of the system if the chance of its time-to-failure to be the same as the failure time of a system is higher than that of any other minimal cut sets (see Roychowdhury[6]). In other words, the maximum time-to-failure of a component, Y_i, of the ith minimal cut set corresponds to the most likely minimal cut set if its chance of being least among all such Y_i-values is maximum, i.e., if

$$P(Y_i \le c) \ge P(Y_h \le c), \text{ for all } c \text{ and all } h \ne i,\ i, h = 1, 2, \ldots, m. \qquad \ldots (2)$$

From (2) we can say that the ith minimal cut set will be the most likely minimal cut set of the system if its time-to-failure is stochastically smaller than the time-to-failure of the any other minimal cut set of the system. Thus the risk of failure of a system by time c is same as $P(Y_i$ d” $c)$, if Y_i, the maximum time-to-failure of a component of the ith minimal cut set, is the most likely minimal cut set.

The times-to-failure of the components can be dependent on each other in various ways. For different forms of dependence Lehmann[2] may be referred to.

The random variables $X_1, X_2, \ldots, X_n$ are said to be positively upper or than t dependent if

$$P(X_1 > x_1, X_2 > x_2, \ldots, X_n > x_n) \ge \prod_{i=1}^{n} P(X_i > x_i), \text{ for all values of } (x_1, x_2, \ldots, x_n)$$

and they are called positively lower or than t dependent if

$$P(X_1 \le x_1, X_2 \le x_2, \ldots, X_n \le x_n) \ge \prod_{i=1}^{n} P(X_i \le x_i), \text{ for all values of } (x_1, x_2, \ldots, x_n).$$

If $X_1, X_2, \ldots, X_n$ are the times-to-failure of components $1, 2, \ldots, n$ of an n-component series system, the risk of system failure (at time t) will be

$1 - P(X_1 > t, X_2 > t, \ldots, X_n > t)$,

or $P(X_1$ d” t or X_2 d” t or … or X_n d” $t)$,

and the risk of system failure (at time t) of an n-component parallel system will be

$1 - P(X_1 > t$ or $X_2 > t$ or … or $X_n > t)$

or, equivalently, $P(X_1$ d” t, X_2 d” $t, \ldots, X_n$ d” $t)$.

Here we discuss some important results (see Roychowdhury and Bhattacharya[8]), which show the effect of dependence on series and parallel systems. The results reveal that if independence of components is assumed while actually the components are dependent, then the risk of system failure will be either underestimated or overestimated.

The risk of failure of a series system with dependent components is smaller than a similar system with two independent components, when the times-to-failure of the components are positively dependent (positively lower or than t dependent or positively upper or than t dependent).

The risk of failure of a parallel system with dependent components is higher than the similar system with two independent components, when the times-to-failure of the components are positively dependent (positively lower or than t dependent or positively upper or than t dependent).

The above results can be extended to a higher order series or parallel system too.

The risk of failure of a series system with n dependent components is smaller than its corresponding series system with n independent components, when the times-to-failure of the components are positively upper or than t dependent.

The risk of failure of a parallel system with n dependent components is higher than its corresponding parallel system with n independent components, when the times-to-failure of the components are positively lower or than t dependent.

Effect of Dependence on System Performance

Let us consider a positive dependence model. In our model with the failure of one component the remaining times-to-failure of the other components decrease by a random factor r. We will study how dependence of components affects overall system performance. Let the random variables $X_1, X_2, \ldots, X_n$ be the times-to-failure of the components of an n-component coherent system. In this section we carry out a simulation to see the effect of dependence on the failure time of the system and in the next section we discuss the risk of system failure for different probability distributions of the failure times of the components. Depending on the type of failure rate curve, the appropriate failure time distribution can be chosen. Failure rate is constant in time for exponential distribution of time-to-failure, while for the lognormal distribution for the time-to-failure the failure rate curve starts at zero, then go up to its peak and finally moves toward zero, asymptotically. When the distribution of time-to-failure is Weibull, the failure rate curve is monotonically increasing (decreasing) for its shape parameter value greater (smaller) than unity. At the early life (wear-out) phase, when failure rate decreases (increases) with time, a Weibull distribution with shape parameter value less (more) than unity will be the most appropriate distribution. At steady state phase, a Weibull distribution with shape parameter unity will be appropriate. Actually a Weibull distribution can have different shapes based on the value of its shape parameter. We can get an exponential, a beta or a gamma distribution from a Weibull distribution for its different parameter values. Here we observe how these life distributions influence the variation in change in the time-to-failure of the system and the risk of system failure for different system designs.

A bridge system or a hi-fi system, as pictured in Figs. 1 and 2, is a 5-component system. The minimal cut sets of a bridge system are $\{1,2\}$, $\{4,5\}$, $\{1,3,5\}$ $\{2,3,4\}$. The minimal cut sets of a hi-fi system are $\{1,2\}$, $\{3\}$, $\{4,5\}$. For a bridge system, the time-to-failure of the system, $T_1 = \min\{\max(X_1, X_2), \max(X_4, X_5), \max(X_1, X_3, X_5)\}$. The time-to-failure of a hi-fi system is $T_2 = \min\{\max(X_1, X_2), X_3, \max(X_4, X_5)\}$, where times-to-failure of the components X_1, X_2, X_3, X_4, X_5 are assumed to follow a Weibull distribution. Let the random factor r by which the remaining times-to-failure of the components reduce after the failure of a component follow a uniform distribution between è and 1, where $0 <$ è <1.

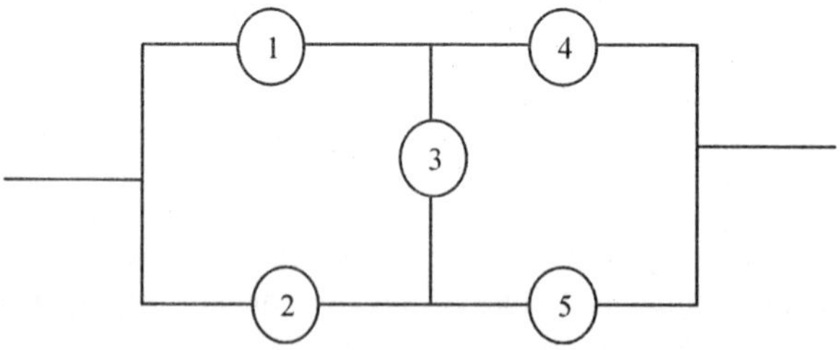

Fig.1 : System 1 (Bridge System)

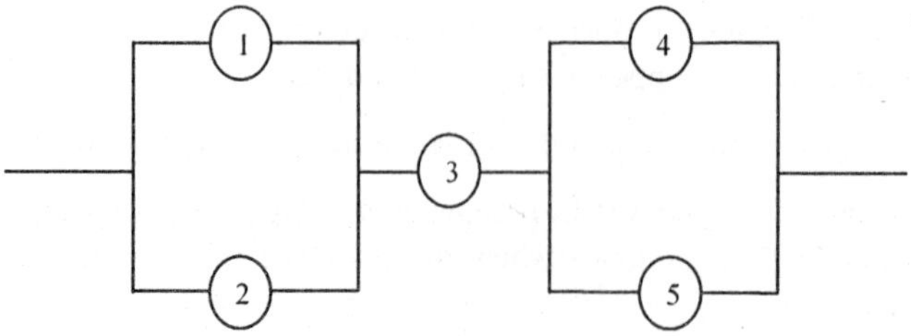

Fig. 2 : System 2 (Hi-fi System)

Let us draw a random sample of size 5 from a Weibull distribution having shape parameter 4 and scale parameter 2 for the times-to-failure of the components of a bridge system. Let $(X_1, X_2, X_3, X_4, X_5) = (2.75189, 2.428505, 1.813506, 2.259444, 1.973540)$ be a random sample drawn from the said population. Here component 3 fails first at time 1.813506. Here the system does not fail with the failure of component 3. So we proceed as follows: a random sample, (0.9526010, 0.9171080, 0.9983486, 0.9295437, 0.9083337), of size 5 is drawn from a uniform distribution having parameters è = 0.9 and 1, for the random factor r by which the remaining times-to-failure of the other components decrease. Then the reduced failure times of the components will be $(X_1, X_2, X_3, X_4, X_5) = (2.707392, 2.377527, 1.813506, 2.228025, 1.95887)$, which indicates that after the failure of component 3, component 5 will fail, and it fails at time 1.95887. The system will still function. We draw another random sample, (0.9412097, 0.9443361, 0.9764843, 0.9249544, 0.9940138), of size 5 from the uniform distribution with parameters (0.9, 1) for r, which gives the reduced failure times of the components as (2.663386, 2.354223, 1.813506, 2.207826, 1.95887). From this we observe that component 4 will fail next, at time 2.207826, and with this failure the system fails. Hence failure time of the bridge system is $T_1 = 2.207826$, under dependent set up.

If the system worked under independent set up, then the time-to-failure of the system would have been $T_1 = \min\{\max(2.75189, 2.428505), \max(2.259444, 1.973540), \max(2.75189, 1.813506, 1.973540), \max(2.428505, 1.813506, 2.259444)\} = 2.259444$. Hence, due to dependence, the percentage loss in failure time of the system is 2.28444%.

It may be noted that if the sample times-to-failure, as drawn earlier, corresponds to the hi-fi system, then there would not be any loss. The time-to-failure of the system will be same for dependence and independence set ups, because component 3 fails first and the system fails with the failure of component 3 there.

Now let us draw another sample of size 5 from the Weibull distribution having shape parameter 4 and scale parameter 2 for the times-to-failure of the components of the hi-fi system. Let $(X_1, X_2, X_3, X_4, X_5) = (0.6237454, 1.3251238, 1.7688247, 2.5985788, 2.6444809)$ be the failure times of the components. Here component 1 fails first at time 0.6237454. With this failure the system does not fail. As before, draw a random sample of size 5 from a uniform distribution with parameters (0.9, 1) for the random factor r. Let (0.9085119, 0.9507358, 0.9213588, 0.9861542, 0.9139768) be the sample. Then the reduced failure times of the components are (0.6237454, 1.290571, 1.678774, 2.571236, 2.470651). Next fails component 2, with which the system fails at time 1.290571. Hence the time-to-failure of the system under dependent set up is $T_2 = 1.290571$.

Under independence set up the time-to-failure of the system would be $T_2 = 1.325128$. Thus the percentage loss in failure time of the system is 2.607515%.

Comparison of Risks of Failure of the Systems having Positive Dependent Components

Let us consider a positive dependence model where failure of one component increases the risk of failing to meet a target life for the remaining components by a common factor. Under this model two (or more) coherent systems are compared by evaluating their risk of failure. We select the system whose risk of failure is minimum.

For determining which of the systems is better (best) in the sense of having less risk of failure to meet a target life the most likely minimal cut sets of the systems are obtained and their sizes are compared. The following rule suggests which system is to be selected, based on the size of their most likely minimal cut sets (see Roychowdhury and Bhattacharya[7]).

Rule: When we compare two (or more) coherent systems with positive dependent components (under the model stated above), the system having most likely minimal cut set of larger (largest) size will be better (best) in the sense of having less (least) risk of failure to meet a target life.

An Example

The minimal cut sets of a bridge system are $\{1,2\}$, $\{4,5\}$, $\{1,3,5\}$ and $\{2,3,4\}$. The minimal cut sets of a hi-fi system are $\{1,2\}$, $\{3\}$, $\{4,5\}$. Since the sizes of minimal cut sets of a bridge system are 2 and 3, and that of a hi-fi system are 1 and 2, the most likely minimal cut set of the bridge system is 2 and most likely minimal cut set of the hi-fi system is 1. Hence a bridge system with positive dependent components is better than a hi-fi system with positive dependent components.

A Simulation Study

Let us draw a random sample of size 5 from a Weibull distribution for the times-to-failure of the components. Let (1.045310, 1.116336, 2.527368, 2.040003, 1.907704) be a random sample of times-to-failure of the components from a Weibull distribution with parameters (shape =) 4 and (scale =) 2. We draw 10^5 such samples and compute the proportion of cases a component fails before time $t = 2$, which estimates the probability that a component fails before time $t = 2$. For a bridge system, we obtain the proportion of cases where minimum of maximum of X_1, X_2 and maximum of X_4, X_5 is less than less than time $t = 2$, which comes out to be 0.9434. For a hi-fi system, we obtain the proportion of cases when component 3 fails before time $t = 2$, which comes out to be 0.9712. We repeat this for different values of t, such as $t = 0.5, 1.0, 1.5, 2.5$, and in all cases the former proportion comes out to be smaller than the latter one, which supports our decision. We repeat this for other failure time distributions of the components, such as exponential(2), gamma(4,3), lognormal(3, 1), for different values of t, and in all cases we find that the proportion of times the system fails before time t is smaller for bridge system, which indicates that the bridge system is better than the hi-fi system.

The simulation results are tabulated below:

TABLE 1 – Simulation results showing the proportion of times the system fails before time t

t	Weibull		exponential		gamma		lognormal	
	Bridge system	Hi-fi system	Bridge system	Hi-fi system	Bridge system	Hi-fi system	Bridge system	Hi-fi system
0.5	0.00278	0.00389	0.41787	0.63212	0.04983	0.06564	0.00009	0.00011
1.0	0.04152	0.06059	0.85075	0.86466	0.28727	0.35277	0.00099	0.00135
1.5	0.11252	0.27124	0.91497	0.95021	0.58396	0.65770	0.00361	0.00474
2.0	0.42559	0.63212	0.92118	0.98168	0.73985	0.84879	0.00898	0.01053
2.5	0.75927	0.91296	0.98005	0.99326	0.90517	0.94085	0.01701	0.01859

Conclusion and Discussion

The effect of dependence of components on time-to-failure of a system and the risk of its failure for different system configurations and for different distributions of failure time of the components of a system has been studied in this paper. If times-to-failure of the components are actually dependent, but assumed to be independent, the risk of system failure will be under- or over-estimated. The extent of the change in risk of system failure or its time-to-failure depends on the distribution of the failure time of the components and on the designs of the system. A simulation study reveals that a bridge system is better than a hi-fi system under dependent set-up, in the sense of having less risk of failure to meet a target life. The study has been done considering different distributions of failure time of the components of those systems, and the same findings have been observed.

References

1. C. Ma, Uniform stochastic ordering on a system of components with dependent lifetimes induced by a common environment, *Sankhya* **61** (1999), Series A, 218-228.
2. E.L. Lehmann, Some Concepts of Dependence, *Ann. Math. Statist.*, **37**(1966), 1137-1153.
3. G. G. Roussas, Positive and negative dependence with some statistical applications, *Asymptotics, Nonparametrics, and Time Series: A Tribute to Madan Lal Puri*; (S. Ghosh, Ed.), Marcel Dekker, Textbook Monograph, **158** (1999),757-788.
4. M. Shaked, A concept of positive dependence for exchangeable random variables, *Ann.Statist.* **5**(1977), 505-515.
5. R.E. Barlow and F. Proschan, *Statistical Theory of Reliability and Life Testing: Probability Models*, Silver Spring, MD (1981).
6. S. Roychowdhury, A Generalized approach to comparing the systems of different order, *Advanced Modeling and Optimization*,**12** (1) (2010), 57-69.
7. S. Roychowdhury and D. Bhattacharya, On Selection of Best System from a Group of Systems with Dependent Component Lives, communicated (2010).
8. S. Roychowdhury and D. Bhattacharya, Effect of Dependence of Components on the System Performance (2011), To appear.

◈◈◈

ISBN – 978-93-5024-769-3

12

A Study of Impact of Tax Holiday on IT/ITES Industries

Mandeep Kaur Gondara
Asst. Prof. Jayawant Institute of Management Studies, Pune.

Introduction

The Software Technology Park India (STPI) scheme was introduced in the formative years of the Information Technology (IT) industry in India. It provides certain concession in duties, levies and taxes to companies that export IT and IT-enabled services which are named as Tax-Holiday. These include exemptions from customs and excise duty, as well as reimbursement of Central Sales Tax. However, the largest concession is the exemption from corporate tax for the initial ten years, from when a business "unit" is set up, all being subject to certain provisions of the Indian Income Tax Act. This initial ten-year tax holiday helped the fledgling IT industry grow rapidly as companies churned back earnings into investments in expansion and growth. The growth of IT industry has made a huge impact on economic scene of India; it has now become a significant sector contributing to India's GDP, Employment, and ancillary Industries. In this paper, first I have presented the contribution of IT/ITES sector to our economy in terms of statistical processed data after the Tax Holiday given to IT industry. Secondly, I have presented the opinion of IT professionals regarding continuation of Tax Holiday. I have also compared the STPI scheme with SEZ and highlighted the benefits of STPI. The study of my research will provide insights to the government of India into making decisions involving Continuation or End of TAX Holiday for IT/ITES industry.

Background

One of the major factors of excellent and consistent growth of Indian software industry can be attributed to continuous liberalization of policies of the Government of India. The Software Technology Park India (STPI) is a society set up by the Ministry of Communication and Information Technology, Government of India in 1991, with the objective of encouraging, promoting and boosting the Software Exports from India. It provides certain concession in duties, levies and taxes to companies that export IT and IT-enabled services. These include exemptions from customs and excise duty, as well as reimbursement of Central Sales Tax. However, the largest concession is the exemption from corporate tax for the initial ten years, from when a business "unit" is set up, all being subject to certain provisions of the Indian Income Tax Act [1]. With the IT industry growing at a fairly rapid pace, it is imperative that the extension in time lines for tax exemptions offered by section 10A - under the STPI Act be reviewed. The primary benefit under STPI act is the tax exemption under section 10 A which states a software unit registered as a STPI unit - into exports - does not have to pay tax for revenues it makes out of its exports. Software Technology Park [STP] Scheme is a 100% export oriented scheme for undertaking software development for export using data communication links or in the form of physical media including export of professional services [4].

The TAX Holiday is nearing end which has prompted me to take up the study of impact of TAX Holiday on IT and ITES industry during the formative years till the current state of IT/ITES industry. When the Software Technology Parks of India (STPI) tax benefits go away in March 2011, effective tax rates (tax as a percentage of profits before tax) could go up from the average 15-17 per cent now. The decision of continuation or end of TAX HOLIDAY for IT/ITES industries is particularly Important for business process outsourcing (BPO) companies and the small and medium segment that have been greatly impacted by the rupee appreciation, inflation and signs of slowdown of the U.S. economy. The study outcome of my research will be helpful in deeper understanding of impact of Tax Holiday on IT/ITES Industry and on our economy

Objectives of the Study

- The objective of this particular study has been to highlight the significant economic and social contribution of the 'for profit' activities of the industry.
- To study the impact of TAX HOLIDAY on IT/ITES industry in terms of contribution to Indian economy.
- To find out the impact of TAX HOLIDAY in employment generation by IT/ITES Industry.
- To study the contribution of TAX HOLIDAY in building brand image of Indian IT/ITES industries globally.
- The study outcome will be helpful in deeper understanding of impact of Tax Holiday on IT/ITES Industry.
- The study will provide insights into making decisions involving Continuation or End of TAX Holiday for IT/ITES industry

Research Approach

The research approach involved a combination of primary and secondary survey of IT/ITES companies.

Primary survey

1. As a first step, Two-page questionnaire was designed to capture some basic information about the companies and their relevant activities and to know the views & ideas of employees about impact of TAX HOLIDAY on IT/ITES Sector.

Secondary Survey

2. Past study reports and information available with NASSCOM
3. Annual Reports, websites of IT companies and documented information shared by companies who had participated in the survey
4. Articles, newspaper clippings, reports available in public domain.

Contribution of IT/ITES to Our Economy After TAX-HOLIDAY

The Indian IT / ITES industry has been one of the great success stories of modern India[3]. In the last two decades, the Indian IT/ITES industry has contributed significantly to Indian economic growth in terms of GDP, foreign exchange earnings and employment generation.

Export Earnings of the IT/ITES industry (USD billion) due to TAX HOLIDAY

If export earnings of the industry are considered as an indicator of contribution to foreign exchange reserves of the country, the IT/ITES industry has clocked an impressive growth of 31.9% in FY07. Export earnings for FY09 stood at approximately USD 46.8 billion as compared to USD 18.3 billion in FY05.

Fig. 1 : Export Earnings of the IT/ITES industry

Contribution of IT/ITES industry to GDP

In the last two decades, the Indian IT/ITES industry has contributed significantly to Indian economic growth in terms of GDP, foreign exchange earnings and employment generation. However, equally significant though not as tangible, has been the ripple effect[3].

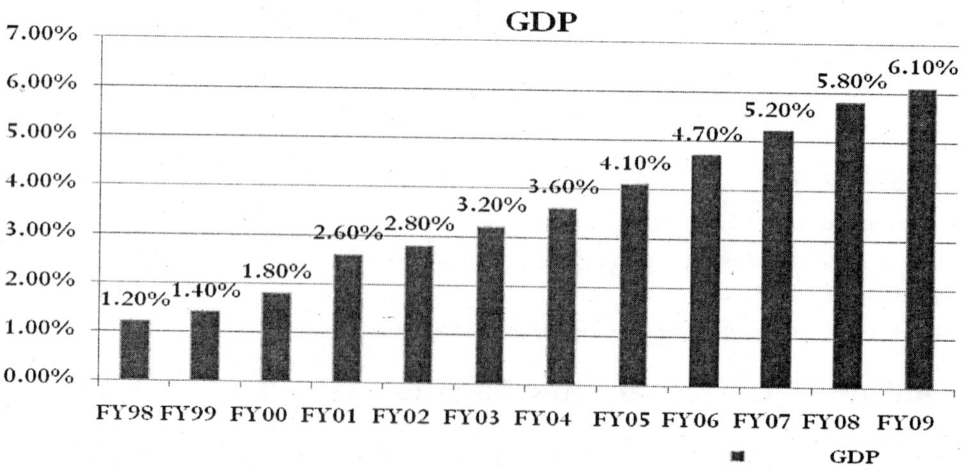

Fig. 2 : Contribution of IT/ITES industry to GDP

Direct Employment in IT/ITES industry

Direct employment in the sector of IT/ITES is around to be 2.28 million by end of FY09, making it the largest employer in the organized private sector of the country. From the figure 3, it is evident that IT sector has contributed in the employment generation at a rapid rate. This growth was possible due to huge earned profits after the TAX concessions given by the government of India.

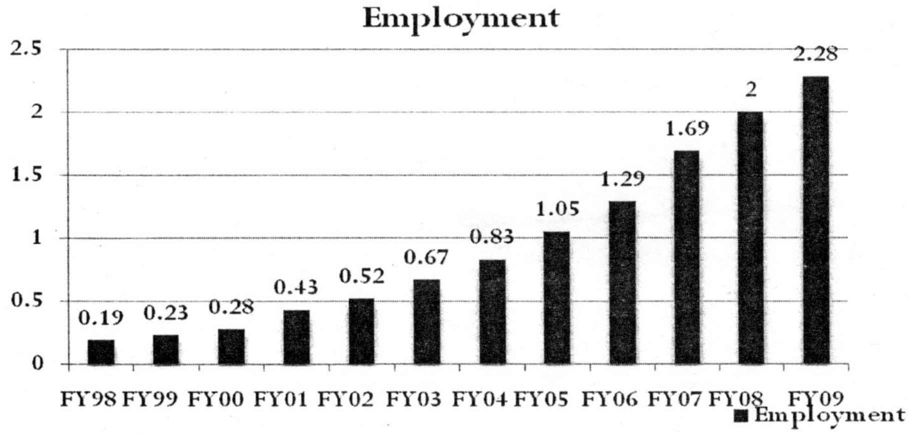

Fig. 3 : Direct Employment in IT/ITES industry

Promoting women empowerment

The growing trend [3],[6], in the number of women employed in IT/ITES sector indicates that not only does the industry offer equal opportunity to women but also has in place proactive and sensitive mechanisms which counter the common causes that discourage women from pursuing employment in the corporate sector. In 2006, the ratio of men and women employees was 76% and 24%. In 2008, men employees were 65% and women 35%. In 2010, men employees are 45% and women are 55%.

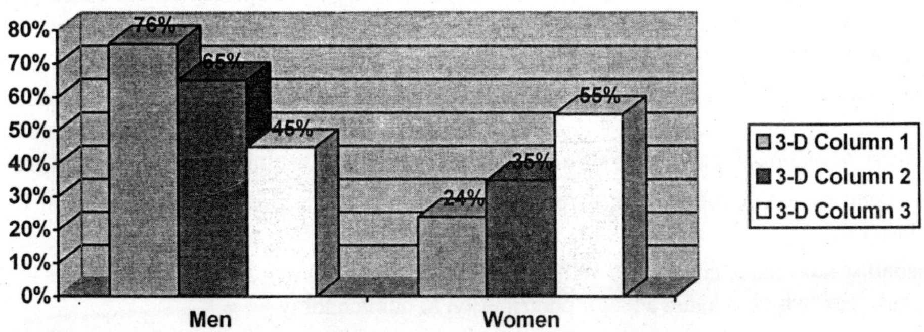

Fig. 4 : Women employees Vs Men employees in IT sector

IT Professionl's Opinion About Continuation of Tax Holiday

As figure 5 depicts, 80% IT professionals are in the favor of continuation of Tax holiday whereas 20% say no for continuation of Tax holiday.

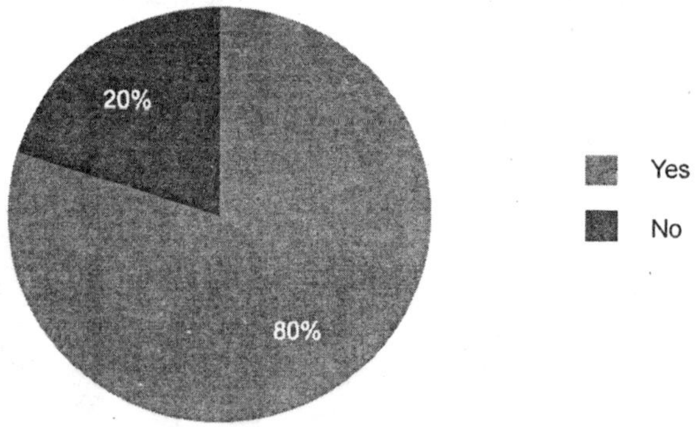

Fig. 5

4.1 Reason to say "No"

- The existing tax holiday under the STPI scheme is set to expire in 2011. This means all IT companies will have to pay 30+% corporate tax as well as indirect taxes like any other company. While this would result in a major revenue boost to the central and state governments
- The problem is the tax holiday enjoyed by IT companies. Like other things in India, the exception always seeks to become the rule [2]. Once benefits are given they cannot be taken back or cut down
- SEZ (Special economic zone) scheme is there till 2020, why to stress upon the continuation of STP scheme.

4.2 Reason to say "Yes"

- The IT/ITES industry has contributed to the growth and development of the country in terms of various economical and social aspects through its "for-profit" as well as "not-for-profit" activities but just because of TAX HOLIDAY [3].
- The infant IT companies could not deal with the astronomical cost of tele-communications, archaic customs duty rules, and a high rate of taxation. So the initial 10-year tax holiday helped an infant industry to attain critical mass[6]. Still the industry is in its immature stage; it needs to grow more
- The contribution of the STPI tax holiday is the reason behind the overall success of the IT/ITES industries.
- Secondly, most of the employees of the companies are contributing 30% of their salaries in the form of Income Tax; which is again a major contribution to our economy.

Advantage of STPI Over SEZ Scheme

Sr.No	*STPI(Software Technology Park India)*	*SEZ(Special Economic Zone)*
1.	The software Industry has attained global recognition primarily because of STPI scheme; an autonomous society under Ministry of communication and Information Technology [5].	The Special Economic Zones (SEZs) Policy was announced in April 2000 and implemented with effect from April 2005 with a view to attract larger foreign investments in India [4].
2.	An STP unit may be a standalone unit by itself or it may be one of such units located in any area designated as STP Complex.	SEZ unit has to be located within the specified zones developed; there is no liberty to set up a unit like STPI scheme
3.	The STPI Unit is Exempted from payment of Income Tax U/s 10A upto 31.03.2011	An SEZ Unit will be exempt U/s 10AA from 100% Tax exemption for First 5 years after commercial production- & 50% of profits are exempt for the next 5 years (subject to certain conditions)[4].
4.	Even though an STPI Unit is exempted from payment of tax as aforesaid in point 1- It still needs to pay Minimum Alternate TAX (MAT)- In effect 10% of its books profit effectively will be paid out as MAT which can be treated as advance tax and set off when it pays regular income tax after 01.04.2011	An SEZ unit will be exempted even from payment of MAT. This scheme won't contribute in terms of minimum alternate tax.
5.	Even Small scale industries can be a part of STPI scheme	A Small company wanting to grow to less than 25-30 people, would find it difficult to get an area in SEZ of about 3-4K sq ft Area. The rentals are also on the higher side.
6.	An STPI unit when Distribute dividends to its shareholders will have to pay a Dividend Distribution Tax (DDT)@12.5%	An SEZ unit is exempted from payment of DDT.

It is evident from the above mentioned points that STPI is more fruitful scheme for the growth of IT industries and our economy.

Conclusion

The tax holiday is a precious tool. If used right, it will help such as the case with the Software Technology Park India (STPI). The IT/ITES industry has contributed to the growth and development of the country in terms of various economical and social aspects through its "for-profit" as well as "not-for-profit" activities due to Tax holiday given by the government. Indian IT/ITES industry still needs a space and support from the Indian government for its growth. IT industry is still immature at the current stage and needs certain concession from our government in terms of Tax holiday. I conclude my research paper with the decision of continuation of TAX HOLIDAY for IT/ITES industry on the basis of facts of survey.

References

1. Thomas J. Sebastian, Project Director, TPI "India Service Provider Tax Holiday End Draws Near: Cause for Concern" at http://www.tpi.net/
2. http://www.realitycheck.wordpress.com/
3. www.nasscom.in/
4. www.sezadvisors.in/
5. www.stpiconsultancy.com
6. www.dateyvs.com

◇◇◇

ISBN – 978-93-5024-769-3

13

The Role of Technology in Improving Services Quality, in a Banking Sector

Rupa D. Jajoo
Research Fellow.
Dr. Vani N. Laturkar
School of Commerce & Management Sciences S.R.T.M. University, Nanded.

Introduction

Banking environment has become highly competitive today. To be able to survive and grow in the changing market environment banks are going for the latest technologies, which is being perceived as an 'enabling resource' that can help in developing learner and more flexible structure that can respond quickly to the dynamics of a fast changing market scenario. Information Technology enables sophisticated product development, better market infrastructure, implementation of reliable techniques for control of risks and helps the financial intermediaries to reach geographically distant and diversified markets. Internet has significantly influenced delivery channels of the banks. Internet has emerged as an important medium for delivery of banking products and services.

Most of the banks have been in the credit card business having tie-ups with entities such as Visa, Master card, etc. sometimes during online transaction snoopers may get hold of the private information transacted through these lines. Hence banks should take preventive steps towards preventing violation of such private information.

The information technology (IT) has various aspects of our life. It has transformed the repetitive and overlapping systems and procedures into simple single key pressing technology resulting in speed, accuracy, and efficiency of conduction business. Thus, the implementation of IT has left an indelible impression almost on all the vistas of our life and activities. The IT is emerging as a strong tool to manipulate figures to its last precision. The large computing powers have given mankind a major tool to generate MIS and other relevant information which can be used effectively to improve both product and service.

During the last few years the global scene of banking and finance has changed rapidly largely due to deregulation and liberalization and coupled with increased use of Information Technology. It would thus be proper to infer the IT can be best utilized in banking and related services. The banks generate tremendous amount of data, reports and files that need to be converted into key information. Voluminous transaction are conducted within and across branches and advancement in IT provides better delivery channels to meet the ever increasing demand of customers.

Computerization and automation of banks and financial institutions is a key focus area today and is receiving prime attention as it touches everybody's work in some way or the other. Banks also looked at new avenues to improve operational efficiency and provide better customer satisfaction. Technology enabled some of the banks to introduce innovative products to their customers in the form of ATM facility, tele-banking, home banking, And Credit cards etc.

Banks as well as other financial entities in India have recently taken to the world of information technology and computer networking in a bigger way. No doughtily technology up gradation is taking place in public sector banks in a phased manner. Computerization is increasingly being applied in day to day operations. At present 40-45% of banking business has been computerized. Banks perform several important functions in the financial sector. In performing all these functions IT helps banking business at great level.

The customers can view the accounts; get account statements, transfer funds and purchase drafts by just punching on few keys. The credit cards have added new dimension to the scenario. Collection of Electricity bills and telephone bills has become easy. The up gradeability and flexibility of internet technology after unprecedented opportunities are for the banks to reach out to its customers. No doubt banking services have undergone drastic changes and so also the expectation of customers from the banks has increased greater.

Many banks have modernized their services with the facilities of computer and electronic equipments. The electronics revolution has made it possible to provide ease and flexibility in banking operations to the benefit of the customer. The e-banking has made the customer say good-bye to huge account registers and large paper bank accounts. The e-banks, which may call as easy bank offers the services like Credit Cards/Debit Cards, ATM, E-Cheques, EFT (Electronic Funds Transfer), De-MAT Accounts, Mobile Banking, Telephone Banking, Internet Banking, EDI (Electronic Data Interchange) to its customers.

Customer management is a strategy and methodology adopted by management of the banks and other financial institutions, which help them to manage proper information about customers that helps bank to serve customer better than competitors. Customer management also provides banks and card companies, leverage in their marketing and other strategies. It also assist card companies in proper tracking of customer behavior for developing marketing and relationship-building processes that bond the consumer to the bank or the company's brand. Proper customer management strategy ultimately helps in increasing sales and satisfaction level of customer hence increasing customer retention. In simple language Customer management is a "customer focus approach" by the company.

Role of Technology

Information Technology has basically been used under two different avenues in Banking. One is Communication and Connectivity and other is Business Process Reengineering. Information technology enables sophisticated product development, better market infrastructure, implementation of reliable techniques for control of risks and helps the financial intermediaries to reach geographically distant and diversified markets. In view of this, technology has changed the contours of three major functions performed by banks, i.e., access to liquidity, transformation of assets and monitoring of risks. Further, Information technology and the communication networking systems have a crucial bearing on the efficiency of money, capital and foreign exchange markets. Internet has significantly influenced delivery channels of the banks. Internet has emerged as an important medium for delivery of banking products & services. Detailed guidelines of RBI for Internet Banking has prepared the necessary ground for growth of Internet Banking in India. The Information Technology Act, 2000 has given legal recognition to creation, trans-mission and retention of an electronic (or magnetic) data to be treated as valid proof in a court of law, except in those areas, which continue to be governed by the provisions of the Negotiable Instruments Act, 1881. As stated in RBI's Annual Monetary and Credit Policy 2002-2003: "To reap the full benefits of such electronic message transfers, it is necessary that banks bestow sufficient attention on the computerisation and networking of the branches situated at commercially important centres on a time-bound basis. Intra-city and intra-bank networking would facilitate in addressing the "last mile" problem which would in turn result in quick and efficient funds transfers across the country".

Advantages of Technology

1. From both customer and banking perspectives it shows that the Internet is a convenience tool available whenever and wherever customers need it. It is also found that the Internet has improved the factors in service quality like responsiveness, communication and access. It is concluded that the Internet has an important and positive effect on customer perceived banking services and the service quality has been improved since the Internet has been used in banking sector.
2. It's generally secure. But make sure that the website you're using has a valid security certificate. This lets you know that the site is protected from cyber-thieves looking to steal your personal and financial information.
3. It gives twenty-four-hour access. When the neighborhood bank closes, you can still access your account and make transactions online. It's a very convenient alternative for those that can't get to the bank during normal hours because of their work schedule, health or any other reason.
4. It allows us to access our account from virtually anywhere. If we're on a business trip or vacationing away from home, we can still keep a watchful on our money and financial transactions – regardless of our location.
5. Conducting business online is generally faster than going to the bank. Long teller lines can be time-consuming, especially on a Pay Day. But online, there are no lines to contend with. You can access your account instantly and at your leisure.
6. Many features and services are typically available online. For example, with just a few clicks you can apply for loans, check the progress of your investments, review interest rates and gather other important information that may be spread out over several different brochures in the local bank.
7. Technology has opened up new markets, new products, new services and efficient delivery channels for the banking industry. Online electronics banking, mobile banking and internet banking are just a few examples.
8. Information Technology has also provided banking industry with the wherewithal to deal with the challenges the new economy poses. Information technology has been the cornerstone of recent financial sector reforms aimed at increasing the speed and reliability of financial operations and of initiatives to strengthen the banking sector.
9. The IT revolution has set the stage for unprecedented increase in financial activity across the globe. The progress of technology and the development of worldwide networks have significantly reduced the cost and time of global funds transfer.
10. It is information technology which enables banks in meeting such high expectations of the customers who are more demanding and are also more techno-savy compared to their counterparts of the yester years. They demand instant, anytime and anywhere banking facilities.
11. IT has been providing solutions to banks to take care of their accounting and back office requirements. This has, however, now given way to large scale usage in services aimed at the customer of the banks.
12. IT also facilitates the introduction of new delivery channels—in the form of Automated Teller Machines, Net Banking, Mobile Banking and the like.
13. Use of de-mat account and online trading enables a person to buy and sell shares any time. The share trading companies and AMC's can give improved and faster service with help of technology.
14. There are many useful features and services available online besides for the usual transactions. For example, you can apply for credit cards, manage investments, and pay bills through your online account portal. You can also perform more mundane tasks such as ordering new checks, requesting additional deposit slips, or reporting a lost or stolen debit card.

Certainly the above mentioned advantages if technology have improved the quality of service in a banking and financial sector.

Technology Products in A Banking Sector

1. Net Banking
2. Credit Card Online
3. Instant Alerts
4. Mobile Banking
5. e-Monies Electronic Fund Transfer
6. Online Payment of Excise & Service Tax
7. Phone Banking
8. Bill Payment
9. Shopping
10. Ticket Booking
11. Railway Ticket Booking through SMS
12. Prepaid Mobile Recharge
13. Smart Money Order
14. Card to Card Funds Transfer
15. Funds Transfer (e-Cheques)
16. Anywhere Banking
17. Internet Banking
18. Mobile Banking
19. Bank @ Home "Express Delivery"

Some of common available banking products are explained below:

(1) **Credit Card:** Credit Card is "post paid" or "pay later" card that draws from a credit line-money made available by the card issuer (bank) and gives one a grace period to pay. If the amount is not paid full by the end of the period, one is charged interest. A credit card is nothing but a very small card containing a means of identification, such as a signature and a small photo. It authorizes the holder to change goods or services to his account, on which he is billed. The bank receives the bills from the merchants and pays on behalf of the card holder. These bills are assembled in the bank and the amount is paid to the bank by the card holder totally or by installments. The bank charges the customer a small amount for these services. The card holder need not have to carry money/cash with him when he travels or goes for purchasing. Credit cards have found wide spread acceptance in the 'metros' and big cities. Credit cards are joining popularity for online payments. The major players in the Credit Card market are the foreign banks and some big public sector banks like SBI and Bank of Baroda. India at present has about 3 million credit cards in circulation.

(2) **Debit Cards:** Debit Card is a "prepaid" or "pay now" card with some stored value. Debit Cards quickly debit or subtract money from one's savings account, or if one were taking out cash. Every time a person uses the card, the merchant who in turn can get the money transferred to his account from the bank of the buyers, by debiting an exact amount of purchase from the card. To get a debit card along with a Personal Identification Number (PIN). When he makes a purchase, he enters this number on the

shop's PIN pad. When the card is swiped through the electronic terminal, it dials the acquiring bank system – either Master Card or Visa that validates the PIN and finds out from the issuing bank whether to accept or decline the transaction. The customer never overspread because the amount spent is debited immediately from the customers account. So, for the debit card to work, one must already have the money in the account to cover the transaction. There is no grace period for a debit card purchase. Some debit cards have monthly or per transaction fees. Debit Card holder need not carry a bulky checkbook or large sums of cash when he/she goes at for shopping. This is a fast and easy way of payment one can get debit card facility as debit cards use one's own money at the time of sale, so they are often easier than credit cards to obtain. The major limitation of Debit Card is that currently only some 8000-10000 shops country wide accepts it. Also, a person can't operate it in case the telephone lines are down.

(3) **Automatic Teller Machine:** The introduction of ATM's has given the customers the facility of round the clock banking. The ATM's are used by banks for making the customers dealing easier. ATM card is a device that allows customer who has an ATM card to perform routine banking transaction at any time without interacting with human teller. It provides exchange services. This service helps the customer to withdraw money even when the banks ate closed. This can be done by inserting the card in the ATM and entering the Personal Identification Number and secret Password.

ATM's are currently becoming popular in India that enables the customer to withdraw their money 24 hours a day and 365 days. It provides the customers with the ability to withdraw or deposit funds, check account balances, transfer funds and check statement information. The advantages of ATM's are many. It increases existing business and generates new business. It allows the customers. ATM's can be installed anywhere like Airports, Railway Stations, Petrol Pumps, Big Business arcades, markets, etc. Hence, it gives easy access to the customers, for obtaining cash.

The ATM services provided first by the foreign banks like Citibank, Grind lays bank and now by many private and public sector banks in India like ICICI Bank, HDFC Bank, SBI, UTI Bank etc. The ICICI has launched ATM Services to its customers in all the Metropolitan Cities in India. By the end of 1990 Indian Private Banks and public sector banks have come up with their own ATM Network in the form of "SWADHAN". Over the past year upto 44 banks in Mumbai, Vashi and Thane, have became a part of "SWADHAN" a system of shared payments networks, introduced by the Indian Bank Association (IBA).

(4) **E-Cheques:** The e-cheques consists five primary facts. They are the consumers, the merchant, consumer's bank the merchant's bank and the e-mint and the clearing process. This chequing system uses the network services to issue and process payment that emulates real world chequing. The payer issue a digital cheques to the payee ant the entire transactions are done through internet. Electronic version of cheques are issued, received and processed. A typical electronic cheque transaction takes place in the following manner:

- The customer accesses the merchant server and the merchant server presents its goods to the customer.
- The consumer selects the goods and purchases them by sending an e-cheque to the merchant.
- The merchant validates the e-cheque with its bank for payment authorisation.
- The merchant electronically forwards the e-cheque to its bank.
- The merchant's bank forwards the e-cheque to the clearing house for cashing.
- The clearing house jointly works with the consumer's bank clears the cheque and transfers the money to the merchant's banks.
- The merchant's bank updates the merchant's account.

- The consumer's bank updates the consumer's account with the withdrawal information.
- The e-chequing is a great boon to big corporate as well as small retailers. Most major banks accept e-cheques. Thus this system offers secure means of collecting payments, transferring value and managing cash flows.

(5) **Electronic Funds Transfer (EFT):** Many modern banks have computerised their cheque handling process with computer networks and other electronic equipments. These banks are dispensing with the use of paper cheques. The system called electronic fund transfer (EFT) automatically transfers money from one account to another. This system facilitates speedier transfer of funds electronically from any branch to any other branch. In this system the sender and the receiver of funds may be located in different cities and may even bank with different banks. Funds transfer within the same city is also permitted. The scheme has been in operation since February 7, 1996, in India. The other important type of facility in the EFT system is automated clearing houses. These are the computer centers that handle the bills meant for deposits and the bills meant for payment. In big companies pay is not disbursed by issued cheques or issuing cash. The payment office directs the computer to credit an employee's account with the person's pay.

(6) **Telebanking:** Telebanking refers to banking on phone services. A customer can access information about his/her account through a telephone call and by giving the coded Personal Identification Number (PIN) to the bank. Telebanking is extensively user friendly and effective in nature.

- To get a particular work done through the bank, the users may leave his instructions in the form of message with bank.
- Facility to stop payment on request. One can easily know about the cheque status.
- Information on the current interest rates.
- Information with regard to foreign exchange rates.
- Request for a DD or pay order.
- DeMat Account related services.
- And other similar services.

(7) **Mobile Banking:** A new revolution in the realm of e-banking is the emergence of mobile banking. On-line banking is now moving to the mobile world, giving everybody with a mobile phone access to real-time banking services, regardless of their location. But there is much more to mobile banking from just on-lie banking. It provides a new way to pick up information and interact with the banks to carry out the relevant banking business. The potential of mobile banking is limitless and is expected to be a big success. Booking and paying for travel and even tickets is also expected to be a growth area. According to this system, customer can access account details on mobile using the Short Messaging System (SMS) technology where select data is pushed to the mobile device. The wireless application protocol (WAP) technology, which will allow user to surf the net on their mobiles to access is anything and everything. This is a very flexible way of transacting banking business. Already ICICI and HDFC banks have tied up cellular service provides such as Airtel, Orange, Sky Cell, etc. in Delhi and Mumbai to offer these mobile banking services to their customers.

(8) **Internet Banking:** Internet banking involves use of internet for delivery of banking products and services. With internet banking is now no longer confirmed to the branches where one has to approach the branch in person, to withdraw cash or deposits a cheque or request a statement of accounts. In internet banking, any inquiry or transaction is processed online without any reference to the branch (anywhere banking) at any time. The Internet Banking now is more of a normal rather than an exception due to the fact that it is the cheapest way of providing banking services. As indicated by McKinsey

Quarterly research, presently traditional banking costs the banks, more than a dollar per person, ATM banking costs 27 cents and internet banking costs below 4 cents approximately. ICICI bank was the first one to offer Internet Banking in India.

(9) **Demat:** Demat is short for de-materialisation of shares. In short, Demat is a process where at the customer's request the physical stock is converted into electronic entries in the depository system. In January 1998 SEBI (Securities and Exchange Board of India) initiated DEMAT ACCOUNTANCY System to regulate and to improve stock investing. As on date, to trade on shares it has become compulsory to have a share demat account and all trades take place through demat.

Disadvantages of Technology

1. Yes, online banking is generally secure, but it certainly isn't always secure. Identity theft is running rampant, and banks are by no means immune. And once your information is compromised, it can take months or even years to correct the damage, not to mention possibly costing you thousands of dollars, as well. This generally does not happen in case of traditional method of banking.
2. Some online banks are more stable than others. Not all online setups are an extension of a brick-and-mortar bank. Some operate completely in cyberspace, without the benefit of a branch that you can actually visit if need be. With no way to physically check out the operation, you must be sure to thoroughly do your homework about the bank's background before giving them any of your money.
3. Before using a banking site that you aren't familiar with, check to make sure that their deposits are FDIC -insured. If not, you could possibly lose all of your deposits if the bank goes under, or its major shareholders decide to take an extended vacation in Switzerland.
4. Customer service can be below the quality that you're used to. Some people simply take comfort in being able to talk to another human being face-to-face if they experience a problem. Although most major banks employ a dedicated customer service department specifically for online users, going through the dreaded telephone menu can still be quite irritating to many. Again, some are considerably better (or worse) than others.
5. Not all online transactions are immediate. Online banking is subject to the same business-day parameters as traditional banking. Therefore, printing out and keeping receipts is still very important, even when banking online.
6. If your bank operates only online or simply does not have a branch office in your local area, you will not be able to reach a representative in person for discussion of account issues. Normally this is not a problem, but sometimes customer service by telephone or email can be spotty and may prove to be more of a hassle if you have a serious issue that is not easily resolved. Some banks are better than others in this department, so you will need to do some research if this is an important consideration for you.
7. Using online banking effectively requires some basic computer literacy and familiarity with navigating the Internet. While this is not a problem for people like me, those who are afflicted with technophobia or are simply inexperienced with this particular genre may not be comfortable with this concept. There are also a significant number of people who are suspicious of anything having to do with the Internet because it is outside of their comfort zone. Others are simply too stubborn to acquire the relevant knowledge and skills.

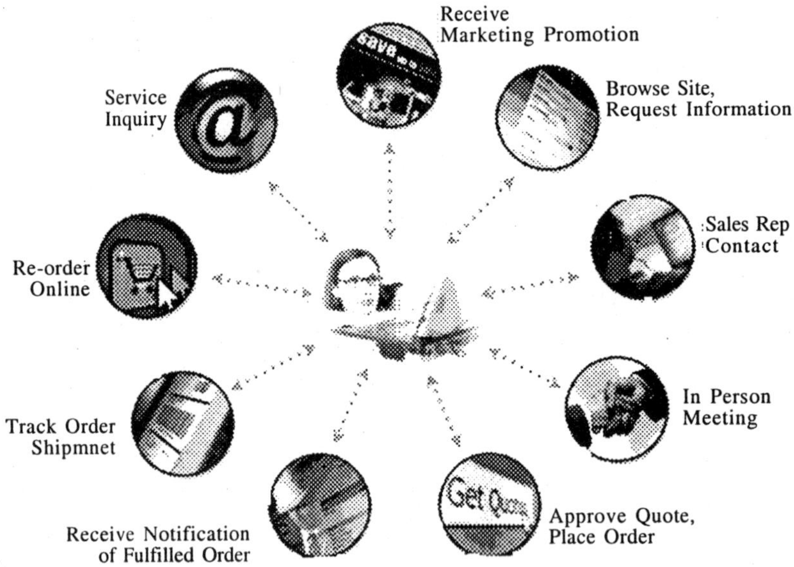

Benefits to the Customer

- Anywhere Banking no matter wherever the customer is in the world. Balance enquiry, request for services, issuing instructions etc., from anywhere in the world is possible.
- Anytime Banking – Managing funds in real time and most importantly, 24 hours a day, 7days a week.
- Convenience acts as a tremendous psychological benefit all the time.
- Brings down "Cost of Banking" to the customer over a period a period of time.
- Cash withdrawal from any branch / ATM
- On-line purchase of goods and services including online payment for the same.

Benefits to the Bank

- Innovative, scheme, addresses competition and present the bank as technology driven in the banking sector market
- Reduces customer visits to the branch and thereby human intervention
- Inter-branch reconciliation is immediate thereby reducing chances of fraud and misappropriation
- On-line banking is an effective medium of promotion of various schemes of the bank, a marketing tool indeed.
- Integrated customer data paves way for individualized and customized services.

Impact of IT on the Service Quality

The most visible impact of technology is reflected in the way the banks respond strategically for making its effective use for efficient service delivery. This impact on service quality can be summed up as below:

With automation, service no longer remains a marketing edge with the large banks only. Small and relatively new banks with limited network of branches become better placed to compete with the established banks, by integrating IT in their operations.

The technology has commoditizing some of the financial services. Therefore the banks cannot take a lifetime relationship with the customers as granted and they have to work continuously to foster this relationship and retain customer loyalty.

The technology on one hand serves as a powerful tool for customer servicing, on the other hand, it itself results in depersonalizing of the banking services. This has an adverse effect on relationship banking. A decade of computerization can probably never substitute a simple or a warm handshake.

In order to reduce service delivery cost, banks need to automate routine customer inquiries through self-service channels. To do this they need to invest in call centers, kiosks, ATM's and Internet Banking today require IT infrastructure integrated with their business strategy to be customer centric.

Impact of IT on Privacy and Confidentiality of Data

Data being stored in the computers is now being displayed when required on through internet banking mobile banking, ATM's etc. all this has given rise to the issues of privacy and confidentially of data are: The data processing capabilities of the computer, particularly the rapid throughput, integration, and retrieval capabilities, give rise to doubts in the minds of individuals as to whether the privacy of the individuals is being eroded. So long as the individual data items are available only to those directly concerned, everything seems to be in proper place, but the incidence of data being cross referenced to create detailed individual dossiers gives rise to privacy problems.

Customers feel threatened about the inadequacy of privacy being maintained by the banks with regard to their transactions and link at computerized systems with suspicion.

Aside from any constitutional aspect, many nations deem privacy to be a subject of human right and consider it to be the responsibility of those who concerned with computer data processing for ensuring that the computer use does not revolve to the stage where different data about people can be collected, integrated and retrieved quickly. Another important responsibility is to ensure the data is used only for the purpose intended.

Conclusion

Banks face increasing pressure to stand out from the crowd. On the Internet, this means offering your target customers an increasingly broader range of services than your competitors and that too in unique way.

Already electronic transfers, clearings, settlements have reduced translation times. To face competition it is necessary for banks to absorb the technology and upgrade their services. However use of High-Tech sophisticated technology leaves the predominantly rural, poor and even illiterate mans in the lurch to which the level of automation and efficiency of services are immaterial.

References

1. Kalakota and Robinson, Consumer Relation Management, Elsevier, 2001
2. Information Technology: Jonathan Shearman, 2006
3. Modern Banking Technology - Dr. Firdos T. Shroff – 2007.
4. www.rbi.com
5. www.toodoc.com
6. www.google.com

◈◈◈

ISBN – 978-93-5024-769-3

14

CRM: A Tool for Gaining Competitive Advantage with Special Reference to Organized Retailing

Prof. Shweta Sharma
Dhole Patil College of Engineering & Management.

Introduction

Over the last few years, retail has become one of the fastest growing sectors in the Indian economy. Though the country has highest retail outlet density in the world, Indian reta il sector is highly fragmented and organized retail in the country is at very nascent stage. Organized retailing accounts for less than 5% of the retailing industry in India. Therefore, there is no real retail revolution in India since the industry is still in the stage of infancy. The organized retail industry in India is expected to grow 25-30 % annually and is projected to attain USD 23 billion by 2010 (FCCI, 2005). Retailing is gradually inching its way towards becoming the next boom industry.

The "Retailing is the final step in the distribution of merchandise- the last link in the supply chain connecting the bulk producers of commodities to the final consumers. "One undergoing this process is referred to as Retailer. Retailing includes diverse products such as apparel, footwear, consumer durables, financial services and leisure. However in India retail trade remains in the backward state but at the same time is poised to expect a rapid growth in tandem with the economic growth. India's $350-400 ban retail market -$7.5 ban organized retail is growing about 25-30% annually against economic growth of around 8% a year.

With this onset many players are entering the market with various products and strategies to cash upon this development in retail sector, thereby increasing competition. Similarly there are various retail formats coming up to grab the opportunity in the retail sector. One of the most prominent retail formats coming up is "Shopping Malls" which can be defined an arrangement of retail stores and providing the right mix of shopping, food courts and entertainment and parking facilities. The retail space is shared by anchor stores and other retailers (tenants), who will pay the developers of the mall-rent or lease payment for putting up the shop within the mall premises.

Sarang Panchal, Executive Director Customized Research A C Nielsen South Asia says, "With increase in the sheer numbers of malls and modern format stores shopping has almost become a national pastime in our country especially in the cities. Strong economic growth along with booming young adult populations with unprecedented levels of disposable incomes has made people more conscious of the latest trends and fashions. No one wants to be left behind, Indian consumers are ever willing to upgrade their knowledge where latest trends are concerned and these definitely helped in increasing the footfalls in all these modern malls mushrooming across the city. "And there are a large number of Shopping Malls and various other retail formats coming up in Metros, Tier I and II cities giving tight competition to the existing ones. And because of this, the retailers are the main focus today and they are totally engrossed in knowing their customer and consumer.

There are several malls coming up in metros among which Mumbai, Bangalore, Delhi, and Pune rank among the top cities in country for retail growth. In case of Mumbai, malls comprise of 90% of total retail development in the pipeline. The success of mall in tier I cities is definitely influencing tier II cities and smaller towns to replicate the mall model. Thus the next logical step for a retailer is to tap this huge latent demand in tier II cities and establish a strong presence in such cities. So keeping this in mind, I decided to study the CRM in reference of the shopping Malls (organized retailing).

Purpose of the Study

Consumers are the major beneficiaries of the retail boom. The Indian consumer is changing rapidly. They now have a choice of wide range of products, quality and price. Retailing is changing the whole concept of shopping in terms of consumer buying behavior. In such a scenario, consumer decision making is of great interest for consumer educators and marketers interested in serving the consumer. Therefore, there is clearly a need for research on this issue in India. number of Shopping Malls and various other retail formats coming up in Metros, Tier I and II cities giving tight competition to the existing ones, perfect ground for investment prospects. As Pune have such huge investment opportunities and is looking forward to retail revolution many players are trying to cash upon it. They are understanding the need of the present age and the demand of the growing changing lifestyle and the increasing affluence of the society; realizing the potential of Pune and the need of planned retailing, and hence they are bringing a new era that reflects itself with upcoming projects.

Objectives Of The Study

- To investigate the consumer decision making style in shopping mall.
- Challenges faced by organized retailing Outlets.
- The study tries to understand the implications of the strategy used by the retail organizations under the headings of Customer Relationship Management.

HYPOTHESES

Hypotheses developed based mainly on the comments cited in the literature and reasonable assumptions.

- **Hypothesis 1:** Consumers who visit the shopping mall are likely to spend more time and money shopping at mall stores and department stores as compared to consumers who do not visit the shopping mall .
- **H2:** Shopping lifestyle of the consumers has a strong association with the buying behavior of the consumers in shopping mall.
- **H3:** Fashion involvement of consumers has a strong association with the impulse buying behavior of the consumers in shopping mall.
- **H4:** People are happy to purchase the product on shopping mall.
- **H5:** People are interested to visit the different market.
- **H6:** The main value provided by the malls to people is the convenience of housing so many facilities and brands under one roof. It is a one stop shop and entertainment for them where they enjoy as well as fulfill their shopping needs."

Research Methodology

Secondary Research -Published data of Organized Retailing (Shopping mall) in India regarding food and grocery retail sector has been analyzed and collected on the basis of identified literature on this particular subject for the last 3 years i.e. 2006 to 2009.

Primary Research -To carry out the primary research, structured questionnaires was design. These questionnaires was fill personally from respondents representing various stakeholders connected with special reference to Shopping mall in Pune City.

Primary data collection was through the Questionnaire method where in a structured questionnaire was used for recording the feedback of respondents. Respondents include consumers, front office staff of the shopping mall, opinion leaders in shopping mall and management staff (corporate &finance/ strategy managers) of the shopping mall separate questionnaires was administered to all the above respondents.

Sample Type - Non probability stratified samples have selected with the assumptions that they are truly representatives of the population even though not statistically. The behavior of these samples can then be used to predict the behaviour of the entire population.

(B) Retail outlets- Under this heading two types of samples used

(I) Non probability Area samples; Different retail outlets spread over Pune city was selected.

(II) Non probability purposive sampling; the retail outlets covered included food and grocery, ready made garments and others. Samples accordingly selected so that we have all representative types of outlets.

Sample size was as follows;

(A) Consumers – 200

(B) Shopping mall- 08

Data Analysis and Interpretation

The two questionnaires, viz one for the consumers and the other for the organized retailers are analyzed. The tables are prepared for the sample selected in the same order as they appear in the questionnaire.

No statistical significance is provided where the answer are straight forward in the form of " Yes" and "No". However, wherever possible, statistical significance has been offered.

(1) Compare your earlier experiences of retailers with the present generation of organized retailers.

Old Retailers

Ambience	24	12%
Courteous & trained staffs	64	32%
Choice of products	56	28%
Personal attention	72	36%
Home delivery	136	68%
Credit facilities	108	54%
Use of technology	32	16%
Discounts/ offers	68	34%

Personal service	76	38%
Payment terms/credit facilities	116	58%
Taking back of goods	132	66%
Telephonic order systems	76	38%
In case of stock-outs are branded products procured on order	88	44%

Sample 200

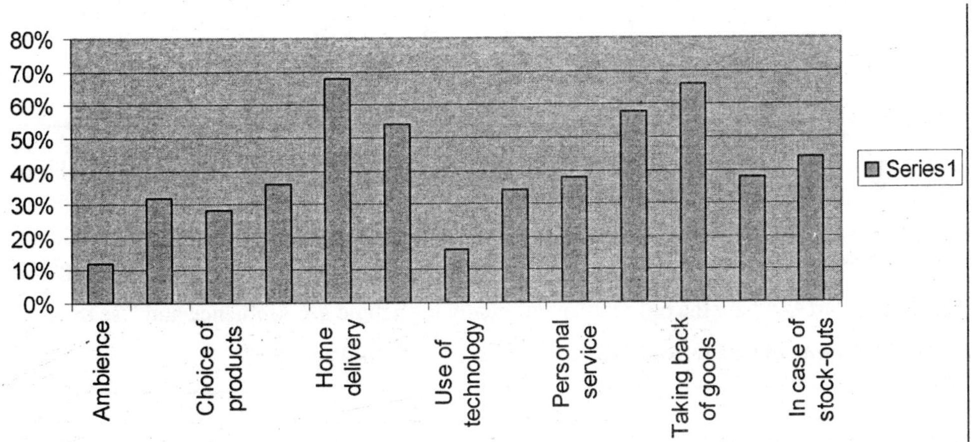

New Retailers

Ambience	192	96%
Courteous & trained staffs	172	86%
Choice of products	192	96%
Personal attention	132	66%
Home delivery	112	56%
Credit facilities	120	60%
Use of technology	184	92%
Discounts/ offers	152	76%
Personal service	124	62%
Payment terms/credit facilities	96	48%
Taking back of goods	112	56%
Telephonic order systems	120	60%
In case of stock-outs are branded products procured on order	140	70%

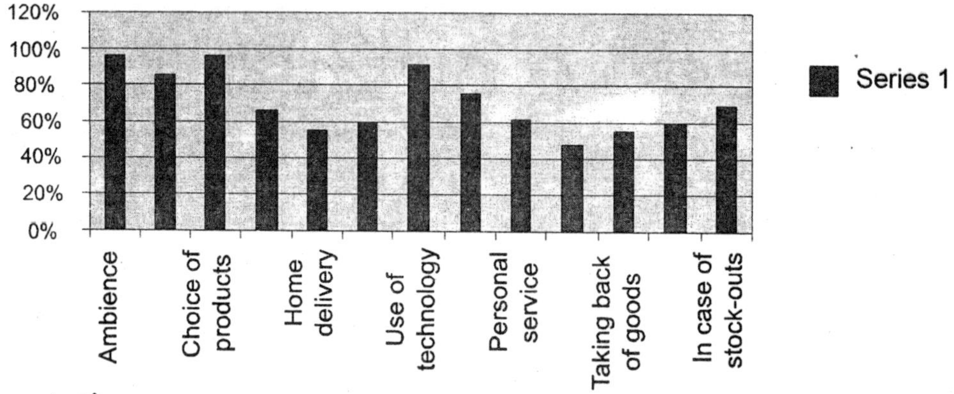

Intrepretation

It is clear that new or organized retailers have a clear upper hand. People feel that they are far better then old retailers in ambience, Courteous & trained staff, choice of product, personal attention, Use of technology, Discounts & offers, telephonic order system. But old retailers are also giving them a good fight or are even better in some areas such as home delivery, Credit facility, payment terms, easy taking back of goods.

The two main areas where the old retailers are really far behind are Ambience and Use of technology.

(2) How is the new retailer treating you as compared to the old retailer?

	New	*Old*	*New*	*Old*
Keeps you on mailing list	48	—	24%	0%
Informs you of the special offers	164	—	82%	0%
Gives you a credit card?	52	—	26%	0%
Greats you by personal name	56	20	28%	10%
Gives home delivery	156	100	78%	50%
Has intimate knowledge about you	56	10	28%	5%
Recommends merchandise to you	172	20	86%	10%

Comparison

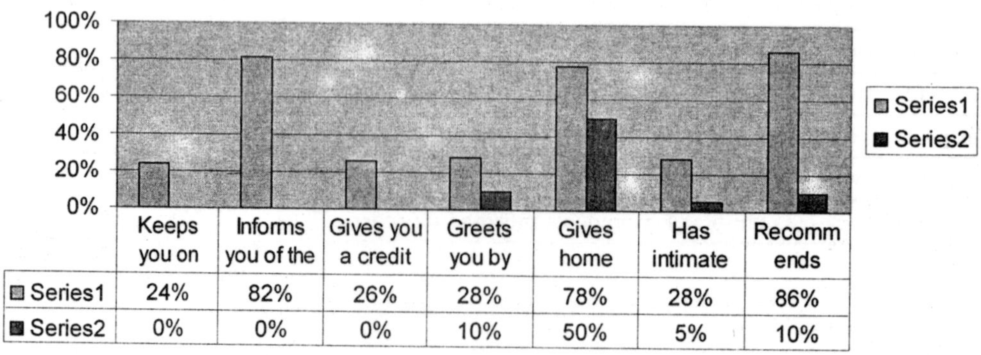

Interpretation

According to the data we easily recognized that new retailer is keeping customers on mailing list, informs them of special offers and gives a credit card, has intimate knowledge and recommends merchandise.

(3) How often does the new retailer obtain your feedback as compared to old retailers ?

	New	*Old*	*New*	*Old*
Once a month	68	20	34%	10%
Once in 6 months	60	40	30%	20%
Never	72	140	36%	70%

Interpretation

Here the data generated is of serious cause for concern for the new retailers. Majority (36%) of people said that they never asked for feedback (by the new retailers). About 30% said that they have been asked once in 6 months. This is really bad because customers feedback is the main source of data for them to up to date themselves and change according to the market demand.

(4) How does the new retailer compare with that of the old retailer in acting on your suggestions?

	New	*Old*	*New*	*Old*
Always	28	40	16%	20%
Occasionally	128	40	64%	20%
Never	40	120	20%	60%

Comparison

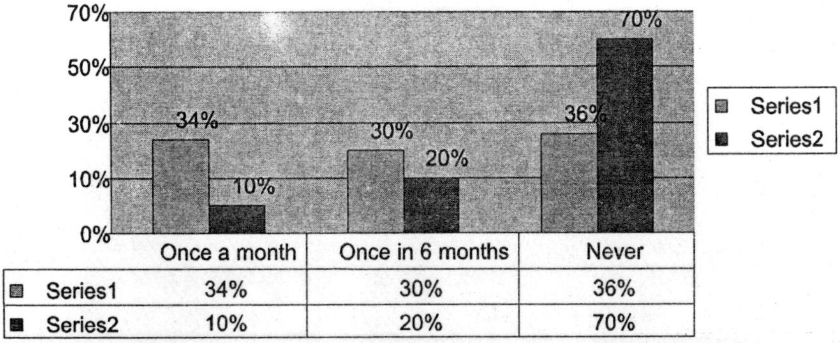

Interpretation

The data founded here is also not very good for the new retailers. People go to new retail shop because at the rush time their own *gali kiranawala* don't even bother to listen to them. But from this data it seems that in the new retail outlets also there is nobody to listen to them. About two-third of customers (64%) think that occasionally they listen to their suggestions.

(5) Are you happy with your present retailer?

Yes	48	92%
No	32	8%

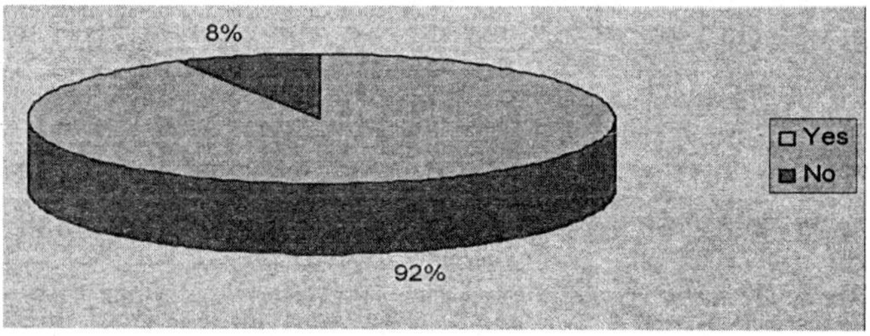

Interpretation

Now this will be the happy finding for the new retailers. It seems that almost everybody like the new retailers. All want that these should be open in their nearby market area. People like their ambience, cleanness, their approach to customers, etc.

(6) Does your present retailer offer good value for money as compared to old retailer ?

	New	*Old*	*New*	*Old*
Always	76	40	38%	20%
Occasionally	84	80	62%	40%
Never	00	80	0%	40%

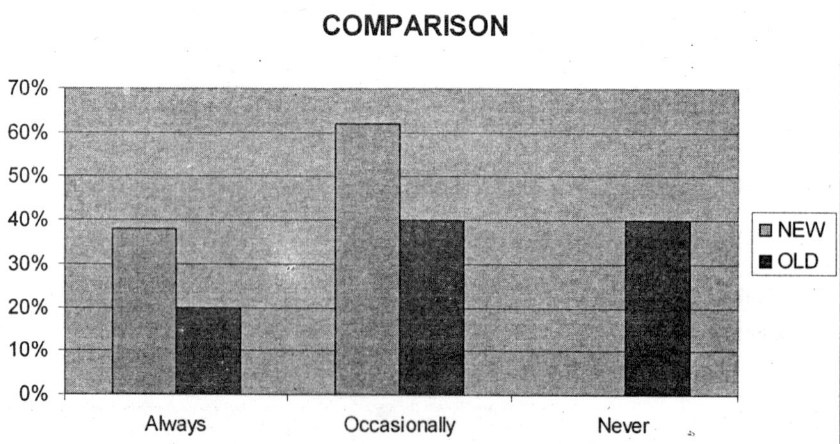

Interpretation

Here also people go with the new retailers. 100% feel that these new retailers give them good value for money either occasionally or always. But nobody feels the other way. For the retailers 62% feel that they got value for money occasionally is good cause of thinking. They should try to change them into better part.

(7) (a) Is it easy to access this new retail outlet as compared to the other old retail outlets?

	New	*Old*	*New*	*Old*
Yes	188	140	94%	70%
No	12	60	6%	30%

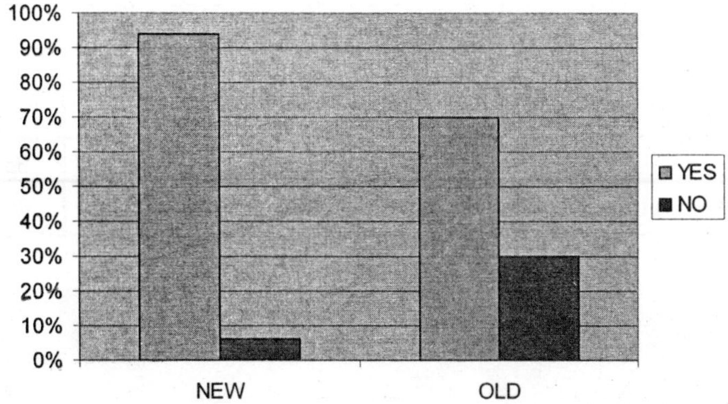

Interpretation

94% customers feel that their retail outlet is relatively easy to access than others. This is also a good sign for the new retailers, because it shows a sign of loyalty in their customers toward their respective retail outlets. They feel that products of their respective stores are customized for them so they use to come to that store. Only 6% feel that other stores are easier to access than their retail store.

(b) Do they (new retailer or old retailer) serve or meet you properly?

	New	*Old*	*New*	*Old*
Yes	172	120	86%	60%
No	28	80	14%	40%

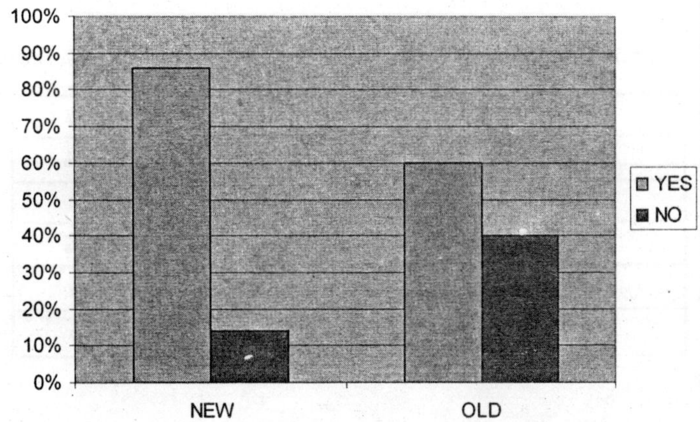

Interpretation

Most of the customers (86%) think that new retailer's approaches to meet and greet the customers are very good. They are well trained, well dressed, and have good product knowledge. At this front they are far ahead of old retailers.

(c) How many times do you visit this new retail outlet in a week as compared to old retail outlets?

	New	*Old*	*New*	*Old*
Every day	-	-	-	-
Once	112	10	56%	5%
Twice	52	40	26%	20%
Thrice	16	68	8%	35%
Monthly	20	80	10%	40%

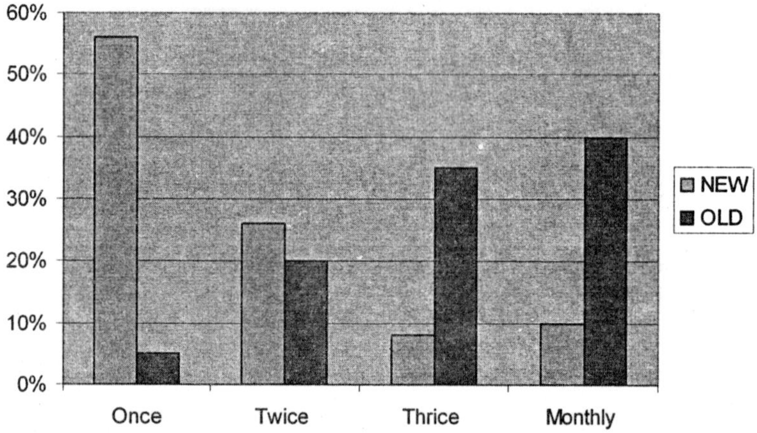

Interpretation

More than half (56%) of the people used to go to new retail outlets once in a week. Another 26% visited even twice in a week. This seems to be a healthy frequency for the new retailers as only 10% of the customers visit monthly.

(d) How quickly do the service staffs respond to the customer problems, request and question?

	New	*Old*
Quick response	120	60%
As problem occurred	36	18%
Take some time	20	10%
Slowly	16	8%
Don't know	8	4%

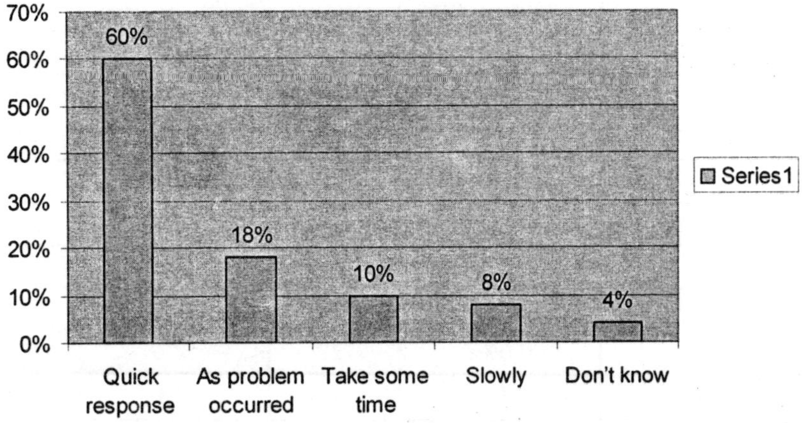

Interpretation

According to the data 60% people feel that new retailer staffs are more conscious about customers problems, requests and questions. They take very quick action when the problem occurs while 10% think that they take time when customer complained. 8% people feel they are very slow in taking action and some don't want to comment. It means generally people are happy with the staff of new retailer.

(e) Is the service described clearly and accurately in terms of discounts and offers?

Yes	144	72%
No	56	26%
Don't know	4	2%

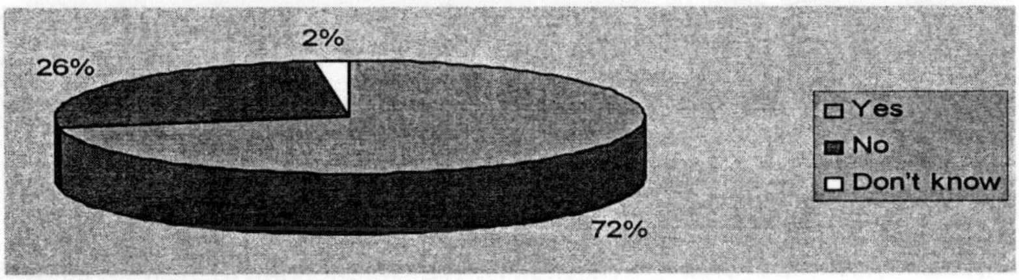

Interpretation

72% people are agreeing with the new retailer's service as described clearly and accurately in terms of discounts and offers. While 26% people are not satisfied, they feel that the discounts and offers are very complicated, in the case of new retailer always they mention **condition apply**.

(9) Rank this retail outlet on the following attributes given below on a 5 POINT SCALE (according to their importance with respect to customer's services expectations) .....

1- Below average, 2-average, 3-above average, 4-good, 5-exceptional

	Below average	*Average*	*Above average*	*Good*	*Exceptional*
Reliability	0%	14%	38%	46%	2%
Responsiveness	6%	16%	42%	24%	12%
Assurance	6%	8%	42%	40%	4%
Empathy	6%	10%	48%	34%	2%
Tangibles/physical evidence	2%	12%	44%	40%	2%
Accessibility	0%	10%	24%	62%	4%
Security	4%	8%	18%	60%	10%
Communication	0%	2%	54%	32%	12%
Competence	4%	4%	46%	36%	10%

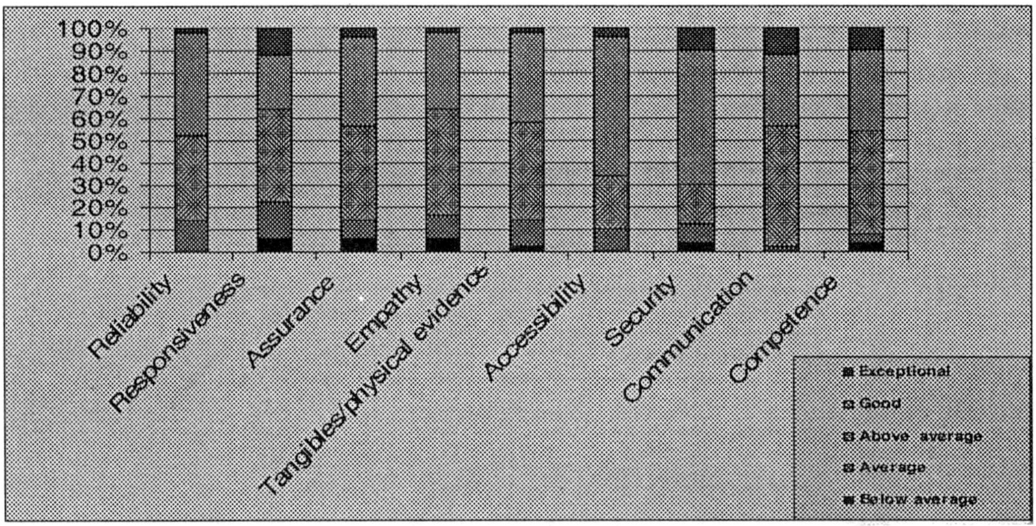

Interpretation

In this question we are going to generate the data from different point of view about the weightage rating for the new retail outlets. These data is based on the rating given by the customers on the different aspects.

Reliability: People rather have a good feeling for the retailers on the reliability factor. Most of them (46%) rate as "good" and 38% rate as above average. Only 7% rate as average and not a single percent rate as below average. This is really good for the retailers.

Responsiveness: On this front most of people (42%) have given the rating as above average. Percentage of "good" (24%) is lower than this. Here 6% also rate them as below average or "bad". But almost double of the people have gave them exceptional rating.

Assurance: Here there is good feeling in the people about the new retailers 40% give them "good" and 42% give them as average rating. Here also about 7% of customers rate the new retail outlet as below average.

Empathy: Here almost half (48%) of their customer give them above average rating and 34% of customers as good. But here also 6% of them rate as below average.

Physical evidence: Here also the scenario is almost similar to above aspects. 44% rate as above average and 40% as good. But only 2% rate as below average.

Accessibility: New retail outlets got the best rating at this front. About 62% rate as good and 24% rate as average. But the main thing is nobody rates them as below average.

Security: 62% customers rate the new retail outlets as good on the security point of view. 18% rate as above average and 10% also rate them as exceptional.

Communication: At this front only 32% give the retail outlets "good" rating. But 54% rate them as "above average". The main point of concern is that not a single percent rate them "below average" while 12% rate them as exceptional.

Competence: at this front the data generated is much similar to the above one. 36% rate the new retailers as good and 10% as exceptional.

The overall scenario is that the customers rate in the favour of new retailers. Most of the customers rate them as above "average", "good", and "exceptional". That is a good sign for the new retailers.

Questionnaire for the Retailers

1. What is your nature of retailing- food, clothing? Is it a part of any large group? or independent retailer ?

Sr. No.	*Retailers*	*Retailers*	*Percentage*
1.	Independent	05	10%
2.	Part of the large group	45	90%

- Most of the new retailers are large retail chains. They are backed up either by their own parent company (like Shopper Stop and Big Bazaar have their parent company, RPG and Future group respectively). Only few players are independent on their own.

  In the retail chain segment also, some are really very large players (Big Bazaar, Food Bazaar, Reliance Fresh, Shopper's Stop, etc.) and some are small players like Subhiksha, Vishal mega mart, Trumart, etc. The latter has now been acquired by Indiabulls and may result in all India chain.
- Most of the players in the market mainly focus on the food products & utensils whether it would be Big bazaar or Food bazaar or Reliance fresh. The food items sell most in India. After that ,they focus on garments and Home accessories.

2. Who are your customers?

Sr.No.	Type	Segment (Income wise)
1.	Reliance	Upper middle & middle class
2.	Big Bazar	Upper, Upper Middle, Middle and lower middle class

- Reliance Fresh has the segment of upper middle and middle class. Big bazaar has the segment of upper, upper middle, middle, and lower middle class.
- They also segment their customers by location like neighbour colony, nearby society, local residential area, etc. Some (Nike, Adidas) segments their customer on the basis of their occupation such as student, businessman, job professionals, etc.

3. How do you attract customers to the stores?

	Strategy to attract customers	*Retailers*	%
1.	Discounts	30	60%
2.	Membership Cards	45	90%
3.	Lucky draws	25	50%
4.	Scratch cards	25	50%
5.	Free shopping to customers	20	40%
6.	Collaboration with neighborhood society	15	30%
7.	Advertisement supplement in newspaper	40	80%
8.	Handouts thru newspapers vendors	35	70%

- Every retail outlet has their own strategy to attract their customers. Most of them use promotional activities for attracting the customers, some use discount as a tool, some use membership card to attract their customers.
- Promotional activities include lucky draws, scratch cards, free shopping to certain number of customers like 100th or 500th. Collaboration with the neighborhood society is also used by some retailers. In this, the members of those societies are given some extra discount by that retailer.

4. What do you do to satisfy/delight your customers?

	Retailers	%
Rs. 100 discount on every purchase	30	60%
Discounts and offers	45	90%
Membership cards	45	90%
Credit facilities up to certain limits	10	20
Others	20	40%

- The data we generated suggested that discounts and offers remain the main tools that the companies use to satisfy or delight their customers. But the membership card which has come into use very recently seems to be the most effective tool to delight their respective customers.
- The companies give first the temporary card when the customer makes the first purchase. Then, the permanent membership card is issued. By this card, different companies give different offers. Some give Rs. 100 discount on every purchase, some give credit up to the certain limits without any interest between 25th to 10th of the month and some also give personalized basket after observing the pattern of purchase of particular customers.
- It can be seen that, the overall scenario of the current retail market industry is to give as much focus on to retain the old customers as much as to make new customers.

5. Where do you use technology?

The retailers use the technology mostly for two things.

a. For data warehousing and mining,

- Under these headings, they use the technology to store the information about their customers and to generate the data when ever required. This is used to study the customers purchase pattern and buying behavior. And also to analyze what the customers want at what time, how the service could be upgraded or enhanced. It also helps to track the good customers and enables the retailers to change them into loyal customers. It also helps them to track the occasional buyers or who have not visited the shop for a substantial period. So that they could approach these customers to know about the reason and then try to solve their problems and maintain them as good customers. For this, they use latest SQL software or CRM, SCM, Management Control System, software's.

6. What customer feedback mechanism do you use?

	Retailers	*%*
Feedback Forms	45	90
Suggestion Box	40	80
E mails to customer care office or corporate office	35	70

- Majority of the retailer maintain approximately the same process for getting the feedback from the customers. They provide the feedback forms and the suggestion box at their every outlet. Customers can directly approach to the manager if they have a point of concern.
- But now days, they are giving more emphasis on e-mails. They encourage the customer to send their feedback through e-mails directly to the corporate office or customer care office so that immediate action could be taken.

7. Strategies on CRM

	Retailers	*%*
Customer data base	40	80
Loyalty card	35	70
Customer satisfaction surveys	20	40

Even though a lot is written about CRM in popular journals as well as in text books, the most commonly used practices observed were maintaining customer data base, analyzing their purchase patterns, conducting periodically customer satisfaction measurement surveys and issuance of loyalty cards. We feel that some newer creative ideas are required to be developed on this subject.

Conclusion

Research study of this nature should be a contribution to the knowledge. At the same time, this knowledge should have practical utility. My work will be useful to organized retailers i.e. shopping mall in the following manner;

Understanding the Buyer behaviour so that he can take strategic decisions with respect to Product, Price, Place, and Promotion (4 P's) & satisfy the today"s customer needs, wants & desires.Old retailer new the new technology & maintain the good customer relation to the customer

It should help the organized retailers on information management through data mining and data warehousing.CRM is most important strategy to attract new as well as exiting customer.

With the increase in competition, the study should help the organized retailers in developing competitive strategy.

◈◈◈

ISBN – 978-93-5024-769-3

15

Understanding the Rural Markets "A Competitive Edge in Tapping the Potential in Rural Areas of Ahmednagar District"

Prof. Anand Padle
SGREF's IMR, Chas, Ahmednagar.
Dr. O. P. Haldar
SMS, Kondhapuri, Pune.
Prof. Satish Ubale
Matrix School of Business Vadgaon, Pune.

Introduction

The popular image of a rural consumer is of one who has limited educational background, is exposed to limited products and brands, choose price over quality, and is influenced by word-of-mouth communication. There is also the view that a rural consumer is no different from his urban counterpart. Changing consumption pattern reflects the evolving life style of rural consumers. The influences on the behavior of the rural consumers are also changing. The life style of rural consumers is influenced by:

- Increasing income and income distribution
- Marketer's efforts to reach out and educate potential consumers.
- The situation in which the consumer utilizes the product.

The last point is usually an overriding factor. Understanding the product-use situation creates opportunities for marketers. This is because the rural environment does not have the infrastructure facilities available in urban areas, which affects the consumption of both durable and non-durable products.

Buying Decision Process

The buying decision process follows a logical sequence of steps as follows :

(1) ***Need recognition***: When the buyer recognizes the gap between his desired state and the actual state, buying process starts. Such recognition may be caused by stimuli either internal (self) or external (by environment or marketer). At this stage, marketer should help consumers identify their current and future problems. For this, marketers have to research on consumer problems and needs.

(2) ***Information search***: Consumers try to find information pertaining to their want satisfying products to make the right choices. The amount of information depends upon :

- Type of the product- convenience, shopping or speciality good.
- Nature of the product- complex, high-tech or simple and easy to distinguish.
- Availability of sources- the consumer may obtain information from one or more of the following sources

a. Personal- family, friends, neighbours
b. Commercial- advertising, sales people, displays
c. Public- TV, radio, internet and print media
d. Experiential- handling, examining, using the product

Keeping in mind the information needs of consumers, marketers should design the communication programs to reach the consumers and provide adequate and relevant information.

(3) ***Evaluation of alternatives***: How do consumers evaluate the brands, which they have come to know and like to consider? The evaluation process may be done more carefully and logically in some cases, for example consumer durables. In case of convenience goods, which are purchased for one-shot consumption, the evaluation may be very less. Evaluation requires designing and application of suitable criteria.

(4) ***Purchase decision***: Through information search, consumer will become aware of some brands which are available in the market. Awareness set consists of brands which the consumer is aware of the brands, which meet initial, buying criteria, will be considered for final criteria, the consumer evolves his choice set. All the brands in this set are acceptable to consumers. However, the final choice will be made in favour of the brand. The choice is dependent upon the factors influencing the mind of consumer at this final stage.

Purchase decision comprises answers to the following questions:

- Which brand?
- Which dealer?
- How much quantity?
- Buy when?
- Which payment mode?

(5) ***Post-purchase behavior***: Marketers should know the answers to the following:

- What are the feelings of the buyer after buying and using of the product?
- What are his reactions when satisfied? When dissatisfied?
- How does he dispose of the product after use?

Post-purchase feeling: A buyer feels satisfied when the perceived product performance is close to his/her expectations, if it exceeds expectation, the consumer is delighted. If it falls short of expectations, the customer is disappointed. He develops cognitive dissonance.

Objectives of the Study

1. To study the consumer- decision- making process of rural consumers with reference to 'two-wheeler' in selected villages of Ahmednagar district.
2. To identify the factors which influence the decision-making process of rural consumers.

Methodology

Sample: A sample of 50 consumers who had purchased two-wheelers within last two years was selected from five villages of Ahmednagar district, for the purpose of the study.

Sources of Data and Information

Data and information were gathered from both primary and secondary sources. Information related to the growth of the rural market, market potential etc., presented earlier above, was obtained from text books, news papers, magazines and websites. The data relating to the behavior of rural customers in the context of two-wheeler was obtained with the help of a structured questionnaire. The questionnaire consists of multiple choice questions.

Data Analysis: The data is analysed in terms of percentage and also presented in the form of pie chart.

Respondent Profile

- Age Group: 25-50 years
- Education: 50% of the respondents were educated upto Xth standard.
- Occupation: agriculture (60%), private service (20%), small entrepreneurs (16%), others 4%.
- Income profile: 70% of the respondents had annual income less than Rs. 1,50,000/-.
- Source of finance: 25% of the respondents purchased the two-wheeler on cash payment and remaining opted for loans.

Data representation

1. To study need recognition of the respondent.

Members	*Number of respondents*	*%*
Self	42	84
Family members	05	10
Friends	03	6
Total	50	100

2. To study the information search of the respondents.

Particular	*Number of respondents*	*%*
Previous Experience	11	22
Friends	31	62
Adds, showroom	08	16
Total	50	100

3. To study the brand selection decision of the respondent.

Members	*Number of respondent*	*%*
Media	05	10
Sales person	04	8
Family members	30	60
Friends	11	22
Total	50	100

4. To study the factors influencing choice of show room.

Location	*Number of respondent*	%
Semi-urban	37	74
Urban	13	26
Total	**50**	**100**

5. To study the factors influencing purchase decision.

Factors	*Number of respondent*	%
Looks	28	56
Quality	11	22
Mileage	06	12
Price	05	10
Total	**50**	**100**

6. To study the post purchase behavior of the respondents.

Problems faced	*Number of respondent*	%
Spares not available	07	14
Service not available	06	12
Frequent breakdown	04	8
No problem	33	66
Total	50	100

Observations of the Study

1. ***Recognition of the need:*** 84% of the respondents reported that the need for owning a vehicle was triggered one's own felt need, 10% respondents says that family members and 6% says friends helped them to arrive at need recognition.
2. ***Sources of information:*** 62% of the respondents say that their friends/ relatives provided them the required information, 22% respondents has got previous experience where as 16% says information is gathered from show rooms and advertisement. It is important to note that advertisement through public media and showrooms, which are expected to play fairly important roles in urban areas, are not quite pertinent here.
3. ***Influencing roles on brand selection:*** 60% of the respondents say that their family members helped them in brand selection and 22% says, friends/ relatives are important influencers in making the final choice. It is once again noteworthy that media influences 10% and sales person at the showrooms influences only 8% of the respondents.
4. ***Choice of showroom location:*** 74% of the respondents purchased at the showroom located in the semi-urban area closed to their place of residence and rest 24% purchased from urban area. This suggests that, there is no fascination for going to urban areas, if similar facilities are available in proximity.
5. ***Factors influencing Purchase decision:*** factors like price, design, mileage, quality, service availability etc., affects purchasing decision of two- wheeler. For the respondents, looks 56%, quality 22%, mileage 12% and price 10% are the factors which effect their purchasing decision while selecting a two wheeler.

This stands contrary to one's expectations that price would play a very important role. Looks of the two wheeler is more crucial factor than price.

6. ***Post purchase behavior:*** the major problems were non-availability of spares 14% and non-availability of service 12%. 66% of the respondents are satisfied with their vehicles and have no intention of changing the same. The loyalty levels are evidently quite high. Even among those who intend to change, the overwhelming reason (95%) is the attraction of newer models.

Conclusions

Conclusions emerging from responses to the structured questionnaire are already discussed above. Listed below are some additional observations that emerged during the course of discussions with the respondents-

1. Customers are influenced by financing facilities; company should try and make available loans to increase the sale in rural market.
2. Two wheeler marketers should develop customer relationship programs in rural markets to gain loyalty and organize mobile service camps in these areas.
3. There is a good demand for two-wheelers in rural areas but availability of factual and comparative information to the potential customer is limited. Marketers should therefore focus on developing an effective communication strategy to reach the rural market.
4. The rural consumers first become aware of the product during the launch of a durable. Interest is generated in the product when he hears his neighbours and friends discuss the new product. He learns more about the product and then on the advice of the others decides on its purchase. The decision to purchase the product and its model and type is made by the consumer after deliberating with the retailer and other users.
5. Two wheelers and television in particular are fast moving goods in rural area. Hence, a study relating to the decision making process of purchasing of two- wheeler in selected rural areas of Ahmednagar district was taken and the findings are presented.

References

1. **Marketing mastermind**, December 2008, January 2009.
2. **Rural Marketing-**Text and cases, *C.S.G. Krishnamachryulu & Lalitha Ramkrishnan,* 2006, Pearson Education,
3. **Marketing Management**, *Rajan Sexena*, 3rd Edition, Tata McGraw Hill Publishing Company Ltd.,
4. **Marketing Management-** planning, implementation & control (Global perspective IndianContext), *V. S. Ramaswamy & S. Namakumari*, 3rd edition, Pearson Education,
5. **Marketing Management** (Text & cases in Indian Context), *Dr. K. Karunakaran*, 2009, Himalaya Publishing House Pvt. Ltd.
6. Business Standard, *newspaper*- 2nd March 2010

◈◈◈

ISBN – 978-93-5024-769-3

16 Identifying the HR Functions for Outsourcing: The Human Angle!

Dr. Lalit Khullar
Tirpude College of Social Work, Nagpur.
Prof. Carol Poonekar
Tirpude Institute of Management Education, Nagpur.

Introduction

In today's dynamic world, all employers need to search for ways to reduce costs while maintaining or improving functionality. Various theories and processes abound on how to achieve the above. But by far the most cost effective, and naturally then, the most attractive option is to go in for HR outsourcing. In the words of a leading entrepreneur "*Employers are constantly on the lookout for an opportunity for improving HR performance through HR outsourcing.*"

The moot questions are primarily the most basic; what to outsource? Who to outsource? When to outsource? Why to outsource? Where to outsource? How to outsource?

The answers to these and more such questions are the ones that entrepreneurs and decision makers are looking for across the SME sector.

The researchers are trying to understand the various benefits of outsourcing the HR functions as well as to identify the various functions within the HR vertical which can be easily outsourced while keeping the timber of the function intact.

Key Issues in HR Function Outsourcing

When choosing to outsource a function as critical as human resources, trust is the most critical factor. People Are Human Resources! In fact, employees can become a company's sustainable competitive advantage if they are considered talent rather than labor. It is a general belief that the synergy created from informed and involved Team Building can have an exponential impact on the bottom line of a company's success.

Why Human Resource Outsourcing

HR is an essential partner in developing and executing organizational strategy. As is evident HR is something that is really critical to an organizations functioning. Human Resources (HR) responsibilities includes all the related functions that work towards employee well-being in the organization including payroll, benefits, hiring, firing, and keeping up to date with statutory requirements, etc.

The competitive challenges of the global marketplace are creating demand for Expert human resource outsourcing (HRO). HRO providers in order to manage non-value adding administrative business function of their businesses, tend to outsource certain activities thereby facilitating the businesses to concentrate on their core competencies.

Some of the more common reasons for outsourcing are given below:

Reason for Outsourcing

- Cost saving
- Focusing on core strategy
- Improve compliance
- Improve accuracy
- Lack HR experience in house
- Take advantage of technological advances
- Offer services that the company otherwise could not
- Focus on core business

Who do HR Outsourcing Companies Service?

In most situations HR outsourcing companies are working with small to medium sized businesses. The reason why such companies would outsource human resources stands in cutting costs combined with not being able to handle the processes in a correct way. Most companies prefer to outsource instead of working on HR themselves because they can gain a lot more time to focus on core activities that are generating money. Also, a lot of companies use HR outsourcing companies in order to take in better employee benefits. This can only happen if one is working with an experienced company. Others usually want to outsource just part of the human resources services that they need to manage.

Most of the SME organizations end up trying to outsource their HR activities starting with recruitment to recruitment consultants in their region. These recruitment consultants over a period of time graduate on to becoming HR process consultants and so on.

Apart from these are a large number of HR consulting organizations which have started providing HR consulting services. Even quite a few ISO related consultants have also started offering HR consulting services. Another way of taking HR consulting services is by way of tying up with various educational institutes for conducting HR interventions.

An increasing number of major businesses are outsourcing their human resource operations today. Some of the services on offer are Payroll operations, benefits administration, employee data records and management, asset management services. Human Resources Outsourcing helps in boosting organizational performance with many strategic benefits like eliminating the redundant non-core HR functions, increasing cost competitiveness effectiveness and helps in maintaining strategic HR focus.

How to Identify Which HR Functions to Outsource?

A typical area of concern for most SMEs is related to the type of HR activities to be outsourced and the level of activities that need be outsourced.

The researchers have proposed that for SMEs to better understand and distinguish between functions that can be outsourced and which cannot be; a clear distinction needs to be established between the two.

Thus an organization needs to ascertain as to which activities are value adding and which activities are Non-Value Adding.

These can be segregated as under:

TABLE 1

Value Adding Activities	**Non-Value Adding Activities**
Employee Induction	• Annual review and revision of employee handbook
Training	• Audit of HR strategies, policies and procedures
Team Building **Job Rotation**	• Job description process • Exit interviews • Employee development program • Performance management process • On-site support • Employee retention programs • Long term incentive/equity stock option programs • Employee Morale Building • Compensation plan review • Maintenance of personnel records
Performance Appraisals	
Multi-Skilling	**Recruiting services**
Compensation Planning	• Retained Search • Job Description Development Strategy • Advertisement Placement • Applicant Screening • Reference and Background Check • Candidate Interviews and Evaluations • Placement of Offer • Integration/Induction of New Employee **Payroll services** • Employee self-service features • Payroll processing and reporting • Payroll tax reporting • Time off tracking • Online benefits enrollment
Talent Management	
Succession Planning	
Enhancing Responsibilities	

Employee Induction

Induction can be defined as 'a systematic process of familiarizing the employee to the organization, the job and other employees so that they quickly become productive. Induction is a follow-up action of recruitment and concerned with the problem of introducing or orienting a new employee to the organization.

Training

Training is the systematic process of imparting skills to the employee which enable him/her to perform his/her job to the desired level of performance. Training as an activity is provided in many ways including classroom training, On-the-Job training, Role Plays, etc.

Team Building

Team building is an important factor in any environment since it plays an essential role towards the overall organizational performance. It focuses on to get the best out of the employees by working closely with each other towards the accomplishment of 'combined tasks'. It is highly imperative for the management to communicate its importance to the employees working in teams. This way, employees can learn a lot from each other's experiences as it also ensures self development.

In any Organization, and at any level, a facilitated Team Building workshop will be a possible route to boost the Team and to foster high performance. A Team could be a powerful entity. A high performing Team not only achieves success, but conjointly has dynamism and an energy that nurtures individual high achievement and a high degree of job satisfaction. Teamwork is the approach we tend to work along to achieve our goals. It includes our values, attitudes, relationships, and Team processes.

Job Rotation

A Job rotation is the systematic movement of employees from job to job within an organization, with job assignments usually running for a year or more. Rotation programs can vary in size and formality, depending on the organization.

There are many reasons for implementing a job rotation system. They include the potential for increased product quality, the opportunity for employees to explore alternative career paths, and, perhaps most important, the prevention of stagnation and job boredom. Employees who participate in job rotation programs develop a wide range of skills, and generally they are more adaptable to changes in jobs and career and more engaged and satisfied with their jobs in comparison with workers who specialize in a single skill set or domain.

Performance Appraisals

Performance Appraisal is a powerful tool designed to test the competencies of the employees, for people to know each other and set benchmarks for the company and its competitors. It is a form of translating organizational strategic goals into workable measures.

It is carried out in the presence of a neutral body like a consultant and the immediate boss or the supervisors that the employee reports to. This performance appraisal gives the employees dues, states their rewards and sometimes even states their penalties.

Multi-Skilling

Multi-skilling is the process of training maintaining employees in specific skills that cross the traditional trade or craft lines, and then ensuring that the work is performed. The advantage of multi-skilling is that particular jobs which historically require more than one craft – not necessarily more than one individual – are now performed by just one person.

The advantage to the company in multi-skilling comes with the ease of scheduling work which, in the past, required two or more crafts or skill distinctions. The advantage to the worker is usually an incremental increase in pay for the additional skills learned and used.

Compensation Planning

Compensation is what you pay someone to entice them to continue to do work for a company. Compensation includes many things beyond straight salary. It also includes benefits, perks, stock options, etc. Also, to balance what these cost against what the employees perceives as their value, and that varies by employee. A company needs to measure compensation levels against other employees in the company, against other employees in other companies in similar positions, and against performance.

Of late, compensation planning has taken up an added dimension. Strategic compensating planning ensures the achievement of organizational goals and objectives and aligning with the mission and vision of the organization. Enabling employees to perform beyond their potential and wealth sharing are some of the other key value adds that compensation planning brings with itself.

Talent Management

Talent management refers to the skills of attracting highly skilled workers, of integrating new workers, and developing and retaining current workers to meet current and future business objectives. Talent management does not refer to the management of entertainers. Companies engaging in a talent management strategy shift the responsibility of employees from the human resources department to all managers throughout the organization. The process of attracting and retaining profitable employees, a means of optimizing the performance of each employee and the organization as it is increasingly more competitive between firms and of strategic importance.

Succession Planning

Succession planning is a process where in an organization ensures that employees are recruited and developed to fill each key role within the company. Through the succession planning process, a company can recruit superior employees, develop their knowledge, skills, and abilities, and prepare them for advancement or promotion into ever more challenging roles. Succession planning ensures that employees are constantly developed to fill each needed role.

As the company expands, loses key employees, provides promotional opportunities, and increases sales, the succession planning guarantees that the employees on hand ready and waiting to fill new roles. Effective, proactive succession planning leaves the organization well prepared for expansion, the loss of a key employee, filling a new, needed job, employee promotions, and organizational redesign for opportunities.

Through the succession planning process, a company can retain superior employees because they appreciate the time, attention, and development that the company has invested in them. Employees are motivated and engaged when they can see a career path for their continued growth and development. To effectively do succession planning in the organization, you must identify the organization's long term goals. You must hire superior staff.

A company needs to identify and understand the developmental needs of your employees. A company/ organization must ensure that all key employees understand their career paths and the roles they are being developed to fill. The organization / company should focus on resources on key employee retention.

Enhancing Responsibilities

Organizations today need to have systems and processes in place to ensure that employees role in the organization can be revised upwards. Most HR departments tend to ensure that the potential of an employee is developed by giving additional responsibilities to an employee or at times even offering responsibilities to an employee which are of a better or higher position than the employee is in at the moment.

Apart from these there are countless measures that organizations can undertake to ensure that the potential of an employee can be gauged as well as developed over a period of time.

Non-Value Adding Activities

These are all those activities which are by their very nature such that they can be safely outsourced without causing any immediate harm to the overall strategy of the organization.

The list given in Table 1 indicates the activities and the sub-tasks within those activities which by their very nature are non-critical in nature. Also these are those activities which are mostly non-value adding or add little value to the Human Resources of the organization.

However, apart from the activities listed in the Table 1, there are some more activities within the HR vertical which can be easily outsourced. A sampling of these is given below:

- Brokerage Services
- Custom Benefit Plan Strategies and Design
- Benefit analysis, cost control and reduction recommendations
- Development of Employee Communications
- Eligibility and Enrollment Services
- Employee claims resolution
- Monthly invoice audit and reconciliation
- On-line employee access to benefits information

HRO as a Vital Component of HR Strategy

HR Outsourcing is generally considered very vital and important to the overall strategic imperatives of an organization. Some of the reasons why it is thought so are given below:

- HRO enables structural reduction of the Human Resource Management (HRM) cost base, by identifying the non-value adding activities and eliminate the hidden HR operations costs.
- It helps in identifying the inefficient Human Resources (HR) Administration processes and HR practices.
- It facilitates streamlining the processes and make it more transparent to the employees
- Organizations tend to focus on human resource performance.
- It ensures that organizations serve their employees better and helps preserve the sanctity of information between employee and employer.

Some Advantages and Disadvantages of HR Outsourcing are Mentioned Below

Outsourcing and Its Advantages:

- Outsourcing is the practice of using outside firms to handle work normally performed within a company.
- HR plays a major role in any organization, but let's face it—the HR department is a cost center that does not deliver a tangible return on investment (ROI). It is a necessary component of every organization/ company; the key to increasing the HR department's value is to purchase software that meets the company's needs and enhances its capabilities while at the same time keeping costs down. This can be achieved by purchasing only the functionality that is needed.

- Making the decision to outsource HR processes is a major step for an SMB, yet these companies routinely outsource their HR and accounting processes because they can't afford to match the in-house support services that large enterprises can, since they are working with smaller budgets. By outsourcing these processes, costs can be reduced, and these savings can be allocated to employee services. This reallocation of funds benefits an SME in that it is better able to pay for skilled manpower, such as payroll and compensation professionals and lawyers.

Disadvantages of Outsourcing:

- Outsourcing is not for every SME; not all companies are comfortable having a third party vendor handle its HR functions and run its day-to-day operational protocols relating to personnel management. By outsourcing any business process, a company gives up a significant amount of control over that process.
- Secondly, the third party vendor assumes and manages all the risk for the SME company. It is therefore essential for the business to ensure that the third party vendor is aware of compliance issues and regulations the company must meet, and that the vendor abides by the company's security and privacy policies. This is especially true when dealing with sensitive data, such as bank information and employees' social security numbers.

Benefits of Outsourcing HR Services

- Low cost of service
- Higher level of service
- Time saving & controlling of hassle factors

Low Cost of Service

One of the most crucial factors that cannot be ignored while making outsourcing HR decision is cost - both operating cost & cost avoidance.

Expected Higher Level of Service

Perceived higher level of service is associated with HR outsourcing companies. They specialize in providing efficient and cost effective services. With their highly skilled team of consultants; employers can expect a better career path for employees, and the ability to better retain them for a specified job.

Time Saving

Senior HR people are more interested in the business of their company than the business of human resource that is they are more concerned in the growth of the business in the long run. The only way they can save their time is by outsourcing them.

Controlling the Hassle Factors

There are loads of "hassle factors" like keeping track of all people, managing technology budgets, managing service level agreements etc. all these core competencies of business are really required, but these factors can easily be taken care by outsourcing HR company, to give employers ease from managing such complex functionalities.

Comprehensive HR Outsourcing Services that you can Outsource

Measures of Successful Outsourcing

The HR department by tradition has been a cost-consuming function, but now gradually is contributing significantly to a company's bottom line. This has led to outsourcing tasks like payroll, benefits, education/training, rccruiting, personnel administration, organizational development and workforce management.

The outsourcing market is beginning to see HR as a preferred choice. Only those companies ready to address the necessary transformation of their HR processes will find that outsourcing will bring access to world-class processes, competitive advantage, and increased shareholder value.

Technology compatibility, confidentiality and cost are other challenges that both sides should work on. A clear understanding of requirements and expectations from both sides is an important platform in building the relationship. Compatibility in culture and values along with an open and flexible approach go a long way in ensuring that the outsourcing venture is a successful one.

A few measures that would help the outsourcing relationship remain contemporary and relevant are:

- Saving process time and cost
- Levels of satisfaction
- Updates on mandatory practices
- Effective implementation of workflow and policy changes
- Continuous feedback mechanisms

Conclusion

HRO is a strategic imperative of any organization and as such has to be treated with due care. Decisions related to HRO need to be evaluated at the highest of levels as they can be more a 'make or break' decisions in the long run due to their strategic long-term impact.

HRO as a process needs to be carefully evaluated and it would vary from organization to organization. Depending upon the needs of the organization and their strategic fit along-with their business mission, different organizations may define Value adding and Non-value adding activities differently. What, however, cannot be disputed is the various benefits that HRO accrues for an organization. These benefits by their very nature could be short term or long term; many a benefits may even be sustainable in the long term and hence bring about enormous strategic advantages to the organization.

As a part of the strategic process of an organizations growth, HRO is here to stay. Particularly so it is true for SMEs for whom it works like a charm and is more of a boon than a bane. To sum up SMEs need to streamline their businesses in case if they want to grow in an unhindered environment. HRO enables them to break their internal shackles and prevents them from straitjacketing themselves.

References

Human Resource Management, By – Jyothi Ventakesh

Human Resource Management, By – Snell and Bolander

Human Resource Management, By – V.S.P . Rao

The essential HR Handbook, By – Barbara Mitchell

HR Outsourcing, By- Karen V Beaman

HR Business process outsourcing, By Edward E Lawler
Human Resource Management, By – Mondy
www.outsource2india.com/
www.hrprofessor.com/
www.humanresources.about.com/
www.humanresource.com/
www.ictstandards.com/
www.referenceforbusiness.com/
www.go4bpo.com/
www.thethrivingsmallbusiness.com/
www.humanresource.com/

◈◈◈

ISBN – 978-93-5024-769-3

17

E-Banking: Technological Challenge in Banking Sector

Dr. D. B. Bharati
Pratibha Institute of Business Management Chinchwad.

Introduction

I.T. in Banking Industry

Technology has opened up new markets, new products, new services and efficient delivery channels for the banking sector. Online electronics banking, mobile banking and internet banking are just a few examples. Information technology has been the cornerstone of recent financial sector reforms aimed at increasing the speed and reliability of financial operations and of initiatives to strengthen the banking sector. The IT revolution has set the stage for unprecedented increase in financial activity across the globe. The progress of technology and the development of worldwide networks have significantly reduced the cost of global funds transfer. It is information technology which enables banks in meeting such high expectations of the customers who are more demanding and are also more techno-savvy compared to their counterparts of the yester years. They demand instant, anytime and anywhere banking facilities. IT has been providing solutions to banks to take care of their accounting and back office requirements. This has, however, now given way to large scale usage in services aimed at the customer of the banks.

IT also facilitates the introduction of new delivery channels - in the form of Automated Teller Machines, Net Banking, Mobile Banking and the like. Further, IT deployment has assumed such high levels that it is no longer possible for banks to manage their IT implementations on a stand-alone basis with IT revolution, banks are increasingly interconnecting their computer systems not only across branches in a city but also to other geographic locations with high-speed network infrastructure, and setting up local area and wide area networks and connecting them to the Internet.

Objectives

The objectives of the article are

- To understand the evolution, concept and meaning of e-banking.
- To observe the exposure to growing number of technology products in e-banking.
- To know about the services offered by e-banking.

- To find out the benefits of e-banking.
- To assess the impact of I.T. on banking industry.
- To study the challenges in e-banking.

Methodology

This article is based on the secondary data. The secondary data has been collected from magazines, journals, Internet searches; libraries etc.

Evolution, Concept and Meaning of E-banking

E-banking made its debut in UK and USA 1920s. It becomes prominently popular during 1960, through electronic funds transfer and credit cards. The concept of web-based baking came into existence in Europe and USA in the beginning of 1980.

In India e-banking is of recent origin. The traditional model for growth has been through branch banking. Only in the early 1990s has there been a start in the non-branch banking services. The new private sector banks and the foreign banks are handicapped by the lack of a strong branch network in comparison with the public sector banks. In the absence of such networks, the market place has been the emergence of a lot of innovative services by these players through direct distribution strategies of non-branch delivery. All these banks are using home banking as a key "pull' factor to remove customers away from the well entered public sector banks.

The banks using the electronic technology to meet ever increasing competition in banking has converted the traditional banking into e-banking. E-Banking can be described as delivery of bank's services to a customer at his home or office by using electronic technology. Many banks have modernized their services with the facilities of computer and electronic equipments.

Technology Products

As a result, information systems and networks are now exposed to a growing number. Technology Products:

(1) Net banking: It is also known as online banking or Internet banking. It allows customers to conduct financial transactions on a secure website operated by their bank.

(2) Credit Card Online: A credit card is a plastic card that contains identification information such as a signature or picture, and authorizes the person named on it to charge purchases or services to his account — charges for which he will be billed. This card can be used to obtain cash, goods or services up to a stipulated credit limit. The credit granted can be settled in full by the end of a specified period or in part, with the balance taken as extended credit. Interest may be charged on the transaction amounts from the date of each transaction or only on the extended credit where the credit granted has not been settled in full.

(3) One View: If you have accounts with at least five banks, One View gives you a single platform to manage them all centrally. The benefits of one view are: No need to individually log on to internet banking of every account, Manage up to 5 accounts in different banks, Remember only ONE password, and this service is available absolutely FREE.

(4) Insta Alerts: This facility provides you to update your bank account on your mobile phone or email-ID. Just register for Insta Alert service and receive updates on your account as and when the select transaction happens - all this without visiting the branch or ATM!

(5) Mobile Banking: It is also known as M-Banking, mbanking, SMS Banking etc. It is a term used for performing balance checks, account transactions, payments, credit applications etc. via a mobile device such as a mobile phone or Personal Digital Assistant (PDA). The earliest mobile banking service was offered via SMS. With the introduction of the first primitive smart phones with WAP support enabling the use of the mobile web in 1999, the first European banks started to offer mobile banking on this platform to their customers. Mobile is a simple and secure way to transact 24x7; view account details, transfer funds, pay bills and much more.

(6) Net Safe: Net Safe, the latest technology offering from many banks, is a unique service which makes online shopping completely secure. With Net Safe a customer of the bank can create a virtual card (Net Safe Card) from your Bank Visa Credit / Debit Card or Master Card Credit / Debit Card number that provides you with complete security while shopping online. There are many benefits of Net Safe.

As an added safety feature, the virtual card number is valid only up to the expiry date of the virtual card. And, the limit of the card is the amount as chosen by you.

(7) e-Monies Electronic Fund Transfer: Computer-based electronic funds transfer (EFT) has revolutionized the way banks and consumers transact financially. To avoid the security risk of handling millions in cash, financial institutions prefer electronic transactions; and depositors are following suit. Television commercials extolling the virtues of a society which operates solely on credit cards versus cash may be fictional, but not far from reality. As e-commerce and e-banking increase, consumers and corporations are finding that making purchases, paying bills, and making installment payments is much easier and more secure when transacted electronically. From electronic money transfer (EMT) and online banking, to wire transfers and cash advances, savvy spenders have moved away from paper to digital dollars; and it just makes plain sense.

(8) Online Payment of Excise & Service Tax: e-Payment facilitates online payment of Excise Duty and Service Tax by an assessee. To avail this facility the assessee is required to have a net-banking account with any of the banks listed below.

(9) Phone Banking: Telephone banking is a service provided by a financial institution, which allows its customers to perform transactions over the telephone. Most telephone banking services use an automated phone answering system with phone keypad response or voice recognition capability. To guarantee security, the customer must first authenticate through a numeric or verbal password or through security questions asked by a live representative (see below). With the obvious exception of cash withdrawals and deposits, it offers virtually all the features of an automated teller machine: account balance information and list of latest transactions, electronic bill payments, funds transfers between a customer's accounts, etc.

(10) Bill Payment: Discover a Simple, Secure and Convenient way to make Bill Payments Online for all your Utility Bills like mobile, landline, electricity, etc

(11) Railway Ticket Booking through SMS

(12) Card to Card Funds Transfer

(13) Funds Transfer (e Cheques)

(14) Anywhere Banking

(15) Bank @Home

(16) Cash on Tap: (i) Express Delivery (ii) Normal Delivery.

(17) EFTPOS: Electronic funds transfer at point of sale (EFTPOS) is a payment system for purchases through debit cards within the store itself.

(18) ECS: Electronic clearing system (ECS) is a paperless mode of effective payment for handling bulk and repetitive payment transactions.

Services Offered by E-Banking

The electronics revolution has made it possible to provide ease and flexibility in banking operations to the benefit of the customer. The e-banking has made the customer say good-bye to huge account registers and large paper bank accounts. The e-banks, which may call as easy bank offers the following services to its customers:

- Credit Cards/Debit Cards
- ATM
- E-Cheques
- EFT (Electronic Funds Transfer)
- De MAT Accounts
- Mobile Banking
- Telephone Banking
- Internet Banking
- EDI (Electronic Data Interchange)

Benefits of E-Banking

E-banking Enable Better Business Anywhere, Anytime. E-banking represents a tremendous opportunity in India. However, Factors such as illiteracy in India, availability of cheaper labor force, reluctance to change by the existing staff of banks and slow growth of technology in India are responsible for slow growth of e-banking in India. Development and acceptance of standards by financial institutions will clearly have a positive impact on the level of security achieved by banks and bank customers. Since opportunities foregone are opportunities lost, the banks have to rise ahead of time so as not to lag behind in the e-banking era.

(A) To the Customers

It is possible to operate the banking transactions from anywhere wherever the customer is in the world. Balance enquiry, request for services, issuing instructions etc., can be made possible from anywhere in the world.

- Anytime Banking – There will be no restrictions on the timings. It is easier to manage funds in real time and most importantly, 24 hours a day, 7days a week.
- Convenience acts as a tremendous psychological benefit all the time.
- It is possible to bring down "Cost of Banking" to the customer over a period a period of time.
- Customer can withdraw cash from any branch / ATM
- On-line purchase of goods and services including online payment for the same.

(B) To the Bank

Innovative, scheme, addresses competition and present the bank as technology driven in the banking sector market

- Reduces customer visits to the branch and thereby human intervention
- Inter-branch reconciliation is immediate thereby reducing chances of fraud and misappropriation

- On-line banking is an effective medium of promotion of various schemes of the bank, a marketing tool indeed.
- Integrated customer data paves way for individualized and customized services.

Impact of IT on the Service Quality

- The most visible impact of technology is reflected in the way the banks respond strategically for making its effective use for efficient service delivery. This impact on service quality can be summed up as below:
- With automation, service no longer remains a marketing edge with the large banks only. Small and relatively new banks with limited network of branches become better placed to compete with the established banks, by integrating IT in their operations.
- The technology has commoditizing some of the financial services. Therefore the banks cannot take a lifetime relationship with the customers as granted and they have to work continuously to foster this relationship and retain customer loyalty.
- The technology on one hand serves as a powerful tool for customer servicing, on the other hand, it itself results in depersonalizing of the banking services. This has an adverse effect on relationship banking. A decade of computerization can probably never substitute a simple or a warm handshake.
- In order to reduce service delivery cost, banks need to automate routine customer inquiries through self-service channels. To do this they need to invest in call centers, kiosks, ATM's and Internet Banking today require IT infrastructure integrated with their business strategy to be customer centric.

Impact of IT on Banking System

The banking system is slowly shifting from the Traditional Banking towards relationship banking. This suggests the importance of customer's relationship management. Traditionally the relationship between the bank and its customers has been on a one-to-one level via the branch network. This was put into operation with clearing and decision making responsibilities concentrated at the individual branch level. The head office had responsibility for the overall clearing network, the size of the branch network and the training of staff in the branch network. The bank monitored the organization's performance and set the decision making parameters, but the information available to both branch staff and their customers was limited to one geographical location.

E-Banking – Major Challenges

There is a tremendous change in every aspect of banking industry. In future the success of the banking industry will depend on the services that they provide to their customers. The banks, which are capable of providing qualitative service to their customers, will acquire competitive advantage. The banking industry had to face certain challenges arising out of e-banking that are discussed below:

- Challenge of investment: The banks will have to invest to invest huge amount in technology and people.
- Challenge to update data: Due to huge investments in Research and Development continuous monitoring of current trends in technology will be a difficult task.
- Challenge from hackers: The banks will have to safeguard the system and software from the hackers.
- Challenge of Law: The banks will face several emerging legal issues that must be addressed through the evolving legal and regulatory framework of e-banking.

- Challenge of Better Service: The real challenge is how to offer better services with value addition while implementing e-banking.
- There is a chance of unauthorized copy of data.
- Frauds in e-banking are increasing day by day. The number of frauds is increasing with the development of technology.

Conclusion

Technology has been one of the most important factors for the development of mankind. Information and communication technology is the major advent in the field of technology which is used for access, process, storage and dissemination of information electronically. Banking industry is fast growing with the use of technology in the form of ATMs, on-line banking, Telephone banking, Mobile banking etc., plastic card is one of the banking products that cater to the needs of retail segment has seen its number grow in geometric progression in recent years. This growth has been strongly supported by the development of in the field of technology, without which this could not have been possible of course it will change our lifestyle in coming years.

References

1. E-banking, Vasu Deva.
2. E –banking in India – Challenges and Opportunities, Edited by R. K. Uppal, Rimpi Jatana.
3. IT in Banks – Strategic Issues, edited by Kasturi Nageswara Rao.
4. E – Commerce in Indian Banking, T. M. Bhasin
5. Internet Banking – The second Wave, Sanjiv Singhal.
6. www.banknetindia.com
7. www.rbi.org.in.

◈◈◈

ISBN – 978-93-5024-769-3

18

Work-life Balance – HR Strategy for Sustainable Growth of Organization

Prof. Ekta Talwar
Institute of Business Management & Rural Development, Ahmednagar.

Introduction

In today's competitive world, there has been a substantial increase in work which is felt to be due, in part, by information technology and by an intense, competitive work environment. Long-term loyalty and a "sense of corporate community" have been eroded by a performance culture that expects more and more from their employees yet offers little security in return.

The change in the life style of the society and the priorities and career plans of the individuals are setting new trends and demands in life. Devotion of long hours in the office, gives little time to the personal life. More often than not, employees complain about social boycott, because they do not find time for themselves. In organizations, today, employee stress is of great concern which is because of high performance pressure. People employed in organizations are stressed out from the work loads they have and also the long hours they are required to put in. This is specifically true in the case of people who are in the field of sales and marketing. The scorching heat, the dominant boss, the targets, the commitments, so on and so forth, are the underlying factors, which cause strain, tension, difficulty, anxiety and depression. With globalization being the buzzword, organizations implementing the latest technology, processes to satisfy the needs of the customer which increases the pressure on the workforce and they are literally working 24 X 7, particularly in this service oriented economy.

In these changing scenarios, an employee is required to create a balance between the professional and personal affairs. This drives the need for strategic role of HRM in maintaining a "Work- Life balance". The expression was first used in the late 1970s to describe the balance between an individual's work and personal life. In this knowledge based business economy it is the prime responsibility of the HR team to maintain the work life balance of their workforce which is most valuable asset.

Through designing and implementing various effective HR strategies that led organizations to align the long term business objectives and vision with an optimum utilization of manpower resources that successfully help employees maintain their status quo at work place and in personal life is an emerging challenge of the hour. As rightly quoted- "An happy worker is definitely productive worker".

Work life balance is the term used to describe those practices at workplace that acknowledge and aim to support the needs of employees in achieving a balance between the demands of their family (life) and work lives.

Individual Approach

The employee himself takes the responsibility for maintaining the work life balance, by implementing time management, increasing physical exercise, adopting relaxation techniques, and expanding his social network.

Organizational Approach

The organizational support is for maintaining the flexibility of work and life of the employees. These entails the dissemination of the culture of work flexibility, HR strategy, HR policies and other organizational regulations that allow the employees to maintain a good blend of personal lives with their careers.

Necessity

The role of work has changed throughout the world due to economic conditions and social demand. Originally, work was a matter of necessity and survival. Throughout the years, the role of "work "has evolved and the composition of the workforce has changed. Today, still it is a necessity but it should be a source of personal satisfaction as well. One of the vehicles to help provide attainment of personal and professionals goals is work-life benefits programmes demand for work-life-balance solutions by employees and managers is expanding at an unprecedented rate. As a result, work-life balance is an increasingly dominant topic in boardrooms. Over the coming decade it will be one of the most important issues that executives and human resource professionals will be expected to manage.

To be competitive in today's increasingly complex and rapidly changing environment, organization must retain personnel and promote the well being of the employees. Organizational changes such as globalization, competition, advancements in information technology, a changing workforce and changes in the expectations and capabilities of employees have resulted in the need to increase our focus on human resource practices. Although retaining employees and keeping them healthy always has been invaluable to organizations, the retention and the health of personnel takes on increased importance during such unstable organizational times.

Today's organizations face competition relative not only to the item produced, but also in retaining the personnel required to produce the items. In order to retain employees, leaders must look beyond traditional issues such as pay and benefits. They must consider the well being of the employees. This includes examining the issue of work life balance and what he organization can do relative to the challenge employees' face as they struggle with competing demands for their limited time. Expending the effort to look after employees' organizational commitment and loyalty, this will increase employee retention. This includes encouraging employees to maintain a healthy work-life balance.

Work Life Balance as defined as a state of equilibrium in which the demands of both a person's job and personal life are equal. From an employee point of view it is solution to the dilemma of managing work obligations and personal/ family responsibilities. Whereas from an employer point of view; it is the challenge of creating a supportive company culture where employees can focus on their jobs while at work.

In a society filled with conflicting responsibilities and commitments , work life balance has become a predominant issue , work life balance have become a predominant issue in the workplace.. Three major factors that contribute to the interest in and importance of the work life balance:

1. Global Competition
2. Renewed interest in personal lives and family values
3. An aging workforce

Research suggests that forward-thinking human resource professional seeking innovative ways to augment their organizations competitive advantage in the market- place may find that work life balance challenges offer a Win- Win solution, as per Rosa Beth Moss KanterOs seminal book (1977), Work and Family in the United States. A critical Review and Agenda for Research brought the issue of work life balance to the forefront of research and organizations.

In their highly acclaimed book, Work and Family Allies, Friedman and Greenhaus (2000), two leaders in work life balance bring forth new evidence to help us understand choices that we make as employers and individuals regarding work and family. Their study of 800 professionals revealed. Their research reveals a compensatory effect between two forms of psychological interference: work to family and family to work. Specifically, support from two domains (partner and employer) has a significant impact on one another. The impact of partner support when business professionals feel that their employees are unsupportive of their lives beyond work. Conversely for employees with relatively partners, the employer family- friendliness reduces role conflicts more than partners. Thus one support compensates for the lack of the others.

Industries have realized the importance of the above. Organizations are setting up policies for maintaining a work life balance. They are going in for innovative methods to keep their employees happy and satisfied, as it makes office a better place to work and also positively impact productivity. The concept of work-life balance (WLB) is not a new but with the changing pace of life and increase in stress levels, negatively affecting the quality of work, has made many organizations think about the strategies for maintaining a work life balance.

Objectives of Work-life Balance

1. **Minimize the Recruitment cost:** The people on whom you have invested time, money and training in. Recruitment is expensive and staff turnover is significantly lower in those organizations that have initiated various work- life balance programmes.
2. **Reduces Absenteeism:** In a recent survey, a public sector organization established that more than 50% of its staff admitted to using sick leave as a means of managing family commitments, resulting in overall attendance rates of 87%. When improved improved flexible working options were introduced, the attendance rose to 96%.
3. **Motivate Staff:** Employees who can designate the times they would like to work , their less preferred times, times when they are not available, and so on , are likely to be more productive, have higher attendance rates and less likely to seek another job. Lack of work life balance is one of the top reasons stated by employees to resign a job. The employee feels more committed to its work.
4. **Improve customer service:** More productive, happier employees also mean better customer service. Having the right people with the right skill in the right place at the right time improves operational efficiency and performance- increasing average revenue and sales, reducing time spent managing customer complaints and so on.
5. **Reduces stress on employees at the workplace:** Employees who maintains the work life balance himself through yoga, meditation helps to reduce stress.

Strategies for Work-life Balance

Work Life Balance is about creating supportive, healthy work environment for employees who are striving to better integrate their work and personal responsibilities.

The objective of this study is to contribute to the work-life balance research by exploring the fit between companies' human resource practices and higher managers' actual perceptions and needs. In order to gain different perspectives, our empirical research consists of a series of interviews with both HR managers and members of higher management. By implementing proactive programmes and initiatives that support employees, organization can strengthen employee commitment and loyalty, resulting in higher productivity, improved customer satisfaction.

Individual Approach

The employee himself takes the responsibility for maintaining the work life balance, by implementing time management, increasing physical exercise, adopting relaxation techniques, and expanding his social network. Stress is essentially an outcome of mismanagement of time. Most of the people manage their time very poorly. Those last minute report preparation, those last minute rushes to meet the target, which when not done often lead to anxiety, that in turn leads to depression and therefore stress. Whenever we encounter a stressful event, our bodies undergo a series of hormonal and biochemical changes that put us in 'alarm mode.' Our heart rate increases, adrenaline rushes through our blood stream, and our digestive and immune systems temporarily shutdown. If the stressors continue and we stay on high alert for a prolonged period of time, we experience exhaustion and bum-out. None of us can avoid stress, but we can return to a state of balance and regulation through a variety of means, including deep breathing, meditation, yoga and exercise. These activities provide calming and relaxing sensory input for stress relief and can be selected according to ones lifestyle and preference.

When you're facing a stressful situation, you can reduce your stress simply by deep breathing. Deep breathing involves not only the lungs but also the abdomen. To experience abdominal breathing, sit comfortably with your back straight. Put one hand on your chest and the other on your stomach. Inhale through your nose and the hand on your stomach should begin to rise. Your other hand should move very little. Exhale as much air as you can while contracting your abdominal muscles. Once again, the hand on your stomach should move in as you exhale, but your other hand should move very little.

Meditation

When you meditate you bring together all of the mind's energies and focus them on a word, a sound, a symbol, a comforting image, or your own breathing. The optimal setting for meditation is a quiet, clean place. People typically meditate sitting on the floor or in a chair with their eyes closed.

A variation of traditional meditation involves guided imagery or visualization. If you use this method, you'll imagine a scene in which you feel at peace, able to let go of all concerns and tensions. In guided imagery, audio instructions help you visualize the scene, focus your thoughts and relax.

Yoga

The term yoga is a Sanskrit word meaning "to unite." Yoga teaches you a series of stationary and moving poses called asanas and a form of breath control known as pranayama, as well as concentrate on techniques.

Benefits of Yoga

Health Benefits of Yoga: Improves flexibility and joint mobility, Strengthens and tones muscles, Increases stamina, Improves digestion. Lowers cholesterol and blood sugar levels

Improves circulation, Boosts immune response.

Mental Benefits of Yoga: Increases positive body awareness, Relieves chronic stress patterns in the body, Relaxes the mind and body, Centers attention, Sharpens concentration, Frees the spirit.

Yoga postures are designed to balance the different systems of the body, including the central nervous, the endocrine (glandular, and the digestive systems. By slowing down your mental activity, taking your mind off the causes of stress, and having you gently stretch your body in ways that massage your internal organs; yoga helps you create dynamic peacefulness within yourself.

Basic physical exercises such as aerobics, walking, jogging, swimming and riding bicycle could be the ways to deal with excessive stress levels. Expanding your social network like having friends, family, or colleagues to talk to, also provides an outlet when stress levels increase.

Drawing an appropriate schedule for the day, week or the moth is dividing time between work and family. Engaging himself in a hobby, Utilizing the permissible off's available at workplace as per the prevailing priorities between demands of profession and demands of mind, family and society. Ensuring that, his family participates in all social occasions sponsored by the organization. Being in tough with family, even while working, during the day through telephone, email, etc. Avoiding the loads of office work to home, Simplify Life, Learn to distress, Distribute the workload, and Manage time.

Organizational Approach

Work/life initiatives fall into different areas depending on an organization's perspective, Barrington said. They can be part of the recruitment strategy for an organization wanting to become an employer of choice; a diversity strategy to promote women's advancement; a total rewards strategy; a strategy to retain top talent; or a health and wellness strategy if the focus is stress reduction, he said.

To influence leaders in your organization, Barrington recommended:

Make the business case for work/life initiatives through data, research and anecdotal evidence.

Train managers on how to use flexible management approaches.

Use surveys and focus groups to demonstrate the importance of work/life in retaining talent.

Train all managers and subordinates in career-life planning.

Support pioneer leaders and enlist them in making the case for work/life balance

Striking a balance between work and life is as difficult for the corporate as it is for the employees. Work life balance is an employment practice that is concerned with providing scope for employees to balance their work with the responsibilities and interests they have outside work. Research has shown that better work life balance leads to better employee satisfaction and satisfied employee contribute a lot to the organization in terms of productivity. Organisations supporting towards maintaining the flexibility of work and life of the employees is the prerequisite. The top management of the company should communicate that it values the personal lives of its employees. Work life balance is about introducing flexibility in the workplace that takes account for the diverse needs of employees at the various stages in the lives. Changing the way we work can enhance family life, leisure time and education. People work life balance will enable those with disabilities to draw up a suitable work schedule as they cannot cope with the regular 9-5 office hours. Thus it will ensure their participation in the labor market without difficulty. But it doesn't just benefit he employee, the employer gains too. The employer gains is more contented workforce, which boast productivity and reduces staff turnover. The rise in the flexibility of working patterns in recent years has been fuelled as much by employers as employees. Many companies has started working on this issue for example; IT companies like IBM and Infosys gives enough time to work after childbirth, time-off for personal needs without loss of pay, time for education. Pepsico not allowed the outstation meetings on Sunday and Nestle is not rewarding to an employees who put in long hours at work. To maintain the worklife balance amongst the employee Ford Motor has taken initiatives to start offering the Flexitime, Childcare consultation, Eldercare consultation, etc.

Flexitime

Flexitime is that staff members vary their timings about commencing, ceasing and meal break times while still maintaining the total number of hours worked over a period. Flexi-time enables the arrangement of working hours to suit personal or family commitments, particularly staff with dependent children. A flexitime policy also may permit employees to adjust their work hours in order to utilize time for doctor's appointment, to continue education, children's activities, hobbies or voluntary work. For example, by commencing work at a later time or finishing work at an earlier time enables many parents to drop their children off to school in the mornings or pick them up in the afternoon. Accumulating additional hours then having long stretches of time off work allows employees to more effectively pursue broader career/personal/social and community responsibilities and interests. Employees who are better able to manage their work-life balance more effectively are more likely to have high staff morale, greater employee satisfaction and work commitment resulting in a more enriched working environment and a correspondingly more vibrant, creative and productive workforce.

Flexitime refers to allowing the employee to adjust the arrival and departure times of his/her standard work schedule to meet their transportation or other work/life needs, while still maintaining an 8-hour work day. Flexible start/end times typically fall within "core" department operating hours (e.g. 9:00 a.m.-3:00 p.m.) and must not conflict with the department's needs

Telecommuting

Telecommuting is an increasingly popular work option which has the potential to provide significant benefits for both employers and employees. Telecommuting offers a flexible work arrangement in which selected employees work remotely for a predetermined number of days per week. It has been described as "moving the work to the workers, instead of the workers to work." The number of companies that are developing and implementing formal telecommuting programs has increased. Telecommuting programs support business and human resource needs, including attraction and retention of talented employees and work-life balance. Telecommuting is also known as, remote work, virtual work, and mobile work are the most commonly used terms to refer to work done outside the traditional on-site work environment. These terms are defined in different ways and used in different contexts to refer to anything from jobs that are completely virtual or mobile, to arrangements that enable the employee to work from home a few days per week or per month.

At Accenture, they believe that telecommuting is one of the key tools for attracting and retaining employees especially women employees. Our employees have the flexibility to exercise a need based work from option as it helps them more in maintaining balance between work and home. The benefits of telecommuting include increased productivity, lower attrition, less number of leaves taken, cost savings on infrastructure and of course an extremely happy workforce.

Benefits of Telecommuting

Many benefits of telecommuting have been identified:

- Increased productivity
- Expense savings
- Decreased turnover
- Decreased absenteeism
- Increased labor pool
- Improved morale
- Decreased commuting time

- Increased flexibility in work schedules
- Decreased rush hour traffic (and therefore decreased air pollution)
- Reduced need for office space

Increasingly, employers and insurers are relying on telecommuting as a return-to-work strategy for injured employees who have workers' compensation or group benefits (short term disability or long term disability) claims and who typically experience delayed return to work at the job site.

Job Sharing

Job sharing is an employment arrangement where typically two people are retained on a part-time or reduced-time basis to perform a job normally fulfilled by one person working full-time.

For employees seeking more free time for themselves, job sharing may be a way to take back more control of their personal lives. Employees who job share frequently attribute their decision to "quality of life" issues. Studies have shown that net productivity increases when two people share the same.

Job sharing is a type of work arrangement in which more than one person works in a position meant for one employee. Having a job partner to share work and alternate schedules with isn't something that can be decided and arranged by workers themselves, but rather must be approved by the employer. Like other types of flexible work arrangements, such as telecommuting and shorter summer hours, job sharing is a non-traditional work choice that continues to grow in popularity. In many cases, two employees in a shared job alternate the work week, such as each person working two days and then alternating the fifth day, but there are many different scheduling possibilities for shared work arrangements.

Some shared jobs involve the workers alternating entire weeks or even months. The type of work schedule used in job sharing depends on the needs of the employer as well as the employees. It's important to realize that having a job partner affects many employees and not only the ones directly involved in job sharing. Unless the job partners work in a cohesive way, it can be difficult for other employees to coordinate their efforts as part of a company team. To help avoid communication problems, individuals sharing the same job may find tools such as a log book system helpful.

Partners in a job sharing position can write important details either by hand in a notebook or in a computer file to create the log. This way, the other worker can be kept aware of what happened at work when he or she wasn't on the job. Both communication and organization in a shared job is essential and job partners must be committed to making the arrangement workable for everyone in the company. Many job sharers communicate daily at shift changes and have each other's contact information for regular as well as emergency communication. They must usually cover each other in emergencies as well as for vacations and other agreed upon hours.

As long as the two or more employees sharing a job are strong, knowledgeable workers committed to making the job sharing arrangement work, the employer usually benefits. Hiring temporary workers without a relationship with the company can usually be avoided in shared job arrangements. Employees in flexible work arrangements tend to appreciate being able to work on a schedule that fits their lives and are often top performers who exhibit loyalty to the company. Workers interested in job sharing may be older workers wanting to work part-time before retirement or they may be parents who need to balance employment with family life.

Job sharing is a somewhat controversial alternative to telecommuting, flexible working hours, compressed work weeks, and other arrangements used by small businesses looking to offer their employees a bit more flexibility while maintaining productivity. It is aimed at the small number of employees in the work force who do not have a problem with earning less money if it offers them the opportunity to pursue the other interests in life that are important to them. A job sharing position should not to be confused with a part-time job. These types of employment opportunities are usually ones that require all the attention and dedication that is standard to the typical work day and week.

Job sharing offers small businesses a chance to retain valued employees that they would normally be in danger of losing if not for the flexible schedule. It can also help eliminate the need to train new employees if a valued employee were to leave the company. Job sharing can seem intimidating to managers, who may fear that it could lead to confusion, more paperwork, and a host of other hassles. If a proper plan is in place and each job sharer is held accountable for their duties, however, these issues can be avoided.

Job sharing occurs when two or more employees share one or more positions or set of duties. It should be clear before starting how these arrangements affect pay, benefits, and holidays. It is very important that those in a job sharing arrangement work effectively as a team and communicate well.

Shift Swapping

A common way for employers to give employees some flexibility in their working hours is to allow them to swap shifts with colleagues.

Compressed Work Week

Compressed work week is a form of flexible scheduling that gives the employee the benefit of an extra day off by allowing the employee to finish the usual number of working hours in fewer days per pay period. The most common practice would be the "4/40 schedule," where the employee would work four 10-hour days with one day off each week. The Compressed Work scheme is compressing the number of workweek from the conventional 5- day workweek to a fewer working days (see Giuliano et al., 1990; Bhattacharjee et al., 1997; Tanaboriboon, 1994). This working arrangement of Compressed Work scheme allow the employees to work in a fewer days, let say, 3 days or 4 days a week but extending their working time duration to compensate the hours lost due to the extra free days (Hung, 1996; Latona, 1981; Nollen, 1981; Ronen and Primps, 1981; Gerwig, 1996). Many literatures related to Compressed Work scheme focused mainly on the benefits and problems it brings to the employers and the employees (Nollen, 1981; Ronen & Primps, 1981). Other similar studies on Compressed Work scheme relates to the impact in transportation like reduced work commuting (Hung, 1996), and increased weekend commuting (Allen & Hawes,1979; Gavney et al., 1979). Evidence also shows that compressed workweek or staggered working hours also brought a significant change in travel conditions (Giuliano and Golob, 1990). Infosys is on the verge of rolling out policy for young mothers who have been on sabbatical. Firm realized that for some women it is difficult to work as full time employees, so it will allow them to work either three full or five half days a week.

Part-time Employment

In this arrangement employees are permitted to meet both job and personal needs.

Example:- Mind Tree announced a policy called 'Part pay part work'.

Benefits of Work-life Balance

Infact work life balance is an issue that is more concerned with the employee rather than the employer. Work life balance is more individual issue that affects the organization than it is an organizational issue that affects the individual.

Improvement in the productive capacity of the employee.

High sense of commitment of an employee to the organizations welfare.

Development of high level of confidence in an employees.

Retention of skilled workforce.

The employees benefits physically and mentally, the employer benefits business and profit wise.

Conclusion

To implement the work life balance practices, the organizations will have to scan the external and internal environment by identifying he work life balance practices being used by other like organization and what is working well for them for this they should have the clear picture of the needs of the staff, what sort of business it is in, kind of work life conflicts their employees are exposed to.

References

HRM review 2007

www.google.com

www.2dix.com

HRM practices in Industry by H.L Kalia, S Ravishankar, J K M nair, Thomaskutty, Himalaya Publishing House Pvt. Ltd.

Strategic Human resource Management, Tanuja Agarwal, Published - Oxford University.

◈◈◈

ISBN – 978-93-5024-769-3

19 Competencies of Successful HR Professionals in Today's Changing Scenario

Prof. Anjan Kumar Maiti
Sterling Institute of Management Studies, Navi Mumbai.

Introduction

At the dawn of industrialization skilled labor force was not abundant. To respond to the growing need of rapid industrialization working force used to be drawn from surplus from the farm. These unskilled hands fresh from the countryside had little education. To train them was an uphill task. As a way out complex industrial operation was fragmented into multiple tasks. The workers were given training only to work in an extremely limited area of operation and their tasks were mainly repetitive. The workforce was not expected to apply their minds. They were supposed to use their hands only. Command and control used to be the main mantra for maintaining order and discipline in the steadily growing workforce.

'The old model of management was formed to deal with a very different set of circumstances than the ones organizations face today. Industrial workers were proliferating at the turn of the 19th century. Many knew only craft or home based labor and was unfamiliar with working in large organizations. Most were relatively uneducated; many were motivated to work hard only by external pressure: (Davenport, 2001)'.

Transition from industrial age to knowledge age after riding many peaks and troughs industrial age reached knowledge age. This change in the industrial scenario has brought about far reaching changes in the mindset of the employees, employers and the society. The bureaucratic layers have dismantled to a great extent. The vertical organizational structure has given way to flat, flexible structure. Numerous layers in a typical vertical structure numbering more than 10 even 20 have come down within 10 even in world famous organizations like GE where Jack Welch, the legendary chairman declared a virtual war against bureaucracy and practiced delivering ruthlessly. Jack Welch also introduced a system of workout where the managers and the departmental heads had to sit with the workers regularly to take feedback/ suggestions from them about improvement in the process, product, marketing, supply chain etc to improve the operational efficiency. They had to report within a timeframe the acceptability or otherwise of the suggestions from the employees. Experiences of post 2nd world war Japan in enacting exemplary reconstruction of a war ravaged economy and ushering in a revolution called total quality management have established that the workforce can work miracles if they are empowered sufficiently. Imbued with the quality doctrine preached by Deming the Japanese have brought about the resurgence of their economy and reached the pinnacle of quality movement to surpass the highly industrialized nations, even the mighty U.S.A in productivity and quality. The supremacy of Japan in Industrial world has been heralded by their highly motivated, dedicated quality conscious work forces who have worked with their heads, hands and hearts.

Globalization has brought the world closer but made the competition stiffer Internet has changed the rules of the game. Now even a small firm can compete globally. The organizations have to be proactive, prompt, and agile to respond to any development or likely development in the market. They have to visualize what may lurk from invisible. The efforts to produce the present products in new ways, produce new products, enhance product features, discover new markets, diversify product range, enhance market share, bring about process improvement and economy through business process reengineering and pursuing best practices and even going beyond that to invent better practices than best practices are to be pushed without interruption. Any relaxation or complacence will force the organization to shed their supreme position or market share, if not going to total oblivion, in the days of abundance physical resources like material, money, and machine may be available. The physical resources may no longer constitute the competitive advantages. What distinguish one organization from another are the commitment, skill, involvement, and knowledge of the employees. But the superior knowledge level flows from the talent and dedication of the concerned employees who have minds to do the right application.

'Managing with knowledge, managing knowledge work, and managing knowledge itself all require that most of the assumptions about management must change.... In the United States and Europe we have reached the point of critical mass at which knowledge drives the way we think about management. (Davenport, 2001)

The Rise of Knowledge Worker

'Because knowledge is an invisible asset that resides largely in the minds of human beings, management can no longer be about close observation and monitoring. Because knowledge work can and is done by managers as well as workers, strict separations between workers & manager no longer make sense. Because knowledge work has become the key to growth and differentiation in today's economy the differential in cost and value between knowledge work and management has decreased. Management in the knowledge economic is a different game with different rules. ...... By the end of the twentieth century in these advanced economies more than 50 percent (40 percent salaried managerial and professional workers in the United States, and more than 20 percent in other knowledge work categories) of workers are 'knowledge workers' whose primary tasks involve the manipulation of knowledge and information. Even before they became a majority, they had the most influences on the economy they are paid the most economic value, and they are the greatest determinant of the worth of their companies. Companies with a high proportion of knowledge workers- let's call them knowledge intensive- are the fastest growing and most successful in the U.S. economy, and generate most of its growth in the past decade '(Davenport, 2001)

'Recruiting will have to become a fulltime continued process for most managers. Instead of beginning to look for a knowledge worker when there is an opening, it will become important to look all the time'. (Davenport, 2001)

'Given the coming shortage of knowledge workers, the efforts to retain knowledge workers will be as difficult as that to recruit them- and, of course recruitment and retention policies are related. It will undoubtedly be expensive to retain the best workers, but cheaper than having to recruit new ones. It is also heartening that knowledge workers say that money is not the primary factor in retention (Davenport,2001). Finding effective ways to attract, develop, and retain key talent in today's challenging marketplace includes proactively managing leadership development and succession planning, understanding emerging skill requirements and the impacts of workforce demographics and technology, and creating a high performance culture where people at all levels are engaged and energized. (Graddick Weir 2005)

Industrial revolution is a few hundred years old, but the awakening of the supremacy of the employees is of recent origin. If you focus on the early motivation theories it seems as if the whole purpose of motivation was to prevent subordinates from obstructing the intentions of their superiors. When management aims merely to minimize the employee's ability to interfere with its aims, either through old fashioned pressure tactics or by means of the more sophisticated gambit of keeping him contented, it is in effect acknowledging as a sort of necessary evil whose potential contribution to the organization is at best rather small. The underlying assumption would seem to be that organization can accomplish things only because management guides and energizes it and employees serve merely as instruments for handling details and dirty work. Such a management would seem to regard its function in the organization as being very much that of a master puppeteer (Gellerman). The concept is the best on the notion that the role of management is to control behavior of their subordinates which can be done by creating a situation that induces the worker to fall in line with management purpose. 'These is traditional theory what workers are like and what organization must do the manage them, a rather uncomplimentary but allegedly hardened theory that Mayo and many others have described'. (Gellerman) Countering this notion McGregor has contended that 'a lot of management policies are bucking against human nature.' McGregor has referred to the puppeteering or authoritarian point of view as theory X where 'management appears to have concluded that the average human being is permanently arrested in his development in early adolescence. Theory X is built on the least common human denominator; the factory hand of the past. Theory X is based on three cornerstones. One is that most people just don't like to work, the second is that some kind of club has to be held over their heads to make sure that they do work, and the third is that the ordinary mortal would rather be told what to do than have to think for himself.' (Gellerman)

Over the years people started realizing the deficiencies of puppeteering or authoritarian view of management. Management literature got over the misunderstanding over the negative role of the workforce and started acknowledging that employees with abundant freedom and choice can be creative and innovative and ensure supremacy of any organization. McGregor propounded theory Y which upholds first of all, that people do not like or dislike work inherently but rather develop an attitude towards it based on their experiences with it. Second, while authoritarian method can get things done, there is nothing inevitable about them and their undesirable side effects do not have to be tolerated. Third, people select goals for themselves if they see the possibility of some kind of reward, be it material or purely psychic, and once they have selected a goal they will pursue it at least as vigorously as they would if their superiors were trying to pressure them into doing the same thing. Fourth, under the right circumstances people do not shun the responsibility but seek it (Gellerman) Theory Y claims at integrating individual's aspiration with the organizational goals. McGregor has placed his faith on people and believed that when people are positively motivated, they can actually be a lot more cooperative and efficient without controls' (Gellerman)

Lawler111 (2001) has talked about three 'major sources that when combined can produce organizations that are likely to be winners. These three are all concerned with the human side of business: human capital, organizational capabilities, and core competencies. These three go together in the sense that organizational capabilities and core competencies require the right kind of human capital in order to be created the sustained by corporations. (Lawler111, 2001)

Importance of people side of an organization on innovation and creativity is reflected in the following sentences in 'organizing Genius':

Jack Welch once said of his role in the General Electric : ' Look, I only have these things to do .I have to choose the right people, allocate the right number of dollars and transmit ideas from one division to another with the speed of light (Bennis and Biederman, 1997)'

Work Place Diversity

'Today workforce diversity is global topic - a global work place topic, and a global market place topic. Any business that intends to be successful must have a borderless view and an underlying and an unyielding commitment to ensuring that workforce diversity is part of their day to day business conduct. (Childs, 2005). The complexity of diversity has assumed a new dimension as a sequel to more tolerant and liberal acceptance of gay, lesbian and transgender (GLT) population in the workforce. According to Mc Rae (1994) some countries and Britain is a good example. The pace of social change has been quite remarkable. 'In 1960, 6 percent of children born in the UK were born to unmarried parents (The parenting deficit, Amitai Etzioni, Demos, 1993 cited in Mc Rae, 1994). 'In 1990 it was 28 percent up from 12 percent a decade earlier and by 1992 had risen to 31 percent. Similar though in most cases less dramatic, rises occurred in most industrial countries. True, not all children who are born to unmarried parents are born to single parents-roughly three - quarters are born to what are called consensual unions, where both parents live together but have decided not to have legal union (21 percent are joint registrations, and 8 percent are single parent registering the birth; UK office of population censuses and surveys, (1990); cited by McRae, 1994)'. The position highlights a phenomenal increase in consensual unions away from legal marriages, but discernible breakups are also there in consensual unions. Rejection of marriage as an age old social and legal institution and breakup in families leading to steady rise in the number of single parent families have thrown new challenges to HR professionals.

The situation is getting more complicated with the entry of increasing number of women in work force to constitute source of new labor in many developed countries as with a stable population the number of people of working age will dwindle and proportion of aging population will increase. This will induce increase in retirement age, higher pension burden. Changes in employment pattern will necessitate changes in the terms of employment. With telephone and internet connections becoming cheap working from home will be common .With complexity in the nature of work teamwork would be preferred. Part-time and contract employment will proliferate. Obligation of child and old care will go up. This would reduce the need for huge brick and mortar structure. Office premises with sleek staff strength would be utilized more for meeting or occasional get together of the team members. Huge office premises in central locations will be redundant. The concept of virtual office will gain currency.

'Some of the features noted above are already evident. Every member of the EU is increasing the retirement age or is considering doing so: by 2020 the normal retirement age may well have risen to 67 or even 70 in most industrial countries. The main motive for this in Europe is cost to the state: (McRae, 1994)'

Workplace diversity contributed by workforce drawn from varying locations-even countries, languages , religions, ethnicities , social orientation, physical disabilities and large scale entry of females in workforce will throw the challenge of synthesis and harmony to HR professionals.

'If we are to address the complex issues in the twenty - first century such as continuing core issues of race and gender, the growing issues of child and elder care, the emerging issues of multiculturalism, tolerance of religious practices, and the full inclusion of people with disabilities in the work force, diversity professionals have to play the key role to respond to the challenge.

'The final and most pressing challenge is for HR to rise up to truly live, model , and promote the values that have historically characterized our profession but that are also necessary for long term organizational success. To do so will continue to increase in difficulty as organizations become more and more cost focused and demand more accountability from HR '(Wright and Snell, 2005)

'In his cogent analysis of the HR function, Human Resource champions, Dave Ulrich (1999) speaks of four primary roles for HR : administrative efficiency, employee advocacy , strategic execution (via HR strategy) and culture change (a component of workforce strategy) are critical to delivering strategy in the future, we advocate that most HR's time efforts and professional development be devoted to these areas . This is where HR can truly differentiate itself and become a player. (Beaty and Schneier, 2005)

In fast changing scenario HR has a major role to play as 'firms don't change; people do and it's people who change the organizations. HR therefore has a major role to facilitate the change process' (Beaty and Schneier, 2005' It facilitates the development of a workforce that delivers and executes the firm's business strategy.

Managing diversity in workforce will warrant extraordinary understanding and appreciation. HR often advocates promotion of a high performance culture. HR has, at times been described as the important keepers and analysts of an organization's culture. Culture is a crucial determinant of many dimensions of organizational performance, and HR's cultural role is significant--- HR needs to be concerned with the mental models and mindsets of the people in the company and particularly its leaders. Because what we do comes from what and how we think, intervening to uncover and offer mental models may be the most important and high leverage activity that HR can perform (Pfeffer, 2005).

HR has to meet the cost containment and governance issues by 'managing the rising costs of healthcare, dealing with the implications of increased regulatory scrutiny. (Graddick-Weir)

Summary of HR Competencies

With emphasis on the creativity and innovation of individual employees their talent will be the major distinguishing factors of the organizations. As the demand for talented knowledge workers far exceeds the supply and as the mobility of talent is global the organizations have to pay serious attention to the issue of attracting and retaining the talent. HR professionals must develop the competencies to identify the desirable human capital, desirable length of their hiring and the type of employment deals for attracting and retaining the desirable employees. Organizations would be required to judge the merit of HR professionals on the basis of their competency to attract and retain the best employees The position has been lucidly explained by Charles Handy (2003) 'If you are going to employ people who are intelligent, and who like to think for themselves, then you've got to give them a lot of responsibility, a lot of power. Otherwise they will leave you, because nobody wants to be a robot or an instrument.' Handy (2003) has further added that 'One of the challenges for organization, therefore, is to give people space for their initiative, but also to be able to define success, this brings another dimension to the competency of HR professionals. He has also predicted changes in the job profile of individual employees. In the twenty first century, we will see more and more people adopting a 'Portfolio' approach to their lives and to their work. What I mean by this that life will be a collection of different activities, almost like a share portfolio. A part of the portfolio will be the core activities for providing the essentials for living, where as the rest will be other things that we think of as personal fulfillment as responsibilities towards other people or even just as fun,

Instead of having a career in the traditional sense, you will for part of a life, have a portfolio career, where part of your time will be spent earning wages or fees, and the rest will be for community work of some form, even it much of it is unpaid and it will all go to make up a portfolio of a activities will increasingly define you.

HR professionals should have the competencies to arrange for different kinds of work within the same organization to bring out people's diverse talents.

Handy (2003) also highlighted that 'the very definition of work is changing work used to mean having a job with an employer. But today it increasingly means working for yourself and by yourself.'

Strategic Business Partner

'In the near future, half of the workforce of the developed world will be working 'outside' the organization. Traditional organizations now employ only 55 percent of the work force on the full time basis. The rest are temporary, part time or contractual workers. Our portfolios will increasingly be collections of different work for different clients (Handy, 2003) The massive restructuring of organizations in the 1990s saw the first large scale outsourcing of transactional HR activities (Payroll, benefits administration, some types of training) (Cascio, 2003)

A compilation of the comments of the leaders and their insights reflect a fourth stage of development of the HR field, namely strategic business partners. The idea was, and is that if transactional activities are being eliminated, the survival of in house HR talent depends on a demonstrated ability to add value to the business, (Cascio, 2003). Cascio (2003) relies on the views of HR business leaders expressed in HR Role models and believes that to add value to an organization a number of key competencies are necessary. These competencies include proficiencies in areas such as organization's business model, basic business literacy (corporate finance, marketing , accounting , information technology , and general management), functional areas within HR (legal requirements, recruitment, staffing, training and development, performance management, compensation and benefits, labor and employee relations, occupational safety and health), listing skills, skills as strategic business partner. Creating an overall talent or people mindset; creating an HR strategy that aligns people, process and systems; developing human capital metrics that are aligned with the strategy of the company; the ability to assess talent during the due diligence phase of a proposes merger or acquisition ensuring that ethical standards are practiced.

Managing Human Resource outsourcing has brought a new dimension to the HR functioning. The growth rate between 1999 and 2004 was 32 percent and the current market opportunity is over $60 billion- with 30 percent future growth rate (Dataquest, Inc) (cited from Graddick-Weir, 2005). Companies are resorting to HRO in different scales, either a fraction of their HR functions like benefits enrollment, recruitment and selection or the entire range of HR functions. The reason for outsourcing are well documented ; organizations hope to achieve significant cost savings, greater efficiency, increased value creation, and better leverage of capital investments in HR Systems; create career opportunities for HR employees; and enable HR focus on more strategic activities. (Graddick-Weir, 2005). Improvement in technologies has replaced many core HR functions. HR has been vested with a critical role to choose among the competing outsourcing vendors. Determination of what is core to the organization and what can be outsourced constitutes an important HR function. Making the right choices requires partnering with line managers and facilitating the development of an overall workforce strategy aligned with the business priorities' (Graddick-Weir, 2005). Given the increasing trend towards HR outsourcing one vital HR competency is managing virtual resources, managing a virtual network of resources across traditional and nontraditional organizational boundaries, while ensuring results are achieved, when you do not directly control the resources. Becker, Huselid and Ulrich (2001) made three large scale HR competency studies and observed six vital domains. Table (Cited in Graddick-Weir) below describes these competencies along with the views of Graddick-Weir (2005) on what is particularly critical in today's fiercely competitive market place.

Building HR Competency

To qualify for the glorious role HR has been entrusted with matching their newly acquired status HR professionals need to be endowed with these competencies.

HR competencies	*Becker, Huselid and Ulrich findings*	*Application in a highly competitive market.*
Knowledge of the business	Understanding the financial, strategic, technological and organizational capabilities.	Having a relentless focus on financials, understanding customer needs, and demonstrating strong business acumen.
Delivery of HR practice	Ability to deliver state of the art, innovative HR practices. Mastering the theory of HR and adapting the theory to unique situations.	Demonstrating flexibility and nimbleness by quickly adapting innovative policies and practices to meet changing business requirements.
Management of Change	Ability to diagnose problems, build relationships, set a vision, solve problems, and implement goals	Increasing the velocity of implementing large-scale change interventions aligned with evolving business strategies.
Management of culture	HR as "keepers of the culture"- champions cultural transformation and reinforces desired behaviors.	Preserving core values while driving the adoption of new policies, practices and cultural attributes to respond to changing market place dynamics.
Personal Credibility	Living the values, establishing relationships built on trust, and having a point of view	Demonstrating the ability to win in a competitive environment while maintaining integrity, candor, credibility, trustworthiness and courage.
Strategic HR Performance management	Orchestrating the firm's strategy implementation through balanced performance measurement systems	Developing metrics to quantify the impact of HR initiatives and people strategies on delivering tangible results that contribute to the bottom line.

References

1. Beaty, Richard & .Schneier, Craig Eric; Work Force strategy: A missing Link is HR'S future success' The Future of Human Resource Management 'edited by Michael Losey, Sue Meisinger, Dave Ulrich; 2005, John Wiley & Sons, Inc'New Jersey'.
2. Cascio, Wayne F.; From Business Partner to Driving Business Success' The Future of Human Resource Management'edited by Michael Losey; Sue Meisinger, and Dave Ulrich' 2005, John Wiley & Sons, Inc, New Jersey.
3. Childs Jr., J.T., Workforce Diversity A Global HR topic that has arrived; 'The Future of Human Resource Management' edited by Michael Losey, Sue Meisinger, & Dave Ulrich; 2005, John Wiley & Sons, Inc. New Jersey.
4. Davenport, Thomas H; Knowledge work and the Future of Management; The future of leadership; edited by Warren Bennis, Gretchen M.Spreitzer, Thomas G. Cummins; Jossey-Bass, 2001, A Wiley Company, San Francisco.
5. Graddick-Weir, Mirian M; Life after outsourcing: Lessons learned and the role of human resources as a strategic business partner 'The Future of human resource management' edited by Michael Losey, Sue Meisinger; Dave Ulrich; 2005, John Wiley & Sons, Ine, New Jersey.

6. Gellerman, Saul W; Motivation and productivity; D.B.Taraporevala Sons & Co. Private Ltd.' Mumbai
7. Handy, Charles; Finding sense in uncertainty; Rethinking the future; edited by Rowan Gibson; 2003, Nicholas Brealey Publishing, London.
8. Lawler III, Edward E.; From Human Resource Management to organizational Effectiveness: The future of Human Resource Management edited by Michel Losey, Sue Meisinger,: Dave Ulrich; 2005, John Wiley & Sons, Inc; New Jersey.
9. Pfeffer, Jeffry ; Changing Mental Models : HR'S most important task . The future of Human Resource Management edited by Michael Losey, Sue Meisinger and Dave Ulrich; 2005, John Wiley & Sons, Ine, New Jersey.
10. Tsui, Anne S; and Wu, Joshua B.

    The New Employment Relationship versus the Mutual Investment Approach; Implications for Human Resources Management: 'The Futures of of Human Resource Management' edited by Michael Losey; Sue Meisinger and Dave Ulrich; 2005, John Wiley & Sons, Inc New Jersey.
11. Wright, Patrick M and Snell, Scott A: Partner or Guardian? HR'S challenge in Balancing value and values: The Future of Human Resource Management edited by Michel Losey, Sue Meisinger, Dave Ulrich: 2005, John Wiley & Sons, Inc, New Jersey.

◈◈◈

ISBN – 978-93-5024-769-3

20 Information and Communication Technology in Indian Co-operative Banks

Dr. (Mrs.) Rajani Jadhav
Sinhgad School of Business Studies, Narhe, Pune – 41.

Introduction

Financial Institutions are the backbone of the Indian economy. Today Indian banking industry is in the midst of an IT revolution. Nowadays nearly all nationalized banks have implemented IT based solutions for their day to day transactions and to provide better services to their customers. The applications of IT in banks have reduced the scope of traditional or conventional banking with manual operations. The Banks are using new tools and techniques to find out the needs of the customer and accordingly offering tailor made products and services. IT has enabled the banking industry to not only come out with new products and services but also enhanced the turn around time by bringing efficiencies in the backend processes.

As per the norms of RBI the computerisation is compulsory for organized banking sector. Computerisation in banking has its own importance. It is time saving, efficiency oriented and practically convenient process of modern banking. The co-operative banks have limited area of operation. However these are the segments of modern Indian banking system and hence cannot function independently on traditional method as it brings failure to them in new era of competition after globalization. The impact of automation in the banking sector is difficult to measure. The present study focuses on technological revolution in co-operative banks. The aim of this research is to focus on automated banking system and its service efficiency, problems faced by co-operative banks while implementing different types of computerization techniques namely back office application, total branch automation and core banking solutions. The researcher also offered some recommendations based on the study for improving the service efficiency and working process of the bank.

Automated Banking System and Service Efficiency of Banks

For the past three decades India's banking system has several outstanding achievements to its credit. The banks are the main participants of the financial system in India. Indian banking sector is divided into different components from which co-operative banking sector is one. Co-operative banking is retail and commercial banking organized on a co-operative basis. Co-operative banking institutions take deposits and lend money in most parts of the world. Information and network technology plays a very important role in the development of banking sector. The banking sector is still accepting and adopting the technological developments and innovations into their banking operations.

According to the study of the literature it can be stated that 95% of the commercial i.e. Private and public banks, are computerised but co-operative banks have not reached up to their level of computerisation.

The information technology in cooperative banks plays a significant role in establishing and maintaining contact with potential customers. Rapid developments in communication and network system are set to change the operational environment of cooperative banks. An effective and efficient management information system (MIS) can make a major impact on deposits, loans and other services provided by cooperative banks. Technological innovations, both internal and external, brought about changes in cooperative banks. Its adoption has resulted in development of e-banking, on-line banking internet banking, telephone banking and automated teller machine. Cooperative banks shall have to change their vision, mission, strategy and governance in the context of information technology. Information technology has a lot of influence on cooperative banks and it will help them to face competition and new challenges to meet customer's expectations in the context of globalization and structural readjustment.

Computerisation of cooperative banks is a very difficult task. Very few states like Maharashtra, Karnataka, Gujarat and Goa are leading in computerisation. Computerised urban cooperative banks have online branches and have succeeded in taking almost all the operational activities. Urban cooperative banks are leading in implementing information technology, but state and district cooperative banks are still lagging in computerisation drive and are still in their infancy. Few urban cooperative banks in Maharashtra have started their customer services through tele-banking, inter branch transaction and providing 24 hours services through ATM. Measuring productivity of emerging information technology in cooperative banking sector is difficult, due to difficulty of measuring output accurately when quality of service is changing.

Types of Automation in Banking Sector

As per the norms of RBI the computerisation is compulsory for organized banking sector. Computerisation in banking has its own importance. It is time saving, efficiency oriented and practically convenient process of modern banking. The co-operative banks have limited area of operation. However these are the segments of modern Indian banking system and hence cannot function independently on traditional method as it brings failure to them in new era of competition after globalization.

From the IT perspective, the banking industry can be classified into three categories:-

- Banks where all the processes are automated.
- Banks that are in the process of implementing core banking software and setting up their networking infrastructure.
- Banks that are in the process of identifying the core solutions

The banks have started following stepwise automation process to survive themselves in the technology based competitive environment-

Back Office Application

The first step of RBI towards bank computerization, was implementation of the Back office application in the banking sector. The Back office application uses computers only for data entry operations and a few calculative operations. It also stores customer's data and uses dos base FoxPro to calculate interest and develop the pay roll system to calculate the employees' salary. This application was not beneficial to the banks customers because it was not providing them any kind of service.

Total Branch Automation

Another step taken by RBI was Total Branch Automation in which the bank should have TBA s/w being used in branches that are covering 80% of the total business of a bank. These branches should have a single customer ID concept using which all the accounts of the customer can be retrieved. The bank should start collecting the customer-related information for customer information system. Also training the employees in the areas of customer relationship, marketing at the customer touch points should be started. In case of TBA bank can also provide ATM facility, but that ATM facility is restricted to that branch only which is providing ATM centers. Because in TBA data centre is not established so customer's data is available only at particular branch. So customer can withdraw their cash only at particular branch's ATM centre in which the customer has his/her account. Due to this restriction although the ATM facility is available customer can not take the advantage of any where banking.

Core Banking Solution

After the turn of consolidated databases (Back office Application) and networks (Total Branch Automation) the next term is core banking applications. Core banking applications (CBS) in Banks provide the complete front-end and back-end automation of banks. These applications also help the banks to achieve centralized processing of each and every service of the customer. "Core banking applications provide anywhere, anytime 24 by 7 non-stop services, which is not possible with traditional localized branch automation systems. These applications also provide automation across multiple delivery channels. Core banking is a centralised system that provides accounting, customer information management and transaction processing functions. It provides a central operational database to bank's assets and liabilities, a transaction processing engine and a system for the financial management of the bank. In core banking, a branch will become a service outlet like an ATM booth. Thus, the importance of physical branches will be reduced. In case of core banking, customer can operate their account from various locations like- customer can open an account at one location and can deposit a cheques, check bank balance, withdraw cash, get demand draft, get account statement, transfer funds, other transactions from various different locations of different cities. Implementation of core banking in banking sector allows inter connectivity of branches with the centralised data centre. Core banking is just one part of a fairly complex architecture of today's banking which takes care of the essential banking activities. The major Banks in India, both in the private and public sectors are moving towards core banking solutions. Core Banking Solutions offered some transactional modules like - *Customer information files management, Deposit management, Loan management, Security management, Reserve for bad debts, Limit management, Financial accounting, Complementary third-party products* etc. Advanced electronic services provided by banking organization are – ECS, EFT, Internet banking, ATM, Mobile Banking, Telephone Banking, Credit cards/Debit cards etc.

Problems Faced by Banks While Implementing Automated Services

To study the problems about computerization of co-operative banks the researcher has collected data from co-operative banks of Pune city. The status of the co-operative Banks in Pune city reflects the position of co-operative banks in general. In Pune, a total of 55 co-operative banks exist. Out of which only 18% co-operative banks are well established and have implemented core banking solution (CBS) to provide automated services to their customers. About 46% co-operative banks have implemented the total branch automation (TBA) and 36% co-operative banks are still working on back office application (BOA) and have neither implemented TBA or nor CBS. The researcher has selected 18 co-operative banks for the purpose of study.

The process of computerisation in banks begins with Back Office Application (BOA), which is followed by Total Branch Automation (TBA) and Core Banking Solutions (CBS). The implementation process of selected co-operative banks of Back Office Application (BOA) was started in 1988 and completed in 2003, even though RBI made it mandatory for the co-operative banks to adopt it between the periods of 1984-85. As regards adoption of Total Branch Automation (TBA), it has been observed that in the last decade of twentieth century 61% co-operative banks have adopted the TBA, whereas in the cases of the implementation of CBS it has been observed that only 22% banks have implemented CBS during the period 2003-2008. This analysis represents that the co-operative banks are slow in adopting the process of computerization as compare to other banks. Co-operative banks faced some problems while implementing stepwise automation process. These problems are listed below-

Problems Faced by Co-operative Banks During Back Office Application

At the time of implementing the back office application (BOA), banks use computers only for storing their daily transactional information. In this the bank needs to do manual data entry. At the same time, the bank needs to take daily/weekly/monthly back up of saved data. Thus the back office application does not provide any type of service to the bank's customers. While implementing the back office application (BOA) in the banking sector, banks faced various problems out of which a few important problems are listed below -

TABLE 1 – Problems of Co-operative Banks During Back Office Computerisation

Sr. No	*Particulars*	*Percentage*
1.	Duplication of Work	77.80%
2.	No benefit to customer	61.10%
3.	Limited functions covered	66.70%

Source : Field Work

Problems Faced by Co-operative Banks While Transferring from Back Office to Total Branch Automation

After back office application (BOA) was implemented, RBI has taken a new stand/step about the implementation of total branch automation (TBA) in the banking sector. Due to compulsion from RBI, the banks moved from back office application to total branch automation. At the time of the implementation of total branch automation (TBA), co-operative banks faced various problems as listed below-

TABLE 2 – Problems Faced by the Co-operative Banks While Transferring from Back Office Application to Total Branch Automation

Sr. No.	*Particulars*	*Percentage*
1.	As human nature / tendency of staff	55.60%
2.	Y2K technical problem	22.20%
3.	Data back up (daily/weekly/ monthly)	88.90%
4.	Antivirus updating problem	72.20%
5.	Limited services provided by the bank	33.30%
6.	Lack of computer knowledge to staff	27.80%
7.	Data conversion	72.20%

Source: Field work

Problems Faced by Co-operative Banks in Implementing Core Banking Solution

The Back office application and Total Branch Automation provides only certain functions to the banks about their banking transactions. Nowadays, the focus of banks is on core banking solution (CBS). Core banking solution provides, anywhere anytime banking facilities, to the bank customers. Besides the customer, core banking solutions are beneficial to the bank as well as bank employees. While implementing CBS, the banks faced the following major problems as listed below -

TABLE 3 – Problems Faced by the Co-operative Banks While Implementing Core Banking Solution

Sr. No	*Particulars*	*Percentage*
1	Huge investment in infrastructure	94.40%
2	More dependability on outside service providers	94.40%
3	Very complex software and hardware used in CBS	88.90%
4	Highly qualified professionals are to be employed and hence salary burden increase.	66.66%
5	Difficulty to detect problem from number of stages	72.20%
6	Consumers are not ready to use CBS	61.10%
7	Any other (Health problem)	61.10%

Source: Field work

From the above analysis it has been observed that the present cooperative banking scenario is far from the anywhere and anytime banking due to the level of awareness amongst the customers, consciousness of the banks for extending such facilities to the customers is very low, so the Indian co-operative banking sector has not yet considered the anywhere and anytime banking as one of the important parameters for their customer service.

Conclusion

Although technological developments and infrastructural improvements are coming up very fast, it needs a huge amount of investment for any individual bank to reap the full benefits of such developments. Many of the cooperative banks are not in a very sound position financially as the profitability of those banks is on a decline. Thus many banks in the country may not be in a position to invest such huge amount in the technological areas although it is highly necessary for their survival as the private sector banks and the foreign banks are posing stiff competition to them particularly in the areas of customer service, business growth and profitability. These banks (private, public, foreign) because of their sound capital base can invest huge funds for technological developments and are optimally using the IT tools for their benefit. In comparison with this, the cooperative banks are falling behind in this area due to their poor capital base.

The banks should also take steps for enhancing the level of knowledge and skill of their employees at all levels including top executives on IT by imparting training. The employees of all categories should be motivated through training on behavioural science so that there is a perceptible change in their attitudes about the new technologies that they are going to handle in the future. At the same time, the banks have the responsibility of educating their customers so that they are accustomed to the new environment.

References

1. http://www/banknetindia.com
2. http://www.rbi.org.in/scripts/PublicationsView.aspx?id=10991
3. www.rbi.com
4. D. Joe Edwinraj, "Information Technology: The emerging driving force in cooperative banks", Cooperative Perspective, Vol.40 No1. April – June 05.
5. Mittal R. K. and Dhingra Sanjay, "Technology in banking sector: issues and challenges", Vinimay, Vol. XXVII, No. 4, 2006-07.
6. A Subbiah & S Jeyakumar, "Customer service in commercial banks in India: a study with reference to core banking", Vinimay, Vol. XXIX, No. 3, 2008-2009
7. Field work of co-operative banks.

◈ ◈ ◈

ISBN – 978-93-5024-769-3

21

Efficient Leadership During Complexity and Change

Dr. B. D. Kolekar & Dr. Sangita R. Devhare
JSPM's JIMS

Introduction

In the face of seemingly endless stream of disruptive technologies, increases customer expectations, new competitors coming out of nowhere, on relenting globalization, and increasing shareholder expectations, a leadership must be sensitive to change the organization to meet these new demands.

Leadership is the influencing process of leaders and followers to achieve organizational objectives through change.

Effective leaders influence followers and their followers influence them. If you want to be an effective follower, you need to share your ideas. Also, as a leader you need to listen others and implement their ideas to be effective.

Influencing is the process of a leader, communicating ideas, gaining acceptance of them, and motivating followers to support and implement ideas through change. Influencing includes power, politics, and negotiating.

Leadership's actions are devoted to helping a group to attain its objectives. Leadership is the ability of management to induce subordinate to work towards group goals with confidence and keenness. Leadership also implies that the leaders accept responsibility for the achievement of the group objectives and it is, therefore, essential for trust and cooperation for both sides to be evidence all the time.

Lord Montgomery – in his book "Path to Leadership" described Leader as, '……one who can be looked up to, whose personal judgment is trusted, who can inspire and warm the hearts of those he leads, gaining their trust and confidence and explaining what is needed in language which can be understood'.

A leaders should have the following attributes—skill, technology, perception, knowledge, physique, memory, imagination, determination, endurance and courage. (Chester I. Barnard, - "Functions of an Executive".)

Leadership qualities that are needed in a particular situation are not usually found in any one individual. From this it can be seen that, if a particular vacancy has to be filled, the strength and weaknesses of the person who is being appointed should be considered along with those of the people he will be working with.

It must be carefully noted that the successful leadership therefore can be considered to be perceptible and flexible and able to act appropriately, i.e. in one situation he is strong, in another he is permissive. It is worth noting, also that the formal status of an individual does not indicate the ability he has to influence others, and as such ability is rather a combination of his position and his personality.

Research by R. Tannenbaum and W. Schmbit, found that managers/leaders were often uncertain, how to handle specific problems. Leaders need to consider various issues such as: their own values, their inclinations towards leadership, the level of confidence they had in their subordinates, subordinates' needs for responsibility and independence, their knowledge and interest of the problem and the amount they desired to be involved in solving problems, concern for the nature of problem, the competence of the group in handling the problem, the time available and the type and history of the organization.

Change: Speed the New Reality

Change should emphasis speed of deployment, which can be major competitive advantage in all industries. Change process should be dynamic, interactive and fluid. Central conclusion of research by Elspeth J. Murray and Peter R. Richardson, is that the more focused the process and faster deployment occurs the greater the likelihood of success.

In the past century, some of the most successful military campaigns have been based around speed and mobility. The German invasion of France at the outset of the Second World War and the successful Allied campaign to close the Gulf War come to mind in this respect.

These are parallels in business. For example, the beauty of acquisition is that if they work, they can rapidly produce profitable growth. The deal can be concluded within the first 100 days and initial benefits can be secured within second 100 days. That, at least, is the theory. However many companies can move fast to make the deal but move slowly when it comes to integration and generating value from the acquisition.

The unfortunate reality is that many companies are neither organized nor structured to move at the necessary pace. This poses particular challenge when change arises not from a comfortable, slowly evolving environment, but from abrupt discontinuous change, the cause of which may be external or internal. True, there can be important developments that happen overnight and demand a strategic response, such as the surprise launch of a new product by a major competitor or a major acquisition that restructures the industry.

The reality in many large companies, however, is that external development that give rise to the need for significant changes in strategy all too frequently do not even appear on the radar screen of the executive team until there is no time to even to react thoughtfully. Sometimes, off course, the developments are internal: for example, the sells force may come up with a major new market opportunity or R & D team may develop a breakthrough product or service opportunity.

What is required for success is to make decisions, commit resources and achieve results quickly.

Winning condition for successful change means that a critical mass of resources must be brought together quickly to build momentum.

Shared Understanding

Usually, organization change is associated with a high level of uncertainty, disagreement and lack of understanding about what to do.

Richard Daft, R. Lengel, and L. Trevino writing on this challenge, observed: managers are not certain what question to ask, if questions are posed, there is no store of objective data to provide an answer...... The organization reduces equivocality by pooling opinions and overcoming disagreement. This leads to a shared understanding and social agreement about the correct response.

The experience of researchers has lead them to the realization that the problem is often not with the vision itself. Many executives are with powerful and articulate visions. The challenge has been to turn these in to tangible actions.

Bringing a vision to life also requires an operational commitment that rests on growing foundation of shared understanding. It may be easy to get people excited about vision and to get an intellectual commitment. However, bringing a vision to life also requires an operational commitment that rests on growing foundation of shared understanding which goes beyond vision incorporating three other elements:

- Agreed-to measures of success
- Clear definition of projects and programs required to bring the vision in to reality
- A set of enabling process that continually deepen the team's understanding of its challenges and what needs to be done.

A Role of Efficient Leadership in Strategy

It takes little imagination to come up with strategy. In fact, all most all leaders can easily identify any number of strategic options for their firms. The problem is often not with in itself. The challenge has been turn the vision in to tangible actions. Popular strategic options are:

- Grow larger
- Downsize
- Diversify into new markets
- Dominate a niche
- Outsource the production process
- Integrate the productions process
- Become the cost leader, even if quality is sacrificed
- Become the quality leader, even if cost increase
- Drive rivals from the market
- Cooperate with rivals
- Be an innovator
- Be an imitator

While dealing with complexity and change its primary role of the efficient leadership is to develop and analyze strategies. Leadership has to answer to principal questions:

1. Does the firm possess advantage that will translate into profit?
2. Does the firm's business environment permit these advantages to turn in to profits?

The firm must have a unique and defensible value creation proposition.

Any initiative must be understood in the context of converting shareholder resources into profits over the long run.

The efficient leadership during complexity and change must define the firm's uniquely valuable role in the industry.

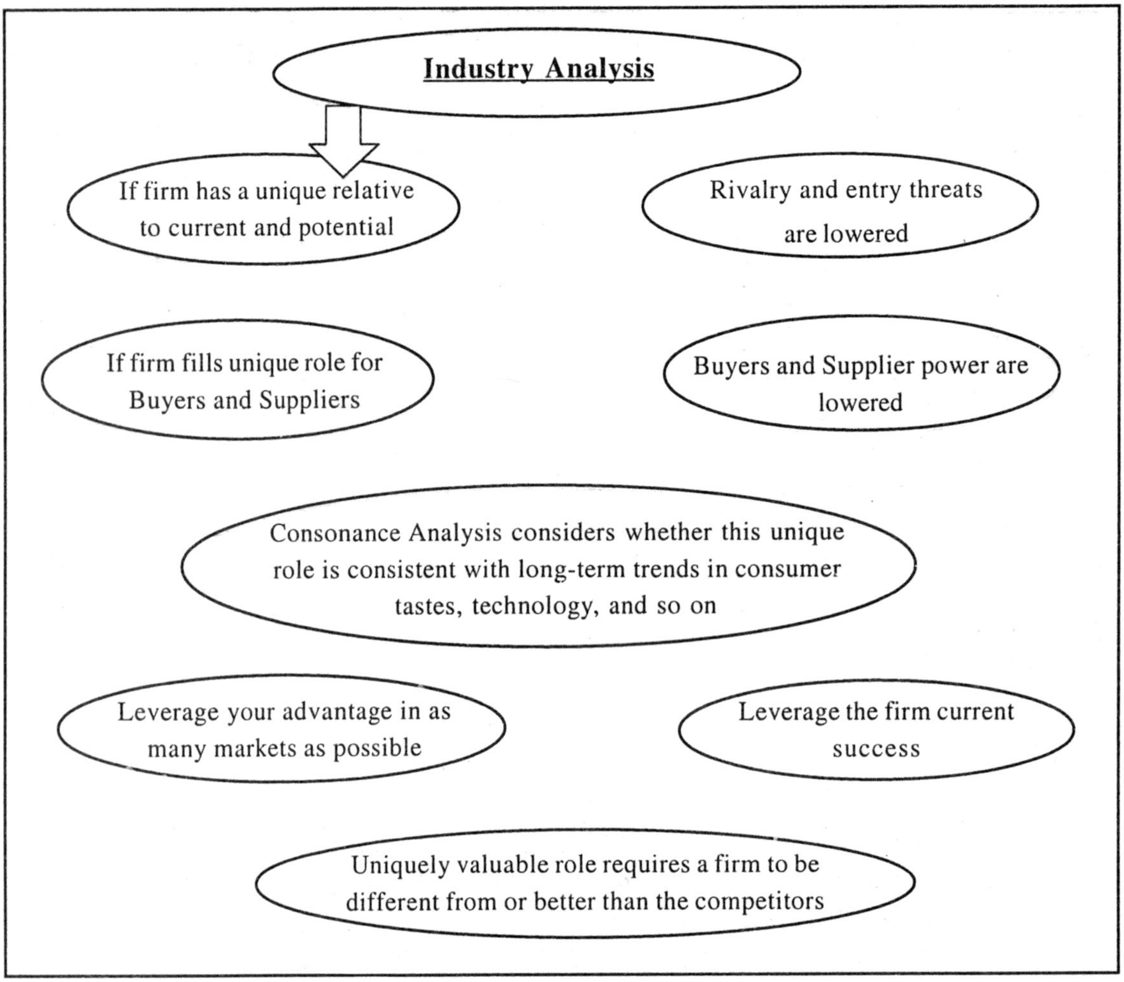

Fig. 1 : Figure showing Industry Analysis and Consonance Analysis

If the firm's uniquely valuable role is that it is better at something, it should leverage this advantage in as many markets as possible. Be sure to identify all the markets in which you can leverage your advantage.

The best opportunities are not necessary in the same market, but do leverage the source of the firm's current success. Firms should grow into new markets or new activity only if there are synergies with their existing activities.

While doing so firms must avoid destructive price competition which is always a loose-loose proposition. Each firm has uniquely valuable position, price competition is minimized, and each firm profits by serving its role. If not, you must find way to soften price competition.

In developing strategy never take competitors' position as given or fixed. While it can be tough to anticipate action and reactions of rivals, it is important to make intelligent conjectures by steeping into their shoes.

In situation of high risk, evaluate strategies more on the extent to which they create or destroy options and less on single prediction of their expected value. Does taking a hit in the near term give you a vantage point in the future?

There are situations in which building market share is strategically important for future profits. These are first-mover advantages: learning curves, reputation effects, switching cost and network effects. Firm's must recognize when these situation do and do not exist, to avoid choosing the wrong tactics.

Value is the difference between the benefits enjoyed by the firm's customers and it's cost of production (The amount of value that a firm creates is equal to B – C.)

If achieving a competitive advantage is difficult sustaining that advantage may be even harder the firm must produce more profits than its rivals, survive competition and entry, and minimize the effects of the imitation. Isolating mechanisms such as reputation, switching cost and early-mover advantages can help but they are not panaceas.

New Management Paradigm

In a situation of a common peril- and every institution is likely to encounter it sooner or later- survival of all depends on clear command. If the ship goes down, the captain does not call a meeting, the captain gives an order. And if the ship is to be saved, everyone must obey the order, must know exactly where to go and what to do, and do it without "participation" or argument. "Hierarchy," and unquestioning acceptance of it by everyone in the organization, is the only hope in a crisis.

In is implied in the new paradigm, in organization, individuals will have to be able to work at one and same time in different organization structures. For one task they will work in a team. But for another task they will have to work-and at the same time-in a command and control structure. The same individual who is a "boss" within his or her own organization is "partner" in an alliance, a minority participation, a joint venture and so on. Organizations, in other words, will have to become part of the executive's tool box.

Instead of searching for right organization, management needs to learn to look for, to develop, to test

The Organization that Fits the Task

The productivity of the knowledge worker is likely to become the center of the management of the people, just has the work on the productivity of the manual worker became the center of managing people a hundred year ago, i.e. since Frederic W. Taylor. This will require above all where different assumptions about people in organization and their work:

One does not "manage" people

The task is to lead people

And the goal is to make productive the specific strengths and knowledge of each individual.

Management now has to start out with the assumption that there is no one technology that pertains to any industry and that, on the contrary, all technology are capable- and indeed likely- to be of major importance to any industry and to have impact on any industry. Management similarly has to start with the assumption that there is no one given end use-for any product or service and that, a conversely no end use is going to be linked to any one product or service.

Management in other words, will increasingly have to be based on the assumption that neither technology nor end use is a foundation for management policy. They are limitations. The foundations have to be values and customer decision on the distribution of their disposable income. It is with those that management policy and management strategy increasingly will have to start.

The new assumption on which management will increasingly have to base itself is that the scope of management is not legal.

It has to be operational. It has to embrace entire process. It has to focus on results and performance across the entire economic change. The boundaries have to be defined operationally rather than politically.

Management exists for the sake of institution's results. It has to start with intended results and has to organize the resources of the institution to attend these results.

The centre of modern society, economy and community is not technology. It is not information. It is not productivity. It is the managed institution as the organ of society to produce results. And management is the specific tool, the specific function, the specific instrument to make institution capable of producing results.

This Requires a Final New Management Paradigm

Management's concern and managements responsibility are every that affects the performance of the institution and its results- whether inside or outside, whether under the institution control or totally beyond it.

Change Strategy

What can strategy be based on in a period of rapid change and total uncertainty, such as the world is facing from the turn of the 21st century? There are indeed FIVE phenomena that can be consider certainties. They are not essentially economic. They are primarily social and political:

1. The Collapsing Birth Rate in the Develop World.
2. Shifts in the Distribution of Disposable Income.
3. Defining Performance.
4. Global Competitiveness.
5. The Growing Incongruence Between Economic Globalization and Political Splintering.

One cannot Manage Change. One can only be ahead of it

It is central 21st century challenge for management that its organization becomes a change leaders. A change leader sees change as opportunity. A change leader looks for change knows how to find the right changes and knows how to make them effective both outside the organization and inside it. This requires:

1. Policies to make the future.
2. Systematic methods to look for and to anticipate change.
3. The right way to introduce change, both within and outside the organization.
4. Policies to balance change and continuity

The change leader puts every product, every service, every process, every market, every distribution channel, every customer and end use' on trial for its life.

How the Effective Leadership Deals with Change?

The policy for the change leader to build in to the enterprise is systematic policy of innovation, that is, policy to crate change.

To be a successful change leader an enterprise has to have a policy of systematic innovation. The main reason is that a policy of systematic innovation produces the mind set for an organization to be a change leader. It makes the entire organization see change as an opportunity.

Windows of Opportunity

This requires a systematic policy to look, every Six to Twelve months, for changes that might be opportunities- in the areas "the windows of opportunities".

- The organization's own unexpected successes and unexpected failures, but also the unexpected successes and unexpected failures of the organization's competitors
- Incongruities in the process of production and distribution or in customer behavior
- Process needs
- Changes in industry and market structure
- Changes in demographics
- Changes in meaning and perceptions
- New Knowledge

Making the Future

One thing is certain for developed countries and probably for the entire world: we face long years of profound changes. The changes are not primarily economic changes. They are not even primarily technological changes. They are changes in demographics, in politics, in society, in philosophy and, above all, in world view.

Conclusion

Theories tried to ignore the changes and to pretend that the tomorrow will be like yesterday, only more so. This, however, is the positions that existing institution tend to adopt in such a period-businesses as well as non businesses. It is, above all, the policy likely to be adopted by the institutions that were most successful in the earlier period before the changes. They are most likely to suffer from the delusion that tomorrow will be like yesterday, only more so. Thus it can be confidently predicted that a large number of today's leaders in all areas are unlikely still to be around thirty years hence and certainly not in their present form. But to try to anticipate the changes is equally unlikely to be successful these changes are not predictable.

The only policy likely to succeed is to try to make the future. Changes of course have to fit the certainties (mentioned earlier) within these restraints, however, the future is malleable. It can still be created.

The efficient Leadership must try to clarify the complex future.

To try to make the future is highly risky. It is less risky, however, than not to try to make it.

References

1. Jagdish Bhagwati "The Winds of the Hundred Days How Washington Mismanaged Globalization', (2000), MIT Press.
2. Berenbeim, R.E. "Ethics Programs and Their Dimensions". (1992), Journal of Business Ethics.
   Niall Ferguson "The Cash Nexus The Money and Political Power", Allen Lane, (2002) , the Penguin Press.
3. Francis, David R. "Asking for Help: A Guide to Using Socially Responsible Consultants". (1991, January/February), Business Ethics Magazine.

◈◈◈

ISBN – 978-93-5024-769-3

22 KPO Opportunities in India – Current Trends and Future Outlook

Prof. N. S. Goje & Prof. R. R. Ubale
Institute of Management and Research Kamptee, Nagpur.
Prof. Mrs. Sheetal N. Goje
Principal Arunrao Kalode College Nagpur.

Introduction

After the success story of business process outsourcing (BPO), India will emerge as a "key player" in the knowledge process off shoring space considering its large base of talented professionals, according to global consultancy firm Price water house Coopers (PwC). "India will be a key player on KPO supply side, as it is a country with a large base of highly qualified professionals," PwC Executive Director Joydeep Datta Gupta said unveiling the report 'Global Integration through KPO'.

In this knowledge era, our success depends on what we know and what we do with what we know. The changes that we are going through are mind-boggling. The evolution and maturity of the Indian BPO sector has given birth to yet another wave in the global outsourcing scene: KPO or Knowledge Process Outsourcing. The success in outsourcing business process operations to India has encouraged many firms to start outsourcing their high-end knowledge work as well. Cost savings, operational efficiencies, access to a highly talented workforce and improved quality are all underlying expectations in off shoring high-end processes to India.

What is KPO?

Knowledge process can be defined as high added value processes chain where the achievement of objectives is highly dependent on the skills, domain knowledge and experience of the people carrying out the activity. And when this activity gets outsourced a new business activity emerges, which is generally known as Knowledge Process Outsourcing.

Knowledge Processing Outsourcing (KPO), calls for the application of specialized domain pertinent knowledge of a high level. The KPO typically involves a component of Business Processing Outsourcing (BPO), Research Process Outsourcing (RPO) and Analysis Process Outsourcing (APO). KPO business entities provide typical domain-based processes, advanced analytical skills and business expertise, rather than just process expertise. KPO Industry is handling more amount of high skilled work other than the BPO Industry. While KPO derives its strength from the depth of knowledge, experience and judgment factor; BPO in contrast is more about size, volume and efficiency.

Characteristics of KPO

A business process that is repeatable, scalable and that does not require the physical presence of a worker near the client can theoretically be outsourced and offshored; this forms the basis of Business Process Outsourcing or BPO. A Business Process Outsourcing or Offshoring firm's function can be simply defined as follows: it acquires a process from the end-client and runs it at its site until the process has reached its logical conclusion, after which it sends the results - if any - to the client. In contrast, a KPO or Knowledge Process Outsourcing firm functions at a higher level and can be differentiated from BPO firms in the following ways:

- A KPO firm requires substantially more domain expertise. In fact, Knowledge Process Outsourcing and Offshoring is an area where professionals continue to learn, just as doctors and lawyers undergo continuous training to learn new treatments and procedures and newer interpretations of existing laws.
- Not surprisingly, experienced professionals can leverage their expertise to generate more revenues for the KPO firm. Such professionals can earn anywhere between $80 and $500 per hour in the US, Canada or the UK and between $20 and $100 per hour in India. Clearly, the more experience its professionals have, the more the firm can earn.
- Since domain expertise is the key factor, not only companies but also countries can easily differentiate themselves from each other. The countries that will emerge as strong contenders in the KPO business are those that have large numbers of engineers, medical doctors, graduates in sciences and technology (including biotech and pharmaceuticals), MBAs, certified financial analysts, accountants, statisticians, lawyers, etc. Low-wage countries that seem to have these professionals in large numbers include India, China, Russia, Poland, the Philippines, Hungary, and many republics from the erstwhile Soviet Union.
- Most KPO projects are smaller by a factor of 5 to 10 than the corresponding BPO projects. Furthermore, the salespeople selling KPO services need to be well versed in these services and to have the required domain expertise in order to be credible.
- The fifth facet of a KPO is the scalability factor of the process wherein the methodology is similar but there is a premium placed on domain expertise.
- The last but probably the most important distinction between a KPO firm and a BPO firm is that in a KPO firm, the client is involved during the entire execution process.

Potential in India

In fact, it is the evolution and maturity of the Indian BPO sector that has given rise to yet another wave in the global outsourcing scenario: KPO or Knowledge Process Outsourcing. The success achieved by many overseas companies in outsourcing business process operations to India has encouraged many of the said companies to start outsourcing their high-end knowledge work as well. Cost savings, operational efficiencies, availability of and access to a highly skilled and talented workforce and improved quality are all underlying expectations in outsourcing high-end processes to India

India has a large pool of knowledge workers in various sectors ranging from Pharmacy, Medicine, Law, Biotechnology, Education & Training, Engineering, Analytics, Design & Animation, Research & Development, Paralegal Content and even Intelligence services.

This talent is soon being discovered and tapped by leading businesses across the globe resulting in the outsourcing of high-end processes to low-wage destinations. Hence Knowledge Process Outsourcing involves offshoring of knowledge intensive business processes that require specialized domain expertise.

Here are some KPO services that can be outsourced to India:

- Research & Development
- Business and Technical Analysis
- Learning Solutions
- Animation & Design
- Business & Market Research
- Pharmaceuticals and Biotechnology
- Medical Services
- Writing & Content Development
- Legal Services
- Intellectual Property (IP) Research
- Data Analytics
- Network Management
- Training & Consultancy

Comparison of Opportunity in BPO and KPO Markets

Low-end outsourcing services have an expected Cumulative Annual Growth Rate (CAGR) of 26% by 2010. In contrast, the global market is poised for an expected CAGR of 46% by 2010. The following figure demonstrates the expected growth in the BPO and KPO markets within seven years.

Source: Evalueserve Analysis

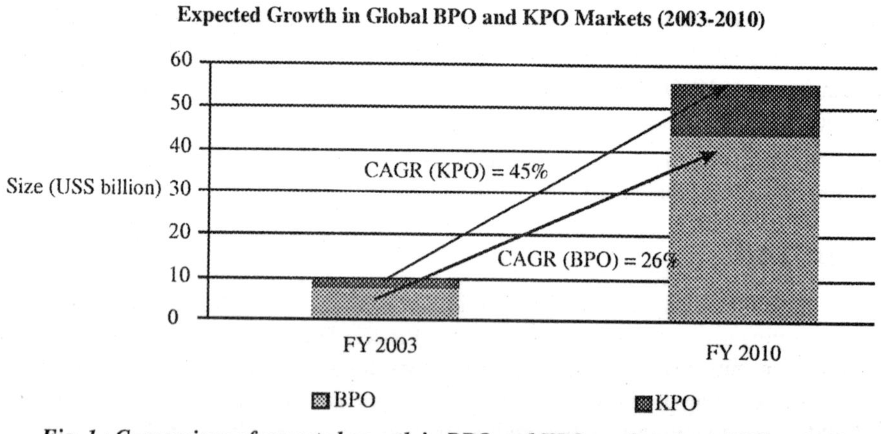

Fig. 1 : Comparison of expected growth in BPO and KPO markets from 2003 to 2010

Critical Success Factors in Outsourcing Knowledge Work

As organizations determine which of their critical, high-end and strategic functions can be performed in an outsourcing environment, a number of factors will influence their experience with KPO:

- ***Ease of Process Portability:*** Just how well knowledge work can be divided into smaller, manageable segments will determine what can be performed and managed in an outsourcing environment. KPO processes are typically fragmented across geographies and business groups, and are difficult to disengage and cluster for porting outsource. Success in this activity requires significant outsource experience and the deployment of rigorous methodologies.

- ***Availability of Skills:*** It is not just the availability of skills at the macroeconomic level but also the availability of differentiated skills in a specific location that is important. Hence, determining the availability (and subsequently locating) specific mathematical modeling skills or radiologists is more complex than the ITO/BPO practice of estimating the talent pool based on the number of Engineering or English-speaking graduates. Additionally, as potential "destination" economies also grow, a number of industries will compete for the same talent to cater to their own domestic markets.
- ***Potential for Economies of Scale:*** A small section of the organizational pyramid performs high-end critical knowledge work and, because of this, KPO generally does not achieve the economies of scale of ITO and BPO in an offshored or outsourced environment.
- ***Legal and Licensing Issues:*** Traditional barriers to entry employed by professions such as medicine, law and accounting will limit the extent of services that can be offshored. The litigious environment that surrounds these professions further limits the risk appetite for using blended global delivery. In some cases, there could even be licensing implications to processes being offshored.
- ***Protecting Intellectual Property Rights (IPR):*** Many functions and processes, such as certain strategic marketing ideas or financial functions, are core to the organization. For example, some proprietary databases, models, and algorithms in equity research would be critical to an organization. Similarly, the databases and findings of a clinical trial from a pharmaceutical company would need to be protected. Therefore, protecting IPR would be one of the key considerations in outsourcing knowledge functions.

Challenges in KPO

KPO delivers high value to organizations by providing domain-based processes and business expertise rather than just process expertise. These processes demand advanced analytical and specialized skill of knowledge workers that have domain experience to their credit. Therefore outsourcing of knowledge processes face more challenges than BPO (Business Process Outsourcing). Some of the challenges involved in KPO will be:

- Maintaining higher quality standards,
- Investment in KPO infrastructure,
- The lack of talent pool,
- Requirement of higher level of control,
- Confidentiality and enhanced risk management.

Current and Expected Growth of KPO

According to expert research, the revenue earned by the Knowledge Process Offshoring industry worldwide was approximately US $1.2 billion in 2003-04 and US $4.4 billion in 2006-07; this implies an annual growth rate of 54 percent. Furthermore, the Knowledge Process Offshoring industry employed approximately 34,000 and 106,000 professionals in 2003-04 and 2006-07 respectively. Our forecasts also show that the industry is expected to grow to US $16.7 billion in revenue in 2010-11 (which would imply an annual growth rate of 39 percent during the next four years) and to employ approximately 350,000 professionals globally. In contrast, the rest of the Business Process Offshoring industry worldwide grew from revenue of US $7.7 billion in 2003-04 to US $15.8 billion in 2006-07, which corresponds to an annual growth rate of approximately 27 percent. During the next four years, the BPO industry is expected to grow annually at 26 percent, thereby earning US $39.8 billion in revenue during 2010-11.

Following Fig. 2 depicts according to Evalueserve's current forecasts with respect to the revenue earned by this sector upto 2010-11, as well as the number of billable professionals it employs.

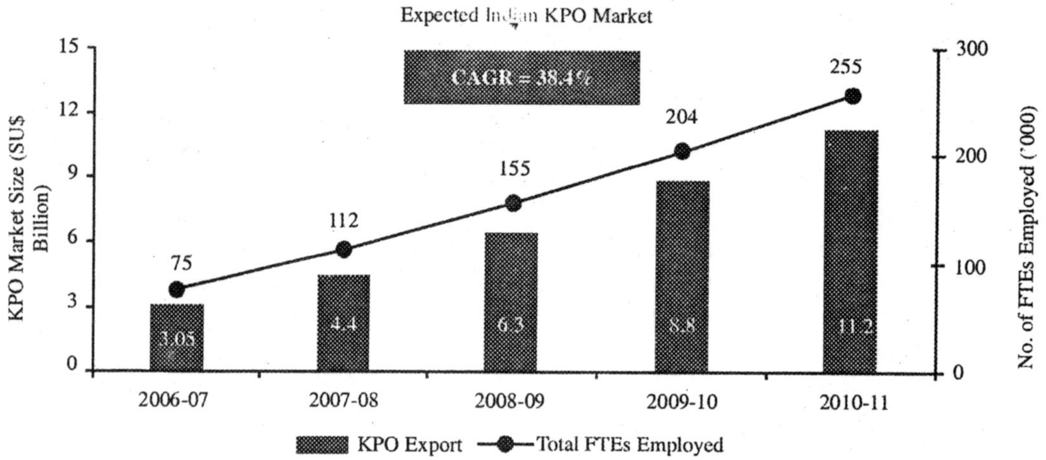

Fig. 2 : Indian KPO Market (US $ Billion)

Findings and Conclusions

From the above analysis following good things are found about Indian KPO sector

- The Indian BPO industry includes basic data and market research, equity research, management, engineering design, animation and simulation, medical content & services and education and publishing.
- India as a major KPO player in the world has inherent advantages because of its intellectual and Internet resource.
- The resulting economic success of the BPO industry has taken many firms to their advanced knowledge work to off shore destinations

Comparing the different challenges with the Indian IT and ITES service providers, it is not surprising that India has been ranked the most preferred KPO outsourcing destination owing to the country's large talent pool, quality IT training, friendly government policies and low labor costs. India is well equipped to meet this emerging sector's challenges and all set to be the global KPO hub.

References

1. Parthasarathi Swamy & Meenu Sekhar , "From BPO To KPO", (2005), Business India, PP.46-52.
2. Tiwana A , The Knowledge Management Toolkit, (2002), 2nd ed., NJ:Prentice Hall.
3. Sveiby K.E and Simons R, "Collaborative Climate and Effectiveness of Knowledge Work - An Empirical Study", 2002, Journal of Knowledge Management, Vol.6, No.5, PP.420 - 433.
4. Evalueserve The Future of Knowledge Process Outsourcing. (2005), EVS Media Relations.
5. Dow Jones Newswire. Infosys BPO to focus on knowledge services. (2008)

6. Gearing for KPO – Some issues related to Transition, Delivery & Commercials. report by WNS global services.
7. Knowledge Wharton Article. Indian BPO Firms Step Out of the Back Office, toward Knowledge Process Outsourcing and Beyond. (2007).
8. Evalueserve, Indian Offshore IT Services, (2009), EVS Media Relations.
9. Evalueserve, The Next Big Opportunity-Moving up the Value Chain-From BPO to KPO. (2004), EVS Media Relations.
10. Falguni Sen and Michael Shiel, From business process outsourcing (BPO) to knowledge process outsourcing (KPO) some issues, (2006).

◈ ◈ ◈

ISBN – 978-93-5024-769-3

23 4G – A Real Time Technology

Prof. Mrs. Parul H. Bhalotra
G.H.R.C.E.M. Pune.
Prof. Mr. N. N. Ghuge
E & TC Engg, M.I.T.R. Pune.

Introduction

The first operational cellular communication system was deployed in the Norway in 1981 and was followed by similar systems in the US and UK. These first generation systems provided voice transmissions by using frequencies around 900 MHz and analogue modulation. The second generation (2G) of the wireless mobile network was based on low-band digital data signaling. The most popular 2G wireless technology is known as Global Systems for Mobile Communications (GSM). The first GSM systems used a 25MHz frequency spectrum in the 900MHz band. Planning for 3G started in the 1980s. Initial plans focused on multimedia applications such as video conferencing for mobile phones. When it became clear that the real killer application was the Internet, 3G thinking had to evolve. As personal wireless handsets become more common than fixed telephones, it is clear that personal wireless Internet access will follow and users will want broadband Internet access wherever they go.[2]

Given the technology at large, 4G mobile technology as an example, will give people a more convenience and ease in lifestyle. With the "anytime, anywhere, anything," capability, 4G wireless technology will benefit every individual regardless of time and place. The objective of the 3G was to develop a new protocol and new technologies to further enhance the mobile experience. In contrast, the new 4G framework to be established will try to accomplish new levels of user experience and multi-service capacity by also integrating all the mobile technologies that exist (e.g. GSM - Global System for Mobile Communications, GPRS - General Packet Radio Service, IMT-2000 - International Mobile Communications, Wi-Fi - Wireless Fidelity, Bluetooth)

Migrating to 4G

The fact that 4G mobile networks intend to integrate almost every wireless standard already In use, enabling its simultaneous use and interconnection poses many questions not yet answered. The research areas that present key challenges to migrate current systems to 4G are many but can be summarized in the following: Mobile Station, System and Service. [3] To be able to use 4G mobile networks a new type of mobile terminals must be conceived. The terminals to be adopted must adapt seamless to multiple wireless networks, each with different protocols and technologies. Auto reconfiguration will also be needed so that terminals can adapt to the different services available. This adaptation may imply that it must download automatically configuration software from networks in range. Moreover terminals must be able to choose from all the available wireless networks the one to use with a specific service. To do this it must be aware of specifications of all the networks in terms of bandwidth, QoS supported, costs and respect to user preferences. Terminal mobility will be a key factor to the success of 4G networks. Terminals must be able to provide wireless services anytime, everywhere. This implies that roaming between different networks must be automatic and transparent to the user. There are two major issues in terminal mobility, location management and handoff management [5]. Location management deals with tracking user mobility, and handling information about original, current and (if possible) future cells. Moreover it must deal with authentication issues and QoS assurances. Handoff management primary objective is to maintain the communications while the terminal crosses wireless network boundaries. In addition, 4G networks, in opposition to the other mobile generations, must deal with vertical and horizontal handoffs, i.e., a 4G mobile client may move between different types of wireless networks (e.g. GSM and Wi-Fi) and between cells of the same wireless network (e.g. moving between adjacent GSM cells). Furthermore, many of the services available in this new mobile generation like video conference have restrict time constraints and QoS needs that must not be perceptible affected by handoffs. To avoid these problems new algorithms must be researched and a prevision of user mobility will be necessary, so as to avoid broadcasting at the same time to all adjacent antennas what would waste unnecessary resources. Another major problem relates to security, since 4G pretends to join many different types of mobile technologies. As each standard has its own security scheme, the key to 4G systems is to be highly flexible.

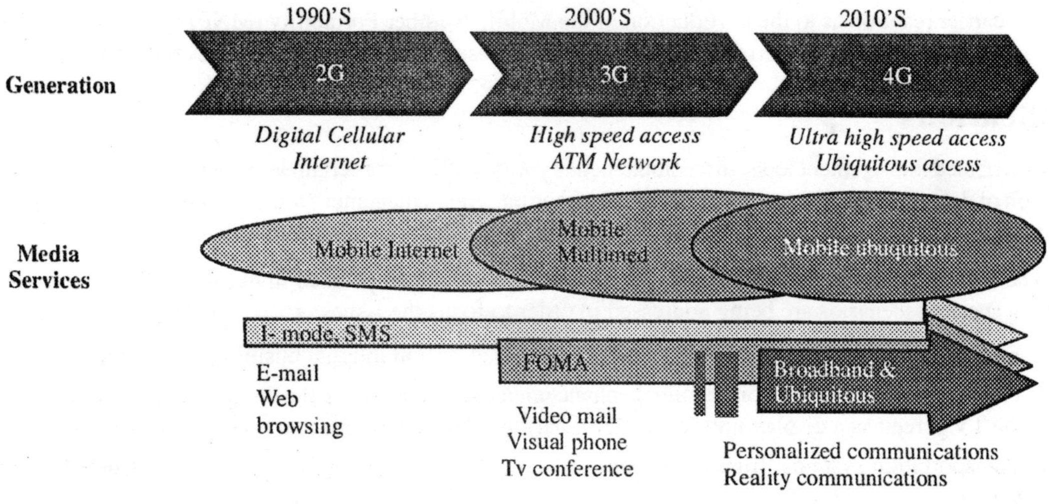

Evolution of the Mobile Communications Systems

Fig. 1 : Evolution of the Mobile Communications Systems

4G Characteristics

(a) Convergence Services: The idea of convergence means that the creation of the atmosphere that can eventually provide seamless and high-reliable and quality broadband mobile communication service and ubiquitous service through wired and wireless convergence networks without the space problem and terrestrial limitation, by means of ubiquitous connectivity. Convergence among industries is also accelerated by formation of alliances through participation in various projects to provide convergence services. 4G mobile systems will mainly be characterized by a horizontal communication model, where such different access technologies as cellular, cordless, wireless LAN type systems, short-range wireless connectivity, and wired systems will be combined on a common platform to complement each other in the best possible way for different service requirements and radio environments [6].

(b) Broadband Services: Broadband is a basis for the purpose of enabling multimedia communications including video service, which requires transmission of a large amount of data; it naturally calls media convergence aspect, based on packet transport, advocating the integration of various media on different qualities.

(c) Flexibility and Personalized Service: The key concern in security designs for 4G networks is flexibility. 4G systems will support comprehensive and personalized services, providing stable system performance and quality of service. To support multimedia services, high-data rate services with good system reliability will be provided. At the same time, a low data rate transmission cost will be maintained. In order to meet the demands of these diverse users, service providers should design personal and customized services for them. Personal mobility is a concern in mobility management.

Personal mobility concentrates on the movement of users instead of users' terminals, and involves the provision of personal communications and personalized operating environments.

The goal of 4th Generation (4G) mobile communications technologies is to realize wireless communications at the same high data rate as is made possible through use of the fiber-optic transmission systems that are available today. Realization of 4G mobile communications is foreseen in the early 2010s, but various precursor technologies and services have been appearing as of late. A scrutiny on the market trends, along with a close watch on carrier reaction as to the introduction of the Mobile Number Portability (MNP) system planned for October 24, 2006, is of vital importance at this time for all those interested in this business field. [6]

Applications

Distributed management tools, in a complementary way, will allow a certain level of monitoring (including collection of data for analysis), control and troubleshooting. The management tools currently available do not encompass mobility efficiently and hence this is another important area of research.

The aim of the research in this area is to develop tools that can be used in 4G software systems. The following specific scenarios are being addressed in order to focus the issues:

- E-commerce, including micro transactions, share trading and internal business transactions
- Home services, ranging from terminal enhancements (e.g. enhancing the display capabilities by using the TV screen as a display unit for the terminal) to security systems and housekeeping tasks
- Transportation systems: Itinerary support, ticketing and location services are to be targeted in this area.
- Infotainment on the move: This will demonstrate the need for software and terminal reconfiguration and media-adaptation.
- Telemedicine and assistance services: Emergency team support, remote/virtual operations and surveillance of heart patients are possible stages for this scenario.

Mobile financial services : In the USA, brokerage firms like Fidelity and TD Waterhouse already provide a wireless internet service, so that their customers receive real-time quotes, quote lists, market updates, news and other extensive research.[2] Applications such as access to real-time equity information for traders on the floor are driving mobile middleware vendors' sales. Professional services companies are also investing in mobile middleware as opportunity costs revolve around a connected remote workforce.

Conclusion

It is always dangerous to predict too far ahead in a fast- moving field such as mobile communications. Almost by definition the eventual 2010 scene will not match exactly that depicted in the 4G vision described herein. However, the key elements—fully converged services, ubiquitous mobile access, diverse user devices, autonomous networks and software dependency—will persist. The 4G Vision is a living document which intends to update and amend as time and knowledge progress. It will act as the umbrella vision to a large research programme and place in context the detailed research work that will take place in the various areas. In this respect it will help to continuously steer the research as it progresses and, therefore, to make it more relevant and beneficial.

References

1. Hui, Suk Yu, and Yeung, Kai Hau, "Challenges in the Migration to 4G Mobile Systems", IEEE Communications Magazine, December 2003, pp. 54-59.
2. Tachikawa, Keiji, "A perspective on the Evolution of Mobile Communications", IEEE Communications Magazine, October 2003, pp. 66-73.
3. http://www.cnn.com/2001/TECH/ptech/03/08/4G.world.idg/
4. ITU Report, "Broadband Mobile Communications Towards a Converged World", ITU/MIC Workshop on shaping the future mobile information society, March 2004.
5. WiMAX Forum, "Mobile WiMAX: The Best Personal Broadband Experience", June, 2006.
6. ETRI Paper, "Broadband Mobile Communications towards a Converged World", ITU/MIC Workshop on Shaping the Future Mobile Information Society, March 4-5, 2004.

◈◈◈

ISBN – 978-93-5024-769-3

24 Efficiency and Effectiveness of SHRM in Healthcare Organization

Prof. Saptaranjan Kadam
Institute of Business Management & Rural Development, Ahmednagar.
Dr. Rachana Dubey
Dr. D Y Patil Institute of Management Studies, Akurdi, Pune.

Introduction

The healthcare landscape in India is changing quiet fast. Health care systems across the world have undergone significant changes in the last few years. New management systems, technologies, drugs along with increased skill manpower with in the sector, have been driving improvement in the healthcare outcome. With the rising demand in facilitating better health care services, health care system struggle to reconcile three competing objectives: equitable access, high quality and low cost. Management has always been the weakest aspect of healthcare organization as a result health care organizations have lagged far behind industry in development of management policies and strategies and there is greater need for efficient organization management based on planned and scientific methods. Human resource is the most important resource, and its effective utilization assumes vital significance in terms of organizational effectiveness. Effective utilization of human resource, right employee selection, training, balanced remuneration system and cordial employee management relations can bring out efficiency and effectiveness in health care organization. Main challenge to the healthcare organizations is appointing and retaining quality healthcare professionals.

It is critical to manage human resources in today's scenario, as they are considered as assets in line with other physical resources such as use of technology. Especially in a knowledge based sector like health care, human resource is the key for its existence, sustenance, excellence and competitive advantage. The National Organizations survey of profit and non-profit firms showed positive association between human resource management practices and organizational outcome. In the healthcare environment the need for quality output, requires people to work in teams to achieve learning and development. The human factor is central to the healthcare. The fit between organizational strategy and HRM increase the organizational effectiveness. Strategic Management of HR in healthcare is important in delivering high quality patient care. Health care organizations irrespective of profit & non-profit firms can achieve performance standard by adopting SHRM practices through external orientation to customer demand's and a commitment to employees. The objective of the paper is to study the relationship between Strategic Human Resource Management and Health care outcome by considering the suitable variable and suggest the various HR strategies such as flexi time, telemedicine, etc. that increases the organizational effectiveness in terms of outcome.

Strategic Human Resource Management

Since 1990 there has been an increased focus on the strategic role of human resource management. The strategic approach to HRM refers to the relationship between human resource practices and the strategic objective that is the long term goal of the organization. With the increasing recognition of the potential of the human resources in providing competitive advantage, organizations have begun to consider employees as valuable asset or investment. This view has become more significant in today's knowledge economy that depends on the skill and knowledge of the workforce. From being a routine, administrative, and reactive function, the HR function today has evolved to being proactive and strategic.

The human resource management that aims to improve the productive contribution of individuals while simultaneously attempting to attain other societal and individual employee objectives has undergone drastic change with the passing of years. We all know that HRM is concerned with the "people" & keeping the fact in mind that HRM helps in acquiring, developing, stimulating & retaining the outstanding employees as it gives both effectiveness & efficiency to the working of the organization, it has been started being used strategically & is now termed as strategic human resource management. Organizations are facing problems like managing people, motivation to adopt new technology changes, recruitment and training, performance management, development, and compensation management. Earlier the role of HR managers was confined to administrative functions like managing manpower requirements and maintaining rolls for the organization. Now it is more strategic as per the demands of the industry.

Perhaps the most significant feature of HRM is the importance attached to strategic integration, which flows from top management's vision and leadership, and which requires the full commitment of people to it. David Guest (1987, 1989a, 1989b, 1991) believes that a key policy goal for HRM is strategic integration, by which he means the ability of the organization to integrate HRM issues into its strategic plans, to ensure that the various aspects of HRM cohere, and to provide for line managers to incorporate an HRM perspective into their decision making. Karen Legge (1989) considers that one of the common themes of the typical definitions of HRM is that human resource policies should be integrated with strategic business planning.

Strategic HRM is a process that involves the use of overarching approaches to the development of HR strategies, which are integrated vertically with the business strategy and horizontally with one another. These strategies define intentions and plans related to overall organizational considerations, such as organizational effectiveness, and to more specific aspects of people management, such as resourcing, learning and development, reward and employee relations.

Definition and Components

Given the increasingly significant role of human resources in an organization, HRM has become strategic in nature. Strategic human resource management (SHRM) is concerned with the relationship between HRM and strategic management in an organization. Strategic human resource is human resource management relationship, recruitment, training, development, performance management, reward, and employee relations. Wright and McMahan (1992) defined SHRM as the pattern of planned human resource deployment and activities intended to enable the firm to achieve its goals'. This definition implies the following four components of SHRM.

1. It focuses on an organization's human resources (people) as the primary source of competitive advantage of the organization.
2. The activities highlight the HR programmers', policies and practices as the means through which the people of the organization can be deployed to gain competitive advantage.

3. The pattern and plan imply that there is a fit between HR strategy and the organization's business strategy (vertical fit) and between all of the HR activities (horizontal fit).
4. The people, practices and planned pattern are all purposeful, that is , directed towards the achievement of the goals of the organization.

On the whole, SHRM is concerned with people issues and practices that affect or are affected by the strategic plan of the organization.

From HRM to SHRM: in Focus

The dynamic and competitive business environment resulting from globalization has led management to bring a new focus on how human resources should be organized and managed. The HR function now has to develop a more strategic role. The early 1980s saw the emergence and increases in the use of the term strategic HRM. The late 1980s and early 1990s witnessed a visible convergence between HRM and business strategy. In the 21st century this convergence has become startlingly obvious with the use of terms, such as 'knowledge', 'networked', 'knowledge –base firms', and 'the virtual organization'. When the adjective strategic is prefixed to HRM it puts an emphasis on the way in which HRM contributes to the organization effective.

Strategic human resource management focuses on the relationship of HRM with the strategic management of the organization, as defined earlier. It goes beyond the functional role of HRM and emphasizes proactive HRM at the strategic level of the organization effectiveness and performance, changes in structure and culture, matching resources to the present and future requirements of the organization, capability development employment relationship, and change management. Since corporate plans are implemented through people and because human resources provide competitive advantage to the organization, it is important to integrated HR considerations with the development of the strategic corporate/business plans.

Objectives of SHRM

The major objective of SHRM is as follows:

- To ensure the availability of skilled, committed, and highly motivated workforce in the organization to achieve sustained competitive advantage.
- To provide direction to the organization so that the business needs of the organization and the individual and collective needs of its workforce are met. This is achieved by developing and implementing HR practices that are strategically aligned.

The extent of application of SHRM organization, as well as the form and content of SHRM, vary from one organization to another. Strategic human resource management is practiced in only those organizations that have a clearly articulated corporate or business strategy. Organization that lacks a corporate plan cannot have SHRM. Rather, in such organization, HR personnel carry out the traditional administrative and service roles and are not concerned with strategic business issues.

Benefits of a Strategic Approach to HR

- Facilitates development of high-quality workforce through focus on types of people and skills needed
- Facilitates cost-effective utilization of labor, particularly in service industries where labor is generally greatest cost
- Facilitates planning and assessment of environmental uncertainty, and adaptation of organization to external forces
- Successful SHRM efforts begin with identification of strategic needs

- Employee participation is critical to linking strategy and HR practices
- Strategic HR depends on systematic and analytical mindset
- Corporate HR departments can have impact on organization's efforts to launch strategic initiatives

Factor Linkages of HR Plans and Strategies

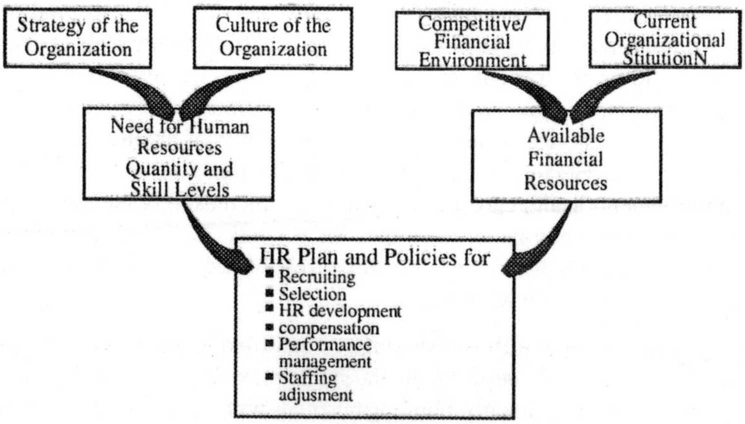

Factors determining HR Plans & Strategy

Given diagram presents various factors that have an impact on HR plans and Strategy and how are they interlinked with each other. Their interactions and impact on each element and the resulting change in HR Plan and policy is also indicated clearly.

Overview of Healthcare Organization

Corporatisation of healthcare delivery is definitely bringing investments to the industry and in last few years the bed to patient ratio has increased for the affordable class of patients. The affordability has also gone up with the increase in per capita income and improving GDP, availability of easy and affordable healthcare insurance and increasing penetration of the third party payers. Unfortunately, the availability of the trained manpower has failed to match the state of the art buildings and the cutting edge technology available with these hospitals.

Most of the healthcare professionals agree that today institutions are facing a challenge in terms of finding the right man. The healthcare delivery mechanism is facing a huge trained talent pool deficit. Healthcare cannot be the sole responsibility of one sector alone. The emphasis of the planning machinery in the coming decades of this century would be in the health sector. Although there have been some spectacular achievements in the health sector, the overall picture is rather grim. While we have sophisticated world-class tertiary care facilities, our primary healthcare is riddled with problems due to a resource crunch and poor management of manpower and equipment. Even though there has been an increase in the resource allocation, because of the rising population and as a percentage of the GDP, allocation has actually dwindled. The State has not been able to provide healthcare for the masses. Even now, 80 per cent of healthcare is under the domain of private sector.

Challenges in Healthcare

Hospital management is becoming increasingly difficult in today's market. The demand is growing and the challenges are increasing. From inadequate reimbursement and productivity management to rising insurance costs and patient satisfaction concerns, hospital management demands smart minds and smart technologies to keep the healthcare system running smoothly. Health sector being a manpower driven industry, the challenges with regards to human resource management is increasing day-by-day. The healthcare industry is currently grappling with human pool deficit. "It is a very challenging issue in today's scenario, where the opportunities available to the healthcare workers are plenty and the talent is hardly available. Recruiting human resource is becoming a greater and greater challenge. Even if hospital management attracts the right talent to fill the shifts, turnover is a major issue in the healthcare industry, especially nursing staff. Hospital management is also tasked with keeping overtime costs in check. With too few medical staff, the available personnel tends to work long hours and has to be paid for it. Hospital management also entails quality compliance and patient safety, managing premium labor costs, revenue enhancement and governmental regulations and mandates. In the health care industry, as in other service-related business, the benefits of having engaged, empowered, loyal employees can lead to increased retention, lower costs, enhanced reputation, and a profitable business picture. In this competitive environment, health care administrators are increasingly feeling the pressure to manage costs and provide new treatments and better outcomes for patients. In an industry where success is being driven more and more by patient satisfaction scorecards, reliable access to and retention of top talent is essential to meet the demand for quality patient care.

India's hospital industry faces significant shortage of qualified manpower in all categories of doctors, nurses and paramedical staff. This is perceived to be the single most important challenge that Indian hospital industry will have to reckon with. Additionally, building hospitals without a mandatory 'needs analysis' in light of catchment area requirements will lead to an uneven development of healthcare delivery infrastructure and hamper optimal utilisation of scarce resources. Affordability of the high cost of technology by consumers of healthcare in India will necessitate significant adaptations to technology in the context of Indian markets. This is especially important in light of the escalating costs of material and equipment.

When Peter Drucker remarked- 'Hospitals are perhaps the most complicated business enterprise ever created by mankind', he was bang on target. There are other businesses and there is healthcare delivery business. Both are not the same thing.

The complexities are many. Here are some factors that make healthcare delivery a complicated business to be in.

- It is a both labour and capital-intensive business. Most businesses are either dependent on manpower or money. Healthcare delivery is dependent on both. Not only it requires a huge amount of investment to set up hospitals, it also requires lot of skilled people to be able to run it. Add to this the global shortage of such professionals.
- Business of healthcare is evolving with every passing day. Healthcare providers are learning to cope with these complexities. The riddles may never be cracked fully, but the incremental progress is being made.

Many healthcare providers are faced with cutting costs while maintaining high quality services. Patients, employers, business groups, health plans, and insurers are scrutinising the delivery of care from the perspective of quality and cost. Determining what matters most to employees and aligning expenditures with priorities are strategic challenges for HR. "For organisations to be successful at competing for new talent and retaining employees, they have to know what workers want, what keeps them happy, and what makes them stay, fair compensation, valuable benefits, and the ability to balance work and life are crucial components of an organisation's overall retention strategy. Organisations must not only create a mix of benefits that retain and motivate what are often very diverse workforces, but they must also continually fine-tune that mix. Hospitals that know how to create an organisational culture that accommodate the needs of their targeted workforce will have the advantage in the competition for talent.

Research has proven that wholly engaged employees tend to be more self-motivated, reliable, and have higher levels of organisational loyalty. Additionally, studies have revealed that an engaged personnel tends to retain employment and is less absent Besides, these engaged employees have higher levels of customer approval and service quality and they regularly achieve, and often surpass, goals. Survey conducted at Rockland Hospital However, the only dimension that reflected the dissatisfaction of employees was compensation and benefits.

Despite temporary hiring freezes in certain health care markets, industry growth is expected to continue. Additionally, health care organizations are looking beyond financial performance measures, giving more focus on how to deliver higher quality care. While some improvements in care quality can be reached through investments in technology and infrastructure, *the most dramatic improvements are achieved through people.*

- Identifying, recruiting, and retaining the right talent and continuously training them.
- Better lucrative compensation offers from the competing organisations for attracting the ready made talent resulting in pressure on the compensation plans of the hospital.
- Opportunities available with the competing domains for the talent like TPA trying to hire experienced nurses for claims verification and clearance.
- Ensure clinical excellence & improved quality of patient care. Decrease cost of operations & administration: As hospitals grow to become large enterprises, managing functions of their operations, administration and finance departments in themselves become extremely difficult to manage.
- Acquire & retain quality staff and develop a career path for each and every employee, Talented professionals, especially doctors. Amidst rising competition, retaining talent is one area companies are always struggling to cope with.
- Strategic Management of Health Care Organizations is a comprehensive text on strategic management as it applies to a variety of healthcare organisations, across the healthcare spectrum. The strategic management can improve the success of healthcare organisations in a turbulent environment. Strategic planning has been defined as the set of organisational processes for identifying the desired future of the organisation and developing decision guidelines (Ginter, Swayne and Duncan, 1995).
- "Today healthcare organisations that do not have a clear strategy are doomed to mediocrity at best - and failure at worst - resulting in poor quality of life for the community." Health care organisations that did not develop that clear strategy

Measures to Improve Efficiency & Effectiveness of Healthcare Organisation Through Strategic Management

Planning the Compensation Strategy:- Compensation plays an important role in not only recruiting and retaining employees but also increasing their satisfaction, rewarding and encouraging star performers and reducing turnover and enhancing employee loyalty. "Compensation package can be linked to business structure, employee recruitment, retention, motivation, performance, feedback and satisfaction.

There are some basic principles of compensation strategy senior managers need to understand. The alignment of compensation with business needs, the goals of the compensation system, reward system levers and basic choice managers need to make are among these principles. A foundation of knowledge will help senior managers use compensation as an important tool for managing the business. The idea that money doesn't motivate employees has been around since decades. It received its most famous formulation in the work of Fredrick Herzberg. He claimed that intrinsic sources of motivation rising from the design of work are much more important than the extrinsic sources, such as pay, in determining the level of employee motivation. In Herzberg's view, extrinsic sources are "hygiene" factors that can have a negative effect but not a positive effect on motivation, while intrinsic sources are true motivators. However, while Herzberg is remembered for his emphasis on the importance of intrinsic motivation, contemporary motivation in scholars almost universally reject his claim that extrinsic rewards do not motivate.

For retention of staff at the middle and lower level, the compensation package is an important factor but the higher you go, though the compensation package is an important factor, aspects like working conditions and the general job satisfaction also plays an important role for retention of staff. For doctors especially compensation package alone might not be the factor for retention of staff. What does a doctor need? What is his comfort level? He wants to practice in an environment where he has good support structure and best of equipment. Instant rewards and recognition, offering stocks and retention bonus are few approaches applied by the Hospitals today with the way compensations are offered. Tremendous growth plans are being chalked out across various sectors and hospitals is one of them. Private equity firms have also started getting interested in this sector and there have been a few investments. Stock options have been very popular in the west for quite some time now and have gained a significant importance in the Indian markets since the last few years. "The whole idea behind Employee Stock Ownership Plan (ESOP) is to incentivise the people to create a huge value, which they too get to share as stock option holders. Listed Hospitals like Fortis have started offering ESOPs to its medical staff also.

Paying for Performance

BM Birla Heart Research Centre, Kolkata is well-known for its HR practices have adopted a philosophy of 'pay for performance'. Due to privatisation and corporatisation of the Indian healthcare industry there has been a big boom in the last 10 years. The base salary of all levels of healthcare workers has gone up probably because of two reasons - firstly because of the demand supply gap and secondly the sector is now offering more opportunities. Hence, retention of manpower and restricting HR budgets has become a very challenging job. Identifying the criticality attached to compensation packages and incentives in the manpower driven healthcare industry, Indian hospitals are today seen gearing up to attract and retain the best available talents and they are bound to do this, to remain afloat, from both point of view— their own sustenance as well as to protect their customer base. Compensations amount to 30-50 per cent of operating expenses of a Hospital and its impact on profitability is undeniable. "Compensation models help in bringing uniformity in the salary and helps remove disparity." According to experts compensation model or structure primarily plays the same role in healthcare as it plays in any industry or domain for its overall management and functioning. And the approach to compensation management is said to be the key to success or failure of any enterprise. It may vary from industry to industry, depending upon the criticality of the human resource requirements irrespective of the fact whether it is a manufacturing industry or service sector. However, health sector being primarily a human resource driven domain, the role of compensation model or structure becomes all the more important for its successful functioning. "The compensation model or structure actually affects the quality of services directly or indirectly. In Wockhardt Hospital, compensation model practiced is a normal combination of basic salary with addition of incentives, bonuses together and other benefits. In Max Healthcare the compensations given to consultants are based on their consult fees, practice base and the speciality they work in.

Compensation and benefits are important to employee job satisfaction. However, there are more important factors that contribute to job satisfaction, such as relationships with immediate supervisors, management recognition of employee job performance, and communication between employees and senior management. The information garnered from such surveys can give the management knowledge that directly impacts the bottom line and fosters positive employee relations.

Performance Management System

A well-defined performance management system (PMS) with focus on talent development, career progression and succession planning can be a good HR practice to establish an organisation as preferred employer. The PMS should be implemented at all levels of hierarchy with very clearly defined reward and recognition system. This not only motivates the employees, but also creates an environment for healthy competition for performance improvement. PMS should be used to assess the achievements / failures of the employee concerned in the areas of his responsibilities. It should also help to know the strengths and weaknesses of the employee and suggest for his training to strengthen his positive qualities and overcome his weaknesses.

Training and Development

Since the basic objective of the hospital is to provide quality healthcare service to the patients, a very high degree of professional skill, knowledge and dexterity is called for on the part of its knowledge workers, viz; doctors, nurses and technicians. The administrative staff is equally required to contribute to this. For the above purpose, the hospital should be fully aware of its responsibilities in providing the necessary training inputs to employees at all levels. These programmes should be need based and should be organised with due care, thought and planning. An organisation is as strong and successful as its employees are. By measuring employee satisfaction in key areas, organisations can gain the information needed to improve their satisfaction, motivation, retention and productivity.

Term-Time Working: When someone on a permanent contract can take unpaid leave during school holidays.

Part-Time Working: Employees work a reduced number of hours, usually with working times agreed in advance.

Flexi-Time: Gives employees a choice about when they work.

Job-Share Schemes: Two people share the duties of a post that would normally be done by one person. Both work part-time and share the salary, holidays and any other benefits.

Compressed Working Hours: Allows staff to work their contracted hours over a shorter number of days, *e.g.*, a four-day week.

Shift Swapping: Employees re-arrange shifts among themselves to suit their needs, as long as the business needs are met.

Telecommuting: Employees do their jobs from home, often using a telephone and computer to stay in touch.

Staggered Hours: Employees have different start, finish and break times that cover longer working days.

Suggestions for Healthcare Organization

- Hospital departments that have higher levels of employee satisfaction provide better experiences for patients.
- Patients that have higher levels of satisfaction are most likely to recommend the hospital to others when they are treated in the high employee satisfaction departments, compared to those treated in the low employee satisfaction departments. Word of mouth, more than any other source of marketing / promotion, is a primary driver in patient health care decisions.
- Individual employee recognition, as well as the need and value of increasing recognition of staff members in higher positions were identified as a key contributor to employee satisfaction.
- In addition, recognition at the hospital was not only viewed as acknowledgement for a job well done, but also as being able to participate in decision making, and being listened to by management and

fellow professionals. This practice results in "more respect and visibility," which in turn enhances employee satisfaction.

- Programs and activities at the hospital which are designed to contribute to employee satisfaction need to be viewed strategically, rather than offered as short-term efforts, or efforts initiated on multiple fronts, which weakens the overall impact of the program. In addition, multiple programs may be distracting to meeting the demands for patient care.
- Some major employers have long-standing and sophisticated wellness programmes. For example: Wipro runs a number of wellness programmes covering its employees from both the IT and BPO sector. The programmes rolled out include aspects such as nutrition consulting, arena (health centres), medical camps, employee well being events, mitr (friend) initiative to provide counseling for employees of the company etc.
- Infosys has taken a holistic approach to promote a positive environment through collaborative care and wellness management among its employees. The initiative is seen as a catalyst to improve the health standards of the employees thereby reducing absenteeism and increasing productivity.
- PepsiCo worked with the ILO to raise awareness about HIV/AIDS with the company's own employees, and those working for its business partners.
- The upshot is clear – more satisfied employees lead to more satisfied patients. A key aspect of this study is that health care administrators can add "quality of patient care" to the list of benefits of having satisfied employees.

Conclusion

In order to be successful the employees should be developed in such a manner that they can be the competitive advantage, & for this the human resource management must be an equal partner in both the formulation & the implementation of the corporate & competitive strategies. Recent study found that health systems suffer from poor HRM, resulting in absence of effective recruitment and retention strategies, poor HR planning, lack of proper performance evaluation mechanisms, and absence of a policy for re-licensing of medical staff . HRM challenges in HCOs should be valued by policy makers and managers and developing effective HR strategies should become a priority.

Reference

1. 'Strategic Compensation: A Human Resource Management Approach' by Joseph J Martochhio. Published by Pearson Education.
2. G.N Sumathi & T.J. Kamalanabhan, Strategic Human Resource Management (Key to Bring Out Healthcare Outcomes) (Creating Wealth through Strategic HR and Entrepreneurship, Nirma University) pp. 83-91.
3. Shivender M. Singh, The Healthcare Sector, Business Standard India 2009, Business Standard Books, pp. 153-181.
4. 'Strategic Human Resource Management by Tanuja Agarwal. Published by Oxford University.
5. www.google.com.
6. www.2dix.com.

◈◈◈

ISBN – 978-93-5024-769-3

25 Business Ethics : An Essential Tool for Success

Dr. Anukrati Sharma
Biff & Bright College of Technical Education, Jaipur (Raj.)

Introduction

'Value have gone down; 'Morals have been destroyed; "Society is stinking; "Corruption in public life has reached scandalous proportions"; such statements have been making newspaper headlines with frustrating regularity in recent times. What may be ethical behavior to 'X' may be unethical to 'Y'.

Business ethics has come to be considered a management discipline, especially since the birth of the social responsibility movement in the 1960s. In that decade, social awareness movements raised expectations of businesses to use their massive financial and social influence to address social problems such as poverty, crime, environment protection, equal rights, public health and improving education. An increasing number of people asserted that because businesses were making a profit from using our country's resources, this business owed it to our country to work to improve society.

Ethics issues are important for mangers for various reasons. If ethics are missing, business and society as a whole cannot flourish. Likewise, when job values are in conflict with individual expectations, productivity suffers. The job holder remains unhappy and discontented. If the organization fails to project a healthy image of itself in society – its quality, service and customer satisfaction – its quality, service and customer satisfaction – its very existence may be in danger. In short, ethical concerns are of vital importance to individuals, organizations and the society in general and cannot be discounted or slighted away as unimportant and unnecessary.

Globalization brought huge benefits, based on opportunities for trade and increased access to market and technology, to the millions of masses of East Asian countries. It has brought better awakening in its wake for an active global civil society, fighting for more democracy and greater social, justice. The world is a complicated place. Each group in the society focuses on the part of reality, which affects it the most. Workers worry about jobs and wages while financiers worry about interest rates and being repaid. The workers see high interest rates as inducing economic slowdown, and for them, this means unemployment. High interest rates are good for creditors whether long term or short-term provided they paid back. They are very much worried about inflation. Inflation, for them, means that dollars they get paid will be worth less than what they lent. The problem is that the international institutions like the IMF, World Bank and the WTO have come to reflect the mind-sets of those to whom they are accountable. The Central Bank Governors begin their day worrying about inflation statistics, not poverty statistics while the Trade/Commerce ministers worry about export numbers, not pollution indices.

The emergence of business ethics is similar to other management disciplines. For example, organization realized that they needed to manage a more positive image to the public and so the recent discipline of public relations was born. Organizations realized they needed to better manage their human resources and so the recent discipline of human resources was born. As commerce became more complicated and dynamic, organizations realized they needed more guidance to ensure their dealings supported the common good and did not harm others and so business ethics was born.

Myths about Business Ethics

Business ethics in the workplace is about prioritizing moral values for the workplace and ensuring behaviors are aligned with those values – its values management. Yet, myths abound about business ethics. Some of these myths arise from general confusion about the nation of ethics. Other myths arise from narrow or simplistic views of ethical dilemmas.

1. Our employees are ethical so we don't need attention to business ethics.
2. Business ethics and social responsibility are the same thing.
3. Business ethics is more a matter of religion than management.
4. Our organization is not in trouble with the law, so we're ethical.
5. Business ethics is a discipline best led by philosophers, academics and theologians.
6. Business ethics is superfluous – it only asserts the obvious: "Do good".
7. Business ethics in the new policeperson on the block.
8. Ethics can't be managed.
9. Business ethics is a matter of the good guys preaching to the bad guy.
10. Managing ethics in the workplace has little practical relevance.

Roles and Responsibilities of Management Towards Ethics

Many ethical questions may remain unresolved in day-to-day life. What is 'fair' profit? What is a 'just' price for a product? How 'honest' should a company be with the union? Determining what is or what is not ethical is often a difficult task. According to the size of the organization, certain roles and responsibilities may prove useful in managing ethics in the workplace. The following points shows responsibilities that should be included somewhere in the organizations -

1. The Organization's chief executive must fully support the program.
2. Consider establishing an ethics committee at the board level.
3. Consider establishing an ethics management committee.
4. Consider assigning/developing an ethics officer.

Ethical Guidelines for Managers

In this world, not everyone has the same ethical standards. It is not possible to lay down hard and fast rules for every possible business condition because situations differ from one another. However, certain of common sense guidelines – offered by James o 'Toole – may be kept in mind:

- **Obey the law:** When in doubt, follow the laws of the land, preferably both the letter and the spirit of the law.

- **Tell the truth:** Telling the truth is important in building trust with relevant stakeholders.
- **Show respect for people:** Treating people with respect has deep roots in the study of ethics. Value their contributions, involve them, take them into confidence, encourage them to do well and see the impact of treating them with fairness and justice on the overall organizational performance.
- **Stick to the golden rule:** The golden rule, "Do unto other as you would have them do unto you" provides a benchmark for evaluation ethical issues in business.

While resolving questions involving ethics, a manager needs to evaluate the consequences on society, on the company and self carefully.

Benefits of Managing Ethics in the Workplace

Many people are used to reading or hearing of the moral benefits of attention to business ethics. However, there are other types of benefits, as well. The following list describes various types of benefits from managing ethics in the workplace.

1. Attention to business ethics has substantially improved society.
2. Ethics programs help maintain a moral course in turbulent times.
3. Ethics programs cultivate strong teamwork and productivity.
4. Ethics programs support employee growth and meaning.
5. Ethics programs are an insurance policy – they help ensure that policies are legal.
6. Ethics programs help avoid criminal acts "of omission" and can lower fines.
7. Ethics programs help manage values associated with quality management, strategic planning and diversity management – this benefit needs far more attention.
8. Ethics programs promote a strong public image.
9. Overall benefits of ethics program.
10. Last and most formal attention to ethics in the workplace is the right thing to do.

Benefits of Managing Ethics as a Program

There are numerous benefits is formally managing ethics as a program, rather than as a one-shot effort when it appears to be needed. Ethics programs:

1. Establish organizational roles to manage ethics.
2. Schedule ongoing assessment of ethics requirements.
3. Establish required operating values and behaviors.
4. Align organizational behaviors with operating values.
5. Develop awareness and sensitivity to ethical issues.
6. Integrate ethical guidelines to decision making.
7. Structure mechanisms to resolving ethical dilemmas.
8. Facilitate ongoing evaluation and updates to the program.
9. Help convince employees that attention to ethics is not just a knee-jerk reaction done to get out of trouble or improve public image.

Consider the following Guidelines when Developing Tools of Ethics

1. Review any values need to adhere to relevant laws and regulations.
2. Review which values produce the top three or four traits of a highly ethical and successful product or service in your area.
3. Identify values needed to address current issues in your workplace.
4. Identify any values needed, based on findings during strategic planning.
5. Consider any top ethical values that might be prized by stakeholders.
6. Example of ethical values might include
7. Compose your code of ethics; attempt to associate with each value, two example behaviors which reflect each value.
8. Include wording that indicates all employees are expected to conform to the values stated in the tool of ethics.
9. Obtain review from key members of the organization.

Market Fundamentalism of Ethics

Over the last more than fifty years, economic science has explained why and what are the conditions under which, markets work well and when they do not. It has shown why markets lead to underproduction of some things, like basic research and the over production of others, like pollution. The most dramatic market failures are the periodic slumps, recessions and depressions that have marred capitalism over the past two hundred years that leave large number of workers, unemployed and a large fraction of the capital stock, underutilized. The developing countries repeatedly ask why, when US faces a downturn, does it argue for expansionary fiscal and monetary policy, and yet when they face a downturn, just the opposite is insisted upon.

Assumptions underlying market fundamentalism do not hold in developed countries, let alone in developing countries. But advocates of market fundamentalism still argue that inefficiencies of the market are relatively smaller than the inefficiencies of the governments. They see government more as part of the problem than the solution; unemployment is blamed on government for setting high wages, or allowing much power to the unions. Democracy means freedom to choose. Much of the developing world feels as if it is being deprived of making its own choices, and even being forced to make choices that the countries like the USA have rejected. Washington Consensus policies, which international financial institutions impose on developing nations, provide for billions of dollars to corporate and financial bailouts in countries facing economic crises, leaving nothing for those forced into unemployment. The basic business of loaning of the IMF and the World Bank is concentrated in developing countries globalization, by increasing the interdependence among the people of the world, has enhanced the need for global collective action and the importance of global public goods. There are global environmental issues, especially those that concern the oceans and the atmosphere. Global warming caused by industrial nations' use of fossil fuels, leading to concentrations of greenhouse gasses (CO2), affects those living in pre industrial economies, whether in South Sea island or in the heart of Africa. The hole in the ozone layer caused by the use of chlorofluorocarbons (CFCs) similarly affects everyone, not just those who made use of these chemicals. As the importance of these global environmental issues has grown, various international conventions have been signed. The one directed at the ozone problem (the Montreal Protocol, 1987) has so far worked remarkably well, while others such as those that address global warming, having yet to make a significant dent.

On global health issues, the WHO has succeeded in eradicating a few diseases, like colour blindness and small pox but in many global public health issues like AIDS, the challenges ahead are enormous. Under TRIPs agreement of the WTO, the inventors of life saving-drugs are to be paid huge amounts for their inventions, by way of royalty which a large number of developing nations are unable to pay. As a matter of fact, the IPR regime overwhelmingly reflects the interests and perspectives of the producers, as opposed to the users, whether in developed or developing countries. It was under the pressure of Western industrial nations that the global pharmaceutical giants had to reduce prices of AIDS controlling drugs. Knowledge itself is an important global public good, the fruits of which can be of benefit to anyone, anywhere at no extra cost. But the knowledge edge-rich North hardly parts with it for knowledge-poor South. Even the general news one gets is censored news. The developing nations should know only what the West wants them to know. If they come to know some thing more, it is because of the leak over which they had no control.

Conclusion

The whole human society has progressed by following certain ethical values and principles. Indian culture and heritage is unparalleled in this respect. At the time of independence, we had only two big names i.e., Tatas and Birlas in the filed of industry. Over the last five decades, India has made tremendous holistic development. Now, our own Indian multinationals like Modis, Goenkas, Mahindras, Singhanias, Thapars Ambanies, Mittals and the businesses like Ranbaxy, Cipla, Reliance, HCL, Infosys, Wipro, Telco, Oracle NIIT, TISCO, Sundhram Fasterners are some of the names we can rightly be proud of. They have reached the present heights only after putting into practice, certain ethics and values. Attention to ethics in the workplace sensitizes leaders and staff to how they should act. Perhaps most important, attention to ethics in the workplace helps ensure that when leaders and managers are struggling in times of crises and confusion, they retain a strong moral compass. However, attention to business ethics provides numerous other benefits. Let all of us take a decision right now that we shall act upon certain ethical principles in our life.

References

1. Jagdish Bhagwati "The Winds of the Hundred Days How Washington Mismanaged Globalization', (2000), MIT Press.
2. Berenbeim, R.E. "Ethics Programs and Their Dimensions". (1992), Journal of Business Ethics.
3. Niall Ferguson "The Cash Nexus The Money and Political Power", (2002), Allen Lane, the Penguin Press.
4. Francis, David R. "Asking for Help: A Guide to Using Socially Responsible Consultants". (1991, January/February), Business Ethics Magazine.
5. V.S.P. Rao & V. Hari Krishna "Management – Text and Cases" (2007), Excel Book.
6. General business ethics resources at the Center for Applied Ethics.
   (http://www.ethics.ubc.ca/resources/business/)
7. Center for Applied Ethics at http://www.ethics.ubc.ca/
8. Dr. Anukrati Sharma, Vice Principal, Biff & Bright College of Technical Education E-mail: editor.proficient@gmail.com & anukratisharma81@gamil.com

◈◈◈

ISBN – 978-93-5024-769-3

26 Nano Computing — Advancement of Microelectronics

Deepmala Sihint
Jayawant Institute of Mgt. Studies, Tathwade.

Introduction

Nano Computing technology has the potential for revolutionizing the way that computers are used. However, in order to achieve this goal, major progress in device technology, computer architectures, and IC processing must first be accomplished. It may take decades before revolutionary nano Computing technology becomes commercially feasible. All computers must operate by basic physical processes. Contemporary digital computers use currents and voltages in tens of millions of complementary metal oxide semiconductor (CMOS) **transistors** covering a few square centimeters of silicon. If device dimensions could be scaled down by a factor of 10 or even 100, then circuit functionality would increase 100 to 10,000 times.

History

The invention of Germanium transistor way back in June 1946 was the starting point of microelectronics technology. The history of computer technology has involved a sequence of changes from gears to relays to valves to transistors to integrated circuits and so on. Today's techniques can fit logic gates and wires a fraction of a micron wide onto a silicon chip. Beginning in about 1946, researchers began to utilize this knowledge base, and most of the basic semiconductor devices used over the past half-century were developed within the next 15 years:

- 1948: bipolar transistors;
- 1953: Field-Effect Transistors (FETs);
- 1955: Light-Emitting Diodes (LEDs);
- 1957: tunnel diodes;
- 1959: Integrated Circuits; and
- 1962: semiconductor lasers.

The semiconductor industry has already entered the nano technology world. In 2000, it introduced the 130-nm node with a 70-nm gate-length feature size, followed in 2002 by the 90-nm node featuring a critical dimension of 50 nm. Industry leaders see new scalable technologies emerging from the novel alternative architectures and devices being proposed today that will take us through multiple processor generations for another 30 years or so.

Definition of Nano Computing

Nano Computing is defined as," The use of the distinct properties of structures on the scale of 100 nanometers or smaller to solve complex mathematical or logical problems, or to accomplish any of the tasks that we expect of modern computers."

To begin with, general desktop computing has made the transition into nano technology, with the advent of nanotransistors. Also, carbon nanotubes and silicon nanowires are now being tested for use in computers to speed up connections between nanotransistors. The technology that has been used so far has been CMOS (complementary metal oxide semiconductor) Technology. This involves the use of semi-conductors, which forms gates and transistors. A gate is the structure that takes many different inputs and produces one output. In today's computers, an n-type semiconductor is used along with a p-type semi-conductor to form each gate. Gates can be AND, OR, XOR, NOT or a combination of these like NAND, NOR etc. There is bits (0's and 1's). A 0(off position) and 1(on position) are the directions that pass through these gates.

Emerging Research Architecture Levels

3D Heterogeneous Integration- It is clear that emerging technologies beyond scaled CMOS **(complementary metal oxide semiconductor)** offer the potential for greatly improved performance by mixing and matching technologies for particular applications. The combination of technologies requires the 3D integration of functionally dissimilar technologies beginning with microprocessors, ASICs, and DRAMs and extending to RF, analog, optical, and MEMS. These dissimilar technologies may later include 3D integration of molecular, plastic, rapid single-flux quantum superconductors and other emerging technologies

(a) Quantum Cellular Automata (QCA)

A locally interconnected architecture consists of a regular array of cells containing several quantum dots. Electrostatic interactions, not wires, provide the coupling between the cells. Two bistable states representing 1 and 0 align themselves in one of two directions, with the electrons populating the opposite corner of the cell. Although electronic QCAs are predominant, magnetic QCAs are another recent development for which the performance cannot yet be assessed. Combining these QCAs allows performing circuit functions that are quite different from using Boolean logic gates.

(b) Defect-tolerant Architecture

The possibility of fabricating nanometer-scale elements that probably will not satisfy the tolerance and reliability requirements typical of larger-scale systems creates the need for defect-tolerant hardware. Systems consisting of molecular-size components are likely to have many imperfections, and a computing system designed on a conventional zero-defect basis would not work. For a conventional integrated circuit, designers describe the chip function, then they construct the hardware. The general idea behind defect-tolerant architectures is conceptually the opposite: Designers fabricate a generic set of wires and switches, and then they configure the resources by setting switches that link them together to obtain the desired functionality. A cornerstone of defect-tolerant systems is redundancy of hardware resources—switches, memory cells, and wires—which implies very high integration density.

(c) Quantum Computing

Quantum computers are characterized as something between a device and architecture. There are many different ways to instantiate quantum computing, including a solid-state proposal by Bruce Kane and colleagues at the University of Maryland. Other options include liquid state, nuclear magnetic resonance, linear ion traps, or quantum dots. Essentially, three different approaches have been taken to the implementation of quantum computers:

- Bulk resonance quantum implementations including NMR (Nuclear Magnetic Resonance), linear optics, and cavity quantum electrodynamics
- Atomic quantum implementations including trapped ions and optical lattices and
- Solid-state quantum implementations including semiconductors and superconductors

Nanocomputing Technologies

(1) From microelectronics to Nanoelectronics

The rapid growth of microelectronics has been based on the continuous miniaturization of electronics components over decades. The invention of transistors; electronics circuits have evolved the concept of IC **(Integrated Circuits).** They are complex circuits which have been etched onto tiny chips of semiconductor (silicon). The first integrated circuits contained only up to a dozen components. The process that produced these early ICs was known as small scale integration (SSI). By the mid-960s, medium scale integration (MSI), produced ICs with hundreds of components. This was followed by large scale integration techniques, or LSI, which produced ICs with thousands of components and made the first microcomputers possible.

(2) From Nanoelectronics to Nanocomputing

The architecture of the IC's and the systems must be suitable for implementations in nanoelectronic devices. In other words, architectures must be optimally making use of the proprieties and at the same time deal with drawbacks of the devices. The unreliability of nanoelectronic devices comes from two sources. One is the bottom-up manufacturing process of self-assembly and it is almost inevitable that a large number of defective devices will appear due to this fabrication process. The other source of errors is the environment in which the devices will be operating.

(a) Silicon Nanowires

Another material being looked at for help in creating future transistors are silicon nanowires. It results in great mobility than bulk silicon. The silicon nanowires connect the source and drain contact points, but with different gate structures: a back gate, a metallic gating structure separated by an oxide and a coaxial structure. Currently there are nanotransistors about 35 nanometers wide with a 1.2nm thick gate oxide. Transistors now allow only 35% of the current that flows through them to get from the source to the drain, losing the rest to the insulator surface around it. At 35nm though, the electrons migrate ballistically means they do not bump into anything. This cause only a 15% loss from start to finish.

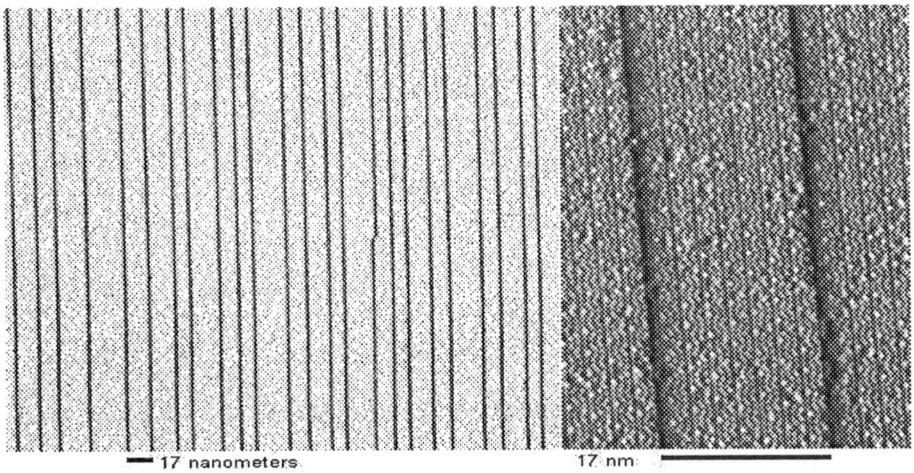

Fig. 1 : Silicon Nanowires

(3) Alternative to Transistors Technology-Quantum Computing

The next step is to go on a whole new route altogether with computing-Quantum Computing, which is different from computing we do today. It is still a part of nanocomputing, because it uses the properties of single atoms to do computing which is certainly the realm of nanocomputing.

It is highly promising outlook in nanocomputing. Current nanocomputing involves the study of very small electronic devices and molecules, their fabrication, and architectures that can benefit from their inherent electrical properties. Nanostructures that have been studied include semiconductor quantum dots, single electron structures, and various molecules. Very small particles of material confine electrons in ways that large ones do not, so that the **quantum mechanical** nature of the electrons becomes important.

(a) Quantum dots

It behave like artificial atoms and molecules in that the electrons inside of them can have only certain values of energy, which can be used to represent logic information robustly. Another area is that of "single electron devices," which, as the name implies, represent information by the behavior of only one, single electron. The ultimate scaled-down electronic devices are individual molecules on the size scale of a nm.

- In addition to this there is one potential architecture, called **cellular neural networks (CNN)** in which devices are connected to neighbors, and as inputs are provided at the edge, the interconnects cause a change in the devices to sweep like a wave across the array, providing an output at the other edge.

(b) Quantum-dot cellular automata

An extension of the CNN concept is that of **quantum-dot cellular automata**. This architecture uses arrangements of single electrons that communicate with each other and arrangement of electrons at the edges provides the computational output. The electron arrangements of QCA are controlled by an external clock and operate according to the rules of Boolean logic.

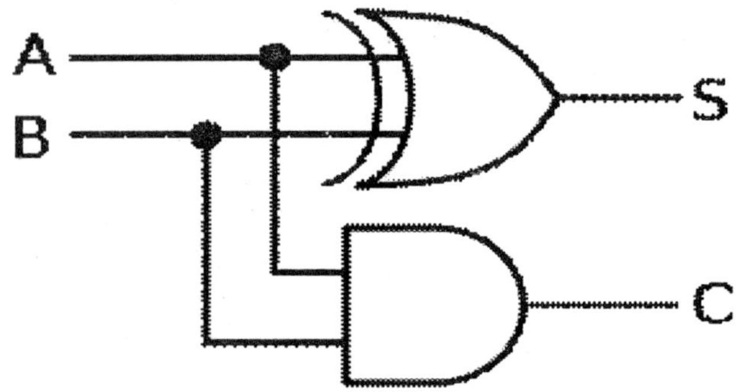

Fig. 2 : Half Adder using logic gates

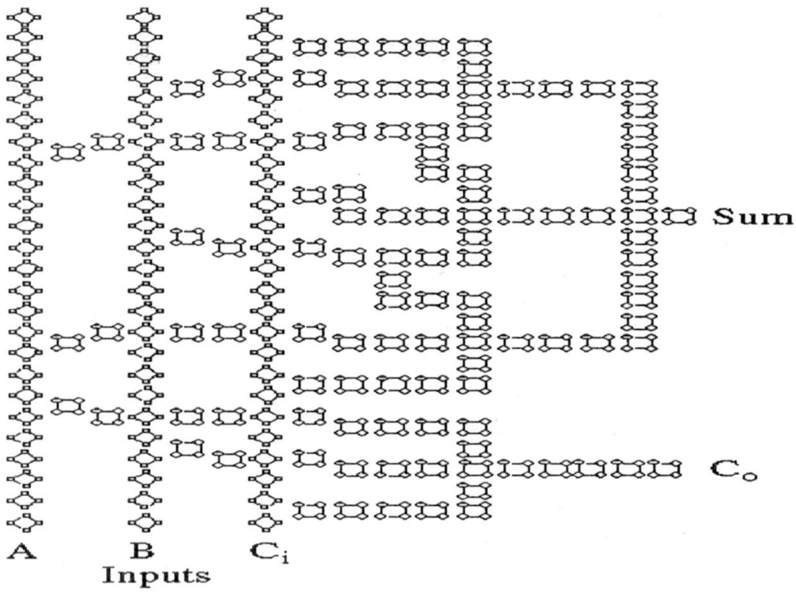

Fig. 3 : Quantum-dot cellular automata (Half adder using cells)

(c) Quantum Communication

The research carried out on quantum computing has created the spin-off field of quantum communication. This area of research aims to provide secure communication mechanisms by using the properties of quantum mechanical effects.

How quantum communication works? Quantum communications makes use of the fact that information can be encoded as the polarisation of photons (i.e. the orientation of a photon's oscillation). An oscillation in one direction can be thought of as 0 and in another as a 1. Two sets of polarisations are commonly used, rectilinear and diagonal)

The property that quantum communication exploits is that in order to receive the correct information, photons have to be measured using the correct filter polarisation e.g. the same polarisation that the information was transmitted with. If a receiver is in rectilinear polarisation, and a diagonally polarised photon is sent, then a completely random result will appear at the receiver. Using this, property information can be sent in such a way as to make it impossible for an eavesdropper to listen undetected. The mechanism by which this works is as follows:

The sender transmits information to the receiver using random polarisations.

1. The receiver detects this information (also at random polarisations) and records it.

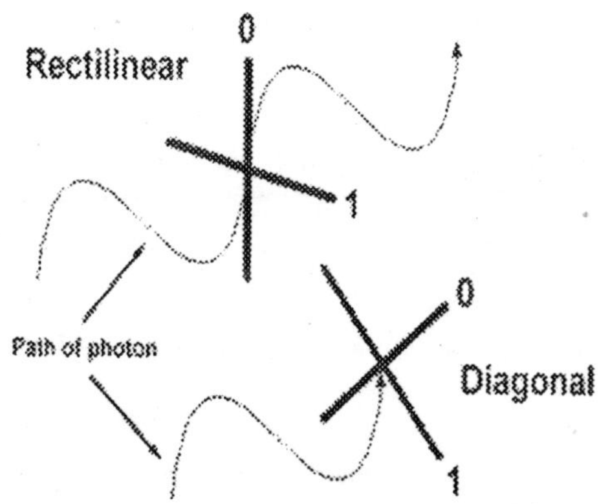

Fig. 4 : The polarisation of photons can be used to encode data. In order to receive the data, the polarisation of the filter must match that of the photons.

The sender then informs the receiver of the polarisations that he used over a public channel.

1. The receiver and sender compare a random selection of the information that was received at the correct polarization.
2. If an eavesdropper has intercepted and forwarded the information, the receiver and sender will be alerted as a higher percentage of errors will be present than expected.
3. If an eavesdropper has been detected, then the whole process has to be repeated.

Future of Nanocomputing

Computing at the nanoscale is set to revolutionize computing and our way of life. Nanocomputing will help technologists to meet the quest to pack power of computing into the smallest possible device without compromising on speed or accuracy. Future nanocomputers could be evolutionary, scaled-down versions of today's computers, working in essentially the same ways and with similar but nanoscale devices. Or they may be revolutionary, being based on some new device or molecular structure not yet developed. Research on nanocomputing is aimed at learning the physical properties of very small structures and then determining how these can be used to perform some kind of computing functions.

Conclusion

Nanocomputing technology has the potential for revolutionizing the way that computers are used. However, in order to achieve this goal, major progress in device technology, computer architectures, and IC processing must first be accomplished. Within the next twenty years nanotechnology will advance greatly, and may be fully capable of producing tiny complex machines.

References

1. "The Future of Microelectronics." Nature 406 (2000): 1021–1054.
2. Coontz, Robert, and Phil Szurami, eds. "Issues in Nanotechnology."
3. National Nanotechnology Initiative. <http://www.nsf.gov/home/crssprgm/nano/nni.htm>
4. Bernstein, Gary H.; Porod, Wolfgang. "Nanocomputing."
5. James Heath, Philip J. Kuekes, Gregory S. Snider, and R. Stanley Williams, A defect-tolerant computer architecture: Opportunities for nanotechnology.
6. Ellenberger, J. (1998). A Brief Overview of Nanoelectronic Devices.
7. Debayan Bhaduri and Sandeep Shukla, Nanolab: A tool for evaluating reliability of defect-tolerant nano architectures, IEEE Transactions on Nanotechnology (2004)
8. Lisa Durbeck and Nick Macias, The cell matrix: An architecture for nanocomputing, Nanotechnology (2001), 217-230.
9. Jie Han and Pieter Jonker, A system architecture solution for unreliable nanoelectronic devices, IEEE Transactions on Nanotechnology 1 (2002), no. 4, 201-208.
10. Jie Han and Pieter Jonker, A defect- and fault- tolerant architecture for nanocomputers, Nanotechnology (2003), 224-230.
11. Zhibin Ren, Nanomos, http://nanohub.purdue.edu/NanoHub/tools/info/- nanomos.php (2004).
12. Y. Cul and C.M. Lieber, "Functional Nanoscale Electronic Devices Assembled Using Silicon Nanowire Building Blocks."
13. W. Porod, et al., "Quantum-Dot Cellular Automata: Computing with Coupled Quantum Dots"
14. B.E. Kane, "A Silicon-Based Nuclear Spin Quantum Computer".
15. Y. Huang, et al, "Logic Gates and Computation from Assembled Nanowire Building Blocks".

ISBN – 978-93-5024-769-3

27

Smart Phone Banking: Threats and Opportunities

Ramesh Bandu Kakad & Phad Chandrakant Ramrao
Sharadchandra Pawar Institute of Management, Dumbarwadi, Junnar.

Introduction

Liberalization, privatization and globalization have completely changed the customer relationship management in banks. The process of globalization and our move towards global standards have changed the perception of customer service, and the banking endeavor to serve the customer better has resulted in innovative banking services and products. The future of any business lies in its excellent management of customer relationship. Customer focusing is not to be viewed as jus a business strategy but should become a corporate mission (Shankar, 2004 p.5). Corporation Bank and Tata Teleservices have launched the first pan-India mobile-based financial inclusion service called 'Green'("The Analyst" Jan. 2010 p.67). Initially, it is for mobile money transfer between migrant workers working in metros and tier-1 cities sending money back to their families in Karnataka and Kerala. This is a simple model where both the sender and the beneficiary open 'no frills' account at PCO's and than are able to remit money. The service is powered by the brand is owned by Paymate. As of on starting of 2010 there were 32 banks which have been approved by the RBI for some form of mobile banking/ payment service.

Many believe that mobile users have just started to fully utilize data capabilities in their mobile phones. Service providers are every day coming up with new services, providing methods to make the solution more easy to use, implementing techniques to improve security, launch of 3G is providing higher data transfer rate and invention of new phones more frequently is driving mobile users towards subscribing to mobile banking services. In India, where mobile subscribers far exceed fixed line subscribers because of better mobile infrastructure in comparison to fixed line infrastructure has made mobile banking much more appealing in India today. Various players involved in providing mobile banking services (banks, financial institutions, service providers, operators etc) are therefore expecting a potential growth in mobile banking industry in India.

Learning Objective

After reading this paper, readers will come to:

1. About mobile banking.
2. About various threats and opportunities of mobile banking.

About Mobile Banking

Over the last few years, the mobile and wireless market has been one of the fastest growing markets in the world and it is still growing at a rapid pace. Mobile phones have become an essential communication tool for almost every individual. Advent of mCommerce has managed to take mobile VAS to next level, adding tremendous value to telecommunication industry. Mobile banking which is an integral part of mCommerce has become very popular among mobile users ever since its existence in 2007. It creates new, convenient communication and fast financial transactional channel for mobile users which is accessible from anywhere, anytime.

Checking account information, balance available, credit/debit card information, cheque status, setting alerts , payment reminders, locating ATMs and bank branches, accessing mini statement, accessing loan and equity statements, insurance policy management, placing orders for cheque books etc via mobile phones are some of the services offered in mobile banking. With multiple access channels such as SMS, down loadable client, mobile Internet (WAP) mobile banking is encouraging mobile users more to explore the service.

Along with the increasing usage of mobile phone handsets globally, the handset is becoming an excellent primary digital channel for the banking and financial players in the markets - mostly being emerging markets. These include m-banking, money transfers, m-wallets, and remittances.

This trend currently is growing at a very fast rate and is said to reach 1 billion people by the end of 2015. According to Berg Insight, an insight agency, in April 2010 estimated that users of m-banking and related services (including money transfers) almost doubled between 2008 and 2009 to 55 million, and also stated that it will double again in 2010.

In 2015 there will be 894 million users globally. This growth is mainly being driven by efforts of operators and banks in developing countries (particularly in the Asia region) to bank the unbanked. Global Industry Analysts (GIA) in February 2010 predicted the global customer base for m-banking will reach 1.1 billion by the year 2015 whilst ABI Research in January 2009 forecasted that in 2013 there will be nearly half a billion customers of MFS.

Mobile Banking in India

Business information provider Dun & Bradstreet (D&B) says it expects mobile technology to drive the next leg of banking sector growth, which in turn would support the Reserve Bank of India's thrust on financial inclusion.

In a report on the outlook for Indian banking sector in 2011, D&B, says, "Mobile technology is expected to widen the reach of the banking network on one side along with providing for ease of transactions on the other. Corroborated with the business correspondent model and UID, the same is expected to making banking services accessible to very small habitations by utilising mobile technology where setting up a branch is unfeasible."

There were around 525.9 million mobile connections as of November 2010, compared with around 69,160 bank branches and 60,153 ATMs across the country. According to the Reserve Bank of India (RBI), around 90% of public sector branches have been updated with core banking software, while around 97.8% of public sector banks' branches have been fully computerised. The trend of transactions is also seen to be shifting from paper-based to electronic. In FY10, the share of electronic transactions to total transactions stood at around 89% in value terms and around 40% in volume terms, the information provider said.

3G's likely impact As telcos start rolling out 3G on a mass scale across the country, VAS players will see better days. Once 3G becomes a mainstream technology, there will be faster access to content over the Internet on the phone.

"3G is likely to give a significant push to the overall VAS business. As customers get comfortable accessing the mobile Internet through their feature phones, smartphones and tablet devices (iPad from Apple or Galaxy Tab from Samsung), the VAS industry is likely to grow significantly," said Badri Sanjeevi, COO, Mauj Mobile.

Agreed Nitish Mittersain, CEO of Nazara Technologies, "With 3G, there would be a huge thrust by telecom companies to grow their slice of the data services pie. To put it in perspective, mobile Internet traffic in India was growing at a rate of nearly 300-400% annually in India prior to the 3G launch."

"Mobile data services consumption in India has increased to 4% of the total Internet usage. The number of subscribers using the mobile Internet has increased by 104% in 2009," according to Abhishek Chauhan, Senior Consultant, ICT Practice, Frost and Sullivan, South Asia and Middle East.

Most Popular Banking Service on Mobile

Checking account balances is the most popular banking service used by urban Indians with almost 40 million users followed by checking last three transactions, 28 million and status of cheques with 21 million users.

Most Popular Bank

ICICI bank maintains its position as country biggest private lender on mobile screen as well with more than 17.75 million users. HDFC accounts for second most subscribers with more than 9.1 million subscribers followed by State Bank of India with more than 6.13 million subscribers.

Opportunities of Mobile Banking

Banking the Unbanked

According to Pavola and Nokia, with more than 4.6 billion people already using a mobile phone globally and less than 2 billion people having a bank account (out of a world population of 6.8 billion), it's clear that a larger populations is left without bank accounts mostly being in developing economies. Being able to do transactions in a secured way, as well as from anywhere in the world, is a key part for people's life as it enables them to build and grow their own life and business.

This is where mobile wallets (m-wallets) come into play as it meets the needs of cellular customers who don't have a bank account for themselves. In Indonesia for instance, there are only 40 million banking customers but there are 160 million mobile-phone subscribers. Of all mobile financial services (MFS), the one with the biggest potential is remittance services, particularly the sending of cash from abroad according to statistics of Putra and Indosat.

Mobiles will play a significant part in the quest to provide banking or banking-like services to those at the bottom of the pyramid. Mobiles are fairly simple to understand and roll out; it's also cheaper and more accessible to everyone according to Avendano/GXI.

Realizing the Potential

Banks and other financial institutions throughout the globe are now realizing the added values, improved customer convenience, speed of information availability and cost savings resulting from mobile integration of consumer and enterprise services.

These simple notifications services which are available to customers not only improves customer satisfaction levels but also results in savings for banks as customers do not call centers or walk into bank branches for such routine information, thus saving the traffic by minimizing it - being green and responsible. It's almost the moment to cut as much things as possible that are confusing the customers - it's much better to be simple.

Benefits to the banking and financial institutions

This will strengthen customer loyalty by offering new and better services by attracting new customers to one-on-one bank-customer relationships, expanding the institution's brand presence in the marketplace, extend the bank's reach by turning cell phones into ATMs, increasing market presence using new, flexible and ubiquitous channels, reducing the cost of direct teller interactions while maintaining the level of high quality service, increasing usage through availability, providing 24/7 services, creating direct marketing channels and also creating new revenue sources by offering new transaction.

Benefits to Mobile Network Operators (MNO's)

This increases the provider's brand presence attracting new customers and by strengthening customer loyalty levels through better service offerings, increases ARPU (Average revenue per user) by opening up new revenue streams and boosting the usage levels of the network, widens the provider's services portfolio, providing subscribers with instant access to airtime purchase. This also increases the cost-benefit ratio by reducing per-service costs, and overall it allows Mobile Network Operators in playing a leading role in the convergence of services and breakthrough technology. Some mobile banking programs even offer electronic bill pay and ATM locators. More innovations are on the way. The only limitation banking representatives foresee for mobile services is an inability to dispense cash, ATM-style. Globally, India ranks behind China in the number of mobile subscribers. As users start maturing in their mobile usage behavior, there could be a different trend that could shape this industry. Instead of the stakeholders pushing their content on the users, users could pull services or content according to their needs. According to Chauhan, mobile VAS revenues represented 7.2% of the total mobile services revenues in India in 2009 and are expected to touch $5 billion by 2016.

Threats of Mobile Banking

To create a safe environment, all parties involved must understand the threats unique to and inherent in the mobile environment. The mobile ecosphere is rife with a range of threats ranging from nuisances to fraudulent. The threats include:

Security

Security experts generally agree that mobile banking is safer than computer banking because very few viruses and Trojans exist for phones. That does not mean mobile banking is immune to security threats, however. Mobile users are especially susceptible to a phishing-like scam called "smishing." It happens when a mobile banking user receives a fake text message asking for bank account details from a hacker posing as a financial institution. Many people have fallen for this trick and had money stolen through this scam.

Online banking is usually done through an encrypted connection so that hackers cannot read transmitted data, but consider the consequences if your mobile device is stolen. While all banking applications require you to enter a password or PIN, many people configure their mobile devices to save passwords, or use insecure passwords and PINs that are easy to guess.

Compatibility

Mobile banking is not available on every device. Some banks do not provide mobile banking at all. Others require you to use a custom mobile banking application only available on the most popular smart phones, such as the Apple iPhone and RIM Blackberry. Third-party mobile banking software is not always supported.

If you do not own a smart phone, the types of mobile banking you can do are usually limited. Checking bank account balances via text message is not a problem, but more advanced features such as account transfers are generally not available to users of "dumb phones."

Cost

The cost of mobile banking might not appear significant if you already have a compatible device, but you still need to pay data and text messaging fees. Some financial institutions charge an extra fee for mobile banking service, and you may need to pay a fee for software. These extra charges quickly add up, especially if you access mobile banking often.

SMS Spam

Between 3 to 5 percent of all SMS traffic is spam. These messages contain a broad range of content - from those designed to elicit a purchase to extraction of money or information from a user by faking an origin.

Mobile Viruses

There are currently more than 400 mobile virus variants in the world. While some render a device useless, others are more sinister, designed to grab and send data stored on a device.

Malware

Malware targets corporations and consumers often charging a one time fee when users open a link or respond to an email.

Rogue Applications

While not technically an intended threat, poorly written or rogue applications can create annoyances and damage a brand. The mobile environment is different from the PC world in terms of protection. PC vendors use a bait and test method for viruses, spam and other forms of threats. This method is not feasible in mobile, given the need for handsets to be in active engagement with all user communities across the globe. For this and other reasons, the mobile operator should be the first line of defense for mobile banking, to protect consumers and businesses as well as brand reputation and mobile transactions. Only the operator can filter a number of communications on a granular level to determine what is spam, what poses a real threat and which information can be released to which business. Working closely with financial institutions, the mobile operator can provide the level of security that will allow a seamless, safe mobile banking experience.

Conclusion

Asia-Pacific is by far expected to become the most important regional market, accounting for more than half of the total user base. Furthermore by 2015, Berg Insight forecasts that mobile banking will attract 115 million users in Europe and 86 million users in North America. It's time up for marketers across banking and financial services, telecommunication sectors as well as mobile payment entities to realize the potential it holds and leverage this opportunity before it's too late. The Coastal Bank, a locally owned and operated community bank headquartered in Savannah, recently launched mobile banking and Text Message Banking.

References

1. The Analyst (Jan 2010).
2. http://www.npr.org/2011/01/04/132657646/Smart-Phone-Banking-On-The-Rise-But-Is-It-Safe.
3. www.the coastalbank.com.
4. http://www.pluggd.in/mobile-banking-in-india-market-report-297/
5. http://www.telecomindiaonline.com/telecom-india-daily-telecom-station-mobile-banking-in-india-perception-and-statistics.html.
6. http://www.ehow.com/list_6683378_disadvantages-mobile-banking.html#ixzz1AIOWh2Nm
7. Expressindia.com.

◈◈◈

ISBN – 978-93-5024-769-3

28 "Financial Stability: The Challenge for Global Economy"

Prof. V.M. Tidake
SRES's College of Engg. Dept. of MBA, Kopargaon.

Introduction

Does financial stability require the soundness of institutions, the stability of markets?

The absence of turbulence, low volatility, or something more fundamental? Can it be achieved? and maintained through individual private actions and unfettered market forces alone? If not, what is the role of the public sector in fostering financial stability, as opposed to private collective action: is it just to make way for the private sector to achieve an optimum on its own, or is a more proactive role necessary for achieving the full private and social benefits of finance? Is there a consensus on how to achieve and maintain financial stability? The last three questions are not likely to have clear answers without a useful answer to the first question. Likewise, without a good working definition, the growing financial stability profession will continue to find it difficult to develop useful analytical frameworks for examining policy issues. Unfortunately, there is no single, widely accepted and used definition of financial stability. Thus the various definitions of Financial Stability can be listed as follows-

1 According to **Deutsche Bundesbank-**

"The term financial stability broadly describes a steady state in which the financial system efficiently performs its key economic functions, such as allocating resources and spreading risk as well as settling payments, and is able to do so even in the event of shocks, stress situations, and periods of profound structural change."

2."Financial stability is a condition in which an economy's mechanisms for pricing, allocating, and managing financial risks (credit, liquidity, counterparty, market, etc.) are functioning well enough to contribute to the performance of the economy"

3. "Financial stability refers to the smooth functioning of the key elements that make up the financial system."

4. According to **Michael Foot (U.K. Financial Services Authority)-**

"We have financial stability where there is: (a) monetary stability; (b) employment levels close to the economy's natural rate; (c) confidence in the operation of the generality of key financial institutions and markets in the economy; and (d) where there are no relative price movements of either real or financial assets within the economy that will undermine (a) or (b).

5. According to **Norges Bank**-

"Financial stability means that the financial system is robust to disturbances in the economy, so that it is able to mediate financing, carry out payments, and redistribute risk in a satisfactory manner."

Global and Indian Perspective Towards Financial Stability

The global financial crisis has changed the way policy maker's view and approach the issue of financial stability. The crisis has shown that even with price and macroeconomic stability, financial instability is a distinct possibility. Financial stability, therefore, needs to be pursued as an explicit policy variable. The emerging paradigm, post-crisis, is aimed at a more holistic approach to financial sector regulation with focus on systemic interconnectedness among various financial sector entities, apart from micro prudential surveillance of individual institutions and use of macro prudential instruments to address the systemic risks. Many countries are in the process of redefining the regulatory objectives and mandates of various regulators. The Financial Stability Board has been set up, under a broadened mandate from the G20 Leaders, with the objective of co-ordinating, at the international level, the work of national financial authorities and international standard setting bodies in order to develop and promote the implementation of effective regulatory, supervisory and other financial sector policies.

In the Indian context, the multiple indicator approach to monetary as well as financial sector management has implicitly imbued the policy approach with the elements of financial stability.

India's Response to the Crisis

The nature and intensity of the impact of the global crisis on India was very different from those in some of the developed economies. The financial sector remained resilient and functioning, despite of some volatility. There was no material stress on the balance sheets of banks and non-banking financial companies on account of toxic financial instruments. There were no solvency issues with any of the financial institutions requiring direct financial support from the Government.

The prudential policy framework for institutions and markets evolved over the years and the unconventional measures taken in response to emerging risks are now widely acknowledged to have played a significant role in protecting the Indian financial system from key vulnerabilities.

Though the direct impact of the crisis on India was relatively muted, the knock-on effects on the Indian economic and financial system were discernible, indicative of India's rapid and growing integration into the global economy. The economy experienced a significant slowdown in 2008-09 in comparison with the robust growth performance in the preceding five years. The Indian rupee also weakened significantly and the equity markets experienced sharp corrections.

However, quick and aggressive policy responses both by the Government and the Reserve Bank in the post-Lehman scenario mitigated the adverse impact of the global financial crisis. A number of conventional and unconventional measures were swiftly taken to improve domestic and foreign exchange liquidity and to contain excessive volatility. The domestic markets returned to normalcy much ahead of the global markets with a significant reduction in risk and a rebound in market activity. There was also an early recovery in economic growth.

Global Outlook

The forceful and coordinated global policy response to the crisis has facilitated the relative stabilisation of global markets and easing of credit risk concerns after the financial turmoil, especially in the second half of 2009. Uncertainties about growth prospects and financial stability, however, persist. The unevenness of the global recovery adds to this uncertainty.

Concerns about sovereign credit risk have also intensified in the light of the fiscal woes of Greece and some other Euro zone nations. Advanced economies are facing challenges in tackling high public debt which may not be addressed with just unwinding of existing stimulus measures.

Shortening of the maturity profiles of bank liabilities during the crisis has created large refinancing needs during the coming few years. International banks will need to take advantage of every opportunity to lengthen the maturity profile of their liabilities and to diversify their liability structure to include more customer deposits.

While global imbalances declined somewhat due to contraction of demand in advanced economies during the financial crisis, the structural problem associated with the imbalances remains.

Domestic Outlook and Assessment

There are evident signs of recovery in the growth increasingly taking hold. Data on industrial production, currently available up to January 2010, show that the uptrend is being maintained. The manufacturing sector, in particular, has recorded robust growth. The acceleration in the growth of the capital goods sector points to the revival of investment activity. After contracting for 13 straight months, exports have expanded since November 2009. Sustained increase in bank credit and the resources raised by the commercial sector from non-bank sources also indicate a revival.

The process of monetary policy exit has already begun. Sector-specific liquidity facilities were discontinued and the Statutory Liquidity Ratio (SLR) of scheduled commercial banks was restored to the precrisis level. The cash reserve ratio was raised by 75 basis points in January 2010. With the intensification of inflationary pressures, a hike of 25 basis points each in repo and reverse repo rates was announced on March 19, 2010.

Early steps to exit from the fiscal stimulus measures have also been initiated with the Union Budget for 2010-11 committing a return to the process of fiscal consolidation.

Inflation

Inflationary pressures have intensified in the recent past. Even as food prices are showing signs of moderation, they remain elevated. More importantly, the rate of increase in the prices of non-food manufactured goods has accelerated. Furthermore, increasing capacity utilisation and rising commodity and energy prices are exerting pressure on overall inflation.

Regulatory Environment

There is an effort underway at the global level to realign the regulatory framework to make the financial system safer, less vulnerable to crises of the recent kind and more focussed towards the needs of the real sector. The key themes on which there is broad agreement are: a) Tighter regulatory standards on capital, liquidity and leverage for banks; b) Providing oversight/bringing into the regulatory fold hitherto unregulated systemically important financial entities; c) Addressing the systemic risks arising from the interconnectedness among financial sector entities; and d) Regulation of financial markets and market infrastructure from a systemic risk perspective.

Regulation of Financial Markets

The crisis has demonstrated the need for effective regulation of financial markets not merely from a conduct of business perspective but also from a financial stability perspective. This becomes particularly relevant for markets involving key macroeconomic variables such as exchange rates and interest rates in the context of emerging countries like India.

Institutional Arrangements for Financial Stability

A High Level Coordination Committee on Financial Markets exists for addressing inter-regulatory and other policy related issues and for monitoring the systemically important institutions (financial conglomerates). The Committee is headed by the Governor, Reserve Bank, and has representation from the Government and other major financial sector regulators viz., SEBI, IRDA and PFRDA. The Government has also announced the establishment of an institutional arrangement for financial stability in the form of a Financial Stability and Development Council (FSDC) to monitor macro prudential supervision of the economy, including the functioning of large financial conglomerates, and to address inter-regulatory co-ordination issues without compromising the independence of individual regulators.

Banking and Financial Sector

Indian banks have remained resilient even during the height of the subprime crisis and the consequent financial turmoil. The banking sector is adequately capitalised, the dominant component being loss absorbing common equity. In fact, the migration to Basel II (Standardised Approach for credit and market risk and Basic Indicator Approach for operational risk) has resulted in an increase in the capital adequacy ratio of the banking system.

Despite a relatively strong outlook, it is clear that the economic slowdown has decelerated growth in the balance sheet of the banking system. This could have a lagged effect on the credit quality and profitability of banks. In fact, after showing a declining trend till 2007- 08, there was some increase in NPA levels in 2008-09. Prudential regulations for restructured accounts were modified as a one-time measure and for a limited period in view of the extraordinary external factors, in order to preserve the economic and productive value of assets which were otherwise viable. Several accounts were restructured under this dispensation.

Given the emergent pressures on the inflation front and the large fiscal borrowing programme, there are likely to be pressures on yields, which may have some impact on the cost of funds of banks. Banks may also need to make provisions towards depreciation in value of investments depending on the duration of their portfolio.

Though there has been some increase in banks' duration of equity in recent months, the same is relatively low. This is a pointer to active interest rate risk management by banks and suggests that the banks' vulnerabilities to interest rate increases will not be very significant.

Banks in India have been actively managing their asset liability mismatches based on guidelines which cover interest rate risk and liquidity risk measurement / reporting framework and prudential limits.

Other emerging issues include over-reliance on bulk deposits in certain institutions, which remain at elevated levels, and this could impact the cost and stability of the deposit base. With a fast expanding corporate sector and extant exposure norms, the headroom available to banks is constrained and needs to be addressed.

Liquidity stress tests indicate that some banks face liquidity constraints under the stress scenarios. Though the scenarios developed have very stringent assumptions, the results of the stress test suggest that banks need to continuously monitor their contingency liquidity plans while also strengthening systems for management of liquidity risk. The stress tests assume that assets available to meet the funding gaps are those maturing within one year. However, as banks maintain a minimum of 25 per cent of their net demand and time liabilities (NDTL) in SLR securities, it would be possible to raise additional liquidity when required.

The ratio of the credit equivalent of off-balance sheet (OBS) items to the balance sheet size of banks is low at around 3 per cent. However, such exposures, particularly those related to complex derivatives, are concentrated in a few foreign banks, which could be a cause for concern.

Excessive growth of non-insured deposits in the banking system also bears watching. This could make deposit insurance less effective and have a destabilising impact on the system. While there has been a significant element of cross-subsidisation in the settlement of deposit insurance claims, introduction of risk-based premiums at this juncture may not be feasible.

Co-operative Banks

India's co-operative banking sector constitutes approximately 7 per cent of the banking sector's total assets. The duality of regulatory control between the Registrar of Co-operative Societies and the Reserve Bank affects the quality of supervision and regulation of cooperative banks. To an extent, this has been addressed through the MoU entered between the State Governments and the Reserve Bank. While the financials of Urban Co-operative Banks have shown improvement, the financials of the rural co-operative sector remains a concern.

Non-banking Financial Companies

The non-banking financial sector was able to manage the fallout of the crisis without creating systemic issues. Though an arrangement for providing liquidity support to meet the temporary liquidity mismatches for eligible non-deposit taking systemically important NBFCs was put in place, the actual arrangement through this window remained minimal.

Another aspect necessitating close monitoring is the interconnected flows between NBFCs and other financial sector entities. While exposure of banks to NBFCs is prudentially capped, the movement of funds between NBFCs and their group entities in the financial sector (especially in the capital market) could be relatively significant. Close and holistic monitoring of exposures between banks, mutual funds, NBFCs and other entities in the sector is important to prevent build up of systemic risks and to plug opportunities for regulatory arbitrage.

Accounting Framework

Policy proposals to improve valuation of financial instruments and transparency in financial markets have assumed greater importance in the aftermath of the global financial crisis. The IASB has announced an accelerated timetable for replacement of IAS 39 dealing with the recognition and measurement of financial instruments. Further, IASB and the US FASB are working towards convergence between IFRS and the US GAAP.

In India, the ICAI had announced the mandatory convergence of Indian Accounting Standards with IFRS from 1st April 2011. Subsequently, the Ministry of Corporate Affairs has announced a roadmap for mandatory convergence of corporate in a phased manner commencing from 1st April, 2011. A separate roadmap for convergence of banks and insurance companies is under preparation. The convergence programme could be a major challenge for the Indian banking system in view of the rigorous requirements for skill up gradation, changes in IT systems, maintenance of parallel accounts during the transition period and implementation issues.

Concluding Remarks

To sum up, India has been relatively less impacted by the global financial crisis and its financial institutions, markets and infrastructure remain healthy and robust. While robust regulatory and supervisory policies ensured the strength and resilience of the financial sector, a range of fiscal, monetary and prudential measures were utilised together to maintain financial stability, once the global disturbances touched Indian shores. This synergistic approach has been possible because of the close co-ordination between the Government and the Reserve Bank and other financial sector regulators, coupled with the fact that the Reserve Bank is both the monetary authority and the regulator of banks, non-banking financial companies and certain segments of financial markets.

However, the recent financial turmoil has clearly demonstrated that there is no place for complacency in the pursuit for maintenance of financial stability. No country is immune from any financial instability anywhere in the world. Maintenance of financial stability involves trade-offs and raises a number of challenges. It requires constant vigilance, especially during 'peace' times, to detect and mitigate any incipient signs of instability.

Bibliography

1. Financial stability Report by RBI from www.rbi.gov.in
2. Definition of Financial stability from www.imf.org
3. www.google.com
4. www.researchpapers.com
5. www.wikipedia.org

◈ ◈ ◈

ISBN – 978-93-5024-769-3

29 Theme – Great Managers have Different Control over Employees
Sub Theme – Manager Empowers Employees

Prof. Savita D. Uppali
SIBM Kamlapur.

Prof. Amarnath Patne
SKNSBS Pandharpur.

Prof. Vaisali Palankar
SBS Solapur.

Introduction

Managers are the backbone of the business today. In the era of globalization various competencies are needed by the managers for survival and growth of the business. They should able to incorporate all the sub-systems in HR and help them in achieving the ultimate goal - exceptional performance. Creating an environment that stimulates the creation of knowledge and its sustenance throughout the organization is big challenge. No longer can the HR department carry on with its traditional functions. However, Human Resource Information Systems (HRIS) is to be put in place - to build and sustain a performance - driven culture. The role will shift to that of facilitator. HR will have to involve the whole organization in this process and act as a counselor and facilitator and that is the most gigantic challenge the HR of any organization faces. Average managers treat all their employees the same. HR managers will have to accommodate employees in their virtual work locations and find ways to manage corporate culture, socialization and employee orientation. In order to obtain and maintain a competent workforce, they must act as organizational performance experts and shape employees behavior without face to face meetings. Great managers discover each individual's unique talents and bring these to the surface.

Empowerment is the process through which managers enable and help others to achieve influence within the organization. Sharing information is a necessary precondition and another important feature found in successful work systems. Encouraging the decentralization of decision making and broader employee participation and empowerment in controlling their own processes. By definition, employee empowerment is giving your staff the freedom to make decisions without the authority of a manager, after they have been properly trained. Make no mistake, abdicating responsibility to employees because you are too busy, too lazy, or too important to do it yourself is not empowerment - that's what we call "dumping". While true employee empowerment comes with many valuable benefits, few leaders use it as a means of raising the bar and driving excellence within their team. So, why don't managers empower their employees? Well there are four fundamental reasons:

They are too busy. Too often managers are so involved in "doing the work", that they lose sight of the fact that they may very well have a team of talented employees who can perform those duties with just a little coaching and direction - freeing you up to be the visionary leader you were hired to be.

They think it takes too much time. Many managers feel that in the time it takes them to train an employee on a new task, they could have very well taken care of it themselves. Unfortunately, this is short-sided thinking because your employees "never learn to fish" this way, and must continually interrupt you for insignificant matters that they should be capable of resolving on their own.

They think it's too risky. Some managers are fearful their employees will make costly mistakes; in essence these managers are unwilling and afraid to take the risk. They don't want to suffer the consequences of a poorly executed decision, even if it is a valuable learning experience for the employee.

They are secretly intimidated. Some managers question, "what if the employee makes a decision that makes them look smarter than me?" These type managers don't want to arouse any movers or shakers within the department; thus, mediocre to marginal employee performance is just fine -- and is the most they get out of the team. So, if you've noticed that your boss rarely empowers you to make decisions or delegates challenging tasks to you, there may be an underlying reason. On the other hand, if you are the boss who rarely empowers the staff to handle routine issues within the department, you might identify with our top four reasons outlined above.

Bottom-line, creating and sustaining a culture of excellence cannot be achieved without fully engaged employees who feel a part of the organization, and that they are truly valued contributors to the success of the organization. For tips and coaching strategies on properly empowering your team, effectively delegating new tasks, and gaining back your valuable time, check out some of the best practices posted on my website.

Research Objectives

1. To study the role of managers in the world of globalization for achieving the organization objectives.
2. To know the views of the employees towards manager's role.
3. To find out the different strategies how manager can empower the employees.

Research Methodology

The following research approach was adopted for this research paper.

Primary Data: The primary data is the data which is collected freshly or first time from direct communication with person to person. Primary data which is collected from the sample size of 50 employees in different areas. Questionnaire was including closed ended and open ended questions to get the broader look for the study.

Secondary data: Secondary data was collected through the internet and books.

Sample Size: 50 respondents.

Limitations of Study

(1) The study is restricted only in Solapur city

(2) Information is based on the sample size of 50 respondents

(3) The opinion may be varies from person to person

Discussion

A survey was conducted and discussion was made with 50 respondents regarding the importance of manager in the organization and the competencies required by the manager. Following questions were asked and the result of the discussion was as under.

TABLE 1 – Impact of globalization on manager's role.

Response	*No. of Respondents*	*Percentage*
Strongly Agree	40	80
Agree	10	20
Strongly Disagree	0	0
Disagree	0	0
Neutral	0	0

(Source: Survey)

The researcher has asked the first question to the respondents regarding the impact of globalization on manager role and it was found out that 80 Percent of respondents were strongly agree and 20 percent of respondents were agree.

TABLE 2 – Success of every organization is depending on the manager.

Response	*No. of Respondents*	*Percentage*
Strongly Agree	15	30
Agree	35	70
Strongly Disagree	0	0
Disagree	0	0
Neutral	0	0

(Source: Survey)

Success of every organization is depending on the manager and 30 percent respondents were strongly agree with this and 70 percent respondents were agree.

TABLE 3 – Various competencies required for manager.

Response	*No. of Respondents*	*Percentage*
Strongly Agree	45	90
Agree	5	10
Strongly Disagree	0	0
Disagree	0	0
Neutral	0	0

(Source: Survey)

The above table indicates that 90 percent of respondents were of strong opinion that manager requires various competencies while 10 percent were agreeing.

TABLE 4 – Manager should try to identify individual's strengths and weaknesses.

Response	*No. of Respondents*	*Percentage*
Strongly Agree	50	100
Agree	0	0
Strongly Disagree	0	0
Disagree	0	0
Neutral	0	0

(Source: Survey)

The researcher has tried to focus on the very important function and it was observed that 100 percent respondents were strongly agree that manager should try to identify individual employee's strengths and weaknesses.

TABLE 5 – Manager should do continuous evaluation of individual's work.

Response	*No. of Respondents*	*Percentage*
Strongly Agree	30	60
Agree	20	40
Strongly Disagree	0	0
Disagree	0	0
Neutral	0	0

(Source: Survey)

It was found that 60 percent respondents were strongly agreed that manager should do continuous evaluation of individual's work and 40 percent were agreed.

TABLE 6 – Manager should have problem solving approach

Response	*No. of Respondents*	*Percentage*
Strongly Agree	25	50
Agree	20	40
Strongly Disagree	5	10
Disagree	0	0
Neutral	0	0

(Source: Survey)

As per 50 percent of respondents, manager should have problem solving approach and 20 percent were agreed while 10 percent were strongly agree.

TABLE 7 – Manager should try to be flexible or accept the changes in the working.

Response	*No. of Respondents*	*Percentage*
Strongly Agree	50	100
Agree	0	0
Strongly Disagree	0	0
Disagree	0	0
Neutral	0	0

(Source: Survey)

The above table indicates that 100 percent respondents were strongly opined that manager should be flexible as well as he has to accept the changes in working.

TABLE 8 – Fix specimen for evaluation of employee performance.

Response	*No. of Respondents*	*Percentage*
Strongly Agree	50	100
Agree	0	0
Strongly Disagree	0	0
Disagree	0	0
Neutral	0	0

(Source: Survey)

The above table indicates that 100 percent respondents were strongly agree that manager should have fix specimen for evaluation of employee performance.

TABLE 9 – Close relation between employee satisfaction and empowerment.

Response	*No. of Respondents*	*Percentage*
Strongly Agree	45	90
Agree	5	10
Strongly Disagree	0	0
Disagree	0	0
Neutral	0	0

(Source: Survey)

When the researcher has tried to find out the relation between employee satisfaction and empowerment then it was observed that 90 percent of respondents were strongly agree and opined that there is very close relation between employee satisfaction and empowerment and 10 respondents were agree.

TABLE 10 – Manager empowers employees.

Response	*No. of Respondents*	*Percentage*
Strongly Agree	30	60
Agree	20	40
Strongly Disagree	0	0
Disagree	0	0
Neutral	0	0

(Source: Survey)

The views of the respondents were taken regarding the empowerment of employees by the managers and the result was 60 percent of respondents were strongly agree and 40 percent were agree on the same.

TABLE 11 – Empowerment leads more productivity.

Response	*No. of Respondents*	*Percentage*
Strongly Agree	45	90
Agree	5	10
Strongly Disagree	0	0
Disagree	0	0
Neutral	0	0

(Source: Survey)

The researcher has asked the question regarding the result of empowerment of employees and 90 percent respondents strongly opined that certainly empowerment increases the productivity of the employees while 10 percent agreed on the opinion.

Results

From the above survey and the discussion carried out with 50 respondents from different organizations, the researcher got following results.

1. More than 2/3'rd of respondents believes that today, in the era of globalization the role of manager has been changing and also they feel that manager's are responsible for the success or failure of any business organization up to certain extent.
2. Majority of employees have strongly opined that manager requires various competencies in order to achieve the organizational goals and objectives. These competencies include good communication skill, sincerity, honesty, hard work, innovation, co-operative and understanding others etc.
3. As per the 100 percent respondent, every manager should know his team in detail and he should try to identify individual employee's strengths and weaknesses. So that he can assign the responsibilities and held accountable to the employee.
4. More than 60 percent employees strongly agree that manager should do continuous evaluation of individual's work, try to rectify the mistakes of the employees also he should appreciate the employees time to time and he should have open mindedness to accept the ideas of the employees. Also he

should welcome the ideas of the employees and should treat problems as opportunities. He should create have learning organizations. He should have good problem solving approach.

5. All the employees have the firm opinion that manager should be flexible as well as he has to accept the changes in working and he needs to update himself time to time.
6. As per the employees opinion manager should have firm policies regarding the evaluation of employees and he should not have any bias for the employees.
7. When the researcher has tried to find out the relation between employee satisfaction and empowerment then it was observed that 90 percent of respondents were strongly agree and opined that there is very close relation between employee satisfaction and empowerment and 10 respondents were agree. For empowering the employees the manager should satisfy the employees.
8. More than 50 percent respondents strongly agree that manager's can empower the employees and there is a direct relation between employee empowerment and increase in productivity. If the organization wants to increase the productivity than manager plays an immense role.

Conclusion

Empowerment is difficult to establish in an organization due to the ambiguous feelings of management and employees about the implementation of the concept. In depends on the individual managers how to empower the employees and up to what extent they have to be empowered. As manager has to play key role in the attainment of organizational objectives and goals, in the present knowledge based economy surely empowerment of employees will helpful to the managers. It is vital to have a work force with potential, but how do you get your employees to perform at their highest ability? A work environment consisting of empowerment will help keep top employees and will attract new, high quality employees. Empowering employees can be the key in turning an average employee into an exceptional one. Empowered employees are usually happier; and, therefore, more likely to stay (Blanchard, O'Connor & Ballard (2003). The job of an empowering manager is more similar to that of a coach than that of a traditional manager. The manager's mission is to unlock the potential of every person within the organization. Motivated, empowered employees are more productive. They are able to use their own innovation to streamline inefficient processes and policies, saving both you and your customers' money.

Great managers have different control over employees through employee empowerment. With the empowerment manager can find not just effect but efficient way for work in 21'st century.

Bibliography

1. http://ezinearticles.com/?4-Reasons-Managers-Dont-Empower-Employees&id=3096546.
2. http://humanresources.about.com/od/managementandleadership/tp/empowerment.htm.
3. http://blogs.hbr.org/goldsmith/2010/04/empowering_your_employees_to_e.html.
4. http://www.ehow.com/how_5836815_encourage-empower-employees.html.
5. http://www.themanagersguide.co.uk/how-empower-staff-delegating.html.
6. http://www.1000ventures.com/business_guide/crosscuttings/employee_empowerment.html.
7. http://www.highbeam.com/doc/1G1-166935380.html.
8. Human Resource Management S. S. Khanka, S. Chand Publisher.
9. Human Resource Management, Aswathappa K, Tata McGraw-Hill.
10. Dynamics of Industrial Relations, Dr. C.B. Mamoria, Dr. Satish Mamoria and S.V. Gankar, 2003, Himalaya Publishing House.

ISBN – 978-93-5024-769-3

30

Training and Development Needs of Generation Y Workforce

Prof. Gopa Das & Prof. Archana Patil
Department of Management. Sinhgad Institute of Management, Pune.

Introduction

Workplace in the India has been changing in recent times. Thus making Training and development an inevitable part of any organization. The fundamental aim of training is to help the organization achieve its purpose by adding value to its key resource – the people it employs. Training means investing in the people to enable them to perform better and to empower them to make the best use of their natural abilities. But with the ever changing dynamic environment, the demands and expectation of the present workforce is also changing. And here lies the challenge for the employers to meet the demands of the present workforce i.e. Generation 'Y'. Generation Y or Gen Y employees are born between 1981 and 1995. This segment of the employee population includes entry level workers that are new university grads as well as employees that have been in the work force 15 years or more. To design training for entry level workers, middle managers or young executives, it is important to consider the values of this generation and how they impact learning and professional development choices.

Objectives of the Study

1. This paper seeks to provide a clear understanding of the youngest generation in the corporate world.
2. It examines their traits, what attracts them to an organisation and what keeps them with a particular employer, as well as their career aspirations and the implications for employers trying to attract and develop them.
3. The paper provides a unique perspective of the Generation Y. It gives a blueprint for employers while recruiting, developing, engaging and retaining the future of the profession in today's workplace.

Overview of the Research Methodology

The methodology employed in this research endeavor was primarily qualitative research combined with a historical review of the literature. This method was chosen because it provided in-depth data about basic views and assumptions of generation Y from their own perspective through interactions, direct observation and written documents. Extensive literature review of Generation Y books, articles, and other studies was incorporated to provide comprehensive background information.

The Power of Now; Generation Y

Gen Y is considered the nurtured generation. Gen Y employees have a high tolerance for diversity, are optimistic, collaborative, open-minded and driven. They have a sense of entitlement and indispensability. Gen Y's attention span is short due to the advent of technology and instant gratification. They are interested in technology and its applications. Gen Y wants to understand the big corporate picture – strategy, goals, and values. Gen Y strives for success and takes time to define their career path.

Gen Y has a pull towards brand image and lifestyle of any company, making it one parameter to choose a company or organization based on a link between corporate and personal values. Gen Y prefers a flat organization where they will be heard and open doors give them the freedom to talk to upper management. Gen Y enjoys clear goals and direction and prefers a management style that respects their knowledge but at the same time guides their career development. Gen Y have a strong desire to work in teams and will form teams at will. Shift of today's Generation has to be taken in consideration by an employers while engaging and retaining Gen Y which leads to corporate culture

As Generation Y makes up an increasing proportion of the global workforce, tapping into the knowledge, skills and talents of the new generation will be critical to organizations' success. But why does this generation matter so much? In many developed countries birth rates are declining significantly, and the older baby-boom generation is retiring, which means that the youngest working generation will make up an ever larger proportion of the workforce. With Generation Y also having to work longer because of dwindling pension security, a heavy burden is being placed on young shoulders. It is not just developed economies where Generation Y has huge significance: this generation is important to the fortunes of emerging markets too, and in the working population an increasing proportion of qualified workforce belongs to Generation Y.

What Attracts the Generation Y Professionals to Work for a Particular Organization and how do They Like to Learn?

The attraction of Gen Y talent to organisations will be a key competitive differentiator in the future, and will require employers to ask themselves what attracts the younger generation into particular organizations.

Chart 1: Top-five factors attracting potential employees

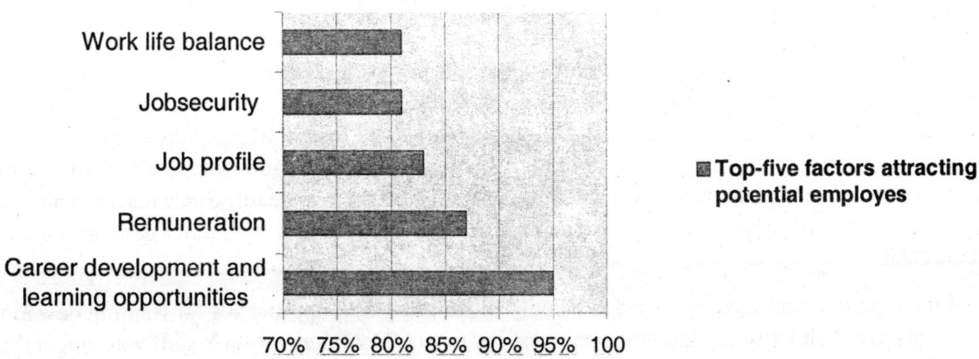

The figures from the study of Generation Y overwhelmingly demonstrates that career development and learning opportunities are the primary factors in deciding to join a particular organization (chart 1). The perception that career development is the key to attracting Generation Y is universally shared with the employers also.

Chart 2: Top-five preferred learning methods of Generation Y

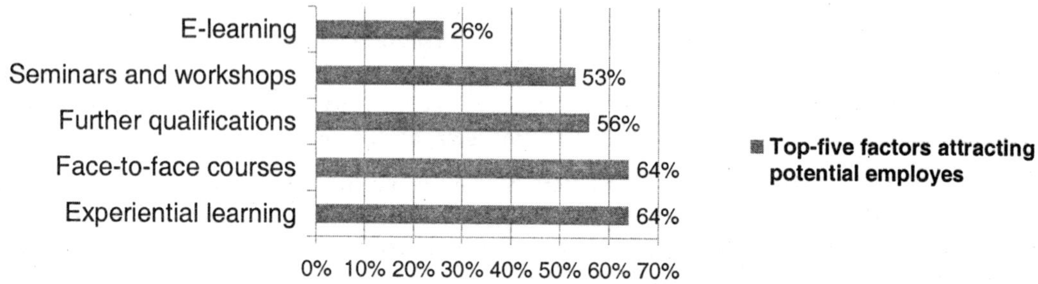

According to a survey, Generation Y is a hands-on generation that wants dynamic career progression supported through experiential learning (learning through experience) and other more formal training approaches. Experiential learning gives trainees the knowledge and skills they need and when planned in a formal, structured way it underpins career paths. Alongside experiential learning, face-to-face learning is identified as a preferred learning method for this generation. Face-to-face learning interventions provide knowledge and skills to complement the workplace experience of Generation Y. There has been a paradigm shift in the field of educational which has a direct or indirect impact on the individual mindset of Gen Y. In yester year having a graduation degree sufficed the Indian mindset but now the trend has changed. Merely a bachelors degree is considered to be outdated masters degree along with professional course is the need of the hour. Thus giving rise to a new benchmark in the educational field due to various reasons the dimensions has taken a complete switch and today Gen Y is expected to have a in-depth knowledge of any core field thus making them multitasking now in this scenario Gen Y is expected to have a distinctive skill to carry out such multitask in which training aids to a large extent. Training trends change accordingly to have the competitive edge. Knowledge and higher educational qualification gives a better understanding of learning which is a plus point for Training in any process of organization. Our overall conclusion is that organizations need to adopt various approaches to develop and deliver their training offerings, and that experiential learning supported through face-to-face interventions is the key to engagement, with e-learning having a specific role to play such as imparting information.

Training Generation Y

Within the field of Training & Development the learning style of generation Y employees is a hot topic. The central question is how to prepare these youngsters for their role in the workforce. In traditional instructor-led courses this generation growing up with Social Networks and Instant Messaging will be bored within 10 minutes. Should we adapt training approaches to this new continuously multitasking and thrill seeking target audience or should we stick to our traditional approach and bore them to death? Since research has shown that most traditional training approaches have generated disappointing results with other generations as well, the answer is clear.

Many organizations already invested heavily in adopting new approaches for training new employees. Researchers have found that the time-to-competency of most of their generation Y staff was longer than it used to be. That is why it shifted from traditional Human Engineering approach towards Technology-Enhanced Hands-on Training. A shift from theory oriented instructor-led training towards instant practice in a safe environment with technology support was useful. No computerized simulations or videogames, but a real-life experience in a film set like training center. According to researchers the new generation can be seen as Generation Why? They don't like following instructions and always question assumptions.

The youngest generation seeks out career paths which are aspirational, fluid and evolving quickly. The generation is divided between those seeking to follow traditional career routes and those wishing to embark on much broader career paths outside their mainstream roles. To understand the training needs of generation Y it is important to understand their traits

10 Tips while Training and Managing the Generation Y Workforce

Generation Y is the fastest growing segment of the workforce. If the common stereotypes are true, Generation Y employees are easily bored, impatient and disloyal. Yet they're also open-minded, collaborative and keen multi-taskers. The trick is to understand what makes Gen Y employees "tick" and to address both the positive and negative characteristics of Generation Y.

To get the most from your Gen Y employees — both in training and in day-to-day operations — you need to understand the values of Generation Y.

1. Reassure Gen Y Employees That What They do Matters

Be quick to praise them for their outstanding efforts, and look for opportunities to recognize them in public (Employee of the Month Award, for example).

2. Share Your Vision

Gen Y is not the type to fade into the background. They're interested in the bigger picture like the company's goals, strategies and values etc. and will be more loyal if they understand how their job relates to the whole.

3. Recognize That Gen Y Employees are Tech-savvy and Interested in all of its Applications

Provide the latest technological resources for their career development, and consider computer-based training that involves quizzes, online videos and even virtual "games."

4. Be Open to Their Feedback

Even though they're younger, Generation Y employees want to be heard and treated with respect. At the same time, you'll earn their respect not by your title, but by your actions, honesty and positive influence.

5. Let Them Work in Teams

Gen Y employees like working in groups, preferably with peers, where they can share their ideas and talents. In training, they'll respond favorably to group discussions, projects and experiential.

6. Multitasking

Generation Y-ers are exceptional multi taskers, from surfing the internet since a young age. They've been brought up in the Microsoft Windows world, where you have multiple things on the go at once. By setting them multiple complex tasks, all at once, you'll get more out of them and get tangible results.

7. Comprehensive Management

Just as generation Y-ers don't like mundane tasks, they don't like mundane management, so it is a need to manage them comprehensively. This style will be disliked and de-motivate the staff. Instead, set boundaries from the start, but make them wide. It's important with this new generation of workers to let them know from the start that they have considerable autonomy. Making it clear that they need to manage their own deadlines and volunteer for tasks.

8. Developing Leadership Traits

One final, but important, way to harness this generation's power is allowing them to do some leading. They have unique skills to bring to the workplace: exceptional social networks, excellent multi tasking, and vision. Allow them to share some of this rather than keeping them in their place.

9. Effective Communication is the Key

It is a need to focus on communication and trust building. Managers must institute some one-on-one, face-to-face communication. They also need to learn how to get two-way communication flowing because it's really the first step to building relationships and trust with Gen Y employees.

10. Allowing Flexibility

Generation Y expects more open and flexible working experience, where careers don't necessarily just advance up the corporate ladder but rather move laterally too, depending on changing personal and professional ambitions and needs. They want to be successful in their jobs, but just in a different way. It doesn't mean being in the office every day 9 to 5, it means getting your job done no matter whatever the job is.

Conclusions and Suggestions

Generation Y actively seek out those organizations that can meet their career development aspirations, so it is imperative for organizations to ensure they understand what career paths are available, and communicate these clearly to prospective employees. Experiential learning, combined with face-to-face learning interventions, underpins effective career development. Many other learning interventions are also rated by this generation, although e-learning, a learning medium most often associated with this generation, appears to have less traction. Certain tips especially like technological advancement, leadership qualities and flexibility must be borne in minds of the employers while dealing with this generation.

This is a confident generation that wants to be committed to organizations but it appears to be prepared to walk away if the career promise is not being delivered. Generation Y is a demanding generation to manage, but for employers that can offer great and interesting careers, it contains a wealth of untapped talent waiting to be unleashed.

References

1. Pull you our Strings – Dr. Wayne W Dyer
2. Bacal, Robert, Performance, McGraw Hill
3. file:///H:/training%20and%20dev%20call%20paper/employee-training.html
4. file:///H:/training%20and%20dev%20call%20paper/t%20ad%20d%20articles.htm
5. file:///H:/training%20and%20dev%20call%20paper/training-and-or.html
6. file:///H:/training%20and%20dev%20call%20paper/t%20ad%20d.htm
7. T+D;mlaff@astd.org

◈ ◈ ◈

ISBN – 978-93-5024-769-3

31

Effectiveness of Differential Pricing Strategy in Pharmaceutical Marketing – An Overview

Prof. Vidya Arun Nakhate
Assistant Professor, Sinhgad Institute of Business Administration & Research, Kondhawa (BK), Pune.

Introduction

The pharmaceutical industry is the world's largest industry due to worldwide revenues of approximately US$2.8 trillion. Pharma industry has seen major changes in the recent years that place new demands on payers, providers and manufacturers. Customers now demand the same choice and convenience from pharma industry that they find in other segment. Indian Pharmaceutical Industry is poised for high consistent growth over the next few years, driven by a multitude of factors. Top Indian Companies like Novartis , DRL, CIPLA and Dabur have already established their presence. The pharmaceutical industry is a knowledge driven industry and is heavily dependent on Research and Development for new products and growth. However, basic research (discovering new molecules) is a time consuming and expensive process and is thus, dominated by large global multinationals.

There are 24,000 licensed pharmaceutical companies. Of the 465 bulk drugs used in India, approximately 425 are manufactured here. India has more drug-manufacturing facilities that have been approved by the U.S. Food and Drug Administration than any country other than the US. Indian generics companies supply 84% of the AIDS drugs that Doctors without Borders uses to treat 60,000 patients in more than 30 countries.

However total pharmaceutical market is as follows:

Therapeutic Area wise Total Pharma Market

Category	*Value Market Share%*
Antidiabetics	16.4
Gastrointestinal	10.9
Cardiac	10.3
Respiratory	10.2
Vit./Minerals/Nutrient	9.6
Pain/Analgesics	9.5
Dermatologics	5.4

Gynecology	5.3
Neuro psychiatry	5.3
Antidiabetics	4.4
Opthologicals	1.7
Others	11.0
Total	100.00

By differential pricing is meant the adaptation, in some measure, of prices to the purchasing power of consumers in different countries.

Literature Review

Some economists (Danzon, 1997) have argued that, under the right market conditions, the prices charged for patented pharmaceuticals would be inversely related to the price sensitivity of the consumers in different markets and thus, differential pricing would resolve the dilemma that arises in the debate on prices of patented medicines for poor countries about how to ensure a fair allocation of joint R&D costs.

Multiple studies starting from Schmalensee (1981) have shown that differential pricing by a single profit-maximizing manufacturer leads to improvements in overall social welfare, if as a result of the differential pricing the total sales increase. However, it is important to note that an increase in sales due to differential pricing is only a necessary but not a sufficient condition for enhancements in welfare. Similar findings are reported in Varian (1985) and Schwartz (1990). However, it is less clear as to how much of an increase in sales would be sufficient to increase social welfare.

Danzon (1997) compares the welfare effects of differential pricing for pharmaceuticals in the United States and the European Union (EU). Danzon and Chao (2000) compared the prices of a limited sample of drugs across countries. Several other studies by Danzon and co-authors have explored the issue of differential pricing between the United States and other countries primarily to inform policy about pharmaceutical pricing in the United States.

Dumoulin (2001) examines the pricing of essential innovative medicines by comparing a single global price with differential prices based on country income. Using a simulation model, the author calculated the pharmaceutical manufacturer's profit and the affordability of drugs to the population. The analysis shows that differential pricing maximizes both indicators and increases access by a factor of roughly 4-7 times.

Danzon and Towse (2003) show that differential pricing can enhance access while preserving incentives for innovation. Thus, it would benefit patients in both developing and developed countries in the long run. They conclude that one possible way of implementing sustainable differential pricing is to bilaterally negotiate discounted prices between individual companies and governments through a system of confidential rebates.

The Concept of Differential Pricing

Differential pricing define as the adaptation, in some measure, of prices to the purchasing power of consumers in different countries. In the context of access to essential medicines, this would mean that pharmaceutical companies would charge lower prices in poorer countries. Since such pricing relates prices to consumers' ability to pay, it can also be seen as addressing issues of equity and is sometimes referred to as equity pricing. Again, since such pricing divides consumers into different groups or tiers, it is sometimes called tiered pricing.

The principle of differential pricing is based on the economic concept of price discrimination.

Price discrimination describes the situation where a profit-maximizing seller sells the same product to different consumers at different prices and where the price differences bear no relation to differences in supply cost but rather reflect the differing willingness and ability of consumers to pay. For this to happen, three conditions need to be fulfilled:

- The seller must have some control over price, i.e. some degree of market power.
- The seller must be able to identify and segregate consumers according to varying price sensitivities.
- Opportunities for re-sale from low-priced markets to high-priced markets must be unstrained or, in other words, market segmentation must be assured.

The counterfactual to differential pricing is uniform pricing wherein the seller sets one price, adjusted for transport, distribution and other costs, for all consumers and markets. Under such pricing, the seller maximizes his profits against global demand or an aggregation of each market's demand. The seller will continue global sales up to the point where costs of producing and selling an additional unit of the product exceed revenues from such sales anywhere in the world.

If the conditions for price discrimination can be fulfilled, economic theory suggests that it would be more profitable for pharmaceutical companies to charge lower prices in highly price sensitive markets, such as the poorer countries, than in less price sensitive markets, such as the richer countries. The seller would continue sales in each segmented market up to the point where costs of producing and selling an additional unit of the product exceed revenues from such sales in that market. Compared to uniform global pricing, the additional volume from selling at a lower price in the more price-sensitive market would more than offset the lower unit margins received there.

Objectives of the Study

To study the Differential Pricing Strategy in Pharmaceutical Industry.

To study the effectiveness of the Differential Pricing strategy.

To analyze the existing literature on differential pricing, examines successful and unsuccessful examples of differential pricing and recommends actions for improvement.

Key Findings from DifferEnitial Pricing Theory

- Differential pricing may lead to overall welfare benefits only when the overall sales increase as a result of differential pricing.
- Social welfare is enhanced when differential pricing permits the pharmaceutical companies to open new markets in countries where the affordability for the drug is significantly lower than the prevailing price in existing markets.
- Under a market-driven differential pricing scheme, countries with a high degree of wealth concentration will face a higher price because in such countries companies would choose to price for the rich market rather than the numerically larger (in terms of people) lower income market.
- Whether the benefits of differential pricing accrue more to the pharmaceutical company or to the patient/payer depends on the elasticity of demand and the market structure.
- Differential pricing is not a panacea to ensuring access. For patients with affordability levels lower than the marginal cost of manufacturing, donor subsidies and government support will continue to be required.

- Theoretical models of differential pricing do not explicitly differentiate between manufacturer's price and end-patient price.
- Existing literature inadequately captures the impact of differential pricing when the markets have heterogeneity in the purchasing market structure (e.g. out of pocket vs. organized group purchasing).

The Welfare Effects of Differential Pricing

A key question is what is the allocation of the welfare effects of a move from global uniform pricing to differential pricing in markets characterized by the requisite degree of market power, i.e. who are the winners and are there losers from such a change. In analyzing this, there are three groups who are primarily affected:

- The consumer in the less price-sensitive (richer) market;
- The consumer in the more price-sensitive (poorer) market; and
- The producers.

With regard to the latter group, the producers, economic theory would suggest that, where the conditions for price differentiation are met, they will benefit from adopting such pricing. Indeed, in an environment where prices are set by the market, it can be expected that as a general rule they will only engage in such pricing to the extent that it is beneficial. Thus, in principle, differential pricing should also enhance incentives for research and development into new drugs and, to this extent, be in the long-term interests of consumers, in rich and poor countries alike.

With regard to the short-term interests of consumers in terms of access to existing drugs, much depends on the extent to which uniform pricing takes into account demand in more price-sensitive as well as less price-sensitive markets. If it does, then differential pricing may lead to an increase in prices in the less price-sensitive (wealthier) markets, and thus a loss of consumer welfare there, while leading to lower prices and increased welfare in the more price-sensitive (poorer) markets. If, on the other hand, the uniform world price is set with only the conditions in the wealthier markets taken into account, there should be no increase in prices in those markets from a shift to differential pricing, but only a reduction in prices in the poorer markets. In this situation, a move from uniform pricing to differential pricing should yield unambiguously positive welfare effects; that is to say, it should be a win-win situation in that the welfare of the consumer in the poorer countries is enhanced, and that of the consumer in the rich countries is not adversely affected but may actually, in the long term, increase as a result of enhanced incentives to R&D.

An important question therefore is whether the global pharmaceutical market corresponds to the second of the two situations described above. There would appear to be good reasons to believe that it does and that, in practice, where uniform prices are set, they are set without significantly taking into account the more price-sensitive markets. The reality of the global pharmaceutical market is that sales in poorer countries constitute a very small part of total sales. Moreover, sales in those countries may well be targeted primarily at the more well-to-do segment of the population which has a lower degree of price sensitivity than the poor in those countries. Further, since in many developed countries prices are not set by the market but are subject to some form of price regulation, there is no reason to expect a market-driven effect on these prices from a shift to differential pricing.

Reason for not having differential pricing so common:

If, as economic theory suggests, differential pricing can be a win-win situation which is good or at least not harmful to consumers and beneficial to producers, the question arises as to why it is not more commonly practiced. It might be helpful for the Workshop to explore this issue, since it may provide guidance as to what needs to be done to promote differential pricing. A number of possible explanations can be advanced. One of course is that there may not, in practice, be effective market segmentation between countries. For market segmentation to be effective for the purposes of differential pricing, it is necessary that not only should there be adequate means to prevent the diversion of the lower-priced product into the higher priced markets, but also an insulation of prices in the higher-priced market from any materially significant psychological or political effects that might flow from the existence of lower prices in the other markets. Another factor could be that the main market of interest in the poorer countries lies with the well-to-do minority and that it is difficult to adequately separate this market from the market represented by the poorer parts of the population. A third consideration may be that of administrative simplicity. These factors tending towards uniform prices, when combined with price controls in developed countries, may help explain the "anomaly" sometimes observed of higher prices in poorer countries.

Giving Operational effect to the differential pricing :

If indeed differential pricing can be generally welfare enhancing, the question arises as to how it should be given operational effect. Three main types of approach would appear to have been advanced:

- Establishing the right conditions and leaving it to the market.
- A combination of the above with negotiated price discounts and some degree of moral suasion.
- The establishment of a global system of differential pricing. Where patented products are concerned, it may be recalled, when examining each of the above approaches, that under the legal environment in which the relevant markets work the supply of differentially priced products can be effected either through direct supply by the patent owner or through voluntary licensing.

The Market-driven Approach

Some economists (Danzon, 1997) have argued that, under the right market conditions, the prices charged for patented pharmaceuticals would be inversely related to the price sensitivity of the consumers in different markets and thus, differential pricing would resolve the dilemma that arises in the debate on prices of patented medicines for poor countries about how to ensure a fair allocation of joint R&D costs.

Key Drivers for Differential Pricing

Research has looked at the effects of differential pricing on access, societal welfare and the profits of the pharmaceutical companies. At a more pragmatic level, there are several other reasons that prompt the pharmaceutical industry to engage in differential pricing. Although many of these are strong drivers, the innovative pharmaceutical industry has historically been cautious of experimenting with pricing models because of the potential of eroding margins in the developed markets. Typically, differential pricing is less central to the business models of generic manufacturers, who serve multi-source product markets and compete on cost and other product attributes. Admittedly, there are instances of multi-sourced products where generic manufacturers charge differential prices in different markets.

(a) Socially Responsible Pricing

Differential pricing allows pharmaceutical companies to signal that their pricing policies are socially responsible and consistent with their obligations to society and not merely geared towards maximizing their profit. New initiatives such as the Access to Medicine Index monitor highlight the efforts of pharmaceutical companies to increase access to medicines in developing countries.

(b) Opening New Markets

Many low and middle-income markets could not be served earlier due to lack of overall affordability and demand across an overall drug portfolio. Differential pricing on select drugs opens opportunities to serve these markets and creates economies of scope for pharmaceutical companies. Differential pricing can provide opportunities to tap the new consumers and help build relationships that will continue to last when these consumers reach higher levels of income/ability to pay.

(c) Threat of Compulsory Licensing

Compulsory licensing is authorization permitting a third party to make, use, or sell a patented invention without the patent owner's consent. The TRIPS agreement allows compulsory licensing wherein the patent holder is forced to allow a local entity to produce the patented product in a number of circumstances. Differential pricing with lower prices in low and middle-income countries is a good strategy to thwart such a threat and risk having strong price pressures on an important product.

(d) Competition from Generic Producers

Generic competition acts as a catalyst for price reductions and the start of differential pricing programs. The fall in the price of first-line combinations of stavudine (d4T), lamivudine (3TC), and nevirapine (NVP) from over $20,000 in 2000 to $90 in 2010 and the start of multiple tiered pricing programs by large ARV manufacturers is attributed largely to generic competition by some authors. (Wilson P 2010).

Differential pricing would allow maintaining a fairly significant market share in key therapeutic segments in the domestic markets of generic manufacturers, and could act as a mechanism for entry deterrence in high income markets. Little evidence exists to understand the impact of differential pricing on the price of first entry generic producers (Waning et al. 2009)

The biggest benefit potential from differential pricing holds for single-sourced drugs where the pharmaceutical company has a clear incentive to maximize its profits and enter new markets through lowered pricing.

Prices for pharmaceuticals are typically measured at three points in the distribution chain: the ex-manufacturer price, the ex-wholesale price, and the retail price. In low and middle income markets, the wholesale and distribution markups constitute a larger portion of the end patient cost for both multi-sourced generic and single sourced patented products. For such products the societal benefits of differential pricing at the manufacturer price level are only of a limited measure.

A key prerequisite for inter-country differential pricing is the existence of two distinct markets: one with higher income and affordability and another with lower income and affordability. Throughout this paper researcher use the term ?products with dual markets.

For products that have a higher income as well as a lower income market. However, there are single and multi-sourced drugs e.g. anti-malarial that are used exclusively in low income countries. For drugs that treat almost exclusively diseases of the developing world, the prices that the average patient in a low income country can afford to pay are sometimes insufficient to cover even the marginal costs of production, leave alone the R&D expenses. Thus, a combination of external subsidies on the supply side such as grants to Product Development Partnerships (PDPs) to reduce amortization of R&D costs in drug pricing.

However, there are significant opportunities for differential pricing under many of these new and innovative mechanisms.

TABLE 1 – Drivers for Inter-Country Differential Pricing for Different Categories of Drugs

Category	*Drivers for Differential Pricing*	*Theoretical Welfare Gains from Differential Pricing*
Single Source Dual Market	· Profit Improvement · Corporate social responsibility · Opening new markets · Threat of compulsory licensing · Competition from generic producers	High
Single Source Low Income Market Only	· Corporate social responsibility · Threat of compulsory licensing · Learning about low income markets for other more profitable drugs	Moderate
Multi source Dual Markets	· Corporate social responsibility · Opening new markets · Profit improvement	Marginal

Differential Pricing - New Horizon

Interviews with manufacturers conducted during this study revealed that they choose different prices based on a combination of factors, most importantly:

- affordability of the market
- buy side market structure
- volume of purchase
- security of financing (in the case of public sector or institutional buyers)
- transaction cost associated with selling to that buyer

It is noteworthy that income/affordability is only one of the variables used in the pricing model. In instances where there are strong natural relationships between the other variables and the income/affordability of the market segment, this may lead to welfare maximizing differential pricing. In instances where the other variables are negatively correlated with the income and affordability of the market, the pricing model could lead to potentially adverse outcomes from the standpoint of social welfare maximization.

Conclusion

Differential pricing can enhance access to medicines, improve quality of medicines and achieve higher profits for pharmaceutical manufacturers. However, differential pricing can be sustainable only if it aligns the incentives of the different stakeholders: pharmaceutical manufacturers, national governments, end patients and civil society organizations. Pharmaceutical manufacturers would want become more receptive to differential pricing if the risks of physical arbitrage could be managed collectively together with national governments, international donors and large NGOs. In addition, firms could develop contractual agreements with group purchasers who receive lower priced products to ensure that the product is only used in the market for which it is intended and administer certain drugs only in clinics to avoid the leaking of these drugs to other markets. Intra-country differential pricing in lower middle and middle income countries would help avoid political pressure from middle income tier countries in to reduce prices. To avoid the problem of formal or informal external referencing, firms could nudge countries to use pharmaco-economic assessments instead of reference pricing. Additional empirical research is needed to understand the welfare impact of external reference pricing. Implementing the recommendations in this paper would require inputs and collaboration from several parties in addition to those who are recommended to lead each of the specific recommendations. The national governments of low and middle income countries have a key role to play in providing the political will and objectively determined reimbursement policies to enable differential pricing.

References

1. Lu, J.L., and W.S. Comanor : "Strategic Pricing of New Pharmaceuticals", Review of Economics and Statistics, (1998), 80 pp. 108-118.
2. Maskus, Keith E., and Denise Eby-Konan : Trade-Related Intellectual Property Rights: Issues and Exploratory Results. In Analytical and Negotiating Issues in the Global Trading System, ed. by Alan V. Deardorff and Robert M. Stern. Ann Arbor, (1994), MI: University of Michigan Press.
3. OECD : "Pharmaceutical Policies in OECD Countries: Reconciling Social and Industrial Goals", DEELSA/ELSA/WD(2000)1, April.
4. OXFAM : Cut the cost: Patent Injustice: How world trade rules threaten the health of poor people, (2001), February, London.
5. Pavcnik,N. "Do Pharmaceutical Prices Respond to Potential Patient Out-of-Pocket Expenses?," 2002, RAND Journal of Economics, vol. 33(3), pp. 469-487.
6. Redwood, Heinz : New horizons in India: The Consequences of Pharmaceutical Patent Protection, (1994), Oldswicks Press, Felixtowe, England.
7. Redwood, Heinz : Brazil - The Future Impact of Pharmaceutical Patents, (1995), Oldswicks Press, Felixtowe, England.
8. Ramsey, F., A Contribution to the Theory of Taxation, 1927, Economic Journal, pp. 47-61.
9. Reich MR, Bery P. "Expanding Global Access to ARVs: The Challenges of Prices and Patents," in Mayer KH, Pizer HF, eds., The AIDS Pandemic: Impact on Science and Society, New York: Academic Press, 2005, pp. 324-350.
10. Scherer, F. M. & Watal, J. ?Post-TRIPS Options for Access to Patented Medicines in Developing Countries?, Commission on Macroeconomics and Health Background, (2001), Paper, p. 45.

◈ ◈ ◈

ISBN – 978-93-5024-769-3

32 The Pyramid of Corporate Social Responsibility: Managing Stakeholders Ethically

Mrs. Manisha N. Paliwal
Associate Professor Sinhgad Institute of Management, Vadgaon Pune-41
Email: mnpaliwal@gmail.com
Ms. Jyothi Pawar
Assistant Professor Sinhgad Institute of Management, Vadgaon Pune-41
Email: pawar_family@yahoo.co.in

Abstract

One of the most significant changes to affect the business environment, in recent years, has been the growing interest in questions to do with the scope and nature of corporate social responsibility. Corporate social responsibility remains an embryonic and contestable concept. CSR spells out an organization's commitment towards society and is a measure of the organization's social responsiveness. This article will explore the nature of CSR with an eye toward understanding its component parts. This discussion will be framed by a pyramid of corporate social responsibility. Carroll designed a four-part conceptualization of CSR that included economic, legal, ethical and philanthropic elements. Furthermore, these four categories or components of CSR might be depicted as a pyramid. This paper assesses four key approaches of CSR and offers a perspective gauging little prospect of theoretical synthesis and ways that might be useful to executives who wish to reconcile their obligations to their stakeholders with those to other competing groups claiming legitimacy.

Key Words

Corporate Social Responsibility, Social Responsiveness, Stakeholders

Introduction

Business is facing challenging times world-wide. Increased competition and commercial pressure are combining with rising regulatory standards and consumer demand to create a whole new playing field for business. Traditional expectations of business are also changing. It is no longer enough to simply employ people, make a profit and pay taxes. Companies are now expected to act responsibly, be accountable and benefit society as a whole. This is the new agenda of corporate social responsibility (CSR). From a trickle, it has become a wave sweeping boardrooms across the world. In this age of global competition, corporate are beginning to realize the stake that they have, as a part of the society. There is a growing realization that they should contribute to social activities globally with a desire to improve the immediate environment where they work and many companies are taking keen interest in such activities. Companies that pay genuine attention to the principles of social responsibility are also favoured by the public who prefer to consume their goods and services. This has given rise to the concept of Corporate Social Responsibility (CSR). By social responsibility, we mean a doctrine that claims that an entity whether it is state, government, corporation, organization or individual has a responsibility to society. According to Infosys founder, Narayan Murthy, 'social responsibility is to create maximum shareholders value working under the circumstances, where it is fair to all its stakeholders, workers, consumers, the community, government and the environment'. Commission of the European Communities (2001) stated that being socially responsible means not only fulfilling legal expectations, but also going beyond compliance and investing 'more' into human capital, the environment and the relation with stakeholders. The focus in this paper will be on how businesses and managers can deal with the topic of CSR and business ethics vis-a` -vis their stakeholders.

CSR: An Introduction: Corporate social responsibility (CSR) is:

- An obligation, beyond that required by the law and economics, for a firm to pursue long term goals that are good for society
- The continuing commitment by business to behave ethically and contribute to economic development while improving the quality of life of the workforce and their families as well as that of the local community and society at large
- About how a company manages its business process to produce an overall positive impact on society

Business's major stakeholders include consumers, employees, owners, the community, government, competitors, and the natural environment. The literature of CSR has produced many definitions and many concepts over the past half century since its emergence and formalization on the business scene. CSR has been defined as a function that transcends but includes making profits, creating jobs and producing goods and services (Oketch 2005).

Some researchers claim that it has come to mean the positive actions that a company takes to help discharge its responsibilities to external stakeholders (Rushton 2002).

Still other definitions include financial performance as an aspect of CSR. In line with this, a wide range of behaviours are classified under CSR including cause-related marketing, sponsoring charitable events, offering employee volunteerism programs, making charitable donations, utilising environmental initiatives and demonstrating a commitment to health and safety issues (Maignan & Ralston 2002).

Keith Davis suggested that social responsibility refers to businesses' "decisions and actions taken for reasons at least partially beyond the firm's direct economic or technical interest." At about the same time, Eells and Walton (1961) argued that CSR refers to the "problems that arise when corporate enterprise casts its shadow on the social scene, and the ethical principles that ought to govern the relationship between the corporation and society."

Perhaps the most oft-cited definition of CSR is that of Carroll's model (1979). Carroll's famous three dimensional conceptual model of CSR depicted the multilayered nature of CSR as something over and above meeting the basic economic and legal responsibilities. Carroll designed a four-part conceptualization of CSR that included economic, legal, ethical and philanthropic elements. According to this model, all business responsibilities rely upon the economic responsibility, which includes maximizing profitability and maintaining a strong competitive position. Legal responsibilities include complying with laws and regulations. Ethical responsibilities reflect societal standards, expectations and norms that have not been specifically legislated. Finally, philanthropic responsibilities encompass actions that are in response to society's expectation that businesses be good corporate citizens. These are distinguished from ethical responsibilities in that they are of a charitable nature and, as such, a company is not considered unethical if it does not provide them (Carroll 1991).

The basic definition of CSR is as follows: "The social responsibility of business encompasses the economic, legal, ethical, and discretionary (philanthropic) expectations that society has of organizations at a given point in time."14 This notion of CSR is both a stakeholder model and a contingency model. It is a stakeholder model in the sense that various stakeholder groups each send expectations to management about what they expect the organization to do under the banner of economics (profits), law, ethics, and philanthropy. It is a contingency model in several respects, but the most important is that society's views or expectations of business performance change and evolve over time. The expectation that firms will be good corporate citizens in the global sphere is one of the latest mandates of CSR.

A Pyramid of CSR as a Framework

Having a framework and context for business's social and ethical responsibilities to global stakeholders is an initial best practice. The Pyramid of Corporate Social Responsibility (see Figure 1) is presented as a helpful way to graphically depict the four kinds of social responsibility that business has with respect to global business.

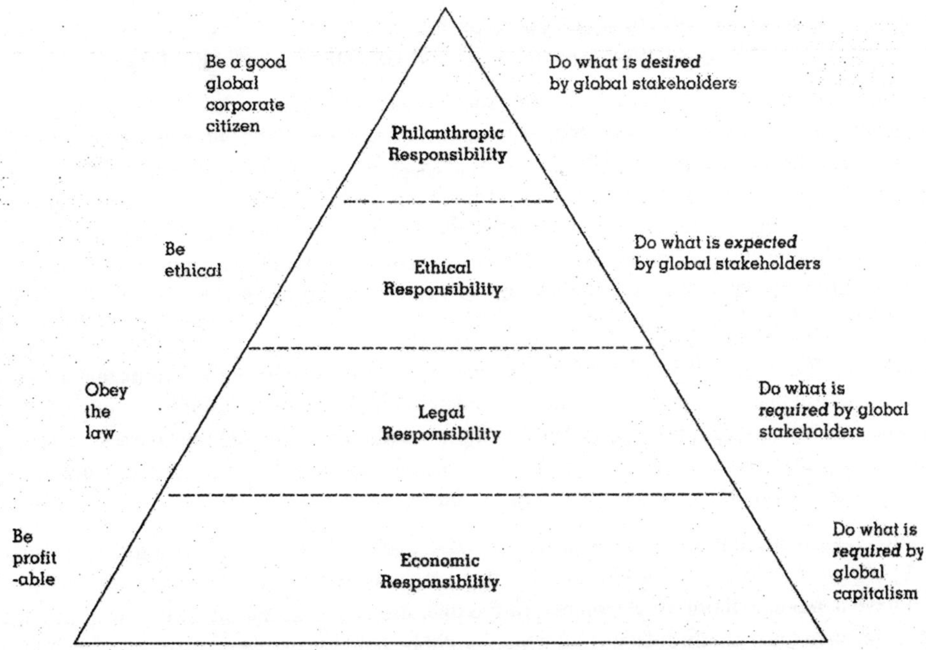

Fig. 1 : Pyramid of Global Corporate Social Responsibility and Performance

To be sure, all of these kinds of responsibilities have always existed to some extent, but it has only been in recent years that ethical and philanthropic functions have taken a significant place. Each of these four categories deserves closer consideration.

Economic Responsibilities: Historically, business organizations were created as economic entities designed to provide goods and services to societal members. The profit motive was established as the primary incentive for entrepreneurship. Before it was anything else, the business organization was the basic economic unit in our society. As such, its principal role was to produce goods and services that consumers needed and wanted and to make an acceptable profit in the process. At some point the idea of the profit motive got transformed into a notion of maximum profits, and this has been an enduring value ever since. All other business responsibilities are predicated upon the economic responsibility of the firm, because without it the others become moot considerations. Figure 1 summarizes some important statements characterizing economic responsibilities. Legal responsibilities are also depicted in Figure 1, and we will consider them next.

Legal Responsibilities: Society has not only sanctioned business to operate according to the profit motive; at the same time business is expected to comply with the laws and regulations promulgated by federal, state, and local governments as the ground rules under which business must operate. As a partial fulfillment of the "social contract" between business and society, firms are expected to pursue their economic missions within the framework of the law. Legal responsibilities reflect a view of "codified ethics" in the sense that they embody basic notions of fair operations as established by our lawmakers. They are depicted as the next layer on the pyramid to portray their historical development, but they are appropriately seen as coexisting wit economic responsibilities as fundamental precepts of the free enterprise system.

Ethical Responsibilities: Although economic and legal responsibilities embody ethical norms about fairness and justice, ethical responsibilities embrace those activities and practices that are expected or prohibited by societal members even though they are not codified into law. Ethical responsibilities embody those standards, norms, or expectations that reflect a concern for what consumers, employees, shareholders, and the community regard as fair, just, or in keeping with the respect or protection of stakeholders' moral rights.

In one sense, changing ethics or values precede the establishment of law because they become the driving force behind the very creation of laws or regulations. For example, the environmental, civil rights, and consumer movements reflected basic alterations in societal values and thus may be seen as ethical bellwethers foreshadowing and resulting in the later legislation. In another sense, ethical responsibilities may be seen as embracing newly emerging values and norms society expects business to meet, even though such values and norms may reflect a higher standard of performance than that currently required by law. Ethical responsibilities in this sense are often ill-defined or continually under public debate as to their legitimacy, and thus are frequently difficult for business to deal with.

Philanthropy Responsibilities: Philanthropy encompasses those corporate actions that are in response to society's expectation that businesses be good corporate citizens. This includes actively engaging in acts or programs to promote human welfare or goodwill. Examples of philanthropy include business contributions of financial resources or executive time, such as contributions to the arts, education, or the community. A loaned-executive program that provides leadership for a community's Unite.

CSR and Organizational Stakeholders: By now most executives understand that the term "stakeholder" constitutes a play on the word stockholder and is intended to more appropriately describe those groups or persons who have a stake, a claim, or an interest in the operations and decisions of the firm. Sometimes the stake might represent a legal claim, such as that which might be held by an owner, an employee, or a customer who has an explicit or implicit contract. Other times it might be represented by a moral claim, such as when these groups assert a right to be treated fairly or with due process, or to have their opinions taken into consideration in an important business decision. The challenge of stakeholder management is to ensure that the firm's primary stakeholders achieve their objectives while other stakeholders are also satisfied. Even though this "win-win" outcome is not always possible, it does represent a legitimate and desirable goal for management to pursue to protect its long-term interests.

The important functions of stakeholder management are to describe, understand, analyze, and finally, manage. Basically, there are five major stakeholder groups that are recognized as priorities by most firms, across industry lines and in spite of size or location: owners (shareholders), employees, customers, local communities, and the society-at-large. Although the general ethical obligation to each of these groups is essentially identical (protect their rights, treat them with respect and fairness), specific behaviors and orientations arise because of the differing nature of the groups. At this juncture we would like to expound upon the link between the firm's ethical responsibilities or perspectives and its major stakeholder groups. Here we are isolating the ethical component of our CSR pyramid and discussing it more thoroughly in the context of stakeholders. One way to do this would be to use major ethical principles such as those of justice, rights, and utilitarianism to identify and describe our ethical responsibilities. We will take another alternative, however, and discuss stakeholders within the context of three major ethical approaches - immoral management, amoral management, and moral management. These three ethical approaches were defined and discussed in an earlier Business Horizons article (Carroll 1987). There are numerous examples of moral management. When IBM took the lead and developed its Open Door policy to provide a mechanism through which employees might pursue their due process rights, this could be considered moral management. Similarly, when IBM initiated its Four Principles of Privacy to protect privacy rights of employees, this was moral management.

When McCullough Corporation withdrew from the Chain Saw Manufacturers Association because the association fought mandatory safety standards for the industry, this was moral management. McCullough knew its product was potentially dangerous and had used chain brakes on its own saws for years, even though it was not required by law to do so. Another example of moral management was when Maguire Thomas Partners, a Los Angeles commercial developer, helped solve urban problems by saving and refurbishing historic sites, putting up structures that matched old ones, limiting building heights to less than the law allowed, and using only two-thirds of the allowable building density so that open spaces could be provided.

The stakeholder management perspective provides not only a language and way to personalize relationships with names and faces, but also some useful conceptual and analytical concepts for diagnosing, analyzing, and prioritizing an organization's relationships and strategies. Effective organizations will progress beyond stakeholder identification and question what opportunities and threats are posed by stakeholders; what economic, legal, ethical, and philanthropic responsibilities they have; and what strategies, actions or decisions should be pursued to most effectively address these responsibilities. The stakeholder/responsibility matrix provides a template management might use to organize its analysis and decision making.

Throughout the article we have been building toward the notion of an improved ethical organizational climate as manifested by moral management. Moral management was defined and described through a contrast with immoral and amoral management. Because the business landscape is replete with immoral and amoral managers, moral managers may sometimes be hard to find. Regardless, their characteristics have been identified and, most important, their perspective or orientation towards the major stakeholder groups has been profiled. These stakeholder orientation profiles give managers a conceptual but practical touchstone for sorting out the different categories or types of ethical (or not-so-ethical) behavior that may be found in business and other organizations.

Corporate Social Responsibility In India: Indian companies are now expected to discharge their stakeholder responsibilities and societal obligations, along with their shareholder-wealth maximization goal. In India as in the rest of the world there is a growing realization that business cannot succeed in a society which fails. An ideal CSR has both ethical and philosophical dimensions, particularly in India where there exists a wide gap between sections of people in terms of income and standards as well as socio-economic status. However, the concept of CSR is not new in India. The idea of social responsibility in the Indian society, bounded by notion of caste and fate, dates back to the time of British Rule when Indian reformers launched reform movements which slowly became more socially responsible. During the independence struggle Indian companies, which began to proliferate and proper from the mid 19th century, throw in their lot with **Mahatma Gandhi** and the resulting concern for the nations caused many of them to be involved in providing education, health service and even clean water. The research says that CSR was no longer an exclusive domain of the government and

CSR is much more than "passive philanthropy, beyond the private sector, corporate players in India's public sector too have been actively involved in corporate social responsibility initiatives. Most public sector units in the heavy engineering industry have not only set up a township around the plant, but also established a school, a hospital and several other civic facilities for its employees and those that live in that area. Private sector companies have been encouraged to undertake rural development programmes down the years through fiscal incentives by the government. For instance, special benefits are offered in the industrial policy to companies that set up industries in backward areas and tax incentives are also offered to companies that set up water purification projects. It is well-known that the development indices in India are still not where they should be. For example, the most recent World Bank Report (2009) shows that the 'Below Poverty Line' ratio in India is still significant with 28% people in rural regions and 26% in the urban areas surviving below the poverty line. The Infant mortality rate (per 1,000 live births) in 2009 was 57, maternal mortality (per 100,000 live births) was 450, the percentage of underweight children (below 5 years) was 46, male adult literacy rate (15-year and older) was 73%, female adult literacy rate (15-year and older) was 48%, access to pure water source (% of pop) at 89% and access to improved sanitation was 33%. Most of those children who were not enrolled in school belong to marginalized society. India's Integrated Child Development Services (ICDS) Scheme is trying to undergo drastic changes to address the wide scale malnutrition crisis in India.

India has a vibrant and very enterprising business community, some with long family traditions of being in business. CSR, as it is known in the western hemisphere, is considered to be more of a nascent activity in the Indian corporate sector than an established trend in general. Still, one can identify visible efforts among Indian businesses as a tradition to take up socially-relevant causes, either collectively or individually (such as setting up schools or charitable dispensaries).

The concept of CSR was never new to India; it was built into the traditional fabric of the country from time immemorial. In ancient times, especially the Vedic period marked the guilds to be working for social development. The guilds represented a network of socio-economic-political-religious institutions which affected the state machinery. They exercised an advisory role to the king and took part in political and administrative issues of the state as well. A guild had the function to oversee that the revenues of the state were diverted to social work. At times guild members acted as representatives of the government administration. The influence and the power of the guilds were such that they even withstood the destruction of kingdoms. The head of the guild was supposed to know the *Vedas*; the wisdom of the *Vedas* was not thought to be incompatible with the economic prudence. Good corporate citizenship and CSR initiatives are inextricably linked with improved brand reputation, which is one of the most important drivers of CSR identified by the respondent companies. The other key drivers of Corporate Social Responsibility in India were diverse ranging from stated philosophy of founding fathers to improving relationship with local communities to enhanced shareholder value.

So, social responsibility may not have been new to India, but it was in the hands of those in power. Collective decision making and stakeholder relations were not present, however, everything was voluntary and charity was trickling down from the king. In recent times, Mahatma Gandhi introduced the concept of 'Trusteeship' as a practicable norm for Indian business community. He wanted to propagate the idea that businesses were similar to trustees of the wealth of society for its well-being (Mitra, 2007). According to him 'Trusteeship' means leveling of the disparity in wealth in society, a nonviolent way to make the capitalists the trustees of the wealth of society and partners in community welfare activities. Thus, though CSR is considered primarily a concept which is western in origin but India too had her own visualization of social responsibility of business.

In the modern times, the initiatives taken by Confederation of Indian Industry (CII), one of the oldest business associations in India, and its own 'CII-social code for business' be taken as instances of an industry effort. They consider principles of equality in gender representation in employment, documentation of all the contributions of learning experience to all stakeholders, striving for partnerships and synergizing all the opportunities to bring community development and companies learning from each other how to become better corporate citizens. CII claims to emphasize on broad socially-relevant issues such as development of social infrastructure, women empowerment, control and prevention of HIV/AIDS.

Similarly, Federation of Indian Chambers of Commerce and Industry (FICCI) proclaims that along with competitiveness and quality of business, business-government-civil society relationship and the effort of business to improve the quality of life of people also must be upheld has a business value. FICCI also claims to have a 'Resource Conservation & Management Group' (RC&M) which tries to improve the competitiveness of business for long-term by adopting sustainable strategies with environmental and natural resources. The effort is not a one-sided activity generated purely from the side of business. Mitra (2007) claims that though the GOI earlier may have been skeptical about the role of business in developmental work, the recent trends show that the Government is also showing some interest in encouraging the formulation and implementation of development-oriented CSR policies in the private sector.

Moreover, it is somewhat understood that the claim by both CII and FICCI is that they should balance the existing developmental realities and the expectation from business with operational constraints.

Apart from these, they claim to engage in collective efforts as a fraternity of business. If we look closely at the individual efforts of Indian companies, we find that development oriented CSR policies are present in the agenda of many of the leading corporations. For example, providing education for the local community, health facilities for children & mothers, sustainable development etc., are already included in Tata Steel's policies. There are other corporations such as Hindalco (Birla group) which also claims to follow the ten principles of GC as laid down by the UN. Indian Tobacco Company (ITC) claims to have aligned its CSR actions with the Global Reporting Initiative (GRI) standard for social reporting.

Infosys, another global leader, claims to follow the world economic forum policies for social and economic development since 1997. Developmental activities by the companies are usually taken to include initiatives towards societal upliftment or community improvement. However, we must note that developmental effort also means efforts to sustain the natural environment for the long term . Apart from societal concerns, with the looming threats of global warming and climate change, development-related responsibilities of businesses now must include a bigger responsibility of nurturing and protecting the natural environment and the natural resources. With this kind of expanded understanding of developmental effort, the environmental integration strategies of some prominent Indian companies are discussed below. The data are obtained from their explicitly publicized sustainability reports or from their environmental reports. Some are implicitly involved in environmental work towards aiding sustainable development. Here implicitness means that certain 'green' ventures were never pronounced but in turn always been latent as a part of company's philosophy.

Reliance Industries claims to be involved in promoting training facilities for employees and enhancing their responsibilities towards environment, and supposedly follows relevant environmental laws, reduces emissions and encourages recycled products. The company also claims to promote awareness among their supply chain and quality improvement with research and development facilities. Hindustan Unilever Limited has implemented environment policy at the plant level (in products, design and production). The company is trying to increase the understanding of environmental issues and disseminate good practice. The e-Choupal of ITC supposedly helps the farming communities, contributing to health issues and supporting vulnerable communities. Dabur India Ltd. has initiated some significant programs for ecological regeneration and protection of endangered plant species. The company claims to be committed to ecological conservation and regeneration, and uses state-of-the-art technology to preserve, produce and also encourage the local people to cultivate rare herbs. Wipro claims to recognize its responsibility as a global citizen to assess and minimize the impact of its business activities to reduce environmental impact and protecting ecosystems. The company improves its triple bottom line by integrating marketplace, workplace, environment and community concerns with business operations. In recent times Indian Public Sector Units (PSUs) apart from abiding by the Planning Commission are taking self-motivating initiatives to foster developmental activities for the local community. For example, Oil and Natural Gas Corporation Limited (ONGC), India gives more impetus on use of cleaner technologies and follows the Kyoto Protocol. ONGC complies with the GC principles and involves in community development while following the best environmental practices around the world. Steel Authority of India Limited (SAIL) claims to integrate good environment and good practices. Cleaner technologies and energy efficient methods of production are incorporated, also improvement in environmental performance by setting targets and measuring the progress. NTPC India claims to be involved in incorporation of environmental provisions into machinery design. The company helps in empowering people, resettlement and rehabilitation, also involves in environmental impact assessment monitoring eco-friendly technologies.

In 2008, a survey was carried out by TNS India (a research organization) and the Times Foundation which claimed that all major Indian organizations surveyed were involved in CSR initiatives. In fact, the private sector was found to be more involved in CSR activities such as livelihood environment, and women empowerment promotion, education and health, . The Social Initiatives Group (SIG) of ICICI Bank Ltd works with a mission to build the capacities of the poorest of the poor to participate in the larger economy. The group identifies and supports initiatives designed to break the intergenerational cycle of poor health and nutrition ensure essential early childhood education and schooling as well as access to basic financial services. Thus, by promoting early child health, catalyzing universal elementary education and maximizing access to micro financial services, ICICI Bank believes that it can build the capacities of India's poor to participate in larger socio-economic processes and thereby spur the overall development of the country. The SIG works by understanding the status of existing systems of service delivery and identifying critical knowledge and practice gaps in their functioning. It locates cost effective and scalable initiatives and approaches that have the potential to address these gaps and supports research to understand their impact. This is undertaken in collaboration with research agencies, nongovernmental organisations (NGOs), companies, government departments, local stakeholders and international organisations.

The K. C. Mahindra Education Trust was established in 1953 by late Mr. K. C. Mahindra with an objective to promote education. Its vision is to transform the lives of people in India through education, financial assistance and recognition to them, across age groups and across income strata. The K. C. Mahindra Education Trust undertakes a number of education initiatives, which make a difference to the lives of deserving students. The Trust has provided more than Rs. 7.5 Crore in the form of grants, scholarships and loans. It promotes education mainly by the way of scholarships. The Nanhi Kali project has over 3,300 children under it. We aim to increase the number of Nanhi Kalis (children) to 10,000 in the next 2 years, by reaching out to the underprivileged children especially in rural areas.

In future, the trend, if sustained properly and with GOI encouragement, can deliver many of the developmental aspirations that this huge country with teeming millions has always hoped to achieve. The idea of 'public-private partnership' (PPP) in achieving developmental targets and Indian corporate sector joining hands with GOI in national development is an idea that deserves serious consideration. The GOI policy framework and the programs undertaken by companies may be studied together to investigate the possibility of better coordination among the efforts. A sector-wise study of Indian management decisions could be undertaken to find out the impact of these efforts on meeting the needs of the underprivileged, and the disadvantaged, in the country.

India's main problem lies in underdevelopment of the masses, so there arises the question of tapping more skilled-resources and money to meet the challenge. The private sector in India, even before Independence, showed interest in community development. However, such activities were scattered and often depended on the caprices of the management. Some companies were successful enough to institutionalize CSR work into policies and strategies, while others continued with philanthropy.

Conclusion

The business of the 21-st century will have no choice but to implement CSR. The sooner corporate houses realize this and aggressively pursue this process, the better off they will be. The laws need to be formulated to help in reinforcing CSR practices.

Indian CSR has traditionally been a matter of classical paternalistic philanthropy, financially supporting schools, hospitals and culture institutions. However, far from being an add-on motivated by altruism and personal glory, the philanthropic drive has been driven by business necessity. With minimal state welfare and infrastructure provision in many areas, companies had to ensure that their workforce had adequate housing, healthcare and education and simultaneously the country grows at a fast pace.

The CSR should not be merely a statement of intent. It should be made compulsory for the corporate operating in India. This will definitely help in upholding human rights. In this context, the following measures may be made mandatory to ensure participation of the corporate in social development:

- Incorporation of a section on social actions in annual reports of companies
- Appointment of an independent social accounting committee to measure, monitor, evaluate and report impact of CSR in annual reports
- Separate department to look after the CSR
- Periodic training programmes and awareness camps to train personnel on CSR
- Linkage between CSR and financial success should be established a certain percentage of profit should be earmarked for social development that should reflect in the annual balance sheets of companies.

With the economy witnessing gradual recovery from the global meltdown, the country's corporate sector should go for redefining their corporate social responsibility and accountability. There is a need to make development sustainable, and this is possible only when CSR is internal to businesses. The government would prefer to opt for a liberal route in an enlightened role involving dialogue and partnerships.

When inspiration and initiatives do not result in improvement, the role of instructions from the government is inevitable. The government does not want to be like moral policeman, and businesses must try to convert CSR from a philosophy to real deliverables. The companies should take an inclusive approach to undertake their CSR activities, corporate India should include the rural and agricultural sectors to ensure benefits of economic growth percolates to all sections of the society and the companies can think of being innovative in creating a multiplier so that people can live in a sustainable manner.

References

1. Carroll AB, "A Three Dimensional Conceptual Model of Corporate Performance", (1979), *Academy of Management Review* 4 (4): 497-505.
2. Carroll AB, "The Pyramid of Corporate Social Responsibility: Towards The Moral Management of Organizational Stakeholders", (1991), *Business Horizons* July-August: 39-48.
3. Carroll AB, "Corporate Social Responsibility Evolution of a Definitional Construct", (1999), *Business & Society*, Vol. 38, No. 3, pp. 268-295.
4. Freeman R E, *Strategic Management: A Stakeholder Approach,* (1984), Pitman, Boston.
5. Garriga E and Mele D, "Corporate Social Responsibility Theories: Mapping the Territory", (2004), *Journal of Business Ethics*, Vol. 53, Nos. 1/2, pp. 51-71.

6. Hoffman W M, "Business and Environmental Ethics", (1991), *Business Ethics Quarterly*, Vol. 1, No. 2, pp. 169-84.
7. Knox S, Maklan S and French P Corporate Social Responsibility: Exploring Stakeholder Relationships and Programme Reporting across Leading FTSE Companies, (2005), Journal of Business Ethics 61: 7-28.
8. Maignan I and Ralston DA Corporate Social Responsibility in Europe and the US: Insights from Businesses' Self Presentations, (2002), *Journal of International Business Studies* 33(3): 497-514.
9. Min-Dong P L, "A Review of the Theories of Corporate Social Responsibility: Its Evolutionary Path and the Road Ahead", (2008), *International Journal of Management Reviews*, Vol. 10, No. 1, pp. 53-73.
10. Mitra M, *It's Only Business India's Corporate Social Responsiveness in a Globalized World*, (2007), Oxford University Press, New Delhi.
11. Oketch MO The Corporate Stake in Social Cohesion, (2005), *Peabody Journal of Education* 80(4): 30-52.
12. Rushton K Business Ethics: a sustainable approach, *Business Ethics: A European Review* (2002), 11(2): 137-139.
13. Smith NC Corporate Social Responsibility: Whether or How? (2003), California Management Review 45(4): 52-76.
14. www.emeraldinsight.com/0306-8293.htm

◈ ◈ ◈

ISBN – 978-93-5024-769-3

33

Data Mining for Churn Management in Telecom Industry

Jayalekshmi K.R.
Sterling Institute of Management Studies, Nerul.

Introduction

Customer acquisition and retention are one of the most significant concerns of businesses. In the telecommunication industry, customers are able to choose among multiple service providers and actively exercise their rights of switching from one service provider to another. In this fiercely competitive market, customers demand tailored products and better services at lesser prices, while service providers constantly focus on acquisitions as their business goals. Given the fact that the telecommunications industry experiences an average of 30-35 percent annual churn rate and it costs 5-10 times more to recruit a new customer than to retain an existing one.

Churn prediction aims to identify subscribers who are about to transfer their business to a competitor. The telecommunications sector endures an annual rate of churn, ranging from 25 per cent to 30 percent this churn rate could still continue to increase in correlation with the growth of the market. It would seem reasonable to invest more on churn management rather than acquisition management for mature companies because; the cost of acquiring a new customer is more than retaining an existing one.

Consequently, in order to tackle this problem we must recognize the churners before they churn, so developing a model which predicts the future churners seems to be vital. In this study a predictive model using data mining is developed. This model should be able to recognize the customers which tend to churn in close future. But, due to the nature of pre-paid mobile telephony market which is not contract based, customer churn is not easily traceable and also definable, thus building a predictive model would be of high complexity. To achieve such goal in prepaid market segment the initial step is to define the churn and a churner and then designing the predictive model. In this study, I developed a dual step model building approach, utilizing data mining techniques, which consists of clustering phase and classification phase. The new model will be able to recognize the customers which tend to churn in near future.

Literature Review

The mobile telephony market is one of the fastest-growing service segments .In order to support telecommunications companies manage churn reduction, not only do we need to predict which customers are at high risk of churn, but also we need to know how soon these high risk customers will churn. Therefore the telecommunications companies can optimize their marketing intervention resources to prevent as many customers as possible from churning. In other words, if the telecommunications companies know which customers are at high risk of churn and when they will churn, they are able to design customized customer communication and treatment programs in a timely efficient manner.

Data Mining and its Application in CRM

Data mining has become an area of research with an increasing importance. Data mining techniques are the result of a long term research and product development and their origin have roots in the first storage of data on computers, which was followed by improvement in data access. Data mining is "the process of selecting exploring and modeling large amount of data to uncover previously unknown data patterns for business advantage". It also can be defined as:" the exploration and analysis of large quantities of data in order to discover meaningful patterns and rules" (Berry & Linoff, 2004) and it involves selecting, exploring and modeling large amounts of data to uncover previously unknown patterns, and finally comprehensible information, from large databases. What data mining tools do is to take data and construct a model as a representation of reality. The resulted model describes patterns and relationships, present in the data. The broad application of data mining falls in two major categories

1. Descriptive data mining: aims at increasing the understanding of the data and their content;
2. Predictive or perspective data mining: aims at forecasting and devising, at orienting the decision process. The following sections gives a brief review of data mining techniques that were utilized in this research for building the model.

Classification

Classification is the most frequent learning model in data mining, especially in CRM field. Classification can be defined as the process of finding a model (or function) that describes and distinguishes data classes or concepts, for the purpose of being able to use the model to predict the class of objects whose class label is unknown. Classification process is the process of dividing a data set into mutually exclusive groups such that the members of each group are as "close" as possible to one another, and the members of different groups are as far" as possible from one another. Also we can define the classification as "examining the features of a newly presented object and assigning it to one of the predefined set of classes" .The objective of the classification is to first analyze the training data and develop an accurate description or a model for each class using the attributes available in the data.

Decision Tree

Decision Tree is a tree-shaped structure that represents sets of decisions and is able to generate rules for the classification of a data set. The Decision Tree technique is suitable for describing sequence of interrelated decisions or predicting future data trends. Three types of nodes in the decision tree are root node, internal node and terminal node or leaf node. A record enters the tree at the root node. The root node applies a test to determine which internal node the record will encounter next. There are different algorithms for choosing the initial test. This process is repeated until the record arrives at a leaf node. All the records that end up at a given leaf of the tree are classified the same way, and each leaf node is assigned a class label.

Clustering- A cluster is a collection of data objects that are similar to one another within the same cluster and are dissimilar to the objects in other cluster. Cluster analysis encompasses many diverse techniques for discovering structure within complex bodies of data. It is an approach by which a set of instances (without a predefined class attribute) is grouped into several clusters based only on information found in the data that describes the objects and their relationships. The objective is to group either the data units or variables into clusters such that elements within a cluster have a high degree of "natural association" among themselves while the clusters are "relative distinct" from one another.

Cluster analysis divides the data based on similarity among them. There exist different types of clustering from different point of view. The need for cluster analysis arises in natural ways in many fields such as life science , medicine, engineering, agriculture, social science, etc .In biology, cluster analysis is used to identify diseases and their stages. In marketing cluster analysis is used to identify persons with similar buying habits. By examining their characteristics it becomes possible to plan future marketing strategies more efficiently.

Objective

From the literature review that was done, it was observed that customer churn is the focal concern of most companies, which are active in industries with low switching cost. Among all industries which suffer from this issue, telecommunications industry can be considered as the topper of the list with approximate annual churn rate of 30% churn. So developing a model which predicts the future churners seemed to be vital.

The objective of this research is to develop and design an effective and efficient model for customer churn prediction in telecommunication industry (Pre-paid mobile telephony market).

Methodology

It is the basic plan for conducting the data collection and analysis phase. Studies generally fall into the following three categories: Descriptive, Explanatory (causal), and Exploratory (Saunders, Lewis, & Thornhill, 2000). The primary purpose of exploratory research is to shed light on the nature of a situation and identify any specific objectives or data needs to be addressed through additional research. Exploratory research is most useful when a decision maker wishes to better understand a situation and/or identify decision alternatives. Based on the definition given for data mining, such approach aims at describing the process of discovering knowledge from databases stored in data warehouses. The purpose of data mining is to identify valid, novel, useful, and ultimately understandable patterns in data. Data mining is a useful tool, an approach that combines exploration and discovery with confirmatory analysis. Since the focus of this study is data mining, thus the purpose of this research is exploratory. Since the aim of this research is data mining and data were collected from service provider's databases, the strategy, which fits this study, is a secondary data analysis.

Data Collection

The examined data of this research is the call records of a particular service provider, which has been gathered and stored in Oracle data base software. Since telecom company's data base is a dynamic one that is being updated and extended every second, the call records' data base is a huge data base with millions and thousands million of records. The working data of this research is extracted from the company's data base in a period of 3 months from 1 December 2008 to 28 February 2009 and it contains the call records of 33623 customers of the Company. The number of records is 18500504. Among various data types that are being saved and gathered in company's database I extracted the following one in order to utilize them in building the required and targeted features:

Date of Call

Time of call

Duration of call

Incoming call / Outgoing call

Data Mining — The data mining phase was conducted in two steps and in these steps both descriptive **and predictive** data mining techniques were utilized. Firstly, the customer base was clustered based on their usage behavioral feature (RFM).

In the second step and for executing the predictive data mining approach, classification technique was utilized. Classification is the process of finding a model or function) that describes and distinguishes data classes or concepts, for the purpose of being able to use the model to predict the class of objects whose class label is unknown. The derived model is based on the analysis of a set of training data (ie data objects whose class label is known). Among the existing classification method Decision Tree is used due to its ease of interpretation and more understandable logic.

Model Building for Churn Prediction

The first task in constructing a classification model which is capable of predicting the churners in telecommunication segment (pre-paid mobile market) to define the "Churn" and "Churner" so that we can label churners from non-churners. Giving a definition of churn is the initial step prior to the model building phase. So the two steps taken here are

1. Defining the churn
2. Constructing the Predictive Model

Defining the Churn

Pre-paid telecommunication service providers, who does not have contract between the company and the clients, anyone can simply purchase the SIM Card and become a user. On the other hand, any customers at any time can just stop using the provided services by the company, and become a churner without leaving an immediate trace. Churn in such cases happens with no tracking point such as terminating the contract or not renewing it and its recognition becomes complicated.

The data base of customers consisting a number of customers with different calling behaviors some of them use their cell phone every day, but the others use it every 2, 3,… or 20 days. Now if we define a churner as "A person who has not used his/her cell phone for 7 days" a considerable part of our customers who use their cell phone occasionally (i.e. every 8, 9,….., 20 days) would be considered as a "churner", mistakenly. On the other hand if we take a longer time span for prediction period and define a churner as "A person who hasn't used his/her cell phone for 25 days" our model may suffer from inability in recognizing the real churners. To Tackle this problem, I tailored the RFM features and constructed the following set of 12 RFM related variables, which has been extracted from customers' calling records data by the use of Microsoft SQL Server software, in order to segment the customer base, based on their calling behavior

1. Call Ratio: proportion of calls which has been made by each customer with more than one day time distance to his/her total number of calls.
2. Average Call Distance: the average time distance between one's calls
3. Max Date: the last date in our observed time period in which a call has been made by a specific customer
4. Min Date: the first date in our observed time period in which a call has been made by a specific customer
5. Life: the period of time in our observed time span in which each customer has been active
6. Max-Distance: the maximum time distance between two calls of a specific person in our observed period

7. No-of-days: number of days in which a specific customer has made or received a call
8. Total-no-in: the total number of incoming calls for each client in our observed period
9. Total-no-out: the total number of outgoing calls for each client in our observed period
10. Total-cost: the total money that each customer has been charged for using the services in the specific time period under study
11. Total-duration-in: the total duration of incoming calls (in Sec) for a specific customer in our observed time span
12. Total-duration-out: the total duration of outgoing calls (in Sec) for a specific customer in our observed time span

By the use of Two Step Cluster technique the customer base was divided into 6 individual clusters with the following specifications.

Cluster No	Call ratio		Avgcall distance		Life		Max distance		Max date		Min date		No of days		Total no of IN		Total no of Out		Total cost		Total duration In		Total duration of Out				
	Mean	Sd	Mean	Sd	Mean	Sd	Mean	sd	Mean	Sd	Mean	Sd	Mean	Sd	Mean	Sd	Mean	sd	Mean	sd	Mean	Sd	Mean	Sd			
Cluster1	0.037	0.193	0.0	0.0	87.7	6.27	3.874	5.3	89.54	4.98	1.67	3.05	83.378	3.062	1200.26	1030.15	550.58	450.65	576051.	543675.	131100.	96957.8	55046.7	55745.60			
Cluster2	0.134	0.52	0.0	0.0	87.32	5.51	3.87	4.27	91.02	4.54		1.713	3.08	83.04	11.00	11.03	410.18	236.80	349.90	135.75		243567	104065.	38093.18	29535.45	23515.9	11211.00
Cluster3	3.89	6.25	0.08	0.28	25.05	18.63	5.72	6.55	52.64	30.33	52.46	27.99	19.53	15.38	65.09	110.28	41.53	65.10		35183.	59928.	6245.5	11705.	3496.82	5585.49		
Cluster4	6.98	6.42	0.06	0.26	84.17	8.28	16.33	12.521	87.66	6.94	3.496	5.3	45.56	12.27	90.74	93.2	55.81	55.50	40815	46030	9244.5	15792.4	3863.78	4487.45			
Cluster5	31.89	12.45	3.309	4.02	56.05	21.6	24.88	17.19	67.5	18.499	11.36	15.409	14.8	10.905	11.80	12.29	7.822	8.521	5679.6	10269.	788.18	995.14	640.89	1009.72			
Cluster6	1.67	1.89	0.0	0.0	89.16	2.956	3.902	2.514	92.54	2.297	1.42	1.883	82.119	8.253	229.11	150.11	105.02	64.578	65789.	42352.	21494.	19057	6295.1	4368.12			

Max-Distance is found to be a suitable representative for normal usage frequency of the customers. This feature addresses in what time distance the majority of cluster members uses their mobile phone and thus provides us with the regular usage behavior of customers. Max-Distance feature for all extracted clusters is as follows

Cluster label	Max-distance
Cluster1	3.874 Days
Cluster2	3.87 Days
Cluster3	5.72 Days
Cluster4	16.33 Days

Cluster5 24.88 Days
Cluster6 3.902 Days

Max-distance value for each cluster by considering the max-distance the clusters are redesigned to 4 out of the 6 existing ones as follows

Cluster1
Cluster2 ⇒ Cluster1
Cluster6

Cluster3 ⇒ Cluster2

Cluster4 ⇒ Cluster3

Cluster5 ⇒ Cluster4

Then by considering the prediction period as twice as the max distance , and defined the prediction, retention and observation periods as shown below.

Cluster label	Max-distance	Prediction period	Retention period	Observation period
Cluster1	3.76 Days	7	7	30
Cluster2	5.15 Days	10	7	30
Cluster3	17.33 Days	34	7	30
Cluster4	25.10 Days	49	7	30

Prediction, retention and observation period for each cluster

Constructing the Predictive Model

From the previous research works it is observed that the predictive accuracy of the model would be in its highest level when the number of sub-periods is equal to two. Two sub periods of 15 days are selected and the following features are made for each cluster.

1. IMOU initial : Incoming MOU of a subscriber in the first sub-period
2. IFOU initial : Incoming FOU of a subscriber in the first sub-period
3. OMOU initial: Outgoing MOU of a subscriber in the first sub-period
4. OFOU initial: Outgoing FOU of a subscriber in the first sub-period
5. "IMOU2: The change in Incoming MOU of a subscriber between the sub-period 1 and 2 and is measured by "IMOU2=("IMOU2-"IMOU1+0.01)/"IMOU1+0.01where, IMOU1=MOUinitial
6. "IFOU2: The change in Incoming FOU of a subscriber between the sub- period 1 and 2 and is calculated as "IFOU2=("IFOU2- "IFOU1+0.01) / "IFOU1+0.01 where IFOU1=FOU initial
7. "OMOU2: The change in Outgoing MOU of a subscriber between the sub- period 1 and 2 and is measured by "OMOU2=("OMOU2-"OMOU1+0.01)/"OMOU1+0.01 where OMOU1=OMOU initial
8. "OFOU2: The change in Outgoing FOU of a subscriber between the sub- period 1 and 2 and is calculated as "OFOU2=("OFOU2-"OFOU1+0.01) / "OFOU1+0.01 where OFOU1=OFOU initial
9. Churn: binary churn labels for each client according to their churn status in prediction period

Using the first 8 features as the input features to the tree, the "churn" feature as the output of the tree, and the hit ratio= 1:2 (churner : non-churner), we built different predictive models for each cluster. At first, based on 75% of data (Training Dataset) and by utilizing Decision Tree (CART algorithm) the predictive models were constructed on each of the four developed clusters. The following table shows the performance of the developed predictive model based on gain values.

Cluster No	*Appropriate Algorithm*
Cluster1	Decision Tree C5.0 Algorithm
Cluster2	Decision Tree CART Algorithm
Cluster3	All Tested Algorithms
Cluster4	Decision Tree CHAID Algorithm

Cluster No	*% Gain for percentile=10*	*% Gain for percentile=20*
1	45.3	76.8
2	53	66.7
3	15	31
4	17	44.5

Performance Based on Gain Measures

Performance evaluation of the constructed model with different decision tree algorithms (like **CART**, C5.0, and CHAID) on the clusters based on gain measure is done and observed that a multi- algorithm approach is beneficial for building the model. Depending on the gain measure the following algorithms were found best for each cluster.

Suitable Algorithm for Each Cluster

The following table depicts that the developed model is able to bring the gain factor of %80.2, %67.2, %31.6, and %80 for the top %20 of the customer base of our four developed clusters, respectively. This implies that by applying the developed multi algorithm predictive model, choosing a sample size of only %20 of each cluster's customer base is enough for identifying %80.2,%67.2,%31.6 and % 80 of the total number of churners in each of our four developed clusters respectively.

Cluster No	% Gain for percentile=10	% Gain for percentile=20
1	78.7	80.2
2	52	67.2
3	15	31.6
4	41	80

Gain measures for each cluster

Conclusion

The problem that the service provider was dealing with is to recognize the customers with high probability of churn in close future and target them with incentives in order to convince them to stay, but due to the absence of an accurate model for monitoring their client's behavior the company was unable to distinguish the churners from non-churners. Consequently the developed models are considerably able to distinguish the churners from non-churners and help the service provider to conduct a more efficient retention campaign. In fact by utilizing this approach the company would be able to not only reduce the marketing cost and churns rate simultaneously.

References

1. Wei, C. and Chiu, I. Turning telecommunications call details to churn prediction: a data mining approach. (2002), Expert Systems with Applications. 23(2) pp. 103-112.
2. Ahmad, S. Applications of data mining in retail business. (2004), Information Technology, 2, pp. 455-459.
3. Ahn, J., Han, S., & Lee, Y. Customer churn analysis: Churn determinants and mediation effects of partial defection in the Korean mobile telecommunications service industry (2006), Telecommunications Policy, 30, pp. 552-568.
4. Ansari, S., Kohavi, R., Mason, L., & Zheng, Z. Integrating e-commerce and data mining: architecture and challenges. WEBKDD'2000 Workshop on Web Mining for E-Commerce Challenges and Opportunities (2000).
5. Berson A., Smith S. and Thearling K. Building Data Mining Applications for CRM. (2000), New York: McGraw-Hill.
6. Booz,Allen & Hamilton. Winning the Customer Churn Battle in the Wireless Industry. (2001), Information Technology Group, 1(1), pp. 1-12.
7. Thearling, K. A Introduction of Data Mining. (1999, Feb.), Direct Marketing Magazine pp. 28-31.
8. Wei, C. P., Chang, H. T., and Lee, Y. H. Telecommunication Data Mining for Target Marketing. (2000), Journal of computer.
9. Hui, S.C., and Jha, G. Data mining for customer service support.(2000), Information & Management, 38, pp. 1-13.
10. Au, W., Chan, K., & Yao, X. A novel evolutionary data mining algorithm with applications to churn prediction. IEEE Transaction on Evolutionary Computation, (2003), 7 (6), pp. 532-545.
11. Ahn, J., Han, S. and Lee, Y. Customer churn analysis: Churn determinants and mediation analysis: Churn determinants and mediation effects of partial defection in the Korean mobile telecommunications service industry. (2006); Telecommunications Policy. 30(10-11) pp. 552-568
12. Hung, S., Yen, D. and Wang, H. Applying data mining to telecom churn management. (2006), Expert Systems with Applications. 31(3) pp. 515-524.
13. Adomavicius, G., & Tuzhilin, A. Recommendation technologies: Survey of current methods and possible extensions. Working paper, Stern School of Business, (2003), New York University, New York.
14. Lejeune, Miguel A.P.M. Measuring The Impact of Data Mining on Churn Management. Internet research: Electronic Network Applications and Policy, (2001), 11(5), 375-387.
15. Sohn, S. and Kim, Y. Searching customer patterns of mobile service using clustering and quantitative association rule Expert Systems with Applications. (2008), 34(2) pp. 1070-1077.
16. Coussement, K., & Van den Poel, D. Improving customer attrition prediction by integrating emotions from client/company interaction emails and evaluating multiple classifiers. Expert Systems with applications, (2009), 36, pp. 6127-6134.

ISBN – 978-93-5024-769-3

34 Role of Technology in Banking Sector and Effective E-Banking in 21st Century

Prof. Reetuja Deshpande & Prof. Yogesh Gharpure
Department of Management Studies & Research, Tirpude College of Social Work, Civil Lines, Sadar, Nagpur.

Introduction

Present era is of information and communication technology. Electronic revolution in this 21st century is leading to establish and ensure a better, easy and comfortable way of management, communication and development with the use of information technology. As the information technology is growing day by day it offers opportunities for developing nations to leapfrog earlier stages of development. Information technology (IT) is becoming a powerful tool driving development, supporting growth, promoting innovation, and enhancing competitiveness. If information and communication technology is coupled with knowledge management becomes a promising tool for the development process.

The banking sector is an example in which information-technology infrastructures have had implications on the economic development of many nations in the developing world. It is important to note that the banking industry was one of the very first to utilize information technology, and has thus a record of influencing the development process through the technology. The banking sector today is fast paced and is constantly in the throes of change, with new regulations, new processes and new policies in place.

Technology has played a critical role in the past in shaping the way things are today, and will continue to do more than ever before. Competition makes it difficult for banks to show differentiation and even harder to show profits. In this situation, competitive advantage will be derived by those banks that effectively leverage their processes and systems around customers and channels in order to deliver innovative products and services, retain the customer and enhance lifetime value. Apart from just attaining the competitive edge, several new initiatives have been taken up by banks towards sustainable development encompassing environment friendly initiatives to rural initiatives for financial inclusion.

E-banking implies performing basic banking transactions by customers round the clock globally through electronic media. Today's banking is virtual banking denotes the provision of banking and other related services through the extensive use of IT, without direct resource to the bank by customers. The silent feature of virtual banking is the overwhelming reliance on IT and absence of physical bank branches to deliver banking services to customers.

Advantages of E-banking

1. **24 × 7 Banking:** E-banking has made possible to transact 24 × 7 days. There is no binding on the number of working hours.
2. **Easy Banking:** Customers can perform any banking transactions sitting in their office or from home as no longer personal visit to customers is required,. Customers has a facility that they can get drafts sitting at their door steps through a e-mail call.
3. **Low Cost Banking (Services):** The operational costs have come down due to technology adoption. The cost of transactions through internet banking is much less than any other traditional mode.
4. **Profitable Banking:** The increased speed of response to customer's requirements under E-banking enhances customer satisfaction and consequently can lead to higher profits via handling a large no of customer accounts.
5. **Low Cost Banking (Establishment):** Brick and mortal structure of banking gets converted into click and portal banking. Banks can access to a greater number of potential customers without the commitment costs of physically opening branches. Hence, there is much saving on the cost of infrastructure and the requirement of staff at banks gets reduced to a great extent.
6. **Quality Banking:** E-banking opens a new vistas for providing efficient, economic, enlarged number of services and quality service to the customers.
7. **Speed Banking:** The increased speed of response to customer requirement under E-banking will lead to greater customer satisfaction and handling a larger number of transactions at a lesser time, thus increases customers convenience to a greater extent and facilitates better customer retention.
8. **Service Banking:** E -banking creates strong basic infrastructure for the banks to embark upon many cash management products and to venture in the new fields like E-commerce, EDI etc. Instant credit, immediate payment of utility bills, instant transfer of funds etc, would be made possible under e-banking.

Constraints in E-Banking

Although the advantages of e-banking are more but still there are some constraints in this regard:-

1. **Huge Establishment Cost:** Banks has to incur huge establishment expenses or initial set up cost for venturing in to E-banking. It includes :-
   a. The connection cost to the internet or any mode of electronic communication. The network should be secured, efficient and scalable with inhibit redundancy.
   b. The cost of sophisticated hardware/software and other related components include Modern routers, bridges, network management system etc.
   c. The cost of maintenance of all equipments, websites, skill level of employees etc.
   d. The cost to set up organizational activities to implement E-banking.
2. **The Trust Problem:** India counts some 81 million internet users. While only 16% of the users in India are expected to be banking users in the short term, that number can grow rapidly if banks are able to establish trust with and understandably wary public.
3. **Training And Maintenance And Lack Of Skilled Personnel:** E banking involves 24 x 7 support environment, quality service to end users and other partners which world necessitate a well qualified and robust group of skilled people to meet external and internal commitments. The banks have to spend much on training and retaining the trained staff.

4. **Security:** According to NASSCOM more than 80 Indian banks lack the security safeguards that they need to thwart attacks from phishes and identity thieves. If the security check are not there, cheques, passbooks can be easily be modified without leaving any traces.
5. **Legal Issues:** Legal framework should be devised for E-banking activities. If suppose it happens that very sensitive data falls in to the wrong hands or if his account shows a nil balance all of a sudden without his knowledge, there comes legal issues regarding unauthorized access, unauthorised modification of data or wrongful communication. To prevent these crimes banking legislation should make some provisions with consultation and proper discussion with the legal and technical experts.
6. **Prize Mechanism:** As all prices are easily available at a mouse click. Customers go on comparing prices of each and every products and services offered to them. As a result competition increases and disturbs the prize mechanism.
7. **Restricted Clientele And Technical Problems:** It is not necessary that each and every person has computers at their home or work place or knows how to access these services. Majority of the population of the rural areas mostly prefer traditional banking than e-banking.

The development of IT in Indian Banking commenced from the mid eighties of the twentieth century when the Reserve Bank took upon itself the task of promoting automation in banking to improve customer service, book keeping, MIS and productivity.

The Role Played by the Reserve Bank has Continued over the Years. Some of the Major Landmarks in this Regard are

1. **MICR:** Cheque Clearing represents an important milestone in the development of an efficient payment and settlement system. Manual processing of cheques has undergone a sea-change when mechanised processing of cheques using Magnetic Ink Character Recognition (MICR) technology was introduced. This technology was first used in India in the late eighties at the four major metropolitan cities of Mumbai, Chennai, New Delhi and Kolkata. These centres were set up and are managed by the Reserve Bank of India. The success of these MICR based local clearing processing centres has spurred initiatives on the part of commercial banks for setting up of many more MICR based Cheque processing centres at commercially important centres of the country with the latest state-of-the-art technology. Some centres have also got the facility for 'Imaging' which enables capturing of the digital images of the cheques. Mechanised cheque processing using MICR technology has brought in its wake quicker realisation of cheques, improved customer service and more effective housekeeping at banks
2. **Computerisation of branches of banks:** An activity which commenced from the late eighties with the introduction of ledger posting machines (LPMs), advanced ledger posting machines (ALPMs), followed by stand alone computer systems which metamorphosised into network based systems and the latest development pertaining to the installation of Core Banking solutions;
3. **IDRBT:** The setting up of the Institute for Development and Research in Banking Technology (IDRBT), Hyderabad in the mid nineties, as a research and technology centre for the Banking sector;
4. The commissioning in 1999, of the Indian Financial Network as a Closed User Group based network for the exclusive use of the Banking sector with state-of-the-art safety and security. The network supports applications having features such as Public Key Infrastructure (PKI) which international networks such as S.W.I.F.T
5. Commencement of Certification Authority (CA) functions of the IDRBT for ensuring that electronic banking transactions get the requisite legal protection under the Information Technology Act, 2000;
6. Ensuring Information Systems Audit (IS Audit) in the banks for which detailed guidelines relating to IS Audit were formulated and circulated;

7. Enabling IT based delivery channels which enhance customer service at banks, in areas such as cash delivery through shared Automated Teller Machines (ATMs), card based transaction settlements etc.;
8. Providing Guidelines for Internet Banking, which facilitated the banks to ensure that common minimum requirements relating to Internet Banking offerings were provided for;
9. Providing detailed specifications to banks on the configuration of systems relating to critical inter-bank payment system applications such as Real Time Gross Settlement (RTGS) System, Negotiated Dealing System (NDS), Centralised Funds Management System (CFMS) etc.;
10. Implementation of the National Financial Switch (NFS) to ensure interconnectivity of shared ATMs and to provide for funds settlement across various banks.
11. Establishment of e-payment gateways for the benefit of customers (such as the gateways for funds transfers and other account related transactions) and for facilitating e-commerce.
12. Sharing of information through the secured internet website for the Centralised Data Based Management System-Internet (CDBMSi) project.
13. Providing a platform for transmission of electronic messages across banks using common standards, for facilitating 'Straight Through Processing' (STP) in the form of the Structured Financial Messaging System (SFMS), which will be similar to the SWIFT messaging pattern;
14. Setting up connectivity of all clearing houses of the country so as to enable the introduction of the National Settlement System (NSS)

Technology has completely transformed the way we do banking today. Centralised banking system implementations have computerized all the banking processes, ATM's dispense cash to customers 24 × 7 and internet banking has enabled customers to transact from the convenience of their homes. No long queues at the bank counters or multiple trips to the local branches at HO's. Transactions, bill payment, trading, investing, ordering cheque books, transferring funds, setting up FD's etc., can now all be accomplished with a few mouse clicks.

While internet banking offers benefits, it is still and extremely unsafe place to conduct financial transactions. Cyber criminals use a variety of methods to capture the customer's credentials authentication information (login ID/ password, one-time passwords and even personal digital certificates) and use this information to commit fraud.

Customers today have no way to ascertain whether their banks website being displayed in their browser is authentic or not, whether the transactions they are transacting is reaching the bank correctly or not. Additionally, the customers computer is typically infected by some malware or the other such as key-loggers, screen-scrappers and Trojans that can capture the keystrokes and mouse-clicks of the customer and send it to a fraudster for later (ab)use. Most of the customers are not technically qualified to know what malicious programs are resident on their systems and how to remove them in order to ensure a safe environment for doing transactions online.

Some of the Solutions Available in the Market that Claims to Provide Security to Internet Banking are as Follows

1. **SSL Certificates:** At present majority of the banks are using SSL certificates and HTTPS for providing access to their internet banking applications. SSL does provide an encrypted channel between the customer's browser and the banks server, it does not provide authentication of the website that the customer is going to. The browser only validates whether the SSL certificate is valid or not and does not authenticate whether the certificate indeed belongs to the bank. The customers might see the "lock" icon in his/her browser and still may be connected to a malicious website that can steal their credentials.

2. **One - Time Password (OTP) Tokens:** OTP Tokens generate a single-use password that the customer has to enter in addition to the regular Internet Banking password for authentication. OTP may be generated on a hardware device, a software program on PC or a mobile handset or may be generated by the authentication server and sent to the user using SMS, E- Mail or automated IVR systems. The limitation with OTP systems is that the customer still enters this OTP on an unauthenticated page and on an insecure communication channel. The OTP cannot assist the user in authenticating the server hence it is prone to man-in-the middle attacks. OTP have to be distributed to the customers and have to be renewed between every 3 to 5 years.
3. **Challenge – Response Mechanism:** In this the server sends a challenge to the client, and the client sends a response based on a pre-shared algorithms. Based on the response the server decides whether the client is authentic or not. Some banks have also implemented challenge response mechanism on banks the customer as well as the server side for additional security.
4. **Client-side Digital Certificates:** Some banks have issued digital certificates to their customers. The customer installs the digital certificate on a USB token. The client side digital certificate is used to authenticate the customer and to encrypt and sign the data being communicated between the bank and customer.

Some Solutions for having Secure Internet Banking are

Following are the security essentials for any internet banking technology in order to qualify as the next generation internet business channel:

1. Ensure the security and integrity of the access device being used for accessing internet banking and that no malicious program has access to the banking environment on the access device.
2. Ensure that the client authenticates the client and the server and the server authenticates the client before any identity credentials are shared - this means providing connection level authentication rather than application level authentication.
3. Ensure that a secure network is created and maintained between the client and the server over which banking services are provided. Essential characteristics of such network are mutual authentication, and end to end encryption and ability to create a private network on the internet.
4. Ensure that the data being transmitted is not revealed in clear at any point in time to any network element.
5. Ensure that the access device cannot connect to any other server except the banking server.

Conclusion

Today's business environment is very dynamic and undergoes rapid changes as a result of technological innovation, increased awareness and demands from customers. Information technology has not only simplified the operation but it has also given a great comfort an individual who does not have a good knowledge of IT but need to access banking in an optimum manner. Technology has helped the banks to deliver to deliver the services to customers not only in quick fashion but with a great degree of efficiency and effectiveness. Banks are constantly facing challenges like data management front, in managing technology and in keeping pace with the rapid strides in technology. If the technology is not understood properly, it adds to risk. E-banking is becoming immensely popular globally and India is no exception to it.

References

1. http://www.banknetindia.com.
2. http://www.rbi.co.in.
3. http://www.indianbankassociation.org.
4. http://www.polaris.co.in.
5. www.sbi.com.
6. www.canarabank.com.
7. www.bankofindia.com.
8. www.mindbranch.com.
9. Sugan C. Jain, "E-Banking".
10. Abhay Jain and B S Hundal, "Barriers in Mobile Banking adoption in India".
11. Premkumar. N B and Esther Gnanapoo. J "E-Banking the essential need of today" Kisan World, March 2008.
12. Vasudevan V., "Theory of banking", S.Chand & Company Ltd., Delhi.
13. "A study of the Trends and issues in implementation of E- Banking," Dr.Meena Mathur, Zakiya Khan.
14. E-Banking In India: The Paradigm Shift- Jayshree Bose.
15. Modern Banking Technology -Dr. Firdos T. Shroff.
16. E-Banking in India: challenges and opportunities- Rimpi Jatana.
17. Indian Banking in Electronic Era- S.S. Kaptan.
18. "Online fraud in Asia" Asian Channels, June 2009.

◈◈◈

ISBN – 978-93-5024-769-3

35

Strategic Competitive Advantage through Customer Relationship Management

Prof. Jyoti Meshram & Prof. Gajendra Pawar
JSPM's Jayawantrao Sawant Institute of Management & Research, Hadapsar, Pune-4.

Introduction

Organizations attempt to satisfy consumer needs by offering the right merchandise, at the right price, at the right place, as & when the consumer wants, but is that the only criterion to satisfy the customer? No, the today's customer expects something extra. **Customer relationship management** is a series of activities designed to enhance the level of customer satisfaction. Where competition flourishes, customer relationship management is essential to an organization's long-term viability. It must be central to its strategy. An organization can outperform its rivals only if it can establish a difference that it can preserve. Customer relationship management can make is such a difference. Good relationship management keeps customers brand loyal, and generates positive word-of-mouth communication, which attracts new customers. The challenges of maintaining consistent relationship with the customers provide an opportunity for an organization to develop a sustainable competitive advantage.

This paper deals with the challenges and opportunities for the organizations while they are trying to obtain Strategic competitive advantage through customer relationship management, the approaches organizations use to develop a sustainable competitive advantage, and few of the customers' experiences with the customer relationship strategies followed by organizations in various sectors. The customer's both the good and the bad experiences about the relationship techniques adopted by various organizations and whether the customer thinks that these techniques are sufficient for winning the customer's heart and build a brand loyalty over a period of time. The respondents will also share whether relationship management can be used as a tool for obtaining a sustainable competitive advantage from a customer's perspective.

Strategic Competitive Advantage Through Customer Relationship Management

The new millennium is in the midst of explosive change witnessing rapidly changing market conditions, volatile equity markets, reconstructed value chains and new global competitors. And Customers themselves are changing – natural customer loyalty is a thing of past. Little wonder then, the concept of customer relationship management (CRM) has taken center stage in the business world for sustainable business advantage. Long-term success requires a great Customer Relationship Management strategy. A technology-enabled CRM strategy to meet Customer-focused objectives involves the vast majority of any organization's activity. No doubt about that Customer relationship management (CRM) has become a top priority for companies seeking to gain competitive advantage in today's stormy economy. However, confusion reigns about exactly what CRM is, how to best implement it, or even what role it should play in enhancing customer interaction.

Customer Relationship Management (CRM) is a process by which a company maximizes customer information in an effort to increase loyalty and retain customers' business over their lifetimes.

The primary goals of CRM are to-

- Build long term and profitable relationships with chosen customers.
- Get closer to those customers at every point of contact.
- Maximize your company's share of the customer's wallet.

Customer relationship management is a widely-implemented strategy for managing a company's interactions with customers, clients and sales prospects. It involves using technology to organize, automate, and synchronize business processes—principally sales activities, but also those for marketing, customer service, and technical support. The overall goals are to find, attract, and win new clients, nurture and retain those the company already has, entice former clients back into the fold, and reduce the costs of marketing and client service. Customer relationship management describes a company-wide business strategy including customer-interface departments as well as other departments

Acquiring new customers is always important, but holding on to existing customers is crucial. After all if existing customers are satisfied they will help in acquiring new ones by spreading the news of your outstanding customer services i.e. word of mouth publicity. Let's take a look at these statistics:

- Repeat customers spend 33% more than new customers
- Referrals among repeat customers are 107% greater than new customers
- It costs 6% more to sell something to a prospect than to sell that same thing to a customer.

What is a Strategic Competitive Advantage?

A company with a strategic competitive advantage consistently outperforms their competition through its strategic competitive advantage(s) which is that company's unique value proposition wherein it produces better products or services than anyone else.

When the firm earns the profits that exceed the average for its industry the firm is said to possess the competitive advantage over its rivals/competitors . The goal of the business strategy is to achieve a sustainable competitive advantage for the firm.

There are Two Types of Competitive Advantage

(A) Cost advantage- when the firm is able to deliver the same benefits as the competitors but at the lower costs.

(B) Differentiation advantage- when the firm delivers the benefits that exceed those of competing products

In these ways the firm would be able to create superior value for its customers and superior profits for itself.

Top 3 Top Customer Service Objectives

Customer Experience — People evaluate their business relationship every time they contact a company; therefore, making this experience as enjoyable as possible is essential to customer acquisition and retention.

Cross-Selling and Up-Selling — Generating revenue through cross-selling and up-selling has become just as important in contact centers as providing customer service. Every customer interaction, regardless of channel, must be explored as a sales opportunity and acted on accordingly.

Agent Productivity and Satisfaction — Since the majority of contact center costs lie in employing agents, any increase in their productivity and satisfaction can significantly enhance return on investment.

CRM Business Cycle

As shown in the diagram below, any organization starts with the acquisition of customers.

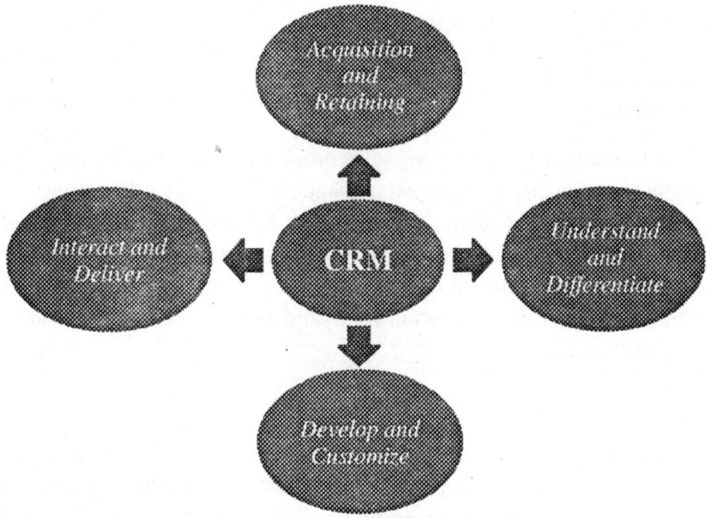

Acquisition and Retaining

Acquisition is a vital stage in building customer relationship. For purpose of customer acquisition an organization is likely to focus its attention the suspects, enquiries, lapsed customers, former customers, competitor's customers referrals, and the existing buyers. From these the organizations need to acquire customers and prospective customers and retain valuable customers.

Understand and Differentiate

Organizations cannot have a relationship with customers unless they understand them.. what they value, what types of service are important to them, how and when they like to interact and what they want to buy. True understanding is based on a combination of detailed analysis and interaction.

Develop and Customize

In the product world of yesterday, companies developed products and services and expected customers to buy them. In a customer – focused world, product and channel development has to follow the customer's lead. Organizations are increasingly developing products and services, and even new channels based on customer needs and service expectations.

Interact and Deliver

Interaction is also a critical component of a successful CRM initiative. It is important to remember that interaction doesn't just occur through marketing and sales channels and media; customers interact in many different ways with many different areas of the organization, including distribution and shipping, customer service and online. With access to information and appropriate training, organizations will be prepared to steadily increase the value they deliver to customers.

Use of Technology in CRM

The application of technology is the most exciting, fastest growing and changing the way customers get information about products and services. Technology includes all the equipment, software, and communication links that organizations use to enable or improve their processes. The mostly used tools are explained below:

Sales Force Automation

These systems help in automating and optimizing sales processes to shorten the sales cycle and increases sales productivity. They enable the company to track and manage all qualified leads, contacts and opportunities throughout the sales cycle including customer support. They improve the effectiveness of marketing communications programmes for generating quality leads as well as greater accuracy in sales forecasting. The Internet can be used by the company in imparting proper training to its sales force. In depth product information, specialized databases of solutions, sales force support queries, and a set of internal information on the Internet can improve the productivity of the sales force.

Call Centres

Call Centre helps in automating the operations of inbound and outbound calls generated between company and its customers. These solutions integrate the voice switch of automated telephone systems with an agent host software allowing for automatic call routing to agents, auto display of relevant customer data, predictive dialing, self –service Interactive Voice Response systems, etc. These Systems are useful in high volume segments like banking, telecom and hospitality. Today, more innovative channels of interacting with customers are emerging as a result of new technology, such as global telephone based call centers and the Internet. Companies are now focusing to offer solutions that leverage the internet in building comprehensive CRM systems allowing them to handle customer interactions in all forms.

Data Warehousing

A data warehouse is an implementation of an informational database used to store shareable data that originates in an operational database-of-record and in external market data sources. It is typically a subject database that allows users to tap into a company's vast store of operational data to track and respond to business trends and facilitates forecasting and planning efforts.

Data Mining and OLAP

Data mining involves specialized software tools that allow users to sift through large amounts of data to uncover data content relationships and build models to predict customer behavior. Data mining uses well-established statistical and machine learning techniques to build models that predict customer behavior. OLAP (Online Analytical Processing), also known as multi-dimensional data analysis, offers advanced capabilities in querying and analyzing the information in a data warehouse. In some CRM initiatives, OLAP plays a major role in the secondary analysis that takes place after initial customer segmentation has occurred. For example, in CRM –based campaign management systems, OLAP is an excellent tool for analyzing the success or failure of the promotional campaigns.

Decision Support and Reporting Tools

Web enabled reporting tools and executive information systems are used to deploy the business information that has been discovered. This enhanced customer knowledge is distributed to executive decision-makers as well as to the operational customer contact points. Applications equipped with some of the same sophisticated modeling routines developed in the data-mining phase are applied to individual contacts in real time.

Electronic Point of Sale (EPOS)

The main benefit of EPOS and retail scanner systems is the amount of timely and accurate information they deliver. Advances in the technology have significantly aided the scope for data analysis. In addition to the original scanner-related data on sales rate, stock levels, stock turn, price and margin, retailers now have information about the demographics, socio-economic and lifestyle characteristics of consumers.

Challenges Ahead the Organizations in Implementing CRM

Tools and workflows can be complex, especially for large businesses. Previously these tools were generally limited to contact management: monitoring and recording interactions and communications. Software solutions then expanded to embrace deal tracking, territories, opportunities, and at the sales pipeline itself. Next came the advent of tools for other client-interface business functions, as described below. These tools have been, and still are, offered as on-premises software that companies purchase and run on their own IT infrastructure.

Often, implementations are fragmented—isolated initiatives by individual departments to address their own needs. Systems that start disunited usually stay that way: soiled thinking and decision processes frequently lead to separate and incompatible systems, and dysfunctional processes.

Business reputation has become a growing challenge. The outcome of internal fragmentation that is observed and commented upon by customers is now visible to the rest of the world in the era of the social customer, where in the past, only employees or partners were aware of it. Addressing the fragmentation requires a shift in philosophy and mindset within an organization so that everyone considers the impact to the customer of policy, decisions and actions. Human response at all levels of the organization can affect the customer experience for good or ill. Even one unhappy customer can deliver a body blow to a business.

Approaches of CRM

Satisfaction

Relationship marketing relies upon the communication and acquisition of consumer requirements solely from existing customers in a mutually beneficial exchange usually involving permission for contact by the customer through an "opt-in" system. With particular relevance to customer satisfaction the relative price and quality of goods and services produced or sold through a company alongside customer service generally determine the amount of sales relative to that of competing companies. Although groups targeted through relationship marketing may be large, accuracy of communication and overall relevancy to the customer remains higher than that of direct marketing, but has less potential for generating new leads than direct marketing and is limited to Viral marketing for the acquisition of further customers.

Retention

A key principle of relationship marketing is the retention of customers through varying means and practices to ensure repeated trade from preexisting customers by satisfying requirements above those of competing companies through a mutually beneficial relationship. This technique is now used as a means of counterbalancing new customers and opportunities with current and existing customers as a means of maximizing profit and counteracting the "leaky bucket theory of business" in which new customers gained in older direct marketing oriented businesses were at the expense of or coincided with the loss of older customers. This process of "churning" is less economically viable than retaining all or the majority of customers using both direct and relationship management as lead generation via new customers requires more investment.

Many companies in competing markets will redirect or allocate large amounts of resources or attention towards customer retention as in markets with increasing competition it may cost 5 times more to attract new customers than it would to retain current customers, as direct or "offensive" marketing requires much more extensive resources to cause defection from competitors. However, it is suggested that because of the extensive classic marketing theories center on means of attracting customers and creating transactions rather than maintaining them, the majority usage of direct marketing used in the past is now gradually being used more alongside relationship marketing as its importance becomes more recognizable.

It is claimed by Reichheld and Sasser that a 5% improvement in customer retention can cause an increase in profitability of between 25 and 85 percent (in terms of net present value) depending on the industry. However Carrol, P. and Reichheld, F. dispute these calculations, claiming they result from faulty cross-sectional analysis. Research by John Fleming and Jim Asplund indicates that engaged customers generate 1.7 times more revenue than normal customers, while having engaged employees and engaged customers returns a revenue gain of 3.4 times thc norm.

According to Buchanan and Gilles, the increased profitability associated with customer retention efforts occurs because of several factors that occur once a relationship has been established with a customer.

- The cost of acquisition occurs only at the beginning of a relationship, so the longer the relationship, the lower the amortized cost.
- Account maintenance costs decline as a percentage of total costs (or as a percentage of revenue).
- Long-term customers tend to be less inclined to switch, and also tend to be less price sensitive. This can result in stable unit sales volume and increases in dollar-sales volume.
- Long-term customers may initiate free word of mouth promotions and referrals.
- Long-term customers are more likely to purchase ancillary products and high margin supplemental products.
- Customers that stay with you tend to be satisfied with the relationship and are less likely to switch to competitors, making it difficult for competitors to enter the market or gain market share.
- Regular customers tend to be less expensive to service because they are familiar with the process, require less "education", and are consistent in their order placement.
- Increased customer retention and loyalty makes the employees' jobs easier and more satisfying. In turn, happy employees feed back into better customer satisfaction in a virtuous circle.

Customers' Experiences

We have collected the experiences of few customers related to the CRM techniques followed by various organizations in different sectors-

1. **Kotak Mahindra Bank: -** Mr. Anurag Sharma an IT professional says- I am quite impressed with the relationship this bank has maintained with me. Once I forgot to make payment of my credit card on time, so I was charged with the late payment charges. It kept on piling up and my payment due reached to the double of initial amount. Unaware of all this, I was under impression that I have already made the

payment. The case was diverted to the collection agency and those people started calling me for payment, I refused to make complete payment which was double the amount I have utilized. Finally when I got in touch with the bank officials , considering my relationship as a regular customer, they reverted the complete charges and I was asked to pay only the sum I have utilized & moreover they promised me that my name will not come in defaulters list. I appreciate this bank. I receive wishes for festivals on my mobile. The customer care is also fine, so overall I believe that this bank won my heart with its relationship techniques and I will always prefer it over the other banks.

2. **Domino's Pizza:-** Mrs. Dhruvi Uchil, a working woman says- I work on 6 days of the week, when I get only Sunday off I don't feel like cooking food at home. Usually fast food becomes the first choice, and so Domino's is one of our favorite joint. Initially I felt that the prices are too high, but when we became regular customers we started receiving SMS alerts for special offers and even the offers sent through couriers. These offers may not be very special but they certainly give us the feeling that we are special for the organization. The company is taking an extra step to maintain the communication with us in order to improvise the relationship. From my point of view Domino's is doing pretty well in relationship maintaining. And my overall satisfaction level is excellent. When it comes to pizza, Domino's would always be my first choice.

3. **Jai Hind Collections:-** Mr. Abhishek Mukherjee says- I had a really nice purchase experience with this store. The sales people are really nice, they guided me throughout the purchasing process, and they were cordial and pleasant. The hospitability is excellent, the services are prompt & the ambience is plush. I think that the products are excellent, the service is very good. Jai Hind is famous for its products. What I feel is that they should be maintaining the records of their customers and be in touch with them. There are festival sales offers on clothing, which the customers should be made aware of. Jai Hind definitely is better than many of the competitors but, implementing few CRM techniques will definitely help the store in gaining sustainable competitive advantage.

4. **Reliance Mart:-** Mrs. Rupali Chatterjee says- shopping the necessities of home is a routine process. I work five days a week and hence I get only two days for my family and all other works including shopping. I cannot really visit different shops so I prefer to shop from malls. Reliance Mart is one of the best options I can think of. I get everything under roof, rates are pretty good. They provided me with a membership card, & have my database with them. I keep on getting updates from them & the membership cards gets me points on every purchase I make. These points can be redeemed. I feel this gives a personal touch to the relationship. I am anonymous entity for them, but they know me personally. Though this is nothing new as other retail formats like Aditya Birla's More also follow the same. But, it is certainly something that differentiates it from many other retailers in the market.

5. **Life Insurance Corporation of India:-** Mr. Sameer Tupe, an Engineer by profession says- I like and trust LIC like many other people do. But the customer relationship techniques LIC has started using like maintaining complete database of the customers, keeping track of their premium payments is really appreciable. LIC is symbol of trust for a mass, but the private players in the insurance sector provide many personalized service. To face this competition, LIC certainly need to implement CRM techniques. Apart from the quality, CRM is an important tool to gain a competitive advantage.

Conclusion

In summary, to implement CRM successfully, you'll have to reorganize your customer and change your organizational mindset. When CRM works, it helps to solve this problem by meshing everyone together and focusing the entire organization on the customer. Like all strategic initiatives, CRM requires commitment and understanding throughout the company, not just in marketing. In all, it adds to a sense of expectation and loyalty being instilled within the consumer and the development of a relationship between company and customer that competitors find hard to break. Business decisions based on complete and reliable information about your customers are very difficult for your competitors to replicate and represent a key to the ***sustainable competitive advantage.***

Bibliography

Books

1. Leading Through Relationship Marketing- Richard Batterley.
2. Relationship Marketing - S. Shajahan, TMGH, 1st ed., 2006 reprint.

Websites

1. www.quickmba.com.
2. www.Wikipedia.
3. www.crm-daily.com.
4. www.twocrows.com.
5. www.businessdictionary.com.
6. www.realmarket.com.
7. www.tricityretail.com.

◈◈◈

ISBN – 978-93-5024-769-3

36

CRM: A Tool for Gaining Competitive Advantage

Anurag Avinash Padoley, Rahul Sahu & Sneha Wankhede
Institute of Management and Research, (ITM) Nagpur.

Introduction

In the present scenario, no organization can exist without customer. This is the soul reasons which leads the organization to strive a strong bond with its customer an to utilize a lot of efforts care and attention to achieve it. Hence customer satisfaction has been the need of the hour for all organizations around the globe which leads to:-

- Increased revenue and growth rate
- An efficient and effective utilization of organizations resources to enhance customer satisfaction
- An improved customer loyalty which leads to increase profit margins.

India today is looked at as one of the most attractive market in the world. The recent visit of the united states president BARAK OBAMA to India in search of tie-ups and opportunities for foreign direct investment is just an evidence of the customer relationship. When enterprises start out in business, keeping track of customer, order and leads may not have been that difficult. Customer relationship management (CRM) technology allows for accumulation of information regarding all customer related activities, including marketing, sales, accounting, support and mode. With the click of button, you can find which leads responded to the direct mail campaign or which customer needs to be notified about outstanding bills. Everything is right where you need it to be.

Customer relationship management (CRM) has a collected customer data can be used to help you learn which types of people to target with your marketing or to keep of their buying habits that could be vital information for future sales and marketing campaign. The applications can also be used to manage new needs and to track their progress from first contact to first purchase. customer relationship management(CRM) program can even alert you when it is time to follow up with lead or a current customer. Customer relationship management can be affected by as many as nine different types of cycles. These include macro cycles such as economic and industry cycles, as well as company-specific cycles such as budget and inventory cycles. CRM systems can be an essential tool for effectively tracking and managing these diverse cycles. This white paper discusses the impact of each of nine different types of cycle on a business, and shows how CRM software can be used to mitigate the negative impacts of those cycles, while making the most of the opportunities that cycles present. Before an organization can start to manage its operations and relationship with its customers. It must have a known-how about its potential customers.

Definition of Customer

"A customer is the most important visitors of our premises. He is not dependent on us we are dependent on him. He is not an interruption in our work; he is a purpose of it. He is not an outsider in our business he is part of it. We are not doing him a favor by serving him; he is doing us a favor by giving us an opportunity to do so".

ISO 9001 standard defines the term 'customer' as an organization or a person that receives the product. A customer is often called as consumer, client, end user retailer, beneficiary, and purchaser. Hence ion simple terms, a customer is one which receives a product a service provided by an organization or individual. Basically there are two stages that should be taken into account in order to improve the customer relation:-

- general: Management of organizations' operations.
- specific: Customer relationship oriented process.

Hence it is a primary goal of a structure he process is systematically taking into account the customer-centric approach it should clearly describe the product and services the organization offer extra attention to be devoted to 'customer satisfaction and organizational culture' .

Hence, benefits of implementing an appropriate business solution for customer relationship management helps to achieve several business benefit for the organization.

The potential benefits are:

- enhanced customer satisfaction.
- large market share
- increased profit margin and revenue
- immediate and prompt access to customer information account history etc
- better ability to meet customer requirement
- an optimized and efficient approach through cost reduction of customer handling

Customers are now in charge. Thanks to the growth of the Web, it is easier than ever to comparison shop and switch from one business to another with the click of a mouse. However, research has found that in the online market, customers yearn for trustworthiness more than ever.

Customer relationships are a companies most valuable asset - worth more everything else combined as no customers = no business. Getting and keeping more customers who stay with you longer is crucial. If your customers are loyal to your business, they will be much more likely to choose you over your competitors. Loyal customers will be much more likely to tell their friends about you. Loyal customers spend more and bring in even more new customers. Loyalty is immensely valuable. Research has shown that a 5 percent increase in customer retention rates results in a 25 percent to 95 percent increase in profits.

Its easy to say customers are our most important assets but turning CRM strategy into bottom-line results is hard work. It means winning the battle for customers? hearts and minds every day, with each interaction at every customer touch point. Long-standing relationships only arise from trust gained over many transactions and by customers' belief that the company wishes to keep them around rather than drive them away.

The Customer Relationship Lifecycle

Traditionally defined as "before you realized what the Internet was all about"? Enterprise employees were the primary users of applications designated "CRM." Then e-business or a buzzword flavour of the month" applications were introduced to allow enterprises to interact directly with customers via corporate web sites, e-commerce storefronts and self-service applications. Starting in 1999, partner relationship management applications hit the market, designed to support channel partners and other intermediaries between an enterprise and its end customers.

These applications support the following business processes involved in the customer relationship lifecycle:

- **Marketing.** Targeting prospects and acquiring new customers through data mining, campaign management and lead distribution. Remember, the emphasis here is on long-term relationship value, not quick hit.
- **Sales.** Closing business with effective selling processes using proposal generators, configurations, knowledge management tools, contact managers and forecasting aids? all without uttering The Eight Words That Kill A Sale: "Let me get back to you on that."
- **E-commerce.** In the Internet Age? welcome to it? selling processes should transfer seamlessly into purchasing transactions and be done quickly, conveniently and at the lowest cost. All customers should have one face with your company, no matter which touch-point they choose to use.
- **Service.** Handling post-sales service and support issues with call centre applications or web-based customer self-service options. We said "handling," not "sloughing off to an inadequate FAQ page."

CRM is a business strategy to create and sustain long-term, profitable customer relationships. Successful CRM initiatives start with a business philosophy that aligns company activities around customer needs.

Customer relationship management (CRM) is a business strategy to acquire and manage the most valuable customer relationships. CRM requires a customer-centric business philosophy and culture to support effective marketing, sales and service processes. CRM applications can enable effective customer relationship management, provided that an enterprise has the right leadership, strategy and culture.

CRM is about customer value creation. Company objective is not to generate maximum revenue from customer transaction, but rather to build lasting relationship with customer. Building customer relationship is creating the process, which could help customer to create value for them selves. The advantage of CRM is the company responsibilities are not only creating the product base on price, but also to help customers to create value for themselves.

CRM sees the product as a process. The transaction between producer and customer is become, how to deliver company competence into customer value creation. This mean company could differentiate value creation to build customer relationship.

Company as a provider is not enough to satisfied customer need, but also responsible to build relationship by creating customer possibilities to create value for themselves.

It is important for the company to understand its knowledge of how customers create value for themselves. It is easier for the company to evaluate how it can support the customer with the competence it has. Without understanding of value creation, it is difficult for the company to develop a good relationship, which brings good value for customer and company.

Success Factors of a Business Solution

The key success factors which boost the business of an organization are :

- the faith of the entire staff including top management on the CRM
- promotion of CRM based business solution
- the vitality of connection interfaces and interaction between the process.
- the influence of the software and support staffs
- the understanding of CRM implementation as a continuous process

As more firms embrace CRM as a core business strategy, it is getting more important to assess firms' CRM readiness and performance for diagnosing, guiding, managing, and evaluating their current CRM practices. Previous CRM studies have been limited to extracting a few success factors or focus only on specific implementation methodologies without any theoretical underpinning. In this paper, we suggest a performance measurement framework called CRM scorecard as an integrative organizational artifact to diagnose and assess a firm's CRM practice. The CRM scorecard was developed through comprehensive literature review and in-depth interviews with CRM practitioners, with specific objective and subjective instruments added to measure corporate CRM capability and readiness. Additionally, we conducted an analytic hierarchy process (AHP) analysis to prioritize the evaluation factors in the CRM scorecard.

Challenges

Tools and workflows can be complex, especially for large businesses. Previously these tools were generally limited to contact management: monitoring and recording interactions and communications. Software solutions then expanded to embrace deal tracking, territories, opportunities, and at the sales pipeline it. Next come to the advent of tools for other client-interface business functions, as described below. These tools have been, and still are, offered as on-premises software that companies purchase and run on their own IT infrastructure.

Addressing the fragmentation requires a shift in philosophy and mindset within an organization so that everyone considers the impact to the customer of policy, decisions and actions. Human response at all levels of the organization can affect the customer experience for good or ill. Even one unhappy customer can deliver a body blow to a business.[5]

Strategy

For larger-scale enterprises, a complete and detailed plan is required to obtain the funding, resources, and company-wide support that can make the initiative of choosing and implementing a system successful. Benefits must be defined, risks assessed, and cost quantified in three general areas:

- **Processes:** Though these systems have many technological components, business processes lie at its core. It can be seen as a more client-centric way of doing business, enabled by technology that consolidates and intelligently distributes pertinent information about clients, sales, marketing effectiveness, responsiveness, and market trends. Therefore, a company must analyze its business workflows and processes before choosing a technology platform; some will likely need re-engineering to better serve the overall goal of winning and satisfying clients. Moreover, planners need to determine the types of client information that are most relevant, and how best to employ them.[2]
- **People:** For an initiative to be effective, an organization must convince its staff that the new technology and workflows will benefit employees as well as clients. Senior executives need to be strong and visible advocates who can clearly state and support the case for change. Collaboration, teamwork, and two-way communication should be encouraged across hierarchical boundaries, especially with respect to process improvement

- **Technology:** In evaluating technology, key factors include alignment with the company's business process strategy and goals, including the ability to deliver the right data to the right employees and sufficient ease of adoption and use. Platform selection is best undertaken by a carefully chosen group of executives who understand the business processes to be automated as well as the software issues. Depending upon the size of the company and the breadth of data, choosing an application can take anywhere from a few weeks to a year or more

Obstacles and Risks

Before the implementation of major concepts or idea, its vital to analyses and assess the risk, obstacles or effect that may get generate as consequences which is associated with the process. Some major obstacles during the implementation of a business solution can be:-

- organizations are mostly much focused on the product sale or geographical segmentation of markets and give least attention towards the operational factors of the business solution.
- lack of commitment and faith for the top management on the CRM business solution
- weak functional organization of company can cause confusion among customers and employee.
- new technology and solution are often implemented without essential analysis, necessary frame work for extensive strategy.

Risk Management and CRM

Some risks associated with realizing CRM benefits are common to all technologies or business initiatives in organization. There is for example a risk that appears because CRM solution are new. CRM has only taken of in the last few years. These means that CRM solution are not enough tested, tried and implemented in details. They are used only across few areas that are not necessarily comparable with the area of organization willing to introduce CRM solution. Further more an organization implementing a CRM solution is exposed also to independent variables. This could be motivation of employees (employee motivation has a significant influence an customer satisfaction), quality of products, offer competitiveness etc.

There are already developed CRM software solutions on market today. The most popular and very similar to each other we find at Siebel Systems, Trilogy, SAP, IBM, Oracle. Majority of them took to consideration the integration between front office and back office tools also.

Conclusion

Properly defined and systematically documented business processes are critical components of any successful online business solution. A proper interface between marketing, sales and customer support is also taken into account. Further more for all organizations including small and medium enterprises following things are essential:

- motivational level of employees
- quality of products
- faith in human and other vital resources of the organization
- faith in the integrated business solution system
- highly focused on the concept of the social marketing.

Hence our paper emphasizes on the basics of customized business solution which can be used by any organization with a structural approach. For further study we would consider the requirements of information architecture analyses the various business models available contemporarily in market.

References

1. An e-commerce and marketing dictionary of terms Online: http://www.udel.edu/alex/dictionary.html [12.1.2004].
2. Information systems audit and control foundation: CRM -managing benefits Realisation; Prince waterhause coopers llp; 2003.
3. Wang Jiyu,Wang Jintao and huang Zhichao."Modern enterprise management system", journals scientific and technological progress and countermeasures, 2002(12): 15-17.
4. Ma Li. "Staff relationship management based on CRM Theory", Journals, Human resource development, 2008.2: pp. 172-173.
5. Zhou Jieru,Customer relationship management and value creation[m].Shangai:Shangai Jiaotong university press, 2006.

ISBN – 978-93-5024-769-3

37 Customers Value in Marketing: Customer Servicing is Fuelling Steady Growth in the Indian Retail Industry

Mr. Prashant Kadam
SBS, Korti, Pandharpur.

Introduction

The retail industry is becoming one of the most competitive in India, with supermarket chains and malls mushrooming all over .People are making a beeline for shopping experience at FOOD World, Fabmall, Family Mart, BIG BAZAR, Forum, Shopper's Stop and the like ,who are competing to woo them. Some persue the strategy of providing better customer service and more variety of goods, while others try to make shopping more pleasant by investing in entertainment. Some offer bargains to customers while others provide store-specific brands. In general, retailers are competing to provide superior value and a better shopping experience to customers. All over the world, retail marketing is growing and becoming highly competitive (e.g.: Tesco).

Retailing consists of business activities involved in selling goods and services to consumers for their personal, family or household use. It includes every sale of goods and services to final consumer, ranging from automobiles to apparel to meals at restaurants to movie theater tickets. Retailing is the final stage in distribution process. With the popularity of the Internet, retailing is becoming popular using the website and a new form e-tailing is developing.

Retailing is not restricted to tangible products. It covers services also. Airline travel, dry-cleaning, training programmes, and the like come under retailing's purview. Retailing is not also confined to a store. Web purchases (like Amazon.com and Fabmart), mail and phone orders, direct marketing and vending machine sales all fall within the scope of retailing.

While the leader retailer in India, PANTALOONS, is on an expansion spree today (2006), Reliance Industries planning an entry into organized retail with massive investments.

The development of organized retailing in India will benefit a majority of the population, as it will bring about increased employment, efficiency in agriculture and exports study by CII and Price WaterHouse Coopets (PWC)has said.

According to study,' The Rising elephant: Benefits of modern trade to Indian Economy', the development of organized retail will generate an additional eight million jobs, directly and indirectly. It is expected that by 2020 India will have lead in the organized retailing sector. The demographics of the country are such that nothing can stop it from becoming the leader.

Allaying fears of FDI in retail creating unemployment by wiping out 'Kirana'stores , the study said only those working in one lakh mid-category stores were likely to be displaced in the mid-term as against the workforce working in 12 million retail outlets across the country. In the long run ,the metamorphosis of this sector will lead to the redeployment of this workforce also. Experts feel that unless India allowed FDI in retail it would not enough even be on the reader of potential investors.

Organized retailing in India was expected to touch Rs.1.1 lakh crore by 2010, but for that to happen it would need about Rs.20000 crore of investment.

The study says development of organized retailing will result in increased efficiency in agricultural sector and remove intermediaries in the food supply chain. With the investments in upgrading technology and practices in the entire value chain, including production, packaging, grading, storage and logistics, the current level of wastage ranging between 24% and 40% are expected to come down, it said.

Highlighting the impact of entry of foreign players in retail on sourcing from India, the study said it would result in a significant increase. All the global players source 95% of merchandise locally wherever they are present . Hence the same would be applied to India, and the local industries are bound to benefit.

The study, however, said for the retail sector to develop in India ,the Government will have to consider legislative reforms such as allowing FDI and granting industry status to the retail sector along with infrastructure development.

It also said that the private sector would need to invest in supply chain and manpower development.

Objectives

(1) To understand the different strategies used by D Mart.

(2) To find out how purchase decision changes by infrastructure and value addition by D Mart.

(3) To know how customer servicing is fuelling to retail industry

Research Methodology

Researcher collected the primary data using questionnaire method in a Solapur city. Although having large population size of customers in Solapur city, researcher prefer 50 as a sample size and collect the data in simple random sampling way without replacement.

Thus, sample area – Solapur
Sample size- 70
Valid sample size-50
Sampling method-Simple random sampling
Statistical tools used - test and weighted average method
Scaling techniques- Likert scale.

Data Analysis

(A) DemogrAphic Factors

(1) Monthly income pattern of customers :

Income in Rs	*No.of respondents*	*Percentage*
0-5000	10	27
5000-10000	7	19
10000-20000	10	27
20000-above	10	27
Total	37	100

The above table shows that 27% respondents have their income below Rs-5000. 19% respondents have their income group more than Rs-5000 but less than 10000. 27% respondents have their income group more than Rs-10000 but less than Rs-20000. 27% respondents have their income group more than Rs-20000 and above.

(2) Monthly expenses in retail :

Monthly expenses in Rs	*No.of respondents*	*Percentage*
0-1000	1	2.7
1000-2000	6	16.2
2000-3000	8	21.6
3000-5000	10	27
5000-above	12	32.4

From the above table it can be seen that , 2.7% of the respondents spending Rs-1000 on monthly expenses on retail. Where as 16.2% respondents can spend Rs-1000 to Rs-2000. About 21.6% respondents can spend Rs-2000 to 3000 on their monthly retailing. There are 27% respondent who can spend in between Rs-3000 to Rs-5000. There are 32.4% with their spending power upto Rs-5000 and above.

(3) Educational Qualification:

80 % of the customer's visits to the store are Graduates. Other 20 % includes customers are undergraduates.

(B) Opinion about Customer Service at Retail Store

B	Attributes	SA	%	A	%	D	%
1	Visual presentation helps get more information	41	82	9	18	0	
2	Proper treatment by sales people at store	37	74	7	14	6	12
3	sales promotion activity changes purchase decisions	35	70	13	26	2	4
4	Value added services helps to come back to store	33	66	14	28	3	6
5	Get all varieties of goods in the store	39	78	8	16	3	6
6	Is free home delivery in favor of the customer	34	68	10	20	6	12
7	Credit card facility for payments	49	98	0		1	2
8	Agree that SMS alerts helps to get more information	43	86	6	12	1	2
9	Retailers taking efforts to visit the store again	27	54	15	30	8	16
10	Satisfied with in all aspects of customer service	49	98	1	2	0	0

The above table shows that:

(1) 82% respondents strongly that visual presentation helps to get more information about the products details and offers, whereas 18% respondents are agree for the same.

(2) 74% respondents are strongly agree that proper treatment by sales people at the store motivates them to visit the store frequently, whereas 7% respondents are agree for the same and 12% respondents are disagree.

(3) 70% respondents are strongly agree that sales promotion activities changes the purchase decision regarding purchase , whereas 20% respondents are agree for the same and 4% respondents are not agree with the same.

(4) 66% respondents are strongly agree that value addition services helps to come back to the store whereas 28% respondents are agree with the same and 6% of the respondents are disagree .

(5) 78% respondents are strongly agree that they get all varieties of goods at the store, whereas 16% respondents are agree with the same and 6% respondents are disagree with the same.

(6) 68% respondents are strongly agree that home delivery in favor of the customers, whereas 20% respondents are agree with the same and 12% respondents are disagree with the same.

(7) 98% respondents are strongly agree that credit card facility is available , whereas 2% respondents are disagree with the same.

(8) 86% respondents are strongly agree that SMS alerts help them get information about new offers, product information, whereas 12% respondents agree with the same and 2% respondents are disagree.

(9) 54% respondents are strongly agree that retailer is taking efforts to visit the store again, whereas 30% respondents are agree with the same and 16% respondents are disagree.

(10) 98% respondents are strongly agree that are satisfied with the retail store in overall aspects of customer service, whereas 2% respondents are agree that they are satisfied .

(C) Purchase Decision of the Customers

(1) Planning for purchase decisions

Particular's	*No.of respondents*	*Percentage*
Yes	35	70
No	13	26
No comment	2	4
Total	50	100

Above table indicates that 70% of the respondents are well planned for their purchases whereas 26% respondents are not planned for their purchases. Only 4% respondents were unable to answer the question.

(2) Getting impression by infrastructure of store

Particular's	*No.of respondents*	*Percentage*
Yes	46	92
No	3	6
No comment	1	2
Total	50	100

The above table shows that, 92% respondents are impressed by the infrastructure of the store whereas 6% respondents were not impressed. Only 2% respondents were no comments.

(3) Willingly increasing budget at the time of purchase

Particular's	*No.of respondents*	*Percentage*
Yes	43	86
No	7	14
Total	50	100

From the above table it can be seen that 86% respondents willingly increasing their budget at the time of purchase, whereas 14% respondents remaining unchanged.

(4) Purchasing power changes with display of the products

Particular's	*No.of respondents*	*Percentage*
Yes	43	86
No	4	8
No comment	3	6
Total	50	100

The above table shows that, 86% respondents agree that their purchasing power changes with display of products, whereas 8% respondents don't change their purchasing and 6% respondents were of null opinion

(5) Allowing retailer you to handle the objects, things and others

Particular's	*No.of respondents*	*Percentage*
Yes	48	96
No	2	4
Total	50	100

The above table indicates that 96% respondents say that retailer allowing to handle things, whereas 4% respondents say that retailer doesn't allow to handle things.

(6) Assertive about the giving contact number

Particular's	*No.of respondents*	*Percentage*
Yes	39	78
No	10	20
No comment	1	2
Total	50	100

The above table shows that there are 78% respondents are willing to give their contact number to the retailer, whereas 20% respondents are not ready to give their contact number to retailer, still there are 2% respondents who are of null opinion.

(7) Special offers change purchase decisions

Particular's	*No.of respondents*	*Percentage*
Yes	41	82
No	8	16
No comment	1	2
Total	50	100

Above table indicates that 82% of the respondents are of the opinion that special offers can change their purchase decisions, whereas 16% respondents are not of the same opinion. Only 2% respondents were unable to answer the question.

(8) Do you know that you are raising your customer basket

Particular's	*No.of respondents*	*Percentage*
Yes	47	94
No	2	4
No comment	1	2
Total	50	100

The above table shows that there are 94% respondents agree that they are raising their customer basket whereas 4% respondents are disagree with the opinion, still there are 2% respondents who are of null opinion.

Findings

From the above research the researcher find the fact that 1) when the question was asked regarding visual presentation that majority of the respondents were impressed with the physical infrastructure and the display which motivates them to get more information and inturn change their purchase decision. 2) when the question was asked about treatment by sales people that majority of the respondents were impressed with the same and handling the things at own. 3) when the question was asked about sales promotion activity change your purchase decisions that majority of the respondents were strongly agreed for the same. 4) when the question was asked regarding value added services and variety of goods that majority of respondents were delighted with the same. 5) When the question was asked regarding the credit card facility and SMS alerts that majority of the respondents were strongly in favour of these services. 6) Customers willingly raises their customer baskets & purchase decision changes as per attributes. 7) Expense pattern of the customers is positively skewed. 8) When question was asked regarding efforts taken by retailer that majority of the respondents were delighted with the efforts as well as satisfaction on account of overall aspects of customer service particularly in this store.

Conclusion

With studying all relevant aspects in detail the researcher arrived to the conclusion that, presently Indian retailers are taking care of all aspects which are very important from customer service is concerned. The deliberate systematic and planned way to deal with customers in through visual presentation, trained sales people to handle the queries ,sales promotion activities, value added services, getting all varieties of goods in the store, Credit card facility ,SMS alerts and in general all aspects making customer feel homely and at ease so as to boost the sales at highest level of customer satisfaction. Store is focusing on the benefits of Customer servicing and ultimately fuelling the steady growth.

Bibliography

1. Dr.K.Karunakaran, Marketing management, 2nd ed.,2010, Himalaya publishing House,.
2. Deepshikha Punj , Dec-2010, India Today Aspire.,
3. Susan Ward, 8 Rules For Good Customer Service- Good Customer Service Made Simple, About.com Guide.

◈ ◈ ◈

ISBN – 978-93-5024-769-3

38 An Article on: "Competencies of Successful HR Professional in Today's Changing Scenario"

Patel Sazia & Hudli Nilofer
Allana Institute of Management Sciences.

Introduction

Today is the world of challenges and opportunities, a successful HR professional has many tasks to accomplish. One of the most important task is to keep the employees happy. HR has to take care of various activities in the organization like recruitment & selection, training & development, competency mapping, performance evaluation, compensation management, labour relations and labour welfare.

HR should be competent enough to handle the sudden changing situations in the organization and should be able to put forth the following.

Workplace Flexibility, Creative employment contracts will support more time off, flexibility in hours and work location, technological job aids and more pay at risk with significant upside potential, developing the training and development tools.

At Global level-The role of corporate HR will change to that of creator of overall values and direction, and will be implemented by local HR departments in different countries. Technology, especially the Internet, will enable more businesses to enter the global marketplace. HR professionals will have advanced acumen in international business practices, international labor laws, multicultural sensitivities and multiple languages. HR professionals will need to be knowledgeable of other cultures, languages and business practices to help their companies find and enter more markets.

Problems faced by HR while handling sudden changing situations in the organization.

Retaining the Trained Workforce

Is retention a bigger challenge than skills shortfall?

For 60% of HR managers, retention is a bigger challenge than skills crunch. Hiring is on the rise but problems with available talent pool still continue. Skills are at a premium and extremely hard to find in almost every industry. Furthermore, retaining the current employees is an uphill task for HR managers across industries. In a poll conducted by TJinsite, 60% of HR managers responded that for them, retention is a bigger challenge than skills crunch. India Inc is taking several initiatives to provide growth opportunities to current employees

- training being on top of the agenda. Problem arises when by the time an organisation trains an employee, he/ she shifts jobs. Other than monetary investment, time and effort is also involved in training an employee. To arrest attrition many organisations, especially IT companies, are moving toward contracts/bonds. Hiring itself is composed of many challenges – hiring new employees (considering that HR managers are struggling with skills shortfall) and soaring expectations of the workforce being some of them. Offering a steep pay hike may ensure getting people on board quickly, but does not guarantee a long stint with the organisation. It is the non-monetary benefits that give an organisation the extra edge over competition. According to industry experts, while monetary measures do help in controlling attrition, it is not a long-term sustainable measure, since an organisation cannot continue paying above industry standards to all employees. A series of polls and surveys conducted by TJinsite revealed that though attrition is a problem and companies are focusing energies on retention, they are largely hiring for business expansion. The industry is initiating various measures to provide growth opportunities to employees. Organisations are engaging employees through regular in-house trainings, employee appreciation programs, and fun-at-work initiatives. Overall, employee engagement through training and recreation is the buzz word for corporates, to deal with attrition.

Employee engagement through training-based programs and cultural initiatives is the mantra that India Inc is banking on to retain its talent. The rate of attrition is highest at executive and manager levels. The expectations of this group are very high - ranging from good salary packages to impressive job profiles/ designations. Giving a salary hike can be a short term means to hold an employee to an organisation. To offer employees a sustainable career, providing opportunity for growth by way of trainings and recognition of employee achievements are considered as more effective measures. A dynamic succession planning, strong engagement focus and building a sense of belonging helps in controlling attrition to a greater extent.

The Business Needs It

Corporates today are mainly hiring for business expansion. Attrition is a problem but hiring is for more productive reasons Corporates today are mainly hiring for business expansion. Attrition is a problem but hiring is for more productive reasons. According to the survey approximately 80% of all organisations are hiring for business expansion or new business projects. Attrition is a problem but companies are initiating programs to attend to this issue. As corporates want to focus on positives, they are hiring for productive reasons. In the BPO sector, almost 30% said that they were hiring due to attrition, vis-à-vis 20% in other sectors.

Attrition in BPO's

In BPOs hiring is maximum at fresher level; so is attrition. One reason is that this set of workforce is easily lured by slight hike in compensations. In the BPO industry hiring is highest at the fresher level and so is attrition. One reason is that this set of workforce is easily lured by even a slight hike in salary. The reason why this is so is not far to seek. In the BPO and Knowledge Outsourcing industries, nearly 60% of the companies are hiring freshers, whereas this proportion is about half in the other industries. Freshmen as a group are far more prone to job hopping in an industry where demand (given that 100% of them are hiring) seems to be greater than Supply. In all other sectors, the demand is for people with at least 3-5 years of experience or more. This is in line with the finding that for nearly 80% of the organisations, business expansion or business projects are the reasons for hiring. Experience and familiarity with the business process is critical in these areas and recruiting and training freshers to take on the mantle of an executive level position would not work for companies in these industries. 51 % of employers surveyed said that they are hiring for business expansion. 70% of the organisations across industries prefer to use internal resources over hiring outside help in the form of consultants or others. While hiring is on the rise, the problems with the talent pool available still continue. To work out the problem of skills shortage, corporates are resorting to training as a means of providing growth opportunities to employees and to retain them.

Sources of Hiring

Online recruitment portals are the most preferred source of hiring across industries. On an average, recruitment portals seem to be the most popular source for hiring of resources, followed by both recruitment agencies and word-of-mouth. However, this changes drastically when analysed by industry type. Print is the most popular source among the IT companies, 63% of them said that they rely on print media. Among the other industries, the BFSI favours word-of-mouth and the CRMs/Call Centres/BPOs favour recruitment agencies. Among all sectors, recruitment portals come second, with between 30-40% of the respondents stating that they use these portals. 36 % of the employers voted recruitment portals as the preferred hiring channel.

Conclusion

Competencies of Successful HR Professional in Today's Changing Scenario The War for Talent is Back

It's a known fact that the economy is once again on a growth trajectory. But amidst all the optimism that is dominating India Inc currently, the war for talent is gaining momentum. In terms of hiring, India Inc seems to have come back to where it was two years ago. In the new economy, competition has gone global, capital is abundant, ideas are developed quickly and people are willing to change jobs more frequently. Another high point is the dearth of employable talent. So, on one hand, there are more jobs in the market and people are changing jobs more often and on the other, organisations are facing a shortage of employable talent.

HR should be competent to hire talented and dedicated workforce.

Big pay days are back.

Higher level employees are now moving from one sector to another more frequently, say headhunters, and are negotiating more than just salary. Stock options, performance-linked incentives, cash incentives and long-term payouts are now discussed more than just basic salary. HR should maintain internal and external equity while structuring the salary components. Some of the leading technology companies such as Google is raising the compensation for its employees, which also reflects the entities' improving business performance. A newspaper reported that some of the world's largest technology firms are

Lifting pay rates apart from taking other measures to retain employees. This reflects improved performance in the companies' businesses and heightened competition for workers with the right experience.

At global level HR should train and develop employees by effective use of technologies, cross cultural training and crisis handling as employees have to deal with people from diverse sectors while working as a team.

If more Indians turn skilled in future, they would be employable which in turn would create savings, investments and ultimately growth.

Sources

1. Times of India Nov., 2010.
2. Economic Times Dec., 2010.
3. www.timesjob.com.
4. Human Resource Management by C.B. Mamoria.
5. Human Resource Management by Gary Dessler.
6. Human Resource Management by Ashwathapa.

◇◇◇

ISBN - 978-93-5024-769-3

39

Financial Leverage and Effective Value of the Firm: Financial Stability

Rashmi Sundriyal Gairola
Pune Institute of Business Management, Pune.

Introduction

In finance, leverage is a general term for any technique to multiply gains and losses. Common ways to attain leverage are borrowing money, buying fixed assets and using derivatives. The basic objective of financial management, i.e., the maximization of shareholders wealth requires the maximization of market price of the share by maximizing the Earnings Per Share (EPS). So given the level of operating profit i.e., Earnings Before Interest and Taxes (EBIT), the financial manager should strive to maximize the EPS and for this purpose the understanding of financial leverage is essential. However, as the level of EBIT depends upon the sales revenue, the operating leverage should also be analyzed though the financial leverage is more important and directly relevant. Moreover, the operating leverage and financial leverage are related to each other.

Therefore,

Operating Leverage = (Revenue – Variable Cost) / Operating Income, where Operating Income is EBIT, and Financial Leverage = Operating Income / Net Income, where Operating Income is EBIT and Net Income is Profit After Tax (PAT).

This implies that, Combined leverage = (Revenue – Variable Cost) / Net Income

Financial leverage measures the relationship between the EBIT and the EPS and it reflects the effect of change in EBIT on the levels of EPS. The financial leverage measures the responsiveness of the EPS to a change in EBIT and hence the Degree of Financial Leverage (DFL) can be defined as:

DFL = % Change in EPS / % Change in EBIT

It has been argued that presence or absence of financial leverage in a firm's capital structure affects the value of the firm. Value of firm can be defined in more than one ways. One of the definition states, Value of firm = Total Equity + Total Debt. According to Modigliani-Miller (MM) theory, the market value of a firm is determined by its earning power and the risk of its underlying assets, and it's independent of the way it chooses to finance its investments or distribute dividends. As per MM, (assumptions given)

ke = ko = D/E (ko – ke), where,

ke is the required rate of return, or cost of equity.

ko is the company unlevered cost of capital (i.e. assume no leverage).

kd is the required rate of return on borrowings, cost of debt.

D/E is the debt-to-equity ratio.

ke is the required rate of return on equity, or cost of equity.

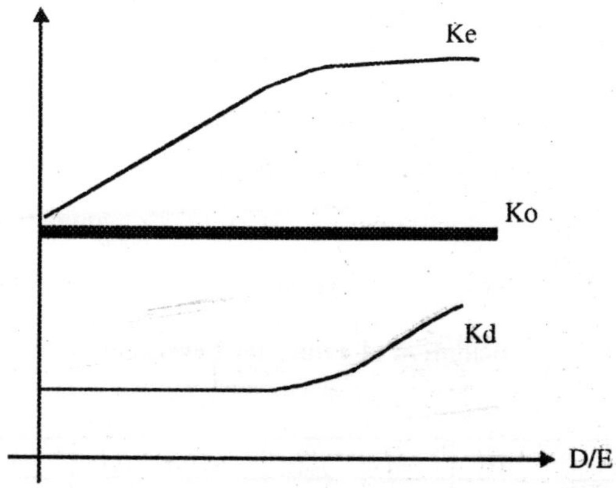

As the above diagram shows that ko remains constant even when the D/E ratio rises. The D/E ratio here determines the deferent levels of leverage and ko ultimately indicates the value of the firm. The higher debt-to-equity ratio leads to a higher required return on equity, because of the higher risk involved for equity-holders in a company with debt. The formula is derived from the theory of weighted average cost of capital (WACC). It is to be noted that the theory is subject to many limitations.

Objective of the Study

The main objective of the research is to investigate whether capital structure (debt-equity ratio or degree of financial leverage) influences the value of the firm.

Research Methodology

1. Scope of the Study

- A random sample of 1 company, each from the following industries, viz., FMCG, Banking, IT, Aviation and Manufacturing will be selected.
- The financial leverage will be calculated for the past 5 years on the basis of which the value of the firm will be ascertained.

2. Type of Data

- Secondary data will be used.

3. Data Source

- Company websites and other published data.

Calculations

For the purpose of the study the following formulae have been used.

1. Financial Leverage = Operating Income / Net Income

   Operating Income = Earnings Before Interest and Taxes (EBIT)

   Net Income = Profit After Tax (PAT)
2. Degree of Financial Leverage (DFL) = % Change in EPS / % Change in EBIT

   EPS = Earning Per Share
3. Value of Firm = Total Equity + Total Debt

   Total Equity = Equity share capital + Reserves & Surplus

   Total Debt = Long term loan + Preference share capital

Let us calculate the above mentioned variables for different companies from different sectors <u>FMCG</u>

Dabur India Ltd. (Refer to Appendix I)

Calculation of Financial Leverage

(Rs. crore)

	Mar ' 10	*Mar ' 09*	*Mar ' 08*	*Mar ' 07*	*Mar ' 06*
Adjusted PBDIT	564.78	452.24	399.36	307.80	242.01
Depreciation	31.91	27.42	25.75	21.98	19.05
EBIT	532.87	424.82	373.61	285.82	222.96
Adjusted PBT	513.93	406.41	357.01	274.90	212.97
Tax charges	93.70	51.44	48.40	32.15	25.78
Adjusted PAT	420.23	354.97	308.61	242.76	187.19
Financial Leverage = EBIT/PAT	1.26	1.19	1.21	1.17	1.19
EPS	4.99	4.32	3.67	2.92	3.30

Calculation of Degree of Financial Leverage

	Mar '10	*Mar '09*	*Mar '08*	*Mar '07*	*Mar '06*
% Change in EPS (%)	15.50	17.71	25.68	-11.51	-
% Change in EBIT (%)	25.43	13.70	30.71	28.19	-
DFL= % Change in EPS / % Change in EBIT	0.60	1.29	0.83	-0.40	-

Calculation of Value of Firm

(Rs crore)

	Mar ' 10	*Mar ' 09*	*Mar ' 08*	*Mar ' 07*	*Mar ' 06*
Total Equity					
Equity share capital	86.76	86.51	86.40	86.29	57.33
Reserves & surplus	662.48	651.69	441.92	316.90	390.54
Total Debt					
Secured loans	24.27	8.26	16.45	19.28	19.23

Unsecured loans	81.80	130.72	0.24	0.26	1.25
Value of Firm = Total Equity + Total Debt	855.31	876.46	545.01	422.73	468.35

Aviation

Kingfisher Airlines Ltd. (Refer to Appendix II)

Calculation of Financial Leverage

(Rs crore)

	Mar ' 10	*Mar ' 09*	*Mar ' 08*	*Jun ' 07*	*Jun ' 06*
Adjusted PBDIT	321.80	41.24	-276.54	-232.42	-104.98
Depreciation	162.80	133.20	18.28	17.67	13.34
EBIT	159	-91.96	-250.70	-250.21	-118.32
Adjusted PBT	-2,141.08	-2,159.68	-747.57	-742.39	-387.99
Tax charges	-770.69	-546.38	-494.45	3.40	3.75
Adjusted PAT	-1,370.39	-1,613.30	-253.12	-745.79	-391.73
Financial Leverage = EBIT/PAT	-0.11	0.05	0.99	0.33	0.30
EPS	-61.95	-60.50	-13.85	-30.97	-34.69

Calculation of Degree of Financial Leverage

	Mar '10	*Mar '09*	*Mar '08*	*Mar '07*	*Mar '06*
% Change in EPS (%)	2.39	336.82	-55.27	-10.72	-
% Change in EBIT (%)	-272.90	-63.31	0.19	111.46	-
DFL= % Change in EPS / % Change in EBIT	-0.008	-5.32	-290.89	-0.09	-

Calculation of Value of Firm

(Rs crore)

	Mar ' 10	*Mar ' 09*	*Mar ' 08*	*Jun ' 07*	*Jun ' 06*
Total Equity					
Equity share capital	265.91	265.91	135.80	135.47	98.18
Reserves & surplus	-4,268.84	-2,496.36	52.99	249.23	125.95
Total Debt					
Secured loans	4,842.43	2,622.52	592.38	716.71	448.16
Unsecured loans	3,080.17	3,043.04	342.00	200.00	3.50
Preference share capital	97.00	97.00	-	-	-
Value of Firm = Total Equity + Total Debt	***4016.67***	***3532.11***	***1123.17***	***1301.41***	***675.79***

Banking

ICICI Bank Ltd. (Refer to Appendix III)

Calculation of Financial Leverage

(Rs crore)

	Mar ' 10	*Mar ' 09*	*Mar ' 08*	*Mar ' 07*	*Mar ' 06*
Adjusted PBDIT	5,857.66	5,738.55	5,772.43	4,102.73	3,735.96
Depreciation	619.50	678.60	578.35	544.78	623.79
EBIT	5238.16	5059.95	5194.08	3557.95	3112.17
Adjusted PBT	-12,354.42	-17,665.98	5,194.08	3,557.95	3,112.17
Tax charges	1,600.78	1,830.51	1,611.73	984.25	556.53
Adjusted PAT	3,890.47	3,740.62	4,092.12	2,995.00	2,532.95
Financial Leverage = EBIT/PAT	1.34	1.35	1.27	1.18	1.22
EPS	**36.10**	**33.76**	**37.37**	**34.58**	**28.55**

Calculation of Degree of Financial Leverage

	Mar '10	*Mar '09*	*Mar '08*	*Mar '07*	*Mar '06*
% Change in EPS (%)	6.93	-9.66	8.06	21.12	-
% Change in EBIT (%)	3.52	-2.58	45.98	14.32	-
DFL= % Change in EPS / % Change in EBIT	**1.96**	**3.74**	**0.17**	**1.47**	**-**

Calculation of Value of Firm

(Rs crore)

	Mar ' 10	*Mar ' 09*	*Mar ' 08*	*Mar ' 07*	*Mar ' 06*
Total Equity					
Equity share capital	1,114.89	1,113.29	1,112.68	899.34	889.83
Reserves & surplus	50,503.48	48,419.73	45,357.53	23,413.92	21,316.16
Total Debt					
Secured loans	-	-	-	-	-
Unsecured loans	2,02,016.60	2,18,347.82	2,44,431.05	2,30,510.19	1,65,083.17
Preference share capital	-	350.00	350.00	350.00	350.00
Value of Firm = Total Equity + Total Debt	***2,53,634.97***	***2,68,230.84***	***2,91,251.26***	***2,55,173.45***	***1,87,639.16***

Information Technology

Infosys Technologies Ltd. (Refer to Appendix IV)

Calculation of Financial Leverage

(Rs crore)

	Mar ' 10	*Mar ' 09*	*Mar ' 08*	*Mar ' 07*	*Mar ' 06*
Adjusted PBDIT	8,279.00	7,782.00	5,642.00	4,559.00	3,211.00
Depreciation	807.00	694.00	546.00	469.00	409.00
EBIT	7472.00	7088.00	5096.00	4090.00	2802.00
Adjusted PBT	7,472.00	7,086.00	5,095.00	4,089.00	2,801.00

Tax charges	1,717.00	895.00	630.00	352.00	303.00
Adjusted PAT	5,755.00	6,191.00	4,465.00	3,737.00	2,498.00
Financial Leverage					
= EBIT/PAT	1.29	1.14	1.14	1.09	1.12
EPS	**101.10**	**101.73**	**78.15**	**66.14**	**87.72**

Calculation of Degree of Financial Leverage

	Mar '10	*Mar '09*	*Mar '08*	*Mar '07*	*Mar '06*
% Change in EPS (%)	-0.61	30.17	18.15	-24.60	-
% Change in EBIT (%)	5.41	39.08	24.59	45.96	-
DFL= % Change in EPS / % Change in EBIT	-0.11	0.77	0.73	-0.53	-

Calculation of Value of Firm

(Rs crore)

	Mar ' 10	*Mar ' 09*	*Mar ' 08*	*Mar ' 07*	*Mar ' 06*
Total Equity					
Equity share capital	287.00	286.00	286.00	286.00	138.00
Reserves & surplus	21,749.00	17,523.00	13,204.00	10,876.00	6,759.00
Total Debt = 0					
Value of Firm = Total Equity + Total Debt	***22,036.00***	***17,809.00***	***13,490.00***	***11,162.00***	***6,897.00***

Manufacturing

Godrej Industries Ltd. (Refer to Appendix V)

Calculation of Financial Leverage

(Rs crore)

	Mar ' 10	*Mar ' 09*	*Mar ' 08*	*Mar ' 07*	*Mar ' 06*
Adjusted PBDIT	75.91	48.47	117.50	91.20	83.79
Depreciation	28.39	26.46	25.47	24.26	22.59
EBIT	47.52	22.01	92.03	66.94	61.20
Adjusted PBT	-12.90	-36.50	53.75	27.92	36.89
Tax charges	-0.80	-2.83	2.22	2.23	14.99
Adjusted PAT	-12.10	-33.67	51.53	25.69	21.90
Financial Leverage = EBIT/PAT	-3.9	-0.65	1.78	2.60	2.79
EPS	**2.55**	**0.60**	**3.57**	**2.67**	**2.44**

Calculation of Degree of Financial Leverage

	Mar '10	*Mar '09*	*Mar '08*	*Mar '07*	*Mar '06*
% Change in EPS (%)	325.00	-83.19	33.70	9.42	-
% Change in EBIT (%)	115.90	-76.08	37.48	9.37	-
DFL= % Change in EPS / % Change in EBIT	2.80	1.09	0.89	1.00	-

Calculation of Value of Firm

(Rs crore)

	Mar ' 10	*Mar ' 09*	*Mar ' 08*	*Mar ' 07*	*Mar ' 06*
Total Equity					
Equity share capital	31.76	31.98	31.98	29.19	29.19
Reserves & surplus	978.07	981.05	1,009.73	363.17	319.25
Total Debt					
Secured loans	204.19	232.82	249.48	330.92	249.11
Unsecured loans	343.42	368.14	186.19	136.77	78.03
Value of firm = Total Equity + Total Debt	*1,557.44*	*1,613.99*	*1,477.38*	*859.30*	*675.58*

Findings & Analysis

Company		*Mar '10*	*Mar '09*	*Mar '08*	*Mar '07*	*Mar '06*
Dabur India Ltd.	Financial Leverage	1.26	1.19	1.21	1.17	1.19
	Value (Rs.crore)	855.31	876.46	545.01	422.73	468.35
Kingfisher Airlines Ltd.	Financial Leverage	-0.11	0.05	0.99	0.33	0.30
	Value (Rs.crore)	4,016.67	3,532.11	1,123.17	1,301.41	675.79
ICICI Bank Ltd.	Financial Leverage	1.34	1.35	1.27	1.18	1.22
	Value (Rs.crore)	2,53,634.97	2,68,230.84	2,91,251.26	2,55,173.45	1,87,639
Infosys Technologies Ltd.	Financial Leverage	1.29	1.14	1.14	1.09	1.12
	Value (Rs.crore)	22,036.00	17,809.00	13,490.00	11,162.00	6,897.00
Godrej Industries Ltd.	Financial Leverage	-3.90	-0.65	1.78	2.60	2.79
	Value (Rs.crore)	1,557.44	1,613.99	1,477.38	859.30	675.58

The following conclusions can be drawn from the above analysis:

1. From the year 2006 to 2008, the value of Dabur India Ltd. moves with the financial leverage of the firm. For example, the financial leverage in 2007 drops to 1.17 from 1.19 in 2006. The value also drops from 468.35 in 2006 to 422.73 in 2007.
2. It can be said that the value if Dabur India Ltd. is dependent on the financial leverage except for the years 2009 and 2010.
3. For Kingfisher Airlines Ltd., there seems to be no correlation between the value of the firm and the financial leverage.
4. Similarly in case of ICICI bank Ltd., the financial leverage and value of the firm do not behave in the same manner, i.e. as the financial leverage increases, the value of the firm not necessarily increases and also not at the same rate.
5. Infosys has zero debt content. So it is hard to say that whether the value of the firm is affected by the financial leverage since the leverage arising out of fixed cost borrowings is missing in this case.
6. In case of Godrej, it can be again said that the value of the firm doesn't depend on the financial leverage.
7. Overall, it can be concluded from the above analysis of the companies taken into consideration, is that the **Value of the firm does not depend on the Financial Leverage.**

Limitation

1. Limited data. Whatever conclusion that has been drawn for the analysis is based on just 5 companies for a period of 5 years only.
2. It is hard to generalize the result for the whole industry on the basis of just 1 company randomly selected.
3. There is more than one method available for calculation purpose. For example, for calculating value of firm, there can be many ways. The answer might differ in case some other method is selected, in which case the conclusion of the analysis also might differ.

Despite the above limitations, the result of the above analysis can be supported by the argument given by Modigliani and Miller (MM) in the capital structure theory given by them. The MM model states that the total value of the firm is independent of the financing mix, i.e. the financial leverage.

Conclusion

Financial Leverage occurs when a firm's capital structure contains obligation with fixed financial charges. It is defined as the ability of a firm to use fixed charges to magnify the effects of changes in EBIT on the firm's EPS. As we have already seen, it occurs when a firm's capital structure contains obligation of fixed charges, such as, interest on debentures, dividend on preference shares etc., along with owner's equity to enhance total earnings of equity shareholders. Financial leverage also helps in designing the appropriate capital structure. The debate on capital structure has been pertinent for decades with plausible arguments both for and against increased levels of financial leverage. As presented by Modigliani and Miller, under a given set of assumptions, the capital structure and its composition has no effect on the value of the firm. However, financial leverage is a double edged sword. On the one hand it increases earning per share and on the other it increases financial increases. A high financial leverage means high fixed financial cost and high financial risk. Thus financial manager has to bring a balance between risk and return for determining the appropriate amount of debt in the capital structure of a firm.

Bibliography

1. Financial Management Theory, Concepts and Problems, R.P. Rustagi, 1999, Galgotia Publishing Company.
2. Financial leverage and firm value, Kuben Rayan, 2008, Gordon Institute of Business School.
3. Financial Management (A Planning And Control Approach), Dr. M.K. Rastogi, 2010, University Science Press.
4. http://en.wikipedia.org/wiki/Leverage_(finance).
5. http://www.investorwords.com/1952/financial_leverage.html.
6. http://en.wikipedia.org/wiki/Modigliani%E2%80%93Miller_theorem.
7. http://money.rediff.com/companies/dabur-india-ltd/12540103/balance-sheet.
8. http://money.rediff.com/companies/kingfisher-airlines-ltd/16600017/balance-sheet.
9. http://money.rediff.com/companies/icici-bank-ltd/14030056/balance-sheet.
10. http://money.rediff.com/companies/infosys-technologies-ltd/13020007/balance-sheet.
11. http://money.rediff.com/companies/godrej-industries-ltd/12520018/balance-sheet.

◈ ◈ ◈

ISBN – 978-93-5024-769-3

40

HR Competencies Required in Todays World

Mr. Yogesh Raut & Mr. Sachin Vyavhare
STES's Sinhgad School of Business Studies, Narhe, Pune – 41.

Business Context

In the world of business, familiar themes continually surface. Globalization has made the world a global village and new markets (particularly in China, India, Brazil, and Russia) offer new challenges and opportunities. Global issues like trade barriers, exchange rates, tariffs, and distribution become important elements of managerial choice. Technology has increased accessibility, visibility, and connection. The connected world is smaller, changing rapidly, and transparent. Customers have become increasingly segmented, literate, and demanding. Investors have become increasingly attuned to and actively concerned about not only financial results, but also intangibles. Competitors come from both traditional large global players and increasingly smaller inventors. Employees represent increasingly diverse demographic backgrounds. In some parts of the world, employees are aging more than in others. Employee expectations are constantly rising as they gain in education and skills. Most of these trends are outside the control of any one individual or any one company. They occur in both predictable and unpredictable ways. They affect all aspects of business from how to fund a firm to how to position the firm in customer minds and how to engineer and deliver products. They also affect human resources. HR practices are becoming more integrated, aligned, and innovative. HR departments are operating more like a business within the business with a clear strategy and channels of distribution. HR professionals are being asked to help businesses compete, and to do so, HR professionals must not only observe, but also understand and adapt to these business trends. HR professionals are expected to contribute by the competencies they possess. The functions of Human Resource Management vary from organization to organization both in nature and degree. So, the qualities required of an HR manager differ from organization to organization depending on its nature, size, location, etc. However, the qualities which will be applicable in general have been discussed in this study.

HR Competencies Overview

For HR professionals to respond to changing business conditions, they must demonstrate new competencies. HR professionals who would have been successful in previous decades would not be effective today. We have worked for the last 20 years to identify the competencies that enable HR professionals to respond to the business conditions. HR competencies are the values, knowledge, and abilities of HR professionals. HR professionals with the right competencies will perform better. They will be more likely to engage employees, to serve customers, and to create intangible shareholder wealth. HR competencies define what is expected from those who work in HR and form the basis for assessment and improvement in the quality of HR professionals.

We recommend an HR competency framework in this study, which is structured into the following building blocks:

- Personal Attributes;
- Leadership and Management Competencies;
- HR Core Competencies; and
- Role-Specific HR Competencies

Each of the four building blocks represents success factors that are responses to different sets of environmental requirements for HR professionals.

This framework is modular in design so that it can serve as a flexible engine to drive excellent performance. The competencies are arranged in building blocks or clusters that can be grouped into profiles necessary for a specific individuals current position, as well as future positions in an individuals potential career path. Each person can select competencies according to individual, functional, and organizational needs. This approach enables individuals and organizations to create a variety of robust models quickly.

1. Personal Attributes

Our interaction with mangers from industry has revealed that every contemporary organization, more than ever, needs honest, committed employees who can continuously learn and adapt to change. These basic, but critical, requirements translate into a set of **Personal Attributes** encompassing four competency areas (see Figure 1 below).

Challenge	*Personal Attributes, Competencies and Definitions*
• Producing a valuable product and/or service	• **Results Orientation**: Maintains focus on those activities that have the greatest impact on meeting work commitments
• Energetically supporting the organizations vision and strategy according to the highest standards.	• **Commitment**: Demonstrates initiative and personal accountability to meet work demands
• Taking personal responsibility to grow and change	• **Continuous Learning**: Proactively seeks performance feedback and identifies approaches to improve own and others performance and learning.
• Exhibiting highest day-to-day work standards	• **Honesty and Integrity**: Demonstrates the highest level of business ethics and consistently adheres to and promotes key values and principles in all business and personal transactions.

Fig. 1

2. Leadership and Management Competencies

Our research indicates that leadership and management excellence depends on adaptive behavioral responses to the shifting focus, scope, scale and complexity of organizational demands. Excellent performers apply competencies according to various dimensions, such as:

- Strategic vs. tactical needs
- Person vs. task demands
- Demands related to opening vs. closing system boundaries
- Efforts related to initiating vs. completing processes.

Developing individuals who can both master individual competencies and apply them situationally are critical success factors.

The diverse needs of organizations can be encompassed in eight universal processes, defining key types of interventions that occur at different levels. Half of these processes focus primarily on motivating, energizing and leading people; half focus on managing operational or task issues.

In addition, some of these universal processes are more strategic in nature and are more predominant requirements for mid-level managers and executives. Others are more tactical in nature and are more often the primary responsibility of frontline supervisors, team leaders and individual contributors. To articulate how excellent performers behave situationally to support these processes and various leadership dimensions, we have translated them into eight Leadership and Management Competencies (see Figure 2 below).

Organization Level	*Strategic vs .Tactical Dimension*	*Behavioral Focus*	*Leadership and Management Processes*	*Leadership and Management Competencies & Definitions*
Whole Organization	Strategic ↑	Person ↑	Creating a Compelling	**Visioning and Alignment**: Creates and communicates a Vision for Change vision of the organization that inspires and aligns the workforce.
		Task ↓	Developing a Competitive Strategy	**Strategic Thinking**: Actively pursues strategies and high potential opportunities for the benefit of the organization
Operations		Person ↑	Generating an Integrated Network	**Networking**: Creates and diverse range of key relationships to leverages a improve access to resources and expertise
		Task ↓	Mobilizing and Leveraging Resources	**Resource Management**: Identifies, mobilizes and tracks resources to fulfill key objectives and plans.
Group	Tactical ↓	Person ↑	Building Motivated Teams	**Teamwork**: Develops collaborative work groups that maintain focus on a monopurpose and leverage the unique talents of its members.
		Task ↓	Defining and Implementing Core Processes	**Process Excellence**: Continuously improves processes and work products.
Individual		Person	Maximizing	**Performance Development**:

		Individual Performance	Consistently coaches and develops team members to maximize performance
	Task	Reaching Critical Goals	**Goal Setting**: Develops and tracks challenging goals aligned with organization strategies

Fig. 2

3. HR Core Competencies

While the Personal Attributes and Leadership and Management Competencies presented above can apply equally for all functions, a distinct set of emerging challenges driving the current business climate represent factors that require each function to contribute uniquely to an organizations success.[1]

For the HR function, this means mastering an array of new capabilities, each requiring many new behavioral requirements (see Figure no. -3 below for key challenges, HR impact and related Core HR Competencies).

Challenges	*HR Impact*	*Core HR Competencies and Definitions*
Leveraging Talent	• Increased focus on employee value proposition. • Greater emphasis on maximizing the impact of human assets	**Talent Management**: Generates consistent a approaches across the enterprise for hiring, selecting, retaining, valuing and leveraging key talent
Streamlining and Automating Key Activities	• Re-engineering processes· • Work re-design Shift to HR self-service models	**Technology Expertise**: Helps to identify technology needs and mobilize technologies that provide easy access to HR services and methods for enhancing learning and personal productivity.
	• Making appropriate make vs. buy decisions	**Vendor Management**: Selects and manages vendors in a manner that maximizes benefit to the organization
Access to Information and Expertise	• Identification and leveraging of soft assets· • Developing and leveraging expert networks • Providing online access of key information to everyone	**Knowledge Management**: Demonstrates a conceptual and practical understanding of approaches and tools to help organization groups, units (team, functions, divisions, regions, subsidiaries) capture, share and exploit knowledge to support achieving objectives).
The Virtual Workplace	• Move toward more global organizations· • More cross-team collaboration • Better use of networks	**Virtual Teamwork**: Develops and implements strategies for maximizing the collaboration of non co-located work groups.

	• Creation of communities of practice	
Focus on Metrics	Focus on streamlining processes • More focus on measuring the business impact of people interventions	**Assessment and Measurement Skills** Demonstrates the ability to determine key needs, diagnose and address problems, identify key metrics, and accurately monitor progress of important initiatives and activities.
Making People Feel Safe and Empowered	More focus on leveraging diversity· • Improved HR services • More emphasis on creating a supportive organization culture and practice	**Employee Advocacy**: Maintains focus on supporting a fair and empowering work environment for all employees
Ethical Practices	Facilitating the design of ethical practices and policies • Providing guidance to business leaders about what is right for the business, employees and the community employees	**Stewardship**: Provides advice and support for values, practices and policies that sustain ethical and legal business practices. **Compliance**: Applies an understanding of key legal precedents, policies, and practices to protect the interests of the organization and individual
Demanding Customers	• Increased focus on customer responsiveness • Taking the lead in organizational quality/ process customer interventions that produce customer value	**Customer Focus**: Responds to customers needs in a manner that provides added value and generates significant customer satisfaction
Focus on Core Capabilities	• More focus on strategy, structure, and alignment • More emphasis on process capabilities· • Greater emphasis on best practices and bench marking.	**Coaching and Consulting**: Provides appropriate advice, feedback and development resources to improve the effectiveness of individuals and teams.

Fig. 3

HR Role-specific Competencies

As new challenges drive existing HR sub-specialties to adapt and new HR specialties to emerge, HR departments have responded in various ways to meet new behavioral demands. For smaller organizations, strategist, generalist, and specialist roles are often collapsed. Even in larger organizations, there is no universal agreement about the best way to organize work into specific sub-functions. For example, some businesses combine compensation and benefit activities into one group, while others keep these activities distinctly separate. In many organizations, HR Generalists are the primary driver of organization design and effectiveness initiatives, while in others these efforts are organized into specialized consulting groups. In some enterprises, talent management is defined as a distinct overarching set of activities encompassed in a single sub-function, while in others; separate groups may be responsible for recruitment, staffing, career planning, and succession planning. For the most part, HR Generalists still provide coaching, consulting, as well as access to HR products and services to business partners. However, they are also increasingly asked to lead special projects related to strategy, structure, process, and workforce change initiatives.

HR Strategists are challenged with new requirements too. In particular, business leaders are demanding more rigor from HR in the form of human assets management strategies encompassed through:

- improved ROI of HR interventions and programs,
- improved methods for leveraging people, resources, and
- better metrics to measure, track, and continuously improve the use of human resources.

To capture what makes the HR professionals who interface most directly with different organization clients successful in their specialized roles, we have outlined distinguishing competencies for the HR Strategist, HR Generalist, and HR Specialist roles. The key HR Strategist and HR Generalist competencies stemming from our study are outlined below:

(a) Distinguishing HR Strategist Competencies and Definitions

Business Acumen: Focuses activities and decisions on opportunities that produce significant, strategic business impact.

Strategic Influence: Collaborates with others to build buy-in and support for critical initiatives.

Change Management: Consistently applies change best practices to ensure impact of key programs

(b) Distinguishing HR Generalist Competencies and Definitions

Organization Design, Development and Effectiveness: Performs work and process redesign to improve individual, team and organizational effectiveness.

Relationship Management: Develops positive relationships by demonstrating respect for others perspectives and attention to their needs

Project and Product Management: Plans and implements projects, programs, and product development efforts.

Based on our analysis of top performing organizations, behaviors for all HR Specialist roles can be encompassed in a common set of competencies related to a 4-step process for developing and implementing excellent sub-functional products and services as shown below:

Distinguishing HR Specialist Competencies and Definitions

- **Step 1: Strategy Development**: Develops and leverages perspectives and insights into HR product and service principles and strategies aligned with business strategies.
- **Step 2: Situation Analysis**: Accurately assesses key customer needs related to product/service area.
- **Step 3: Program Design**: Translates data and insights into practical, high-impact program elements, goals, and tasks.
- **Step 4: Product and Service Delivery**: Develops and delivers products and services related to specialty area that produce maximal customer impact and satisfaction.

Our research strongly indicate that organizations most successful at implementing competencies devote the majority of their resources toward aligning competency standards with strategy and integrating them into day-to-day practices[3] The key mistake many HR departments make is to focus too much effort on perfecting rather than institutionalizing the standards. In contrast, best performing HR groups employ change management best practices to ensure new behavioral requirements are accepted and leveraged over time to benefit each professional and the function as a whole.[3] (see below for sample change practices to support competency implementation).[2]

Competency Implementation Best Practices

Model Building

- Ensure linkage between competencies and organization strategies
- Keep models simple at launch, and leverage tools and databases to jump start model building
- Review models frequently to ensure relevancy, add dimensional criteria and keep the momentum

Applications

- Focus on assessment and development applications first, then evaluation and pay applications
- Focus on integration of the competencies with all HR processes
- Improve consistency of applications rather than allowing too many variations
- Automate the processes and tools to minimize paperwork and enable end-users to have ongoing access

Change Management

- Clarify and communicate specific objectives of your applications up front
- Ensure top management and line management buy-in and ongoing support
- Involve managers and employees more deeply in competency development early in the process
- Be focused in implementation (i.e., one function, one pilot group first)
- Provide training and communication more consistently and carefully (building in training at all stages of implementation)
- Develop and consistently apply a measurement system used to evaluate the effectiveness of implementation over time

Conclusion

This study has focused primarily on critical HR competencies required in todays organizational Settings. We have developed a HR competency framework consisting of four blocks and each block represents success factors that are responses to different sets of environmental requirements for HR professionals.

References

1. Marcus Buckingham, Richard M. Vosburgh," The 21st century Human Resources function: It's the Talent, stupid! Identifying and developing Talent, one person at a Time, Becomes our Defining Challenge," Human Resource Palnning, Vol. 24, 2001.
2. Dr. Stephen C. Schoonover,et.al,"Competency-Based HR Applications: Results of a comprehensive survey." Society for Human Resource Management and Arthur Andersen, 2000.
3. Gregory C. Kesler, Julia A. Law," Implementing Major Change In the HR Organization: The Lessons of Five companies", Human resource Planning, Vol. 20, 1997.
4. Dave Ulrich *et al,* "Human Resource Competencies: Responding to increased Expectations".

◈◈◈

ISBN – 978-93-5024-769-3

41 "HR-Competencies-key to Become Successful in the Changing Scenario"

Prof. Mrs. Sushma Kotgiri, Prof. Mrs. Savita Uppalli & Prof. Aesha Aleem
Sinhgad Institute of Business Management, Kamlapur, Sangola.

Introduction

"In the 1990s managers will be judged on their ability to identify, cultivate, and exploit the core competencies that make growth possible - indeed, they'll have to rethink the concept of the corporation it self." (C K Prahalad and G Hamel 1990) This was the main idea about Core Competencies which where developed by C K Prahalad and G Hamel the founder and inceptors of this concept, through a series of articles in the Harvard Business Review. Epsolon's Core Competency is service based with deep proficiency that enables your company to deliver unique value to our customers. It embodies your organization's collective learning, particularly of how to coordinate diverse skills and integrate multiple technologies, this creates sustainable competitive advantage for your company and helps it branch into a wide variety of related markets. Core competency is a specific factor that a business sees as being central to the way it, or its employees, works. It fulfills two key criteria:

- It is not easy for competitors to imitate.
- It can be leveraged widely to many products and markets.

A core competency can take various forms, including technical/subject matter know-how, a reliable process and/or close relationships with customers and suppliers. It may also include product development or culture, such as employee dedication.

Core competencies are particular strengths relative to other organizations in the industry which provide the fundamental basis for the provision of added value. Core competencies are the collective learning in organizations, and involve how to coordinate diverse production skills and integrate multiple streams of technologies. It is communication, an involvement and a deep commitment to working across organizational boundaries. Few companies are likely to build world leadership in more than five or six fundamental competencies.

Literature Review

Competency is-

(a) The quality of being adequately or well qualified physically and intellectually.

(b) An observable, measurable pattern of skills, knowledge, abilities, behaviours, and other characteristics that an individual needs to perform work roles or occupational functions successfully.

Every job has set of competencies. Recruitment of employees should be competency based. While measuring performance of employees, organisation should measure level of competencies as well. Internal placement of employees is based on competencies. Passion is an emotion of feeling very strongly about a person. Passion is an intense emotion compelling feeling, enthusiasm or desire for anything. Passion often applies to lively or eager interest in or admiration for proposal, cause, or activity or love. The dictionary meaning of passion is boundless enthusiasm. (If competencies are compared as locomotive of your career then passion is its fuel. The speed of the locomotive is linked to the amount of fuel you pour in the engine. While competencies can be taught, passion cannot be taught.) Outstanding persons have shown passion in work. While job competencies get success in career, passion gives outstanding achievement in life. Sachin Tendulkar, Amitabh Bacchan and Dr APJ Abdul Kalam could acquire outstanding success in their respective field because of their passion.[2]

Objectives

1. To study the successful professionals in different fields.
2. To know the essential competencies to become successful HR professionals.

Research Methodology

Data Collection Source	Primary and Secondary
Primary Data	Questionnaire
Secondary Data:-	Annual reports published and forwarded to Shareholders, Websites of different industries, Newspapers, opinions of customers and students.
Sampling Technique	Random Sampling
Sampling Size	110 samples
Sampling Tool	Structured Questionnaire
Research Design	Descriptive

Scope of the Study

Researcher found wide scope to study on Competencies which is an effective key to become successful in the competitive World where knowledge and talent are the assets for both companies and employees. In each and every field men is the important element of management and production without which all plans are useless and if companies get employees who have talent in the form of competencies it will definitely turns into success to obtain countable profits.

Limitation of the Study

1. Time is the most important constraints for researcher because it is very tough for researcher to collect primary data on national level in geographically wide area like India.
2. Researcher has to rely on the primary and secondary data for findings and conclusion of the study.
3. Study is limited to Pandharpur taluka in Solapur district.

Analysis and Findings

For the study, researcher took help of different well known personalities within the country and outside the country that is national and international personalities like Barrack Obama, Mahendra Singh Dhoni, Narayan

[2] *http://www.citehr.com/142025-passion-competency.html#ixzz17Q8evWrl*

Murty, and Vishwnath Anand. Considering these personalities questions were asked to respondents and tried to find out that what are the qualities and competencies these personalities have within themselves which make them successful in their life.

Now we will focus on the above mentioned personalities-

1. Barrack Obama, President of the United States
2. Mahendra Singh Dhoni, Captain Indian Cricket team
3. Narayan Murty, founder president Infosys
4. Vishwnath Anand, Grandslam master

Total 110 respondents were selected to collect the information about competencies and other required skills. All respondents were educated, above 35 years of age, working in well reputed industries and good knowledgeable person.

Following information exerted from them and tried to present it in the following manner.

TABLE 1 – Details which shows the views of different people which were taken by the researcher.

Sr.no.	Factors	Strongly agree	Agree	Neither agree nor disargee	Disagree	Strongly disagree
1	Men (employees)are one of the important elements of management	110	0	0	0	0
		100%	-	-	-	-
2	These are well-known personalities and you know them very well.	87	12	0	3	8
		79%	10%	-	3%	8%
3	Scarcity of talented employees in present days	105	0	5	0	0
		95%	-	5%	-	-
4	Every employer is always in search of talented, knowledgeable and competent employees	110	0	0	0	0
		100%	-	-	-	-
5	Today we are living in the knowledge age.	5	48	5	47	5
		4%	44%	4.5%	43%	4.5%
6	Human talent is an asset for institute or organization	0	57	8	45	0
		-	52%	7%	41%	-
7	Competency mapping is the part of knowledge management	110	0	0	0	0
		100%	-	-	-	-
8	Competency and talent are closely related and important elements of knowledge management	0	110	0	0	0
		100%				

9	Competency is an ability for an individual to perform a job properly.	47	51	5	7	0
		43%	46%	04%	07%	-
10	Competencies include *Decision* Making, Influence, Stress Tolerance and	52	28	2	13	15
	Teamwork	48%	25%	1%	12%	14%
11	Competencies are (Plz tick the alternates)	110				
	Knowledge	45				
	Skills		40			
	Behaviors			15		
	Personal attributes				10	
		41%	36%	14%	9%	-
12	These competencies are playing an important role in the organizational and personal development	0	110	0	0	0
		-	100%	-	-	-
13	Human talent that is competency is easily available according to the need of institute	7	48		55	
		6%	44%	-	50%	-
14	If human talent is handled properly, it will increase the individual as well as institutional value	11	43	4	52	0
		10%	39%	4%	47%	-
15	Human resource management is playing an important role for the institute and organization in increasing the value.	0	110	0	0	0
		-	100%	-	-	-
16	In today's competitive edge knowledge management is a remedy for certain difficulties like loyalty, social branding and recruitment and selection process.	9	45	4	52	
		8%	40%	4%	48%	-
17	Knowledge management helps the institutes to build competencies	0	98	10	0	2
		—	89%	9%	-	2%

The table no.1 explains the following facts-

1. The above table shows that men are one of the important elements of management. All the 110 respondents have the positive opinion about the statement.
2. The point two itself explains that all are the well known personalities in their respected field and definitely leadership qualities they have within themselves and they are using it to the maximum level.
3. The statement three explains that there is the scarcities of talented employees in present days.105 respondents are strongly agree with this statement whereas 5 respondents do not want to answer it.

Every employer is always in search of talented, knowledgeable and competent employees, definitely all answers were positive with 100 percent favor.

4. All 100% respondents are agree that every employer is always in search of talented, knowledgeable and competent employees.
5. When the question about present age was asked following responses were found like 5 respondents were strongly agreed, 48 respondents were agree, 5 respondents were not agree and not disagree, 47 respondents were disagree and 5 respondents were disagree. Very surprising responses were got.
6. For knowing the importance of human talent question is asked and 57 respondents were agree with the statement that Human talent is an asset for institute or organization.

7& 8. All positive responses as far as Competency mapping is the part of knowledge management and Competency and talent are closely related one to another.

9. Out of 110 respondents 47 respondents are strongly agree with the statement Competency is an ability for an individual to perform a job properly. 51 are agree, 5 are not for and against and 7 are disagree with the same.
10. When the question arises as competencies include decision making, Influence, Stress Tolerance and Teamwork there was lot of opinions and differences in that opinion like 52 respondents are strongly agree with the statement, 28 are agree while 2 took a stand not to speak on it, 13 were disagree and 15 were strongly disagree.
11. To know the answer of what are the required competencies like knowledge, Skills, Behavior and Personal Attributes we received different answers from each individual like some respondents focused on knowledge, some on skills. But majority was of the opinion that knowledge based skills are more important to consider it as competencies.
12. All 100 percent respondents were of the opinion that these competencies are playing important role in the organisational and personal development.
13. Here mixed opinion got about the availibility of human talent. Some respondents are of the opinion that human talent is easily available according to the need of institute. But major respondents were of the opinion that human talent is not available according to the requirement.
14. When the question arises about handling of human talent, 11 respondents were strongly agree, 43 respondents were agree, 4 were neither agree nor disagree and 52 were disagree on the statement.
15. It is true that all credit goes to the manpower where it is the key element who manage all the things and not only work should be done but also to work in a team as we have to contribute at our level.
16. No doubt today each and every one has to face the competition. It is very difficult to retain talent or build loyalty and honesty. But it is also possible with the help of human resource management. The opinions on this particular point are as 9 respondents are strongly agree, 45 are agree, 4 are neutral and 52 are disagree on above statement.
17. Maximum respondents agree that definitely knowledge management helps institutes to build competencies. Employes are the key factor for the success of any organisation, institute or personality itself.

Conclusion

At last we can conclude that competencies are playing an important role in the success of organisation or institution or as a individual personality. Whether you are individual person and want to get the things in your life or as a politician want to shape your objectives as a leader and contribute maximum to your country or any other person. It is also true that each and every person have certain qualities within himself which will definitely boost him up and whole world will be under his feet.

At last to conclude, competencies are essential to achieve the targeted goals in the life.

References

1. Gregory C. Kesler, Julia A. Law, "Implementing Major Change In the HR Organization: The Lessons of Five companies", Human Resource Planning, Vol. 20, 1997.
2. Dave Ulrich, et al, "Human Resource Competencies: Responding to Increased Expectations".
3. http://www.citehr.com/142025-passion-competency.html#ixzz17Q8evWrI.

◈◈◈

ISBN – 978-93-5024-769-3

42 A Case Study on Competency and Efficiency of HRM in the Acquisition of TC Springs by Mubea Suspension India Ltd.

Prof. Vidya Bhandwalkar, Prof. Kamala Kumari, Prof. Ketaki Phatak & Prof. Shreekala P. Bachhav
Sinhgad Management School, Kondhapuri, Shirur, Pune.

Introduction

Mergers, Acquisition and corporate restructuring are a big part of the corporate finance world. Every day, Wall Street investment bankers arrange M & A transactions, which bring separate companies together to form larger ones. When they're not creating big companies from smaller ones, corporate finance deals do the reverse and break up companies through spinoffs, carve-outs or tracking stocks

The Main Idea

One plus one makes three: This equation is the special alchemy of a merger or an acquisition. The key principle behind buying a company is to create shareholder value over and above that of the sum of the two companies. Two companies together are more valuable than two separate companies - atleast, that's the reasoning behind Mergers and Acquisition..

This rationale is particularly alluring to companies when times are tough. Strong companies will act to buy other companies to create a more competitive, cost-efficient company. The companies will come together hoping to gain a greater market share or to achieve greater efficiency. Because of these potential benefits, target companies will often agree to be purchased when they know they cannot survive alone.

When one company takes over another and clearly established itself as the new owner, the purchase is called an acquisition. From a legal point of view, the target company ceases to exist, the buyer "swallows" the business and the buyer's stock continues to be traded.

In practice, however, actual mergers of equals don't happen very often. Usually, one company will buy another and, as part of the deal's terms, simply allow the acquired firm to proclaim that the action is a merger of equals, even if it's technically an acquisition. Being bought out often carries negative connotations, therefore, by describing the deal as a merger, deal makers and top managers try to make the takeover more palatable.

A purchase deal will also be called a merger when both CEOs agree that joining together is in the best interest of both of their companies. But when the deal is unfriendly - that is, when the target company does not want to be purchased - it is always regarded as an acquisition.

Since mergers and acquisitions are investments taken under conditions of uncertainty, it is not surprising that not all business combinations are successful. Past studies show that successful firms that combine businesses can benefit from economies of scale or economies of scope, whereas diversification for other reasons tends to be successful.

Acquisitions

As you can see, an acquisition may be only slightly different from a merger. In fact, it may be different in name only. Like mergers, acquisitions are actions through which companies seek economies of scale, efficiencies and enhanced market visibility. Unlike all mergers, all acquisitions involve one firm purchasing another - there is no exchange of stock or consolidation as a new company. Acquisitions are often congenial, and all parties feel satisfied with the deal. Other times, acquisitions are more hostile.

In an acquisition, as in some of the merger deals we discuss above, a company can buy another company with cash, stock or a combination of the two. Another possibility, which is common in smaller deals, is for one company to acquire all the assets of another company. Company X buys all of Company Y's assets for cash, which means that Company Y will have only cash (and debt, if they had debt before). Of course, Company Y becomes merely a shell and will eventually liquidate or enter another area of business.

Another type of acquisition is a reverse merger, a deal that enables a private company to get publicly-listed in a relatively short time period. A reverse merger occurs when a private company that has strong prospects and is eager to raise financing buys a publicly-listed shell company, usually one with no business and limited assets. The private company reverse merges into the public company, and together they become an entirely new public corporation with tradable shares.

Regardless of their category or structure, all mergers and acquisitions have one common goal: they are all meant to create synergy that makes the value of the combined companies greater than the sum of the two parts. The success of a merger or acquisition depends on whether this synergy is achieved.

There are many factors that, in combination, explain the success or failure of acquisitions, such as: selectivity or the ability to identify targets where potential synergistic gains are maximized, acquires' skill and ability realized or even exceed expected post-merger gains.

Steps taken in the Process of Acquisition:

- Start with an Offer
- The Target's Response
- Accept the Terms of the Offer
- Attempt to Negotiate
- Execute a Poison Pill or Some Other Hostile Takeover Defence
- Find a White Knight
- Closing the Deal

Company Profile

Reasons for acquisition of the company TC Springs was a Automotive Company, under TACO Group. Specialized in hot coiling. As per the history of the company it was moving in the continuous loss and doesn't grow in last 10 years.

Mubea is a multinational Company having branches all over the world. Specialized in Cold Coiling. Company wanted to spread their Business in India to co-up with Growing Business in India. So the company acquired TC springs on 12 Jan 2010 for establishing their business in India and to compete with the competitors.

Manpower of the company was 209 before the acquisition, and after the acquisition the manpower has reduced to 187. The employees were downsized because of the technological changes introduced by the new company.

Changes Made by New Management

(a) Company set up has been changed by the new Management & Hot coiling plant has been replaced by the cold coiling plant .In the beginning the old TACO policies were in use, but now all the new policies for Mubea Suspension India Ltd. has been prepared by the HR Team & been implemented. Many HR motivational practices has been started & implemented.

(b) New policies has been introduce and implemented by HR department for the improvement and development of the organization.

Role of HRM in the Acquisition

- Development of preliminary organizational designs and identification of the top three levels of management.
- Assessment of critical players and deployment of appropriate resources in the new company.
- Retention of key people and separation of redundant staff.
- Development of a total rewards strategy for the workers.
- Provide appropriate training to workers for improvising the efficiency.
- Standardisation of welfare facilities.
- Communications strategy development and implementation
- Integration of payroll benefits and HR-IS.
- An ability to do all of the above with speed.

Objectives of the Study

- To know the reason for acquisition.
- To study the effect of acquisition of TC spring by Mubea Suspension India Limited on the employees.
- To study the role of the HR manager in making the acquisition successful.

Hypothesis of The Study

"Acquisition of TC spring by Mubea Suspension India Limited is successful."

Research Methodology

Type of Study	Descriptive
Nature of study	Qualitative
Type of questions	Open ended and Close ended
Type of analysis	Statistical

Sample size: 30 Workers and 10 Managers

Sampling method Random method (Personal Schedule)

Sampling source: Mubea Suspension India Limited Ltd, (Formerly TC Spring)

Sources of Information

Primary data:

Primary data for the project was obtained from Workers and manager.

Secondary data:

Secondary data was collected from different websites, manual and documentation of the company.

Methods Used For Collecting Primary Data

(a) Questionnaire

In this study we have used questionnaire method for collecting necessary information. The questionnaire is consisting of both closed ended and open ended questions

(b) Informal discussion

We also made an Informal discussion with the workers and managers to find out the various problems faced by them after acquisition and their reaction about the acquisition.

Limitations

- The time for study was limited.
- The response of the workers could be duplicate.

Analysis and Findings

Question to Workers

(1) Are you satisfied with the acquisition?

Sr. No	*Options*	*Response*	*Response in %*
1	Yes	22	73%
2	No	8	27%
Total		30	100%

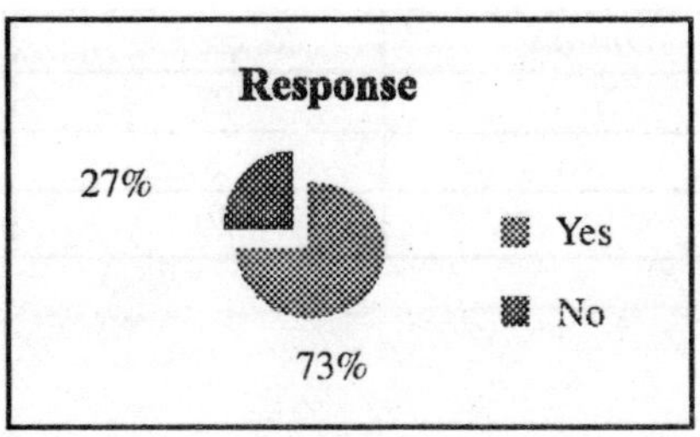

According to the above pie chart maximum of the 73% workers said that they are satisfied with the acquisition.

(2) Do you feel that the new HR management is supportive?

Sr.No	*Options*	*Response*	*Response in %*
1	Yes	25	83%
2	No	5	17%
Total		30	100%

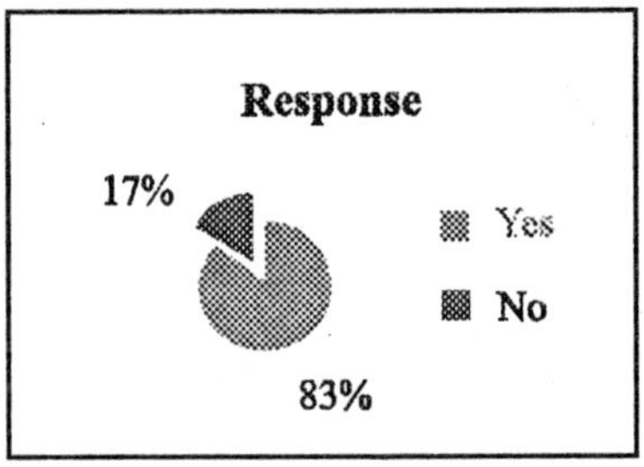

According to the above pie chart maximum of the 83% workers feel that the new HR management is supportive.

(3) Have you faced any problem in working with the new HR department?

Sr.No	*Options*	*Response*	*Response in %*
1	Yes	9	30%
2	No	21	70%
Total		30	100%

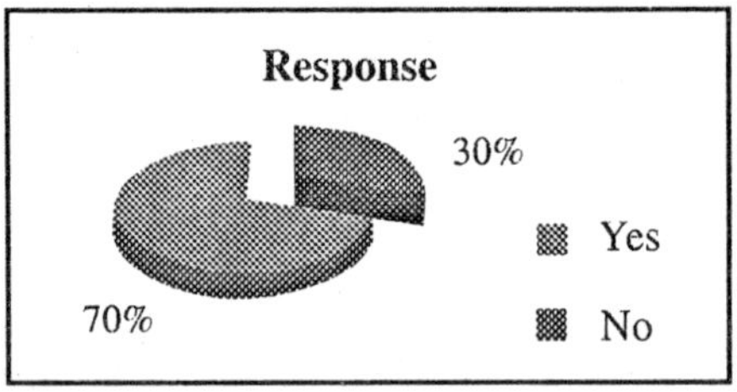

According to the above pie chart maximum of the 70% workers faced problem in working with the new HR department.

(4) Do you feel that the new policies introduce by new HRM are better than the older one?

Sr.No	*Options*	*Response*	*Response in %*
1	Yes	27	90%
2	No	3	10%
Total		30	100%

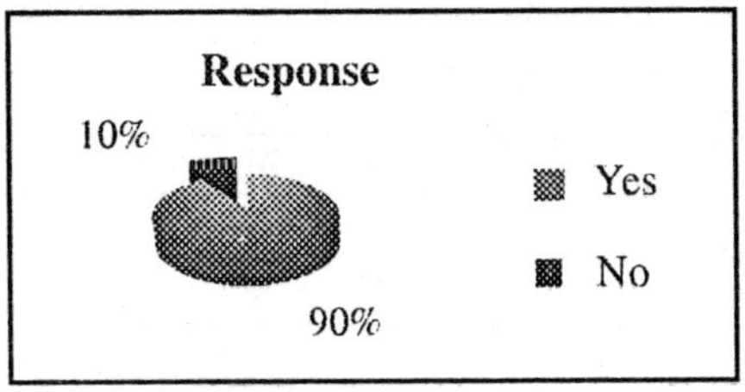

According to the above pie chart maximum of the 90% workers feel that the new policies introduce by new HRM are better than the older one.

(5) Are you satisfied with your new compensation?

Sr.No	*Options*	*Response*	*Response in %*
1	Yes	19	63%
2	No	11	37%
Total		30	100%

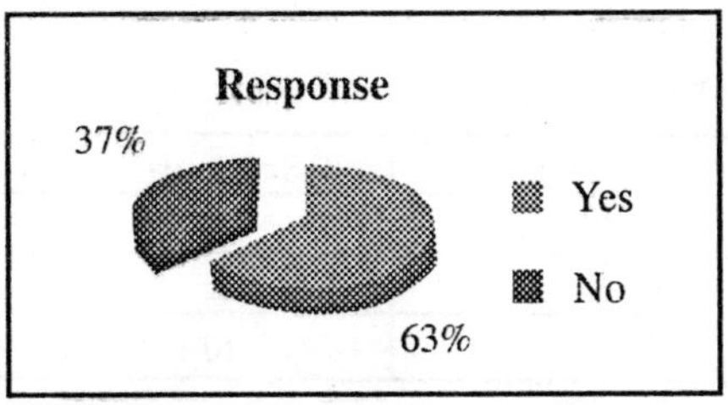

According to the above pie chart maximum of the 63% workers are satisfied with their new compensation.

(6) Do you have healthy relationship with the management?

Sr.No	*Options*	*Response*	*Response in %*
1	Yes	26	87%
2	No	4	13%
Total		30	100%

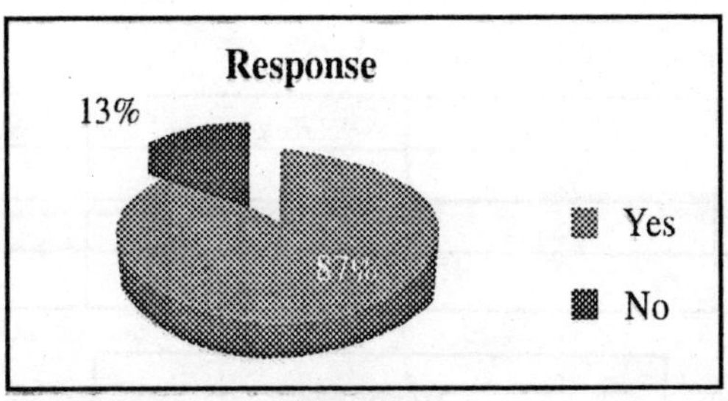

According to the above pie chart maximum of the 87% workers have healthy relationship with the management.

(7) Do you feel that the management is effective in solving your problem?

Sr.No	Options	Response	Response in %
1	Yes	24	80%
2	No	6	20%
Total		30	100%

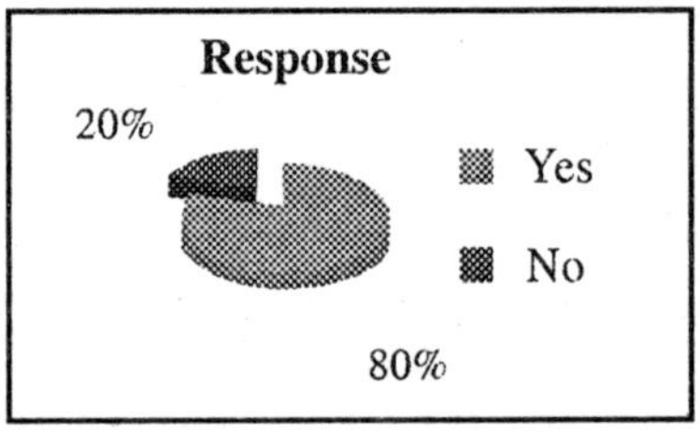

According to the above pie chart maximum of the 87% workers feel that the management is effective in solving your problem.

Question to Management

(1) Do you feel that changes were for good?

Sr.No	Options	Response	Response in %
1	Yes	8	80%
2	No	2	20%
Total		10	100%

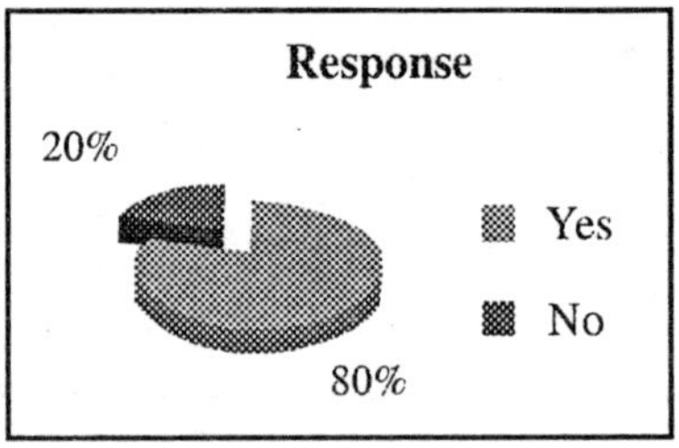

According to the above pie chart maximum of the 80% management feel that changes were for good.

(2) Have you found any opposition from the workers?

Sr.No	Options	Response	Response in %
1	Yes	7	70%
2	No	3	30%
Total		10	100%

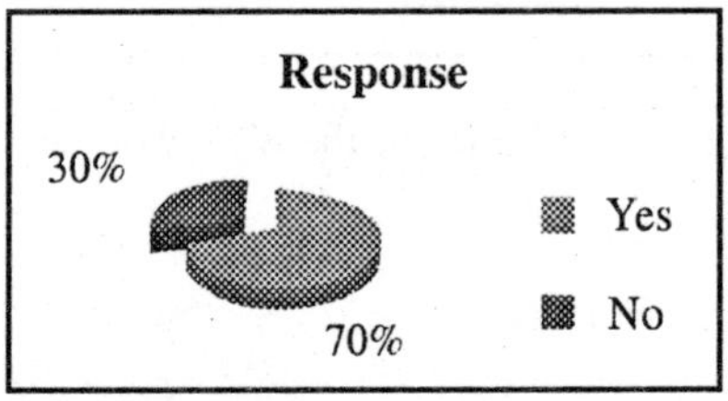

According to the above pie chart maximum of the 70% management found opposition from the workers.

(3) Have you been able to handle the opposition from the workers efficiently?

Sr.No	Options	Response	Response in %
1	Yes	9	90%
2	No	1	10%
Total		10	100%

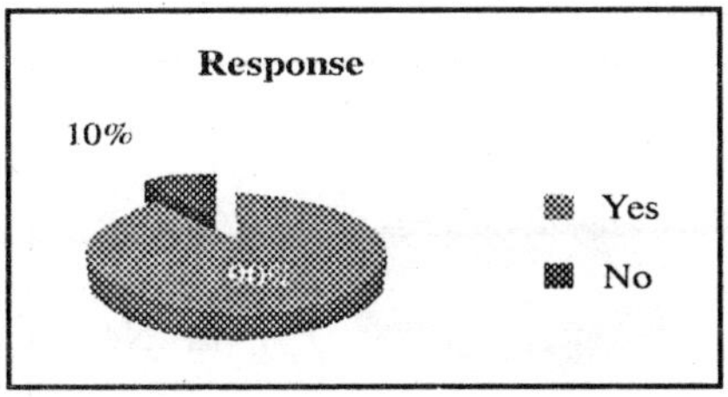

According to the above pie chart maximum of the 90% management able to handle the opposition from the workers efficiently.

(4) Do you have healthy relationship with the workers?

Sr.No	Options	Response	Response in %
1	Yes	4	40%
2	No	6	60%
Total		10	100%

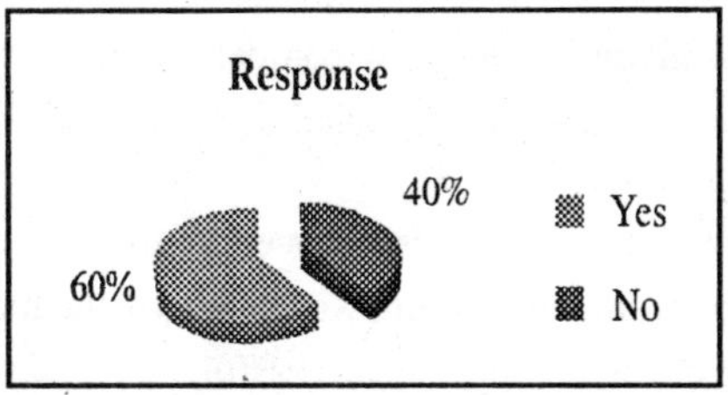

According to the above pie chart maximum of the 60% management don't have healthy relationship with the workers.

(5) Do you feel that you have succeeded in convincing the workers to support the organization?

Sr.No	Options	Response	Response in %
1	Yes	9	90%
2	No	1	10%
Total		10	100%

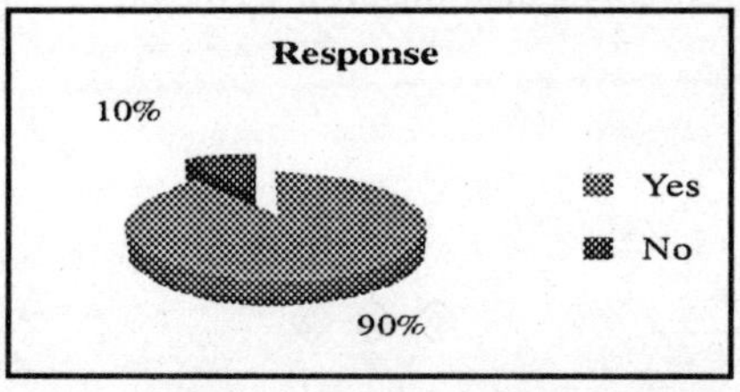

According to the above pie chart maximum of the 90% management feel that you have succeeded in convincing the workers to support the organization.

(6) Do you feel that the acquisition is successful?

Sr.No	*Options*	*Response*	*Response in %*
1	Yes	10	100%
2	No	0	0%
Total		10	100%

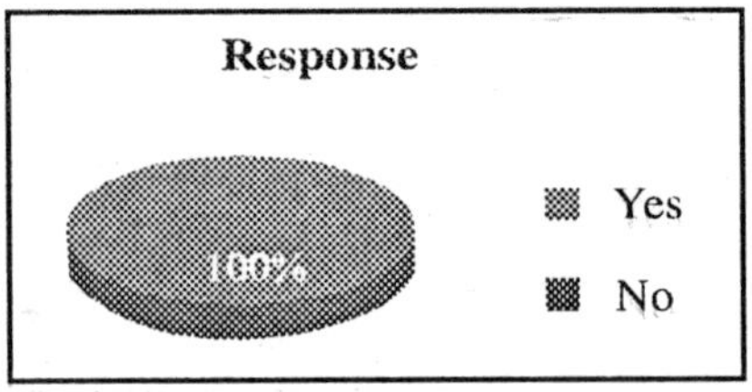

According to the above pie chart maximum of the 100% management feel that the acquisition is successful.

Conclusion

- Technological changes are introduced by the company, and 50% of the machinery is being changed.
- Most of the workers are satisfied with the acquisition.
- They said that the HR management is supportive and they are comfortable in working with them.
- Maximum of the workers feel that the new policies introduced by new HRM are better than the older ones.
- Most of the employees are satisfied by the new compensation.
- Most of the workers said that they have healthy relationship with the management and the management is effective in solving their problems.
- Most of the managers feel that the changes introduced by the new company were for good.
- They said that the opposition from the workers was faced by the management efficiently.
- According to the managers the acquisition is successful.

References

1. Data and documents of the company.
2. Azhar Kazmi,Strategic Management and Business Policy, Third Edition, MC Graw-Hill Companies.
3. Amporn Soongswang,Takeovers and bidding firms' shareholder returns:Thai evidence,September 2008, The Icfai University Journal of Mergers and Acquisitions, Vol.V No.3.
4. James Ang*,Yingmei Cheng**and Gregory Nagel***An Analysis of Acquirers as Dealmakers: Differentiating Acquirers' Timing,Bargain Hunting and Negotiting Skills, December 2008, The Icfai University Journal of Mergers & Acquisitions,Vol. V No. 4 .
5. www.mubea.com.
6. www.wikipedia.com.
7. www.BNET.com.

ISBN – 978-93-5024-769-3

43 "Political Risk and its Impact on Indian Stock Market Performance"

Prof. Vidula Anil Adkar
Sinhgad Institute of Technology (MBA Department) Kusgaon, Lonavala.

Introduction

India being a democratic country, politics is a fundamental element of the economy. Financial market helps the economy to be strong hence market stability is imperative. Stock Exchanges have a vital role to play in an economy. A stock exchange is simply a market that is designed for the sale and purchase of securities of corporations and municipalities. A stock exchange sells and buys stocks, shares, and other such securities. In India Bombay Stock Exchange (BSE) is located in Mumbai, and is considered one of the oldest stock exchanges in Asia, as it dates back to 1875. The exchange lists 3500 companies with a capital of $466 billion. This exchange is considered among the 6 largest in the world. There are various types of risks involved in the Stock Markets, but the most spontaneous is the Political risk. Political risk means, "the risk that an investment's returns could suffer as a result of political changes or instability in a country". Instability affecting investment returns could stem from a change in government, legislative bodies, other foreign policy makers, or military control. Political risk is also known as "geopolitical risk", and becomes more of a factor as the time horizon of an investment gets longer. It is also well established that political events and economic behaviour are closely inter-related. Studies of political risk include political reforms, such as democratization from a military, regulation/deregulation, and nationalization /denationalization of various industrial sectors and their impact on firm valuation. This simply means that political risk is one of the determining factors in stock valuation and companies should pay close attention to any political events.

Political risk is intimately related with „Elections in country like India. Elections, as clearly defined as, "opportunities for large, discrete changes in government and therefore in governing philosophy and resulting policy, constitute a moment when political risk is articulated and determined".

There are many events related to political risk where, general elections not only decide the next government of the country but also the mood and momentum of stock markets as the outcome of polls would be more important factor than even the fundamentals of corporate.

Legislative elections were held in India, the world's largest democracy, in four phases between April 20 and May 10, 2004. Over 670 million people were eligible to vote, electing 543 members of the 14th Lok Sabha (the House of the People, the lower house of the Indian legislature). On May 13, the ruling Bharatiya Janata Party conceded defeat after an unexpectedly strong showing by the Indian National Congress, which while not winning a majority outright was able to put together a stable majority under the new Prime Minister, Manmohan Singh. There is a study of abrupt political changes i.e Legislative elections, on stock markets in this article. The purpose of this study is to conduct analysis of the relationship between the elections and the movement of stock markets in Indian Stock Exchange (BSE-sensex). The study also includes the stock market fluctuations before, during and after the elections. Though the Stock markets in India are well- developed, we are still facing political unrests that are directly or indirectly affecting the stock market. Because of these unrests the companies fail to arrange share capital which may lead to various types of financial problems. Investors may lose interest in the company and may get de motivated with this instability and this may lead to low investments in stock market. The study tells us whether there is any relation between political instability that is Elections and stock market price movement. For this the focus is mainly on Indian stock market. The purpose of the study is to find the negative or positive impact of the Elections on Stock market performance. The relationship between three years events related to elections and its impact on stock market is also studied.

The findings of this study will help the business in emerging market so as to know the relationship between Election and stock market performance, as election is part and parcel of the country. It will help to handle the political risk and minimise its impact on share value. It will also help us understand the elections effects on the stock prices and investors behaviour in expected and unexpected conditions.

Research Methods

The percentage of market returns before and after elections, for past seven years is collected. The collection of major stock market indices is collected for the same year of election. Methodology used is simple comparison method. The relationship of two variables (election and stock market returns) is studied. After relating both the variables that is elections (political risk) and stock market movement, it would indicate that stock market movement is affected by the Legislative elections, which decides the governing body, rules and regulations, different policies etc. This relationship can be useful for prospective investors to make investment decisions. The study of stock market returns before and after the election is carried out for 24 months and past 7 years elections are analysed. Year 2004 election is studied separately. Three years events (related to election) are compared with each other in relation with stock market performance.

Data Source

To study the relationship between two variables that is election and stock market performance on particular dates, BSE index: sensex is studied for twelve months. Table 1 provides the related information. To find the relationship between market returns and elections, the period of seven-year is studied (1984, 1989, 1991, 1996, 1998, 1999, 2004). For detailed news of Legislative elections, the published news in the media helped the most. To collect this information, major newspapers like Economic Times, Hindustan Times, various websites were used. These news events have also been collected for the same time periods.

Data Analysis

Effect of Political Event- „Election on stock market performance

Election is like big carnival in India with entire population from all walks of life gets swayed by it. Everything comes to stand still. School, colleges and offices close on voting day. In India election process is held in multiple phases. Election is, when one will is able to know about the victor and the vanquished. The outcome of the election will also determine the development trajectory of the India incorporate

Election Outcome and Investor

India, the world's largest democracy had an electorate of more than 700 million voters. As long as BJP or a Congress led alliances is in power, investor will likely be reassured of stability in terms of government as well as policies. If a Third Front comes to power, it will create uncertainties in the mind of investor on the development and policies front. Any Third Front government won't be getting investors vote of confidence. According to, an investor survey conducted by Global Financial Services major Morgan Stanley, "the results of the general elections would be the second most important driver for the Indian stocks, after the global market trends". The poll outcome would be more important than corporate fundamentals and the country's fiscal and monetary policies, the survey found.

Election and Stock Market

Returns from the past seven to eight elections have no exact set pattern. The returns in the run up to the elections have been lackluster. Market generally in all the occasion has shown range bound trading or sideways movement. Twelve month return post elections have been positive on four occasions and marginally negative on two occasions. Years when government took bold steps or the mandate swayed in favour of one party has raised the hope of investors and hence good returns were seen. 1984, 1989 and 1991, the market rallied in the first year of the government. After 1996 a significant change has been on the political front in India i.e.; beginning of coalition era. The returns in these times were very moderate as the mandate was clear. The other reason could be Asian crisis, nuclear test, Kargil war, Dotcom bust, etc.

TABLE 1 – Market Returns Before and After the Election

YEAR	*% RETURN BEFORE ELECTION*			*% RETURN AFTER ELECTION*		
	1 MONTH	*3 MONTH*	*12 MONTH*	*3 MONTH*	*6 MONTH*	*12 MONTH*
1984	4.8	4.4	3.8	29.4	68	92.9
1989	–3.9	0.2	11.9	–2.3	13.1	90.8
1991	0	11.7	8.9	44	42.1	142.8
1996	11.8	33.2	6.7	–9.2	–18.9	–1.5
1998	2	–2	14.9	14	–14.5	–3.3
1999	2.9	16.7	–4.5	6.5	6.4	–13
2004	–13.4	9	–10.7	–5.8	6.7	16.7

The table has shown the percentage change in Market Returns:

% Return before election: Year 1984: 12 months before the elections the Market was showing returns of 3.8 percent. 3 months before the elections, percentage rose from 3.8 to 4.4. 1 month before the election again there was a rise from 4.4 percent to 4.8.

Year 1989: 12 months before the elections the Market was showing returns of 11.9 percent. 3 months before the elections the returns drastically fell from 11.9 to 0.2. 1 month before the election again there was negative fall from 0.2 percent to -3.9.

Year 1991: 12 months before the elections the Market was showing returns of 8.9 percent. 3 months before the elections, percentage rose from 8.9 to 11.7. 1 month before the election again there was a fall from 11.7 percent to 0.

Year 1996: 12 months before the elections the Market was showing returns of 6.7 percent. 3 months before the elections the percent rose from 6.7 to 33.2. 1 month before the election again there was fall from 33.2 percent to 11.8.

Year 1998: 12 months before the elections the Market was showing returns of 14.9 percent. 3 months before the elections there was a negative fall from 14.9 to -2. 1 month before the election again there was a rise from 2 percent to 2. Year 1999: 12 months before the elections the Market was showing returns of -4.5 percent. 3 months before the elections the points rose from -4.5 to 16.7. 1 month before the election again there was a fall from 16.7 percent to 2.9.

Year 2004: 12 months before the elections the Market was showing returns of -10.7 percent. 3 months before the elections the points rose from -10.7 to 9. 1 month before the election again there was a negative fall from 9 percent to -13.4.

% Return after election: Year 1984: 3 months after the elections the Market was showing returns of 29.4 percent. 6 months after the elections, percentage rose from 29.4 to 68. 12 months after the election again there was a rise from 68 percent to 92.9.

Year 1989: 3 months after the elections the Market was showing negative returns of -2.3 percent. 6 months after the elections, percentage rose from -2.3 to 14.1. 12 months after the election again there was a rise from 14.1 percent to 90.8.

Year 1991: 3 months after the elections the Market was showing returns of 44 percent. 6 months after the elections, percentage fell from 44 to 42.1. 12 months after the election again there was a rise from 42.1 percent to 142.8. Year 1996: 3 months after the elections the Market was showing negative returns of -9.2 percent. 6 months after the elections, percentage fell negatively from -9.2 to -18.9. 12 months after the election again there was a negative rise from -18.9 percent to -1.5.

Year 1998: 3 months after the elections the Market was showing positive returns of 14 percent. 6 months after the elections, percentage fell negatively from 14 to -14.5. 12 months after the election again there again negative rise from -14.4 percent to -3.3.

Year 1999: 3 months after the elections the Market was showing returns of 6.5 percent. 6 months after the elections, percentage slightly fell from 6.5 to 6.4. 12 months after the election again there was a negative fall from 6.4 percent to -13.

Year 2004: 3 months after the elections the Market was showing negative returns of -5.8 percent. 6 months after the elections, percentage rose from -5.8 to 6.7. 12 months after the election again there was a rise from 6.7 percent to 16.7.

TABLE 2 – a Election Year: 1998 and 1999

Date	*Event*	*Market Movement*
Feb-16 to Feb-28 1998	First to Fourth poll Voting	Up by 12%
March-6 1998	NDA Won the Election	Up by 3%
Overall movement in Feb 1998	Election Month.	Market was up by 12%
Oct-Nov 1999	NDA lost majority & Voting for new government begin.	Market was down by 13%
Nov-Dec 1999	NDA won again with full majority	Market was up by 23%

At the beginning of the year 1998 when the Election round 1 was going on, there was upward market movement. Soon after NDA won the first round market showed less rise. During the election month also the market showed upward growth with higher increase. After the third quarter of the year 1999 NDA lost majority that is, it was a call for new Government. Hence again election and voting formalities but yet market was stable. Soon after the re-victory of NDA there was noticeable rise in market movement.

TABLE 2 – b Election Year: 2004

Date	*Event*	*Market Movement*
Apr-20 to May-10 2004	First to Fourth poll Voting	Up by 6.7%
May-13 2004	Left Front Led UPA won the Election	Down by 6%
May-14 2004	Left Front comments on Stock Market regulation	Black day for Market Down by 12% in a single day
Overall movement in may	Election Month.	Market was down by 13%
Jun-Jul 2004	UPA Govt. Start Economic reform	Market was up by 9%

During the second quarter of the year there was once again a poll voting where market showed downward movement. Left front led UPAs winning but still market was moving downwards. Further due to the comments passed by Left front against the Stock market May 14 2004 was observed as Black Day where there was drastic fall in the market. In the mid of the year during election the market started rising again.

TABLE 3 – Sensex In 2004 Election

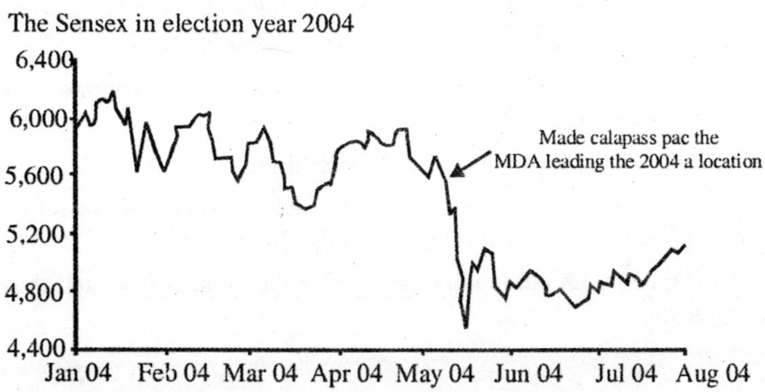

This diagram shows the market movement in the election year. This data is collected from BSE- Sensex where the bearish and bullish candle helps us to know the detailed report. During the year from Jan 04 to May 04 the market was up though there were fluctuations but during and after elections market collapsed.

From the above statistics it is clear that it was tough to predict the market movement, during the Election month and it may continue after the results are been declared, if no one won with clear majority.

Data Interpretation

Table 1: Market returns before elections:

In election year 1984, twelve months before the market was stable and started rising positively till the election month. In election year 1989, twelve months before the markets was stable and started declining negatively till the election month. In election years 1991, 1996, 1998, 1999 the market was stable twelve months before but was fluctuating till the election month. In the election year 2004 market had negative movement twelve months before but was fluctuating till the election month.

Table 2: Market returns after elections:

In all the years there was on average rise in the market performance in long run (twelve months and above) and short run but in short run there were fluctuations in only few cases.

Table 2a: Election Year 1998, 1999

In 1998 and 1999 upward movement was observed in stock market performance. The reason might be that, the same government ruled for both the times

Table 2b: Election Year 2004

In 2004 there was downward movement in stock market performance. As there were many controversies one of the days market suffered a lot. There downward movement but after the election slowly stock markets started recovering.

Table 3: Sensex (BSE index) in 2004 Election

The chart shows the fluctuations in the share prices during elections. Definitely for this election there was a negative movement of stock market performance.

PUBLIC CONDUCT

Though pre-poll predictions were for an overwhelming majority for the BJP, the exit polls (immediately after the elections and before the counting began) predicted a hung parliament. However, even the exit polls could only indicate the general trend and nowhere close to the final figures.

- People were more concerned about issues of their immediate environment such as water scarcity, drought, etc., than national issues.
- The anti-incumbency factor was at work for the BJP allies.
- The BJP government had concentrated more on the market and economic reforms that benefitted the urban people at the expense of the rural poor and the farmers.
- People were concerned with communal issues after the Gujarat riots and thus their mandate for a secular government.

Conclusion

Indian Stock Market has seen lot of positive and negative trends in the Election month. Lot of volatility was seen in the market for past 5 weeks. This process may continue until the election results are clearly visible. Many traders have lost their money in this volatile market, but investors were big gainers.

The stock market (Bombay Stock Exchange) fell in the week prior to the announcement of the results due to fears of an unstable coalition. As soon as counting began, however, it became clear that the Congress coalition was headed for a sizeable lead over the NDA and the market surged, only to crash the following day when the left parties, whose support would be required for government formation, announced that it was their intention to do away with the disinvestment ministry. Following this, Manmohan Singh, the current Prime Minister and the prime architect of the economic liberalization of the early 1990s, hurried to reassure investors that the new government would strive to create a business-friendly climate.

Mostly stock market has reacted positively in long run whereas negatively in short run.

Some Important Points

1. The one thing the equity market hates the most, is uncertainty.
2. Market never accepts the government with left front or third front government. So one thing is very clear, be prepared for big sell off, it that happened.
3. Market will be very comfortable if Congress or BJP will come with full majority. It is investors who will have to take respective decisions.
4. Investor must stay away till the election results don't get declared. Remember cash is the king and if you use it at right time, it will give massive returns in a short span.
5. Traders mostly lose their money in this type of market as fluctuation is always a killer for traders. So quality and timing of calls makes the difference. Most of them generated losses, as they went short at a level of 11000-11500. Trading is always effective in a pure bull or bear market, but not an intermediate market like this.
6. If you will see the investment figures of DII (Domestic Investors), it is very clear they booked the profit slowly and steadily without any panic. Also history suggest that big players stay away during such event and come up with big bull or bear depending upon the poll results.

   Hence it is very difficult to state the exact stock market behaviour. It depends on time and situation as to positive and negative reaction of the stock market performance.

References

1. Economic and Political Weekly.
2. December 4-10, 2010.
3. Business India December 2004 Current Affairs.
4. January 2005 Economic News on the Trading Activity," *Pacific-Basin Finance.*
5. *Journal*, Volume 9, Issue 3, (June 2001), 195-217. Chan, Yue-cheong and K.C. John Wei.
6. "Political Risk and Stock Price Volatility: The Case of Hong Kong," *Pacifi-Basin Finance*
7. *Journal,* Volume 4, issue 2-3, (July 1996), pp. 259-275.
8. Perotti, Enrico C. and Pirter van Oijen, "Privatization, Political Risk and Stock Market Development inEmerging Economies," (February 2001), *Journal of International Money and Finance,* Volume 20, Issue 1, pp. 43-69.
9. Website: Wikipedia Economic times Hindustan times BSE.

◈◈◈

ISBN – 978-93-5024-769-3

44 "Role of Technology in Banking Sector and Effective E-Banking in 21st Century"

Mrs. Smita Mahesh Pachere

Introduction

Business organizations, especially the banking industry of the 21st century operates in a complex and competitive environment characterized by these changing conditions and highly unpredictable economic climate. IT is becoming the backbone of banks' services regeneration in 21st century. The Advanced Information Technology has enough capabilities to enable banks, financial institutions and others to bring about the desired changes. In the traditional banking system a person had to go to a bank branch to deposit or withdraw money and get a bank statement book manually updated by a teller over the counter.

In 21st century Services and products like "Anywhere Banking" "Tele-Banking" "Internet banking" "Web Banking", e-banking, e-commerce, e-business etc. have become the buzzwords of the day and the Banks are trying to cope with the competition by offering innovative and attractively packaged technology-based services to their customers.

IT in the Indian Banking Sector – the Beginnings

The Information technology for Banking in India had their beginnings in the middle of 80s, when the Banks. Spurred on by RBI and the Rangarajan Committee Report, started computerizing the branches in a limited manner to improve customer service, book keeping, MIS and productivity. Institute for Development and Research in Banking Technology (IDRBT), set up by the RBI in 1997, implemented the Indian Financial Network. Most banks in India have used IT to achieve superior business performance, driven mainly by the cost advantage in India, the focus on avoiding legacy systems, superior IT governance that often entails direct CEO involvement and competent outsourcing.

Information Technology in Banking in the New Millennium

- Technological systems of Indian banks in 21 century have rated more advanced than China and Russia; at par with Japan, but less advanced than Singapore, UK and USA. The visible benefits of IT in day-to-day banking in India are quite well known. There's 'Anywhere Banking' through Core Banking Systems, 'Anytime Banking' through new, 24/7/365 delivery channels such as E-Banking Services & Mobile banking which includes following services.

1. ATM (Automated Teller Machines)
2. Debit Cards / Credit Cards / Smart Cards
3. Internet Banking
4. ECS (Electronic Cleaning Systems)
5. EFT (Electronic Funds Transfer)
6. Electronic Data Inter Change
7. INFINET (Indian Financial Network)
8. On-Line Banking
9. SPNS (Shared Payment Network System)
10. Tele Banking
11. Universal Banking
12. 24 Hours Banking
13. Corporate Banking Terminals
14. Online complaint Tracking System

- To know the view of the performance Information Technology in Indian banks, a comparison was made between two dominant categories –

(i) New private and foreign banks

(ii) Old private and public sector banks.

New private and foreign banks focus their IT spends on innovations rather than daily operations. Old private and public sector banks, on the other hand, focus on application development directed more towards augmenting their existing systems that has resulted in low value-addition to their business. New private and foreign banks focus more on value-added activities such as building new infrastructure like ATM networks and modern core banking systems; customer service channels including call centers, Internet banking and mobile banking ; sophisticated risk-assessment and pricing techniques; data warehousing/mining tools; and marketing tools such as customer relationship management. Many companies in India have adopted this strategy and have managed to lower the interaction of the customer with the bank branches. For instance, 10 years ago, 90% of all transactions made by the customers of ICICI bank were through the branches and 10% were through online. Now in new millennium the trend has exactly reversed.

- The Reserve Bank of India is actively involved and took a lead role to create e-payment Some of the e-payments infrastructures are :
  - Electronic Clearing Service (ECS) - Credit and Debit
  - Electronic Funds Transfer (EFT), and Special EFT
  - Centralised Funds Management System (CFMS)
  - Negotiated Dealing System (NDS) for screen based Trading in Government securities
  - Real Time Gross Settlement System (RTGS)

  All these systems have a positive impact on quick, safe and electronic movement of money for various sectors of the economy.

- More technology spends are expected in the near future on areas such as implementation of data centre, expansion of CBS, Business Continuity Plan (BCP)/Disaster Recovery Plan (DRP) installations, IT Security, Electronic Data Interchange (EDI), Storage solutions such as Storage Area Network.

(SAN)/Network Access Storage (NAS) to take care of the hundreds of terabytes of electronic Data being generated, cheque truncation solutions, compliance to regulatory standards like Basel II implementations, customer Relationship Management (CRM) solutions, data ware house and data mining tools, channel integration, global treasury, performance monitoring tools.

- INFINET-Indian Financial Network The 'INFINET' Indian Financial Network is a satellite based wide area network using VSAT (Very Small Aperture Terminal) technology set up by the RBI in June 1999. The hub and the Network Management System of the INFINET are located in the Institute for Development and Research in Banking Technology, (IDRBT) Hyderabad.
- Electronic Authentication and Electronic Signature Banks are now using technology for the proper identification of customers' identity. This methods reduce the speed and efficiency of electronic transactions, financial institutions have adopted alternative authentication methods. There are many global Software Companies/IT solution providers focused on Indian Banking & Finance Industry like Safescrypt Ltd, ICICI InfoTech services ltd, Microsoft corporation, Infosys Technology Ltd, SAP India Pvt Ltd, Tata consultancy Services Ltd, CMC LTD, Dell, Intel corporation, i-flex solution Ltd, IBM etc.

Impact of Information Technology

- Employment and changing skills

  The cost-conscious banks in the country are actively considering using the Internet as a channel for providing services. Liberalization and financial sector reforms during the last one decade have brought the issue of productivity and profitability of banks into the limelight. Liberalization also led to economic growth .It has created job opportunities in abundance for the non-technical, English speaking graduates in the areas like call centre, retail and direct marketing. It has also created opportunities for skilled professionals in the electronic media and Information technology (IT) sector.
- The growth in the range of banking services

  Technology has enabled the banks to conceive deliver, manage and integrate their products in line with the customers' need. A range of services is now provided to both retail and corporate customers covering different financial products, sweep-in/sweep-out facilities, channel financing, straight through processing. Technology has tremendously impacted on marketing activities of Banking Sectors, enterprise resources planning (ERP) systems have shifted the focus to customer relationship management (CRM). There are two types of ECS called ECS (Credit) and ECS (Debit). ECS (Credit) is used for affording credit to a large number of beneficiaries by raising a single debit to an account, such as dividend, interest or salary payment. ECS (Debit) is used for raising debits to a number of accounts of consumers/ account holders for crediting a particular institution. Advantages of the ECS to the ultimate beneficiary is that there will be no risk of loss of Instrument & Fraudulent encashment, eliminates the need to go to the collection centers & no need not track down payments by last dates. The ECS user would monitor the debits. Efficiency of payment systems will no longer be measured in terms of size but also its capability to deliver products matching market expectations.

Following Table explaining the share of paper based versus electronic Transactions.

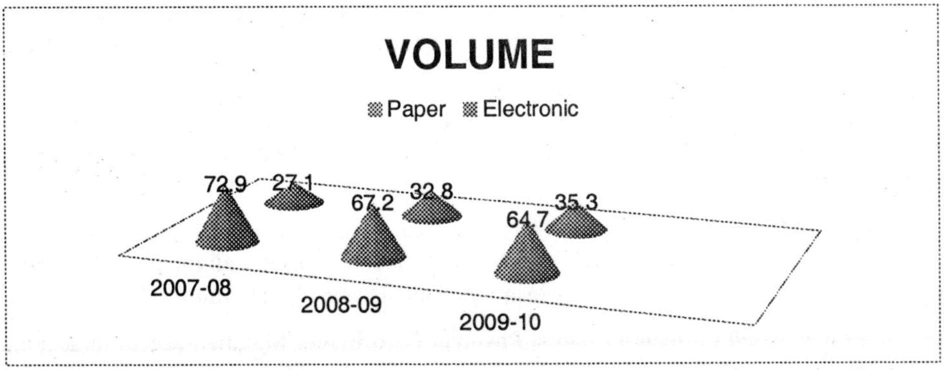

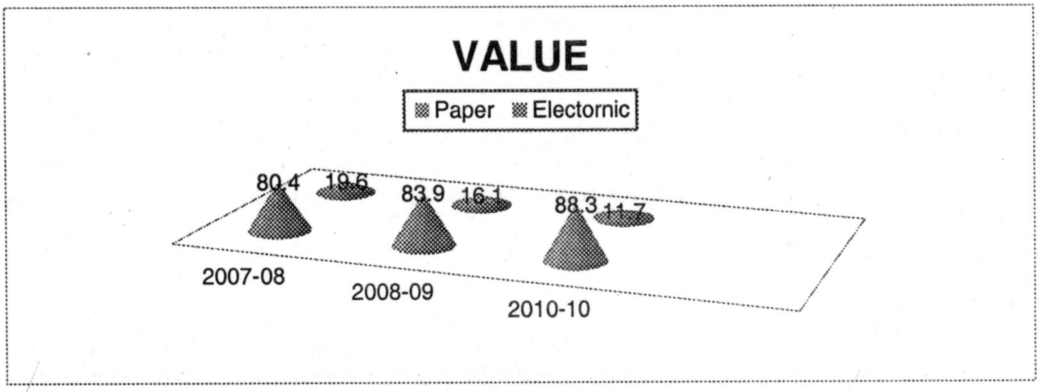

Source: RBI annual Report 2009-10

From the above graph it is clear that due to Implementation Information Technology in banking sector become innovative not only to deliver the services but also to stay in the competition.

Online complaint Tracking System - The Software developed at the request of the ministry of finance, to enable the office of the banking ombudsmen to track the disposal of complaints: access is also available to rural planning & credit department.

ATM transactions and the increased use of **cashless payments** have had a significant impact on cash demand in India and will probably continue to do so in future. Since, however, cash withdrawal and payment habits are changed but this development do not have much impact on monetary policy in India.

- **Optimization of Time & Cost with reference to financial transactions.**

Due to implementation of Information Technology there is reduction in the cost of operations. For example: Assume teller cost at Re 1 per transaction, ATM transaction costs at Re 0.45, phone banking at Re 0.35, debit cards at Re 0.20 and Internet banking at Re 0.10 per transaction. Said V K Ramani, president. information technology, UTI Bank in his special report.

RTGS handles about 150,000 transactions a day for an approximate value of 1,500 billion. The system was launched on March 26, 2004 (on pilot basis by involving 4 banks) by RBI for large value transactions for banks and their clients. As on November 30, 2010 there are more than 72,000 operating their transactions through RTGS.

- **Challenges**

New technologies set off a process of change. That, in turn, poses its own set of challenges to institutions as well as to consumers. IT is not yet a very comfortable choice for the illiterate customers & customers in rural area. Consumer awareness is a major challenge.

The major challenge implementing technology in Indian banks need to introduce innovative, customer friendly products and services for which newer technologies have to be brought in multiple areas to reduce the overall transaction costs.

Deployment of IT offers ample rewards but these rewards can be claimed only by organizations, which successfully address the alignment challenge. Alignment of IT and business, alignment of IT and HR and alignment of IT and organizational structure. These are all critical to derive true value.

Frauds like Frauds based on Identity thefts, Payment Card Fraud, Malafied access to accounts True Name Fraud, Active attacks can be of two types :a) Active on customer's PC b) Active on customer's channel.

Security in an IT-based transaction-processing environment is also critical. Adequate security control is not there. Banks also must have to pass on the benefits of lower costs from technology-based products and services to their customers.

Investment in Information Technology must be made to modernize existing operations, to face competitive challenges, and to meet customer expectations. Information and communication technology is the major advent in the field of technology which is used for access, process, storage and dissemination of information electronically.

Conclusion

Information Technology in the Banking Sector it has graduated from being view from Cost Center to Profit Center. Banks and financial institutions rely on Gathering, processing, analyzing and providing information in order to meet the needs of customers. Technological innovations have enabled the banking sector to open up efficient delivery channels. It is said that IT has helped the banking industry to deal with the challenges the new economy poses. Adoption of a structured IT framework would Enable a bank to perform its business in an orderly and effective manner benefiting the customers and, in the process, aid in its own survival and growth. This needs to be considered against the fact that nearly 70% of all customer defections are a result of poor customer service. After all, it is estimated that its costs 5 times more to acquire new customers than to retain the existing ones and that about 20% of the customers contribute to 80% of the profits. There is a positive impact of implementation of Technology on Employment & Skills. There is Optimization of Cost, Time, and Skills with reference banking operations.

References

1. Seale, G., Branching Continues to Thrive as the U.S. Banking System Consolidates. Federal Deposit Insurance Corporation FYI. October 20, 2004.
2. "Enabling financial sector to leverage on I T for better customer service, improved housekeeping and overall systemic efficiency by DEPARTMENT OF INFORMATION TECHNOLOGY.
3. "Analysis of Impact of Technology on Relationship Marketing Orientation and Bank Performance" Bright C. Opara *Department of Marketing, Rivers State University of Science and Technology Port Harcourt.*
4. Firpo, J. "Banking the Unbanked: Technology's Role in Delivering Accessible Financial Services to the poor", *SEMBA* (2006), *Consulting*: 5.

5. Journal of Internet Banking and Commerce, April 2008, Journal of Internet Banking and Commerce, vol. 13, no. 1.
6. "Innovation of payment system" by R. Mani Deputy General Manager, IDRBT.
7. Secure Internet Banking Authentication, A.Hiltgen, T.Kramp and T.Weigold, IEEE.
8. Security & Privacy, March/April 2006.
9. Two-Factor Authentication: Too Little, Too Late.
10. Bruce Schneier, Communications of the ACM, April 2005, Vol. 48, no. 4.
11. Remote Client Authentication, T.Weigold, T.Kramp and M.Baentsch,
12. IEEE Security and Privacy, 2008.
13. Emerging trends in technology adoption by Indian banks and IT Governance – A practical guide "Trust and reputation can vanish overnight. A factory cannot" by V.G. Sekar, DGM & MoF, CA.
14. Case Study: State Bank of India, World's Largest Centralized Core Processing Implementation by **Robert Hunt** Senior Research Director, Retail Banking Feb. 2009 Reference # V58:06R.
15. Banking sector reforms in India & Performance Evaluation of commercial Banks By Debaprosanna Nandy.
16. Korea IT Times Feb. 2006.
17. The strategic impact of IT on the retail financial services industry by **Derek F. Channon.**
18. Strategies of Banking Technology By Alex Jordon.

◇◇◇

ISBN – 978-93-5024-769-3

45 Market Potential of 20-Litre Water Jar in Pune City for Maestro Trade Link Pvt. Ltd.

Sunil Darawade & Kishor Gaikwad
Sinhgad Management School, Kondhapuri.

Introduction

Water is the most important necessity for life. The drinking-water needs for individuals vary depending on the climate, physical activity and the body culture. But for average consumers it is estimated to be about two to four litres per day. The growing number of cases of water borne diseases, increasing water pollution, increasing urbanization, increasing scarcity of pure and safe water etc. have made the bottled water business just like other consumer items. Scarcity of potable and wholesome water at railway stations, tourists spots, and role of tourism corp. etc. has also added to the growth. The reason for doing this project is to find out the market potential and consumer preferences of Kinley mineral water.

Almost all the major international and national brands water bottles are available in Indian market right from the malls to railway stations, bus stations, grocery stores and even at panwala's shop. Before few years bottle water was considered as the rich people's choice, but now it is penetrated even in rural areas. The growth and status of Indian Bottled Industry in comparison with Western or Asian market, India is far behind in terms of quantum, infrastructure, professionalism and standards implementation. The per capita consumption of mineral water in India is a mere 0.5-liter compared to 111 liter in Europe and 45-liter in USA. Also As per UN study conducted in 122 countries, in connection with water quality, India's number was dismal 120. In comparison to global standards India's bottled water segment is largely unregulated.

Former President Dr. A.P.J. Abdul Kalam has urged youngsters on July 17, 2010 to be aware of water conservation techniques to avoid grave water crisis in future. "It is so sad that today, people are forced to buy water in plastic bottles. I am told that bottled water industry is worth nearly 10000 crore rupees and even big companies like the Coke and Pepsi are involved in this bottling of water and making money. So, it is imperative that we ought to save water," he added.

Do not be surprise if today's bottles water industry becomes next Oil industry by 2025.

Bottled Water Industry in India

Water Shortage and Health Awareness Driving Bottled Water Consumption in India. The Indian market is estimated at about Rs.1,000 Crore and is growing at whopping rate of 40 per cent. By 2010, it will reach Rs 4,000 -5,000 Crore with 33 per cent market for natural mineral water.

According to a national-level study, there are more than 200 bottled water brands in India and among them nearly 80 per cent are local brands. In fact, making bottled water is today a cottage industry in the country. Leave alone the metros, where a bottled-water manufacturer can be found even in a one-room shop, in every medium and small city and even some prosperous rural areas there are bottled water manufacturers.

While India ranks in the top 10 largest bottled water consumers in the world, its per capita per annum consumption of bottled water is estimated to be five litres which is comparatively lower than the global average of 24 litres. Today it is one of India's fastest growing industrial sectors. Between 1999 and 2004, the Indian bottled water market grew at a compound annual growth rate (CAGR) of 25 per cent - the highest in the world. The total annual bottled water consumption in India had tripled to 5 billion liters in 2004 from 1.5 billion liters in 1999. Global consumption of bottled water was nearing 200 billion liters in 2006.

Bottled Water Top Players in India

The top players in bottled water industry in India are the major international giants like Coca cola, Pepsi, Nestle and noticeable presence of national players like Mount Everest, Manikchand, Kingfisher, Mohan Meakins, SKN Breweries , Indian Railways so on. With increasing competition, this sector will register a robust growth in 2010, predict industry analysts.

To take on rivals in this sector, PepsiCo India is drawing up a fresh game plan which includes, investment in capacity enhancement, packaging initiatives and below-the-line activities to pump up volumes in the over-crowded category. Meanwhile, swadeshi major Parle Agro is extending the manufacturing facility for

Bailley from 29 to 60 plants this year. While swadeshi major Bisleri International is beefing up its distribution, manufacturing and marketing operations, Coca-Cola India is sharpening its focus on packaging initiatives of Kinley to woo new consumes. In essence, the packaged water industry in India will soon witness a major tussle between swadeshi and videshi players to gain market and mind share.

The western region accounts for 40 per cent of the market and the eastern region just 10. However, the bottling plants are concentrated in the southern region - of the approximately 1,200 bottling water plants in India, 600 are in Tamil Nadu. But a major problem is southern India, especially Tamil Nadu, is water starved.

Top multinational players such as Coca-Cola and PepsiCo have been trying for the past decade to capture the Indian bottled water market. Today they have captured a significant portion of it. However, Parle Bisleri continues to hold 40 per cent of the market share. Kinley and Aquafina are fast catching up, with Kinley holding 20-25 per cent of the market and Aquafina approximately 10 per cent. The rest, including the smaller players, have 20-25 per cent of the market share.

History of Bottled Water in India

Mineral bottled water in India under the name 'Bisleri' was first introduced in Mumbai by Bisleri Ltd., a company of Italian origin in 1965. Mineral bottled water were in glass bottles in two varieties - bubbly and still in 1965 This company was started by Signor Felice who first brought the idea of selling bottled water in India.

Parle bought over Bisleri (India) Ltd. In 1969 and started bottling Mineral water in glass bottles under the brand name 'Bisleri'. Later Parle switched over to PVC non- returnable bottles and finally advanced to PET containers. Since 1995 Mr. Ramesh J. Chauhan has started expanding Bisleri operations substantially and the turn over has multiplied more than 20 times over a period of 10 years and the average growth rate has been around 40% over this period. Presently it have 8 plants and 11 franchisees all over India. Bisleri command a 60% market share of the organized market.

Currently, Bailley has a national presence in 5 lakh retail outlets across the country. "We plan to increase manufacturing plants for Bailley from 29 to 60, presently 40 plants are operational and few more will be ready for operations over the next few months," informed Nadia Chauhan, joint managing director of Parle Agro.

Variety of Packages

Bottled water is sold in a variety of packages: pouches and glasses, 330 ml bottles, 500 ml bottles, one-litre bottles and even 20- to 50-litre bulk water packs. The formal bottled water business in India can be divided broadly into three segments in terms of cost: premium natural mineral water, natural mineral water and packaged drinking water.

Premium natural mineral water includes brands such as Evian, San Pelligrino and Perrier, which are imported and priced between Rs. 80 and Rs.110 a litre. Natural mineral water, with brands such as Himalayan and Catch, is priced around Rs.20 a litre. Packaged drinking water, which is nothing but treated water, is the biggest segment and includes brands such as Parle Bisleri, Coca-Cola's Kinley and PepsiCo's Aquafina. They are priced in the range of Rs.10-12 a litre.

Bottled water major Bisleri International plans to launch fruit-flavoured water before the start of the festive season this year, a top company official said. Bisleri, which enjoys 65 per cent market share in the branded water segment, is also eyeing a sharp growth in sales during the festive season that begins from August

Market Potential of 20-Litre Water Jar in Pune City For Maestro Trade Link Pvt. Ltd.

Objectives

To find the market potential of 20-litre water jar for kinley mineral water.

To Study the market share of kinley mineral water & its competitors brand.

To analyze consumer market & buying behavior.

To study the customers satisfaction level regarding the product.

To examine the response towards kinley mineral water supplied by the Maestro Trade link pvt. Ltd.

To identify the most preferred brand of mineral water by customers.

To study the market demand for Kinley mineral water.

Scope

The scope of the study not only covers the market share of Kinley mineral water but also the market share of its competitors.

It also provides information about the main outlets of the company.

The information provided shall help the company to know about customer perceptions and their problems and about awareness of Kinley mineral water among customers.

It was also the motive of the company to find out the satisfaction level and priorities of the customers in relation to price and service provided by the maestro trade link pvt. Ltd

Significance

This survey was mainly carried out to study the Market Potential and product preference of Kinley mineral water in Pune city. This study will help the organization to identify current market position and its competitor's Position in the market & current sale and much can be increase in that particular zone by providing better service to the customer.

This study was also carried out to highlight the complaints regarding our product faced by the users. First hand information has been gathered from the respondents, which will help in surmount the complaints. Thus, by improving the total supply chain among distributors and retailers will help in increasing the coverage.

Research Methodology

Type of study: "Descriptive"

Nature of study: "Quantitative"

Type of questionnaire: "Structured"

Type of questions: "Open ended & Close ended"

Type of analysis: "Statistical"

Plan for Secondary data collection

Secondary data was collected from theory books (Marketing management) and website of the company i.e. www.Coca-colaindia.com.

Plan for Primary data collection

Primary data for the project was obtained with the help of structured questionnaire and conducting survey method.

Research Technique: "Survey method"

Contact method: "Personal interview"

Research Instrument: "Questionnaire"

Analysis

I have visited the various areas of Pune city for collecting the data of use of Packaged Drinking Water against the Municipal Water by Various types of Customer & based on that I have done the following analysis.

Why Bottled Water?

Millions of people, both in rural and urban India, suffer from inadequate or no tap water supply. Even some parts of Mumbai, the country's financial capital, get a mere two hours of daily water supply. The city's Virar suburb gets 45 minutes. So bottled water is much in demand by residents - even though the businesses profiting from the sales are thriving from access to public water sources.

Bottled water fills a void created by government failure to address basic services, Peter Gleick of the Pacific Institute writes in its World Water report. "In many parts of the world, tap water is not available or safe to drink," writes . "In these regions, the failure of governments to provide basic water services has opened the door to private companies and vendors filling a critical need, albeit at a very high cost to consumers." The institute reasons that governments should tap into spending on commercial water by consumers to secure funds to provide safe water at fraction of the cost.

Gigi Kellett, US national director of the Think Outside the Bottle campaign, argues that demand for bottled water is due to industry creating "a market by casting doubt on the quality of tap water, when in fact bottled water is subject to far less scrutiny and often comes from the same source".

Bottled Water: How Safe?

The bottled water industry has spent billions over the past decade to sell you on the idea that bottled water is better than tap water. Well the short answer is they are both unhealthy. One of the most ironic parts of the bottled water tragedy is that the water bottling industry gets the water free, filters it, bottles it and sells it back to us at 1,900% profit. The ironic part is that tap water is legislated to be 7.0 pH neutral. They first dump a TON of cholrine in the water to kill off all the bad bacteria, this makes it highly acidic.

In India around 100 companies sell an estimated 424 million litres of bottled water valued at around Rs 200 crore in the country annually . Most bottlers claim that their water is 100 per cent bacteria-free and contains minerals that make it tastier and healthier. But is the water in these bottles really safe to drink? Do they conform to international or national standards?

To find out, the Ahmedabad-based Consumer Education and Research Society (CERS), an independent non-profit institution with a sophisticated product-testing laboratory, recently carried out a detailed study on 13 major brands of bottled water available in the country. The national brands — Bisleri (separate samples were taken from their units in Bangalore, Ghaziabad, Calcutta and Baroda) and Bailley (Mumbai and Surat) — were selected on the basis of their dominant position in the overall market. Bisil (Mehsana), Golden Eagle (Chennai), Aquaspa (Mumbai), Saiganga (Ahmednagar), Nirantar (Thane), Trupthi (Chennai) and Yes (Nadiad) were included because of their regional popularity. To conform to international standards for such testing, 21 bottles of each brand were tested in the CERS laboratory against "analytical" and "sensory" parameters as well as for "microbiological" contamination. To ensure fairness, the results were sent to the individual companies for their comments.

So how safe is bottled water? Not that safe, says the CERS survey. As many as 10 of the 13 brands had foreign floating objects in clear violation of norms. Again during a surprise inspection by the health committee chairman Manjunatha Reddy and team at two mineral water units in the Bangalore on January 11, 2011, it was found that mineral water production unit owners were bottling borewell water. The units were also illegally using several branded labels on the bottles to market the water. The standing committee visited a mineral water production unit called AM Enterprises and found the owner selling water without an ISI mark from the Bureau of India Standards. He was found mixing mineral water with borewell water and selling it in cans to the public.

Water Resources Over-exploited

The majority of the bottling plants are dependent on groundwater. They create huge water stress in the areas where they operate because groundwater is also the main source - in most places the only source - of drinking water in India. This has created huge conflict between the community and the bottling plants.

Private companies in India can siphon out, exhaust and export groundwater free because the groundwater law in the country is archaic and not in tune with the realities of modern capitalist societies. The existing law says that "the person who owns the land owns the groundwater beneath". This means that, theoretically, a person can buy one square metre of land and take all the groundwater of the surrounding areas and the law of land cannot object to it. This law is the core of the conflict between the community and the companies and the major reason for making the business of bottled water in the country highly lucrative.

Take for instance the case of Coca-Cola's bottling plant in drought-prone Kala Dera near Jaipur. Coca-Cola gets its water free except for a tiny cess (for discharging the wastewater) it pays to the State Pollution

Control Board - a little over Rs.5,000 a year during 2000-02 and Rs.24,246 in 2003. It extracts half a million litres of water every day - at a cost of 14 paise per 1,000 litres. So, a Rs.10 per litre Kinley water has a raw material cost of just 0.02-0.03 paise. (It takes about two to three litres of groundwater to make one litre of bottled water.)

On April 7, more than 1,500 villagers defied a police cordon and marched to Coca-Cola's bottling plant in Mehdiganj village, Varanasi, in Uttar Pradesh state, demanding that the company immediately shut down its bottling plant. In January, the New Delhi-based Energy and Resources Institute (TERI) advised Coca-Cola to shut a bottling plant in the drought-stricken state of Rajasthan.

India's Ministry of Water Resources has ranked 80% of ground water resources in Rajasthan as "over-exploited" and nearly 34% resources as "dark/ critical", the gravest ranking across the country.

Bottled Water Companies Earn High Profits

What is amazing is that people are prepared to pay Rs. 12 for a liter of water-in India especially when the cost of material input (0.25 paisa per liter excluding labors cost) pales into insignificance before the price of the product.

Up to 40% of bottled water comes from the same source as tap water, but is sold back to consumers at hundreds of times the cost, says the website of the North American "Think Outside the Bottle" campaign. Not only the Coca-Cola but there are thousands of brands in India's $445 million packaged water industry.

Not just bottlers are involved. In south India, thousands of fuel trucks converted to be water carriers sell ground water to households and establishments at about $10 for 5,000 liters. More than 13,000 tankers carry water drawn from farmland surrounding Chennai, according a social activist R Srinivasan. He estimates a $148 million tanker industry is cashing in on Chennai's acute water scarcity. The story is replicated across India, including in New Delhi.

Plastic Bottles Pollution

Tap water is a local product that needs no packaging. Globally, bottled water accounts for as many as 1.5 million tons of plastic waste annually, according to the Sierra Club. In addition, billions of bottles end up in the ground every year. Sadly, only 20% ever get recycled, according to the Container Recycling Institute. The other 80%? Besides landfills, many bottles end up in oceans, posing a risk to marine life. By purchasing bottled water, you're indirectly raising the price of gasoline and contributing to Global Warming and climate change.

In 2007, the manufacturers of plastic water bottles generated more than 2.5 million tons of carbon dioxide emissions and required the equivalent of more than 17 million barrels of oil, according to the Pacific Institute. Americans drank more than 30 billion single-serving bottles of water last year. Yet the vast majority of us have an unlimited source of clean, EPA-regulated tap water flowing from our faucets.

Plastic Bottles Requires Costly Oil

Making the plastic in the bottles requires 47 million gallons of oil annually. And that doesn't include the jet fuel and gasoline required to transport the bottles- sometimes halfway around the world.

The Anti-bottling Protests

The anti-bottling protests in India against Pepsi and Coca-Cola echo increased concern in Europe and the United States over the proliferation of bottled water, including the creation of billions of soon unwanted plastic containers. In India, protests against the bottling plant in drought-prone Kala Dera near Jaipur focus on the source of the packaged water and how bottling companies are grabbing underground water.

The truth is, many water companies get their water from sources in developing countries, such as India and Fiji. In those places, the companies take water that once belonged to an entire village and buy it for themselves, forcing the villagers to pay for water that they used to be able to use as a community, free of charge. Furthermore, local water sources are polluted in these areas by bottling plants so that the many who cannot afford privatized water have to walk miles and miles, often through intense heat, just to access clean drinking water.

Bottled Water law in India

The term "mineral water" is misleading because our laws do not stipulate the minimum mineral content level required for water to be labelled as such. Ahmedabad-based Consumer Education and Research Society

(CERS), an independent non-profit institution with a sophisticated product-testing laboratory, recently carried out a detailed study on 13 major brands of bottled water available in the country. As many as 10 of the 13 brands had foreign floating objects in clear violation of norms found in the survey. The CERS study indicates that there is an urgent need to revise standards for bottled water.

Health Issue-Purity of Bottled Water

City water systems must issue "right to know" reports about what's in the water. Bottlers successfully killed this requirement for bottled water. Up to 70% of bottled water is unregulated by the Food & Drug Administration. Acceptance of the supposed purity of bottled water is being undermined in India by the government Health Department's warning of pesticides and contaminating organisms being present in some bottled products.

The notion that commercial products taste better has also taken a knock from Decanter, a British magazine, which last December featured top wine tasters testing unmarked samples of water from 22 brands, along with tap water from utility company Thames Water and water from the Decanter office water cooler.

The Decanter panel ranked serviced tap water third in the list, above the world's leading brand, Evian (15th), and the world's most expensive bottled water 420 Volcanic (18th) and Bling H20 (22nd out of 24 brands tasted). 420 Volcanic sells at $99 a liter, and Bling H20 (in Swarovski crystal-studded bottles) at $79 a liter. Decanter editor Guy Woodward said the tasting test exposed the "outrageous" prices of mineral water.

Traditional Indian Methods of Cooling and Purifying Water

Now people of India turning their backs on the country's ancient methods of cooling and purifying water. Stored in earthen pots, for instance, it is not only refreshingly cool and tasty but is said to become bacteria-free. Yet the common summer sight of water matkas (earthen pots) in public offices and spaces is giving way to upturned plastic drums dispensing packaged water.

Rainwater is Safe, Doesn't Bring About Adverse Effects

For centuries people have thought rainwater as unsafe, but contrary to their beliefs, as per an Australian study, drinking of untreated rainwater is safe for human health. The study was conducted under the auspices of eminent researchers from Melbourne's Monash University. The entire team took a look at 300 homes that used rainwater collected in water tanks as their primary drinking source. This endeavor has been described as a world first study that comes in the midst of growing criticism of bottled water.

Findings

During the survey it was found that, Most of the customers prefer to use Packaged drinking water as compared to the Municipal water & Aqua guard water

During the survey it was found that the Cool-spring and Oxyrich are the most popular brands among the users.

Most of the customers say that they are comfortable to pay prices within Rs. 50 to 60.

During the survey it was found that, Most of the customers prefer to use Hot & Cold dispenser as compared to the Plastic dispenser.

During the survey it was found that, Most of the customers prefer to use Rented Hot & Cold dispenser as compared to the Owned Hot & Cold dispenser.

During the survey it was found that, Most of the customers prefer to use Owned Plastic dispenser as compared to the Rented & Free Plastic dispenser.

Conclusion

The survey helps in identifying the lacuna in the distribution as well as the relations maintained by the distributors to the company and to the retailers. Survey helps in identifying the areas of improvement that include distribution, promotion and penetration. It will definitely contribute to the higher sales, higher market share and better growth. Thus, we conclude that the market is still to be explored through penetration and promotion.

Most of the respondents say that the prices of the Kinley mineral water are too high as compared to other brands.

The distribution system is very poor & the product is not readily available so company must stress to make distribution system effective.

Many customers say that they are not aware about the product, so company should advertise the product through newspapers, magazines etc.

Suggestions

Company should advertise & promote its products aggressively. Company should advertise in newspaper, magazines etc. It should adopt new trends of promotion tools to have maximum coverage. Increase customer penetration by increasing brand awareness by bill boards, advertising on road sides along with k.m. sign.

The right distribution channel will have to be chosen to ensure that the market is properly trapped. For maintaining good distribution Channel Company should appoint area sub-distributor who has telephone facility.

A training programme should be organized for salesman & trainees for effective functioning.

The company executive should visit the organizations regularly after a particular interval of time to take the feedback from the market about the problems if any, faced by the organizations.

References

1. Walker & Boyd; Marketing strategy; 2008, 5th Edition, Tata McGraw-Hill, New Delhi.
2. Sheth & Parvatiyar; Relationship Marketing; 2002, 10th printing, Sage Publications, New Delhi.
3. Philip Kotler; Marketing Management; 2008, 10th Edition, Tata McGraw-Hill, New Delhi.
4. Richard Batterley; Leading Through Relationship Marketing; Tata McGraw-Hill.
5. Internet: whereisdoc.com, www//Google.com.
6. Browser and Documents of different Companies and service providers.
7. Vinod V. Sople, Logistics Management, 2008, 2nd Edition, Pearson Education, New Delhi.
8. C.R. Kothari, Research Methodology, 1997, 6th Edition, Prentice Hall India.
9. Company Website: www.Coca-colaindia.com.

◈ ◈ ◈

ISBN – 978-93-5024-769-3

46

Strategic and Efficient Leadership Mantra During Complexity and Change

Prof. Archana Dixit
SKP's Dnyansagar Institute of Management & Research, Balewadi, Pune.

Introduction

Leadership is the act of influencing the behavior on others, so that they perform the functions of the organization in a proper manner. There are various styles of Leadership but there is not any one style which is suites for all organization for each and every situation. Leaders of high-commitment, high – performance organizations refuse to choose between people and profits. Developing Leadership skill is continuous process and those skills have to be developed right through every leader's career's each step and with continuous efforts. Leadership is different from the core management. Leadership is more concerned with emotional and strategic factors while management primarily deals with aspects like control, performance, problem solving etc. For developing Leadership skills the evaluation of present leadership skills should be get done. Organisations should Prepare and arrange training for leaders. Plan for the same get design and implement to enhance more leadership skills. At all level of hierarchy of the organization the Opportunity should get provided for nurturing Effective Leadership Skills. By 'leader', we don't just mean the Vice-Chancellor, the Pro Vice-Chancellors, the Registrar, Deans, Heads of Department, Divisional Heads and Technical and Resource Managers. We mean everyone who leads, manages or supervises groups of staff. Leadership is the fundamental foundation of the way of doing business. Organization should promote the behaviours and leadership capabilities of work force and encourage leadership.

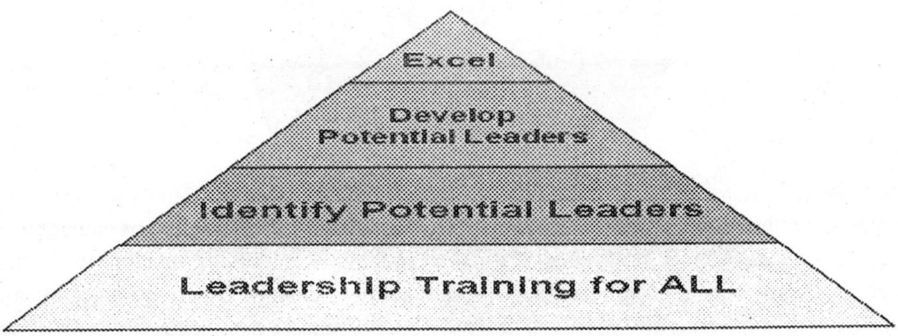

Source: http://www.chijstnicholasgirls.moe.edu.sg/Page/images/primary/LeadershipStru.gif

Characteristics of Efficient Leaders

- Devote their time and energy for achievement of organizational goals.
- Should possess vigor and determination to achieve success,
- Nurturing team spirit and share the success, with due creditability of Team members.
- Set and demand high targets from the employees, as well as for self and keep the follow up of for the achievement of targets.
- Always ready with alternative plans, if failure occurs.
- Boost up the team spirit of Team, though failure occurs rather than to blame or fire.
- Good Listener.
- Enjoy their work and have fun working together with people who are performing well as well as who are up to or below average.
- Should have Empathy
- Positive Thinker
- Excellent Communication skill and who can provide clear direction
- Good Motivator, who can provide the continuous feedback to his team members.
- Who is not bias.
- Create a healthy and joyful work environment.

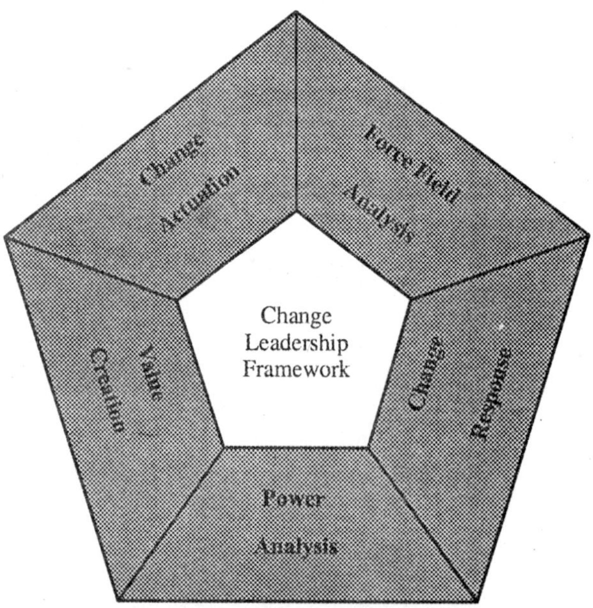

Source: http://changeleadershipgroup.com/images/CLF.jpg

In today's climate of complexity and change there is no ideal structure, strategy, or management approach that guarantees business success. What is most critical to success is leadership capacity to harness people's ideas, enlist highs of performance, build relationships, and adapt to change. Steering an organisation in times of change is no easy feat and frequently involves radically, reconfiguring a complex network of people, tasks, and institutional arrangements. In a climate that demands adaptability, flexibility, and innovation, leadership provides the organisational rudder. When effective, it is pointed in the right direction, it is embracing, it is intelligent, and it is ethical. Leadership is both a position and a process. The quality of leadership can make the difference between a ordinary and a great organisation. Leaders has 'do' leadership effectively. They use the authority accorded them in their position to engage in the process of effective leadership. Effective leaders provide stewardship for the larger purpose that underlies the enterprise. They know where they want to go, and set direction. They establish and drive values, and construct a shared vision and strategy that embraces the interests of important constituencies including shareholders, customers, employees, and the community.

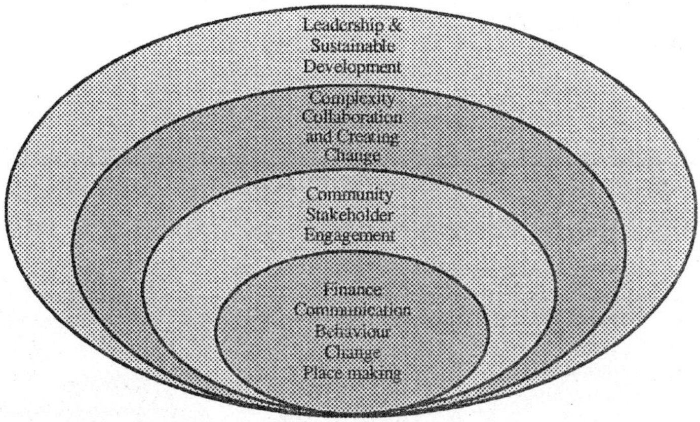

Source: http://www.lead-europe.org/uploads/New-Picture-12.png

Effective Leaders have a sense of moral purpose that guides the decision-making process and is embedded in the vision and its articulation in governance processes, company policies, and behaviours. Effective leaders are able to tap into diverse thinking, asking the right questions and listening to the evidence and argument. They attend not only to the rational, intellectual and factual, but also to the ethical, and emotional. They live comfortably with ambiguity and complexity and avoid simplistic solutions and 'spin' to appeal to short term interests. They are able to distil complexity and articulate a future that is clear and engaging, yet on fronts the challenges of new ways of working, new behaviours, and new relationships. And they are able to communicate, engage and inspire followers, capturing their imagination, aligning them in one direction, and motivating them for action.

Effective leaders construct a shared vision and strategy that embraces the interests of important constituencies, including shareholders, customers, employees, and the community. Leaders have a sense of moral purpose that guides the decision making process and is embedded in the vision and its articulation in governance processes, company policies, and behaviours. They are able to distil complexity and articulate a future that is clear and engaging, yet confronts the challenges of new ways of working, new behaviours, and new relationships. And they are able to communicate, engage and inspire followers, capturing their imagination, aligning them in one direction, and motivating them for action. Leaders get developed by following norms

Be available, Trust people, Be consistent in your behavior, Be decisive, Be fair, Deal with conflict, Set an example. Whether an organization survives a crisis with its reputation, operations, and financial condition intact is determined less by the severity of the crisis than by the effective leadership. Effective crisis response isn't just a matter of protecting reputation. It also allows a company to get on with business faster and more effectively than if it delays its response. More important, effective crisis response has direct impact on a company's productivity, demand for its product, stock price, and other quantitative measures of success. Effective leaders see crisis response not as an interruption in their stewardship of a company, but as the test of stewardship."

Leaders are expected, to act as change agents, who are able to create an atmosphere in organizations which are favorable for implementing change. Change agents don't wait for others to implement changes, rather take initiative and start the change process on their own. They know and accept that change is a power and organization should take the opportunity of Change for the success and prosperity of organization. Effective leaders are always ready to abandon old ideas and accept change with positive thinking as a opportunity. Effective leaders always persist smooth progress of the change process. Plans must be continually updated as new information becomes available. Effective leaders are alert for change and revise the operations plan based on changes in the situation. The impact of the leader on team performance is a function of three things: Personality, Ability, and Leadership Style.

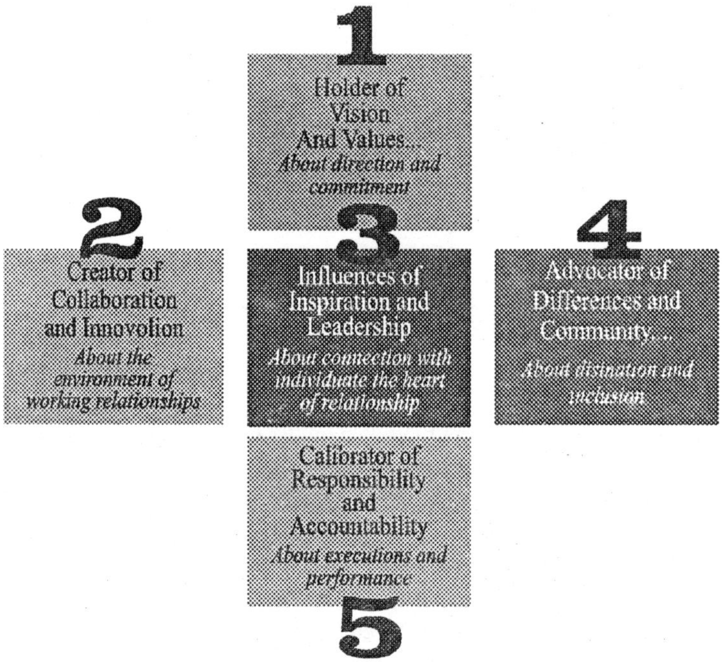

Sources: http://www.coachworks.com/graphics/5BPmodel.jpg

The Seven Traits of Effective Leadership

1. **Proactiveness:-** Instill the belief in all members of the organization that "Quality begins with me, and I need to make my own decisions and be a stakeholder in the success of the organization." Team members must also be responsible for the performance of the organization.
2. **Imagination and Conscience:-**Publicize your vision for your department through the clear expression of your hopes and purpose for your time aboard the unit. Ensure your vision considers the social responsibility you have to the people and their families.
3. **Willpower:-** Maintain a disciplined life that focuses heavily on highly important, but not necessarily urgent activities. Take positive measures to minimize crisis management and maintain high moral values in your professional and personal life.
4. **Think Win/Win:-** Share recognition and power by tapping the capabilities of all people in the department and routinely providing constructive feedback and praise. Attempt to reduce the friction, while recognizing that in an effective team, strength lies in diversity. Create an environment of trust.
5. **Courage Balanced with Consideration:-**Actively listen to subordinates to clearly understand their ideas. Show restraint and respect in dealing with subordinates to maintain two-way communication.

Foster mutual respect and build a complementary team where each individual strength is made productive and each individual weakness is made irrelevant.

6. **Synergy:-** Permit solutions to be formulated through the open communication between respectful individuals. Problem solves using information from those communications. Achieve creativity, improvement, and innovation beyond your own capability.
7. **Continuous Improvement:-**Avoid becoming closed to new ideas. Pursue innovation and refinement in yourself and the department. Broaden cross-functional cooperation and communication; expand trust and synergy within the whole department.

The leader must clearly understand the mission goals and objectives and translate them into team tasks. In assigning tasks, the leader seeks the best match between team resources and tasks.

Team performance is dependent upon each individual. Acknowledging good performance cultivates effectiveness. This type of positive reinforcement also moderates the stress inherent in operational teams. Effective leaders identify others' needs and abilities. They ensure fair and equitable treatment, project high expectations for subordinates and their teams, know their job, express confidence in their abilities, and use reward systems effectively. Leaders appropriately support and assist in professional and personal situations and use formal and informal processes to resolve situations.

When the leader tells the team what his/her understanding of the current state of the mission is, it allows the team to make internal alignment checks. This ensures that all team members share the same mental model. When differences in understanding exist, the effective team resolves the conflict. Feedback is part of the leader's routine. Effective leaders take time at silence in the mission and at the debrief to provide constructive critiques. This includes explaining some of the leader's actions so the team can better understand and anticipate the leader's point of view. It is important to provide both positive and negative feedback.

Positive Feedback: Focuses on what an individual or team does well. Positive feedback lets the person know what they should continue to do.

Negative Feedback: Focuses on problems that one or more team members perceive. Negative feedback lets the person know what they should start or stop doing, or change. Negative feedback is not punishment it is constructive criticism.

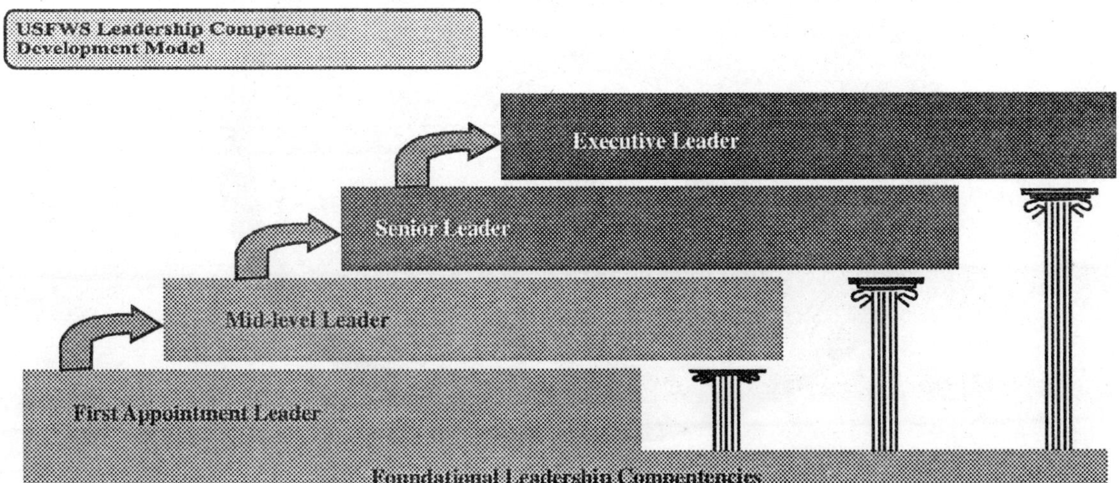

Source: http://training.fws.gov/LED/CompetencyModel/images/model.gif

How Leaders Should Give Effective Feedback

- Descriptive, ***not*** Evaluative.
- Well Intended, ***not*** Hurtful.
- Specific, ***not*** General.
- Well timed, ***not*** Delayed.
- Balanced, ***not*** One-Sided.

Leading a complex organization requires an entirely different mindset. Hierarchy works if every level is doing something distinct and specific. However, due to the interdependence in complexity, this is impossible in today's organizations. By simplifying and clarifying vision and values, core processes and decentralization, and early awareness systems, hierarchy can be complemented by "hierarchy", the interdependent, networked organization in which every part reflects a different perspective of the whole and which is needed in today's global business world. The boss no longer needs to "tell" the team members what exactly to do, but rather depend on their initiative, creativity and competence for success. Leadership in a networked organization means not only providing different leadership roles and styles depending on the situation (but always consistent with the purpose, values, and core processes), but also leading different parts of a networked organization to work together to create value.

The leader of a complex organization must create and communicate understanding of the different roles managers, teams, business units, and bosses play in the inter-dependent structure, otherwise confusion is intensified. Leadership cannot be repetitive, but should be predictable.

Permanent communication is therefore the leadership survival tool in complex organizations, but much more in terms of "storytelling", interpreting context and meaning, and investing in relationships than in transferring dry facts or ultimatums.

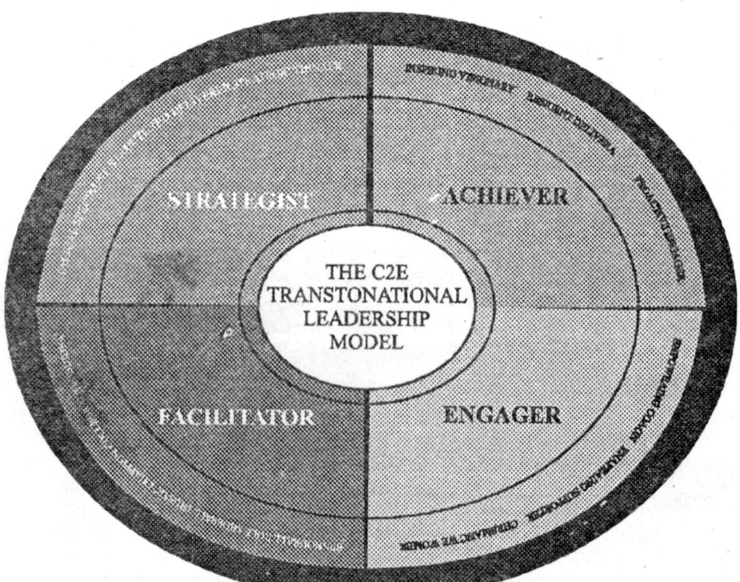

Source: http://www.c2econsulting.co.uk/Media/Images/img_transformational-leadership2.jpg

Conclusion

"Leadership and learning are indispensable to each other." - *By John F. Kennedy* "Leadership is practiced not so much in words as in attitude and in actions" – *By H. S. Geneen.*

Leadership styles exist in India from Ancient times, Leadership Of Shivaji Maharaj is still famous and in use in today's world of Globalization, his Leadership styles got nurture coz, of his Guru – Dadoji Kondev, Guide:- Ramdas Swamy and by his Mother. His Guide Ramdas Swamy's has written famous Grantha " DASBOTH", the qualities of effective leader and how he should plan a strategy is one of the part of "DASBOTH" those strategies getting implemented by today's Effective Leaders it may be the Indian Cricket Team Capt. Dhoni or By CEO of TATA Group Mr. Ratan Tata Or by Infosys Founder Mr. Narayan Murthy. Most large organizations have great managers, and great managers are necessary to get things done properly on time and as per budget. But Management by itself is not sufficient to make a great organisation – a great organisation requires leadership from the top and through all levels. However, leadership does not come naturally for to many people –for most it builds up through learning and experience.

References

1. Team Coordination Training Student Guide.
2. www.icfai.org.
3. STRATEGY & LEADERSHIP, 2006, Vol. 34 No. 1 www.emeraldinsight.com/reprints.
4. Let us know via pwe-feedback@bristol.ac.uk. Advice on organisational change, management and leadership development is available from Personnel Services and Staff Development.
5. National Australia Bank - http://www.genderworx.com.au/resources/LeadershipToday.pdf
6. Harvard Business Review: August 2008.

◇◇◇

ISBN – 978-93-5024-769-3

47 A Paper on Corporate Governance and Corruption

Dr. Manisha S. Bhatt
C. Z. Patel College of Commerce & Management, Vallabh Vidyanagar, Gujarat.

Corporate Governance in India – A Background

The history of the development of Indian corporate laws has been marked by interesting contrasts. At independence, India inherited one of the world's poorest economies but one which had a factory sector accounting for a tenth of the national product; four functioning stock markets (predating the Tokyo Stock Exchange) with clearly defined rules governing listing, trading and settlements; a well-developed equity culture if only among the urban rich; and a banking system replete with well-developed lending norms and recovery procedures. 24 In terms of corporate laws and financial system, therefore, India emerged far better endowed than most other colonies. The 1956 Companies Act as well as other laws governing the functioning of joint-stock companies and protecting the investors' rights built on this foundation.

The beginning of corporate developments in India were marked by the managing agency system that contributed to the birth of dispersed equity ownership but also gave rise to the practice of management enjoying control rights disproportionately greater than their stock ownership. The turn towards socialism in the decades after independence marked by the 1951 Industries (Development and Regulation) Act as well as the 1956 Industrial Policy Resolution put in place a regime and culture of licensing, protection and widespread red-tape that bred corruption and stilted the growth of the corporate sector. The situation grew from bad to worse in the following decades and corruption, nepotism and inefficiency became the hallmarks of the Indian corporate sector. Exorbitant tax rates encouraged creative accounting practices and complicated emolument structures to beat the system.

Changes Since Liberalization

The years since liberalization have witnessed wide-ranging changes in both laws and regulations driving corporate governance as well as general consciousness about it. Perhaps the single most important development in the field of corporate governance and investor protection in India has been the establishment of the Securities and Exchange Board of India (SEBI) in 1992 and its gradual empowerment since then. Established primarily to regulate and monitor stock trading, it has played a crucial role in establishing the basic minimum ground rules of corporate conduct in the country. Concerns about corporate governance in India were, however, largely triggered by a spate of crises in the early 90's – the Harshad Mehta stock market scam of 1992 followed by incidents of companies allotting preferential shares to their promoters at deeply discounted prices as well as those of companies simply disappearing with investors' money. 25 These concerns about corporate governance stemming from the corporate scandals as well as opening up to the forces of competition and globalization gave rise to several investigations into the ways to fix the corporate governance situation in India. One of the first among such endeavors was the CII Code for Desirable Corporate Governance developed by a committee chaired by Rahul Bajaj. The committee was formed in 1996 and submitted its code in April 1998. Later SEBI constituted two committees to look into the issue of corporate governance – the first chaired by Kumar Mangalam Birla that submitted its report in early 2000 and the second by Narayana Murthy three years later. Table 1 provides a comparative view of the recommendations of these important efforts at improving corporate governance in India. The SEBI committee recommendations have had the maximum impact on changing the corporate governance situation in India.

Corruption

Corruption in India is neither new nor limited in scope. India ranks 85th among the 180 countries in a recent study by Transparency International on political corruption.[2] The World Bank ranks India in the 25th to 50th percentile on the ability to control corruption.[3]

Economic corruption in India arose due to state controls of production through licenses and quotas. To gain access to licenses, corporations paid bribes. To gain access to goods and services in short supply, the public paid bribes. Thus, in the public mind, corruption, slow growth, inefficiency, and poor quality became inextricably linked.

A second source of corruption was the misuse of state power. The state has misused power in various ways. These include overstaffing public departments with favored voting groups, reallocating property rights to favored business groups and dispensing privileges in return for campaign contributions. The third source of corruption was inadequate disclosure and enforcement of corporate actions. With a few exceptions, listed companies were run as family firms that viewed their firms as hereditary fiefdoms.

India began reforming its laws from 1991. Licensing for production was eliminated in the 1991 reforms, thus solving the problem of inefficient production and short supply of goods and services.

The state has also shifted from governance by quota to independent regulation. Regulators in finance, insurance, and telecommunications, among others, have been empowered with the right to enforce global best practices and given independence from other organs of the state.

However, corruption in state patronage remains, particularly in land and civic infrastructure allocation, patronage recruitment, and election finance, despite reforms in these areas.

Corporate Governance and Audit

Anti-fraud Culture

Reading Borough Council's culture has always been one of openness and honesty, and its core values of fairness trust and value reflect this. The Council expects that members and officers at all levels will lead by example and ensure comply to legal requirements, standing orders, financial regulations, code of conduct and other applicable Council rules.

Minimizing Risk

The Council has a framework of controls and codes of practice in place to deter fraud from taking place and detect it when it does. It is the responsibility of all members and officers to work within this framework and comply with the Council's rules and regulations.

Managing the risk of fraud and corruption is the responsibility of management. Audit procedures alone, even when performed with due professional care, cannot guarantee that fraud or corruption will be detected. Internal Audit does not have responsibility for the prevention or detection of fraud and corruption. Internal auditors will, however, be alert in all their work to risks and exposures that could allow fraud or corruption. Internal Audit may be requested by management to assist with fraud related work. The Chief Auditor should be informed of all suspected or detected fraud, corruption or improprieties so that he can consider the adequacy of the relevant controls, and evaluate the implication of fraud and corruption for his opinion on the internal control environment.

All internal auditors have/will continue to receive fraud awareness training and basic training on the Police and Criminal Evidence Act 1984 (PACE). All investigations will be undertaken in accordance with PACE legislation.

Detection and Investigation

As well as minimising the risk of fraud, Internal Audit also plays an important role in the detection of fraud and corruption through completion of their risk based audit plan. This process involves reviewing the systems financial controls and specific fraud and corruption tests.

There are numerous system controls in place to deter fraud and corruption, but it is often the vigilance of employees and members of the public that aids detection. In some cases however, frauds are discovered by chance or "tip-off" and arrangements are in place to enable such information to be properly dealt with.

As part of the culture of the council, clear routes by which concerns can be raised by members and officers and those outside of the Council are available. Concerns are treated in confidence and properly investigated in accordance with the Council's whistle blowing policy. Under the Council's code of conduct and financial regulations employees must report and suspected cases of fraud and corruption to the appropriate manager, or if necessary, direct to the chief internal auditor. All suspected irregularities are required to be reported (verbally or in writing) either by the person with whom the initial concern was raised or by the originator.

Transparent Governance/Anti-corruption

Corruption is a problem all over the world, but is particularly prevalent in developing countries and emerging economies where robust and accountable public institutions are often in their infancy. Corruption affects entire societies adversely, and attitudes to corruption become increasingly ambivalent as long as the incidence of corruption remains unchecked. Anti-corruption strategies are therefore inextricably linked to economic and social development in countries where corruption is a problem. ASI's experience of corruption and anti-corruption initiatives is broad and long-standing, and is the result of work on reform projects where corruption has proved to be an obstacle, as well as work on projects specifically designed to combat corruption.

- Reviews of transparency and accountability
- Anti-corruption strategies
- Public information campaigns
- Institutional development
- Design of Citizens Charters
- Design of transparent and accountable procurement procedures
- Organisational reviews to remove gatekeeper posts
- Simplification of business processes

Good Corporate Governance

Good and desirable corporate governance is the one to ensure maximized corporate value and fair distribution of profits to shareholders through transparent business management and appropriate rules of management executives. In general, when the profits of shareholders, who are residual claimants, are maximized, overall business value can be maximized as well. Therefore, companies will focus their management on shareholders. In other words, good corporate governance has the mechanism to ensure transparent business management and appropriate regulations for management executives, thereby effectively realizing management principles focusing on shareholders.

To be more specific, the concept of 'good corporate governance' can be different in each country and company depending on its environment, culture, and industry. However, in terms of general framework and direction, international consensus has been built. In a narrow sense, good corporate governance stresses on protecting the profits of minority shareholders, enhancing transparency in management and accounting information and the role of outside directors. In addition, along with integration of global capital market, importance of external monitoring mechanism through capital market has been highlighted, spreading the efforts to facilitate such monitoring. In addition, discussions on addressing the problems of share pyramid, cross share holdings and multiple voting rights, which often trigger gap between cash flow rights and voting rights, are actively taken place.

Conclusion

The recent surge of interest in corporate governance from institutional investors, international organizations, and governments around the world should be welcome news to the global anticorruption campaign. The empirical results here support a theoretical projection that good corporate governance can lead to reduced level of corruption. More emphasis should be directed to bribe payers instead of focusing solely on bribe takers.

Corporate governance can well become a critical ingredient to break a vicious cycle of bribery and corruption. This vicious cycle starts when firms are forced into bribery practices because of a high level of corruption, but widened participation of firms in bribery practices further feeds into the perception of high corruption, which in turn makes the bribery practices even more uncontrollable. The analysis of the linkage between corporate governance and corruption suggests that the improvement in corporate governance may be a catalyst to break the vicious cycle of bribery and corruption. Shareholders and investors in countries that are experiencing a high level of corruption may receive double dividends from the improvement in corporate governance. Companies with better corporate governance have better prospects of growth and command higher valuation in the market.

At the country level, improvement in corporate governance may help a country with high level of corruption to partially offset the negative impacts of the perception of corruption on the flow of capital (both financial and human), and the additional capital induced by good corporate government serves as catalyst for further improvement in both corporate Governance and the governance of the public sector. On the other hand, bad corporate governance may also undermine the effectiveness of the global anticorruption campaign in an era of globalization. We find that firms from countries with lower corporate governance standards are more likely to be involved in bribery practices when they export goods or services to other nations. Therefore, improving corporate governance in some leading exporting nations should be a top priority.

Bibliography

Books

1. Carrol B.A. *Corporate Social Responsibility,* 2006, Business and Society.
2. Charles Oman, Steven Fries & Willem Buiter, Corporate Governance in Developing, Transition and Emerging Market Economies, Policy Brief No. 23, 2008, OECD Development Center.
3. Friedman, M., The Social Responsibility of Business is to Increase its Profits, 1970, New York Times Magazine.

Internet

1. www.google.com.

◈ ◈ ◈

ISBN – 978-93-5024-769-3

48 Changing Trends in HR as Useful Retention Strategies

Prof. Anand Padle
SGREF's IMR, Chas,
Ahmednagar.

Prof. Deepali Choudaki
Modern College of Engineering,
Shivajinagar, Pune.

Prof. Satish Ubale
Matrix School of Business
Vadgaon, Pune.

Introduction

According to Akio Morita founder of Sony Corporation the success of Japanese Companies in general and Sony in particular is not due to any magic but the secret lies in the way they treat their employees. Nestle's CEO, Peter Brabeck also pointed out the every single person in the organization should ask himself or herself - is there anything I can do to add a little more value to our company? This shows how importantly people are treated in this organization.

Human Resource Management is the efficient utilization of employees in achieving two main goals. The first goal is to effectively make use of the talents and abilities of employees to achieve the operational objectives that are the ultimate aim of the organization. Along with realizing the goals of the organization, Human Resource Management also seeks to ensure that the individual employee is satisfied with both the working environment and the compensation and benefits that he or she receives.

Challenges for HR in India

Then most important challenges before the human resource professionals is the need for team building and managing multidisciplinary , multilinguistic, multicultural and multinational teams in the most cordial and harmonious way so that every individual and every group in an organization will have a sense of belonging. It requires efficient planning, capability to procure best talents available, designing and conducting appropriate human resource development programmes, maintaining and retaining the appropriate manpower, establishing and maintaining a caring organization, carrier planning and succession planning, keeping the people in high spirits through counseling, guidance and motivation, providing an essential direction to all functional areas to manage people with dignity, maintaining cordial industrial relation and organizational climate preventing and setting industrial conflicts. Almost all these aspects are linked with a conductive quality of work life for the establishment of which the HR manager should be instrument.

- Management of knowledge workers
- Technological advances
- Competency Development

- Development in Leadership Quality
- Change Business environment
- Recruitment and Training
- Work life Balance Factor
- Attrition/Retention of the Talent Pool
- Changes in industrial relation

Methodology

An analysis of literature has been done prior to the study. In-depth discussion and interview have been adopted for gaining the empirical understandings which has been analyzed and summarized.

Secondary Data is collected from Journals, Websites and Reference books. To collect primary data about the changing role of HR in today's scenario interview sessions were conducted in the few noted companies in the Ahmednagar MIDC area like ***Atul Electro Formers Limited, Supreme industries private limited, Krishna Soaps Private limited, Chirag industries, Brook Crompton limited, Saideep industries, L&T limited and Sun pharmaceutical limited.***

Changing Role of Human Resource Management Requires Following Measures

Resource Utilization

One of the most common complaints of employees is the lack of resources to effectively perform their job- this can range from access to equipment, insufficient time to do the job well or lack of education and training. In times of cutbacks a review of efficiencies and needs for optimum performance can help HR make the case for programs that support employee efficiency and effectiveness. The right person in the right place with the right tools can be more productive than any number of misplaced and ill-equipped employees. The advantage of this is mutual: the organization benefits and the employees are encouraged to continue their contribution at high levels. Moreover organisation can adopt job rotation technique which will improve multi-skilled work force and can be used in times of absenteeism.

Building Trust

Particularly in a time of uncertainty it is important to foster a culture of trust within the organization, this can range from reviewing situations where employees feel they need to compete for resources and recognition rather than collaborate towards shared corporate goals, to reviewing the management culture and transparency and effectiveness of communications going out to employees.

Cultural Collaboration

Employees who have an understanding of how they fit in with the rest of the organization and the larger goals and objectives tend to remain more committed to the organization. Further more encouraging collaboration between departments and colleague relationships across departments encourages mutual consultation and enhanced creativity.

Motivation & Accountability

Create a culture of recognizing individual and team contributions either through monetary rewards or for instance eligibility for in-house training and career development as well as public platforms for recognition.

Employees who are struggling must be guided with accountability for their performance and their growth. While management must also take accountability for it's shortcomings or failings with regard to individual or team support. Different cultures have different ways of placing accountability up the chain of command to the most powerful employee responsible or down the chain of command to the least powerful employee involved. It may be a valuable exercise to review your organization's natural tendency in this regard.

Improved Communication

The value of effective communication cannot be overstated. Internal and external messages must be clear and effective, taking into account the purpose of the communication, content, the audience and their listening bias and culture, timing and source and modality of delivery. Although effective communication cannot make bad news into good news, it will ameliorate the impact and fallout of bad news as well as the ongoing trust and credibility in the organization and leadership.

Dare to Do Different

If business has wages that are in the lower quartile of wages in the sector this would be an ideal time to make ground with inflation busting wage increases, when everyone else is freezing their wages. You might get two fold advantage. Firstly, you will be signaling to the workforce that they are valued and that you will be keeping as many people as you can, and that the wage increase is designed to help them in difficult times. Secondly, you will be setting your business on a better footing to come out of the recession to attract the best talent into your pool of staff, further reducing recruitment costs, and driving up productivity.

Talent Management

In this era of increasing complexities and cut throat competition people are the last weapon for gaining, competitive advantage. Out of the 4 M's only Men cannot be replicated and can be taken as a lasting weapon of competitive advantage. As it is said it takes talent to spot talent. A deaf will never be able to sense the beauty of a symphony. While there is no magic trick to manage talent, the key is to identify and encourage it. For a HR manager, there is nothing more crucial than to find a right match between the job requirement and the skill set of the job seeker.

Workplace Diversity

The future success of any organizations relies on the ability to manage a diverse body of talent that can bring innovative ideas, perspectives and views to their work. One of the main reasons for ineffective workplace diversity management is the predisposition to pigeonhole employees In order to effectively manage workplace diversity, Cox (1993) suggests that a HR Manager needs to change from an ethnocentric view ("our way is the best way") to a culturally relative perspective ("let's take the best of a variety of ways").

Procedures To Improve Productivity of Human Capital

The HR mandate is sufficiently broad that this department can bring added value to many levels within the organization. Managers need HR support and training to:

- Attract, engage and retain innovators.
- Communicate effectively.
- Negotiate effectively.
- Be flexible.
- Motivate and build team cohesion.
- Deal with:

- Gossip, rumor and uncertainty
- Deliver bad news.

- Deal with their worries and anxieties.
- Have Access to resources and tools.

This will involve implementation of training to develop skills in some companies, in others it may require intervention around culture and attitude by educating managers about the value of human capital and the value of changing their leadership style from authoritarian and disciplinary to transformational and rewarding and implementation of policies and codes of conduct.

Not all initiatives involve more spending. Some may focus on re-envisioning the corporate culture and reputation, reviewing inefficiencies or re-evaluation valuable employee's roles in order to take optimal advantage of their talent and contributions.

Findings

HR Managers could do well by adopting the following in view of the changed conditions:

1. Bring in a transparent work culture.
2. Strong belief in empowering the employees.
3. Communicate effectively and at all times.
4. Appropriate feedback mechanism.
5. Bring in a culture of rewarding people instantly and make everyone know about it.
6. Commitment to organizational and people development
7. Excellent interpersonal skills.
8. Patience to continue with a change program and handle resistance to change
9. Ensure that employees constantly acquire right skills themselves, which not only empowers them but also makes them an asset to the company.
10. Consultation rather than confrontation should be the running theme in exchange of views with the employees.

Conclusion

The ultimate aim for a business and its managers should be to make every employee feel valued and proud of their individual contribution and the specific role that they play. You should strive to develop a work culture that encourages diversity, ingenuity, and commitment. This in turn will assist in the retention of staff and will also serve to improve their performance and productivity. Adopting a strategy for staff retention can be challenging but the results will benefit both the organizations and its employees now and into the future.

Organizations in Ahmednagar, MIDC are accepting this changing role of Human Resource Management. The future is bright for these organizations that adopt innovative efforts to meet the challenging times. To be successful, they need to abandon the traditional innovation approach in favour of pruning the portfolio, wisely managing resources and creating new value. Success will depend not on how much these companies spend on innovation, but on how well they plan and execute their innovation strategies.

References

1. **Human Resource Management**, *K Aswathappa*, 5th Edition, Tata McGraw-Hill.
2. **Human Resource Management**, *Dessler / Varkkey*, 11th Edition, Pearson.
3. **International Human Resource Management**, *Chris Brewster, Paul Sparrow, Guy Vernon*, University Press.
4. **HRM Review**, May 2009, ICFAI University Press.
5. www.whereisdoc.com.

◈◈◈

ISBN – 978-93-5024-769-3

49

"Microfinance: A Strategic View for Rural Economic Development"

Prof. Ganesh S. Lande, Dr. E.B. Khedkar & Prof. Mayura G. Gutal
Sinhgad Management School, Kondhapuri, Pune.

Introduction

Microfinance" is often defined as financial services for poor and low-income clients. In practice, the term is often used more narrowly to refer to loans and other services from providers that identify themselves as "microfinance institutions" (MFIs). These institutions commonly tend to use new methods developed over the last 30 years to deliver very small loans to unsalaried borrowers, taking little or no collateral. These methods include group lending and liability, pre-loan savings requirements, gradually increasing loan sizes, and an implicit guarantee of ready access to future loans if present loans are repaid fully and promptly.

More broadly, microfinance refers to a movement that envisions a world in which low-income households have permanent access to a range of high quality financial services to finance their income-producing activities, build assets, stabilize consumption, and protect against risks. These services are not limited to credit, but include savings, insurance, and money transfers.

Typical microfinance clients are poor and low-income people that do not have access to other formal financial institutions. Microfinance clients are usually self-employed, household-based entrepreneurs. Their diverse "microenterprises" include small retail shops, street vending, artisanal manufacture, and service provision. In rural areas, microentrepreneurs often have small income-generating activities such as food processing and trade; some but far from all are farmers.

Hard data on the poverty status of clients is limited, but tends to suggest that most microfinance clients fall near the poverty line, both above and below.

Most MFIs started as not-for-profit organizations like NGOs (non-governmental organizations), credit unions and other financial cooperatives, and state-owned development and postal savings banks. An increasing number of MFIs are now organized as for-profit entities, often because it is a requirement to obtaining a license from banking authorities to offer savings services. For-profit MFIs may be organized as non-bank financial institutions (NBFIs), commercial banks that specialize in microfinance, or microfinance departments of full-service banks.

The impact of microcredit has been studied more than the impact of other forms of microfinance. Microcredit can provide a range of benefits that poor households highly value including long-term increases in income and consumption. A harsh aspect of poverty is that income is often irregular and undependable. Access to credit helps the poor to smooth cash flows and avoid periods where access to food, clothing, shelter, or education is lost. Credit can make it easier to manage shocks like sickness of a wage earner, theft, or natural disasters. The poor use credit to build assets such as buying land, which gives them future security. Women participants in microcredit programs often experience important self-empowerment.

Empirical studies on the impact of credit are difficult and expensive to conduct and pose special methodological problems. Most impact studies to date have found significant benefits from microcredit. However, only a few studies have made serious efforts to compensate for the methodological challenges. In fact, many studies would not be regarded as meaningful by most professional econometricians. A new wave of randomized trial studies is now in process, which should yield a more definitive picture.

Even so, there is a strong indication from borrowers that microcredit improves their lives. They faithfully repay their loans even when the only compelling reason is to ensure continued access to the service in the future.

Other microfinance services like savings, insurance, and money transfers have developed more recently, and there is less empirical research on their impact. Client demand indicates that poor people value such services. MFIs that offer good voluntary savings services typically attract far more savers than borrowers.

Microfinance System

Above system shows the inter-relationship between the demand and supply of funds available in the market. In this system, there are suppliers of finance as well as parallel effect must be demand for the finance. Intermediaries collect the funds (savings) from the people and such funds must be distributed to the people who are in need of such funds.

Microfinance Can be a Good Tool for Empowering Women

"Microfinance programs have generally targeted poor women. By providing access to financial services only through women-making women responsible for loans, ensuring repayment through women, maintaining savings accounts for women, providing insurance coverage through women-microfinance programs send a strong message to households as well as to communities.

Many qualitative and quantitative studies have documented how access to financial services has improved the status of women within the family and the community. Women have become more assertive and confident. In regions where women's mobility is strictly regulated, women have become more visible and are better able to negotiate the public sphere. Women own assets, including land and housing, and play a stronger role in decision making.

In some programs that have been active over many years, there are even reports of declining levels of violence against women."

Specific Research Objectives

To study and analyse the microfinance schemes which are already working in Shikrapur Village.

To find out the challenges which are faced by the rural people.

To find out government role in development of rural economy as well as study various strategic approaches to microfinance.

Research Methodology

The study would be conducted primarily by surveying the rural area (Shikrapur Village) in view of micro financing. Primary information will be collected by visiting the Shikrapur Village, Self Help Groups, Banks, Credit Co-operative Societies: where the concept is working. The tools would include in-depth interviews- and questions-with the persons affected :and detailed discussions with bankers, other government functionaries.

Microfinance Delivery Models

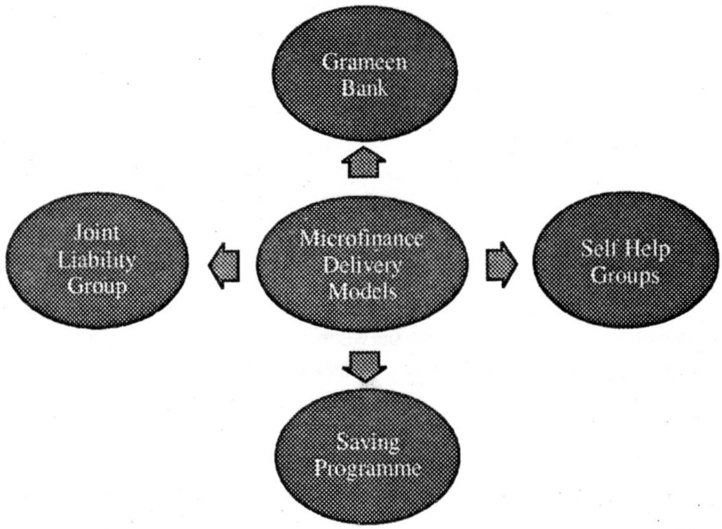

Grameen Bank

The Grameen Bank lending system is simple but effective. To obtain loans, potential borrowers must form a group of five, gather once a week for loan repayment meetings. These decisions incorporate a code of conduct that members are encouraged to follow in their daily life e.g. production of fruits and vegetables in kitchen gardens, investment for improvement of housing and education for children, use of latrines and safe drinking water for better health, rejection of dowry in marriages etc. Though according to the Grameen Bank management, observance of these decisions is not mandatory, in actual practice it has become a requirement for receiving a loan.

Number of groups in the same village are federated into a Centre. The organisation of members in groups and centres serves a number of purposes. It gives individuals a measure of personal security and confidence to take risks and launch new initiatives.

The formation of the groups - the key unit in the credit programme - is the first necessary step to receive credit. Loans are initially made to two individuals in the group, who are then under pressure from the rest of the members to repay in good time. If the borrowers default, the other members of the group may forfeit their chance of a loan. The loan repayment is in weekly instalments spread over a year and simple interest of 20% is charged once at the year end.

The groups perform as an institution to ensure mutual accountability. The individual borrowing member is kept in line by considerable pressure from other group members. Credibility of the entire group and future benefits in terms of new loans are in jeopardy if any one of the group members defaults on repayment.

There have been occasions when the group has decided to fine or expel a member who has failed to attend weekly meetings or willfully defaulted on repayment of a loan. The members are free to leave the group before the loan is fully repaid; however, the responsibility to pay the balance falls on the remaining group members. In the event of default by the entire group, the responsibility for repayment falls on the centre.

The Grameen Bank has provided an in built incentive for prompt and timely repayment by the borrower i.e. gradual increase in the borrowing eligibility of subsequent loans.

Grameen Bank has helped to generate new jobs for a large proportion of the members. Only insignificant portion of the loans (6 per cent) can be diverted for consumption and other household needs.

Savings Programme

It is compulsory for every member to save some money per week which is accumulated in the Group Fund. This account is managed by the group on a consensual basis, thus providing the members with an essential experience in the collective management of finances. Amounts collected from fines imposed on members for breach of discipline is also put into this account. The amount in the Fund is deposited with Grameen Bank and earns interest. A member can borrow from this fund for consumption, sickness, social ceremony or even for investment (if allowed by all group members). Terms and conditions of such loans, which are normally granted interest free, are decided by the group.

Factors behind success of the Grameen Bank are: participatory process in every aspect of lending mechanism, peer pressure of group members on each other, lending for activities which generate regular income, weekly collection of loans in small amount, intense interaction with borrowers through weekly meetings, strong central management, dedicated field staff, extensive staff training willingness to innovate, committed pragmatic leadership and decentralized as well as participatory style of working.

The Grameen Bank experience indicates the vital importance of credit as an entry point for upliftment programme for rural poor. If a programme is to have an appeal for people living in abject poverty, it must offer them clear and immediate prospects for economic improvement. Thereafter, it is easier to sell other interventions of social development, however unconventional they may appear, once improvements in standard of living are demonstrated.

The Grameen Bank clearly shows that lack of collateral security should not stand in the way of providing credit to the poor. The poor can utilise loans and pay them if effective procedures for bank transactions with them can be established. In case of the Grameen Bank, formation of groups with a small group of like minded rural poor has worked well, and group solidarity and peer pressure have substituted for collateral security.

Self-help Groups

Microfinance has the great importance from past 3 to 4 years. In Maharashtra, there is a movement of Self Help Groups (SHG's) and it gives the tremendous growth in the rural economy. The needs and wants of lower income people are to satisfied through the financing.

Formation and Routine Work of SHG

10-20 Members come who's income level is almost same

Members elect the Group leader for the group

Collection of savings regularly (monthly)

Saving Account with Bank in Rural area which provides the special facilities and this account operates the group representatives

Working procedure- Meeting with group members (Weekly, Monthly)

As per requirement of SHG member internal finance is to be provided

Maintain all the details in the separate register

Relationship Between Financial Intermediaries and Self Help Group

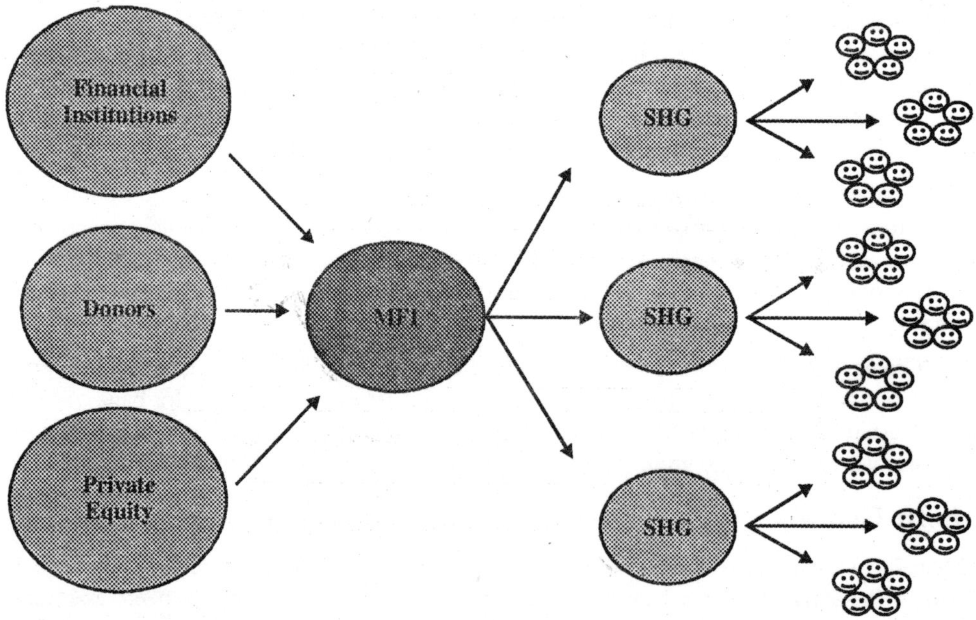

Below poverty line people and who are also nearest to the poverty line, these people formulate the SHG and meet their needs and wants.

In the past few years microfinance is the key area in the rural economy which helps in the development in standard of living of lower income level population.

Types of SHG

1. Women Groups
2. Men Groups
3. Women and Men Group

Self-help Groups (SHGs)

Self-help Group concept has its origin in India. SHGs are now considered to be very important bodies in rural development and are therefore found in almost all parts of the country and their number is still rapidly growing. SHGs are formed by Non-Government Organisations as well as Government agencies and are used as channels for various development programmes.

A Self-Help Group is an association of generally up to 20 members (not exceeding 20 members), preferably from the same socio-economic background. SHGs are facilitated by Government agencies or NGOs for members to come together for discussing and solving their common problems either financial or social through mutual help. An SHG can be all-women group, all-men group, or even a mixed Group. However, it has been the experience that women's groups perform better in all the important activities of SHGs. Mixed group is not preferred in many of the places, due to the presence of conflicting interests.

Some of the Distinct Features of SHGs are

(i) Recognized by government: SHGs are well recognized and accepted by government, SHGs can open bank accounts in the name of SHG. They can also receive government grants and funds for development activities.

(ii) SHGs are social intermediaries: SHGs do not restrict their functions only to financial transactions. SHGs are often involved in many social activities. There are example where SHGs have taken up social issues and fought against social evils like alcoholism, violence, against women, dowry, getting into village politics and being elected as Sarpanch.

(iii) Books of accounts: SHGs maintain their own books of accounts. These are simple books to keep records of their savings, loans income and expenditures. Strong SHGs also make their Balance sheets and Income statements.

(iv) Have office bearers: SHGs gave a structure where there is a Group President, Secretary and Treasure. They are elected by the group.

(v) SHGs are more autonomous as they decide their own rules and regulations.

(vi) SHGs mobilize thrift and rotate it internally.

(vii) SHGs can hold bank account and can also borrow from banks and other financial institutions.

We see that SHGs are groups, which are more autonomous. While they are involved in financial transactions, their role is not just restricted to it. SHGs are also involved in various social issues. As more SHGs are formed they have started federating themselves into clusters and clusters in turn as SHG Federations. The Federations are able to channelise funds to the SHGs and also help in improving the managing and financial skills of SHGs.

Linking Banks with Self-help Groups

Some of the principles underlying the above mechanism and the guidelines that can be issued to the implementing groups are listed below :

- The SHGs are to use part of their funds (almost 60%) for lending to their members and the rest for depositing in a bank to serve as the basis for refinancing from the bank.
- Savings are to come first: no credit will be granted by the SHG without savings by the individual members of the SHG. These savings are to serve as partial collateral for their loans.
- The joint and several liabilities of the members is to serve as a substitute for physical collateral for that part of loans to members in excess of their savings deposits.
- Credit decisions for on-lending to members are to be taken by the group collectively.
- Central Bank refinance is to be at an interest rate equal to the interest rate at which the savings are mobilised.
- All the intermediaries (the Central Bank, banks, NGOs and SHGs) will charge an interest margin to cover their costs.
- Interest rates on savings and credit for members are to be market rates to be determined locally by the participating institutions.
- Instead of penalties for arrears, the banks may impose an extra incentive charge to be refunded in the case of timely repayments.
- The ratio of credit to savings will be contingent upon the creditworthiness of the group and the viability of the projects to be implemented, and is to increase over time with repayment performance.
- SHGs may levy an extra charge on the interest rate for internal fund generation (which would be self-imposed forced savings).

Joint Liability Group – Grameen Model

Grameen model is based on the concept of joint liability. It is the brainchild of Prof.. Muhammad Yunus, founder of Grameen Bank in Bangladesh. Grameen model is the most accepted and prevalent micro-finance delivery model in the world today. Many MFIs have accepted the model as it has high focus on standardization and discipline

Grameen model, as mentioned, is a joint liability group model. Here five-member groups are formed and eight such groups form a Center. Hence, in a full-capacity Center there are 40 members (8 x 5). However, over the years people have experimented with Centers of different sizes and now there are variations of 5-8 groups within a Center. Center is the operational unit for the MFI, which means that MFI deals with a Center as a whole.

Meetings also take place only at the Central level and individual groups do not meet. Group meetings take place only in front of the Field staff of the MFI. A Grameen model is focused on financial transactions and other social issues are generally not discussed. The Group and Center are Joint liability Groups, which means that all members are jointly responsible ('liable') for the repayment. MFI recovers full money from Center, if any member has defaulted: the group members have to pool in money to repay to the MFI. If Group members are unable to do it, Center as whole has to contribute and share the responsibility.

Some Other Features of Grameen Model are

(i) The group meeting take place every week

(ii) Interest rate are charged on flat basis

(iii) MFI staff conducts the meeting

(iv) All transactions take place only in Center meetings

Grameen model is focused on providing financial services to the clients and hence there is an emphasis on standardization and discipline. The model suggests weekly meeting for frequent interaction with the clients to reduce credit risk. The meetings are conducted for carrying out the financial transactions only. The meetings are conducted systematically in a short-time and other social issues are not discussed. Flat interest is charged again for making the system standardized. In flat rate system installment size of repayment remains small for all weeks and hence is convenient and easier to explain. Also, it is easy to break the loan installment into the principal and interest component.

We see that the SHG and Grameen model have originated with two different approaches. SHG model has been developed with holistic view of development and empowerment of society where financial transactions are only one part of it. While Grameen model is specifically focused on providing financial services to the low-income clients.

Grameen model is a particular form of joint liability Group but in India there are other forms of Joint liability Groups as well. MFIs, particularly in urban areas, form JLGs of five-members. These are group of individuals coming together to borrow from the financial institution. They share responsibility ("liability") and stand as guarantee for each other. There is a Group Leader in such JLGs, many MFIs prefer such group in urban business areas. Such JLGs do not hold periodic meetings. Typically members are shopkeepers from same locality. These forms of JLGs are somewhere between Group and Individual lending methods. While lending in such JLGs is to individual members small JLGs still provide some sort of comfort to the MFIs. Also collection can be done from a single point, generally from the Group leader rather than going to each individual. As in urban areas shopkeepers do not have time to hold meeting, these JLGs do not meet.

Credit Mechanisms Adopted by HDFC (India) for Funding the Low Income Group Beneficiaries

- HDFC has been making continuous and sustained efforts to reach the lower income groups of society, especially the economically weaker sections, thus enabling them to realise their dreams of possessing a house of their own.
- HDFCs' response to the need for better housing and living environment for the poor, both, in the urban and rural sectors materialised in its collaboration with Kreditanstalt fur Wiederaufbau (KfW), a German Development bank. KfW sanctioned DM 55 million to HDFC for low cost housing projects in India. HDFCs' approach to low-income lending has been extremely professional and developmental in nature. Negating the concept of dependence, HDFCs' low cost housing schemes are marked by the emphasis on peoples participation and usage of self-help approach wherein the beneficiaries contribute both in terms of cash and labour for construction of their houses. HDFC also ensures that the newly constructed houses are within the affordability of the beneficiaries, and thus promotes the usage of innovative low cost technologies and locally available materials for construction of the houses.
- For the purpose of actual implementation of the low cost housing projects, HDFC collaborates with organisations, both, Governmental and Non-Governmental. Such organisations act as co-ordinating agencies for the projects involving a collective of individuals belonging to the Economically Weaker Sections. The projects could be either in urban or rural areas.
- The security for the loan is generally the mortgage of the property being financed.
- The construction work is regularly monitored by the co-ordinating agencies and HDFC. The loans from HDFC are disbursed depending upon the stages of construction. To date, HDFC has experienced 100% recovery for the loans disbursed to various projects.

Government Role in Rural Economic Development Through Microfinance

1. Setting favourable microfinance policies
2. Launching the schemes for SHG
3. Ensuring the involvement citizens in savings and investments
4. Contribution of people in economy
5. Developing the rural employments
6. Explore the linkage between rural finance and rural development
7. Poverty reduction
8. Subsidies against the loans
9. Strengthening legal framework

Various Microfinance schemes studied in Shikrapur Village, Pune district.

Schemes Implemented Under SHG

Lending short term loans: This is the scheme which provides the short term loan to the members. This scheme needs to have continuous and consistent saving of the members. Whatever the amount is collected by the group from that amount the loan is to be provided. There is a specific rate of interest charged and this loan is provided for shorter period of time, i.e. 3 to 4 months. If members fail to repay the amount in stipulated time then some penalty is taken from the members. Rates of interest of bachat gats working in the Shikrapur are

Shivshakti Bachat Gat- 3%

Shri Bhanoba Mahila Swayamsahayata Bachat Gat -2%

Bhairavnath Mahila Swayam Sahayyata Bachat Gat-2%

Lending long term loans: In this scheme the loan is provided to the members of group. The members can take the loan for a period of more than 6 months. For long term loan the ROI is determined by the group. The rate of interest charged for in this scheme is higher than the rate offered for short term loan. If any member fails to repay the amount within the stipulated time ,penalty is charged i.e. Rs 250 per day. This loan facility can be extended to the outsiders as well .And for outsiders the rate of interest is increased to 8-10%. Rates of interest of bachat gats working in the Shikrapur are

Shivshakti Bachat Gat- 7%

Shri Bhanoba Mahila Swayamsahayata Bachat Gat -3%

Bhairavnath Mahila Swayam Sahayyata Bachat Gat-3%

Bidding for finance: In addition to the above two schemes some bachat gats have implemented this particular scheme as well. In this scheme saving groups collect the money from each member and those members, who are in need of finance, they can participate in the bidding process. Trimurti Bachat Gat is one of the group adopting this scheme.

Bidding Process

Determine the amount for bidding

↓

Basic price for bidding

↓

Members for bidding
(The member who has already taken the long-term loan he is not allowed to participate in bidding process)

↓

Last member who bids higher rate, the bidding process is overs

For example:-

If funds collected from the members is Rs. 10,000/- then base price for the bidding process is decided as Rs. 1,000/-. With this base price bidding is done. The member who bids the higher rate gets that amount and such amount is deducted from the collected fund. In this case, if the bidding is done for Rs.2,000/- then the member is liable to pay in next month Rs.10,000/- plus Rs. 2,000/- as interest.

Interest free loan scheme- This scheme is purely based on government released schemes for BPL population. Interest free loans are distributed to the registered self help group for increasing their standard of living. These loans are strictly repaid within given period by the self help group government. In Shikrapur, PDCC bank, Sampada cooperative credit society works for the groups and government acts as intermediary.

What members of such groups have to say

- We happened to see a TV programme on Bachat Gat (Saving or Self Help Group), and we also wished to form one. But we did not know what this Bachat Gat is exactly and how to form it. We went from pillar to post in many government offices but no one helped. Even the bank was not ready to open our group's account, as we did not come through any scheme. But we kept scouting for it and at last by chance happened to go to ZP office for some work. There, one official – Mr P.Bhujbal - not only gave us the information about SJSRY but also told us all about Bachat Gat. And thus we 15 women formed our Bachat Gat and started saving Rs.100 a month. We decided to take up papad-making and selling, which earns the group Rs.18000 per month i.e. Rs.1200 per month per member."

- a member of Shri Bhanoba Mahila Swayamsahayata Bachat Gat, Landewadi, Shikrapur, Taluka-Shirur, Dist. Pune.

- "We were somehow eking out a living by cutting and selling grass. Once Angan Wadi Sevika Kusum Tai told us about SJSRY for people like us listed under BPL. So under her guidance we started our group saving Rs.200 per month. I took Rs.12000 loan at 2 per cent per month from our Bachat Gat to buy a buffalo. After feeding her for 8-9 months, I sold her for Rs.26000. Even after repaying Bachat Gat's loan with interest, I made a good profit, which would not have been possible had I taken the loan from a moneylender at over 10 per cent a month. Over the last three years, I saved enough through this business and kept Rs.15,000 in fixed deposits for each of my three daughters."

- Manisha Narke ,a member of Bhairavnath Mahila Swayam Sahayyata Bachat Gat, Talegaon Dhamdhere, Tal-Shirur, Dist-Pune

- "Through our Bachat Gat of 17 men saving Rs.1000 per month, a member Rahul Ramane took Rs.20,000 for a welding machine; Sandip Gaikwad took Rs.10,000 for her mother-in-law's operation; Mayur Bhujbal Rs.7,000 for her sister's marriage. We then took over a land on rent for Rs.40,000/acre and nurtured sugarcane crops which after selling in the market we earned Rs.2,10,000, thus making a profit of Rs.1,20,000.

- a member of Shivshakti Bachat Gat, 24th Mail, Landewadi, Shikrapur, Taluka-Shirur., Dist. Pune.

Challenges Faced by Self-help Group

1. Lack of infrastructure
2. Seasonable demand in agriculture sector
3. Less savings
4. Information barriers
5. Natural disasters- Heavy rains, earthquake
6. Limited services allocation
7. Communication and informational gap
8. Domestic politics
9. Poor governance
10. Insufficient capacity of the institute
11. Low productivity
12. Unskilled authorities
13. Lack of Higher Education

Conclusion

In the light of above study it can be concluded that Microfinance has really helped in improving the standard of living of the rural area people.

Some valuable lessons can be drawn from the experience of successful Microfinance operation. First of all, the poor repay their loans and are willing to pay for higher interest rates than commercial banks provided that access to credit is provided.

Even though microfinance is grabbing the attention of government for economic development this sector faces number of challenges such as lack of policy framework, inept management, lack of awareness among people.

Self Help Groups working for women are helping them in getting independent status in the society. Such groups are also improving their capacity of raising and providing finance and have a parallel effect in developing a rural economy. From the conclusions reached the following recommendations are made;

Recommendations

In the view of Microfinance public awareness campaign should be increased in the rural areas by giving lectures, arranging workshops for them.

Students can also take initiative by participating in such schemes and can experience "Earn while Learn".

Rural residing people can use the advanced information technology as a tool for effective management.

As a matter of urgency microfinance institutions should expand increase and diversify in terms of services they render to their numerous targeted customers in more rural areas.

References

1. Udyog Pragati, The Journal of Practicing Managers, Vol. 34, No. 04, Oct.-Dec., 2010, Financial Inclusion through Microfinance Institution-Francis Kehinde Emeni.
2. Journal of Financial Management and Analysis, Vol. 21; No. 1, January- June 2008, Microfinance Institutions in Nigeria: Problems and Prospects: Questionnaire survey Findings-Prakash Singh.
3. The Icfaian Journal of Management Research, Vol. VIII, No. 1, January 2009, Assessing the Performance of the Stakeholders of Microfinance Programs – V. R. Nedunchezian and N. Sivasankaran.
4. The Management Accountant, Vol. 45 No. 1, January 2010, Critical Appraisal of Microfinance in India (Special Reference to UP) – Dr. Ekta Rastogi.
5. Microfinance in India, Publisher-Sage Publications (CA), K.G. Karmakar.
6. Microfinance and Self-help Groups in India: Living Up to Their Promise? Publisher-Practical Action - Author: Frances Sinha, Ajay Tankha, K Raja Reddy.
7. www.microfinancegateway.com.
8. www.indiamicrofinance.com.

◈◈◈

ISBN – 978-93-5024-769-3

50

"Strategies of 4p's & 7p's for Efficient Marketer (With Special Reference to Ahmednagar District)"

Prof. Satish Ubale
Matrix School of Business, Vadgaon, Pune.
Prof. Deepali Choudaki
Modern College of Engineering, Shivajinagar, Pune.

Introduction

The Indian rural market is at once fascinating and challenging. It offers large scope on account of its size and potential. It is also steadily growing, whereas the urban market is highly competitive, the rural market is fairly quiet. In fact, for certain products, it is totally a virgin market. As such, firms can certainly reap big rewards from the rural market. The catch is that market also poses several problems and hurdles. The firms have to face them squarely. They must recognize that rural marketing is primarily is developmental marketing and must be willing to take an approach of 'market seeding' in the initial stages. It is often said that marketers are made, not found. This is particularly true of the rural market of India. It is a market meant for the truly creative marketer. The rural markets have some characteristic features which the corporate and government must analyse properly. They are as follows:

Huge And Scattered Market

The rural market of India is large and scattered in the sense that it consists of over 63 crore consumers from 5,70,000 villages spread throughout the country.

Major Income From Agriculture

Nearly 60% of the rural income is from agriculture. Hence, rural prosperity is tied with agricultural prosperity.

Low Standard of Living

The consumer in the village area do have a low standard of living because of low literacy, low per capita income, social backwardness, low saving etc.

Traditional outlook

The rural consumer values, old customs and tradition, they do not prefer changes.

Diverse Socio-economic Backwardness

Rural consumers have diverse socio-economic backwardness. This is different in different parts of the country.

Infrastructure facilities

The infrastructure facilities like roads, warehouses, communication systems and financial facilities are inadequate in rural areas. Hence, physical distribution becomes costly due to inadequate infrastructure facilities.

Indian Rural Markets and its Potential

Rural markets in India have acquired significant growth and resulted into substantial increase in the purchasing power of the rural communities. Some impulses to go rural are large population, rising rural prosperity, growth in the market, impact of globalization. These markets as part of economy have untapped potential. There are several difficulties confronting the efforts to explore them fully. The concept of rural markets in India is still in evolving stage, and the sector poses a variety of problems like under-developed market, lack of proper physical communication facilities, lack of media for rural communication, many languages and dialects. Further, the markets are dispersed, low levels of literacy, prevalence of spurious brands and seasonal demand hindered the growth of rural market.

Brand consciousness is not important in the rural market as the choices are limited. (For example Chick shampoo and lifebuoy soap, Nirma bar and detergent powder are very popular brands in the rural market as compared to urban market. The success of brands in the rural market is as unpredictable as rain. Many brands, which should have been successful, have failed miserably. This is because most firms try to extend marketing plans that they use in urban area to the rural markets. The unique consumption pattern, tastes, perception, and needs of the rural consumers should be analysed at the product planning stage so that they match the rural people.

Marketers need to understand the psyche of the rural consumers and then act accordingly. Rural marketing needs more intensive personal selling efforts than urban marketing. Firms should refrain from designing goods for the urban market and subsequently pushing them in the rural areas.

Firms should be very careful in choosing the vehicle to be used for communication in the rural market. The advertisement has to be done in the local languages. This gives a powerful impact on the minds of the rural people, grabs their heart by inducing local elements and flavors to the product so that they have some emotional attachment to it. More personalized and relationship based experience should be emphasized in rural marketing.

Marketing Mix for the Rural Markets

Marketer will need to adapt his/her marketing mix to suit rural conditions and the maximum adaptation will have to be in the distribution and media mix.

Product Decision

Products for the rural market will have to be simpler, an easy to use, service, or maintain. The product literature should be simple and well illustrated for the rural customer. Besides, it should be dispensable in single units. A typical rural buyer buys one unit of match box unlike an urban consumer who may buy a full pack of ten or twelve match boxes. Sachet packaging is one alternative which has been successfully used by tea, shampoo and pan masala. Brand identity in rural market is often created through the visual logo of a product, the colour of the product, or the taste of the product.

For example, in one rural market survey, a buyer of Thums Up recognized through its logo and mentioned it as sweet black water that came in a bottle. The generic name was "soda water". But he didn't want just any aerated soda but Thums Up that had a fizz in it and hence he called "soda water". Likewise, Coca-Cola's "Thanda" campaign with Aamir Khan delivered results more than any other slick advertising campaign. Further, price-performance relationship of the product needs to be examined closely. The marketer must attempt to maximize performance in the rural customer's environment without sacrificing any feature which is available to the urban customer.

Pricing Decision

The rural consumer is price sensitive because of his relatively lower income level. The marketers will have to examine the methods by which he can make the product more affordable for the rural consumer. In the case of consumer durables, one way is to work through rural banks and offer hire purchase terms to the customer. Tractor, pump sets, and even televisions have been marketed through this approach.

Another way is to offer a smaller unit or pack size, at a lower price. Toiletries are marketed in rural areas in smaller unit sizes, thus making them more affordable. Thus, while in the urban stores Lux toilet soap is available in 25 gm or even bigger sizes, in rural markets same brand is available in 10 gm sizes at almost half the price. This strategy can help a large firm pass on the benefits of lower costs of a small firm to the customer in the form of lower prices.

Promotion Decisions

As far as rural market is concerned, visual copy has a much greater appeal than just the audio and the print. It is important to note that well-known film stars and models representing the common men, or the man next door, are able to successfully communicate the message. Jingles, folklore, and music can combine to make a message and the brand name memorable. Visual copy has a much greater appeal than just the audio or the print. In terms of the media, television, wall paintings, and even roof painting are effective. So are bus panels and hoardings. Wall hangings and other point of purchase material like stickers and shelf display are also effective in getting the marketer's message through to rural consumers. Rural fairs (mela) haats, Mandi have a special place in the rural consumer's life. Firms like Bajaj Electricals, Hindustan Lever, Parle and ITCs have successfully used them to promote their brands. Personal selling is also important here. But there is no aggressive sales person. Research shows that a simple and subtle salesman can deliver better results here. Hence, many companies use local young people to sell the product.

Distribution

Distribution is the key to penetrating rural markets. It is here that a firm has to deploy a mobile distribution strategy. The firm may either have its own fleet of vans or hire the services of a distributor having one. This is crucial because, today, a firm can no longer afford to wait for the rural buyer to come to the city to buy his requirements. Competition is driving firms to reach out to the buyer. And since no single village can consume the entire van load of products, the firms can derive economies by covering several villages in a single van cycle. Another key to effective distribution is the weekly rural market or haat. It is important that the firm's products are available here either through small petty traders or through its van. The firm should also link the village grocer with the nearest wholesale distributor so that the market is not starved at any given time. Further, the marketer can even consider using the post offices, ration shops, bank branches available in the rural areas for distributing his products. The rural postman and postal vans or vehicles can even be considered for marketing purposes.

However, the marketer cannot afford to ignore the development of organized retail stores ITC's Chaupal Sagar, Mahindra and Mahindra's Shubh Labh Stores and Warana bazaar in Maharashtra. These developments may mark the end of the rural dealer. The marketers need to break the paradigm that urban and rural retail outlets differ in terms of number of product categories stocked by them. The only difference between the two is that urban outlets serviced by more number of companies as opposed to rural markets.

Three Extended P'S of Marketing Mix

People: Customer service and satisfaction lies at the core of service Industries. Even in service Industry, there are some services which involve lot of interaction between the customer and front end employees. BSNL is the best example of service Industry which is doing great job even in the villages. Because of its marvelous job for the villagers and its focus in this particular area, its connectivity to even small villages has taken the place in the heart of rural India. In services, the most important element is people. It is true for the services in which customer interaction is more.

Process: Process includes the procedure, flow of activities or mechanism of work. For a customer, if the products are not delivered on time, customer may get disappointed. To deliver the product or service on time is an important marketing activity. To ensure customer satisfaction in service organization, there are a number of processes involved in making marketing effective. It also involves standardization of service. This is another area where marketers can concentrate on. Marketers can definitely get a wide scope if they focus on the speed and standardization for service which includes insurance, communication industries, hospital, educational institutions, transportation, even restaurants.

Physical Evidence: The environment, or the surrounding of the retails, its ambience may brings a positive change in the minds of the rural customers. Marketers should certainly help the store owners to focus on the physical evidence of the stores. And because of the physical evidence, rural people are attracted toward the urban market. Examples are record store, clothes shop, hair dressing salons by maintaining cleanliness and hygiene etc. not only do they find their way around the store, but they can also offer a good presentation. Though marketers have not paid much attention on the extended P's of the marketing mix in the rural market, one cannot deny the scope of these P's in the near future.

Marketer needs to focus on 4P's and 7 P's of marketing. It is necessary to implement the right strategies for each element of the marketing mix. For this, marketers need to understand the buying behavior of the rural consumers and at the same time their psychology. For this a structured questionnaire was administered to find out the strategies adopted by the marketer. Twelve villages in the Ahmednagar district have been randomly selected and kirana store owners of these villages were asked to fill the questionnaire.

Research Methodology

Research Objective: To study the strategies of 4P's and 7P's of the marketing mix elements in the rural market.

Data Collection Method

Type of Data: Primary data has been used for the research.

Sources of Data: Primary data was collected directly from the 'Kiranas' of various villages of Ahmednagar district using a questionnaire. These villages include Shendi, Kada, Darewadi, Bhalawni, Chas, Nimbodi, Nimblak, Wadgaon, Wakodi, Bhurannagar, Nimgaonwaga and Pimpalgaon.

Research instrument: Questionnaire

Sampling Unit: Small Kirana stores in Ahmednagar district.

Research Area: Twelve villages of Ahmednagar district was selected at random and based on the population of these villages, Kirana stores are selected.

Sample Size: 32 Kirana stores

Data Representation

(1) To study whether rural customer are price sensitive or not.

Price sensitivity	*Number of respondent*	*Percentage*
Yes	29	91
No	03	09
Total	32	100

Interpretation

91% of the respondents say customers are price sensitive and 9% respondents say customers are not price sensitive.

(2) To study whether rural customer prefer branded products.

Prefer branded products	*Number of respondent*	*Percentage*
Yes	24	75
No	08	25
Total	32	100

Interpretation

75% of the respondents say customer want branded products and 25% respondents say customer do not want branded products.

(3) To study the availability of the products throughout the year.

Product availability	*Number of respondent*	*Percentage*
Yes	07	22
No	25	78
Total	32	100

Interpretation

22% of the respondents say that products are available throughout the year and 78% respondents say that products are not available.

(4) To study the promotion activities carried out by companies.

Promotional activity	*Number of respondent*	*Percentage*
Television	10	31
Mobile vans & Posters	17	53
Road shows	05	16
Total	32	100

Interpretation

31% of the respondents say that television helps in brand promotion, 53% respondents say that companies mobile vans & posters helps brand promotion whereas 16% respondents say that road shows help in brand promotion.

(5) To study whether product display helps rural customer to select the product.

Product Display helps in purchasing	*Number of respondent*	*Percentage*
Yes	22	69
No	10	31
Total	32	100

Interpretation

69% of the respondents say that product display helps rural customers to select the product and 31% respondents say that product display do not help rural customers to select the product.

Findings

(1) 91% customers are price sensitive.

(2) 75% customers prefer branded products.

(3) 78% respondent says that distribution is not consistent.

(4) 53% respondent say mobile van & posters helps to improve brand promotion.

(5) 69% respondents say product display helps product selection easy.

Conclusion

1. It is observed from the findings that, rural customers are price sensitive. Therefore, marketers should adopt appropriate pricing strategy like offering the product in small sachet, reducing the price of the product by focusing on the economy packs etc.
2. Rural customers prefer branded products, but these products are not available in the kirana stores and also price of the branded products are high which affects the purchasing decision of the rural customers.
3. It is observed that the products in the rural markets are not available throughout the year. Due to non-availability of the products, customers have no choice for their preferences. Due to poor connectivity of the roads, rail-roads and air, the marketers cannot distribute their products in the rural markets. Therefore, more emphasis has to be given on the infrastructural development which will help the marketers to enhance their businesses, which in turn help the nation to raise the economy and the development of rural India as well.
4. It is observed that visual displays of the posters and banners help the customers to purchase the products. In addition to this, mobile vans also play an important role in promotion of the product.
5. Kirana stores in the rural areas can go for the product displays in the shops which helps the rural people toknow about the product and its information. Merchandising plays an important role in marketing the products like urban market, it helps in attracting the rural customers too.

References

1. **Case studies on Brand Management,** How to break the clutter, *Prof. Naveen Das, and Kumar Satyaki Ray*, 2007, ICFAI books.
2. **Case studies in Strategic Marketing Management,** 2006, ICFAI.
3. **Rural Marketing-**Text and Cases, *C.S.G. Krishnamachryulu & Lalitha Ramkrishnan,* 2006, Pearson Education.
4. **Case Studies in Sales and Distribution Management,** 2006, ICFAI.
5. **Rural Marketing-**Targeting the non-Urban Costumers, *Sanal Kumar Velayudhan,* 2007, II edition, Sage Publications Inc.
6. **Case Studies in International Marketing,** 2006, ICFAI.
7. **Rural Marketing —** Concept and Practices, *Balram Dogra & Karminder Ghuman,* 2008, Tata McGraw-Hill Publishing Company Ltd.

◇◇◇

ISBN – 978-93-5024-769-3

51 Effective and Efficient Cold Chain Management Strategies Adopted by the Few Co. at MIDC in Pune Area

Jyoti D. Desale & Prof. Devika Shinde
Sinhgad Management School, Kondhapuri.

Introduction

In recent years, food supply chains have become more and more complex. As a consequence, the pressure on the industry to produce both high quality and consistently safe products is becoming even greater. Due to increasing long transport routes, safe products and extended shelf life times are paramount for economic reasons. Today's logistics contribute success to the business. It act as backbone for the manufacturing support activities. The cold chain management is a concept came in existence when three was great necessity of transportation of perishable product. The cold chain remains one of the most important ways to preserve perishables and deliver them to market in good condition. The various tools for success in the cold chain are identified, and examples of what can go wrong are given. The main requirements are for education and training and for provision of good operating systems.

The cold chain is generally considered as the transport and storage chain between the initial production and the final consumer of temperature-controlled perishable goods. This is not a complete definition, as there are other items carried under temperature control, for example works of art. There are many types of cold chain. They may be categorized by carriage mode, by commodity, or by location and duration of transport.

Air freight is generally limited to goods at chilled or ambient temperatures. Sea containers are universal in their application. Refrigerated ships carry bulk commodities in their holds, though increasingly these ships also carry containers. International land transport by road and/or rail is able to carry anything. Local distribution generally excludes the movement of bulk frozen goods.

At the present time there are approximately 1300 specialised refrigerated cargo ships, 80 000 refrigerated railcars, 650 000 refrigerated containers and 1.2 million refrigerated trucks in use worldwide. They carry vast amounts of foodstuffs and other perishables and mostly do so very successfully.

Storage is an important part of the overall cold chain. It has been reported by one company that, in the transport of pharmaceuticals during the last five years, critical or major problems arising in storage are more than four times as frequent as problems arising in transport. This emphasizes the point that cold chains should always be considered as a whole, if reliable results are to be obtained.

Objectives

- To get upgraded with latest trends & technologies in the Cold Chain, followed globally.
- To implement best practices for better efficiency learnt from industry leaders.
- To access the advantages by overcoming challenges in the cold chain & being cost effective.
- To upgrade with the innovative tools supporting cold chain management during transportation.

Research Methodology

Population size	:	300
Sample Size	:	120
Area of study	:	(1) Serum institute, Pune
		(2) Katraj Dairy, pune
		(3) Venkey's, pune
Mode of Data collection	:	Primary data – Interviews, Secondary data – Books & Web search

Limitations

- The functional area was limited only to some areas of Pune districts.
- Some of the respondents were reluctant to fill questionnaire & to provide information.
- The study is not extensive study and is done on a selective basis, results are hence derived which are based on the information selected areas.

Analysis and Findings

(1) Serum Institute of India

Serum Institute of India Ltd. has established itself as the world's largest producer of Measles and DTP group of vaccines. It is estimated that two out of every three children immunized in the world is vaccinated by a vaccine manufactured by Serum Institute. In fact, the range of products have been used in 140 countries across the globe.

Cold Chain Strategies:

Tools for Cold Chain Management of Biologicals

Freeze avoidance will become even more critical in the future as more expensive freeze-sensitive vaccines such as DTP-hepatitis B, liquid Hib, pneumococcal, and influenza are introduced into developing-country immunization programs.

Fortunately, accidental exposure to freezing temperatures can be prevented. The following is a list of simple and proven tools available today that could help program managers minimize the potential for freeze damage to their vaccines:

Investigate Vaccine Freezing in Cold Chains

WHO recommends that immunization programs use temperature monitoring studies to identify where problems are occurring so that corrective action can be taken. A WHO protocol has been developed and successfully applied in several countries.

Apply innovative cold chain practices

Using cool water packs instead of frozen ice packs during cold box transport to avoid the freezing commonly associated with improper ice-pack conditioning, storing the more heat-stable vaccines in air-conditioned rooms, and conducting limited transport at ambient temperatures are possible freeze prevention approaches.

Improve Training

Recommended changes in training include educating vaccine managers and handlers about freeze-sensitive vaccines, providing clear guidelines on vaccine handling procedures, and increasing the focus on freeze prevention during supervision.

Update Cold Chain Infrastructure

Improved cold chain equipment is an important aspect of freeze prevention. New refrigerators are being developed that automatically control temperatures and eliminate the possibility of inadvertent vaccine freezing. At a minimum, min/max thermometers can help users better understand the range of temperatures that vaccines are exposed to over time and can prompt mitigation strategies. Electronic temperature monitoring devices are also available to accompany vaccines during transport and storage, including low-cost devices that signal exposure to an established freeze exposure temperature.

Take Advantage of Vaccines' Heat Stability

Freezing temperatures damage freeze-sensitive vaccines more quickly than ambient temperatures. Vaccine vial monitors, heat exposure indicators required on all vaccines distributed by UNICEF, allow vaccine programs to utilize the natural heat stability of some vaccines to expose them to temperatures warmer than 8 æ%C for limited time without risk of heat damage. It may also be possible to allow a slight warming of the recommended cold chain temperatures to reduce freezing without causing heat damage.

Create System-Wide Policy to Avoid Freeze Damage

Policy changes (at the global and country level) are needed to prioritize the prevention of freezing in the cold chain and apply resources to raising awareness, training, and equipment infrastructure.

(2) Pune Zilha Sahakari Dudh Utpadak Sangh Maryadit (Katraj Dairy)

Pune Zilha Sahakari Dudh Utpadak Sangh Maryadit, popularly known as **'Katraj Dairy'** in the local and branded as **"Katraj"**, a district level co-operative organization registered in 1960, involved in processing milk and milk products. The representatives of milk producing farmers based in rurals, encompassing almost the entire Pune District, manage this organization on behalf of the milk producers for their (rural India) socio-economic growth. The objective of **Katraj** is to build a value chain of farmers to source milk at an organized level, manufacture products with high standards and sale these products in the competitive open market place.

The organization has a unique advantage of its strategic location as it is based in Pune city, a place with historic and cultural importance and a major district place in Maharashtra, India with a sound Educational and industrial infrastructure, located about 180 kilometers from Mumbai (the financial capital of India).

Tools for Cold Chain management of Dairy Products

There are many requirements which have to be met for successful handling of Dairy Products. Some of these are as follows:

- Insulated Containers/Vehicles

Insulated shipping containers are used to transport goods at a constant room temperature, no matter how high or low the temperature is outside the insulated container.

- Walk-in Cold Storage

The storage temperature of the walk-in cold storage room is displayed and controlled by digital thermostat for precise control temperature and temperature adjustment to achieve the utmost energy efficiency and perfect storage of food.

- Other Cold Storages

– Refrigerators

– Visi-Coolers

– Deep-Freezers

– Insulated Boxes

1. Produce Temperatures

All refrigerated milk produce deteriorates with time at a rate dependent on the temperature of storage. For most frozen goods at normal storage temperatures of -18°C or below, maximum times for high-quality storage are appreciably longer than transport times, so there are no special difficulties..

Refrigerated chilled and fresh produce, stored and transported at temperatures between -1.5°C and 14°C dependent on produce type, frequently has a high quality storage life measured in weeks rather than months, and the relatively slow pace of marine transport frequently requires much closer control of temperature than is achieved in road, rail or air transport if goods are to be carried successfully.

Many types of chilled and fresh produce have lower temperature limits below which they are damaged. Clearly, for items carried near their freezing points, lower temperatures will give freezing damage, and this is as true for chilled meats as for other more obvious products. There is a temptation if cargoes are loaded at a high temperature to reduce cargo space temperatures to below carriage temperature to achieve more rapid cooling. This can only be done at the risk of damaging part of the cargo.

It must be remembered that, for many cargoes, safe carriage temperatures depend on the variety as well as the type of produce, and may also depend on growing area and on whether early, main, or late harvested produce is being carried. Also, it may be necessary to mix produce with slightly different temperature requirements, in which case the highest temperature must be chosen, with consequent effects on the storage life of the products requiring lower temperatures.

It is essential that the storage characteristics and optimal storage temperature are correctly specified and maintained. Specification is the responsibility of the shipper; temperature maintenance is the responsibility of the carrier. If the shipper specifies the wrong temperature in an obvious way, the carrier will question it, but in less obvious cases the shipper has no reason to over-ride the instructions given. The carriage instructions must be clear and unambiguous

2. Produce quality

At best, refrigerated transport can maintain quality, it cannot improve it. Poor quality produce cannot justify the costs of transportation, and can give the likelihood of an unsuccessful outturn, leading to loss of confidence in the producer. Long-distance transportation should be seen as a means of obtaining premium prices for top quality produce, and never as a means of disposing of second-rate goods for which no local market exists.

The quality of produce may be subject to standards and inspections by producer boards or export control boards in the country of origin. It may also be subject to import requirements in the receiving country, details of which must be determined by potential exporters.

3. Packaging

Packaging has to protect produce, so must have adequate strength. Packaging materials must not contain substances likely to produce taints or odours. Cartons, Bag's must be of a suitable size and to protect the product from movement, wastage and also from external pressure. Successful packaging systems have been developed over the years, and these are frequently more sophisticated in their requirements than is immediately obvious. Changes to such systems should be considered with care.

4. Temperature Control

Temperature control for frozen goods is less critical than that for chilled goods. The former require a maximum temperature (e.g. -18°C) not to be exceeded, whereas chilled goods on long journeys often require temperatures maintained within a band of 2°C or less. In retail display, chilled goods are normally expected to be kept within a 5°C band or less.

The controllability of transport equipment designed for use with chilled cargoes is of necessity good. However, if equipment primarily designed for frozen goods is used for chilled transport, it may be possible to obtain wider temperature swings or lower temperatures than are desirable. Wide swings mean an appreciable time at higher-than-planned temperatures, with consequent loss of storage life. Low temperatures may mean freezing or damage from chilling injury.

5. Journey Time

Marine transport is generally very reliable, but by the nature of things, breakdowns and storms can sometimes create delays. So also can industrial action, often beyond the control of the carrier. Where such things lead to appreciable delays, damage to more perishable produce can occur.

6. Time Without Refrigeration

Goods can be without refrigeration for short periods during land journeys to and from ships, and can occasionally be without refrigeration due to mechanical breakdown of equipment. Breaks in refrigeration of a few hours may be acceptable for many, but not all, produce types. Breaks of a few days are likely to pose problems for all types of produce.

7. Retail sale

Following transportation, the cold chain continues through the wholesale handler and the retail store to the customer. In the store, proper equipment sensibly sited and properly used is necessary. Losses at this stage waste all the effort and energy which has been expended earlier in the chain

(3) Venkateshwara Hatcheries Pvt. Ltd. (Venky's)

The VH group was established in 1971, when motivated by his wife Late Smt. Uttaradevi Rao, our founder Chairman Late Padmashree Dr. B.V.Rao, established Venkateshwara Hatcheries Pvt. Ltd. in Pune (India). Today the group is popularly known the world over as "Venky's". With a unique combination of expertise and experience and supported by strategic collaborations, the company diversified its activities to include SPF eggs, chicken and eggs processing, broiler and layer breeding, genetic research and disease diagnostic, poultry medicine and feed supplements, vaccine production, bio-security products, poultry feed & equipments, nutritional health products, soya bean extract and many more. Today the group is the largest fully integrated poultry group in Asia. The VH group today plays proud parent to a number of reputed organizations under its wide umbrella and successfully caters to poultry and its allied sectors. The pioneering efforts of the VH Group have been well rewarded with several national and international awards.

Cold Chain Strategies:

Tools for Cold Chain Management of Frozen Foods

The vehicle must be provided with a good refrigerated system that remains operating at all times during transportation to keep the product temperature at the required values. During use it is important to keep doors closed, otherwise large quantities of warm air will enter the cold area. Warm air carries moisture that can badly affect the cooling performance Careful attention to delivery routes and the pattern of unloading will help conserve the low temperature environment. The driver's responsibility for the load includes responsibility for the vehicle's temperature; close packing the vehicle will also aid conserve the product temperature. Training may be helpful.

Whilst the vehicle is standing in the depot electric plug in points to operate the cooling systems are a useful method of maintaining temperatures quietly without auxiliary diesel engines running. If a pallet of packaged food is left standing in higher temperatures conditions, those packets at the corners or top edge are especially vulnerable to warming and will thaw quickly. The enemy of all refrigerated transport systems is heat; this will affect the temperature and therefore reduce the quality of the frozen product, which is precisely what we have to avoid. Heat can enter the transport vehicle and the food product in two different ways:

- Through the vehicle insulation – possibly from sunrays.
- Through the air that leaks through badly sealed doors or worse, ingress of water

How to Avoid this Heat Infiltration

- Choose a good insulating material (i.e. a poor heat conductor) and at optimal thickness to minimise the transmission of heat into the interior.
- Construct the body with the best seals possible to reduce hot air ingress.
- Paint vehicles a light colour, preferably white, to reflect the sun's rays and keep them clean..

By fulfilling these conditions and choosing a good refrigeration system it should be possible to achieve a good quality, healthy and safe frozen food product, similar to fresh food.

Conclusion

Global regulatory requirements for the handling, storage, and distribution of thermally labile pharmaceutical, food, dairy products have emphasized the importance of assuring that product quality and integrity are not compromised in the distribution channel. New guidance outline a comprehensive view of cold chain management across the supply chain including: manufacturers, warehouses, distributors, transporters, and retailers.

Trends of recent regulatory inspection citations demonstrate an increased focus on the factors affecting these labile preparations and ensuring their quality and integrity. Due to the presence of multiple uncontrolled variables in the distribution process, developing an appropriate monitoring program is essential.

Trained and experienced logisticians are critical to the effective management of cold chain. Because of the perishable nature of the product, good knowledge of cold chain, close monitoring, timely movement and appropriate storage is highly recommended to minimise risk exposure, avoid wastage and therefore be cost effective and reach the aim of properly satisfying the target population.

Suggestion

- **Reduction in loading & unloading time span**: In the process of loading & unloading the time span should be less. It helps to maintain quality of product if it is less. Atomization also helps to reduce time. So technological up gradation needed in material handling.
- **Maintenance of equipment in transportation to avoid breakdown**: Waste and loss contribute to the cost of the product. And as precaution is better than cure likewise to avoid loss due breakdown in transportation anyone should have to maintain equipments time to time.
- **Temperature monitoring system:** It is very necessary to maintain quality of product and it ensures durability of product by keeping kin observation on temperature. It is very in cold chain.
- **Training and development of manpower in chain management:** Awareness about cold chain management leads to improvement in process of cold chain. It adds value to the product by eliminating waste due to untrained staff. While doing the research paper work the things I noted that there is lack of knowledge among actual line labour e.g how to handle goods in scientifically.
- **Adopting advance technology to reduce deterioration of product :** There is continuous up gradation in technology as growth in this food & medicine industries. Company should adopt new technique to improve quality & to reduce cost. Followings are strategies & tools can be adopted to improve effectiveness of cold chain:

(I) Cold Chain Temperature Monitoring During Transportation

Monitoring of the temperature of sensitive shipments has become more critical than ever before. While methods of shipping have become more reliable, your shipments may pass through several hands before arriving at the final destination, thereby making a permanent record of your products temperature exposure throughout the COLD CHAIN all the more important.

- Despite the best efforts of carriers shipments are still misplaced, misdirected or improperly stored.
- Shipments can be delayed by customs and potentially unpacked or stored incorrectly.
- Tighter regulatory requirements are demanding better record keeping for HACCP (food products) 21 CFR part 11 (pharmaceuticals), ISO 9000 (all industry) and other regulatory standards.
- The use of dataloggers on shipments can lead to significant insurance reductions that will more than offset the cost of the dataloggers in use.
- From a Quality Assurance perspective these records can allow you to improve your Cold Chain leading to improved quality control, reduced customer complaints and improved profit margins.

Types

(1) Thermal indicators

(2) Single use (SU) dataloggers

(3) Multiple use (MU) dataloggers

(4) Wireless (RF) monitoring systems

The above alternatives all offer unique advantages and disadvantages.

(1) Thermal Indicators

Thermal indicator label are frequently used in combination with our dataloggers because of their low cost. Easy to use, you simply observe the color change, or absence of color change upon reaching a specified temperature. With combination of dataloggers this will provides time temperature validation for entire load and temperature validation for each product.

(2) Single use dataloggers

Products such as Tempchecks provide easy to use monitoring of products throughout the shipping process. As these are designed as single use devices there are no returns to your suppliers needed and costing is inexpensive relative to insurance costs and premiums.

(3) Multiple use dataloggers

These are a wide range of reusable dataloggers for most standard shipping applications (temperature, humidity etc.) that can be ideal for customers doing Intra Company or closed loop shipments where you can get most units returned can find these to be a cost effective solution also.

(4) Wireless RF Systems (RFID)

While RF (radio frequency) wireless monitoring systems_are an excellent cost effective method for monitoring warehouses and facilities. Wireless dataloggers is ideal one because that logs data as well as transmitting the data.

The major advantage here is that you do not have to wait for the load to arrive with a datalogger or changed thermal indicators to know your product has potentially spoiled. You will be able to monitor loads live from anywhere and can be proactive instead of reactive. For shipping and receiving personnel there is an extensive line of extremely versatile and cost effective Infrared thermometers, pocket thermometers and other manual monitoring devices to complete your ability to monitor the entire cold chain loop with full confidence.

[II] Innovations for Temperature Control, Monitoring

1. **Vaccine vial monitor (VVM) :** Vaccines must be stored between 2°C and 8°C to prevent spoilage or freezing .VVM is the world's smartest sticker— that adheres to a vaccine vial and changes color when has exposed to change in temperature.
2. **New refrigeration and temperature monitoring technologies** help health clinics and facilities maintain their vaccines at safe temperatures. That also prevent freezing temperatures.
3. **Improve the thermo stability of vaccines :** Vaccines Techniques borrowed from nature and the food industry can stabilize vaccines to protect them from extreme temperatures. This is important for common childhood illnesses such as measles and diphtheria.

[III] Policies and Training for an Effective Cold Chain

- Immunization programs need proper tools for handling vaccines safely, and they need the know-how to effectively operate equipment and store vaccines.
- Use the cold-chain expertise to develop training and manuals on preventing vaccine damage in the cold chain. The World Health Organization (WHO) draft a statement on how to prevent vaccine damage from freezing and evaluating the risks of freezing in the cold chain.
- Implement proper cold-chain policies and in individual countries to improve the reach of vaccines to children in remote areas. For example, in China, Indonesia, and Vietnam, PATH has modeled strategies for taking the heat-tolerant hepatitis B vaccine out of the cold chain and storing it at room temperature to reach newborn babies who are born in rural homes far from health clinics.
- cold chain activities in food product need to implement hygiene practices so that giving training for the same.

References

1. Vinod V. Sople, Logistic management, The supply chain imperative, 2008, 2nd Edition, Pearson Education, page no 57.
2. L. C. Jhamb, Materials and Logistics Management,2008, 10th Edition, Everest Publication House,
3. J. R. Tony Arnold, Stephen N. Chapman, R. V. Ramakrishnan, Introduction to Material Management, 2009, 5th Edition, Pearson Education,
4. David Simchi- Levi, Philip Kaminsky, Edith Simchi- Levi, Designing and managing the supply chain concept strategies and case studies, 2004, 2nd Edition Tata McGraw-Hill.
5. Manual on the Management, Maintenance and Use of Blood Cold Chain Equipment", World Health Organization, 2005, ISBN 9241546735.
6. Clive, D., "Cold and Chilled Storage Technology", 1997, ISBN 0751403911.
7. EN 12830:1999 Temperature recorders for the transport, storage and distribution of chilled, frozen and deep-frozen/quick-frozen food and ice cream.
8. http://en.wikipedia.org/wiki/Cold_chain.
9. http://www.katrajdairy.com/.
10. http://www.seruminstitute.com/.
11. http://www.venkys.com/.

◈ ◈ ◈

ISBN – 978-93-5024-769-3

52 "Effective Element of Promotional Marketing"

Prof. Bhaskar K. Narwate
Arts and Commerce Women's College, Nashik Road, Nashik.

Introduction

Marketing is a process where companies are able to promote their product or service and create a demand for it. One of the instruments to perform a good promotion is an exhibition. Promotion is one of the key of the four Ps in the marketing mix and as such has a key role to play in market success. The Internet's potential to provide an efficient channel for marketing An effective promotion strategy will get you sales by ensuring that customers are aware of you and what you can offer. Get it right and you will become a strong, competitive business. Sales promotion is most important element in the marketing.

Sales promotion is an important component of a small business's overall marketing strategy, along with advertising, public relations, and personal selling. The American Marketing Association (AMA) defines sales promotion as "media and non media marketing pressure applied for a predetermined, limited period of time in order to stimulate trial, increase consumer demand, or improve product quality." But this definition does not capture all the elements of modern sales promotion. One should add that effective sales promotion increases the basic value of a product for a limited time and directly stimulates consumer purchasing, selling effectiveness, or the effort of the sales force. It can be used to inform, persuade, and remind target customers about the business and its marketing mix. Some common types of sales promotion include samples, coupons, sweepstakes, contests, in-store displays, trade shows, price-off deals, premiums, and rebates.

Businesses can target sales promotions at three different audiences: consumers, resellers, and the company's own sales force. Sales promotion acts as a competitive weapon by providing an extra incentive for the target audience to purchase or support one brand over another. It is particularly effective in spurring product trial and unplanned purchases. Most marketers believe that a given product or service has an established perceived price or value, and they use sales promotion to change this price-value relationship by increasing the value and/or lowering the price. Compared to the other components of the marketing mix (advertising, publicity, and personal selling), sales promotion usually operates on a shorter time line, uses a more rational appeal, returns a tangible or real value, fosters an immediate sale, and contributes highly to profitability.

In determining the relative importance to place on sales promotion in the overall marketing mix, a small business should consider its marketing budget, the stage of the product in its life cycle, the nature of competition in the market, the target of the promotion, and the nature of the product. For example, sales promotion and direct mail are particularly attractive alternatives when the marketing budget is limited, as it is for many small businesses.

Objectives

(i) **To introduce new products**: Have you ever heard about distribution of free samples?

Perhaps you know that many companies distribute free samples while introducing new products. The consumers after using these free samples may develop a taste for it and buy the products later for consumption.

(ii) **To attract new customers and retain the existing ones**: Sales promotion measures help to attract or create new customers for the products. While moving in the market, customers are generally attracted towards the product that offers discount, gift, prize, etc on buying. These are some of the tools used to encourage the customers to buy the goods. Thus, it helps to retain the existing customers, and at the same time it also attracts some new customers to buy the product.

(iii) **To maintain sales of seasonal products**: There are some products like air conditioner, fan, refrigerator, cooler, winter clothes, room heater, sunscreen lotion, glycerin soap etc.,

which are used only in particular seasons. To maintain the sale of these types of products normally the manufactures and dealers give off-season discount. For example, you can buy air conditioner in winter at a reduced price. Similarly you may get discount on winter clothes during summer.

(iv) **To meet the challenge of competition**: Today's business faces competition all the time. New products frequently come to the market and at the same time improvement also takes place. So sales promotion measures have become essential to retain the market share of the seller or producer in the product-market

Tools of Sales Promotion

To increase the sale of any product manufactures or producers adopt different measures like sample, gift, bonus, and many more. These are known as tools or techniques or methods of sales promotion. Let us know more about some of the commonly used tools of sales promotion.

(i) **Free samples**: You might have received free samples of shampoo, washing powder, coffee powder, etc. while purchasing various items from the market. Sometimes these free samples are also distributed by the shopkeeper even without purchasing any item from his shop. These are distributed to attract consumers to try out a new product and thereby create new customers. Some businessmen distribute samples among selected persons in order to popularize the product. For example, in the case of medicine free samples are distributed among physicians, in the case of textbooks, specimen copies are distributed among teachers.

(ii) **Premium or Bonus offer**: A milk shaker along with Nescafe, mug with Bournvita, toothbrush with 500 grams of toothpaste, 30% extra in a pack of one kg. are the examples of premium or bonus given free with the purchase of a product. They are effective in inducing consumers to buy a particular product. This is also useful for encouraging and rewarding existing customers.

(iii) **Exchange schemes**: It refers to offering exchange of old product for a new product at a price less than the original price of the product. This is useful for drawing attention to product improvement. 'Bring your old mixer-cum-juicer and exchange it for a new one just by paying Rs.500' or 'exchange your black and white television with a color television' are various popular examples of exchange scheme.

(iv) **Price-off offer**: Under this offer, products are sold at a price lower than the original price. 'Rs. 2 off on purchase of a lifebuoy soap, Rs. 15 off on a pack of 250 grams of Taj Mahal tea, Rs. 1000 off on cooler' etc. are some of the common schemes. This type of scheme is designed to boost up sales in off-season and sometimes while introducing a new product in the market.

(v) **Coupons**: Sometimes, coupons are issued by manufacturers either in the packet of a product or through an advertisement printed in the newspaper or magazine or through mail. These coupons can be presented to the retailer while buying the product. The holder of the coupon gets the product at a discount. For example, you might have come across coupons like, 'show this and get Rs. 15 off on purchase of 5 kg. of Annapurna Atta'. The reduced price under this scheme attracts the attention of the prospective customers towards new or improved products.

(vi) **Fairs and Exhibitions**: Fairs and exhibitions may be organized at local, regional, national or international level to introduce new products, demonstrate the products and to explain special features and usefulness of the products. Goods are displayed and demonstrated and their sale is also conducted at a reasonable discount. 'International Trade Fair' in New Delhi at Pragati Maidan, which is held from 14th to 27th November every year, is a well known example of Fairs and Exhibitions as a tool of sales promotion.

Growth of Sales Promotion

Sales promotion has grown substantially in recent years. There are several reasons for this dramatic growth in sales promotion. First, consumers have accepted sales promotion as part of their buying decision criteria. It provides reluctant decision makers with an incentive to make choices by increasing the value offered by a particular brand. Second, the increasing tendency of businesses to focus on short-term results has helped spur growth in sales promotion, which can provide an immediate boost in sales. Product managers also tend to view sales promotion as a way to differentiate their brand from that of competitors in the short term. Third, the emergence of computer technology has enabled manufacturers to get rapid feedback on the results of promotions. Redemption rates for coupons or figures on sales volume can be obtained within days. Finally, an increase in the size and power of retailers has also boosted the use of sales promotion. Historically, the manufacturer held the power in the channel of distribution. Mass marketers utilized national advertising to get directly to consumers, creating a demand for the heavily advertised brands that stores could not afford to ignore. With consolidation and the growth of major retail chains, however, retailers have gained the power to demand incentives from manufacturers to carry their products. Many sales promotions are designed to provide benefits to the retailers.

Consumer Promotion

Consumer sales promotions are steered toward the ultimate product users—typically individual shoppers in the local market—but the same techniques can be used to promote products sold by one business to another, such as computer systems, cleaning supplies, and machinery. In contrast, trade sales promotions target resellers—wholesalers and retailers—who carry the marketer's product. Following are some of the key techniques used in consumer-oriented sales promotions.

Limitation of Sales Promotion

Although sales promotion is an important strategy for producing quick, short-term, positive results, it is not a cure for a bad product, poor advertising, or an inferior sales team. After a consumer uses a coupon for the initial purchase of a product, the product must then take over and convince them to become repeat buyers. In addition, sales promotion activities may bring several negative consequences, including "clutter" due to the number of competitive promotions. New approaches are promptly cloned by competitors, as each marketer tries to be more creative, more attention getting, or more effective in attracting the attention of consumers and the trade. Finally, consumers and resellers have learned how to milk the sales promotion game. Consumers may wait to buy certain items knowing that prices will eventually be reduced, for example, while resellers have become experts at negotiating deals and manipulating competitors against one another.

Conclusion

Sales Promotion is the important element of marketing .it is the effective factor in the process of marketing without it no one industry can complete the target of selling so each and every industry use the sales promotion to get the success and compete with competitors with in shortest periods .

References

1. Davies, M. Understanding Marketing, 1998, 1st edition. Prentice Hall.
2. Kotler, P, Armstrong, G, Saunders, J and Wong, V., Principles of Marketing: 2001, Third European Edition, Prentice Hall, Harlow.
3. Sales Promotion: How to Create, Implement and Integrate Campaigns that Really Work by Roddy Mullin.
4. Promotional Marketing: Ideas and Techniques for Success in Sales Promotion by William A. Robinson and Christine Hauri.
5. Advertising and Sales Promotions by S.H.H. Kazmi and Satish Batra.

◈◈◈

ISBN – 978-93-5024-769-3

53 Whither Management Education: Developing Competencies or Disseminating Information?

Preeti Shirodkar
MET Institute of Management, Gen. A.K. Vaidya Marg, Bandra Reclamation, Mumbai - 400 050.

Introduction

Education, especially in the Indian context can most often be seen reflecting trends, where a new field or one that has shown promise of employment or gained respect over time attracts the attention of students or those advising them to pursue a particular course. And while this has worked to a certain extent, the flip side is that once the need diminishes, the industry reaches its optimum level of absorption or there is a resultant mass production of graduates in a particular field, leading to stagnation, the stream stands at a crossroad, from where it needs to evaluate its position, before proceeding further; if it is to survive, let alone gain strength. And it is this point at which management education finds itself today.

Yet, if one were to dismiss the importance of a management degree, one could be accused of being naive, as considering the challenges that demography, diversity in industry and expectations from work profiles pose before us, education in general and management education in particular should essentially be going strong.

What then is ailing management education? If analysed carefully, over and above systemic failures, the issue would squarely rest on the industry's complaint that despite being a 'professional' course, management education does not equip its graduates with the ability to function effectively and efficiently, in an organisation. And the cause of this can be primarily seen to be failure of the skills set that they (should) have acquired, during the course.

Objectives

It is time for educationists then to acknowledge, understand, appreciate and act upon this learning and feedback, whether from the industry, the academia or the graduates, who realise this gap. Rather than merely pushing the issue below the carpet, it is important to get it into the open and address it.

Activities to be Analysed and findings over it

In this context at the outset it is necessary to get to the core of management education, as it has evolved over the years, and the various factors that have led to its stagnation/decline, so that the road one charts ahead is one drawn from experience rather than one based purely on a theoretical paradigm.

Followers of management education in India claim that though it has been in place since the early part of the 20th century as a discipline, its sudden growth has been a result of globalisation and the opening up of the Indian economy to the challenges of the world. In fact, in an article written for Advance Edge in April 2003, Mr Ashish Deshpande, Associate Vice President, Kotak Mahindra Mutual Fund remarked how even successful family run organisations had gradually started moving towards professional managers and CEOs, to adapt to the changing order. He remarks, "With the changing dynamics of the business environment indigenous industry realised the need for employees having a formal education packaged with the experience of real life case studies." This is how management education in India moved towards becoming a rage with varied management institutes flourishing, in an attempt to accommodate the desires of those for whom the IIMs were a distant dream. Graduates from all fields flocked to these institutes, who at times offered its graduates packages of up to Rs. 10 lakhs on completion of the course.

Given that most other disciplines with a few exceptions like medicine, engineering, chartered accountancy, company secretary were essentially largely not professional/vocational in nature, management was seen as a burgeoning area that would provide a level playing field for graduates from varied disciplines to compete, with the 'privileged' few, who had pursued a professional course. Institutes are also in an attempt to cash in on this craze, advertised themselves as placement agencies, guaranteeing 100% jobs to all its graduates. This craze in fact gathered such momentum that more than 1000 institutes offering varied approved and autonomous courses in Management sprung up all over the country.

What was ignored or possibly chosen to be ignored was the fact that this bubble was destined to burst, both because there was bound to be a saturation of the number of people that would be required by the industry at 'Higher Positions', as also, that quality would naturally be compromised, if management education became a business rather than a vocation. Against this backdrop, it is no surprise that recession merely proved to be an excuse to lay off the excessive people, who had been absorbed greedily by companies, in an attempt to get the best of the talent, while also serving as both a source of expansion of their business and a show of strength. What was also swept under the carpet was the fact that India was proving to be a hub of cheap but efficient labour, working for MNCs whose actual controls still lay abroad. For Management Professionals, this served as an opportunity to explore the global scenario and travel extensively to foreign lands, which added considerable value to their image.

The bubble burst when layoffs created a panic resulting on the one hand in reverse brain drain and on the other, in creating a cheap experienced labour force being available, as competition to the fresh graduates emerging from Management Institutes. While it created an outburst in both those desirous of pursuing Management Education, who suddenly felt extremely insecure and those who were in the field offering education, who claimed that it was incorrect for Management Institutes to advertise themselves as placement agencies which had lead to this mad rush and attraction to Management Education in the first place, a claim made by an irate IIM faculty, what remains important is the fact that this provided the much needed opportunity to explore where Management Education stood and the course it needs to take, in order to maintain its value in the field of education.

If one were to examine Management Education as it stands today objectively, one can safely arrive at the conclusion that much needs to be done and reworked for it to even maintain its relevance, let alone grow. And this needs to be done in all areas encompassing the Institutes themselves, the Curriculum, the Faculty, the Students, the needs of the Industry and the products that are being churned out under the name of Management Graduates.

In light of the fact that though IIMs earlier never insisted on students with experience for getting into the course and yet managed to produce well informed graduates, who were sought after by the industry and to a great extent still are, it is important to examine whether 'Green Horns' really fit the bill of pursuing Management Courses at a time when Management Education is offered at the 'mass' rather than 'class' level.

If observed carefully, one could easily surmise that very often people who are merely graduates carry with them a temperament, considering the two years of Management Education to merely be an extended holiday, where they can take life easy, while away their time pretending to do a course, keeping at bay either the need to take up a job or to get married. Moreover, given the fact that Undergraduate Education today demands very little commitment, these students carry the same attitude into their Post Graduate Management Course and being large in number, manage to affect the 'Pursuit of Education', which few of the sincere students are attempting to do. Ironically, even the Management Institutes, who often charge a high fee for Autonomous Courses or need to attract students to fill up the seats for University approved Courses, land up making passing a walk over with the only criterion for completing the course, being enrolling for it. The result as can be imagined is disastrous, aided often by random permissions being granted to set up colleges and expand the numbers in existing colleges by the Granting Authorities, often to achieve their own targets.

Given that India's abundant population is only another facet that adds to this self fulfilling prophecy, the result is not really as surprising as it is made out to be. Most students are increasingly getting placed at lower packages or for fairly mundane jobs that would otherwise have gone to Graduates. The only satisfaction that companies derive from this is that they have 'Management Post Graduates' on their roll. In fact as Mr. Dayanand Chandraghatgi, Practicing Industry Professional in Advertising and Visiting faculty in Marketing at the undergraduate and postgraduate levels has pointed out, most companies today are even getting out of this trend, more especially because they have realised that the satisfaction they derive from having hired Management Post Graduates is often lower than the attitude they carry with them and that it is much simpler to hire undergraduates, who can be trained to suit the culture and temperament of the organisation and are more willing to put in much greater efforts since they believe they are 'merely graduates'. In short they become bigger assets being easier to mould, more dedicated, hard working and at a basic level, staying on longer with the organisation to add credibility and value to their resume. The result is that organisations today are looking at hiring such people and offering them the freedom to take up Management Courses as an incentive for their contribution to the organisation and as an indirect means of engaging their loyalty over a longer period of time.

It is thus important for Institutes to assess the Courses they are currently offering in this light and possibly think of tailoring them to absorb such industry requirements, which is even now being done, but to a very small extent. On the other hand, the institutes also need to see whether they should really offer their courses only to students with work experience, so that they come with a thirst for knowledge and are more sincere in what they are studying or at least assess prospective students more on their attitude and temperament to be 'engaged' in a Management Course rather than relying on merely filling up the seats and producing mass graduates who are not really much further at the end of the course than they were when they began it.

So too, the content of what is being offered needs to be seriously assessed to create a knowledge base and a skill set rather than serving as a platform for information reproduction. Currently, most courses offer far too many subjects to be assimilated, let alone in any depth, resulting in a mere lip-service being paid to the various subjects that are proudly listed out on the syllabi of Institutes. A burgeoning flaw that has also emerged in this area, due to the large number of flourishing institutes, is that each institute tries to out-do the other in the 'scope' of Management Education it offers. By trying to provide a maximum range of subjects, at time a ridiculous 40-60 subjects in the course of two years, notwithstanding the holidays, vacations, exam schedules and co and extra-curricular activities that intervene in the teaching-learning process. The result – while most of the students have passed in all the subjects, what at the most they know is the title of the subject that they appeared for. As a senior faculty member states, internal marks are used as a safety valve, to ensure that students pass the course.

Advocates of Management Education and those offering it, would no doubt take offence to such a claim, arguing that there are projects and internships that afford the scope for acquisition of actual exposure to ground realities. However, even this is fairly suspect as students are usually given group projects, which are completed by the most sincere person in the group, while the others only appear on the day of the presentation in order to be marked for their contribution to the project. At other times, even this can be labelled as a sincere attempt as projects are 'bought' or 'downloaded' from various sources, making the exercise of engaging in projects merely a theoretical one. Internships too are taken up with family businesses, friends of parents, or parents of friends or then even when taken up with the industry, what students actually land up doing is data entry or information gathering, with merely 10% of the students engaging in really worthwhile projects. This is because companies who are aware of the ground reality and often have labour easily available, pay no attention to offering internships to the ever increasing number of students seeking it.

To overcome this issue, Institutes hire retired Industry Professionals or those who wish to move out of the rigour of corporate jobs as Placement Officers or Faculty. And to complicate matters, it is the same Faculty who goes Institute hopping, observes Mr. Alok Sharma, Assistant Director, Corporate Relations, United World School of Business. As a consequence, academics becomes a money making business rather than a vocation, with the faculty neither being able to spare the time to update themselves, nor mentor the students, nor having any exposure to the changing trends and realities of the industry, adding to the vicious circle of already existent stagnation and chaos. A huge gap thus exists in what is being delivered and what needs to be delivered and attempts to fill it up through Workshops, Seminars and other such 'additional activities' only prove to be a mere tokenism. Ironically, it is not as if practising industry experts are unwilling to share their knowledge, but the cliques that exist and the attitude of the students has rendered this possible saving grace to a mere theory.

Equipped with mere theoretical inputs and with a false notion of the self, the Industry and their place in it, the students and the Industry have been finding it increasingly difficult to deal with one another. The result is a constant blame game that has never really been discussed, let alone addressed. And while all agree that of the two years allotted to the course, one should be kept for knowledge dissemination and the other for value addition through business impact projects or ones that can help students learn how to apply concepts, it is difficult to find a way to achieve this, as on the one hand, the Industry refuses to offer internships to students, while on the other, there is no other plausible way of acquiring knowledge of the ground realities. As a consequence, instead of changing situations, one only gets caught into a trap, which Bill Beattie warns us of when he says "The aim of education should be to teach us rather how to think, than what to think - rather to improve our minds, so as to enable us to think for ourselves, than to load the memory with thoughts of other men".

One of the solutions offered in this light is the changing of pedagogy, where everyone associated with Management Education agrees that Case Studies and the Role Play methods should be used as a replacement for the current theoretical inputs being provided. However the question still remains whether the students will have the capacity to grapple with it, as also whether the Faculty has the depth required to deliver and sustain it. A related issue is the kind of knowledge that needs to be imparted, while most industry experts prefer General Management to specialisations, arguing that this would provide as Mr. Vikas Shirodkar, Vice President , Human Resource Development, General Motors India says "A broad based application and understanding of interdependence in an organisation, with a willingness to understand and accept how to blend different ideas, concepts and cater to varied departments and functions"; others with a traditional mindset believe that both specialists and generalists are needed and since offering and absorbing generalisations is more difficult, it should be left to the IIMs, while the lesser known Institutes should stick to offering specialisations, as they always have.

Another area that also needs to be focussed on and whose importance is seldom realised by 'Subject Faulty' is the need for development of Soft Skills, which includes Communication, Grooming, Etiquettes, Dressing etc., which are primary to developing the individual with the right attitude and approach to a profession which s/he desires to pursue as most often students are fairly oblivious to these nuances and find it difficult to suddenly adapt themselves to the corporate culture.

Conclusion

Though the issues plaguing Management Education are multi faceted, the fact remains that if it were to continue along the lines on which it is being done today, it is bound to fail. What one needs to focus on is that Management is an Art and not a Science and one therefore needs to develop the right skills in its practitioners, so that they can, as Mr. Vivek Patwardhan, Executive Coach and HR Consultant, Srujan Consulting opines "convert concepts into actionable plans and learn how to influence other using the technique of reflecting on one's experiences".

This would result in fulfilling the true spirit of education which as William Haley puts it can be embodied if one acknowledges that "Education would be much more effective if its purpose was to ensure that by the time they leave school every boy and girl should know how much they do not know, and be imbued with a lifelong desire to know it".

References

1. Walker & Boyd; Marketing Strategy; 2008, 5th Edition, Tata McGraw-Hill, New Delhi.
2. Philip Kotler; Marketing Management; 2008, 10th Edition, Tata McGraw-Hill, New Delhi.
3. Richard Batterley; Leading Through Relationship Marketing; Tata McGraw-Hill.
4. Internet:- whereisdoc.com, www//Google.com.

◈◈◈

ISBN – 978-93-5024-769-3

54

Behavioural Training - A Key to Enhance Organization Climate (A Study in Gabriel India Ltd.)

Ms. Sapna Karia
JDC Bytco IMSR, Nashik.

Introduction To The Topic

Behaviour:

"Any measurable response of an individual, including anything the individual does, says or feels in response to external or internal events. In behavioral training, 'Behaviour' is abroad term that covers the actions, responses and reactions of an individual, team or organization"

Suzanne Skiffington & Perry

Zeus An employee's behavior is one of the major concerns in every organization, thus behavioural training is gaining lot of importance these days.

Objectives of the Study

- To understand the concept of behavioral training & how it is imparted
- To study the role of the trainer in delivering behavioral training in the company
- To understand the importance of behavioral training in the corporate world & its impact on the trainees
- To observe the impact of behavioral training in one of the renowned companies i.e. "Gabriel India Ltd."
- To analyze the data collected and give appropriate suggestions

Research Methodology

A study on Behavioral Training was conducted in the company named "Gabriel India Ltd" only on the managerial level, taking 30 employees as sample size (total management employees are 41 in the company). **Gabriel India** is the flagship company of USD 200 million **Anand Group**. Gabriel is a leading manufacturer of wide range of ride control products in India. The Group consists of seventeen companies spread in eight states of the country, employing 4000 people and supplying components to virtually every vehicle and engine produced in the country, apart from replacement market.

Benefits from Behavioral Training:

- Increased job satisfaction and morale among employees
- Increased employee motivation
- Increased efficiencies in processes, resulting in financial gain
- Increased capacity to adopt new technologies and methods
- Increased innovation in strategies and products
- Reduced employee turnover
- Enhanced company image, e.g., conducting ethics training
- Risk management, e.g., training about sexual harassment, diversity training

Evaluation of Behavioral Training

Evaluation of training means assessment of the impact and effects of training on the employee. A training programme is devised for an employee with some specific objectives in view. These learning objectives can serve as the evaluation criteria for evaluating a training programme and also find out whether the training has helped the employee improve his/ her behavior.

Methods of Evaluation

- Questionnaires (feedback forms) or 'happiness sheets' are a common way of eliciting trainee responses to courses and programmes.
- Different types tests (attitude test/ psychological tests)
- Structured exercise and case studies
- The opinions of those who deliver the training are important
- Interviews
- Observation
- Participation and discussion during training

Data Analysis & Interpretation

1. Identification of Training Needs

Various Needs	*Priority (%)*
Organizational Needs	50
Group Needs	30
Individual Needs	20

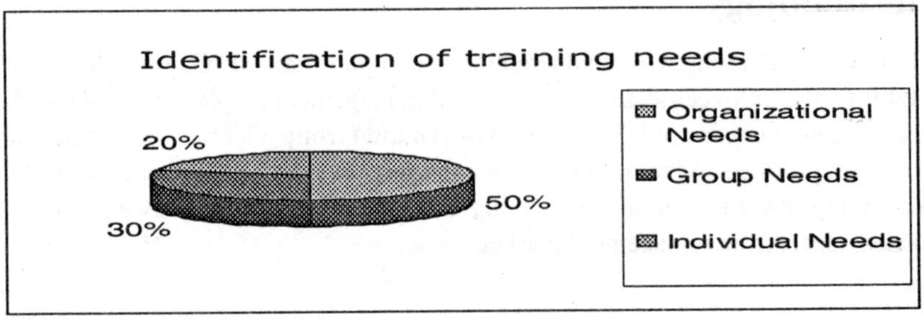

(Ref: Q.3 of the questionnaire)

Interpretation

Behavioral training is a key to enhance organization climate, thus the organization needs are given more priority, followed by the group needs and then the individual nccds.

2. Aspects of training programs

Aspects	Priority (%)
Time constraint	20
Trainer	35
Venue of training	10
Tools & aids for training	20
Number of employees	15

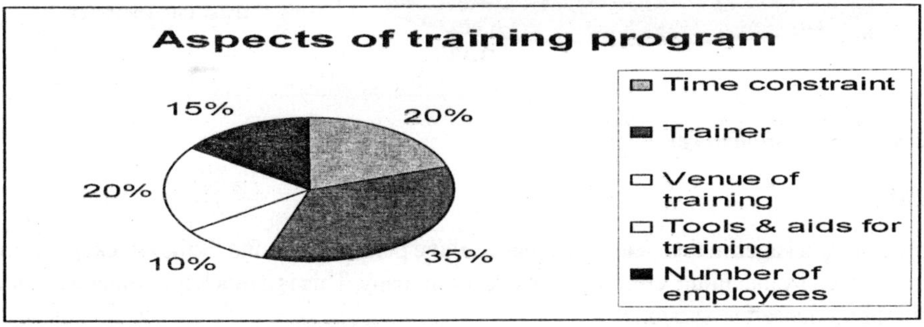

(Ref: Q.18 of the questionnaire)

Interpretation

The HR department has to consider various aspects while designing the training program. The very important aspect is the trainer. The training program should be conducted in an appropriate time span and with the help of essential tools and aids. The venue of training and the batch of employees are also to be previously decided.

3. Aspects related to trainer

Aspects related to trainer	*Priority (%)*
Creating learning environment	30
Facilitating discussions	25
Proper Postures & Communication	25
Audio visual support	20

(Ref: Discussion with HR Manager)

Interpretation

The trainer plays the most important role in the training process. The trainer needs to keep in mind the aspects such as facilitating discussions, use of proper postures & communication, use of audio-visual support; and the most important is creating a learning environment.

4. Learning Skills Blockage

Blockage being faced	*Number of employees*
Employees facing this blockage	25
Employees not facing this blockage	5
Total	30

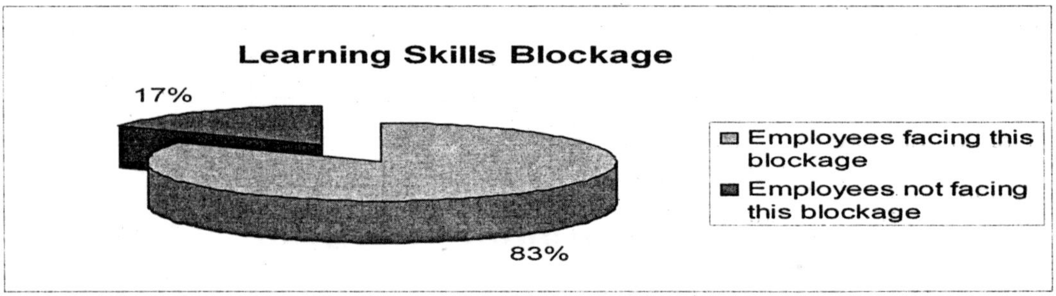

(Ref: Self-assessment questionnaire)

Interpretation

There are four blockages in then learning process of the person; Learning Skills Blockage is one of them and it is generally faced by maximum employees in every company. This is a blockage which we can overcome very easily, through counseling sessions.

5. Distractions/Concentration Blockage

Blockage being faced	*Number of employees*
Employees facing this blockage	15
Employees not facing this blockage	15
Total	30

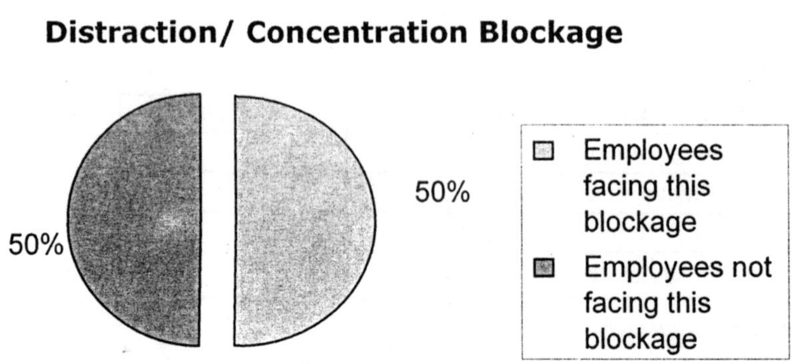

(Ref: Self-assessment questionnaire)

Interpretation

Half of the employees find it difficult to concentrate or we can say they are easily distracted; this kind of blockage can be avoided by using maximum audio-visual means of training.

6. Worries & fears about learning blockage

Blockage being faced	*Number of employees*
Employees facing this blockage	9
Employees not facing this blockage	21
Total	30

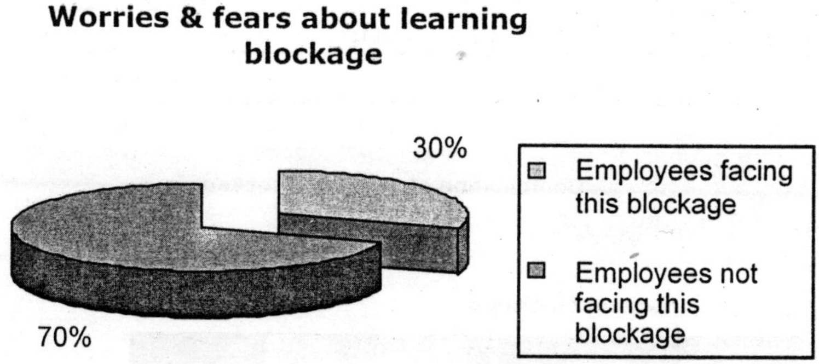

(Ref: Self-assessment questionnaire)

Interpretation

Worries & fears are one of the major barriers in the learning process. But as the company has an open door policy, this kind of blockage is faced only by few employees.

7. Learning from others blockage

Blockage being faced	*Number of employees*
Employees facing this blockage	16
Employees not facing this blockage	14
Total	30

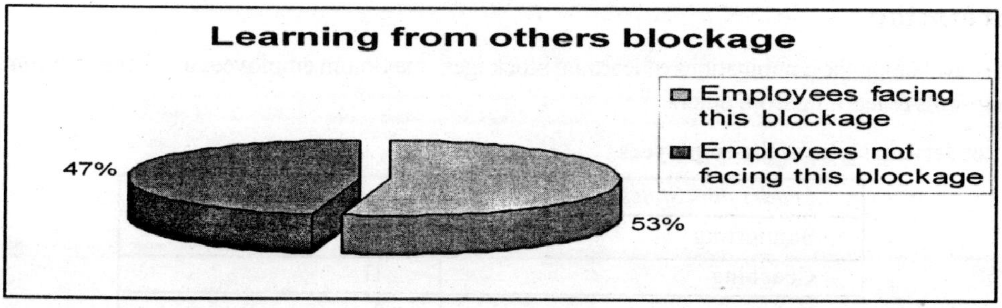

(Ref: Self-assessment questionnaire)

Interpretation

Generally, the employees find it difficult to learn from others, hence this blockage of learning from others is faced. This blockage can be avoided by creating a friendly environment in the company.

8. Combinations of Learning Blockages

Combination of blockages	*No. of employees*
Learning Skills & Learning from others	10
Learning skills & Worries & fears	5
Learning skills & Distractions/ Concentration	5
Worries & fears & Distractions/ Concentration	4
Distractions/ Concentrations & Learning from others	6
Total	30

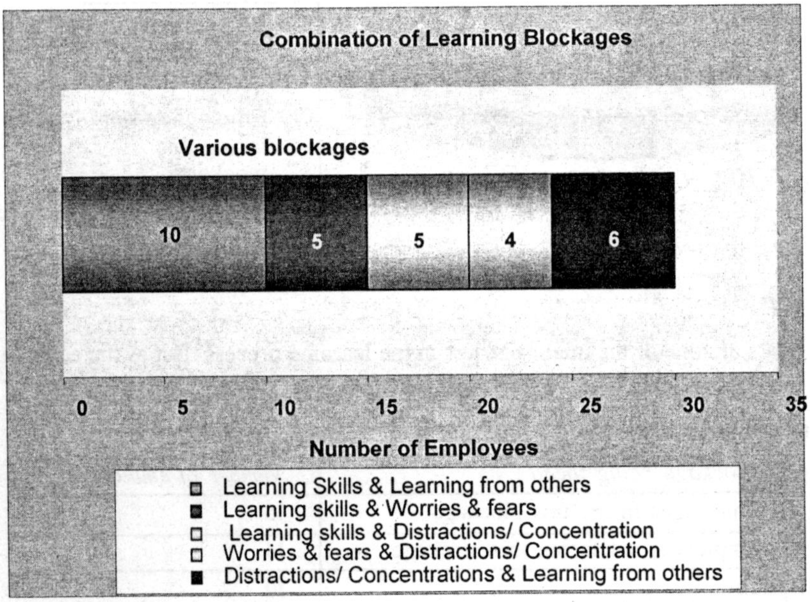

Interpretation

After evaluating the combinations of learning blockages , maximum employees are facing the combination of learning skills & learning from others.

9. Leadership styles of the employees

Leadership Styles	*Number of Employees*
Supporting	5
Coaching	11
Delegating	8
Directing	6
Total	30

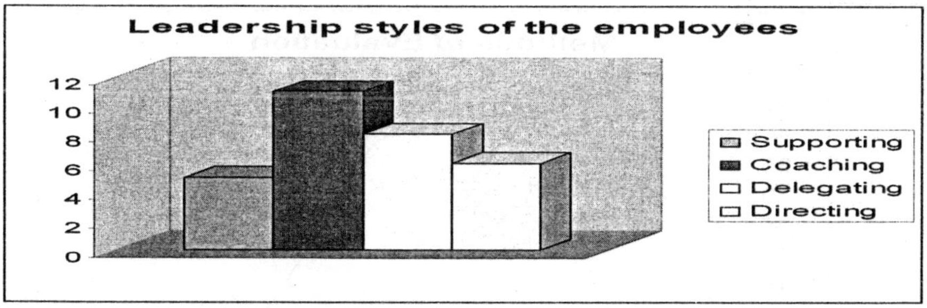

Interpretation

There are four leadership styles, and every employee falls in one of the category. Maximum employees have the coaching approach to leadership in the company. Rest of the employees either believe in delegating the work or directing the employees, and few of them are supporting.

10. Aspects considered for evaluation of training programme

Aspects	Priority (%)
Objectives	40
Methods used	12
Training atmosphere	8
Trainers	25
Time management	15

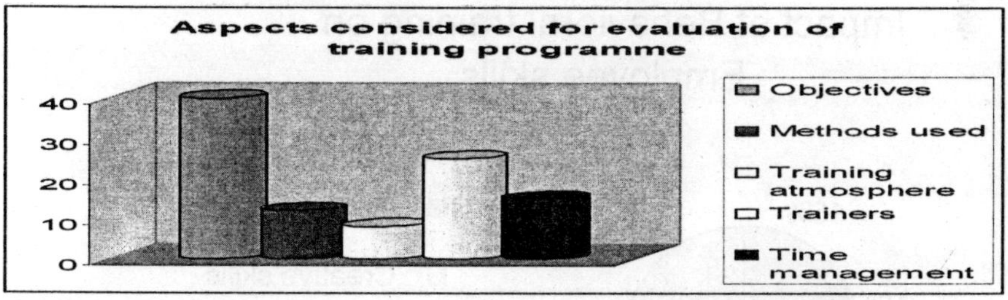

Interpretation

Evaluation of training program is a very important issue for every company and various aspects are considered to evaluate it. To check whether the objectives of the training are achieved or not are to be checked, this is followed by the trainer giving the training, then the methods used and the training atmosphere and to see whether the time management was proper or not.

11. Methods of Evaluation

Methods used	*Priority (%)*
Observation	30
Discussion	20
Questionnaires	40
Interviews	10
Tests	0

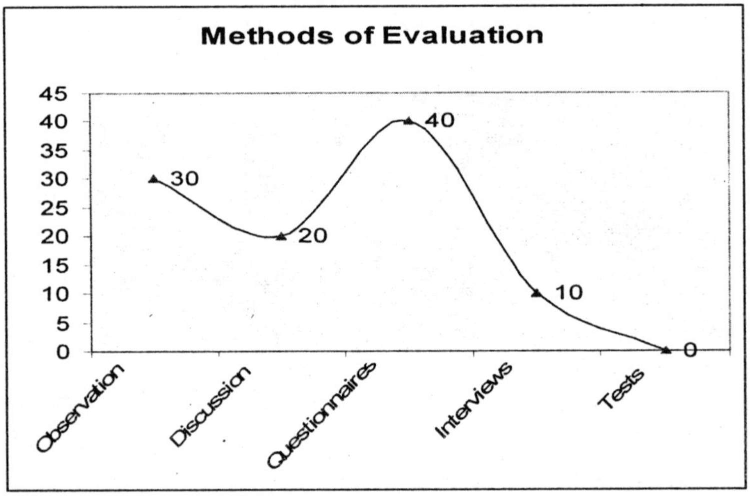

(Ref: Q.16 of questionnaire)

Interpretation

Questionnaires are the most commonly used method for evaluating the training program, observation; discussion and interview methods are also used.

12. Impact of Behavioural training on employee skills

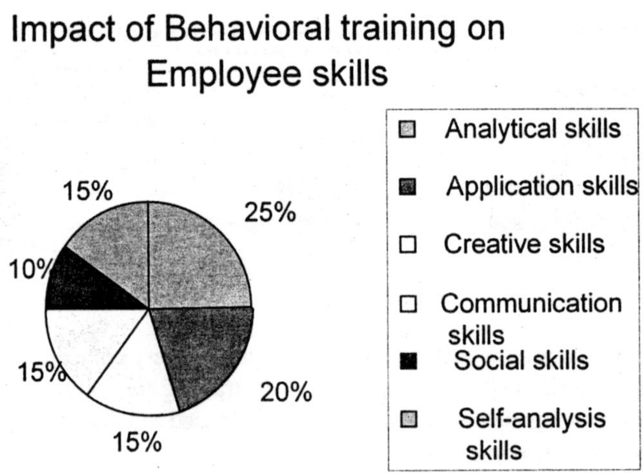

(Ref: Discussion with HR manager)

Interpretation

Behavioral training has impact on various skills in an employee like analytical skills, communication skills, creative skills, social skills, application skills and so on.

Findings

1. Behavioral training – a key to enhance the organization's climate:

Behavioral training is a very essential tool to enhance the organizational climate as it focuses on the improvement of the employees' attitude.

2. Behavioral training focuses on various objectives:

Successful training programs focus on individual, team and organizational business objectives and goals.

3. Self-assessment & learning is the base of Behavioral training:

Through self-assessment, the employees are able to understand their learning blockages and can work on them.

4. Scope for individual differences:

Behavioral training provides lot of scope for the individual differences like personality, values, belief systems and philosophy.

5. Proper evaluation is the base for the next training program:

Evaluation is a very important part in the process of training, on the basis of the evaluation, the next training program can be designed.

Suggestions

1. Use of maximum audio-visual aids for training:

It is said that whatever a person sees remains in his/ her mind for longer time as compared to what the person hears.

2. Organization of workshops:

Various workshops should be organized for the betterment of the employees on various aspects like positive attitude, job satisfaction, co-operation, stress management, etc.

Conclusion

Behavioural training gives a platform to the employees to assess themselves and understand their positives and negatives as well as, Confusions has quoted,

"What I hear, I forget; what I see, I remember;

But what I do, I understand."

Behavioral training facilitates this aspect of every employee, as he/she can enhance their abilities through it.

The effectiveness of Behavioral training also depends on the trainer, and generally this role is of HR manager. Therefore Behavioral training is the most important tool to enhance the organization climate as it leads to an environment of satisfaction in each and every employee.

Biblography

Journals & Magazines: HRM Review; Human Capital

Websites:

www.gabrielindia.co.in

www.anandgroupindia.com
www.lifestrategies.ca/training
www.mindtools.com
www.slideshare.net/hrmanagement
www.emraldinsight.com/journal

Books Referred

1. Behavioral Sciences; Abha Singh & Rajni Arya.
2. Improving Employee Performance through Workplace Training; Earl Carter & Frank McMahon.
3. Training & Development; Steve Truelover.
4. Evaluating Management Development, Training & Education; Mark Easterleysmith.
5. Effective training – Systems, Strategies & Practices; Nick Blanchard & James Thacker.
6. Organize Effective Training – How to Plan & Run Successful Courses & Seminars; James Chalmers.
7. A Handbook of Human Resource Management Practices; Michael Armstrong.
8. Business Research Methods; ICFAI Centre of Management.

◈◈◈

ISBN – 978-93-5024-769-3

55 A New Blueprint for Organizational Business Process: Integration of Knowledge Management and Business Intelligence

Prof. Prakash S Bhongade
Dr. Ambedkar College, Nagpur.
Prof. Sunita Dhote
Ramdeobaba Kamla Nehru Engineering, College, Nagpur.

Introduction

A critical component for the success of the modern enterprise is its ability to take advantage of all available information. This challenge becomes more difficult with the constantly increasing volume of information, both internal and external to an enterprise. It is further exacerbated because many enterprises are becoming increasingly "knowledge-centric," and therefore a larger number of employees need access to a greater variety of information to be effective.

Now a day, economic organizations are subject to external forces that they must live with and react to: increasing sophistication of competitors, customers and suppliers, globalization of business, international competition. It's a real challenge, due to the tremendous flow of information it's facing every day. Also, the nature of information itself has changed, in terms of volume, availability and importance. The data to be considered becomes more and more complex in both structure and semantics. With the Internet, Intranets, Groupware systems the volume of available data increases each day – customer communications, internal research reports or competitors web sites are just some sources of electronic data. Intellectual property and assets, knowledge are contained within the huge volumes of information and leveraging this value is increasingly important in the competitive market. Making sense of all this information, gaining value and competitive advantage through represents real challenges for the enterprise. The IT solutions designed to address these challenges have been developed in two different approaches: structured data management and unstructured content management. We can even think at these approaches in a more general perspective as being information management technologies and knowledge management technologies – being aware in the same time that information management it's a part of knowledge management, as information can be considered a type of knowledge (explicit knowledge). Knowledge management technologies, while less mature than information management technologies, are more and more capable of combining content management systems and the Web with vastly improved searching and text mining capabilities to derive more value from the explosion of textual information. Integrating Business Intelligence and Knowledge Management in order to respond to the challenges the modern enterprise has to deal with represents not only a "new trend" in IT, but a necessity. Over time, techniques from both technologies blended, Competitive Intelligence Systems are a direct result of such integration.

Knowledge Management and Business Intelligence

Knowledge is a fluid mix of framed experiences, values, contextual information, and expert insight that provides a framework for evaluating and incorporating new experiences and information. It originates and is applied in the minds of knowers. In organisations, it often becomes embedded not only in documents or repositories but also in organisational routines, processes, and norms

In addition, Gartner Group defines Knowledge Management as:

"Knowledge Management is a discipline that promotes an integrated approach to identifying, managing and sharing all of an enterprise's information assets. It is the discipline applied to manage intellectual capital."

It can be said that Knowledge Management is a system that includes a process to identify, understand and use knowledge in a creative manner to add value. It is a process to facilitate the efficient flow of knowledge to the right people in a timely manner. A Knowledge Management System therefore includes strategies, tactics, processes and enabling technologies that facilitate and support the creation, capture, process, organisation, delivery and leverage of knowledge within an organisation. Implicit in this definition is the need to encourage the use of knowledge to achieve leverage. For Knowledge Management it is made no sense unless it contributes to improving performance through savings in time, effort and resources. 'A company's choice of Knowledge Management strategy is not arbitrary 'it must be driven by the company's competitive strategy.'

Business Intelligence is the way in which we store and use business information. It encompasses the technologies, applications, and means for collecting, integrating, analyzing and presenting business data. Using data that has been stored in a data warehouse, software applications are able to use this data to report past business information as well as predict future business information, including threats, trends, opportunities and patterns.

Knowledge Management vs Business Intelligence

Business Intelligence and Knowledge Management have the same objective - to focus on improving business performance. The purpose of Knowledge Management is to achieve the maximum degree of understanding of one's operating environment and relevant circumstances that can advance or retard progress toward an objective. However, the same rationale applies to the concept of Business Intelligence. If we agree that Business Intelligence is comprised of Customer, Competitor and Market Intelligence and that the purpose of conducting Business Intelligence is to support strategic decision-making, grow the business and monitor the organisation's competitors, then we recognise that there are definite similarities between Knowledge Management and Business Intelligence. While both concepts share a common high level objective, there are some fundamental differences. These differences are to be found in the manner in which they are applied towards achieving that goal. The value of Business Intelligence and its product, opportunity analysis, is found in its usefulness as a decision making tool; the value of Knowledge Management lies in the ability of the organisation to identify, capture and reuse knowledge and in particular best practices in such a manner that it saves the organisation time, effort and resources -translated and measured in cost.

Enterprise executives understand that timely, accurate knowledge can mean improved business performance. Two technologies have been central in improving the quantitative and qualitative value of the knowledge available to decision makers: business intelligence and knowledge management. Business intelligence has applied the functionality, scalability, and reliability of modern database management systems to build ever-larger data warehouses, and to utilize data mining techniques to extract business advantage from the vast amount of available enterprise data. Knowledge management technologies, while less mature than business intelligence technologies, are now capable of combining today's content management systems and the Web with vastly improved searching and text mining capabilities to derive more value from the explosion of textual information. We believe that these systems will blend over time, borrowing techniques from each other and inspiring new approaches that can analyze data and text together, seamlessly.

Integration of Business Intelligence and Knowledge Management

It is not only a 'new trend' in IT, but a necessity to integrate business intelligence and knowledge management in order to respond to the challenges the modern enterprise. Competitive Intelligence System is a direct result of such integration.

The general opinion about Competitive Intelligence by the business information professionals is that it deals with the collection, selection and interpretation of publicly-held information and emphasizes competitor's position, performance, capabilities and intentions.

Competitive intelligence is nothing but the analytical process, which transforms scattered information about competitors and customers into relevant, accurate and usable strategic knowledge on market evolution, business opportunities and threats. It is mainly focused on environment and uses pubic sources to locate and develop information on competition and competitors, information later used as references, benchmarks or any other basis for strategic analysis. Competitive intelligence is natural exploit of the increasing availability of commercial databases world-wide, the on-line mass-media and development of cutting edge information technologies: business intelligence and knowledge management.

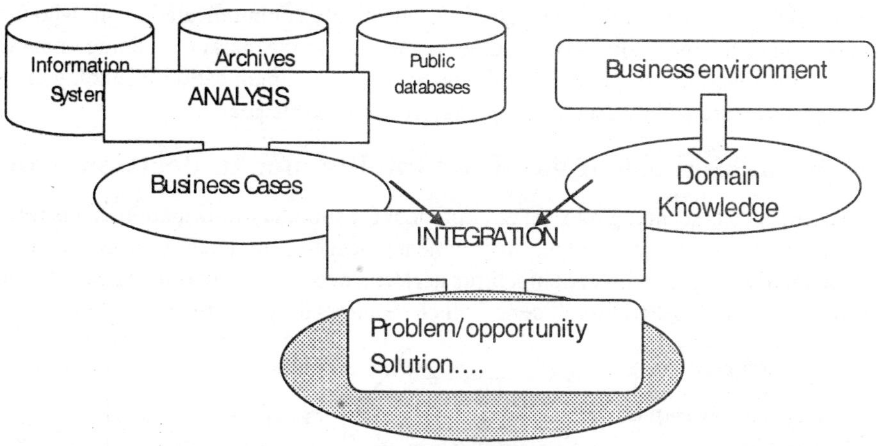

Fig. 1 : Competitive Intelligence Framework

The business deals with customers, suppliers, employees and other stakeholders. Almost all business organizations seeking similar objectives: growth, profit and fame. Competitiveness is natural relationship between businesses. Monitoring competitors worth a lot because it provides necessary knowledge to be able to predict their next moves, exploit their weaknesses and undermine their strengths. According to Arthur Weiss, founder managing partner of AWARE company, there are four stages in monitoring competitors - the four "C"s:

1. Collecting the information
2. Converting information into intelligence
3. Communicating the intelligence
4. Countering any adverse competitor actions

1. Collecting the Information

According to the business decision, different kind of relevant information is required. At this stage the objective is to identify the key areas of concern for the business decision makers and the requested information. Thus, the search needs to be focused and planned and aimed at answering the various intelligence requirements of the business often termed key intelligence topics.

2. Converting Information Into Intelligence

Unfortunately much of collected data will be redundant, out of date, inaccurate or incomplete, even wrong. In fact, there are two basic approaches in knowledge creation:

(i) **Data → Information → Knowledge:** The structured linear view, based on information processing which extracts knowledge from information and information from data. Business Intelligence technologies play the central role in that context. Converting information into intelligence is a process consisting of three steps: collate and catalogue information, analyze and interpret it.

(ii) **Integration:** Integration and communication of tacit (expertise, insight in human mind) and explicit knowledge (documents, databases, data warehouses etc.). Knowledge integration is perceived as being a synthesis of best available evidence with expertise of individuals and customer values.

3. Communicating the Intelligence

Competitor intelligence needs to be evaluated and selectively communicated to all who need to make decisions based on what customers, suppliers, or other companies in the market are doing or are likely to do. Even if this stage seems well understood and well supported by communication technologies, Knowledge Management technologies are widely used in order to fully achieve this goal.

4. Countering (making use of gathered intelligence in decision process)

Business intelligence is scanning internal environment for summary information that is relevant for the decision-making. Current information about the environment is needed in the analysis process to make reference to as industry benchmarks or just as direct competitors performance levels to compare against. This reference information is provided by competitive intelligence which monitors the company environment.

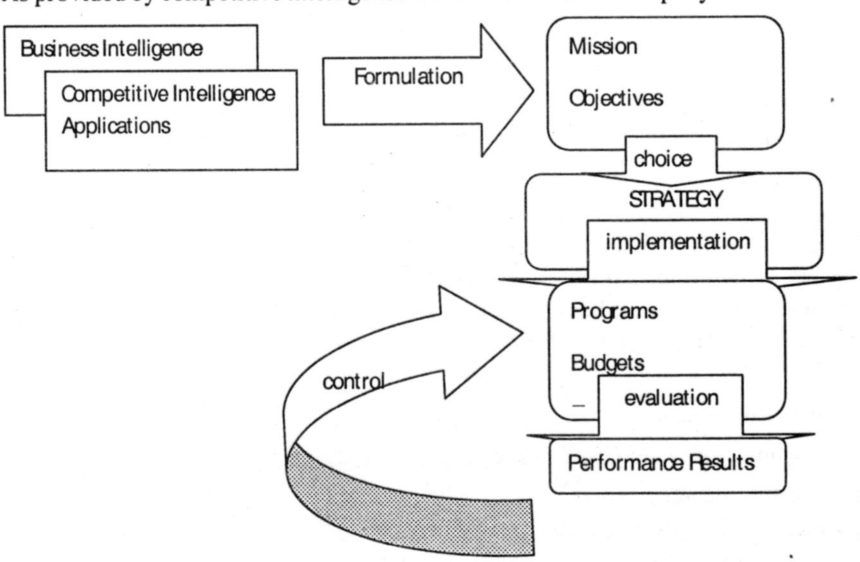

Fig. 2 : Business & Competitive Intelligence Integration in Management Process

As presented in the Fig. 2 above, the integrated technologies of Business and competitive Intelligence are useful in formulating mission and long term objectives for the company; in designing strategies from which the company will make a choice. These are obviously features of strategic management level, the technological support is known as Strategic Management Support System. The implementation of the strategy could also be assisted by Business Intelligence, mostly on operational side – in the planning phase when programs, budgets, procedures, financing plans are to be established and optimized. At this stage, one can rely on Operational Management software support. Once the implementation plan approved and the project start up, Performance Management Systems must enter the scene, in order to evaluate the evolution of the project and keep it under control.

Bibliography

1. IBM Global Business Intelligence Solution "Knowledge Management – Overview", 2006, available on line at www.ibm.com/bi.
2. Turban, E & Aronson, J.E. & Liang, T.P. & Sharda, R. *Decision Support and Business Intelligence System*, 2007, Pearson Prentice Hall, New Jersey
3. www.marketing-intelligence.co.uk.
4. www.scip.org.
5. Dr. B. Rathan Reddy, Knowledge Management, 2nd edition, Himalaya Publication.
6. Ford, N. "From Information- to Knowledge Management," 1989, Journal of Information Science Principles & Practices.
7. Search Engines.
   - www.google.com
   - www.altavista.com
8. Websites.
   - www.wikipedia.com
9. Davenport, T.H. 'Think Tank: The Future of Knowledge Management," 1995, December 15, CIO.
10. Hameed, I., "Knowledge Management and Business Intelligence. What is the difference? 2004, Available at http://onlinebusiness.about.com/.
11. Cook, C. and Cook, M. , The Convergence of Knowledge Management and Business Intelligence, 2000, Auerbach Publications, New York, NY, available at: www.brint.com.

◈◈◈

ISBN - 978-93-5024-769-3

56

Job Sharing: The New Competent Technique for Effective and Efficient Management of Human Resource in 21st Century

Sharad R. Kulkarni
ATS, SB Group of Institutes, Faculty of Management, Tilaknagar, Miraj-416414.
Dist. Sangli (MS)

Introduction

It is worldwide observation that there is a growing skills shortage and combined with the prospect of either ageing or skill deficient workforce. Employers are challenged to examine their approach to retain and develop workforce. At the same time work/life balance is becoming an increasingly important issue. As the shortage of skilled people threatens productivity and growth in many key sectors, sophisticated strategies for the management of human capital has never been more crucial to an organisation's commercial sustainability.

This paper will explore an effective but little understood flexible work solution, job sharing. Job sharing is used in a different way to help organisations in managing a variety of employee related issues. Different employers and job seekers are surveyed to obtain an in-depth understanding about the application of job sharing. Employers were asked about the prevalence and subsequent benefits of providing job share programs, as well as assessing the perceived impact of not providing this flexible work option to current and prospective employees. Job seekers were asked whether their employer offered job share programs. Both employers and job seekers were asked whether they would consider job sharing as an employment option. The results provide a compelling case for employers to provide integrated job sharing programs as a flexible work solution to their employees.

Job sharing

The concept of job sharing is well recognized but its 8999963+63+application may not be so well understood. As a result there are various misconceptions about the topic. In this context, it is necessary to define job sharing as a concept and explain briefly the consequences derived from it, in the organization.

Meaning

Job sharing involves two or more people sharing one fulltime role. The role can be designed and established in many different ways. 'Sharers' can partner with individuals of the same skills or complementary skills. They can share, divide or split the responsibilities of the role. The design is dependant upon the nature of the role, skills of the partners, and each individual's work needs. Job sharing can be applied to most full-time roles, as long as the role has been properly designed and set up.

Concept

Work/life balance is the key driver for looking to share the jobs. Responding to people's key drivers leads directly to improved employee retention. This is why job sharing is an important option to seriously consider for organisations of any size. Some of the reasons why an individual might seek to job share include:

- Balancing family needs which may involve children or providing elderly care.
- Balancing study and work.
- Transitioning mature-aged workers into retirement, by moving from fulltime to part-time employment for an agreed period of time.
- Those seeking improved work/life balance by reducing their working hours.

Individuals choose job sharing to meet many demands of career and life. Job sharing provides the individual with the flexibility required without putting career progression on hold or deskilling. This is otherwise often experienced by individuals who have the part-time employment. Organisations need to engage directly with the issue of work/life balance as part of their overall retention and attraction strategy. Organizations who understand the changing environment will gain a significant competitive advantage over rivals competing in the same pool of skills.

Myths

There are number of myths about concept of job sharing. These are disclosed even during the study. Some of them are described below.

Job sharing is suitable concept only for 'women in administrative roles'

In an international context job sharing has been applied to most roles. As long as the role is properly set up job sharing is equally applicable for administration, client-facing positions, management and operational roles. Job sharing is most valuable when used as a retention tool, particularly to retain senior employees as the cost of replacing senior staff increases exponentially.

A job sharing policy is the same as a job share program.

A job share policy is only a small part of an organisation's job share program. An integrated program focuses on the components which put the policy into practice. A program includes components like business controls, governance, operational processes, education, training and reporting.

Job sharers must have the same skills profile and personality.

It is critical to make job sharing a success only with commitment of job sharers with the job share program and their competencies match the specific needs of the role. Sharers may have the same skills or they may have complementary or unrelated skills. This depends on the role type and the nature of the role.

Jobsharers require twice the amount of time to manage.

In fact, global evidence suggests exactly opposite. Experienced supervisors of jobsharers generally agree that less supervision is required after the job sharing relationship is well established. This is because the emphasis is on the sharers to make the arrangement work, and sharers tend to supervise each other's work. This is an inbuilt form of quality assurance, which reduces errors and encourages self-supervision.

Job sharing costs too much to the business

The full-time salary of jobsharers is split between the employees on a pro-rata basis. Hence there are no additional remuneration costs. The only exception is when there is an agreed overlap time. There are some additional costs such as extra payroll calculations or training. However, the provision of coverage for each other during periods of leave generally adjusts these additional costs.

Objectives of the Study

Present study is focused on following objectives.

1. To study the awareness about the concept of job sharing in selective organizations and sample group of employees.
2. To analyse the experiences regarding job sharing programs among sample employers and employees.

Hypotheses

Null Hypotheses (H0)

(a) Respondents are not aware about job sharing concept.

(b) Job sharing is useful concept for respondents.

Alternate Hypotheses (H1):

(a) Respondents are aware about job sharing concept

(b) Job sharing is not useful concept for respondents.

Methodology

For this study, 50 job seekers were randomly selected for survey. Similarly, 20 employers from five core organizations were surveyed. The number of employees in selected organizations is less than 20. The details about area of work of these organizations are as shown in Table 1.

TABLE 1 – Profile of Respondent Organizations

Sr. No.	*Area*	*No.*	*%*
1	Education	6	30
2	Healthcare	4	20
3	Manufacturing	4	20
4	Retail	3	15
5	Hospitality	3	15
Total		20	100

Source: Field Survey

Data Analysis and Findings

The collected data has been analysed and findings of the survey are deduced as mentioned below.

Do organizations aware about job sharing concept?

TABLE 2 – Awareness about job sharing concept

Sr. No.	Area	Response					
		Yes		Partially Aware		Not Aware	
		No.	%	No.	%	No.	%
1	Education	3	15	2	10	1	05
2	Healthcare	2	10	1	05	1	05
3	Manufacturing	2	10	1	05	1	05
4	Retail	2	10	1	05	0	00
5	Hospitality	1	05	1	05	1	05
Total		10	50	6	30	4	20

Source: Field Survey

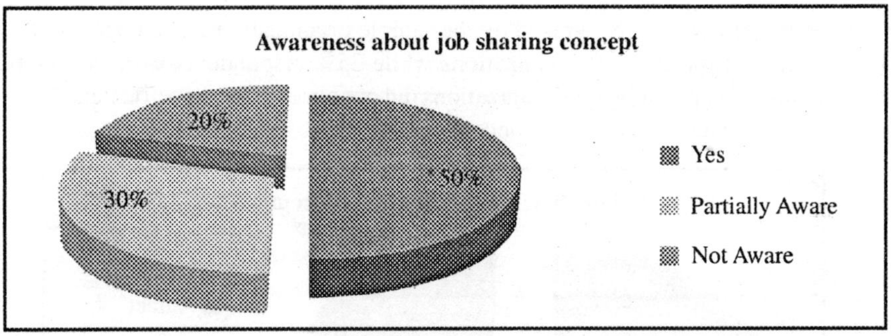

About 50 % of organizations under survey are aware about the concept of job sharing. Out of remaining half of the respondents, 30 % are partially aware but not in position to implement the concept while remaining 20 % organizations are totally unaware. Area wise analysis about awareness is shown in following chart.

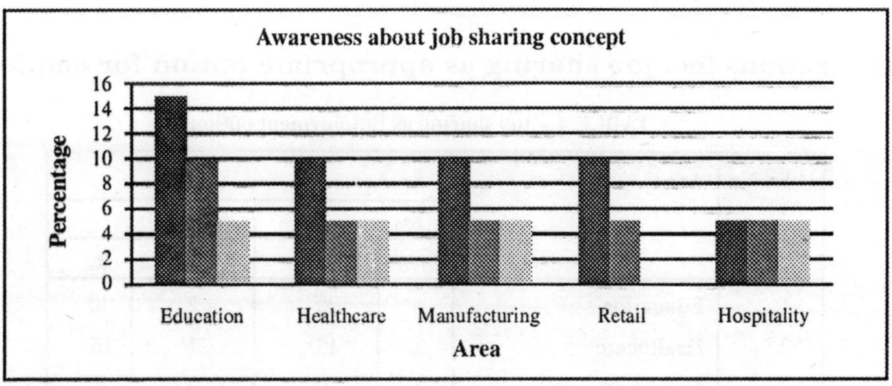

Do organizations experience any benefit from job sharing concept

TABLE 3 – Benefits from job sharing concept

Sr. No.	*Area*	*Response*							
		Attract Employees		*Retain Employees*		*No Benefit*		*Don't Know*	
		No.	*%*	*No.*	*%*	*No.*	*%*	*No.*	*%*
1	Education	2	10	3	15	0	00	1	05
2	Healthcare	1	05	2	10	0	00	1	05
3	Manufacturing	2	10	1	05	0	00	1	05
4	Retail	1	05	1	05	1	05	0	—
5	Hospitality	1	05	1	05	0	00	1	05
Total		7	35	8	40	1	05	4	20

Source: Field Survey

There are two major benefits recognized by the sample organizations. The concept of job sharing was useful to retain employees for 40% of organizations while 35% respondents were successful in attracting employees through this concept. Only 5% organizations did not observe any specific benefit. In addition, 20% respondents were totally unaware about the concept.

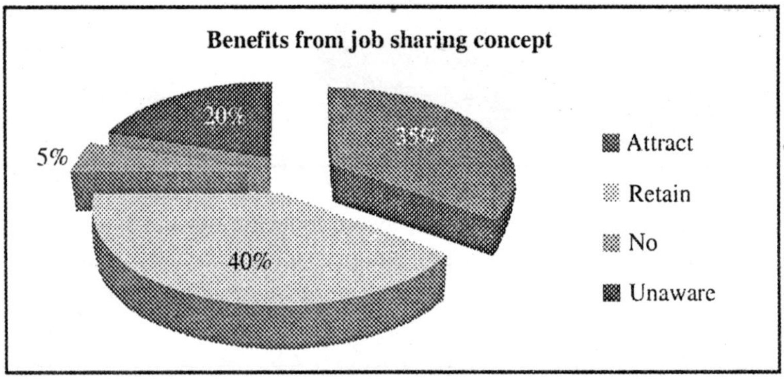

Do organizations feel job sharing as appropriate option for employment?

TABLE 4 – Job sharing as Employment option

Sr. *No.*	*Area*	*Response*			
		Yes		*No*	
		No.	*%*	*No.*	*%*
1	Education	4	20	2	10
2	Healthcare	3	15	1	05
3	Manufacturing	2	10	2	10

4	Retail	2	10	1	05
5	Hospitality	2	10	1	05
Total		13	65	7	35

Source: Field Survey

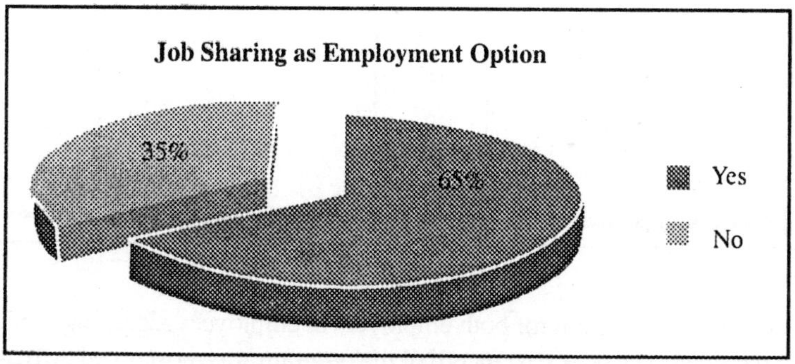

Almost 65 % organizations did not find job sharing as a suitable option for the employment while 35 % respondents had identified the job sharing concept as employment option.

Area wise responses are recorded in table 5. Out of the selected five areas the manufacturing sector alone had equal response (50 % each), healthcare sector had strongly found the positive aspect between job sharing and employment. Remaining sectors namely, education, retail and hospitality were in favour of positive relation between job sharing and employment.

TABLE 5 – Area wise views about Job sharing as Employment option

Sr. No.	*Area*	*Response (%)*	
		Yes	*No*
1	Education	67	33
2	Healthcare	75	25
3	Manufacturing	50	50
4	Retail	67	33
5	Hospitality	67	33

Source: Field Survey

What difficulties organizations face in implementing job sharing programs?

TABLE 6 – Difficulties before organizations in implementing job sharing programs

Sr. No.	*Difficulties*	*Response*			
		Employers (@ 20)		*Employees (@ 50)*	
		No.	*%*	*No.*	*%*
1	Less understanding	14	70	37	74
2	Poor past results	17	85	41	82
3	Rigid job design	13	65	32	64
4	Less confidence	12	60	29	58

Source: Field Survey

Four important difficulties, common for both employers & employees regarding implementation of job sharing programs were recorded. The poor past record of the program was most noted difficulty (85 % & 82 % respectively), followed by poor understanding of concept (70% & 74 %), rigidity in job design (65 % & 64 %) and poor confidence level (60 % &d 58%).

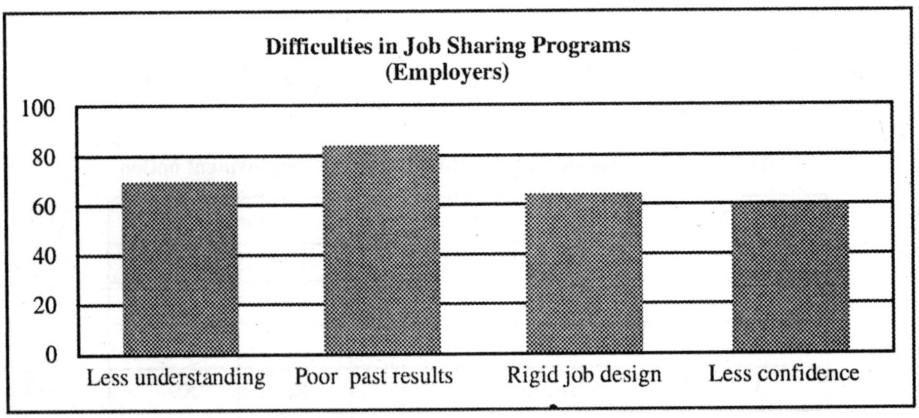

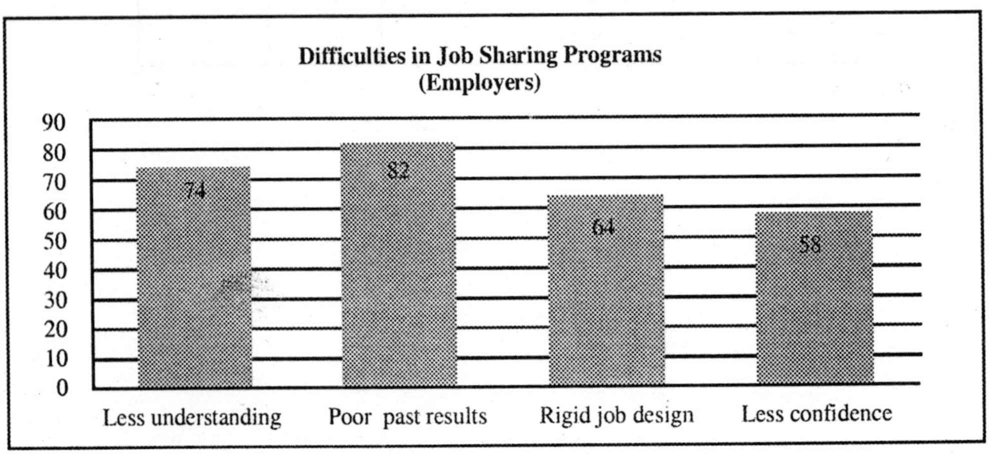

Hypothesis Testing

Fot testing of the hypothesis, the 't' test has been applied. In case of the first hypothesis the values of mean and standard deviation are 5 and 0.98 respectively. The 't' value for 95 % significance (7.3) is greater than the table value (2.78). Hence, the null hypothesis stating that, 'Respondents are not aware about job sharing concept ', is to be accepted.

The values of mean and standard deviation for the second hypothesis are 3 and 1.095 respectively. The 't' value for 95 % significance (6.126) is greater than the table value (2.78). Hence, the null hypothesis stating that, 'Job sharing is useful concept for respondents ', is to be accepted.

Essentials of successful job sharing programs

There are many components to a successful job share program. Out of them, three areas are identified for implementation of this approach. These are,

In-depth definition of the business case

For implementing the job sharing program, like any business initiative, it is essential that the case for change is clearly defined, quantified and understood.

Creation of a sustainable job sharing solution.

The solution should contain three basic building blocks namely, transparent job sharing policy, governance to manage solutions and detail action plan for implementation of job sharing program.

Preparation for change management.

Organisations need to integrate job sharing into the organisation's way of working, culture and behaviours. It is essential that the new work style and process is communicated to all stakeholders, particularly those with whom the jobsharers interact.

Gains from job sharing

A successful result of job sharing appears from the organisation and individuals working together in partnership and sharing their responsibilities. The organisation provides the framework and program for job-sharing, and the individuals work within these parameters. Job sharing can be used as a powerful business tool for organisations to manage people related issues. There must be commitment, clear responsibilities, supporting systems and an understanding for extracting the maximum benefits from a job sharing program. Some significant benefits derived from job sharing program are,

1. Improvement in retention level by providing individuals opportunities to work in challenging environment and fulfilling roles without de-skilling and loosing career achievements.
2. Provision of access to wider pool of skill and expertise.
3. Improvement in productivity and performance by encouraging a sense of loyalty and value from job sharers.
4. Enhancement in abilities to manage the workload of each job sharer.
5. Assurance for better customer service.

Conclusion

Job sharing is the new method for retaining the valuable talent pool in the organisation. The study revels following points in conclusion.

Both employees and employers show a high level of interest in considering job sharing as a viable work option in the future.

- There is absence of a direct link between the level of interest individual's display for job sharing and the quantity of organisations providing a job share program.
- The understanding of job sharing remains limited, with results showing that many are unsure about how job sharing could be applied to their personal roles.
- Employers who have a job sharing program experience a positive impact on their ability to attract and retain staff, with particular emphasis on retention.

Taking into account the survey results and the applications, job sharing can be used by organisations to help in managing real issues related with human resource as well as ensuring ways to attract and retain the employees. If employers are to remain competitive, it is critical that they respond to the changing needs of the workforce. Job sharing is an innovative flexible work solution that, if implemented properly, will help an organisation to attract, engage and retain their workforce intact.

References

1. Chapin, V.J., "*Work Life and Personal Needs: the Job-Sharing Option.*", A background paper, Supply and Services, 1990, Canada. Ottawa.
2. Hudson, "*Employment and HR Trends*", 2006 January-March, Part 3.
3. Singh, S.A, "*Note on the Work Sharing Program: Perspectives on Labour and Income*", (1991), (Statistics Canada), no. 4 (Winter 1991): 56-59.
4. www.entrepreneur.com
5. www.stafco.com
6. www.statcan.gc.ca
7. www.wisegeek.com

◈ ◈ ◈